MW01088302

Harry Ballan

COGNITIVE NEUROSCIENCE AND PSYCHOTHERAPY

COGNITIVE NEUROSCIENCE AND PSYCHOTHERAPY

Network Principles for a Unified Theory

WARREN W. TRYON

Fordham University,
Department of Psychology,
Bronx, NY, USA

Amsterdam • Boston • Heidelberg • London
New york • Oxford • Paris • San Diego
San Francisco • Singapore • Sydney • Tokyo
Academic Press is an imprint of Elsevier

Academic Press is an imprint of Elsevier
32 Jamestown Road, London NW1 7BY, UK
225 Wyman Street, Waltham, MA 02451, USA
525 B Street, Suite 1800, San Diego, CA 92101-4495, USA

British Library Cataloguing-in-Publication Data
A catalogue record for this book is available from the British Library

Library of Congress Cataloging-in-Publication Data
A catalog record for this book is available from the Library of Congress

ISBN: 978-0-12-420071-5

For information on all Academic Press publications
visit our website at www.store.elsevier.com

Typeset by TNQ Books and Journals
www.tnq.co.in

Printed and bound in United States of America

14 15 16 17 18   10 9 8 7 6 5 4 3 2 1

CONTENTS

PREFACE[1]

Psychology is an immature science with a substantial explanatory problem that has set psychologists against one another and created more than 500 psychotherapies distributed across what I refer to as the Big Five clinical orientations: (a) cognitive; (b) behavioral (applied behavior analysis); (c) cognitive-behavioral; (d) psychodynamic (emotion-focused therapy); and (e) pharmacologic, and their variants that corrosively compete for adherents and practitioners. Widespread resistance to using empirically supported treatments caused by these explanatory problems has further fractionated clinical psychologists. ***Cognitive Neuroscience and Psychotherapy*** provides psychotherapy integration via theoretical integration in a way that enables psychology to be practiced as a mature science. The topics of theoretical unification, psychotherapy integration, and how psychology can become a mature science could constitute three separate books, but ***Cognitive Neuroscience and Psychotherapy*** integrates them. Psychotherapists can only be expected to treat people alike when they share a common understanding of psychological science. Hence, theoretical unification provides the most meaningful way to achieve psychotherapy integration. My focus on causal mechanisms enabled me to show how psychology could become a mature science.

The theoretical unification that I offer is a start, not an end. It provides a theoretical foundation upon which to construct a mature psychological science, not a final end point of perfection. The proposed core and corollary principles provide a way to begin to work together rather than in mutual isolation or at competitive cross purposes, as is presently the case. It enables us to understand how cognition and affect interact to produce behavior that is based in contemporary cognitive neuroscience.

Section 1 provides a novel and creative approach to theoretical unification. The recommended approach succeeds where all others have failed because it focuses on causal mechanisms where theoretical unification presently exists by default because psychological theories have not made any claims regarding causal mechanisms. Hence, there are no conflicting positions to unify.

The proposed Bio↔Psychology Network Theory is not a new theory in the ordinary sense of needing to be tested to see if it can be empirically

[1] Additional material added after this book was printed is available at www.fordham.edu/psychology/tryon. This includes an extension to Principle 3: Transformation and a color version of Figure 5.6.

supported. Only its organization in terms of core and corollary network principles is new. Its content consists of the unanticipated, unarticulated, and unacknowledged implications of well-replicated psychological phenomena that can be explained by accepted neuroscience and connectionist mechanisms plus multivariate statistics. While additional research is always welcome, the existing empirical support for the proposed Bio↔Psychology Network Theory is so substantial that future research will likely further support rather than contradict all 12 proposed network principles. Hence, the Bio↔Psychology Network Theory is ready for use today. Only its presentation in the form of core and corollary network principles is new. That a wide variety of psychological phenomena can be explained by the network principles that constitute the proposed theory means that it brings theoretical unification to psychological science. Hence, the subtitle: ***Network Principles for a Unified Theory***.

Chapters 1 and 2 discuss the explanatory problems and impediments to theoretical unification presently faced by psychological science. Chapters 3–6 provide a proposed solution in the form of four core and eight corollary network principles that constitute the proposed Bio↔Psychology Network Theory. Chapter 7 presents criticisms of the proposed solution and rebuttals. It also includes 13 novel features and 7 novel predictions made by the proposed Bio↔Psychology Network Theory, in addition to a call for a paradigmatic shift regarding how we think about psychology. Thinking about psychology and behavior in physical rather than mental terms is what Freud (1895) aimed to do in his *Project for a Scientific Psychology* but could not achieve due to the neuroscience limitations of his day. This book continues and extends Freud's original work. The required paradigmatic shift includes changing psychology from a conscious-centric to an unconscious-centric psychology.

Section 2 shows how the shared understanding provided by the theoretical unification delivered in Section 1 integrates the Big Five clinical orientations to psychotherapy by providing each of them with their conceptual 'must haves'. A novel feature of this section is that it focuses on clinical orientations rather than the theories that generated them. Clinical orientations are much broader than the theories that support them and therefore are easier to integrate. For example, one need not believe everything said by every cognitive-behavioral theorist to have a cognitive-behavioral orientation. Nor does one need to believe everything that has been written by every psychoanalytic author to have a psychodynamic orientation. The proposed Bio↔Psychology Network Theory provides a theoretical basis for a comprehensive clinical practice that incorporates the strengths of each of the Big Five clinical orientations while preserving the requirement that therapies be empirically supported. Therapists' therapeutic goals will expand to include increasing psychological mindedness and emotional regulation, in addition to symptom reduction/removal. Therapists will base their interventions on the core and corollary principles rather than on manuals. Therapists will customize their interventions to their clients' needs. Principles of operant and respondent conditioning are reauthorized as cognitive-behavioral interventions. All of these developments nurture the scholarly motive for doing psychotherapy and consequently are expected to facilitate widespread acceptance of empirically supported treatments into clinical practice.

The theoretical unification required to provide psychotherapy integration entails a paradigm shift precipitated by the following two anomalies: (a) all psychological theories lack causal mechanism information because they are functional theories; and (b) there is no psychological substrate for psychological mechanisms to operate on. Hence, psychological mechanisms based on causal mechanisms do not exist because they cannot exist. The proposed solution is to think about psychology and behavior in physical rather than mental terms. This paradigmatic shift carries several consequences. First, it requires us to embrace neuroscience and reductionism because they provide causal mechanisms that operate on a biological substrate. But reductionism constitutes only half of a complete explanation, because even a complete parts list does not explain how those parts produce psychology. Some assembly is always required! Emergence constitutes the second half of a complete explanation. The four core network principles constitute the explanatory kernel of the proposed emergent Bio↔Psychology Network Theory. Second, the resulting paradigm shift requires psychology to transition from a conscious-centric to an unconscious-centric science. This conceptual shift enables us to understand how neural networks transform stimulus microfeatures into psychological constructs; how mind emerges from brain.

Cults, religions, and immature sciences are organized around august individuals. Sciences are organized around principles. This book is organized around core and corollary principles. Principles 1–4 constitute an explanatory core. They characterize every processing cycle. Principles 5–12 are corollary in that they derive from the explanatory core and greatly expand its explanatory scope. Mathematical proof of the adequacy of the proposed network model is provided.

Cognitive Neuroscience and Psychotherapy addresses all psychologists because it provides a way to practice psychology as a mature science. This includes instructors who wish to teach Introductory Psychology or Foundations of Psychology from a coherent principle-based theoretical perspective grounded in cognitive neuroscience. It includes investigators who wish to construct a mature science organized around basic principles rather than persons. It addresses clinical psychologists' wish to integrate the Big Five clinical orientations and to enter upon an era of truly cooperative and constructive psychotherapy research and practice. It addresses the general population who are, or will be, interested in this paradigmatic shift in psychological science.

The scope of this book is extensive as is required by the comprehensive perspective that it provides. Its content spans multiple fields of general psychology, neuroscience, anatomy, genetics, epigenetics, and some areas of multivariate statistics in a readable and accessible way. Everything that the reader needs to know is explained.

This book is unique in its triple objectives of (a) providing a new perspective, paradigmatic shift, that enables psychology to be practiced as a mature science, that (b) delivers the required theoretical unification (c) to integrate the Big Five clinical orientations regarding psychotherapy in a way that provides a conceptual understanding that supports the scholarly motive for doing psychotherapy, in addition to the need for empirically supported treatments.

I placed the evaluation of the Bio-Psychological Network Theory (BPNT) in chapter 7 as a conclusion to the formal presentation of this theory. When teaching, I skip over Chapter 7 and address it after Chapter 12 because final evaluation of the BPNT depends heavily for clinical psychologists on its contributions to clinical practice that are considered in Chapters 8-12.

I wish to acknowledge Fordham University for providing the four decades of academic freedom and periodic faculty fellowships that enabled me to finally grasp the big picture that I present to you here. I wish to especially acknowledge Elizabeth Tryon, my daughter, who in conversation and editing gave greater focus and clarity of expression to the principles upon which this book is based. Finally, I wish to acknowledge the support of my wife and clinical psychologist colleague Georgiana Shick Tryon.

The figure above is of a neural network drawn by Sigmund Freud in 1895 while writing a text book for neurologists entitled *The Project for a Scientific Psychology*. It is reproduced with permission from Spitzer, 1999, page 5. Freud was trained as a neurologist in medical school by the prominent physiologist Ernst Brücke (1819–1892). Rychlak (1973, pp. 43–4) reported that Breuer and Fleiss encouraged Freud to develop a theory of psychology based entirely on biology. Freud (1895b) complied with these exhortations and wrote the first three chapters, but could not complete his *Project* due to the limitations of neuroscience in 1895.

In this drawing, the left arrow represents incoming energy to the neural network. The small circles represent neurons. The perpendicular double lines represent synapses.

SECTION 1

Theoretical Unification

PART One

The Problem

CHAPTER 1

Introduction

Contents

Cognitive Neuroscience and Psychotherapy
http://dx.doi.org/10.1016/B978-0-12-420071-5.00001-6

Psychotherapy requires one to understand how cognition and affect interact to produce behavior. Psychological science is expected to inform clinical psychologists in this regard but unfortunately it has been of remarkably little help because it has a serious explanatory problem. This problem has prevented psychotherapy integration because it has foiled theoretical unification and precluded psychology from developing beyond its current preparadigmatic state into a mature science[1] (Kuhn, 1962, 1970, 1996, 2012).[2] Clinical psychologists have had to primarily rely on their personal and professional experience to develop the therapies that they use. Clinical science has mainly focused on testing the efficacy and effectiveness of these interventions.[3] Psychological science has not kept pace and this has resulted in an **evidence–theory explanatory gap**. We cannot explain why our empirically supported treatments work, and I believe this has created resistance to their widespread adoption.

This book is about **psychotherapy integration through theoretical unification**. I do this using a slightly expanded version of the **hybrid cognitive neuroscience**[4] **Bio↔Psychology Network Theory** introduced by Tryon (2012). It also provides a way to practice psychology as a mature science. Chapters 3–7 aim to close our explanatory gap as much as

[1] See the section on Mature Science below for further details.

[2] http://en.wikipedia.org/wiki/The_Structure_of_Scientific_Revolutions

[3] Nathan and Gorman (2002) distinguished efficacy from effectiveness. **Efficacy** is concerned with replication of treatment effects that exceed appropriate control conditions. **Effectiveness** is concerned with practical results that can be obtained in clinical settings.

[4] I use the term 'cognitive neuroscience' as shorthand for 'cognitive, affective, behavioral neuroscience' also known as CAB neuroscience or CABN.

is presently possible using connectionist network and neuroscience mechanisms along with multivariate statistics. The four core and eight corollary network principles developed in these chapters provide a way to theoretically unify psychological science. They also enable psychology to be practiced as a mature science. Chapters 8–12 use these principles to provide psychotherapy integration through a Hegelian synthesis of the following Big Five clinical orientations:[5] (a) behavioral (applied behavior analysis); (b) cognitive; (c) cognitive-behavioral; (d) psychodynamic (emotion-focused therapies); and (e) pharmacologic.

The proposed Bio↔Psychology Network Theory is not a new theory in the ordinary sense of needing to be tested to see if it can be empirically supported. Only its organization in terms of core and corollary network principles is new. Its content consists of the unanticipated, unarticulated, and unacknowledged implications of well-replicated psychological phenomena that can be explained by accepted neuroscience and connectionist mechanisms plus multivariate statistics.

OUR EXPLANATORY PROBLEM

Mature sciences explain well-replicated facts and phenomena on the basis of accepted principles and/or laws, using a common vocabulary. Immature sciences provide interpretations by individuals. Teo (2012) revealed this explanatory problem when he commented upon a psychological explanation by a prominent psychologist. 'Lilienfeld (2012) could not rely on general laws or even statistical facts to provide a scientific *explanation* for this question. What is evident from all we know from the philosophy of science is that Lilienfeld offered us an *interpretation*' (p. 807, italics in the original). Psychology presently offers **interpretations** rather than **explanations** because, with a few exceptions, it lacks general principles upon which to base its explanations. If you want a psychological explanation, just ask a psychologist. Some interpretations will make more sense than others. Some explanations will be better grounded in research than others. But in the end, one is faced with choosing among interpretations by individuals because no principled explanation is available. This means that the public has every right to view psychology as a secondary science as Lilienfeld (2012) revealed.

[5] Clinical orientations are broader than are the various theories upon which they are based. For example, one need not endorse everything that Beck, Ellis, Linehan, etc. have said in order to maintain a cognitive-behavioral orientation. Similarly, one need not agree with everything proposed by every psychodynamic theorist to maintain a psychodynamic orientation.

Take a minute to reflect and ponder the devastating implications of this statement for a discipline that considers itself to be a science.

Psychologists tend to form groups based on their affinity for particular interpretations. These groups are frequently referred to by the most prominent psychologist who either originated or best publicized that particular interpretation. Freud and Skinner are two good examples. Individual psychologists who prefer similar, but not necessarily identical, interpretations of events associate with one another to form professional organizations whose main purpose is to advocate for their particular explanatory approach. These groups continue to divide psychologists into opposing schools and camps whose competitions with one another impede the development of theoretical unification and preclude psychology from becoming a mature science. Adherents to each form of interpretation generate their own vocabulary, methods, and findings. They avoid replicating the work of other investigators to appear original. Students of psychology must choose to align themselves with one or another of these schools because there is no overarching principle-based form of psychology to identify with.

Groups of psychologists who provide similar interpretations tend to cluster together and produce larger professional associations such as the American Psychological Association, the American Psychological Society, the Association for Cognitive and Behavioral Therapies, and the American Psychoanalytic Association, among others. These groups are mainly concerned with expanding their membership through 'education' and controlling discourse through journal editorships, grant review panels, and advisory boards. Put bluntly, these groups seem more concerned with perpetuating their particular orientation than advancing psychology as a science.

Mischel (2009) described the reluctance of psychologists to use the work of others as our '**toothbrush problem**': 'Psychologists treat other peoples' theories like toothbrushes – no self respecting person wants to use anyone else's' (p. 3). Kruglanski (2013) described our reluctance to move beyond midlevel theories to more comprehensive explanations as our '**theory shyness**' (p. 871, emphasis added). Gigerenzer (2009) noted that 'much of the theoretical landscape in psychology resembles a patchwork of small territories' (p. 22). Gigerenzer (2010) remarked that 'As a consequence, in some parts of psychology, theories have become replaced by surrogates, such as circular restatements of the phenomenon, one-word explanations, and lists of general dichotomies' (p. 733). McNally (1992) viewed this theoretical diversity as a sign of scientific health, while Staats (1983) considered it to be corrosive, and Spence (1987) worried that it is tearing psychology apart.

Our explanatory problem extends to clinical practice. The therapies we offer are sometimes diametrically opposed to one another. For example, some therapies are based on theories that emphasize unconscious processing while other therapies are based on theories that minimize or deny its very existence. While clinicians can and do appreciate the benefits of theoretical pluralism, eclectic practice is deeply discouraged for at least two reasons. One reason is that the inherent contradictions among supporting psychological theories appears to put patients at risk. A second reason concerns treatment choice. If you are a clinical psychologist and all of your patients respond fully to your interventions then you may continue in the hope that all will remain as successful as it has been. If, on the other hand, some of your patients do not fully respond to your therapies and/or if some of your patients are unresponsive to your interventions then you will need to rethink what you are doing with them. But as an eclectic therapist, what alternative theoretical orientation will you choose? Your theoretical background will always be your primary resource for understanding what went wrong and/or what else needs to be done. But with contradictory choices what decision shall you make?

Science values parsimony. Ideally, we desire a single theory to explain our facts. We do not have, but currently need, a uniform way to understand psychological phenomena and our empirically supported treatments. Our explanatory deficiencies stem in large part from our lack of mechanism information. Currently we can't explain why or how psychological phenomena work. We can't explain why or how our empirically supported treatments work. We lack an understanding of how cognition and affect cause behavior.[6] We also lack a shared vocabulary and a set of core concepts.

There are currently more than 500 therapies.[7] Surely they do not work for 500 different reasons. Such diversity has created a serious training problem in addition to a serious science issue. There is no way to teach students or professionals 500 different therapies. Nor do students and professionals want to learn so many different techniques. There is certainly no way for any clinician to develop a professional level of competence in so many different treatments. Such diversity presents

[6] This book is the first text designed to explain how cognition and affect interact to produce behavior in a theoretically based way. Psychodynamic theory is the only other formal theoretical system that systematically considers how cognition and affect cause behavior but it has its own set of serious problems, as we shall subsequently see in Chapter 9.

[7] http://www.scientificamerican.com/article.cfm?id=are-all-psychotherapies-created-equal, http://apt.rcpsych.org/content/7/4/241.full

potential clients with a confusing array of interventions. How are they to make an informed choice? They expect and deserve greater consensus from psychological science. This book aims to provide theoretical unification in the form of four core and eight corollary network principles that integrate the big five clinical orientations: (a) behavioral (applied behavior analysis); (b) cognitive; (c) cognitive-behavioral; (d) psychodynamic (emotion-focused therapies); and (e) pharmacologic.

MA-level psychologists can be trained to administer structured diagnostic interviews and relevant manualized treatments. If all goes well then no problem exists. If all does not go so well, then the MA psychologist will need to consult with a doctoral-level psychologist whose considerably greater theoretical training may provide helpful suggestions. But which doctoral psychologist should the MA psychologist consult? That depends upon which interpretation the MA psychologist prefers and would like to discuss further. Sadly, psychological science cannot assist because it currently lacks explanatory principles.

Why do we have this explanatory problem? Why has psychological science so long organized itself around august persons rather than principles? I suggest that the reason is that we have been thinking incorrectly about psychology for a long time. It all began with Rene Descartes (1596–1650) who established the concept of mind, which philosophers had long discussed before then, as an entity separate from brain, because he could not imagine, let alone understand, how mind could **emerge** from brain. His conceptual difficulty became our **mind–body problem**. Had he had present-day neuroscience knowledge he almost certainly would never have distinguished 'mind' from brain. Psychology has suffered from and struggled with this self-inflicted problem in various ways ever since. There is no more reason to believe that the mind exists apart from the brain than there is to believe that our behavior is caused by a small dwarf, homunculus, residing inside us. Modern neuroscience has progressed far beyond what it was in the sixteenth century, when behavior was explained in bizarre ways.

I believe that a potential solution exists to our explanatory problem. The solution is to take seriously the need for and provide the missing mechanism information called for by Carey (2011), Gigerenzer (1998, 2009), Kazdin (2007, 2008), and Squire et al. (1993). This missing mechanism information has been gradually accumulating within neuroscience and within psychology especially since McClelland et al. (1986) and Rumelhart and McClelland (1986) published their seminal work showing that connectionist neural network models could effectively simulate a broad range of psychological phenomena.[8] These models contain mechanisms that are currently accepted but are not widely known to psychologists. This information caused me to think about psychological phenomena, including psychological disorders, in **physical** rather than **mental** terms. The result was a paradigm shift, a major qualitative conceptual change, in my thinking that enabled me to see a way towards theoretical unification, psychotherapy integration, and how to practice psychology as a mature science.

At first I thought mainly about applying this new way of thinking to clinical psychology because I am a clinical psychologist. However, I discovered that my new network orientation has an extensive explanatory scope that covers most, if not all, areas of psychological science. The explanatory scope that I discovered is so large that it includes diverse psychological phenomena that normally would not be discussed together, and that may even appear to be unrelated, random, and disjointed. I did not select these phenomena. Instead, these topics emerged as I explored applications of neural network theory to psychology. I intend to show how these seemingly unrelated phenomena arise from common causes in the form of core and corollary network principles. This extensive explanatory scope is remarkable within psychological science and demonstrates the relevance of this approach to general psychology. It greatly enhances our ability to understand how cognition and affect interact to produce behavior. The diversity of topics covered in this book should be understood as strength rather than as weakness. However, a consequence of this topical diversity is that it poses some transition problems.

I refer to my new conceptual orientation as a **Bio↔Psychology Network Theory**. It is a hybrid cognitive neuroscience theory that integrates neuroscience and connectionist mechanisms, well-replicated psychological phenomena, and multivariate statistics. It focuses on well-replicated phenomena because no theory should be expected to explain spurious false-positive findings. Faced with terms such as biopsychology and psychobiology, I chose to hyphenate Bio↔Psychology with a double-headed arrow to emphasize the interactive nature of biology and psychology. I chose to place Bio in the first position to emphasize that biology is the base from which Psychology emerges. The proposed Bio↔Psychology Network Theory

[8] Bressler (2002) discussed the relevance of large-scale cortical networks for understanding cognition. LeDoux (2002) wrote a book entitled *Synaptic self: How our brains become who we are*. Seung (2012) wrote a book entitled *Connectome: How the brains wiring makes us who we are*. Sporns (2011) wrote a book entitled *Networks of the brain* to show how network science enables us to better understand the link between brain structure and brain function.

explains psychological phenomena in **physical** rather than **mental** terms using a combination of widely accepted neuroscience and connectionist neural network mechanisms[9] and multivariate statistics. It constitutes a **paradigm shift** (Kuhn, 1962, 1970, 1996, 2012) to a mature science because it provides a vocabulary and a set of basic concepts that is common to both psychology and neuroscience. This radical reorientation makes psychology more consilient (Wilson, 1998) with neuroscience. The proposed Bio↔Psychology Network Theory consists of four **core** and eight **corollary network principles**. The core principles constitute an **explanatory nucleus** because they always work together during every network processing cycle and cannot be separated. The neural network **cascade** is fundamental to the explanatory nucleus. It **transforms** physical stimuli into psychological concepts. Experience-dependent plasticity mechanisms are activated by the network cascade and physically modify our neural networks, thereby causing them to process differently, thus enabling us to adapt to our physical and social environments. Many such processing cycles generate psychological development. I also formulated eight derivative **corollary principles** that in various combinations and in conjunction with the explanatory nucleus explain a greater diversity of psychological phenomena than I ever imagined was possible.

Each of these network principles was constructed from well-established neuroscience facts and well-replicated psychological phenomena. The resulting Bio↔Psychology Network Theory is therefore already strongly supported by empirical findings long accepted by experimental psychologists and neuroscientists, and is consequently ready to be used today. While further research is always welcome, no further empirical support is needed to warrant our acceptance and use of these principles today. I understand that science is never finished and that additional research is always needed but the extent of contemporary support for each of the 12 network principles strongly suggests that this future research will only refine rather than reject them.

Castonguay and Beutler (2006) used a lesser meaning of the term 'principle' to refer to facts capable of guiding clinical practice such as 'Age is a negative predictor of a patient's response to general psychotherapy'

[9] The front page of *The New York Times* on November 24, 2012 carried an article entitled 'Learning Curve: No Longer Just a Human Trait' by John Markoff that reported on recent progress made by '… deep-learning programs, often called artificial neural networks or just "neural nets" for their resemblance to the neural connections in the brain' (p. A1). These developments alone constitute timely and convincing evidence that this book is on the right track.

(Beutler et al. 2006, p. 27), and 'The more impaired or severe and disruptive the problem, the fewer benefits are noted for time-limited treatments' (Beutler et al. 2006b, p. 112). I counted 216 of these statements across 17 chapters in their book *Principles of Therapeutic Change That Work.* While useful in guiding clinical practice, these are not scientific principles like Archimedes's principle or Bernoulli's principle (http://en.wikipedia.org/wiki/Scientific_law) because they carry no explanatory power, they cannot explain why things work, and therefore cannot facilitate theoretical unification. Greben (2012) cited the following integrative principles regarding psychotherapy: respect, flexibility, inclusion, attention to common factors, patient–treatment matching, stage–treatment matching, and empiricism. While useful in facilitating cooperation among psychotherapists, these are also not scientific principles like Archimedes's principle or Bernoulli's principle. The core and corollary principles presented and elaborated in this book are scientific principles that enable scientific explanation because they carry explanatory force.

Attempts to achieve theoretical unification may seem grandiose and improbable, primarily because theoretical unification is thought to entail an unreachable end-point of near perfection that fully accommodates all conflicting and even contradictory points of view. Clearly, it is not possible to give everyone everything that they want. I therefore now substantially lower this bar, thereby creating a much more modest, realistic, and attainable goal.

It is important for the reader to understand what theoretical unification in psychology is in my view and what it is not. Theoretical unification in psychology need **not** refer to a terminal state of completely correct knowledge that everyone rigidly believes in to the point where dissenting opinions are unwelcomed and not tolerated by authoritarian overseers. Theoretical unification need **not** mean that the theory is completely correct. Theoretical unification can and has been wrong as it was when everyone once thought that the Earth was flat, and again when everyone thought that the Earth was the center of all creation. Theoretical unification can also be partly wrong, or partly correct, depending upon one's perspective, as was the case for Newtonian physics before Einstein. Theoretical unification also does **not** mean that every idea suggested by every theoretician is included. Some concepts are left behind when a science matures. For example, questions and concepts that were highly valued by alchemists were abandoned when chemistry matured as a science. Theoretical unification need only incorporate well-replicated findings because no theory should be asked to explain spurious false-positive findings. Replication is the only way to ensure that findings are not spurious.

Makel et al. (2012) documented that the overall replication rate in psychology is just 1.07%. Chabris et al. (2012) reported that most replications fail. Our exclusive focus on well-replicated psychological findings makes achieving theoretical unification much easier.

Theoretical unification in psychology is about **consensus** regarding **common vocabulary and core concepts** that are sufficient to enable a majority of psychologists to start working together rather than in mutual isolation and/or at competitive cross purposes. Theoretical unification can be a beginning as well as an ending point. Whether or not theoretical unification occurs is determined by personal decisions made by individuals like you to adopt a common vocabulary and core concepts. No committee or authoritarian body can make this determination or enforce it afterwards. If a working majority of us can agree on a shared perspective that enables us to work together then theoretical unification will have been achieved.

The first reason why I believe that theoretical unification is possible is because we are already unified in our ignorance regarding how psychological processes work. All contemporary psychological theories have nothing to say about the physical mechanisms that cause psychological phenomena. Therefore they do not have entrenched contradictory positions to resolve. They have nothing to give up. This is a major step towards theoretical unification. The only remaining barrier to theoretical unification is achieving at least provisional acceptance of the four core and eight corollary network mechanisms that constitute the proposed Bio↔Psychology Network Theory.

The second reason why I believe that theoretical unification is possible is because the proposed Bio↔Psychology Network Theory provides the only contemporary way to explain psychological phenomenon, including psychological disorders in **physical** rather than **mental** terms. No other psychological theory does this. Absent competition, the quest for theoretical unification simplifies to considering reasons for and against adopting the hybrid connectionist and neuroscience mechanisms presented in this book. I aim to convince you that the reasons for adopting the proposed Bio↔Psychology Network Theory far outweigh the reasons against adopting it.

I do not claim completeness, because I know that there is much more to learn than what I offer in this book. I present **a** Bio↔Psychology Network Theory, not **the** Bio↔Psychology Network Theory. This is why I ask only for provisional acceptance of the core and corollary principles, although I think that the evidence I will present warrants full acceptance now. The empirical base supporting each principle is so substantial that subsequent research is unlikely to undercut or falsify any of them. The neuroscience and connectionist mechanisms that I have selected have been firmly established and are currently accepted without question. I therefore believe that the 12 network principles that constitute the proposed Bio↔Psychology Network Theory meet the modest standard that I have set for theoretical unification and warrants contemporary consensus as a mutually beneficial starting point to better understand how cognition and affect interact to produce behavior and to develop psychology into a mature science.

I view this book as a beginning; a start in a new direction; an example of how we should be thinking about psychology and about how cognition and affect interact to produce behavior in physical rather than mental terms. This caveat is aimed mainly at readers who might reject this orientation because of its incompleteness rather than its potential. Instead, I ask that they consider whether or not progress to date and promise of more to come warrants their support.

I also aim to change the way psychologists identify themselves. For example, adopting the proposed Bio↔Psychology Network Theory will enable clinical psychologists to identify with principles of psychological science rather than with people. Religions, philosophies, cults, and preparadigmatic sciences identify with people. Mature sciences identify with principles. Psychologists will also have no further need of 'isms', such as behaviorism and cognitivism. They can refer to themselves as clinical psychologists NOS (not otherwise specified) or as **clinical science psychologists**. I aim to restore clinical psychology to a principle-based practice from its current manual-based practice while preserving its evidence-based approach. I aim to provide a perspective that helps us to better understand how cognition and affect interact to produce behavior.

I am a clinical psychologist and much of this book is therefore directed towards the professional practice of psychology. Clinicians who understand psychology and psychopathology from the same perspective are more likely to treat their clients in similar ways. I aim to provide sufficient mechanism information to provide the required common understanding for psychotherapy integration to occur. I also address general issues that should concern all psychologists because I ground clinical psychology in psychological science.

PREVIEW

In this section terms that refer to major section headings are emboldened and italicized terms refer to minor section headings contained in the remainder of this chapter. Chapters 1 and 2 jointly establish the breadth and scope of our explanatory problem and discuss previous efforts to address it. The main purpose of this first chapter is to convince you that psychological theories lack causal **mechanism** information capable of explaining psychological phenomena in **physical** rather than **mental** terms. This includes our ability to explain why and how our empirically supported treatments work. A related purpose of this first chapter is to document and discuss our present state of theoretical **disunification** and several serious resulting problems in order to show why we need a more unified psychological theory. More than 40 years of teaching graduate clinical psychology students has convinced me that to accomplish these goals I must discuss a variety of **preliminary issues**. My aim in this preview is to provide reasons why I need to address these topics.

The first preliminary issue concerns the *clinical relevance* of my Bio↔Psychology Network Theory because I expect that most of my readers are interested in clinical psychology and this is the first topic that comes to most of their minds. The second preliminary issue concerns *reductionism* and its explanatory complement *emergence* because reductionism is such an emotional issue that the mere hint of it is enough to put off some readers. Therefore I take this opportunity to emphasize that emergence saves us from the ravages of reductionism; emergence is the antithesis, co-equal, and explanatory complement of reductionism.

I document **theoretical disunification** within psychological science and clinical psychology to emphasize the shabby state that we are currently in with regard to theory construction. I assume that most psychologists are aware of this mess, but I discuss this topic because I understand that some psychologists don't see any problem here at all. Unless a reader is concerned over disunification they have no motivation to fix it. I therefore need to generate the required motivation.

The section on our **need for explanation** is aimed at showing that people, including psychologists and their clients, have an inborn strong desire/need to explain phenomena and that this need drives interest in theory construction, theory selection, and mode of clinical practice. I subsequently show that the way empirically supported treatments are practiced and marketed interferes with the scholarly motive for doing psychotherapy and are consequently resisted by many clinicians.

The section on **theoretical issues** is where I discuss 13 topics that stem from and relate to our theoretical disunification. I elaborate upon *three explanatory problems*: (a) our toothbrush problem; (b) our mini-theories with their narrow explanatory scope; and (c) the absence of causal mechanism information that seriously limits our ability to explain psychological phenomena and why empirically supported treatments work. I identify *three defective psychological models* that are commonly used and mistaken for providing legitimate mechanistic explanations of psychological phenomena. They are: (a) ingredient models; (b) box and arrow models; and (c) statistical models. These considerations reveal *two theoretical anomalies*: (a) that our functional theories lack mechanism information; and (b) there is no psychological substrate for psychological causes to operate on. I consider *three possible resolutions* of these anomalies: (a) recall the request for mechanism information that revealed the anomalies in the first place; (b) deny that the anomalies are anomalous; and (c) ignore the anomalies and continue with psychological science as usual. Then I consider *what constitutes legitimate mechanisms*. This leads to a discussion about *integration with neuroscience* and my case for *why psychology needs neuroscience* or at least *why psychology needs some form of network theory*. Neuroscience entails reductionism because it identifies biological mechanisms. However, even a total understanding of these mechanisms constitutes but half of a complete explanation. Psychology must show how mind and behavior emerge from brain function. Emergence is the antithesis and co-equal of reductionism. *Emergence is the explanatory complement of reductionism*. I compare and contrast *cognitive science, neuroscience, and cognitive neuroscience*, favoring the latter perspective.

Finally, I document that **psychology departments are changing their names** in response to the integration of psychology and neuroscience. I take this as serious evidence that psychology is changing in fundamental ways that are discussed and promoted in this book.

PRELIMINARY ISSUES

Clinical Relevance

While it is the goal of all sciences to understand the unity of nature, many of my clinical colleagues seem to be more focused on what concrete practical benefits might result from theoretical unification. I am frequently asked: **what will my clinical practice look like if I endorse the proposed Bio↔Psychology Network Theory? How will my clinical practice change? How can the Bio↔Psychology Network Theory help me to become a better therapist?** I briefly state my responses here and elaborate them in Chapter 12.

1. The way that you think about yourself, your primary professional identity, will change. You will primarily identify with **principles** rather

than **persons** such as august psychologists like Freud, Skinner, Rogers, Beck, Ellis, etc. You will dissociate yourself from all 'isms', such as behaviorism and cognitivism.

2. You will start thinking about psychology and your client's problems in **physical** rather than **mental** terms. This understanding will make seeking treatment more socially acceptable to your clients. It will also increase their tolerance of family members with psychological and/or behavioral disorders. Psychologists who practice in medical settings can now correctly claim to provide biological treatments.
3. Your clinical practice will become more **comprehensive** in at least the following four ways. (a) Your therapeutic goals will expand to include increasing psychological mindedness and emotional regulation in addition to symptom reduction/removal. (b) You will be open to all ESTs regardless of the orientation from which they were developed. (c) You will use multiple ESTs as necessary. (d) You will have a theoretical basis for this eclectic practice.
4. You will base your interventions on the core and corollary principles introduced in Chapters 3 and 4 rather than on manuals. You will customize your interventions to your clients in the way described by Paul (1967) during the early days of behavior therapy. Greene (2012) cited the contemporary trend to replace manuals with principles as an important rapprochement between investigators and clinicians.
5. Interventions based on operant and respondent conditioning will be reauthorized as cognitive-behavioral therapies.

Case Formulation

The following case is intended to illustrate what it means to think about psychological problems in physical rather than mental terms. I consulted on a case where a 16-year-old girl was arrested because of a physical altercation with her father at home. This led to her being placed in a local institution for delinquent youth under court order where she was diagnosed with conduct disorder. Her father was angry with her on the basis that she was just being difficult with him and defiant of his authority. Her father's anger at her, his insensitivity towards her was based on his misunderstanding of her problem in mental rather than physical terms. He thought that her behavior towards him was something she could just change because it was mental not physical. Given her explosive outbursts and major mood swings I recognized that she was suffering from borderline personality disorder.

Her father asked me what was causing her to behave this way. Notice, I said that he asked me for an **explanation** of his daughter's condition. Fortunately, I had just developed the proposed Bio↔Psychology Network Theory to a point where it enabled me to tell him that his daughter likely had a mirror neuron deficit that gave rise to alexithymia; a condition where people have feelings without words for them. He could see that having feelings that she could not describe, or talk about was very frustrating for her. It was also the basis of her not being able to work conflicts out the way normal people do. Talking to her about feelings is like discussing what color to paint a wall with a color-blind person, or talking about intentions with a person who has Asperger's syndrome. Rendering her condition in physical terms enabled her father to see that she was not just being oppositional because she was a teenager. He became more patient, and stopped blaming her when he realized this was an involuntary physical problem on her part. He could also see that her problem was more general and not specific to him. This insight enabled him to be much more understanding of her disability and to calm down in his approach to her. It also reframed her condition from an acute problem to a chronic illness. It enabled him to understand and accept that she needed dialectical behavior therapy and that such treatment typically takes a long time. Like social skills treatment for children with Asperger's, the best outcome that could be expected is that she would be better able to constructively cope with her mirror neuron deficit and resulting alexithymia. Once the correct assessment was provided, she was able to receive the appropriate treatment for her condition and her father was able to take a productive and supportive role because of his new understanding of her condition. Now her family is on board with her treatment and she seems to be responding positively.

Freud's Project for a Scientific Psychology

It seems to be little known that before developing his famous theory, Freud attempted to explain psychology in physical terms. This was a natural course of action for him because Freud was trained as a neurologist in medical school by the prominent physiologist Ernst Brücke (1819–1892) who then led the scientific movement known as Helmholtz's School of Medicine. Jones (1961) reported that in 1842 Brücke pledged a solemn oath along with his colleague Emil Du Bois-Reymond (1818–1896) to accept and provide only natural science explanations. Brücke strongly influenced Freud's approach to medicine. Rychlak (1981b, pp. 43–44) reported that

Breuer and Fleiss also encouraged Freud to develop a theory of psychology based entirely on biology. Freud (1895b) complied with these exhortations and wrote the first three chapters of *The Project for a Scientific Psychology* between September and October of 1895. Lothane (2006) tells us that Freud characterized his book as 'a psychology for neurologists' (p. 48) which also included neuroscientists. Freud mailed his manuscript to Fleiss in October of 1895 and never spoke of it again (Rychlak, 1981a, p. 176). Freud could not complete his *Project* due to the limitations of neuroscience in 1895.

Centonze et al. (2004) documented that Freud was aware of the work of Camillo Golgi, whose stain allowed single neurons to be visualized for the first time in 1873, and the work of Ramon y Cajal who proved the existence of synapses in 1873. Centonze et al. (2004) also reported that Freud anticipated the now well-documented fact that memory is based on synaptic modification. Spitzer (1999, p. 5) presented a figure of a neural network drawn by Freud in 1895.[9a] I believe that the book you are reading now is the book that Freud wanted to write but could not due to the scientific limits of his day. This book also describes psychology in physical rather than mental terms that were unavailable to Freud. Hence, this book continues Freud's original work.

Science Relevance

Psychologists engaged primarily in research may already appreciate the value that theoretical unification brings to every science, including psychological science. It is the goal of every science, to discover the unity in nature. However, some psychologists may worry that the theoretical unification I aim to bring will disrupt and conflict with the research that they wish to pursue. I am sometimes asked: **How will theoretical unification change the psychological science that I am interested in and already doing?** My general answer is that the fact-finding nature of psychological research can continue unchanged with one major exception. Methodological replication will be needed to be funded and published much more than is presently the case if psychology is to become a mature science. I mainly seek to change that part of psychological science that concerns explanation. I seek to change how we explain the facts and functional relationships that psychologists find and replicate. I also seek to introduce new methods aimed at understanding how psychology emerges from biology (see Chapter 6).

[9a] This figure is reproduced just before the beginning of this chapter..

Reductionism vs. Emergence

Students frequently ask '**Is your Bio↔Psychology Network Theory a reductionist theory?'** My answer is yes and no. The proposed Bio↔Psychology Network Theory recognizes that the first half of a complete explanation entails identifying the biological parts, processes, and mechanisms that mediate psychological phenomena. But a complete catalog of such things cannot explain how they produce psychological phenomena. Some assembly is always required. Isolated biological facts cannot explain how psychology emerges from biology. Emergence is the **explanatory complement** of reductionism. Emergence is the science of understanding how complexity arises from the interaction of simple parts. For example, the proposed Bio↔Psychology Network Theory considers how conditioning and cognition arise from networks of interconnected layers of simple neurons. Emergence provides a way for existentialists to endorse the proposed Bio↔Psychology Network Theory because it deals with **transcendence**; how psychology transcends biology in ways studied by human science. I have more to say about this crucial topic in Chapter 2.

THEORETICAL DISUNIFICATION

Psychology was a disorganized science when William James published his *Principles of Psychology* in 1890 and little progress has been made to date. I expect that many readers of this book agree with this claim and therefore my burden of proof here is light because the evidence of the fragmentation of our science and profession is both extensive and obvious. But not all readers think that disunification is bad. Some readers even think that disunification is good and should be preserved, and that theoretical unification should be opposed.

Is Disunification Healthy or Corrosive?

McNally (1992) asserted that theoretical diversity is a sign of health rather than illness and noted that contemporary diversity within psychology is analogous to speciation within biology; i.e., where variation produces new viable forms. While diversity can be a sign of vigor and good health, too much of a good thing can be bad. Diversity for the sake of diversity justifies as many theoretical positions as there are, or will ever be, psychologists. If they all share nothing in common there will be no field of psychology. At some point seeking diversity must give way to finding common ground. To be for theoretical unification is not to be against diversity. It is to be for sufficient common ground that psychologists can begin to work together constructively rather than at cross purposes. Left unchecked, our current course of more and more separatism without limit may completely dissolve our field. Staats (1983) wrote a book regarding the corrosiveness of the current commitment to diversity and separatism.

> Psychology has so many unrelated elements of knowledge with so much mutual discreditation, inconsistency, redundancy, and controversy that abstracting general meaning is a great problem. There is a crisis, moreover, because the disunification feeds on itself and, left unchanged, will continue to grow *(Staats, 1991, p. 899)*.

These comments are over two decades old, and little if any progress has been made to fix this problem. Instead, professional incentives continue to foster separatism to a point where separatism has become corrosive and theoretical unification is actively opposed (see Staats, 1983; Sternberg & Grigorenko, 2001).

Dissolution vs. Integration or Unification

Nearly three decades ago Janet Spence (1987) remarked upon the conclusion of a major doctoral training conference:

> The theme that seems to have almost spontaneously emerged for this conference on graduate training is the issue of **centrifugal** versus **centripetal** tendencies in psychology. Whether psychology is a unitary discipline with a strong central core or a series of relatively independent areas is a question that has implications not only for graduate training but also for the American Psychological Association (APA) as an organization and for psychology as a whole (p. 1052, emphasis added).

Her comments were published just a year before many research-oriented psychologists, including many clinical psychologists, left the American Psychological Association to form the American Psychological Society in 1988, resulting in a major fractionation of organized psychology and evidence that centripetal forces are tearing psychology apart. The subtitle of Spence's (1987) article '**Will the center hold**?' is especially revealing today. I expect that the answer most psychologists would give today is '**what center**?' Spence did not specify what center she was talking about, but having obtained her Ph.D. from the University of Iowa in 1949 where in her dissertation she investigated the effects of anxiety on learning and performance I expect that she was referring to human and animal learning as core psychology. This view is supported by my personal experience where as a first-year graduate student in clinical psychology at Kent State University in 1966 I was required to take ten core courses including a course in animal learning and another in human learning. Learning also featured prominently in other required core courses in abnormal psychology, social psychology, and developmental psychology. Learning was central to the then-new field of behavior therapy. Hence, learning was core psychology for me as it was for the profession in the 1960s. But psychology divorced itself from the study of learning around 1968 (see Tryon, 1995). Learning was subsequently presumed rather than studied by psychologists. How people cognitively processed information became the major focus of study. Inquiry into the basic processes of learning and memory by psychologists was largely abandoned and left to neuroscience. Contemplating Spence's question regarding 'Will the center hold?' the answer now seems quite clearly: '**No, it has not held**'.

A physics analogy is informative. The cosmos is expanding; galaxies are receding from one another at an accelerated rate. One scenario is that this process will continue unabated. The end result is that galaxies will become so distant from one another that light from one will not reach any of the others; i.e., each galaxy will be completely isolated from all others. The American Psychological Association currently has 56 divisions. Division 12 has ten sections. Should all divisions become so fractionated, APA could end up with 560 or more specialized fields. Diversity in methods and findings distance each specialized field of psychology from all others. Unchecked diversity could expand psychology to where each of the potential 560 or more little groups of psychologists are so different from each other that they will have become irrelevant one to another. Readers who view such a result as both extreme and unlikely should perform the following experiment. Select an article from the main journal of any APA division and tally the number of citations that come from the remaining 55 APA divisions. The consistent result is that psychologists rarely cite the work of other psychologists who work outside of their specialized domain. The results are the same if one starts from any article published in any psychology journal. The inescapable conclusion is that psychologists have already become largely irrelevant to each other. Further fractionation does not seem to bode well for the future of psychology as a mature science.

Gardner (1992), Scott (1991), and Slife and Williams (1997) have argued that dissolution of psychology will be the natural end of psychology should the current trend of separatism and fragmentation continue unabated. Kukla

(1992) valued the goal of theoretical unification, but questioned whether psychology could be unified using the following hypothetical scenario:

> For example, consider the empirical lore belonging to the ill-advised science of *bology,* which studies the properties of things that begin with the letter *b.* There is no shortage of empirical work for bologists. They can ascertain whether bisons are benevolent, whether barium is denser than barley water, et cetera. But no one would seriously propose that we apply the philosophy of unified positivism to this domain. The theoretically progressive step in this instance would be to *dissolve* the discipline of bology and to reapportion its empirical results to other sciences that carve nature more closely to its joints (p. 1055, italics in original).

Is psychology like bology? So disparate, fragmented, and diverse that it is ripe for dissolution and the redistribution of its findings to other disciplines because there is no hope of unification? Or, alternatively, will other sciences appropriate psychological findings into their disciplines before psychology can reach maturity as a coherent science with a common vocabulary and knowledge core? The choice to dissolve psychology may not be ours. Our drive towards separatism could do the job for us. Spence (1987) noted:

> In my worst nightmares, I forsee a decimation of institutional psychology as we know it. Human experimental psychologists desert to the emerging discipline of cognitive science; physiological psychologists go happily to departments of biology and neuroscience; industrial/organizational psychologists are snapped up by business schools; and psychopathologists find their home in medical schools. Clinicians, school psychologists, and other health care practitioners have long since gone, training their own in freestanding professional schools or schools of education. Only personality-social psychologists and certain developmental psychologists would have no place else to go. In universities with doctoral programs, departments of psychology would be pale shadows of their former selves, their members outnumbered and outclassed by the natural sciences on the one hand and the humanities on the other hand (pp. 1052–3).

Does any of this sound familiar? The development of new centers to study learning and memory that are unaffiliated with psychology departments is evidence that this shredding and redistribution process is already underway. The following links are to three such programs.[10]

Cacioppo (2007) argued that psychology is a 'hub science' because its findings are relevant to so many other sciences; i.e., psychology functions as a hub and other sciences function as spokes in a wheel of science. Alternatively, the many knowledge products that psychological science has produced can be seen as resources that could well be appropriated by other

[10] http://clm.utexas.edu/, http://www.cnlm.uci.edu/, http://www.iclm.ucla.edu/

sciences. For example, operant and respondent conditioning have become tools for neuroscientists studying memory. Previously standard psychological studies have now become preliminary to conducting fMRI research.

An important part of our theoretical disunification pertains to our models and explanatory mechanisms. We are far from agreement as to what constitutes proper explanatory mechanisms as we shall see in the next section.

Models and Mechanisms

If anything seems, sounds, and feels like a real psychological mechanism to a clinical psychologist it is a **defense mechanism**. Mechanisms by their nature are mechanical. Psychological defense mechanisms are thought to carry the same causal force as physical mechanisms. The mechanical nature of defense mechanisms has been accepted without question since Freud introduced this term.[11] No one has seriously questioned if defense mechanisms are valid psychological mechanisms. That changes right now. The Google command 'define:mechanism' returned the following definition: '(1) A system of parts working together in a machine; a piece of machinery. (2) **A natural or established process by which something takes place or is brought about**'. This second meaning is more relevant to psychology than the first but reveals that defense mechanisms are not mechanisms at all because they do not inform us about the '**process by which something takes place or is brought about'**. Defense mechanisms specify a **functional** effect, but not the causal steps by which that effect is brought about. Defense mechanisms assert **that** something happens but fail to explain **how** that effect occurs by specifying the chain of causal steps that clarifies **why** the functional effect occurs. For example, denial describes that a person refused to acknowledge some fact or event, but does not provide causal details sufficient to explain how this result actually occurs. The same analysis pertains to all other defense mechanisms. None of them inform us about the '**process by which something takes place or is brought about**'. Hence, they are not real mechanisms. One can say that they are 'psychic mechanisms,' but that approach removes them from natural science, the scope of this book, and moves them to the realm of metaphor and literature.

If anything seems, sounds, and feels like a real psychological mechanism to an experimental psychologist it is respondent (classical) and operant (instrumental) **conditioning**. Kirsch (2010, pp. 139–44) used classical conditioning to explain how placebos work. However, classical conditioning

[11] http://en.wikipedia.org/wiki/Defence_mechanisms

concerns a set of procedures for establishing a conditioned response. It does not explain how or why conditioned responses form. The same can be said for operant conditioning. It demonstrates that behavior can be systematically modified, but does not explain how those changes occur by specifying mechanism information that clarifies why behavior changes when reinforced. To ask why a reinforce works is beyond the ability of behaviorism to explain. Neither classical nor operant conditioning inform us about the '**process by which something takes place or is brought about**'. Hence, operant and respondent conditioning are not real mechanisms either. Again, one can say that they are 'psychic mechanisms' because they generate expectations. This defense fails because it offers the functional property of expectation generation as an explanation of how conditioning actually takes place. One functional explanation cannot be used to explain another functional explanation. All functional relationships require explanation in terms of causal steps. We now know many of the physical bases of conditioning, learning, and memory. They are discussed in Chapter 3.

If anything seems, sounds, and feels like a real psychological mechanism to a quantitative psychologist or psychometrician, it is a statistical model such as a structural equation model, path model, or a logistic regression model. Whereas some investigators claim that these models **explain** variation among measured and/or latent variables, it is more accurate to say that they **predict** or **account** for variation among model components. These models do not provide causal mechanism information because they were not designed to do so. They are all based on correlations that cannot prove causation. Statistical models do not specify the causal sequences that give rise to the covariance matrices that they presumably explain. None of these models require random assignment and manipulation; the two defining features of a true experiment which is how causation is demonstrated. None of these models can specify the necessary and/or sufficient conditions for how their identified effects occur, and even if they did identify necessary and sufficient conditions these models could not explain why those conditions and not others are necessary and/or sufficient. **Mediators are not mechanisms**. Hence, statistical models of mediation cannot actually explain why we think, feel, and/or act the way we do. They are several times removed from providing the required mechanism information.

Mechanisms are explained in two ways. (a) Mechanisms entail a sequence of causal events that can be used to show how an observed result came about. (b) Mechanisms have properties that can vary across individuals and within a person over time. These variations can explain variations in observed behavior. For example, nerve growth factor is far more plentiful in infants and children than in adults and elderly people. Such properties causally modify how well the mechanisms of learning and memory work.

This book aims to present as much of the missing mechanism information regarding psychological phenomena as possible within the limitations of a single book and my scholarship. I aim to substantially advance our understanding of how cognition and affect interact to produce behavior in a way that is fully consilient with neuroscience. This includes an explanation of how and why effective treatments work. This latter achievement also advances psychotherapy unification in meaningful ways.

NEED FOR EXPLANATION

The need to understand and explain is as old as myth, legend, and philosophy. Human beings have always had a need to explain the physical and social events that they experience. For example, creation stories have emerged in every culture to explain the origin of the natural world and its inhabitants. Gods and goddesses were imbued with motives that explained, made understandable, events on earth. During bad times in Europe and in Salem MA, the presence of disease and unusual behavior was understood and explained in terms of the devil, witches, incubi,[12] succubi,[13] and pest maidens.[14] The strength of these convictions in Europe motivated the inquisition[15] where untold thousands, perhaps millions, of women were burned alive at the stake. In some villages every woman was burned alive. The 1692 witch hysteria that gripped Salem MA resulted in the deaths of 20 people. Fortunately, the enlightenment,[16] also known as the age of reason, put an end to such thinking and associated barbaric practices, but it did not end our need to explain.

Our irresistible need to explain continues unabated today. Our tolerance for ambiguity and uncertainty is low to non-existent. Our tendency to generate unsubstantiated claims is considerable as long as they appear to explain. We speculate, and sometimes formally hypothesize, but often favor an emotionally congruent position; one where reason justifies how we feel about a topic and other people. Unidentified flying objects

12 http://en.wikipedia.org/wiki/Incubus

13 http://en.wikipedia.org/wiki/Succubus

14 http://jackygilbertson.deviantart.com/art/The-Black-Death-Pest-Maiden-115072829?q=sort%3Atime+gallery%3Ajackygilbertson&qo=10

15 http://en.wikipedia.org/wiki/Inquisition

16 http://en.wikipedia.org/wiki/Age_of_Enlightenment

(UFOs) are not left as unidentified flying objects, but are understood and explained by many as extraterrestrial in origin and manned by aliens. Unidentified means **not** identified, but the strong tendency to render some form of explanation is frequently irresistible. The rise and popularity of pseudoscience illustrates that our need for explanation remains strong and readily rationalizes a wide variety of questionable practices (Lilienfeld et al., 2003). This tendency pertains to clinical psychologists and some uses of projective testing (Lilienfeld et al., 2000). We shall see elsewhere in this book that our need to explain drives a scholarly motive to do psychotherapy that is frustrated by structured diagnostic interviews and manualized treatments.

THEORETICAL ISSUES

To this point I have tried to emphasize the strong need to explain that all people, and especially scientists, have and the disunified way psychologists have gone about explaining cognition, affect, and behavior. I now focus on: (a) our reluctance to build upon theories developed by other psychologists; (b) the narrowness of the theories we construct; and (c) most importantly the absence of mechanism information that psychological science has to offer. This analysis reveals that all psychological theories are functional theories and consequently lack real mechanism information because there is no psychological substrate for such hypothetical mechanisms to operate on. Calls for real mechanism information have revealed two major anomalies that face psychological science with a crisis from which it can either retreat to business as usual, or engage in the recommended paradigmatic shift (Kuhn, 1962, 1970, 1996, 2012).

Three Explanatory Problems

Toothbrush Problem

Our first explanatory problem is that in the absence of general principles, psychologists organized their science around leading investigators and clinicians into competing schools and camps each with its own vocabulary, theoretical orientation, methods, findings, and adherents. Members of each camp even work in relative isolation from each other, as they rarely attempt to replicate the work of other members of their camp. The result is what Kuhn (1962, 1970, 1996, 2012) characterized as preparadigmatic science. Watkins (1984) identified this theoretical diversity as a consequence of our toothbrush problem when he wrote that cognitive theory '... is a bit like someone else's toothbrush – it is fine for that individual's use, but for the rest of us ... well, we would just rather not thank you' (p. 86). Mischel (2009) reiterated that our 'toothbrush problem' was still with us a quarter of a century later when he wrote 'Psychologists treat other peoples' theories like toothbrushes – no self-respecting person wants to use anyone else's' (p. 3). Gigerenzer (2010) subsequently corroborated this problem. Two unfortunate corollaries follow from our toothbrush problem. The first unfortunate corollary of our toothbrush problem is that new investigators are incentivized to repackage discoveries and insights made by previous investigators under new names and without citation in order to appear original. I now provide three disturbing examples of this practice. I expect that other examples exist.[17]

It remains little known that there was a cognitive revolution within psychodynamic psychotherapy that was already about 21 years old when Ellis (1961) wrote his first book on rational emotive psychotherapy, and 47 years old when Tryon (1986) disclosed a remarkable but uncited close parallel between the then-emerging 'new' cognitive behavior therapies and Heinz Hartmann's (1939/1958) ego psychology. Hartmann departed from traditional psychodynamic therapies by putting aside Id/Ego conflicts in favor of focusing on adaptation via the rational problem-solving ego functions of perception, attention, and memory that are responsible for reality testing, impulse control, affect regulation, rational thought, judgment, decision-making, and the ability to develop satisfying relationships with other people. The lack of citation of Hartmann's work is all the more noteworthy given that at least Beck and Ellis were analytically trained at a time not far distant from the publication of Hartmann's book, which means that they almost certainly knew of its existence.[18] Critics may say that this is an isolated event that occurred decades ago but is certainly not happening today.

In response to such doubts I cite the following contemporary example. Tee and Kazantzis (2011, p. 51)[19] discussed the relationship between collaborative empiricism as practiced in cognitive behavior therapy and the working alliance as practiced in psychodynamic therapy. They articulated

[17] Please send additional examples to wtryon@fordham.edu

[18] Albert Ellis received his BA from City University of New York in 1942 and his MA from Teacher's College in 1943 with an emphasis on psychoanalysis. Aaron Beck received his BA from Brown University in 1942 and his MD from Yale Medical School in 1946.

[19] I do not mean to single Tee and Kazantzis out for criticism. Their article just happened to be conveniently available to me at the time I was writing this chapter.

the therapeutic benefits of collaborative empiricism in terms of self-determination theory as follows:

> Self-determination theory states that people have a fundamental propensity toward growth, self-determination, and the resolution of psychological discrepancy *(Deci & Ryan, 1980, 1985; Ryan & Deci, 2000, 2002).*

The 'fundamental propensity toward growth' that they spoke of is pure Carl Rogers (1946), but alas no citation of Roger's work was provided. Rogers (1946) stated:

> But we have not known or recognized that in most if not all individuals there exist growth forces, tendencies toward self-actualization, which may act as the sole motivation for therapy. We have not realized that under suitable psychological conditions these forces bring about emotional release in those areas and at those rates which are most beneficial to the individual. These forces drive the individual to explore his own attitudes and his relationship to reality, and to explore these areas effectively. We have not realized that the individual is capable of exploring his attitudes and feelings, including those which have been denied to consciousness, at a rate which does not cause panic, and to the depth required for comfortable adjustment. The individual is capable of discovering and perceiving, truly and spontaneously, the interrelationships between his own attitudes, and the relationship of himself to reality. The individual has the capacity and the strength to devise, quite unguided, the steps which will lead him to a more mature and more comfortable relationship to his reality. It is the gradual and increasing recognition of these capacities within the individual by the client-centered therapist that rates, I believe, the term discovery. All of these capacities I have described are released in the individual if a suitable psychological atmosphere is provided (p. 418).

Rogers (1946) also wrote:

> The third distinctive feature of this type of therapy is the character of the relationship between therapist and client. Unlike other therapies in which the skills of the therapist are to be exercised upon the client, in this approach the skills of the therapist are focused upon creating a psychological atmosphere in which the client can work (p. 419).

Readers of Tee and Kazantzis (2011), especially students and young professionals, are led to believe that the core concept of self-actualization began with Deci and Ryan rather than Rogers. The motive to be original incentivizes investigators to ignore the historical roots of important psychological constructs. Whereas investigators take care to include the most current citations in their article in order to show that they are on the cutting edge of their field, they frequently ignore the historical basis for the concepts that are central to their theories and findings. Little effort is made to build upon any but the most recent reports. This problem begins in graduate school where so much needs to be learned, typically in just three years, six semesters. The APA-required History and Systems course provides a generic overview of psychology but seems to do little if anything to instill motive to research the origins of one's own field of interest. One might think that opportunities to write master's theses and doctoral dissertations would be a time to do a historical search that could be cited in all future work by the student because history does not change, but alas these documents have become patterned after journal articles where there is little space or reader patience to consider the historical roots of core concepts and properly credit previous generations of scholars.

I try to set a good example. In my 2001 article entitled 'Evaluating statistical difference, equivalence, and indeterminacy using inferential confidence intervals' I cited R. A. Fisher (1925), the person who introduced null hypothesis statistical testing. I also cited later works by Berkson (1942) and Bakan (1966) along with much earlier work by Arbuthnot (1710). In Chapter 4 I begin my brief history of unconscious processing with Galen (c. A.D. 130–200), Spinoza (1632–1677), Wundt (1832–1920), James (1890), and others before getting to Freud (1900/1938) and gradually on to modern times.

Our third and final example of pretending to have discovered something new concerns creating putatively new therapies using elements of existing therapies without acknowledging this fact or crediting the authors of the preexisting therapies. These 'new' therapies are called 'purple hat' therapies because of a hypothetical example provided by Rosen and Davison (2003) where the client is asked to wear a purple hat while engaging in an already-vetted empirically supported treatment. The author of the 'new' therapy attributes successful outcomes to wearing the purple hat. This is currently acceptable practice because the 'new' therapy need only show evidence of efficacy; there is no need to provide evidence of incremental validity for wearing the purple hat. Evidence of efficacy will be met because of the uncited efficacious therapeutic component. The author is entitled to publish reports of this 'new' therapy in top-tier journals and to obtain generous grant support to further investigate its therapeutic effectiveness. We now have over 500 therapies with no end in sight.[20]

The second unfortunate consequence of our toothbrush problem is that investigators are incentivized to develop their 'new' ideas and treatments alongside those of other investigators without citation in order to advance the perception by colleagues that they are an independent investigator.

[20] http://www.scientificamerican.com/article.cfm?id=are-all-psychotherapies-created-equal, http://apt.rcpsych.org/content/7/4/241.full

Dividing larger professional groups into divisions and then further dividing them into sections or special interest groups that meet separately and publish their own journals and newsletters facilitates opportunities for **parallel research** and legitimizes denials of awareness of what other investigators are doing. Mischel (2008) commented that we are 'building a Terminological Tower of Babel across the sub-fields and disciplines that cements their disconnect, carving nature at unnatural joints'.[21] These practices conflict with creating a cumulative science because they avoid connecting one's work with that of others. Mischel emphasized that new investigators are incentivized to avoid the work of others in order to appear original, as this is needed for publishing in top-tier journals, for obtaining grants, and for obtaining positive reappointment and tenure decisions. In short, our current system selects for separatism by excluding those who don't support it.

Kruglanski (2001) directly addressed the issue of what he called 'theory shyness' (p. 871) in social psychology which he referred to as a reluctance to move beyond midlevel theorization to more comprehensive explanations. His section on reasons for theoretical aversion presents the case made by Merton (1957) against high-level theorizing. The primary argument made by Merton is that high-level theories are difficult to test; i.e., difficult to falsify. A corollary point is that proper theorizing requires a rather complete data set. Kruglanski (2001) noted that the history of science shows that major advances in theory were made prior to much supporting data and that the point of a good theory is to direct empirical inquiry, not to merely summarize existing data.

Kruglanski (2001) recognized that avoiding high-level theorizing is not risk-free but comes with its own problems. They include: (a) inventing new names for old concepts; (b) fragmentation of the discipline; (c) declining interest of published articles; and (d) disconnection with the general public who are more interested in theory than supporting data; i.e., the public assumes that scientists have data to support their theories but want to hear their **explanations** rather than review their methodology and/or evidence.

Gigerenzer (2009) observed that 'much of the theoretical landscape in psychology resembles a patchwork of small territories' (p. 22) that substitute surrogates for theory in the form of one-word explanations, circular restatements, and lists of dichotomies. Such theoretical diversity has been interpreted as a sign of scientific health by some (McNally, 1992) and a crisis with corrosive properties (Staats, 1983) that threatens to tear psychology

[21] http://www.psychologicalscience.org/index.php/publications/observer/2008/december-08/the-toothbrush-problem.html

apart (Spence, 1987) by others. Science values parsimony. All else being equal, we prefer simpler interpretations. Parsimony also extends to theory. All else being equal, we prefer to use fewer theories to explain our facts. Ideally, one theory is best. Introductory psychology textbooks demonstrate that we are far from this ideal. A major goal of this book is to introduce an intellectual perspective comprised of core and corollary principles that can transition psychology into a mature and consilient science (Wilson, 1998). We currently need but do not have a uniform way to understand psychological phenomena.

Grand vs. Mini-Theories

Our second explanatory problem is that our theories and models are narrow and limited to a small part of psychology. For example, the Rescorla–Wagner model of classical conditioning (Rescorla & Wagner, 1972) has been successful within the limited domain of classical conditioning, but classical conditioning is a very minor part of psychological science. The Rescorla–Wagner model of classical conditioning does not even generalize to operant conditioning, which was once thought to be an entirely different phenomenon, let alone generalize to other areas of psychology. Festinger's (1957) theory of cognitive dissonance was highly successful within the subfield of social psychology where it was limited to attitude formation and change. Even during its heyday, Festinger's theory was not used in other areas of social psychology, let alone all other areas of psychological science. It no longer drives nearly so much research as it once did and thus its present impact is more historical than contemporary. Other examples of mini-theories that have a limited scope can be found in chapters of introductory psychology textbooks. We currently need but do not have any overarching theory that pertains generally to psychological science.

Psychology went through a **Grand Theory** period from roughly 1900 through 1950 where various attempts were made to construct an overarching theory capable of guiding psychological science. At least two groups of theorists can be discerned. People like Hull, Tolman, Thorndike, and Skinner attempted to explain behavior using data from experimental studies of animal learning conducted in laboratories where all or most relevant variables could be controlled. People like Freud (Sigmund and Anna), Jung, Adler, and Allport attempted to explain human behavior and personality using their clinical experience. Jointly, these efforts resulted in different vocabularies and incommensurate basic concepts; a hallmark of immature science (see Kuhn, 1962, 1970, 1996,

2012). Not only did these efforts to create a grand theory fail, but they left psychology with an aversion for overarching theory. The reactionary backlash was to develop mini-theories whose explanatory scope was intentionally restricted to the particular phenomena under study. The creation of mini-theories appeared to be a more practical achievable goal for psychology.

Theory construction is not formally taught. Gigerenzer (2010) noted that whereas students are taught how to test hypotheses, they are not taught how to construct theories. This means that psychologists are left on their own to develop theory in any way that they see fit without benefit of discussion and possible consensus.

Concern over disunification and the desirability of theoretical unification to create a grand theory has been debated for a long time and has important implications for training and practice. Yanchar and Slife (1997) and Yanchar (2004) provided a general review of the relevant issues. Henriques (2003) noted that Meehl (1978/1992) said:

> It is simply a sad fact that in soft psychology theories rise and decline, come and go, more as a function of baffled boredom than anything else; and the enterprise shows a disturbing absence of that *cumulative* character that is so impressive in disciplines like astronomy, molecular biology and genetics (p. 524, italics in original).

Gigerenzer (2009) noted that 'much of the theoretical landscape in psychology resembles a patchwork of small territories' (p. 22) that substitute surrogates for theory in the form of one-word explanations, circular restatements, and lists of dichotomies. He emphasized the need to specify underlying mechanisms. However, the resulting psychological models merely assert functional relationships without providing details, mechanism information, regarding how these functions are implemented. The computational models presented and discussed in this book aim to provide some of this missing mechanism information.

Explanation and prediction are the two primary goals of science. Theory provides explanations. Recent calls for theory to provide mechanism information constitute calls for a better understanding of how treatments work (cf. Carey, 2011). The accreditation requirement established by the American Psychological Association requires that programs instruct students in the cognitive and affective bases of behavior. One course in cognition and another course in affect may technically meet the letter of the accreditation requirements but not its spirit which entails an understanding of how cognitive and affective factors interact to produce behavior. This is a tall order because it requires a comprehensive understanding of psychology and neuroscience. No contemporary psychological theory can adequately explain these interactions, let alone provide plausible proximal causal mechanism information to support them. Psychological science is presently so disunified that only a bewildering variety of mini-theories and conjectures are available and they provide little to no help at all. No textbooks currently exist that address this degree of interactive complexity. This book aims to address this critical need.

No Mechanism Information

Our third explanatory problem is the most serious by far. It is that our theories currently lack mechanism information, including the absence of consensus regarding what constitutes acceptable mechanisms. Anastasi (1958) was among the first psychologists to directly call for mechanism information over half a century ago when she asked psychologists to answer the question of how environments interacted with heredity. Much more recently, Gigerenzer (1998, 2009) requested the identification of mechanisms that mediate the causal relationships included in psychological models. Kazdin (2007) defined mechanism as 'the basis for the effect, i.e., the processes or events that are responsible for the change; the reasons why change occurred or how change came about' (p. 3). Kazdin (2008) clarified his position: 'By mechanisms, I refer to the processes that explain why therapy works or how it produces change' (p. 151). Kazdin (2008) further clarified his view of mechanism by showing how it requires more than demonstrating a causal link.

> The distinction between cause and mechanism is readily conveyed with the familiar example of cigarette smoking. Cross-sectional and longitudinal studies with humans and experiments with non-human animals have established a causal relation between cigarette smoking and lung cancer. Establishing a causal relation does not explain the mechanisms, that is, the process(es) through which lung cancer develops. The mechanism was shown by describing what happens in a sequence from smoking to mutation of cells into cancer (Denissenko et al., 1996). A chemical (benzo[*a*] pyrene) found in cigarette smoke induces genetic mutation at specific regions of the DNA that is identical to the damage evident in lung cancer cells. This finding conveys how cigarette smoking leads to cancer. The example is one from biology, but biology is not critical to the larger point. Mechanisms of action come from psychological influences as well. For example, the role of corporal punishment in the development and amelioration of child aggression has been demonstrated in cross-sectional and longitudinal

observational studies as well as intervention studies (e.g., Patterson et al., 1992; Reid et al., 2002) (pp. 151–2).

Curiously, Kazdin's second example is not parallel to his first example. While he provided a causal mechanism for cigarette smoking as a cause of cancer, he did not provide a causal mechanism for corporal punishment as a cause of child aggression. The research that Kazdin cited may demonstrate the **causal** role of corporal punishment in the development and amelioration of child aggression, but it does not meet either the previously established definition of **mechanism** that requires knowledge of a '**process by which something takes place or is brought about**,' or Kazdin's own distinctions between cause and mechanism.

The aims and scope of Kazdin's new journal *Clinical Psychological Science* stated on 16 August 2013: 'Among the key topics are research on the **underlying mechanisms** and etiologies of psychological health and dysfunction…' (emphasis added).[22] Squire et al. (1993) stipulated: 'Ultimately, one wants to understand cognition not just as an abstraction, or in terms that are simply plausible or internally consistent. Rather, one wants to know as specifically and concretely as possible how the job is actually done'. (p. 454). Tryon (2012) concluded that 'A mechanism therefore consists of a sequence of causal events that are either necessary or sufficient to bring about the imputed result' (p. 306).

Claims are frequently made about the availability of psychological mechanism information. A PsychInfo search on 26 September 2013 for the term 'mechanism' returned 176,385 results. A PsychInfo search on the same date for the term 'psychological mechanism' returned 2,134 citations. Of special note is the cover of the January 2012 issue of the *Association for Psychological Science Observer* (Volume 25, Number 1) that presented a picture of a human head with several interlocking gears inside the brain area. The associated text reads 'The mechanics of choice'. The table of contents identified the featured article by Wargo (2012) and its title '*The inner workings of decision-making*'. Additional text stated 'After years of tinkering, psychological scientists are figuring out how the gears turn when we make decisions'. Unfortunately, the actual article does not contain any mechanism information that satisfies the definition of mechanism provided above. The following section documents the generality of this problem.

[22] http://www.psychologicalscience.org/index.php/publications/journals/clinical/aims

Three Defective Psychological Models

Ingredient Models

Psychological science recognizes the important roles played by biological, social (culture), and psychological factors in both normal and abnormal development. The popularity of the BioPsychoSocial (BPS) model is documented by a PsychInfo search. Using the term 'biopsychosocial', to allow for articles referring to a 'biopsychosocial approach' as well as to a 'biopsychosocial model', returned 6,028 citations on 26 September 2013. While the BPS model appears to be comprehensive, it is uninformative because it only lists biological, psychological, and social factors without any consideration of how these factors interrelate and/or cause behavior. This model is merely an unstructured list of ingredients. It does not provide any mechanism information. It has the same explanatory value as does a GlassMetalPetroleum (GMP) model of how automobiles work. We should therefore avoid referring to such lists of ingredients as a 'model' of anything, because to do so only augments our illusion of understanding (Lilienfeld, 2012).

Box and Arrow Models

Placing the names of biological, social, and psychological variables in boxes and drawing arrows among these boxes to impute causality adds theoretical structure but does not provide any causal mechanism information. The arrows beg the question of how the functionality they imply is actually implemented in either the mind or the brain. The main contribution of box and arrow models is to augment our illusion of understanding (Lilienfeld, 2012).

Statistical Models

Whereas most 'box and arrow' models are based only on theory, structural equation models (SEMs), path, and regression models are based on data as well as theory. In structural equation models theoretical latent constructs are represented with ovals or circles and their measured empirical indicators are represented with rectangles. The lines connecting indicators to constructs and constructs to each other carry numerical values that quantify the degree of covariation accounted for by the model components. Various indices are used to evaluate how well the model fits the data, including how well the model reproduces the variances and covariances used to construct it. Whereas some investigators claim that SEMs **explain** variation among latent variables; it is more accurate to say that SEMs **predict** or **account** for variation among model components. SEMs do not provide causal mechanism information because they were not designed to do so. The same is true for path and regression models. SEMs, path and regression[23] models cannot specify the required causal mechanism information because: (a) they are all based on correlations that cannot prove causation; (b) they cannot explain how and why the variances and covariances have their observed values. They are silent with regard to the causal sequences that produced the observe variances and covariances; (c) they cannot specify the necessary and/or sufficient conditions for how their identified effects occur; and (d) even if they identified necessary and sufficient conditions, statistical models cannot explain why those conditions and not others are necessary and/or sufficient. Statistical moderators are not mechanisms, despite the strong suggestion that they are by Arch and Craske (2008). Moderators and mediators are not mechanisms. Statistical models are several times removed from explaining psychological phenomena via physical mechanisms. In short, statistical models do not identify sequences of causal events that are either necessary or sufficient to bring about the imputed result, they do not clarify the '**process by which something takes place or is brought about**' and therefore they do not provide proximal causal mechanism information. To conclude otherwise merely fosters our illusion of understanding (Lilienfeld, 2012). Structural equation models are also limited by the ever-present possibility of **model misspecification**; i.e., that alternative models might fit, and predict, as well or better than the advocated model.

Two Theoretical Anomalies

Calls for real mechanism information have revealed two major anomalies that face psychological science with a crisis from which it can retreat to business as usual or engage in the recommended paradigmatic shift (Kuhn, 1962, 1970, 1996, 2012).

Functional Theories Lack Mechanism Information

The first anomaly is that all functional theories/explanations, including those generated so far by psychologists, by definition lack mechanism information. For example, explanations based on reinforcement are claims based on systematic changes in the observed frequency, probability, of behavior following the onset/offset of some event or stimulus. How and why these functional relationships occur is never explained. That requires identifying one or more mechanisms whose properties compel the functional

[23] See Monshouwer et al. (2012) as an example of investigators who mistakenly claim that logistic regression provides mechanism information.

relationship. In this case, the neuroscience mechanism of experience-dependent plasticity explains why reinforcement works: (a) presynaptic terminals may release more neurotransmitter; (b) the number of postsynaptic receptors may increase; and/or (c) present receptors may become more responsive to neurotransmitter (Lombroso & Ogren, 2008, 2009). Structural changes may also occur. Dendritic spines may increase in length (Bear et al., 2007) and/or other spines may grow at the same location (Lombroso & Ogren, 2008, 2009). These mechanisms explain why reinforcement works the way that it does. The mechanisms that mediate psychological phenomena are biological, not psychological.

Psychological explanations are assertions about causal sequences for which no mechanism information is provided. What passes for a psychological explanation is just a claim that one or more functional relationships hold without specifying the physical basis regarding how and why these functional relationships work as they do. Psychological explanations do not actually explain anything because they lack the required mechanism information to show how and why the stipulated functional relationships exist. This makes psychology a soft science. Hard science requires identifying a mechanism whose properties compel the claimed functional relationships.

Biology was once in the same position as psychology is currently in. Darwin's theory of evolution by natural selection began as a functional theory because it was initially published prior to any knowledge of population genetics. Biologists immediately rejected Darwin's theory because it was only a functional theory; because it was based only on associations and covariations. Darwin did not have, and therefore could not present, any proximal causal mechanism information regarding how and why species varied, nor could he provide any proximal causal mechanism information concerning how natural selection worked. He could not **explain** what produced variation and how it actually got selected. Mayr (1982) documented that biologists resisted or rejected Darwin's functional theory for approximately 75 years because his functional theory lacked the required mechanism information; see Tryon (1993b) for further details. Full acceptance of Darwin's theory by the scientific community did not occur until population genetics provided the required proximal causal mechanism information. This made a huge difference. It promoted Darwin's evolutionary theory to a position of preeminence as the theoretical cornerstone and basis of modern biology.

Skinner (1981, 1984a, 1984b) patterned his functional theory of behavior after Darwin's functional theory. He proposed that behavioral variations exist and are selected by events that follow the emission or omission of behavior. Skinner referred to these increases in the probability of behavior as **reinforcement**, but he could not explain why reinforces altered the probability of behavior because he lacked the required proximal causal mechanism information. That behaviors could be reinforced was demonstrated in the laboratory to everyone's satisfaction. Skinner used reinforcement to explain why some behaviors occur more frequently than others. Like Darwin's initial theory, Skinner's explanation was a functional one because it lacked plausible proximal causal mechanism information regarding how reinforcement works. Cognitive psychologists labeled Skinner's functional explanation a 'black box' theory because he could not explain what went on inside of the person. Skinner admitted that he did not have the requisite tools to answer these questions and suggested that they be left for neuroscience to answer; see Tryon (1993b) for further details. Cognitive psychologists rejected this approach, insisting that they could provide the required explanation of these internal events. Sadly, as we have seen, their explanations take the form of ingredients models, box and arrow models, and statistical models, all of which lack the required mechanism information. Skinner (1977) anticipated this problem when he asked 'Why I am not a cognitive psychologist?'

Functional theories provide an excellent basis for behavioral technology because they consist of lawful relationships. That they cannot explain why these relationships hold in no way limits their clinical utility. A highly effective and empirically supported behavior modification technology was built on the functional relationships discovered by Skinner's experimental analysis of behavior. Curiously, this empirically supported behavior change technology was seriously marginalized by clinical psychologists during the cognitive revolution in psychology (Bandura, 1978; Dember, 1974; Gardner, 1985; Mahoney, 1974, 1977; Meichenbaum, 1977) that replaced behaviorism with cognitivism as the dominant explanatory orientation in psychology. The presence of massive supporting empirical evidence of the efficacy and effectiveness of behavioral phenomena and treatments could not keep applied behavior analysis within the mainstream of clinical psychology. It is ironic that the push for, and promise of, psychological mechanism information that inspired the cognitive revolution failed to provide any proximal causal mechanism information. The behaviorist's black box was replaced by functional statements of relationships among hypothetical entities that could not explain those relationships because they lacked proximal causal mechanism information. Why has psychology failed so completely to identify causal mechanisms? The shocking answer is presented in the next section.

No Psychological Substrate

Mechanisms require some form of substrate to operate on. Google defines **substrate** as 'A substance or layer that underlies something, or **on which some process occurs**' (bold emphasis added). The search for mechanism information has led psychologists into a **double denial** that reveals a **second fundamental anomaly** in psychological science; the absence of a psychological substrate for mechanisms to operate on. On the one hand, psychologists deny that psychological mechanisms are entirely mental. Psychologists argue this way to preserve their identity as natural scientists. Otherwise, their psychological mechanisms could be viewed as mere metaphor or philosophical musing if they were purely mental mechanisms. On the other hand, psychologists deny that psychological mechanisms are entirely biological. They do this to avoid, and guard against what Dennett (1995, p. 82) described and Lilienfeld (2007) referred to as **greedy reductionism**; the systematic effort to replace psychology with neuroscience (see Miller, 2010; Miller & Keller, 2000). The alternative less aggressive form of reductionism identified by Dennett (1995, p. 82) is **eliminative reductionism**; a nebulous claim that somehow all psychological events are biological events. Notice the absence of proximal causal mechanism information for how biology gives rise to psychology. This book addresses the question of emergence later in this chapter and in Chapter 2. This double denial reveals that all psychological models make the crucial assumption that some sort of **psychological substrate** exists that enables presumed psychological mechanisms to operate on.

The second anomaly arises from the fact that there is no supporting evidence for the existence of a psychological substrate. It is difficult to imagine a more stark contrast between theory and fact than that between the crucial assumption that an actual psychological substrate exists upon which psychological processes such as thoughts, symbol manipulations, and feelings interact to somehow cause behaviors and the complete lack of evidence for such a substrate. One is reminded of the explanatory role once played by aether/ether; a hypothetical, now considered mythical, material that once was thought to constitute a causal substrate for moving objects. This book is based on the premise that there is no psychological substrate upon which psychological causation intervenes. Such a substrate is no more real than **humanellium**, a hypothetical element that explains human thoughts, feelings, and behavior. Therefore, I conclude that there are no psychological mechanisms per se, nor can there be any such mechanisms because there is no psychological substrate for them to operate on.

A corollary implication is that psychologists should quit wasting time and resources looking for psychological mechanisms that cannot possibly exist. I am **not** supporting reductionism here. On the contrary, I vigorously oppose reductionism (see below) as a complete explanation because I support **emergence** which is the **antithesis of reductionism** and constitutes its explanatory complement. A key theme of this book concerns how psychological phenomena emerge from functioning neural networks. While our neural networks implement biological mechanisms, psychology emerges from them in a way that cannot be reduced to these biological mechanisms. Psychology depends on, is about, entails, emergent mechanisms. Emergence creates new properties. For example, water is constructed from hydrogen and oxygen gases, but the properties of water cannot be explained by the properties of either gas. Table salt, which is necessary for life, is constructed from two poisons; the elements sodium and chlorine. But the properties of salt cannot be explained by the properties of either sodium or chlorine. I resist further efforts to identify psychological mechanisms because such claims are, and must always be, hollow. They suggest that we know more than we do. They promote an illusion of understanding (Lilienfeld, 2012). Searching for psychological mechanisms stands in the way of identifying what is really going on.

An advantage of the network approach presented in this book is that the associated computational models provide some of the missing emergent mechanism information. Processing by an artificial neural network can be mathematically specified in sufficient detail to where it can be simulated on a digital computer. These computational models enable investigators to perform true experiments that support cause-and-effect conclusions, not merely associations because these models allow investigators to create and manipulate neural architectures, provide them with specific learning histories, and damage them in specific ways. Investigators can also examine developmental processes in ways that might otherwise be impractical or unethical. Theoretical synthesis is also possible, as when Read et al. (2010) combined personality structure and dynamics into a single model (see Chapter 6).

Three Possible Resolutions

Serious anomalies, such as those identified above, require resolution even if that entails major changes in methods and theory. Serious anomalies prompt paradigm shifts (Kuhn, 1962, 1970, 1996, 2012). I now discuss three possible resolutions of the anomalies identified above.

Recall Request for Mechanism Information

One way to resolve the two anomalies identified above is to revoke the calls for mechanism information that have revealed them. Perhaps, upon reflection, we may feel that we have over-reached as a science and don't really want to know 'the basis for the effect, i.e., the processes or events that are responsible for the change; the reasons why change occurred or how change came about' (Kazdin, 2007, p. 3). Perhaps we have overstated our interest in mechanisms if we mean '... the processes that explain why therapy works or how it produces change' (Kazdin 2008, p. 151). Maybe we don't really aspire to '... understand cognition not just as an abstraction, or in terms that are simply plausible or internally consistent. Rather, one wants to know as specifically and concretely as possible how the job is actually done' (Squire et al., 1993, p. 454). Perhaps psychological science should be content with more modest explanatory goals that functional theories provide. Restricting our explanatory goals to fit our methods and preferred models will resolve both anomalies, but will also leave us with functional theories based on associations and covariations that we cannot explain. This regressive approach will, I believe, limit psychological science and largely reduce it to a tool used by hard sciences. For example, operant and respondent conditioning were once active fields of inquiry into learning and memory pursued by psychologists. Now operant and respondent conditioning mainly serve as tools used by neuroscientists to activate the neural and biochemical cascades that provide the desired causal mechanism information.[24] What used to be standalone studies of memory have now become preliminary to conducting a brain imaging study. These practices constitute further evidence of the shredding of psychological science and its reallocation to other sciences.

Deny Anomalies

Another possible resolution is to argue that the identified anomalies are not actually anomalous. While such arguments might be valid, it is also possible, and more likely, that they are based on, motivated by, denial and/or self-serving rationalizations. All arguments for maintaining the status quo must therefore be carefully and critically viewed in light of their potential self-serving motives, given that we have lived so long and so comfortably with both anomalies and given how much disruption and change goes with

[24] A few psychologists continue to investigate functional relationships using operant and respondent methods, but they cannot explain why these functional relationships work as they do and will never be able to do so.

recognizing both of them. No argument can falsify the claim that functional theories lack mechanism information, as this is the definition of functional theories. Identifying a psychological substrate that causally mediates psychological mechanisms would do the trick but all indications are that such a discovery will never be made.

Clinical practice will likely remain unaffected by any or all of these resolutions given its long history of being largely based on the clinical experience and recommendations of a few generative clinicians such as Freud, Adler, Beck, Ellis, Linehan, etc., rather than on applications of findings from formal psychological science. Applied behavior analysis is a notable exception given its basis and roots in the experimental analysis of behavior but it constitutes a small proportion of all contemporary clinical practice.

Ignore Anomalies

A third possible way to deal with the identified anomalies is to simply ignore them. I see this as the most likely option because: (a) it is the easiest to implement because editors can simply reject all manuscripts that raise these troublesome issues with few if any supporting reasons; (b) it is probably the most effective way to suppress these radical issues and continue business as usual; and (c) my experience indicates that this practice is already in effect. What follows are three personal examples that I believe demonstrate that there is presently an unwillingness even to discuss these issues let alone deal constructively with them. I submitted a manuscript entitled '*Calls for Mechanism Information Reveal Two Anomalies in Psychological Science*' to three top-tier journals in psychology. The masthead of the first journal I submitted to claims that they are especially interested in publishing information regarding '**underlying mechanisms**'. The editorial decision was to reject my manuscript because the issues I raised were said to be not sufficiently specific to clinical psychology. No justification of this sweeping, and I believe erroneous, statement was provided. This journal subsequently published an article that by title, abstract, and content portended to provide **possible mechanisms** but did not do so. Instead, the authors identified associations and covariations without seeming to understand that correlation does not prove causation let alone constitute mechanism information. The other two top-tier journals specialize in theoretical issues. Both of them rejected my manuscript. Some reviewers provided no justification for their decision. Others claimed that I did not make my case and that a complete rewrite might be in order but neither encouraged me to do so nor directed me as to how I should proceed. In short, the issues I raised were summarily dismissed.

What Constitutes Legitimate Mechanism Information?

We have just seen what does not constitute legitimate mechanism information. The natural dialectical question is what does constitute legitimate mechanism information?[25] Because we have excluded all psychological explanations, we are left with examples from biology, chemistry, and physics including computational simulations. I present two biological examples and one computational simulation example below.

Biochemical Pathways

Biochemical pathways such as those involved in the citric-acid cycle, also known as the Kreb's cycle,[26] are good examples of a causal biochemical sequence where each step gives rise to the next in a compelling causal way. Similar brain-relevant chemical cascades undoubtedly exist. It is important to have a theory-based approach to psychology that can accommodate such mechanism information as it becomes available. The proposed Bio↔Psychology Network Theory is designed to accommodate such mechanism information.

Neural Cascades

Real neural network cascades are complex events that constitute legitimate mechanism information. For example, Krain et al. (2006) published a meta-analysis of neural pathways involved in decision-making. When these results are known with greater precision and specificity they will constitute legitimate mechanism information. The Human Connectome Project[27] is in the process of identifying the major human brain circuits. The process of neural conduction down an axon is well understood. The process of synaptic transmission of neural impulses is well understood. The fact that neural impulses cascade across layers of real neural networks is accepted without question. What remains to be learned is how these events give rise to psychological phenomena; how psychology emerges from biology. The proposed Bio↔Psychology Network Theory discussing this matter in Chapter 3 is designed to accommodate additional emergent mechanism information as it becomes available.

[25] Criticizing mechanism information as too mechanical or machine-like contradicts the call for mechanism information and therefore is not an acceptable criticism of answers to this call.

[26] http://en.wikipedia.org/wiki/Citric_acid_cycle

[27] http://www.humanconnectomeproject.org/

Artificial Network Cascades

Computational simulations provide mechanism information because they provide causal step-by-step details that are far too complex to be fully characterized by words, and thus must be simulated either in software or hardware as discussed below and in Chapter 6 regarding simulations. Parallel Distributed Processing (PDP) Connectionist Neural Network (CNN) models **simulate** rather than **implement** real neural network **dynamics** in an effort to better understand how psychology emerges from biology. Some models simulate more neuroscience facts than others do and no model yet completely reflects all biological processes. Mathematical equations are used to simulate, not implement, biological processes. This method is parallel in principle to the use of mathematics to simulate weather events and supernova explosions. Weather models do not actually rain. Supernova models do not actually explode. PDP-CNN models are not real brains, but they simulate important functional relationships using deterministic mathematical equations in software or using deterministic physical principles in hardware. For example, the forces that drive electrons through transistors are the same as the forces that drive ions through cell membranes. The following link describes how connectionist models are being implemented in hardware.[28]

A related limitation of simulations was identified by Carey (2011). When discussing Tryon's (2005) connectionist explanation of exposure therapy he noted that 'While this might be a model of how exposure *can* work, however, that does not necessarily mean that it is a model of how exposure *does* work' (p. 242, emphasis in the original). Three points deserve emphasis here. First, simulations aim to reproduce functional relationships via mathematical equations. They do not aim to reproduce actual mechanisms. Hence, supernova simulations do not explode. Second, simulations approximate nature's implementations in that they typically do not include every causal element. The objective is for simulations to have enough relevant properties so that valid experiments can be conducted using them. Third, there may be multiple ways to simulate something with the same degree of fidelity and there is no way to know beforehand how many successful simulations of the same phenomenon are possible. I continue to believe that Tryon's (2005) network explanation of how exposure therapy works is correct.

A crucial, key, and central point here, one that is fundamental to most of what follows in this book, is that PDP-CNN models provide causal

[28] http://www.youtube.com/watch?v=mC7Q-ix_0Po

mechanism information, because they trace causal sequences from stimulus to response. The degree to which this causal mechanism information is correct is subject to future study by psychologists and neuroscientists. The more that is learned about the actual physical mechanisms, the more accurate simulations will become and the less this type of criticism will matter.

Simulations enable true experiments to be conducted. All variables are clearly defined. As much neuroscience information as possible can be incorporated to constrain the model. Initial events can be specified in detail. This includes implementing variations of neural architecture which can be 'normal' or damaged to simulate brain trauma. All events are manipulated by the experimenter. Learning histories can be completely specified and varied as desired, thereby enabling the study of developmental processes. Processing cycles can be stopped at will so that intermediate results can be evaluated. Experiments can be exactly replicated by investigators. Firm conclusions about causal mechanisms can result. This methodology provides the required mechanism information for psychological science to deliver causal statements based on true experiments.

Integration with Neuroscience

Barlow (1997), Wilson (1997), and Foa and Kozak (1997) have called for theoretical integration with neuroscience. However, not all behavior therapists share this view. Hayes (1998b) argued that biological, psychological, sociological, and anthropological explanations are each legitimate but distinct perspectives, thereby precluding the possibility of rendering one in terms of another such as a biological (genetic) explanation of psychological and/or behavioral events. Miller (2010) and Miller and Keller (2000) reached a similar conclusion. Their view is comparable to Rychlak's (1993) argument for the independence, but complementarity, of four explanatory bases, which he termed Physikos, Bios, Logos, and Socius. Hayes (1998b) specifically, and I believe correctly, warned against a particular form of biological explanation he called 'biologism' which he defined as '... the belief that the structure of the organism or its parts fully explains its contextually situated actions' (p. 95). He cited instances where findings that the inner ears of lesbians differ from those of heterosexual women are used to explain sexual orientation, and that smokers differ in a nucleotide sequence from non-smokers is used to explain smoking status as examples of biologism. These biological differences do not explain anything let alone explain what they are said to explain. Hayes (1998b) drew attention to the interplay between biology and behavior. Hayes (1998b) recommended that we ask **interactive questions** where the effect of environmental events on biological variables that influence behavior are posed and answered by empirical study. Recognizing current theoretical and methodological limitations, Hayes concluded that these are '... demanding questions that are mostly beyond our current reach...' (p. 96). These comments indicate that contemporary behavioral, cognitive, and/or psychodynamic theories do not inform us about how biology influences psychology and behavior, nor do they explain how experience alters biology. The absence of a truly psychobiological and/or bio-psychological theory leaves a schism between psychology and biology that distorts discussions about nature/nurture issues and behavior genetics. This theoretical deficiency is part of a more general problem that Hayes (1998a) described as the 'Theoretical Emaciation of Behavior Therapy'. Two special volumes of *Behavior Therapy* (Vol. 28, Nos. 3 & 4) further documented and discussed the theory-based problems that continue to face behavior therapists.

The admonition by Hayes (1998b) to ask **interactive** questions emphasizes the **integration** of psychology and neuroscience. Most psychologists are content to study psychology from the psychological orientation that characterized their training. This is not integrative. It is parallel play that masquerades as integration. It presumes that their psychological research somehow contributes to neuroscience. To be truly integrative one must do psychology in a way that bears directly upon neuroscience. Parallel-distributed-processing (PDP) connectionist neural network (CNN) models constitute the most integrative form of psychology currently available. The technical features of the computer simulations that are integral to this approach are unfamiliar to most psychologists. The computer skills required to conduct PDP-CNN simulations are further from their grasp. Integrating psychology with neuroscience therefore depends upon students of psychology who are just learning about our field, are still taking courses, and are willing to invest in a promising future. This book aims to bridge part of this knowledge gap by defining basic terms and clearly describing basic features of the PDP-CNN approach. The simulations presented in Chapter 6 are intended to illustrate that connectionist models can effectively simulate psychological phenomena.

I argue below that psychology needs some form of network theory, but before doing so I address the more fundamental issue concerning why psychology needs neuroscience because a negative view here precludes all interest in integrating psychology and neuroscience.

Psychology Needs Neuroscience

Psychology needs neuroscience because it effectively resolves both anomalies identified above. Neuroscience resolves the first anomaly because it provides proximal causal experience-dependent plasticity mechanism information that explains how learning and memory work. This is crucial because learning and memory are the two fundamental processes that mediate all psychological phenomena, including all psychological development and all psychological interventions. Neuroscience also resolves the second anomaly because these learning and memory mechanisms operate on a biological substrate. The future of psychological science is therefore better served by finding a way to cooperate with neuroscience rather than continuing to criticize and fear it on the basis that neuroscience is reductionistic. Insulating psychology as a science by defining it to be independent of neuroscience and then expecting equal respect and financial support is unreasonable and therefore unlikely to happen.

Miller (2010) and Miller and Keller (2000) presented principled arguments against reductionism. Their claim that reductionism has failed is contradicted by the obvious rapid proliferation of brain-scan-based articles, chapters, and books. Clearly many psychologists are not deterred by their philosophical objections to reductionism. Some level of appreciation of the contributions that neuroscience is making seems to be widespread.

Miller and Keller (2000) also disputed the proposition that neuroimaging research is more fundamental than traditional psychological research even when it comes to providing causal mechanism information, yet Lilienfeld (2012) reported that the public is convinced that biology is a more basic science than psychology. When asked about mechanism information concerning a psychological phenomenon in the presence of relevant brain-scan-based studies it is most unlikely that these studies would not be cited as providing mediating mechanism information. Clearly the intent of brain imaging research is to identify and provide causal mechanism information that is presently missing from psychological science. Why else would one do these studies?

I suggest that my identification of the two anomalies described above has clarified why psychology needs neuroscience. I suspect that subliminal recognition of these anomalies explains why so many psychologists are interested in and supportive of neuroscience. Upon this view, the advancement of neuroscience within psychology is understandable, desirable, and unavoidable. Brain scan technologies have enabled psychologists to see inside the living brain while it processes information, thereby replacing psychological speculation about these processes. This technology replaces introspection with objective extraspective natural science evidence. Neuroscience facts have replaced psychological theories of learning with details about the causal biological mechanisms that mediate learning and memory upon which all psychological phenomena ultimately depend (cf., Bear et al., 2007; Carlson, 2010; Hell & Ehlers, 2008; Kalat, 2009; Lisman & Hell, 2008; Squire et al., 2008). Curiously, with regard to learning and memory, Skinner (1989) prophetically predicted the biological changes that explain learning when he wrote '**The contingencies change the rat, which then survives as a changed rat**' (p. 14, bold emphasis added). Advances in neuroscience have confirmed his speculation and clarified how these changes occur by revealing biological mechanisms that causally mediate learning and memory. We now understand that '*Learning* refers to the process by which experiences change our nervous system and hence our behavior. We refer to these changes as *memories*' (italics in the original) (Carlson et al., 2010, p. 440).

Reviews of neuroscience-based studies have also informed theory associated with the clinical practice of cognitive behavioral therapies. The presumed serial causal sequence of cognition driving affect driving behavior has been completely falsified by Panksepp (1998, 2005, 2008), who has shown that electrical stimulation of subcortical neural networks is sufficient to produce emotions quite apart from any and all cortical influence (see Chapter 5). Moreover, it has been shown that cognitions can function as emotions and emotions can function as cognitions, and that both operate in parallel rather than in sequence (cf., Duncan & Barrett, 2007; Storbeck & Clore, 2007). New journals have been created to explain social, cognitive, and affective phenomena using neuroscience mechanisms. Examples include the journals *Social Cognitive and Affective Neuroscience*[29] and *Social Neuroscience*.[30] These and related developments have been brought about from within by psychologists, as well as from without by neuroscientists, with generous support from Federal and private funding. The Human Connectome Project[31] is well underway towards mapping the major neural networks in the human brain with the expectation that this wiring diagram will facilitate reductionist explanations of psychological phenomena.

[29] http://scan.oxfordjournals.org/

[30] http://www.psypress.com/social-neuroscience-1747-0919

[31] http://www.humanconnectomeproject.org/

Psychology Needs Some form of Network Theory

Resolving Anomalies

The first and most important reason why psychology needs some form of network theory is to resolve the two anomalies identified above. There can be no psychological mechanisms because there is no psychological substrate for them to operate on. There are only biological substrates and neuroscience mechanisms. Psychology needs to show how cognition, emotion, and behavior emerge from these neuroscience mechanisms. Rumelhart and McClelland (1986) and McClelland et al. (1986) have shown how network models can simulate learning, memory, and many other psychological important psychological phenomena. These models and many related parallel distributed processing (PDP) connectionist neural network (CNN) simulations have clearly shown that network models can do psychology (see Chapter 6).

PDP-CNN models are consistent with neuroscience in at least the following ways: (a) they consist of layers of interconnected nodes that can be understood as simulated neurons; (b) processing nodes in all but the input layer receive inputs from many other processing nodes. This simulates dendritic summation; (c) a transfer function relates summed inputs to the probability of firing and thereby further propagation of activation. Simulations use the same sigmoidal transfer function that real neurons use; and (d) connection weights, simulated synapses, are modified by experience. The learning equations used to make these changes simulate well-known experience-dependent plasticity mechanisms. Here we have true integration of psychology and neuroscience. The subtitle of O'Reilly and Munakata's (2000) book *Computational explorations in cognitive neuroscience: Understanding the mind by simulating the brain* tells the basic story. We can understand the mind by simulating the brain because mind emerges from brain. No other theoretical approach taken by psychologists, and particularly by clinical psychologists, accomplishes anything that remotely resembles this degree of theoretical integration of psychology and neuroscience. Hence, psychology needs to embrace some form of network modeling.

Considerable evidence exists that psychology is in fact embracing PDP-CNN models. A PsychInfo search on 6 June 2013 using the term 'connectionism' returned 1,599 references. A PsychInfo search on the same date for 'connectionism' and 'psychological review' in separate search fields revealed that 48 of these articles were published in *Psychological Review* alone. That journal publishes long articles with extensive reference sections. Major reference works, such as the more than one thousand page *Handbook of Brain Theory and Neural Networks* (Arbib, 2002) and similar-sized *Cambridge Handbook of Computational Psychology* (Sun, 2008), further demonstrate that PDP-CNN models can simulate psychological phenomena.

Learning and Memory

A second reason why psychology needs some form of network theory is because it informs us regarding learning and memory; the two pillars upon which all psychological phenomena rest. Psychological research regarding learning and memory markedly decreased around 1968 (Tryon, 1995d), whereas neuroscience research into the biological mechanisms that mediate learning and memory increased. Neuroscientists studied classical conditioning in primitive sea creatures such as *Aplysia*[32] and *Hermissenda*[33] because their limited nervous systems could be studied in detail. Cognitive psychologists such as Rumelhart and McClelland (1986) and McClelland et al. (1986), and their Parallel Distributed Processing (PDP) group began to simulate psychological phenomenon and to study the '**micro-structure of cognition**'; i.e., the underlying mechanisms that gave rise to cognition, using **artificial neural networks** (ANNs). Connectionist network models have subsequently been constructed that can explain classic psychological phenomena such as various operant and respondent conditioning phenomena (Commons et al., 1991; Tesauro, 1990), the Stroop effect (Cohen et al., 1990), affective priming (den Dulk et al., 2002), and cognitive dissonance reduction (Shultz & Lepper, 1996) among other phenomena.

Connectionist network models have also effectively simulated several disorders of interest to psychologists including surface and deep dyslexia (Hinton et al., 1993), dementia (Parks & Levine, 1998), and schizophrenia (Hoffman & Dobscha, 1989; Hoffman & McGlashan, 1993). Connectionist network models have also effectively simulated the effects of aging (Li et al., 2001, 2005; Li & Sikström, 2002). Tryon (2012) organized network principles into three explanatory core principles and eight additional corollary principles that help us better understand a broad range of psychological phenomena. This book adds a fourth network principle to the explanatory core (see Chapter 3).

[32] http://en.wikipedia.org/wiki/Aplysia

[33] http://en.wikipedia.org/wiki/Hermissenda_crassicornis

Unifying Personality Theory

A third reason why psychology needs some form of network theory is because it provides a way to theoretically unify the study of personality. Clinical psychologists are interested in the personality dynamics of individuals. Consequently they have traditionally turned to ideographic research by Freud, Jung, Adler, and related authors. Academic psychologists are interested in personality traits and structures. They have traditionally turned to nomothetic research where factor analysis is commonly used to estimate the number and nature of primary personality traits. Read et al. (2010) developed a connectionist neural network model of personality that integrates both of these long separate and seemingly incommensurate approaches to personality theory. His network model implements the well-documented Behavioral Approach and Behavioral Inhibition Systems. It simulates individual psychodynamics. It also simulates findings of nomothetic research when run with different approach and inhibition settings.

The Orr et al. (2013) article is also of special interest because it provides causal mechanism information that explains how people make personal decisions and why they make particular decisions about health care including smoking cessation, drug use, over eating, and suicidal ideation. The authors replace the typical unscientific 'free will' explanation with a dynamic constraint satisfaction mechanism that incorporates the effects of past experience via learning with immediate social context. This connectionist neural network approach delivers some of the mechanism that Wargo (2012) promised but failed to deliver.

Neuroscience Constraints

Connectionist network models vary greatly in the extent to which they are based on and constrained by neuroscience. Most of these models are constrained in just five principled ways. The first principled constraint is that these network models should consist of at least three layers of simple processing nodes, simulated neurons, because Minsky and Papert (1969) proved mathematically that networks with two layers of processing nodes called **perceptrons** cannot solve problems requiring exclusive-or (XOR) logic (see O'Reilly & Munakata, 2000, pp. 156–8). The second principled constraint is that these processing nodes are highly interconnected into a network by two or more layers of connections that carry continuous activation values that can range from excitatory to inhibitory; a characteristic that one might view as simulated synapses. The third principled constraint is that processing nodes in the middle and/or output layers receive inputs from many processing nodes; a characteristic that might be viewed as simulated dendritic inputs. The fourth principled constraint is that the probability that a receiving node would fire, become active, is a non-linear, preferably sigmoidal, function of the inputs that it receives from other nodes; another characteristic that extends simulated dendritic summation. The fifth principled constraint is a mathematical way of modifying the connection weights in response to a learning history; a feature that might be viewed as simulating experience-dependent plasticity which is a biological basis of learning and memory formation. Other connectionist network models are more heavily constrained by neuroscience facts and findings. The proposed hybrid connectionist approach incorporates additional neuroscience mechanisms.

Traditional connectionist theory and models have assumed that all learning takes place because simulated synapses change from trial to trial. Only indirectly have they acknowledged that network architecture can limit or facilitate network performance. I understand that the challenge of getting artificial networks to learn, form memories, and simulate psychological phenomena was sufficiently daunting that the issue of neural architecture was not pursued beyond the necessary requirement to have at least three layers of processing nodes, simulated neurons, and two layers of connection weights, simulated synapses. However, I favor a hybrid cognitive neuroscience network theory that combines connectionism, neuroscience, well-replicated psychological phenomenon, and multivariate statistics.

Wilson (1998) introduced the term consilience to describe how mature sciences collaborate with each other such as biochemistry that integrates biology and chemistry and quantum chemistry that integrates physics and chemistry. The premise is that consilience is a guide to truth and therefore is to be valued and developed. Doing psychology with formal network models is a form of consilience that may enable psychology to become a mature science that is consilient with biology and neuroscience.

Informal Network Theories

A fourth reason why psychology needs some form of network theory is because informal network theories have already been somewhat useful in understanding psychological phenomena and disorders. Psychology has a long history of informal network theories. The earliest work seems to be in the area of cognitive psychology in the form of a general semantic-network theory. Clinical psychologists have developed network theory to explain symptoms of post-traumatic disorder. I now turn to these two areas.

Cognitive Psychology

Bower (1981) began his article on 'mood and memory' by documenting state-dependent memory. The emotional state that the person was in at the time memory formed is a cue for memory retrieval. Hence, happy people recall more happy events and sad people recall more sad events. Bower argued that a network theory was required to explain state-dependent memory. Bower stipulated that he tailored his network theory to fit within a general semantic-network theoretical context commonly characteristic of cognitive psychology. Bower cited examples of network theories with reference to the following publications: Anderson (1976), Anderson and Bower (1973), Collins and Loftus (1975), and Collins and Quillian (1969).

Bower's model contains several network elements. His model consists of interconnected processing nodes. Activation spreads across this network. The properties of connections among processing nodes vary along an excitation–inhibition dimension. The following quote reveals Bower's basic idea of a network model.

> A relevant analogy is an electrical network in which terminals correspond to concepts or event nodes (units), connecting wires correspond to associative relations with more or less resistance, and electrical energy corresponds to *activation* that is injected into one or more nodes (units) in the network. Activation of a node can be accomplished either by presentation of the corresponding stimulus pattern or by prior activation of an associated thought (p. 134).

Post-Traumatic Stress Disorder

Lang (1977) proposed that PTSD symptoms are mediated by a visual-semantic network. Lang (1979, 1985) suggested that fear is best understood as a network of excitatory and inhibitory connections among a network of associations. Foa and Kozak (1986) extended this line of reasoning to include Rachman's (1980) concept of emotional processing that involved the following treatment. First, activate fear memories by presenting fear-relevant cues. Second, present information that is incompatible with fear. The hypothesized therapeutic result is that fear will become dissociated from the cues presented in the first step. Creamer et al. (1992) suggested that intrusive fear activation indicated the presence of a fear network.

Foa et al. (1989) hypothesized that normal fear networks become exaggerated in persons with PTSD. They claimed that these fear networks were larger, more intense, and more readily accessed than are normal fear networks. Chemtob et al. (1988) proposed a four-level network where Level 1 is concrete and Level 4 is abstract. These authors seem to have some awareness of connectionism because: (a) they cited Grossberg and Stone (1986), Hinton and Anderson (1981), and McClelland et al. (1986); (b) they used the term 'spreading activation'; and (c) their Figure 1 is connected like a feed-forward connectionist neural network. We will see in Chapter 11 that both of these informal theories are fully consistent with the proposed Bio↔Psychology Network Theory in general and Network Principle 6 concerning part–whole pattern completion.

Neural Network Coprocessors

A fifth reason why psychology needs some form of network theory is because it enables us to incorporate important anatomical information. Neural architecture undoubtedly influences processing. For example, it is a well-established anatomical fact that the neural architecture of the cerebellum is markedly different from that of the frontal lobes. This special architecture enables the cerebellum to function as a specialized coprocessor. Its neural architecture enables it to rapidly compute the prodigious calculations required to control the major and minor muscle fibers that enable complex movements such as those that top athletes make during competitions.

The mirror neuron system seems to comprise another coprocessor; one that provides the biological basis of imitation and empathy. It was initially discovered in the ventral premotor cortex and the anterior parietal regions of monkey brains (di Pellegrino et al., 1992; Gallese et al., 1996; Rizzolatti et al., 1996) but has also been found in the pars opercularis of the inferior frontal gyrus, within Broca's area, and in the rostral posterior parietal cortex of the human brain (Iacoboni et al., 1999, 2005).

Broca and Wernike's areas are specialized networks that are crucial for language acquisition and facility. Damage to these specialized neural coprocessors produces expressive and receptive aphasias.[34]

Another way to understand the power of specialized architecture is to consider the role that specialized architecture has played with computers. All computations in the earliest computers were done by a single central processing unit (CPU). Math-intensive computations were relatively slow especially when carried to say ten digits of precision. Intel's math coprocessor greatly speeded up such computations. This chip had a special architecture that rapidly produced computations with 80 digits of precision. This ability was especially appreciated by the people who decomposed complex signals into their component frequencies using Fourier's theorem. Such

[34] http://en.wikipedia.org/wiki/Aphasia

computations are relatively slow when carried out by a generic CPU. A software advance known as the Fast Fourier Transform (FFT) greatly facilitated these computations, but not nearly as much as did the dedicated FFT chip whose architecture enabled hard-wired computation. Graphic displays are relatively slow when implemented by a generic CPU; too slow for today's computerized games. Specialized chips on graphics cards now drive the required high-speed displays. The main point of these examples is that specialized, optimized, hard-wired architecture can produce impressive results. It is therefore understandable that brain evolution should have favored the development of neural network coprocessors. The Human Connectome Project (HNT)[35] is designed to reveal major portions of the wiring diagram of the entire human brain. It is likely that the HNT will reveal a variety of coprocessor networks.

Innateness

A sixth reason why psychology needs some form of network theory is because it provides an understanding of how innateness works. Are infants born with a completely blank slate, table rasa, or do they possess some innate abilities? Psychologists have a long history of interest in innateness, and instinct. The term **psychological nativism**[36] refers to the view that some abilities are hard-wired in the brain and present at birth. This view contrasts sharply with the empiricist belief that infants are born with a blank slate and learn everything in basically the same way. PDP-CNN models provide an integrative perspective. See Chapter 7 for additional comments.

I begin by considering two meanings of innate. The first meaning of innate concerns traits that are observable at birth because there has not been an opportunity to interact with the physical and/or social environment in order to learn these traits. Crying and sucking are two examples of behaviors that are present at birth, and therefore can be considered to be innate. The second meaning of innate concerns traits that will develop in time without specific environmental support. Puberty is a good example of a genetic mechanism that is present at birth but not activated for over a decade, and therefore is innate. Huntington's disease[37] is an example of an abnormal delayed genetic expression. This disease can be considered to be innate in the sense that the genes that cause it are present at birth. In Chapter 7

[35] http://www.humanconnectome.org/

[36] http://en.wikipedia.org/wiki/Psychological_nativism

[37] http://en.wikipedia.org/wiki/Huntington's_disease

we will find that some people believe that language acquisition is also innate in this same delayed sense. That is, while language is not present at birth, the genetic support for language acquisition is present at birth.

Instincts are innate by definition.[38] For example, spiders weave webs, barn swallows build a special kind of nest, and bees construct hexagonal-shaped combs without having to be taught how to do so. How can this be? What mechanisms mediate these behaviors? These questions are more easily answered for simple life forms, so I will continue with spiders. They are fully capable of weaving a complex web soon after hatching. How can this be? My answer requires that I tell you something about how connectionist networks learn. Connectionist network models typically begin 'life' with numerical weights, random numbers between +1 and −1 that tell how strong the connection between processing nodes is. These weights simulate synaptic properties of excitation and inhibition. Positive numbers simulate excitation; negative numbers simulate inhibition. Learning entails modifying these connection weights in ways that enable the system to better perform the task at hand. Ultimately the network optimizes the connection weights over repeated learning trials resulting in 'adult' performance. It seems that spider DNA presets spider synapses to these 'adult' values in addition to constructing the neural network that is the spider's brain. Hence, spiders weave webs upon hatching.

Marks (1969) used the term 'prepotency' and Seligman (1971) and Seligman and Hagar (1972) used the term 'preparedness' to explain why people are commonly phobic regarding heights, the dark, spiders, and snakes, but not puppies, kittens, and bunnies. Evolution has genetically disposed humans to fear these things and that disposition is considered to be innate because no special traumatic history is required to develop these fears (Menzies & Clarke, 1995). The brain consists of multiple interconnected neural networks. It is possible that these evolutionary dispositions come in the form of preset synapses in one or more neural networks.

A major problem with traditional nativist explanations is that they do not actually explain anything because they do not provide plausible proximal causal mechanism information for how innate processes work. So-called support for nativism typically takes the form of criticizing all other explanations. Every inadequacy or limitation of competing explanations such as connectionism is taken as proof that nativism is correct. The unstated assumption appears to be that nativism must be true if no other fully correct

[38] http://en.wikipedia.org/wiki/Instinct

explanation can be given. Entirely absent is any effort to explain how nativism can possibly work. The absence of any mechanism information reveals that nativism is not an explanation at all. Rather, nativism is an assertion that certain things just happen. We are asked to accept this conclusion as a matter of faith, not reason. Hence, this view is literally unreasonable.

Conclusions

By now I hope that it seems obvious to you that some form of network theory is required to make psychology compatible with neuroscience. The major distinctive feature of the proposed hybrid Bio↔Psychology Network Theory is its combination of (a) neuroscience mechanisms, (b) connectionist neural network mechanisms, (c) well-replicated psychological phenomena, and (d) multivariate statistics. This view places special emphasis on emergence; a topic to which we now turn.

Emergence is the Explanatory Complement

Many psychologists, especially clinical psychologists, respond negatively to neuroscience because they believe that reductionism will suck the humanity out of psychology if left unchecked. Other psychologists whose career primarily involves research respond negatively to reductionism because the greedy form of reductionism aims to completely displace and discard psychology once it has been reduced to biology. It would therefore seem that reductionism is the mortal enemy of all psychologists. Such an adversarial approach forces students to study biology or psychology. This choice motivates psychologists and their students to reject reductionism. But I have argued above that psychology needs neuroscience to resolve the two formidable anomalies that keep psychology in its immature state. What is to be done here?

The crucial limitation of reductionism is that identifying neural structures and components cannot explain how those structures and components give rise to psychology. Reductionism can therefore never provide a complete explanation of any psychological phenomenon. Reductionism is just half of a complete explanation. Some assembly is always required. Explaining how psychology emerges from these neural structures and components constitutes the other half of a complete explanation.

Consider visual illusions. Even a complete identification of the neural circuits responsible for visual illusions does not, because it cannot, explain how these neural networks generate illusions. Reductionism will therefore never provide a complete explanation because it cannot account for how psychology emerges from biology. Some form of **synthetic explanation**, the antithesis of reduction, is required to explain how biological mechanisms interact to produce psychological phenomena. This **explanatory complement** to reductionism is needed to obtain a complete explanation. Very likely this synthetic explanatory complement will require some sort of network explanation such as the proposed Bio↔Psychology Network Theory. It is up to psychology to provide this other explanatory half. Doing so will empower psychology with explanatory relevance equal to that of biology. Each science is dependent upon the other. Psychology and biology are equal explanatory partners because each science constitutes the explanatory complement of the other. Markram (2012), a noted neuroscientist, concisely characterized these complementary explanatory roles as follows:

> Reductionist biology – examining individual brain parts, neural circuits and molecules – has brought us a long way, but it alone cannot explain the workings of the human brain ... .We must construct as well as reduce and build as well as dissect. To do that, we need a new paradigm that combines both analysis and synthesis. The father of reductionism, French philosopher René Descartes, wrote about the need to investigate the parts and then reassemble them to re-create the whole (p. 50).

We currently understand the effort to reassemble the results of reductionistic neuroscience as **emergence**. The *APA Concise Dictionary of Psychology* (American Psychiatry Association, 2009) defines emergence as 'the idea that complex phenomena (e.g., conscious experiences) are derived from arrangements of or interactions among component phenomena (e.g., brain processes) but exhibit characteristics not predictable from those component phenomena' (p. 163). Emergent properties can, and often do, differ qualitatively from their constituent elements. Consider how the physical properties of liquid water differ qualitatively from those of hydrogen and oxygen, its gaseous constituents, or how the physical properties of salt differ from its constituent elements of sodium and chlorine. Lilienfeld (2012) tentatively considered the possibility of preserving psychology through the study of emergence citing Chalmers (2006) and Meehl and Sellars (1956) as favorable to this endeavor and Churchland (1984) as doubtful of it. The history of emergence in psychology has been reviewed by Sawyer (2002) and McClelland (2010).

I present the following story reported by Eagleman (2011, pp. 2–4) about the African tribesman who accused Arthur Alberts of stealing his tongue, because it provides an interesting perspective on our understanding of what it means for psychology to emerge from biology. Arthur tape-recorded a villager and played his voice back to him. The native was shocked and concluded that Arthur has stolen his tongue for how else could he have possibly captured his voice so completely? After all, voice is ephemeral and ineffable; it disappears into nothingness after spoken. How could Arthur's machine get hold of his voice except by stealing his tongue! This was no joke to the native and his tribe who wanted to kill Arthur for his terrible deed. Only by using a mirror could Arthur convince the native that he still possessed his tongue. Arthur was lucky that the native did not question the magic of the mirror to show him his tongue. This story may seem simple to us because we understand that Arthur's machine recorded the variations in sound waves that enabled the native's vocalizations to be heard. It did not actually record the native's voice per se nor did it steal his tongue. Voice is the psychological experience of perceiving the sound waves that are generated by humans when they speak. The distinction between a psychological experience such as hearing a voice and the physical basis for its occurrence, sound waves, is critical to the concept of emergence. The physical basis of voice that was recorded is qualitatively different from the subjective experience of hearing a voice. The sound waves provided the physical basis for hearing voice. Understanding this physical basis of voice provides the mechanism information that enables one to understand how it could be mechanically recorded. Voice has been reduced to physical vibrations that were recorded by Albert's machine.

The relevance of this story for emergence is that the experience of hearing a person's voice when exposed to acoustic vibrations generated by the tape recorder can be understood as a form of emergence in that the qualitative experience of hearing a specific person's voice emerged from listening to the sound waves. Stated differently, sound waves entered the ear and the experience of hearing the voice emerged in consciousness. The emergent experience of hearing one's voice is the result of an amazing synthesis. Nothing like reductionism is involved. The central idea of emergence is that a synthetic product results from complex combinations of many simpler processes. Similarly, I discuss in Chapter 2 how thoughts can emerge from neural network cascades in a way that is parallel to how factors emerge during factor analysis.

It is noteworthy that chemistry has long been reduced to physics, but yet we still have departments of chemistry and many professional chemists in business and industry. Hence, the concern over greedy reductionism replacing psychologists with neuroscientists appears to be without merit. Whereas reductionism identifies brain parts and mechanisms, some assembly is required to explain how psychology emerges from biology. I believe that the people who explain how psychology emerges from biology should be psychologists as this seems to be a primary objective and an essential goal of psychology. However, psychologists could refuse this assignment and leave it to other professions. Psychology left the study of learning and memory to neuroscientists who have done a marvellous job at providing causal mechanism information. Clinical psychologists left the issue of diagnosis to the American Psychiatric Association and their *Diagnostic and Statistical Manual* bestseller. These are examples of how our field is fragmenting. Perhaps psychologists are also willing to leave the explanatory complement of how cognition, affect, and behavior emerge from biology to computational neuroscientists. Psychologists may hope that if they leave this issue alone then no one else will engage it, but I firmly believe that such hope is seriously misguided because the explanatory complement is just too important to be ignored by everyone. We have much more to fear from our fellow psychologists than ever we do from neuroscientists. We have a history of being our own worst enemy. Not trying to explain how mind emerges from brain would, in my view, seriously limit the ability of psychological science to actually explain the functional relationships that it has already discovered and will continue to discover.

Cognitive Science, Neuroscience, and Cognitive Neuroscience

Ilardi (2002a) distinguished cognitive science from neuroscience, from cognitive neuroscience. **Cognitive science** is concerned with rules that govern symbol manipulation that presumably occur in the mind. Cognitive science proponents have no interest in the brain. They do not care whether symbol manipulation is implemented in neural tissue or in silicon chips. The same 'psychological laws' are said to apply in both cases. For them psychology has nothing necessarily to do with biology. **Neuroscience** is the polar opposite of cognitive science because its focus is exclusively on neural systems. Neuroscience seeks to fully replace cognitive science through what is called greedy reductionism (see Miller, 2010; Miller & Keller, 2000). **Cognitive neuroscience** seeks a middle position. It is concerned with how mind emerges from brain. It aims to show how processes that seem to require symbol manipulation do so via sub-symbolic network processes. I take a cognitive neuroscience position in this book. The primary contemporary dialectic is between the symbolic approach taken by traditional artificial intelligence investigators and the new sub-symbolic approach taken by connectionist modelers (cf. Sloman, 1996).

Mature Science

According to Kuhn (1962, 1970, 1996, 2012) all mature sciences: (a) explain a set of shared concepts; (b) use a common vocabulary. I add that mature sciences: (c) replicate facts before attempting to explain them; (d) are organized around principles not people; (e) explain phenomena using physical mechanisms; (f) are consilient (Wilson, 1998); and (g) do not retain all concepts that were part of their immature science.

Reported phenomena only become facts when they have been replicated to where they can be trusted. Theoretical unification therefore need only concern itself with trustworthy facts. Kuhn's (1962, 1970, 1996, 2012) description of the maturation of biology, chemistry, and physics reveals that some of the preparadigmatic concepts were discarded during the maturation process as the field focused on different questions that became central to their science. The proposed consilient unification will also not incorporate every preparadigmatic psychological construct. Shedler (2010) complained that:

> Undergraduate textbooks too often equate psychoanalytic or psychodynamic therapies with some of the **more outlandish and inaccessible speculations** made by Sigmund Freud roughly a century ago, rarely presenting mainstream psychodynamic concepts as understood and practiced today (p. 98, bold emphasis added).

While he did not specifically identify these 'outlandish and inaccessible speculations' we can assume that they included the constructs of penis envy, oral, anal, urethral, phallic, latency, and genital personality styles (Rychlak, 1981b, pp. 76–80) plus castration, Oedipal and Electra complexes. The proposed theoretical unification leaves these concepts behind. But, the proposed theoretical unification incorporates, features, and emphasizes unconscious processing which is the cornerstone of all psychodynamic theories.

The proposed Bio↔Psychology Network Theory also leaves behind all unreplicated psychological phenomena because no theory should be expected to explain spurious false-positive findings. Replication is the only way to be sure that findings are real and not artifactual. Makel et al. (2012) documented that the overall replication rate in psychology is a mere 1.07%. Chabris et al. (2012) reported that most genetic associations with general intelligence could not be replicated. All of this makes it easier to achieve theoretical unification than was previously thought.

The proposed Bio↔Psychology Network Theory should be evaluated by what it includes more than by what it excludes. Psychologists who seek a psychology that is independent of neuroscience shall surely be disappointed with my proposal. While this group undoubtedly consists of some psychologists who describe themselves as existentialists, some of them may be pleased to learn about the enteric nervous system described in the next chapter as a biological basis for Gendlin's focusing therapy that they may already be using. They may also like Network Principle 3 concerning transformation. Donahoe (1998), Donahoe and Palmer (1989), and Tryon (1993a, 1993b, 1995c, 1996b, 2002c, 2009b, 2009c) have already discussed the relevance of network theory to the experimental analysis of behavior, despite the reluctance of these psychologists to consider neuroscience mechanism information.

Psychology Departments Change their Names

Departments of philosophy predate departments of psychology. Interest in natural philosophy led to the establishment of separate departments of physics, chemistry, biology, and eventually psychology. Interdisciplinary research emerged as in the case of biochemistry and quantum chemistry. Wilson (1998) used the term **consilience** to describe interdisciplinary research that seeks to integrate scientific knowledge. Psychology has become increasingly consilient in recent years as neuroscience has advanced our understanding of the brain and provided new tools including neuroimaging methods such as fMRI and PET for studying the intact living functioning human brain. **Computational biology**[39] and **computational neuroscience**[40,41] are relatively new fields that seek to understand how neural systems give rise to psychological functions. My concern is that psychology may leave the question of how mind emerges from brain to this new discipline and forfeit the largest part of its historical mission.

On a positive note, the integration of neuroscience and psychology has produced major changes in some prominent psychology departments, including changing their name. Some psychology departments are emphasizing science by their name change. Other psychology departments are emphasizing neuroscience. The American Psychological Society (2011) detailed some of this history in its September 2011 issue (Vol. 24, No. 7, pp. 12–16) in its article entitled 'Identify Shift'. Here are some examples of departments that have included science in their new names:

- Northern Kentucky University now has a Department of Psychological Science http://psychology.nku.edu/

[39] http://en.wikipedia.org/wiki/Computational_biology

[40] The proposed Bio↔Psychology Network Theory can be described as computational neuropsychology.

[41] http://en.wikipedia.org/wiki/Computational_neuroscience

- University of Missouri now has a Department of Psychological Sciences http://psychology.missouri.edu/
- Purdue University now has a Department of Psychological Sciences (http://www.psych.purdue.edu/)
- Ball State University now has a Department of Psychological Science http://cms.bsu.edu/Academics/CollegesandDepartments/Psychology.aspx
- Brown University now has a Department of Cognitive, Linguistic, and Psychological Sciences http://www.brown.edu/Departments/CLPS/

Here are some examples of psychology departments that have changed their names to reflect integration with neuroscience:

- Dartmouth College now has a Department of Psychological & Brain Sciences http://www.dartmouth.edu/~psych/
- Indiana University now has a Department of Psychological and Brain Sciences http://psych.indiana.edu/index.php
- Duke University now has a Department of Psychology and Neuroscience http://psychandneuro.duke.edu/
- The University of Colorado, Boulder now has a Department of Psychology and Neuroscience (http://psych.colorado.edu/)
- Baylor University now has a Department of Psychology and Neuroscience (http://www.baylor.edu/psychologyneuroscience/)
- The University of Pittsburgh and Carnegie Mellon now has a Center for the Neural Basis of Cognition (www.cnbc.cmu.edu)
- The University of California at Berkeley now has a Neuroscience Institute (http://neuroscience.berkeley.edu/)
- The University of California at Davis now has a Center for Mind and Brain (http://mindbrain.ucdavis.edu/)
- Dartmouth College now has a Center for Cognitive Neuroscience (http://ccn.dartmouth.edu/)
- Duke University now has a Center for Cognitive Neuroscience (http://www.mind.duke.edu/)
- The University of Pennsylvania now has a Center for Cognitive Neuroscience (http://ccn.upenn.edu/)

These examples should be sufficient to demonstrate that psychology is changing and departments of psychology are attempting to more accurately reflect these changes by altering their names and by establishing interdisciplinary centers. This book endeavors to participate in this revolution.

The name and content changes noted above are partly, in my view, evidence of the shredding of psychology discussed above. For example, the author of the first chapter in Hell and Ehlers' (2008) comprehensive book on the synapse by Kristen M. Harris reveals that she works in the **Center for Learning and Memory** within the Neurobiology Department of the University of Texas in Austin Texas. Research on learning and memory once were largely the province of psychology, but this is no longer the case. Steven Bressler (2002) wrote about 'understanding cognition through large-scale cortical networks'. He is at the Center for Complex Systems and Brain Sciences at the Florida Atlantic University in Boca Raton, Florida. Arne Öhman (2002) wrote about 'Automaticity and the amygdale: Nonconscious responses to emotional faces'. He is with the Department of Clinical Neuroscience at the Karolinska Institute, in Stockholm, Sweden. Increasingly psychology journal articles are being written by authors who are not part of a traditional psychology department or any department of psychology at all.

The process of changing the name of an academic department is not without conflict because it involves the professional identity and aspirations of its faculty members. The next chapter engages some of these issues.

CONCLUSIONS

Psychology has a serious explanatory problem that this book seeks to resolve. Every science needs to explain its phenomena. Psychology needs to be able to explain how cognition and affect interact to produce behavior. The currently disunified state of psychology has resulted in the development of disparate vocabularies and incommensurate concepts. Mini-theories and interventions organized around persons rather than principles abound. Our functional theories lack a plausible proximal causal mechanism that can provide acceptable scientific explanations because there is no psychological substrate for the presumed psychological mechanisms to operate on. Psychology needs neuroscience because it provides a biological substrate. Psychology needs reductionism because it provides the mechanical parts that form the basis of the emergent explanation that psychology must provide. Reductionism alone can only provide half of a complete explanation. Emergence provides the second half of a complete explanation. Emergence is the explanatory equivalent of reductionism. Psychology needs some form of network theory to provide emergent explanations. The proposed Bio↔Psychology Network Theory is a hybrid cognitive neuroscience theory that aims to provide the required explanations in the form of four core and eight corollary network principles that form the basis for practicing psychology as a mature science and psychotherapy as an integrated applied science. The next chapter considers the issues and impediments that have so far precluded serious progress towards the required theoretical unification for psychology to become a mature science.

Issues and Impediments to Theoretical Unification

Contents

Cognitive Neuroscience and Psychotherapy
http://dx.doi.org/10.1016/B978-0-12-420071-5.00002-8

This chapter continues to consider the problems and challenges faced by anyone who aims to theoretically unify psychology. To begin with, it is important to understand what theoretical unification in psychology is and what it is not. Theoretical unification in psychology is **not** necessarily a terminal state of completely correct knowledge that everyone rigidly believes in to the point where dissenting opinions are unwelcome and not tolerated by authoritarian overseers. Theoretical unification does **not** mean being completely correct. Theoretical unification can and has been wrong, as when everyone once thought that the Earth was flat and again when everyone once thought that the Earth was the center of all creation. Theoretical unification can be partly wrong, or partly correct, depending upon ones' point of view, as was the case for Newtonian physics before Einstein. Theoretical unification also does **not** mean that every idea suggested by every theoretician is included. Some concepts are left behind when a science matures. For example, questions and concepts highly valued by alchemists were abandoned when chemistry matured as a science. Other times reported phenomena are correctly left behind because they cannot be replicated.

Theoretical unification in psychology **is** about **consensus** to where sufficient **common ground** enables a **majority** of psychologists to **start** working **together** rather than in mutual isolation and/or at cross-purposes. It can be a **beginning** as well as an ending point. Consensus is about the **personal decision** to adopt a **common vocabulary** and **core concepts** by a **working majority** in order to provide the required **shared perspective** that enables us to work together rather than against each other. Hence, theoretical unification in psychology, as I see it, is a **modest goal** that I believe can be achieved.

PREVIOUS PROPOSALS

Unified Positivism

Staats (1983, 1991, 1993) proposed building theoretical bridges among existing fields of psychology using a method he called Unified Positivism. This approach was intended to result in a **Psychological Behaviorism** (Tryon, 1990) capable of unifying psychology, but it has not yet done so. Kukla (1992) noted that this approach begins by accepting all research findings and then looks for principles that can unify them. Kukla (1992) cited the astronomical number of psychological facts as a major reason why it is unlikely that any principles could be found that are capable of unifying them. He might have insisted that unification concern only well-replicated psychological facts and phenomena, as that would greatly simplify the task. Kukla (1992) further questioned Staats's assumption that such principles must exist for us to find. The historical argument that other sciences matured through unification does not guarantee that psychology can do so. The approach Staats recommended has been around for nearly 30 years and has not yet had much impact on psychological science. I see no reason why it should begin to have any significant effect now or in the future.

Tree of Knowledge

Henriques (2003, 2008) presented a tree of knowledge (ToK) system that he claimed can integrate physical science, biology, psychology, and the social sciences. He also claimed that Skinner and Freud constitute opposing theoretical poles within psychology that require synthesis. I believe that the proposed Bio↔Psychology Network Theory makes significant progress towards this end. Henriques (2003, 2008) provided a good general review of prior proposals for theoretical integration. In conclusion, the tree of knowledge system has had little impact on psychological science. It is therefore unlikely that it will begin to do so in the near future.

No Single 'ism'

Castonguay (2011) stated that the complexity of psychotherapy is such that it is unlikely that one theoretical orientation will ever provide a comprehensive understanding. One could say as much for psychological science. I agree that no single 'ism' is capable of explaining what psychologists need to know. Freudianism is inadequate, Behaviorism could not do it. Cognitivism has not done it. Connectionism, in my view, is also incomplete because it is not presently highly constrained by neuroscience. While some connectionist models are heavily constrained by neuroscience facts, most are only moderately constrained. I draw deeply upon connectionism because of its network orientation because the brain is composed of interconnected neural networks. I call for greater inclusion of neuroscience facts into connectionist models. I also incorporate multivariate statistics.

I believe that the entire 'ism' approach is misguided because it mainly serves to separate psychologists into competing schools and camps. Instead, we should be looking for **principles**. This book presents a case for principles. My presentation of an explanatory core and corollary network principles is an effort to move psychological science away from isms and towards becoming a mature science based on principles. In doing so we will recover, and reauthorize, conditioning principles as empirically supported cognitive behavioral principles.

CURRENT TRENDS

Norcross and Karpiak (2012) reported that in 1973, 55% of Division 12 members primarily identified themselves as eclectic/integrative. They reported that this number decreased to 22% in 2010.This change appears to be due to the increased popularity of cognitive and cognitive-behavioral orientations. Heatherington et al. (2013) reported data from a survey of theoretical orientations of doctoral programs in clinical psychology demonstrating that the majority of programs now have a cognitive-behavioral orientation. Of the 54 programs that self-designated as clinical science, 80% espoused a cognitive-behavioral orientation. Of the other 116 Ph.D. programs 67% self-designated as cognitive-behavioral. Of the 31 university-based Psy. D. programs, 48% self-designated as cognitive behavioral. Of the 37 free-standing Psy. D. programs, 32% self-designated as cognitive-behavioral. Family systems was the second most frequent self-designation among Ph.D. programs, whereas the second most frequent self-designation among Psy. D. programs was psychodynamic. On average 57% of all doctoral programs self-designated as cognitive-behavioral, which means that a majority of clinical programs have this theoretical orientation.This constitutes a form of theoretical unification.

Heatherington et al. (2013) worried that this trend towards a single theoretical orientation would continue in the future because graduates from these programs will become future professors and clinical training faculty who will operate mainly, if not exclusively, from a cognitive-behavioral orientation. Levy and Anderson (2013) referred to the dominance of CBT as a 'monoculture' (p. 213), and warned against the dangers of monocultures which they claim to include 'the potential for groupthink and loss of innovation' (p. 213). They also feared that biases in judgments and decisions will result. Bjornsson (2013) is less pessimistic. He believes that CBT is a more diverse orientation than Hetherington et al. (2013) indicated. Levy and Anderson (2013) agreed. They claimed that cognitive-behavioral therapy and behavior therapy are becoming more psychodynamic and existential by virtue of placing increased emphasis on emotions, insight, attachment, and the therapeutic alliance. The good news here is that these are trends towards theoretical unification. A major goal of the Bio↔Psychology Network Theory is to integrate psychotherapy by providing the big five clinical orientations (Behavioral (Applied Behavior Analysis), Cognitive, Cognitive-Behavioral, Psychodynamic (emotion-focused therapies), and Pharmacologic) with all or most of their conceptual 'must haves'. This theoretical unification will authorize clinicians to first treat behavioral problems with behavioral methods, first treat cognitive problems with cognitive methods, and first treat emotional problems with emotion-focused methods, with one or more of the empirically supported treatments associated with each treatment modality. Because clients typically present with a combination of these factors, a comprehensive treatment plan will need to be constructed in collaboration with the client as part of establishing a therapeutic working alliance.

IMPEDIMENTS AGAINST THEORETICAL UNIFICATION

Original Research vs. Replication

Replication is the acid test of science. Without replication we cannot discern fact from artifact. Initial scientific reports may be interesting, but they need to be verified by adequate replication before they can be trusted, taught with confidence, ethically applied clinically, and eligible to participate in theoretical unification. The purpose of methodological replications is to determine if an independent investigator can obtain the **same results** by following the **same procedures**. But psychologists rarely attempt to replicate the work of other psychologists which means that most reported findings have yet to be verified and therefore cannot be trusted, taught with confidence, ethically applied clinically, or are eligible to participate in theoretical unification. Makel et al. (2012) documented that the overall replication rate in psychology is a mere 1.07%.[1] Chabris (2012) endeavored to replicate reported genetic associations with general intelligence in three large samples, but most replications were unsuccessful. The combination of a 1% replication rate and a high failure to replicate rate strongly suggest that most of what psychologists have published has not been verified, and therefore cannot be trusted, taught with confidence, ethically applied clinically, or is eligible to participate in theoretical unification. Pashler and Harris (2012) attempted to minimize the problems created by our lack of replication, but serious problems persist.

[1] What constitutes successful replication remains an open question. The rigorous standards presented in this section were not met by studies included in Makel et al.'s (2012) review. Hence, the rate of acceptable replication in psychology is likely a fraction of 1%.

Replication is required because researcher allegiance (RA) has been shown to bias research findings. Munder et al. (2013) reviewed 30 meta-analyses of RA and found that RA exerts a medium effect. Researchers tend to find what they are looking for. Only through replication by investigators who do not share the same allegiance can we trust the reported findings.

Replication is especially important given the large and increasing number of retracted publications. Grieneisen and Zhang (2012) reported finding 4,449 publications that were retracted from the scholarly literature between 1928 and 2011. Fang et al. (2012) reviewed 2,047 retracted biomedical and life-science articles indexed by PubMed. They reported that 67.4% of retracted articles were due to misconduct. Fraud accounted for 43.4% of retractions. Duplicate publication accounted for 14.2% of retractions. Plagiarism accounted for 9.8% of retractions. The only sure way to confidently isolate fraudulent research is through replication. That seemingly important original research will almost certainly not be corroborated emboldens investigators who seek to build their careers on fraudulent research. Replication is required to authorize trust and confidence in the empirical facts that constitute the foundation of all sciences.

Exact methodological replications are difficult to conduct, in part because not all procedural details get published. The quality of such studies is directly proportional to the fidelity with which they have been carried out. Collaboration with the original investigators to confirm all relevant methodological details is likely required. Analyzing the results requires tests of statistical equivalence (Tryon, 2001; Tryon & Lewis, 2008) with which many investigators are unfamiliar rather than popular tests of statistical difference. Both negative and positive results of methodological replications are informative. Positive results confer factual standing of the phenomenon under study. Negative results caution readers that the reported results might be artifactual. Psychometric meta-analysis (Hunter & Schmidt, 1990) is presently the best method for correcting studies for several psychometric limitations, including attenuated reliability and validity in addition to sample size variation before numerically summarizing their findings in order to determine if the 95% confidence interval for the average adjusted effect size exceeds zero. There are other forms of meta-analysis, but they ignore measurement and experimental design issues. These methods were developed by statististicians not psychometricians. They ignore the psychometric properties of the measures used. Combining studies in the absence of correcting for study artifacts gives rise to the valid criticism of lumping good and bad studies together. A great deal of evidence indicates that effect sizes become larger and more homogeneous after correcting for known study artifacts (Hunter & Schmidt, 1990; Schmidt, 1992).

Psychologists rarely conduct methodological replications because reviewers and journal editors are biased against publishing them (Neuliep & Crandall, 1990). Two exceptions are the *Journal of Negative Results in Biomedicine* (www.jnrbm.com) and the *Journal of Articles in support of the Null Hypothesis* (www.jasnh.com). Grant reviewers are similarly opposed to methodological replications. Failure to fund and publish methodological replication studies are two huge disincentives to conducting them. This bias against methodological replications appears to be rooted in a long-held erroneous belief that statistically significant results are necessarily replicable. Carver (1978) identified the belief that $p < 0.05$ implies that the probability of replicability is $p > 0.95$ over 35 years ago. Fifteen years later Carver (1993) reported that this widespread belief was firmly intact. This view continues unabated today. This misunderstanding mistakes statistical power for statistical significance. Only if all studies had a statistical power of 95% could one reasonably expect to replicate their findings 95% of the time. Cohen (1992) reported a median estimate of power of published studies in psychology was 25%, which means that 75 out of every 100 replications would be expected to fail. Cohen (1969, 1988, 1994) provided investigators with the necessary statistical tools to design studies with a recommended power of 80%. Universal achievement of this goal has yet to be realized. If and when this goal is realized, then 20% of all replications can be expected to fail. The resources needed to reach 95%, and especially 99%, power are considerable and in most cases constitute a financial impediment to conducting original research or replications. A corollary issue here concerns how small an effect psychologists are interested in detecting. A convincing rationale is required when designing powerful experiments to detect especially small effects because of the enormous sample sizes required.

That p is evidence of replicability is contradicted by empirical evidence, in addition to being illogical. Cumming (2008) reported that 25 simulated replications of a $p < 0.05$ result yielded p values ranging from 0.001 to 0.76. All p values ranging from 0.051 to 0.76 constitute failures to replicate. Increasing sample size did not remediate this problem. Cumming (2008) generously concluded that p is an unreliable index of replicability. Using p in this way should be discontinued immediately. Grant reviewers and journal editors should revise their views about methodological replications.

Regardless of how much statistical power a study has, it remains open to the risk of a Type I error, also known as an alpha error, which is typically set at 5% when testing for statistical significance. This means that one can expect that 5 out of every 100, which means 1 out of every 20, statistically significant results are expected to be **false** positives. So in addition to failing to find significant results 20–75% of the time, 5% of positive replications will on average be artifactual. Hence, only results that survive multiple significant replications can be trusted, i.e., will be verified. I recommend three successful methodological replications.

To this point I have focused on how facts and phenomena can achieve replicated status by conducting as few as three well-designed studies. Relatively few published studies have 95% statistical power or better because they are so costly to undertake. It is therefore unlikely that efforts to replicate these studies will be any better designed. Funding and editorial priorities would have to change a lot in order to make undertaking these studies possible.

An alternative approach is to conduct a dozen or more underpowered methodological replications using the same sample size as the original study followed by a psychometric meta-analysis to determine if the 95% confidence interval for the average-adjusted effect size exceeds zero. Results that pass this test may be considered to have been replicated.

Another alternative approach is to conduct many different studies that overlap in some important relevant way. A good example of this is the great many studies that have used positive reinforcement to modify various behaviors using different methods. The fact that all of these studies strengthened their target behaviors is evidence that the phenomenon of positive reinforcement has been replicated, even in the absence of any strict methodological replications.

Some journals are occasionally open to publishing conceptual replications. These are inexact replications that contain original features that in principle conform to the journal's aim of publishing original research. These studies suffer from two limitations that frequently preclude their publication. First, reviewers can reasonably and rightfully claim that such studies contribute too little by way of original findings to warrant publication. Second, and more importantly for us, is the fact that every original feature compromises the internal validity of the replication. If positive results are obtained from a conceptual replication it can be argued that they could have occurred because of the new original features, and not because of the previously reported methods. So we cannot conclude anything for sure about the effects produced by the methods that were the object of replication. If negative results are obtained, it can be argued that the new original methods are less effective than the original methods. Again, we cannot conclude anything for sure about the effects produced by the methods that were the object of replication. Hence, both positive and negative results are not helpful with regard to the crucial issue of whether or not the initially reported methods really did produce the reported results. This is reason enough not to publish all conceptual replication studies.

Consider the consequences of prioritizing original research over replications. To be original one must at least appear to have a new idea. This can be done by not citing previously published work on the same topic by other investigators. Originality can also be implied by coining a new term for an existing one. Referring to social and academic support as scaffolding is a good example. It is difficult to keep being original while working on the same topic. Switching topics periodically advances the appearance of originality because new is frequently confused with original. Psychology has a history of hot topics that have come and gone but resulted in little cumulative science.

Genuine original research is rare and should take up relatively little journal space. The following definitions of the word original were found online:[2] '1. belonging or pertaining to the origin or beginning of something, or to a thing at its beginning: The book still has its original binding. 2. new; fresh; inventive; novel: an original way of advertising. 3. arising or proceeding independently of anything else: an original view of history. 4. capable of or given to thinking or acting in an independent, creative, or individual manner: an original thinker. 5. created, undertaken, or presented for the first time: to give the original performance of a string quartet'. Few if any articles published in each issue of top-tier psychology journals are original by these definitions. How many articles present a fresh and novel approach that arises independently of anything else? How many articles are truly reporting on research for the first time? Original seems mainly to mean slightly different or different in some interesting way. But these findings remain tentative until, and cannot be trusted until, they are replicated and consequently verified.

Attempts at theoretical unification need only address well-replicated findings, because no theory should be expected to explain spurious findings. In fact, a theory that can explain spurious as well as valid findings is unacceptable. Consider the following example. Assume that future research will

[2] http://dictionary.reference.com/browse/original

conclusively find that Therapy X is ineffective. Assume also that before this research is conducted someone asks a theory to explain how this treatment works. Rejecting the explanatory request will be held against the theory. Critics of the theory will take this explanatory avoidance to be an admission of what the theory cannot explain. If, on the other hand, the theory provides a convincing explanation of how Treatment X works, that explanation becomes problematic when the future research showing that the treatment is ineffective is published. These findings will reveal that the theory is faulty. Any theory that can explain how an ineffective treatment works is defective. Theories should only be asked to explain well-replicated facts. This reasoning justifies deferring attempts to explain how a therapy works until after the therapy has been shown to be effective. Our exclusive focus on explaining well-replicated psychological phenomena makes theoretical unification much easier. The prominent role played by computer simulations in the proposed Bio↔Psychology Network Theory facilitates conducting exact methodological replications.

Professional Identity

Individual

Psychologists identify themselves by their field of study and specialization such as clinical psychology, developmental psychology, and social psychology. Clinical psychologists further identify themselves by their primary theoretical orientation such as psychodynamic, cognitive-behavioral, or existential. They may further identify themselves by citing a particular school of psychodynamic thought such as Freudian, Jungian, or Adlerian. The Alfred Adler Institute of New York website[3] states 'The Institute has been the primary source of Adlerian psychology training in the Northeast for over 50 years'. And, 'In addition to preserving the traditional Adlerian philosophy and treatment methodology of **Individual Psychology**, we concentrate on demonstrating how Adler's theories remain fresh and applicable to contemporary society' (emphasis in the original). In these ways, clinical psychologists identify with august clinicians.

Each of the world's great religions also identifies with a particular person. Identifying with a person, no matter how great, differs in a fundamental way from identifying with a body of work or set of principles. This is an important way that science differs from religion and philosophy. It is rather more likely that theoretical unification will coalesce around a set of core

[3] http://www.aai-ny.org/home.aspx

and corollary principles than around a single person. The September 20, 1971 issue of Time Magazine pronounced B.F. Skinner as the most influential then-living psychologist,[4] but he primarily divided psychology.

Clinical psychologists identify themselves professionally by referring to their preferred type of therapy such as cognitive-behavioral therapy, rational emotive behavior therapy, dialectical behavior therapy, applied behavior analysis, or acceptance and commitment therapy, to name a few options. These professional identities include the clinician who is primarily responsible for advocating these treatments such as Beck, Ellis, Linehan, Skinner, and Hayes. These professional identities provide personal meaning to being a psychologist and become part of the person's self-concept; i.e., the way they think and feel about themselves. Such identities share similarities with other personal identities such as religious and political party affiliations and may be held as strongly. The probability that a psychologist will change their professional identity approximates the probability that they will change their religious or political identity; i.e., slim to none. The implication here is that calls for theoretical integration will be ignored or opposed most by psychologists whose professional careers have been advanced most by separatism and therefore have the most to lose through unification. It is to be expected that they will continue to advocate for their particular specialization for the remainder of their lives. The corollary implication is that arguments and calls for theoretical unification will mostly influence young students who are beginning to study psychology and have not yet formed their professional identity and may find the prospect of a unified psychology sufficiently attractive to seek and promote it.

Collective

Just as 'birds of a feather flock together' so too do psychologists. Individual psychologists seek membership in organizations that reflect their interests. These organizations have membership committees that seek to identify and recruit like-minded individuals. They target graduate and undergraduate students who are likely to become full members upon graduation and offer them reduced membership fees and trial subscriptions to journals and newsletters. We refer to these practices as marketing and professional development. These groups elect officers, collect dues, publish journals and newsletters, hold conferences and annual meetings where they present awards to members who have promoted the organization or who best exemplify the

[4] http://www.time.com/time/covers/0,16641,19710920,00.html

goals and objectives of the organization. In general, professional groups seek to extend themselves by showing how different they are and how important these differences are. Their existence is directly dependent upon separatism and is threatened by unification. Candidates for office in a professional association whose platform is to disband and join with another group to promote common interests are unlikely to be elected. Candidates who articulate and promote the group's distinctive and separatist mission are more likely to be elected. Tenure and promotion committees look for participation in professional societies as evidence of contributing to and leading one's profession. But this leadership exclusively promotes separatism and the fragmentation of psychology. Ironically, it is just these leaders that are needed to lead their colleagues towards psychology becoming a mature unified science. But like clan leaders who have no concept of nationhood, they lead their kin into xenophobic isolation.[5]

The Association for Cognitive and Behavioral Therapies website[6] states that 'Cognitive and Behavioral Therapies (CBT) use techniques that are based on scientific evidence to understand and treat psychological symptoms'. This professional identification with science has characterized this organization since its inception over four decades ago. The first implication of this professional identification is that allegiance to science distinguishes its members from all other psychologists who presumably provide treatment based on unscientific professional traditions. The second implication is that all practitioners whose treatments are backed by science are welcome.

The extensive and rapidly growing EST literature supporting the efficacy and effectiveness[7] of psychodynamic therapies (PDTs) has considerably complicated professional identification. Meta-analyses by Abbass et al. (2006), Anderson and Lambert (1995), Crits-Christoph (1992), de Maat et al. (2009), Leichsenring (2001, 2005), Leichsenring and Leibing (2003), and Leichsenring et al. (2004) have demonstrated that psychodynamic therapies (PDTs) produce therapeutic effects that are greater than wait list controls, and sometimes equal to those produced by CBT.[8]

5 http://en.wikipedia.org/wiki/Xenophobia

6 http://www.abct.org/Home/

7 Nathan and Gorman (2002b) distinguished efficacy from effectiveness. *Efficacy* is concerned with replication of treatment effects that exceed appropriate control conditions. *Effectiveness* is concerned with practical results that can be obtained in clinical settings.

8 McKay (2011) cited important methodological issues that specifically pertain to Shedler's (2010) presentation and may well apply to other meta-analyses of psychodynamic therapy.

Thoma et al. (2012) assessed the research design quality of 120 randomized controlled trials (RCTs) of CBT covering 10,423 patients and 94 randomized controlled trials of psychodynamic therapy covering 7,200 patients. He found that the quality of both types of RCTs was essentially identical. The mean and standard deviation of quality scores was 25.5 (SD = 9.13) for the CBT trials and 25.1 (SD = 9.04) for the psychodynamic trials. These highly similar means are not statistically or clinically different. Research quality was found to be inversely related to effect size, with better studies showing smaller effects (F (4,91) = 12.6, $p < 0.0001$, adjusted $R^2 =$ 0.525) because they controlled for more sources of variation. Equity in research quality therefore means equity in effect size.

Controlled research also supports Emotion-focused Therapy (Ellison et al., 2009; Goldman et al., 2006; Greenberg & Watson, 1998; Watson et al., 2003). The International Society for Interpersonal Therapy reported that there are currently over 250 empirical studies supporting the effectiveness and efficacy of interpersonal therapy (IPT).[9] I do not cite evidence of effectiveness of CBT because it is so well established. A list of these interventions can be found at the following link: http://www.div12.org/PsychologicalTreatments/disorders.html.

Are all clinicians who base their practice on these ESTs inclined to join or welcomed to join ABCT? Will they be invited and accepted because there are now well-controlled studies demonstrating efficacy and effectiveness of PDT? Will empirically supported PDTs be included in the list of ESTs maintained by APA Division 12 (Clinical Psychology)? Will ABCT and Division 12 promote PDTs with the same enthusiasm as they promote CBTs? Are the explanations for why PDTs are effective to be accepted now that scientific support for their efficacy has been found? I expect that the answer to all of these questions is 'no'. Can allegiance to the scientific method resolve our professional identity fractures? I don't think so, because explanation is such a vital part of science. It is illogical to conclude that the underlying theory of why treatments should work is correct based on the fact that the treatment is effective, for this commits the logical error known as affirming the consequent. Treatments can have their effects for entirely different reasons than those proposed by the theory used to generate them. **Clinicians can be right for the wrong reasons**. Hence, clinicians with equally empirically supported treatments can claim that diametrically opposed theoretical reasons explain why their treatments are effective.

[9] http://interpersonalpsychotherapy.org/about-ipt/

There are few groups whose main goal is theoretical unification. They face the same membership challenges as do all other groups. Fortunately, psychologists often belong to more than one professional organization.

Don't Ask, Don't Tell

Sometimes psychologists ask one another for their theoretical orientation as an implied condition of acceptance. For example, applicants to graduate schools of psychology and applicants for externships and internships in clinical psychology are frequently asked for their theoretical orientation. These questions promote separatism by essentially asking '**what clan are you from**'; the implication being that '**we only care for our own kind here**'. Questions regarding theoretical orientation prime, promote, and activate implicit and explicit issues and controversies that serve to divide rather than unify psychology. I therefore recommend a '**Don't Ask, Don't Tell**' policy.

Personality

Berlin (1953) believed that investigator personality is a major reason why so little progress had been made concerning theoretical unification. He argued that theoretical unification was ego-syntonic for some psychologists and ego-dystonic for others. He labeled the former 'hedgehogs' and the latter 'foxes'. Explaining one's motive for theoretical unification as a personality characteristic suggests that these views are deeply held personal values without further clarification as to why these values are so strongly held, but does suggest that altering psychologists' views about theoretical unification entails personality change that is unlikely to occur.

No Ownership of Scientific Principles

Psychological principles need not be wedded to the particular camp that originated them. For example, reinforcement need not be called a behavioral principle to show that it was created by behaviorists. Reinforcement is a principle for modifying behavior, but that should not confer ownership by one clan thus inviting opposition by other clans. Working alliance need not be called a psychodynamic principle to show that it stems from the psychoanalytic/psychodynamic tradition. It could just be recognized as a principle of clinical psychology. Internal working models need no longer be discussed separately from schemas as if they are completely independent ideas. Tryon and Tryon (2011) took Shedler (2010) to task for attempting to own common factors in psychotherapy; to brand them as psychodynamic. In sum, adding unnecessary ownership labels to psychological principles serves no useful purpose but does promote corrosive separatism in an insidious way.

Psychologists should not have to say whether or not they use empirically supported treatments or have an evidence-based practice. Organized psychology defines itself as a science. Unless enough psychologists vote to redefine psychology as something other than a science, then all those who choose to call themselves psychologists should understand that they are identifying themselves as scientists and therefore as persons who value data and modify their explanations and therapeutic practices accordingly. Let all others who do not believe that clinical practice should be research-driven identify themselves in some other way; perhaps as applied philosophers.

Centering clinical training on psychological principles provides a theoretical foundation suitable for all clinical psychologists, thereby repairing our professional fractionation by emphasizing what we share in common rather than what divides us. Centering on psychological principles entitles one to refer to themself as a clinical psychologist **NFS** (not further specified).

No Incentives for Unification

I am unaware of any incentives for theoretical unification other than the joy of seeing a synthesis emerge from an otherwise fragmented field. Just the wonder that comes with scientific discovery and the belief that future generations of psychologists will appreciate your accomplishment.

REASONS AGAINST UNIFICATION

Concerns over disunification and the desirability of theoretical unification have been debated for a long time and have important implications for training and practice. Yanchar and Slife (1997) and Yanchar (2004) provided a general review of the relevant issues. Some psychologists worry that diversity of opinion will be squelched in an authoritarian drive to achieve uniformity over truth and impose the view of a few on everyone in the name of theoretical unification, putting an end to free inquiry and scholarly exchange. Why this should occur with the unification of psychology when it did not occur with the unification of biology, chemistry, and physics is never stated. Surely no one favors such a future. This irrational nightmarish fear seems intended to scare psychologists into maintaining present-day schisms.

On the contrary, legitimate theoretical unification occurs when a majority of psychologists voluntarily embrace a common perspective as a starting point to cooperatively develop their science. Consider the periodic table of elements. Chemists eagerly embraced this unified perspective. I seek theoretical unification of this kind; one based on intrinsic appeal.

While the goal is also to **end** up with a more correct theoretical unification, that can only happen by **starting** with some common vocabulary and core concepts. Theoretical unification begins more in the hope and promise of what a common perspective can provide than from a demonstration of what has been achieved. A science matures only when its citizens work together. This will not happen as long as they refuse to do so by insisting on separatism and diversity.

Theoretical Unification as Strait-Jacket

Yanchar (2004) noted that concern has been expressed by Green (1992), Koch (1981), Kukla (1992), Rychlak (1988), Toulmin (1987), Viney (1989, 1996), and Yanchar and Slife (1997) that efforts to unify psychology will effectively constrain psychology and place it in a theoretical strait-jacket. Yanchar (2004) cited Henriques's (2003, 2008) fixation on concepts by Freud and Skinner as an example of how other perspectives will be excluded in a rush towards unification. Yanchar (2004) noted that 'A psychology oriented toward truth, for example, rather than unity per se, is not likely to benefit from adherence to a single theoretical perspective set out in advance' (p. 1280). Placing truth and unification in opposition clearly favors the former over the latter. Achieving unification by some arbitrary premature means is particularly unattractive and should rightly set everyone against it now and in the future. The crucial missing element here is that unification should be natural and not forced. It should occur because the proposed synthetic position appeals to most psychologists as a sensible way forward so that it will be voluntarily embraced.

A related matter concerns openness to alternatives once unification occurs. Theoretical unification should therefore **not** mean intolerance of alternative interpretations and perspectives. Adding intolerance to arbitrary authoritarian imposition of a single theoretical perspective irrespective of truth presents an even more undesirable possibility that no one should support now or ever, as it is contrary to academic freedom and scholarly inquiry. So again we see that meaningful theoretical integration must take a form that appeals to most psychologists such that they will voluntarily endorse and subscribe to and support a common perspective.

Theoretical unification raises concern as to whether everyone's favorite concepts will be incorporated. This is not a requirement of theoretical unification and it is unlikely to occur. The history of physics, chemistry, and biology is that quite a few concepts were left behind as these sciences matured. Some concepts and questions will be left behind because they will no longer make sense or be relevant to the emergent perspective. For example, contemporary physicists do not conduct research into and/or ask meaningful questions about aether.[10] Shedler (2010) complained that:

> Undergraduate textbooks too often equate psychoanalytic or psychodynamic therapies with some of the **more outlandish and inaccessible speculations** made by Sigmund Freud roughly a century ago, rarely presenting mainstream psychodynamic concepts as understood and practiced today (p. 98, bold emphasis added).

While he did not specifically identify these 'outlandish and inaccessible speculations' we can assume that they included the constructs of penis envy, oral, anal, urethral, phallic, latency, and genital adult personality styles (Rychlak, 1981b, pp. 76–80) plus castration, Oedipal and Electra complexes. The theoretical unification that I propose leaves these concepts behind, but it provides a central role for unconscious processing which is a core conceptual 'must have' for all psychodynamic theories. Instead of evaluating the unification that I propose by the constructs left behind, it should be evaluated by what is included, which is a lot, and by how consilient the result is. These exclusions will undoubtedly disappoint some people. A unified psychology exists only to the extent that **vocabulary** and **core concepts** are shared by a majority of psychologists. Like political consensus, this means looking to the **center** rather than the extremes. A science matures when a **majority** of psychologists have adopted that vocabulary and core concepts. I seriously doubt that the concepts I have excluded are endorsed by a majority of contemporary psychologists.

Theoretical Impossibility

Some psychologists have argued that psychology can never be unified. Hayes (1998b) argued that biological, psychological, sociological, and anthropological explanations are each legitimate but distinct perspectives, thereby precluding the possibility of rendering one explanation in terms of another such as a biological (genetic) explanation of psychological and/or behavioral events. Kukla (1992) likened psychology to what he called 'the ill-advised science of *bology*, which studies the

[10] http://en.wikipedia.org/wiki/Aether_(classical_element)

properties of things that begin with the letter *b*' (p. 1055) and consequently cannot be unified.

Rychlak's (1968) first edition of *A Philosophy of Science for Personality Theory* discussed the philosophical bases underlying differences among personality theorists. Page 456 of his first edition presents a comprehensive comparison of the philosophical issues that separate the personality theorists who side with John Locke from those who side with Emanual Kant. Rychlak (1981b) subsequently wrote a book on personality and psychotherapy in which he recognized a third camp of mixed Lockeans and Kantians. Rychlak presented these philosophical issues in a way that maximizes their differences and strongly suggests that choice between polar opposites is ultimately required. This presentation minimizes common ground and maximizes confrontation. I intend to do the opposite here. I intend to show that some of these polarities are false dichotomies that should be rejected and thus avoided, or they are not substantive issues.

Rychlak (1993) strongly stated that psychology was faced with four separate explanatory bases that required acceptance because there was no possibility of theoretical integration. They are: (1) *Physikos*, the form of explanation used by physicists; (2) *Bios,* the form of explanation used by biologists; (3) *Socius,* the form of explanation used by sociologists; and (4) *Logos,* the form of explanation used by psychologists. Rychlak (1993) opined that:

> These grounds have been wound – singularly or in combination – into all of our theories in psychology. This is not an exhaustive list. Other grounds might be fashioned in the future. But for now I believe that psychology's complementarity should rely on these four grounds of equal stature, each capable of solitary application to any explanation. Complementarity is called for because these grounding assumptions are no more reconcilable than the wave-particle groundings of physics (p. 936).

Psychotherapy integration is an area where disillusionment regarding theoretical integration also exists. Goldfried (1980) stated how unlikely theoretical integration is:

> At the highest level of abstraction we have the *theoretical framework* to explain how and why change takes place, as well as an accompanying *philosophical stance* on the nature of human functioning. In the search for commonalities, it is unlikely that we can ever hope to reach common ground at either the theoretical or the philosophical level. Indeed, numerous differences can be found at this level within the psychoanalytic, behavioral, and humanistic orientations (p. 994).

Levy and Anderson (2013) concluded 'However, we are still far from a truly comprehensive and integrative theory of psychotherapy that operates across the different aspects of clinical work and the biological, psychological, and social levels of influence and experience' (p. 215). Castonguay (2011), in his presidential address, agreed when he wrote:

> However, considering the complexity of psychotherapy, it is unlikely that one theoretical orientation, method of investigation, or one type of knowledge seeker will ever be able to provide the field with a comprehensive view of therapeutic change and a complete set of interventions to alleviate psychological problems (p. 215).

Beutler and Castonguay (2006) supported this view by citing Goldfried and Padawer (1982) who reiterated that principles of therapeutic change are most likely to be found at a midlevel of abstraction somewhere between theoretical models and techniques. Guided in this way, Castonguay and Beutler (2006) used a lesser meaning of the term 'principle' to refer to facts capable of guiding clinical practice, such as 'Age is a negative predictor of a patient's response to general psychotherapy' (Beutler et al., 2006a, p. 27) and 'The more impaired or severe and disruptive the problem, the fewer benefits are noted for time-limited treatments' (Beutler et al., 2006b, p. 112). I counted 216 of these statements across 17 chapters in their book *Principles of Therapeutic Change That Work*. While useful in guiding clinical practice, these are not scientific principles like Archimedes's principle or Bernoulli's principle,[11] because they carry no explanatory power and therefore cannot facilitate theoretical unification.

I suggest that all of these problems have arisen because we have been thinking in **mental** rather than **physical** terms. I propose that serious progress towards theoretical unification and consequently psychotherapy integration can be made by thinking in **physical** terms instead. We are already united in what we don't know in this regard. We are not seriously divided based on differing views as to how psychology emerges from biology. Tryon (1994) noted that parallel-distributed processing connectionist neural networks (PDP-CNNs) had already made large strides toward integrating Bios and Logos, and to some extent Physikos. Smith (1996) and Read and Miller (1998) subsequently demonstrated that the PDP-CNN models also incorporate Socius. Hence, connectionist models already constitute a partial Hegelian synthesis of these four explanatory bases. The Bio↔Psychology Network Theory introduced in this book integrates connectionism with neuroscience in a way that yields four core and eight corollary network

[11] http://en.wikipedia.org/wiki/Scientific_law

principles that explain psychological phenomena in physical rather than mental terms.

Philosophical Schisms

Earlier in this book I complained that Rychlak's (1968, 1981a) book entitled *A Philosophy of Science for Personality Theory* identified long-standing philosophical issues that seemed to forever block the way forward towards theoretical unification and psychotherapy integration, as well as precluding psychological science from becoming a mature science. In this chapter I show how we can move forward on these issues and make good progress towards diminishing or possibly resolving many of these philosophical conundrums, at least to the point where they no longer require us to segregate ourselves according to positions taken with regard to these matters. I can only introduce my resolutions here because this is a chapter and not a book. I ask that you read this section with this limitation in mind.

In this section I aim to show that the philosophical schisms raised by Rychlak (1968, 1981a) are either false dichotomies that appear to require choice when none is needed or not substantive issues. I aim to maximize common ground and to identify a synthetic position for each schism that understands the two opposing/conflicting positions, thesis and antithesis, as special rare and extreme cases. My goal is to sufficiently diminish, mute, or resolve each schism to the point where it no longer divides most of us into competing schools and camps, thus enabling psychological science to move past these divisive schisms towards common ground upon which to base theoretical unification. Put otherwise, the schisms I address below have yielded much more heat than light. I am to reduce the temperature of these debates to at least a tepid and more manageable degree.

I fully recognize and accept that it is impossible to please all of the people all of the time, and that some psychologists will disagree and even oppose my efforts here. That is OK with me. I certainly do not expect to persuade established psychologists who have built their careers on separatism to agree with me. But as long as I can provide sufficient common ground to convince the majority of contemporary psychologists, and more importantly students of psychology that have not yet identified fully with one camp or another, to work together instead of bickering about these schisms, I will have succeeded.

Adopting the principle-based approach advocated here around the four core and eight corollary principles presented in Chapters 3 and 4 provides an explanatory approach based on empirically supported psychological science rather than philosophical argument. Such an adoption will hopefully remove the associated philosophical issues further to the theoretical background where they might have a lesser impact and no longer be sufficient to define and support schools and camps of psychological scientists. The validity of our core and corollary principles in no way depends directly upon any particular philosophical position regarding these philosophical conundrums, which is why these philosophical issues can be disregarded when explaining psychological phenomena using our core and corollary principles.

The general approach taken here is that of a Hegelian synthesis where opposing positions, **thesis** and **antithesis**, are shown to be special cases of a third synthetic perspective called the **synthesis**. A particular approach taken here is to show that some of the philosophical conundrums that have divided us are actually false dichotomies in the sense that they require choice when a third synthetic alternative is available. In this way the proposed Bio↔Psychology Network Theory satisfies psychologists on both sides of these issues, thereby rendering further debate moot. I address these issues in an order that is most approachable from the proposed Bio↔Psychology Network Theory.

In keeping with my modest definition of theoretical unification that emphasizes a working majority, I seek philosophical positions that a majority of psychologists can accept or have already accepted as my basis for a starting point for a unified psychology. I understand that as long as a single dissenting psychologist remains it can be said that these philosophical issues have not been fully resolved. I find this to be an extreme position and trust that a majority of my readers will also find this position to be extreme and reject it for this reason. I understand that the majority can be wrong, but again I wish to emphasize that theoretical unification is not about being right; it is about consensus. Let's see how much consensus can be generated.

Validating vs. Procedural Evidence[12]

Psychologists, like philosophers, disagree about what constitutes persuasive evidence. Rychlak (1968) defined method as '... the means or manner of determining whether a theoretical construct or proposition is true or false'

[12] Spectral evidence (http://en.wikipedia.org/wiki/Spectral_evidence) was once sufficient to impose the death penalty. It stems from dreams and/or visions where the accused person's spirit (spectre) was 'seen' behaving in a specific way by the witness. Such evidence was accepted without question during the Salem Witch Trials. Science fortunately enabled us to move beyond such explanations.

(p. 43). He then identified two methods that psychologists use. The **cognitive method** is based on what he called **procedural evidence**. **Logical consistency** is considered to be probative. Clinical psychologists use this type of reasoning when they write test reports. Consistent themes that are found across tests are considered to be true, valid, for the person. Their consistency is the primary evidence for their truth. The problem with this type of evidence is that logically derived hypotheses are contradicted, falsified by empirical study, with considerable frequency in all sciences. How can this be if consistency certifies truth? The history of science contains many examples where evidence falsified consistent reasoning. Consistency is necessary but not sufficient evidence of truth.

Rychlak (1968) identified **validating evidence** as the only type of evidence accepted by natural science. Validational evidence requires that research methods be used to collect data and that accepted methods of data analysis be used to analyze data prior to drawing conclusions. Even then we say that a research hypothesis is empirically supported instead of concluding that it has been validated or is true. Our analysis in the final section of Chapter 7 indicates that approximately 98% or more of contemporary psychologists already accept that psychology is a natural science and consequently accept and endorse the need for validating evidence. This means that we have already achieved theoretical unification on this point.

Falsifiability

Falsifiability plays a crucial role in validational evidence and consequently is central to natural science. Some observation made in accordance with accepted research methods must be possible that will falsify the hypothesis, or else it is not a scientific hypothesis. Stated otherwise, not all conjectures form scientific hypotheses. Only those conjectures that can be contradicted by some potential observable result constitute legitimate scientific hypotheses. For natural science this means that a publically observable event, one that could be captured with a video camera, is required. Otherwise the hypothesis remains outside of natural science; perhaps as some part of philosophy or theology. Creation science is not a science of any kind because there is no known way to falsify the creationist hypothesis and conclude that the Bible is wrong. Creation science is simply Bible study and should be recognized as such. That 98% or more of all contemporary psychologists endorse psychology as a natural science means that we already have theoretical unification regarding this matter.

Natural science also recognizes the inductive nature of validational evidence. Having observed one million crows and found them all to be black does not prove that all crows are black. Observing just one white crow will contradict and therefore falsify this hypothesis.

Mind vs. Body (Brain)

The mind–body problem is actually a mistake based in ignorance. Had Rene Descartes (1596–1650) lived and received a doctorate in neuroscience in this twenty-first century versus having no such degree in the sixteenth century it is extremely unlikely that he would have ever proposed that mind is in any way independent of brain. LeDoux's book entitled *Synaptic Self: How Our Brains Become Who We Are* reflects contemporary neuroscience. The bottom-line of this book is '**You are your synapses**' (p. ix, emphasis added).

> My notion of personality is pretty simple: it's that your 'self,' the essence of who you are, reflects patterns of interconnectivity between neurons in your brain (p. 2).

The totality of the interconnections among all neurons in a brain is called a **connectome**. The Human Connectome Project[13] is currently underway. It aims to map all of the major neural network connections in the human brain. Seung (2012) wrote a book entitled *Connectome: How The Brain's Wiring Makes Us Who We Are*, in which he claimed '**You are more than your genes. You are your connectome**' (p. xv, emphasis added). '**You are the activity of your neurons**' (p. xviii, emphasis added). He noted that connectomes are modified by what he refers to as the four Rs: **reweighting, reconnection, rewiring, and regeneration**. All of these are experience-dependent plasticity mechanisms, which means that they modify our connectome throughout our lifespan. The dedication in his book emphasizes this point: '**To my beloved mother and father, for creating my genome and molding my connectome**' (emphasis added).

There is no evidence that mind exists independent of brain and massive evidence that mind is what brain does. For example, people with a flat line for an EEG don't exhibit any properties of mind. Infants born without a brain (anencephaly) do not exhibit characteristics of mind. Anesthesia alters brain function and renders the mind unconscious. Brain damage via strokes, tumors, and/or trauma alters the mind. Many drugs alter the mind.

The mind–body debate also entails the question of whether or not a machine can be constructed that can sufficiently simulate functions of the

[13] http://www.humanconnectomeproject.org/

mind such that one can no longer distinguish the simulation from a real person. This is the essence of the Turin Test. Substantial progress has already been made in this regard. The IBM computer named Watson[14] can process natural language sufficiently well that it beat the human champion at Jeopardy. This accomplishment was considered to be impossible just a few short years ago. There is little reason to doubt that further progress can and will be made. The new Siri Assistant in the iPhone 4S and 5[15] represents another major advance in computer understanding of natural language.

In conclusion, while philosophers such as Van Oudenhove and Cuypers (2010) continue to review philosophical positions on the 'mind–body problem', sufficient empirical evidence exists to effectively resolve this issue. The mind–brain schism was born out of ignorance and continues due to ignorance of the massive body of evidence that clearly demonstrates that mind is an emergent property of brain; mind is entirely dependent upon brain. Natural science has consistently taken the view that the mind is what the brain does. This means that at least 98% of contemporary psychologists believe that the mind is what the brain does. Hence, this formal schism should no longer divide most of us; it should not constitute an impediment to theoretical unification.

Monism vs. Dualism

Psychologists frequently speak of psychological mechanisms where one psychological event or process influences others, such as when cognitions are said to influence emotions, when expectations are said to influence behaviors, or when one decision is said to impact another decision. Psychological mechanisms presume the existence of a **psychological substrate** upon which they can operate. In Chapter 1 we learned that there is absolutely no physical evidence that such a psychological substrate exists. Psychological mechanisms are metaphors that impute causality to the functional relationships that psychologists discover and study. Metaphors are not causal entities. They do not consist of a chain of events that brings about a result.

We rightfully sense a qualitative difference between body and mind that suggests that mind is not physical in the same way that the body is, and therefore the world might well contain two kinds of substances. I refer the reader to Chapter 1 where I presented the example reported by Eagleman (2011, pp. 2–4) about Arthur Alberts who tape-recorded the voice of an African villager who subsequently accused him of stealing his tongue. His

[14] www.ibm.com/watson

[15] http://www.apple.com/iphone/#

machine recorded only sound waves, the physical basis of voice, which is **qualitatively** different from the subjective experience of hearing a voice. So it is with brain and mind.

In conclusion, there is massive evidence that the brain is made of physical matter, and no evidence that a psychological substrate exists upon which psychological mechanisms can operate. Hence, this formal schism should no longer divide psychologists who base their views on empirical evidence. Therefore this schism should no longer stand in the way of theoretical unification.

Reductionism vs. Emergence

Reductionism seeks to replace higher-level constructs with lower-level ones. Wikipedia[16] reports that:

> **Reductionism** can mean either (a) an approach to understanding the nature of complex things by reducing them to the interactions of their parts, or to simpler or more fundamental things or (b) a philosophical position that a complex system is nothing but the sum of its parts, and that an account of it can be reduced to accounts of individual constituents. This can be said of *objects, phenomena, explanations*, theories, and meanings (emphasis in the original).

Rychlak (1968) defined reductionism as 'The procedure of analyzing propositions and constructs into simpler propositions and constructs (i.e., lower-level constructs) has been termed "reductionism"' (pp. 46-47). Miller and Keller (2000) more pointedly stated 'A term defined in one domain is characterized as *reduced* to terms in another domain (called the reduction science) when all meaning in the former is captured in the latter. The reduced term thus becomes unnecessary' (p. 212, italics in the original). Dennett (1995, p. 82) described and Lilienfeld (2007) referred to **greedy** reductionism as the systematic effort to replace psychology with neuroscience (see Miller, 2010; Miller & Keller, 2000). An alternative less aggressive form of reductionism identified by Dennett (1995, p. 82) is **eliminative** reductionism. It consists of a nebulous claim that somehow all psychological events are biological events. Reductionism threatens all psychologists with irrelevance and replacement, which helps us to understand the strong emotion and visceral reactions associated with this issue.

Miller and Keller (2000) endeavored to protect psychology from being reduced to neuroscience using several rationales. One argument was that because we have never done so it is impossible to do so. They did not, because they could not, actually prove what cannot be done. Attempting

[16] http://en.wikipedia.org/wiki/Reductionism

to prove what cannot occur is rather like proving that an effect does not exist; there are many ways to get it wrong; to fail. For example, in the case of demonstrating that an effect does not exist one can seem to succeed by using tests with low reliability and validity coefficients, methods that are inconsistently applied, using small and unequal experimental and control groups. This will minimize statistical power and maximize the probability of a Type II error where the probability of detecting a real effect will be sufficiently small that little or no evidence will be obtained supporting the hypothesized effect. Investigators can confidently, but incorrectly, conclude that the preponderance of the evidence is against the hypothesized effect.

Proof that better methods cannot possibly succeed in supporting the hypothesized effect is even more difficult to establish beyond reasonable doubt. Such proof must stem from deductive reasoning because inductive empirical evidence can always be falsified by the next study. It is also noteworthy that Miller and Keller (2000) endeavored to prove the extreme case where no part of psychology can be reduced to biology. This effort is vulnerable to the same problems and limitations as proving that an effect does not exist.

Another argument given by Miller and Keller (2000) concerns the nature of meaning. 'Because "fear" means more than a given type of neural activity, the concept of fear is not reducible to neural activity' (p. 212). This proof that psychology cannot be reduced to biology is definitional and thus protected from evidence. It is based on asserting a different vocabulary and explanatory scope for psychology and biology. What constitutes a complete explanation for psychology differs by definition from what constitutes a complete explanation for biology. Demonstrating that the vocabulary and basic concepts used by biologists have no bearing on or relevance to vocabulary and basic concepts used by psychologists does not preclude a causal connection between biology and psychology such that at least some part of psychology can be explained by some part of biology by agreeing upon a common vocabulary and explanatory scope. A primary goal of this book is to provide just such a vocabulary and a set of core and corollary concepts. The common vocabulary and set of core and corollary concepts that I have introduced will be used to support the antithesis of reductionism which is **emergence**.

A related argument by Miller and Keller (2000) is that biology and psychology do not interact. For example, 'The concept of "red" does not "interact" with the concept photon-driven chemical changes in the retina and their neural sequelae' (p. 214). This argument also depends upon maintaining separate vocabularies to describe psychological and biological phenomena. Constructing incomensurate definitions and concepts using different vocabularies certainly insulates psychology from biology, but does not preclude the construction of a common vocabulary and shared concepts such as those introduced in this book.

Another argument by Miller and Keller (2000) is that while contemporary brain imaging technology can identify brain areas that are active during psychological tasks, brain imaging cannot provide mechanism information to explain how neural circuits give rise to the psychological phenomena that they mediate. This is true because identification of brain structures in no way addresses the question of how they produce their functions. Dobbs (2005) and Uttal (2001) characterized this use of brain imaging as **modern phrenology**; i.e., attempting to explain psychology by identifying interior brain lobes rather than exterior skull lobes as the original phrenologists did. Connectionist neural network models seek to explain how mind **emerges** from brain by explaining how psychology emerges from neural networks. This explains my interest in these models and why they are so prominently featured in this book and artistically rendered on the book jacket.

Another argument against reductionism by Miller and Keller (2000) questions the connection between biology and psychology. They concluded '**There is an indefinite set of potential neural implementations of a given psychological phenomenon. Conversely, a given neural circuit might implement different psychological functions at different times or in different individuals. Thus, there is no *necessary* identity between psychological states and brain states**' (p. 214 italics in the original; bold face added). One might further argue that the way psychology is implemented biologically is not the same for every person, nor is it implemented the same way across the lifespan. Perhaps one implementation is used during childhood, another during adulthood, and yet another method is used during old age. Miller and Keller's (2000) position advances Fodor's (1968) distinction between *contingent* and *necessary* identity wherein the relationship between psychological and biological states is as follows:

> A person in any given psychological state is momentarily in some biological state as well: There is a *contingent* identity between the psychological and the biological at that moment. The psychological phenomenon implemented in a given neural circuit is not the same as, is not accounted for by, and is not reducible to that circuit (Miller & Keller, 2000, p. 214).

I refer to this as the **psychobiological implementation issue**. An empirical argument can be made for, but mainly against, this issue. The supportive empirical argument is that the avian brain implements color vision differently than does the mammalian brain. Hence, there is no one and only one correct and right neurological implementation of color vision. If there are two neurobiological ways of implementing color vision, then perhaps additional ways of implementing color vision are also possible. And if that is the case with color vision then it might well be the case with other abilities as well.

The contradictory empirical case can currently be made in at least two ways. (a) Whereas there are, in principle, multiple ways to encode genetic information, DNA is used by all invertebrates and vertebrates, including mammals, here on Earth. (b) Whereas there are, in principle, multiple ways to store memories that enable long-term learning, the same experience-dependent plasticity mechanisms are used by all invertebrates and vertebrates, including mammals, here on Earth. In both cases we do not find evidence of the multiple mechanisms that cognitive science posits in order to guard and protect against the possibility of reductionism. It is therefore highly unlikely that there are a large number of indefinite ways of biologically implementing every psychological state. Miller and Keller (2000) do not provide evidence or argument to support their claim that '**There is an indefinite set of potential neural implementations of a given psychological phenomenon**'. If this were true then there should be many other examples of different ways to implement color vision. That there are not undercuts their claim.

By denying that there is any consistent causal connection between biology and psychology, Miller and Keller (2000) have declared **independence** of psychology from biology. But have they gone too far in doing so? They are not alone in this matter because this position has long been widely used to justify cognitive science as an independent discipline. But the argument that psychology and biology are independent rests on the assumption that they are not meaningfully related. The major logical problem with such an argument is that there are a great many ways to not find something. Perhaps the first and most basic problem is that one does not want to find important connections. Half-hearted, poorly funded, poorly designed, rapidly abandoned research programs are sure ways not to find important relationships between psychology and biology.

The second basic problem is that there are so many ways to not find relationships. Perhaps there are but one or two ways to succeed and millions of ways not to succeed. It is much more likely that evidence of no relationship can be found than finding evidence of a relationship between biology and psychology. An important corollary point here is that one, several, or even many unsuccessful efforts to find a meaningful connection between biology and psychology does not prove that no successful relationship exists and therefore cannot possibly be found. One would need a certified complete list of all possible ways that psychology and biology could be related, and would have to show that none of them was viable, in order to definitively make this case. In sum, the conclusion that no meaningful connections between biology and psychology exist cannot be conclusively demonstrated by citing failures to date. This simply is not a convincing proof. It is an inductive argument that can be falsified with a single positive finding. The analogy with statistical power is informative and was discussed above.

One can assume that psychology is independent from biology, but care must be taken when making assumptions because everything that stems from them will be falsified if the assumption proves to be incorrect. Whereas assumptions are made to facilitate some lines of reasoning, unintended consequences may be encountered. The first major unintended problem created by the independence assumption is that it isolates psychology from biology and precludes psychology from joining biology, chemistry, and physics as a consilient science (cf. Wilson, 1998). Wilson's primary thesis is that nature is unified and can only be properly understood by interdisciplinary study. Stated otherwise, mankind has artificially divided nature into pieces and assigned their study to academic departments which have further divided their study into smaller pieces. This process has obscured the larger holistic perspective which Wilson refers to as consilience. Defining psychology in a way that excludes it from integrating with neuroscience rejects Wilson's consilience thesis without examining its merits. Space does not permit a review of all of the arguments advanced by Wilson (1998) in favor of consilience,[17] but these additional advantages are forfeit by declaring the independence of psychology from all other sciences in an attempt to avoid reductionism.

The second major unintended problem created by declaring psychology independent of biology is that psychological models cannot be informed by neuroscience. This allows one to create psychological models that don't pertain to people. **Computer science** is centered on the computer metaphor

[17] http://en.wikipedia.org/wiki/Consilience_(book)

with its separate processor and memory design and its serial processing architecture, whereas **computational neuroscience** is centered on the brain metaphor with is common processor/memory design and parallel processing. Cognitive scientists use their declaration of independence to justify why they do not constrain their psychological models with neuroscience facts. They claim that they do not need to consider how our biology implements our psychology because other methods of implementation are also possible. They reject the possibility of learning about psychology through biological study. Unfortunately, such independence can, and has, led to the development of psychological models that are contradicted by well-established neuroscience evidence. But, psychologists who work in isolation from neuroscience continue to insist their view is correct even though it isn't. Isolation in science comes at a terrible cost.

Cognitive science was originally, and continues to be, based on the digital computer model that has several characteristics that conflict with neuroscience. First, it has separate architectures for memory storage and for processing. Computers store data in separate memory locations and retrieve them for processing as needed with a central processing unit (CPU) that has its own architecture. Processing and memory are done by the same neurons in biological systems. Whereas computers are unchanged by the processing they do, biological systems are modified by the processing they do. Specifically, computer memory remains unchanged by CPU activities, whereas memories are modified by learning that occurs in biological systems. This gives biological systems an adaptive and developmental quality that digital computers currently lack. Computer science understands information processing from a symbol manipulation perspective. Biological systems use a network activation approach. Psychologists who work in isolation of neuroscience confidently continue with their mistaken models.

Processing in computer science models is done one step at a time; in serial rather than in parallel. This approach is demonstrably wrong in at least five ways. First, Grill-Spector and Kanwisher (2005) reported that the time taken to perceptually categorize an object equals the time needed to recognize the presence of the object. Both processes occur simultaneously. The common-sense serial perspective of first recognizing the presence of an object and then categorizing it is falsified by their data that consistently demonstrated equivalent times for both object recognition and categorization. Second, Casey and Tryon (2001) endeavored to measure processing time separate from reading time and discovered evidence that participants were thinking while reading. Participants did not first read and then begin to think; both processes occurred in parallel. Third, humans are organized bilaterally with two eyes, ears, arms, and legs. Information from left and right sides of the body are processed simultaneously by the right and left hemispheres respectively. Innervations of the left and right sides of the body are processed simultaneously by the right and left hemispheres respectively. Fourth, serial processing is several orders of magnitude too slow to account for real-time processing for all functions that have psychological significance. Fifth, computer science understands cognition only in terms of following rules. When asked, experts in many fields report that they do not solve problems by following rules in any step-by-step fashion. Computer science tends to minimize this problem by claiming that they approach psychology '**as if**' people processed information in serial fashion using rules, except this is not how people actually think. Constructing psychological models based on erroneous assumptions and preferences for how people **should** behave seems seriously flawed. Why should we continue with 'as if' models that have already been falsified in fundamental ways?

Miller and Keller (2000) made a practical argument against an important implication of reductionism. If one assumes that psychology can be reduced to biology then why not just fund biologists and not fund psychologists? Isn't it best to always use a biological method to treat a biological disorder? For example, if one understands mental illness as a 'chemical imbalance' then aren't pills the best way to treat it? The answer is no; not always. For example, phenylketonuria (PKU) is a genetic disorder that is presently best treated by a diet that is very low in or free of phenylalanine.

A far more compelling case against reductionism can be made by making the case for its antithesis, its explanatory complement; **emergence**. Emergence, compared to reductionism, concerns the more complex case of two possible relationships between psychology and biology. The *APA Concise Dictionary of Psychology* (2009) defines **emergence** as '**the idea that complex phenomena (e.g., conscious experiences) are derived from arrangements of or interactions among component phenomena (e.g., brain processes) but exhibit characteristics not predictable from those component phenomena**' (p. 163, bold emphasis added). For example, the physical properties of liquid water differ qualitatively and dramatically from those of its gaseous constituent elements of hydrogen and oxygen. We know that water is composed of two molecules of hydrogen gas and one molecule of oxygen gas, but neither of these gases shares any physical properties with water. So it is clearly impossible to reduce the properties of water to some property of hydrogen gas or some property of oxygen gas, or a list of properties of both gases. Water is a new qualitatively different substance that arises from the interaction of hydrogen and oxygen, and therefore cannot be explained in a reductionistic way. The emergent properties of water derive from its physical structure; i.e., how its atoms are interconnected.[18] Similarly, salt is required for life but is constructed from two deadly substances: sodium and chlorine. The emergent properties of salt cannot be reduced to the properties of sodium or chlorine. Emergence is central to chemistry. All complex compounds have some properties that cannot be reduced to the properties of their constituent elements.

Chemists do not fear reductionism. They do not try to avoid reductionism. Chemists are not concerned about being replaced by physicists. Chemists have not found it necessary to declare independence from physics. The field of quantum chemistry[19] blends chemistry and physics. Chemists still have jobs. Chemists embrace and study emergence from a monist position. Likewise, biologists don't fear chemists or physicists. The field of biochemistry has not replaced and displaced biologists or chemists. Instead, it has provided employment for a new group of scientists. Psychologists similarly have nothing to fear from neuroscience as long as they are centrally concerned with emergence.

Several other examples of emergence are illustrated at the following web site: http://www.pbs.org/wgbh/nova/sciencenow/3410/03.html. Consider the example of how birds flock. A reductionist approach would break down the flock into its constituent elements, individual birds, and then analyze each bird in the laboratory for the cause of flocking. This search is doomed for at least two reasons. First, single birds don't flock so the relevant phenomena cannot be studied at the level of the bird. Second, no one bird is in complete control of the flock; i.e., there is no executive bird that can be identified and studied to isolate the cause of flocking. Flocking occurs because each bird is sensitive to the position of neighboring birds; i.e., birds respond to their immediate local environment. Any change in direction by one bird is immediately sensed by the birds to its immediate left, right, above, and below, causing them to change their position to maintain their distances from one another. Such changes **propagate** throughout the group of birds causing the behavior we call flocking. Hence, flocking is caused by every bird to some extent and cannot be reduced to any individual bird

[18] The following URL provides detailed information about the physics and chemistry of water http://en.wikipedia.org/wiki/Water_(molecule)#Physics_and_chemistry_of_water.

[19] http://en.wikipedia.org/wiki/Quantum_chemistry

except in the trivial sense that it takes a group of birds to flock and that each bird is sensitive to its neighbors.

Brain neurons share many functional features with flocking. Each neuron responds mainly to its neighbors via activation and inhibition. Collectively, neurons exhibit intelligence in roughly the same way that bees exhibit a 'hive mind'.[20] This can be seen in the choice of a new nesting site. A bee that finds a suitable new nesting site returns to the hive and performs a waggle dance giving direction to the identified site. This bee's waggle dance **activates** only adjacent bees that do the same dance, causing this dance to propagate throughout the hive from bee to bee. Other bees who find different potential nesting sites return to the hive and perform waggle dances giving direction to those sites. Each bee's waggle dance activates only adjacent bees to do the same dance. These dances also propagate throughout the hive from bee to bee. A dynamic balance is created by these competing activations. The balance eventually shifts in favor of one dance or another and it is at this moment that the 'hive mind' decides on a new nesting site. A similar 'voting' process occurs with neurons as their activations spread across our neural networks. The brain 'decides' based on a majority neuron vote. Both of these examples entail emergence. There is nothing reductionistic about how either the 'hive mind' or real brains make decisions. Likewise, theoretical unification occurs when enough psychologists are persuaded to adopt a common perspective and take the profession in a new direction. The remainder of this book is an effort to seek your vote!

Psychology entails the study of emergent phenomena. For example, functional magnetic resonance imaging (fMRI), and other brain imaging technologies, enable investigators to observe and quantify brain activation occurring during psychological tasks. Cognitive neuroscientists have focused almost exclusively on identifying brain areas that mediate various psychological functions.[21] These methods support biological rather than psychological explanations. Psychologists want to know how these neural networks give rise to cognition. Synthetic, i.e., emergent, explanations are more likely to provide better answers than reductionist explanations. Understanding how the interaction of billions of neurons and trillions of synapses gives rise to consciousness and cognition is more likely to yield positive results than are efforts to reduce psychological functions to neural functioning to chemistry and physics. Our discussion in the next chapter of how the automatic connectionist neural network cascade **transforms**

[20] http://www.youtube.com/watch?v=AonV_MkUFSs

[21] see www.humanconnectiomeproject.org for a map of major brain connections

stimulus microfeatures into latent constructs provides a plausible emergent answer to the question of how networks produce psychology that also conceptually integrates psychology, psychometrics, and neuroscience. Software called **Emergent** is freely available for exploring emergence in simulated neural networks.[22]

An alternative way to make an argument that supports emergence is to note that identifying biological elements such as brain areas/structures, neurotransmitters, and other biological facts supports the construction of biological explanations, but not psychological explanations. Missing is a way to explain how these neuroscience facts give rise to, and thereby explain, psychological phenomena. How do the identified brain areas/structures implement/mediate the psychological functions attributed to them? How can neurotransmitters exert psychological effects? **Showing that brain structures and neurotransmitters mediate psychological phenomena is not the same as explaining how they do it. Description and association do not constitute explanation**. The network approach advocated in this book seeks to provide this missing mechanism information in the form of four core and eight corollary network principles.

Our emergent perspective enables us to also see that **explainable is not equal to reducible**. The Bio↔Psychology Network Theory presented in this book recognizes that the first half of a complete explanation entails identifying the biological parts, processes, and mechanisms that mediate psychological phenomena. But a complete catalog of such things cannot explain how those parts produce psychological phenomena. Some assembly is always required. Isolated biological facts cannot explain how psychology emerges from biology. Emergence is the **explanatory complement** of reductionism. Emergence is the science of understanding how complexity arises from simple parts.

If one can explain complex phenomena as emerging from simpler phenomena in terms of emergence, one has not reduced the complex phenomenon to simpler elements, nor has one replaced the complex phenomenon with simpler ones. It is a concern over replacing psychology with biology that appears to motivate most arguments against reductionism. The argument here is that reductionism alone cannot succeed because psychology emerges from biology. Emergence transforms biology into psychology. Emergence explains how and why psychology exists. The need to provide emergent explanations establishes psychology in its own right.

22 http://grey.colorado.edu/emergent/index.php/Main_Page

In conclusion, I submit that psychologists no longer need to fear reductionism, nor does it need to continue to defend against it. Reductionism provides the components that emergence needs to combine into a synthetic explanation of how psychology emerges from biology; how mind emerges from brain. There is no need to choose here. The schisms of reductionism vs. no reductionism or reductionism vs. emergence are **false dichotomies** and should be dismissed as such. Hence, concern about reductionism should no longer divide most of us and therefore should no longer stand in the way of theoretical unification.

Hard vs. Soft Determinism

Psychologists, like philosophers, disagree about determinism; i.e., the extent to which we are free to make decisions about our behavior. Hard determinism is frequently characterized as meaning that only one outcome is possible; that no choice is possible. Soft determinism is contrasted with hard determinism to essentially mean no determinism. People are thought to freely choose everything. Some people even believe that sexual orientation is a free choice. I aim to show that these hard choices constitute a **false dichotomy** that can, and should, be rejected in favor of an integrative third choice.

I propose the following synthetic perspective. Shannon (1949) defined information as the reduction of uncertainty. Likewise, I define determinism as the **reduction of alternatives**. Determinism can be viewed as a continuum with completely hard determinism at one end and completely soft determinism at the other end. Now we can see that there are many other choices rather than just the two extreme polar opposites. Different people can be at different places along the continuum depending upon the accidents of their birth, including the time in history that they were born, what country they were born into, where their parents were living at the time of their birth, what socio-economic class they are part of, their gender, skin color, sexual orientation, body build, general intelligence, and specific talents for music, math, mechanics, sports, etc. All of these variables and more reduce, or not, the options one has in life. Some people's options are more constrained than others. Some life paths are more probable than others. Some options are completely closed to some people. For example, people who are not born in the United States cannot be President. Very short people will not play professional basketball. Uncoordinated people will not play major league baseball. Retarded people will not win Nobel prizes. All people are not created equal and all people do not have the same advantages and opportunities in life.

Determinism is not constant for a given individual. Infants and small children have little control over their lives. They generally do not control where they are, what they wear, and what they eat. Determinism for them is extreme at this time. Greater choice typically accompanies physical and cognitive development, up to some maximum point reached during their adult life where they are at their occupational and financial peak and are still in good health. Normal aging, and/or disease restrict options and in the end decisions are made for you by your adult children or their surrogates. All such factors increase determinism for particular individuals.

Our society and entire Western tradition of law and Judeo-Christian religion and system of ethics is based on the premise of soft determinism and freedom of choice. Personal responsibility is the basis for holding people accountable for their actions. Some people go so far as to assert that sexual orientation is freely chosen and therefore can be freely rejected if only they want to. People are punished based on the presumption that they wilfully choose to misbehave. Exceptions to such justice are few and include being found not guilty by reason of insanity or diminished capacity. Heaven is the reward for good people who make the right choices and hell is the punishment for sinners who make the wrong choices. Skinner (1971) pursued the social implications of determinism in his book entitled *Beyond Freedom and Dignity*.

In conclusion, I view the choice between hard and soft determinism as a false dichotomy that should be rejected. Determinism is always present to some degree and varies from person to person and across the lifespan. The degree to which behavior is constrained is the real issue. Factors that constrain thoughts, feelings, and actions should be identified so that we can better understand and manage our affairs. Ignoring these controlling factors does not free us from them. Things still fall down even if one chooses not to believe in a universal law of gravitation. We ignore these determinants at our own peril. Ignoring these sources of control makes it possible for other people who recognize them to exploit and control us, while leaving the impression that all outcomes are the result of our 'free' will. Hence, this formal schism should no longer divide most of us and therefore this schism should no longer stand in the way of theoretical unification.

Nature vs. Nurture

Psychologists, like philosophers, disagree about the impact of nature and nurture on psychological phenomena. The nature vs. nurture schism has long divided psychologists. This schism is also based on a false dichotomy.

Nature without nurture predictably ends in early death by starvation or exposure, or results in severe disability depending directly on the degree to which nurture is withheld. Nurture without nature, without a corporal being, is meaningless.

LeDoux (2002) noted that nature and nurture speak the same language in that 'They both ultimately achieve their mental and behavioral effects by shaping the synaptic organization of the brain' (p. 3). He further noted that 'The puzzle of how nature and nurture shape who we are is simplified by the realization that synapses are the key to the operations of both' (p. 5). To illustrate his point he compared nature and nurture to making bank deposits by electronic transfer or by check. Both methods causally influence the account balance. It is meaningless to debate which method of making deposits is more important to the total balance.

Nature and nurture combine to form behavior in essentially the same way that length and width combine to form area. The same area, say 400 square feet, can be created in several ways. One can have a square of 20 feet on a side. Or one can have a 40 × 10 or a 10 × 40 rectangle. Or one can have a variety of other combinations that equal 400 square feet. All have equal area, but different length and width components. So it is with nature and nurture. Various combinations can produce the same result. Being asked to choose between nature and nurture is absurd. Such choice is based on a false dichotomy that should be rejected. Area has no more to do with length than width and discussions that imply this is so are ridiculous.

A more relevant question pertaining to nature and nurture is the question of **how** they interact. Anastasi (1958) prompted psychologists to answer this question over a half century ago, but little progress has been made by psychologists. Behavioral geneticists compute heritability ratios which can assume a wide variety of values depending upon sample characteristics. Heritability statistics can be readily manipulated. By holding environmental factors constant, genetic factors will explain most of the observed variance. By holding genetic factors constant, environmental factors will explain most of the observed variance. Therefore, heritability statistics are largely meaningless unless they are qualified by information regarding how representative the environmental and genetic factors are. And even then, interventions that modify environmental factors can be therapeutic, such as when the inherited disorder of phenylketonuria is treated entirely by diet.

Neural network models provide a way to conduct real experiments in this area. Nature constructs real neural networks. Investigators create artificial neural network architectures. Nurture provides learning histories.

Investigators can specify learning histories with great precision. Nurture sometimes creates trauma. Investigators can damage artificial neural networks in precise ways.

In conclusion, we should now be able to see that the nature vs. nurture schism is a false dichotomy that should be rejected rather than debated. Hence, this formal schism should no longer divide most of us, and therefore this schism should no longer stand in the way of theoretical unification.

Human vs. Animal Learning

Psychologists once considered that their studies of animal behavior enabled them to discover general principles that also apply to people. For example, Skinner's experimental analysis of behavior was based on pigeons and rats. Applied behavior analysts use principles derived from the experimental analysis of animal behavior to effectively treat a wide variety of human behavior disorders.

Prior to about 1968 psychologists rarely questioned the human relevance of research on animal behavior, but the cognitive revolution that began during the 1970s changed all of that (Bandura, 1978; Dember, 1974; Gardner, 1985; Mahoney, 1977). Interest in higher cognitive functions as major determinants of behavior led to the belief that people and animals learned differently. Animals were said to learn by association, whereas people learned via cognition. The processes involved were presumed to be very different. This view has been seriously falsified by compelling empirical evidence. Research summarized by Bear et al. (2007), Carlson (2010), Hell and Ehlers (2008), Kalat (2009), Lisman and Hell (2008), and Squire et al. (2008), among others, has identified learning mechanisms based on animal studies that are phylogenetically general, which means that they pertain equally well to people of all ages; e.g., infants, children, and adults. The human relevance of this animal research is widely accepted.

In conclusion, psychology has had a checkered history with regard to the human relevance of animal research. The brief history presented above shows that with the rise of neuroscience we have come full circle to acknowledging the human relevance of animal research. We can now see that the debate about animal versus human learning is based on a false dichotomy that seems to require choice. This false dichotomy should be rejected rather than debated. Hence, this formal schism should no longer divide most of us, and therefore this schism should no longer stand in the way of theoretical unification.

Network vs. Rule-based

Rychlak (1968, 1981a) did not discuss this issue but it is a central philosophical issue that separates the **subsymbolic** approach taken by connectionists from the **symbolic** approach taken by traditional cognitive psychologists. The central question here is whether the mind is best understood in network terms or in rule-based terms. Sloman (1996) summarized this controversy as follows:

> One of the oldest conundrums in psychology is whether people are best conceived as parallel processors of information who operate along diffuse associative links or as analysts who operate by deliberate and sequential manipulation of internal representations. Are inferences drawn through a network of learned associative pathways or through application of a kind of "psychologic" that manipulates symbolic tokens in a rule-governed way? The debate has raged (again) in cognitive psychology for almost a decade now. It has pitted those who prefer models of mental phenomena to be built out of networks of associative devices that pass activation around in parallel and distributed form (the way brains probably function) against those who prefer models built out of formal languages in which symbols are composed into sentences that are processed sequentially (the way computers function) (p. 3).

Sloman (1996) traced this argument back to James (1890/1950) and the very beginning of psychology. His reference to its raging again for almost a decade, given that Sloman published in 1996, places the resurgence of this issue around 1986. This is the date that McClelland et al. (1986) and Rumelhart and McClelland (1986) published their seminal landmark two-volume work on connectionism. This debate continues to date, modified only by the exponential growth of connectionism as a successful approach to a broad spectrum of psychological phenomenon with a very promising future.

Sternberg and McClelland (2011) discussed this issue and presented evidence regarding what they referred to as 'Two Mechanisms of Contingency Learning'. These two mechanisms were: (a) pathway-strengthening accounts of learning; and (b) inference-based accounts of learning. The first mechanism entails the gradual formation of associations, whereas the second mechanism entails sudden insight. Whereas the abstract to their article suggests that both types of mechanisms exist, the authors concluded that 'It remains possible that some form of associative or pathway-strengthening process is at work in all forms of learning…' (p. 67). It is noteworthy that specific mechanism information was not provided for by either type of learning, as is typically the case when psychologists promise to provide mechanism information.

The debate between pathway-strengthening vs. inference-based accounts of learning can be viewed in terms of possible mechanisms. Learning by pathway-strengthening can readily be understood from a neural network perspective and its causal mechanisms. Activation that repeatedly follows particular pathways through the neural network is likely to recur, given that neurons that fire together tend to wire together. The neuroscience mechanism of experience-dependent plasticity that makes this so is quite well understood. Learning by inference-based accounts implies some sort of psychological substrate, but there is not a shred of evidence that such a substrate exists (see Chapter 1). Nor has any physical mechanism been identified that can implement inference-based learning. Hence the choice is between a pathway-strengthening approach to learning for which causal mechanisms are known, versus an inference-based approach to learning for which no causal mechanisms are known and for which no physical basis for such causal mechanisms exist. This seems to me to be an easy decision in favor of the pathway-strengthening explanation of learning.

I believe that I have already made a strong case for pathway-strengthening learning and could stop here. I continue because of the following 12 **fatal flaws** associated with the rule-governed symbol-manipulating, inference-based approach to cognitive psychology. Network models avoid all of them and thus are to be preferred for at least these reasons.

Consciousness

The **first** fatal flaw of rule-based models is that they assume consciousness; network models do not. One reasons from axioms not too them. Therefore, rule-based models can never explain consciousness, yet consciousness is fundamental to psychology. Alternatively stated, assuming consciousness precludes explaining it. This places a substantial and serious limitation on the scope of psychological science when approached from a rule-based perspective. One can always draw the conceptual boundary here and say that explanations of consciousness belong exclusively to neuroscience. However, explaining consciousness seems like a task that psychologists should be interested in.

A related reason that supports this first fatal flaw is that the extensive literature on unconscious processing reviewed in Chapter 3 contradicts rule-following which has always been considered to be a fully conscious process. One can reply that rule-following was only ever intended to pertain to conscious processing. Given the iceberg analogy, that restricts rule-based processing to around 10% of what people do. Hence, rule-following at best is a minor matter and therefore cannot support a general theory of psychology.

Together these two deficiencies demonstrate that while rule-based models may fit a subset of empirical facts that currently constitute an important field within psychological science, they lack the necessary explanatory scope to be comprehensive psychological models. Network models do not share these limitations. I should be able to stop here as this first fatal flaw in combination with the above-mentioned fatal flaw is sufficient for me to prefer to base psychological science on network models than on rule-based models, but there are ten other reasons that over determine this choice.

Rationality

The **second** fatal flaw in rule-based models is that they treat people as always fully rational and assume that emotions never play a significant role in how people think and behave. People always follow rules. Kahneman (2011) distinguished our slow, deliberate, analytic, rational, step-by-step but lazy effortful System 2 from our fast, automatic, intuitive, irrational, impulsive, emotional, and largely unconscious System 1 that leaps to conclusions that System 2 may or may not examine further. The extensive empirical evidence of illogical, irrational, impulsive, and emotionally driven behavior that characterizes Kahneman's (2011) System 1 reviewed in Chapter 3 falsifies the rationality assumption upon which rule-based models are based. This distinction was not original to Kahneman but has a long history that I review in Chapter 3 as Dual Processing Theories. One can draw a conceptual boundary and declare that psychological science is constrained to deal only with that subset of human behavior that constitutes Kahneman's System 2. This would be unfortunate for clinical psychologists, as System 1 is much more relevant to them than System 2. One can accurately describe cognitive and cognitive-behavioral therapies as an effort to use System 2 to modify the problems created by System 1.

'As if' Models

The **third** fatal flaw is that symbol manipulating cognitive psychologists act **as if** people follow rules like digital computers, even if they don't. One can make models of how people **might behave** rather than how they **actually** behave. This approach is convenient, despite being inappropriate and misguided. '**As if**' models are not just simplifications of complex phenomena but rather are **qualitatively** different. They ignore fundamental characteristics of phenomena being explained to fit a preferred ideology and/or model of human behavior. Hence, serial processing models continue to be preferred by many cognitive psychologists, despite the fact that the brain processes in parallel and that serial models are orders of magnitude too slow to adequately explain how people process information.

Economists also develop 'as if' models for a species that Kahneman (2011) calls **homo economicus**.[23] These mythical beings are always rational. They are always fully aware of every alternative and always process information rationally. This assumption is crucial to the mathematical models economists construct regarding human behavior. Homo economicus has no feelings, or if they do their feelings never distort their thinking. Economists find it easier to develop mathematical models to predict the behavior of homo economicus than to predict the behavior of real people. Kahneman (2011) is a psychologist who won the Nobel prize in economics for his extensive empirical studies of human irrationality that falsifies the assumption that people behave like homo economicus.

Perhaps the most extreme example of 'as if' models comes from the field of animal intelligence. If you search the Internet for 'dogs do calculus' you will find several sources that document the following experiment. Place a person with a stick and their dog together on a beach. Throw the stick diagonally into the water. Observe that the dog runs down the beach to a point roughly perpendicular to where the stick is floating before the dog enters the water and swims to the stick. The conclusion is that dogs do calculus because they minimize the distance that they must swim in the water. This explanation acts 'as if' dogs can actually do calculus based on the fact that a mathematical analysis using calculus would show that the dog followed the best strategy. Dogs may act in ways that can also be described by calculus, but almost certainly dogs really don't perform calculus computations prior to fetching a stick. Alternative explanations are not considered. Likewise, people may act in ways that can be described by rules, but that does not prove that people follow rules any more than the dog experiment proves that dogs do calculus.

Constructing 'as if' models enables one to construct models of any kind and of any degree of complexity. If we are going to act 'as if' dogs are mathematicians, what is to prevent us from acting 'as if' dogs are biologists who perform a metabolic analysis to see which route consumes the fewest calories before retrieving the stick? It is one thing to use simple models of complex processes as when one studies an artificial neural network to learn

[23] http://en.wikipedia.org/wiki/Homo_economicus

something about the brain, but it is quite another matter to act as if brains are computers or as if people don't have emotions.

Learning & Memory

The **fourth** fatal flaw in rule-based models is that they **assume** that people can learn and remember instead of **explaining** how people learn and remember. Rule-based explanations never explain how rules are learned or how rules are remembered. Nor do they explain how rules generate behavior. The rule-based approach merely asserts without explanation that rules are learned and remembered. Parents don't appear to explicitly teach rules to infants and young children. Somehow rules just appear. In fact, rules are generated by investigators to explain observed regularities in what people do. None of this proves that people actually follow rules.

Learning and memory are arguably the two most important basic processes that enable psychological phenomena to exist. If people could not learn and remember then infants would not develop into the children and adults that have served as the subjects in the psychological experiments that have given rise to rule-based models. That rule-based models cannot explain how learning and memory works means that they lack the necessary mechanism information required by a mature psychological science.

Because rule-based models do not address learning and memory, they do not have a developmental component. Are the rules that children follow the same or different than the rules that adults follow? If so, how do rules develop? That these and other seemingly impossible questions arise from a rule-based approach should motivate one to seek alternative explanations. That network models are trained via experience, learned not programmed, automatically provides them with a developmental history; i.e., makes them inherently developmental. This feature fully integrates developmental psychology into network models; a feature not shared by rule-based models. Clinical psychologists, especially those dealing with children and families, need to be informed about development. Because rule-based models ignore development, they fail to benefit from or contribute to developmental psychology and therefore cannot inform clinicians in any meaningful way.

Behavioral Limits

The **fifth** fatal flaw of rule-based models is that they maintain that rationality prevents harming oneself. For example, Sloman (1996) said:

> People are renowned for their willingness to behave in ways that they cannot justify, let alone explain. Instead of performing a complete analysis of their

> interests, people vote for a politician because they have always voted for that person; they buy an item because it is associated with an image that they would like to project. **Most people however only go so far. They would not do something that would be considered irrational if it entailed a real penalty or cost. They would not buy the item if it had been linked to cancer** (p. 19, bold emphasis added).

Except that people do things that harm their health, including causing cancer. People buy cigarettes and smoke, eat too much animal fat, drink too much alcohol, and don't adequately exercise. People also drive drunk, text while driving, take drugs, and don't follow medical advice. All of these activities can cause serious problems including death. Behavioral medicine is aimed at treating a wide variety of destructive behaviors that many people engage in. All of these '**exceptions to the rule**' constitute fatal flaws for rule-based models; especially for clinical psychologists who treat people for these self-destructive behaviors. Network models do not share these limitations as they are compatible with cognitive heuristics and other foibles that can be understood as network properties that evolved long ago when life was very different from modern times.

Emotion

The **sixth** fatal flaw of rule-based models is that there are **no emotional rules** that guide and explain how people feel, nor are there rules that govern how **feelings** influence how people think and behave. This exclusion restricts the explanatory scope of rule-based models to conscious rational processing, which is a small part of what people do. Network models can integrate emotion and cognition.

Brain Damage/Aging/Medications

The **seventh** fatal flaw of rule-based models is that they have mainly been developed on healthy young adults; predominantly college sophomores enrolled in Introductory Psychology courses. These models are silent with regard to the effects of brain damage due to trauma, dementia, and/or schizophrenia. How do these events alter the rules that people follow? Or how do these events alter how people follow the same rules that they used to follow? And how do psychotropic medications alter the rules that people follow? Do effective medications return people to the rules that they used to follow? Or does this not happen? Perhaps medications change the rules. Perhaps medications create new rules or cause the people to follow the old rules in new ways. And what physical mechanism(s) control all of these rule changes? Do animals follow the same rules as people do? If not, how do the rules that animals follow differ from the rules that people follow? Are the rules that dogs follow different from the rules that cats follow? What about birds, fish, and monkeys? These and many related questions stem from a rule-following perspective. It is unlikely that all of these questions can be answered satisfactorily. All of these problems are self-inflicted in that they can all be avoided by just not presuming that behavior is best explained by rule-following. This is like the mind–body problem. It was also a self-inflicted problem that could have been avoided by simply not distinguishing mind from brain. Part of theory construction is avoiding approaches that unnecessarily create unsolvable intractable problems.

Existence of Rules

The **eighth** fatal flaw of rule-based models is that rules are hypothetical constructs inferred by investigators. The evidence that people follow rules is the same as the evidence that dogs do calculus. Namely, rules are invented by investigators to explain their observations. Investigators then mistakenly confuse these rules with causal mechanisms. There is no physical evidence that the brain contains rules. Rules are metaphors. Rules are an analogy that connects two things such as psychology and behavior. Rule-based models imply that experts should be able to specify the rules by which they operate. When experts are asked about how they make decisions like picking a stock or perform surgery, they do not spontaneously provide a list of rules that they follow. When asked for rules, experts frequently deny that they are following rules in any step-by-step way or even in a general way. That they cannot do so seriously questions whether they are really following rules. It is quite possible that neither people nor animals routinely follow rules when they think, feel, and behave. If the testimony of experts that they are not following rules is insufficient to falsify models that assume that they are following rules, then how can rule-based models possibly be falsified? Such complete insulation from falsification renders them unscientific as explanations.

Serial vs. Parallel Processing

The **ninth** fatal flaw of rule-based models is that they were developed on the von Neuman approach to computer design, where a central processing unit (CPU) implements rules in a serial step-by-step fashion. While this may work for relatively simple cognitive tasks, the Watson super computer that beat the top Jeopardy players is a massively parallel machine that explicitly abandoned the rule-based approach for a network approach.[24]

Sensory Processing

The **tenth** fatal flaw of rule-based models concerns sensory processing. What rules do people follow that enable them to see, hear, feel, and taste? If these functions do not require step-by-step conscious rule-following then why should one believe that all other psychological functions require rule-following? Moreover, rule-based cognitive processing of visual stimuli, image processing, is several orders of magnitude too slow to be realistic.

Independence Assumption

The **eleventh** fatal flaw of rule-based models is that a cognitive science based on rule-following assumes that psychology is independent of biology. This is done to avoid the possibility that psychology can be reduced to biology in general and neuroscience in particular. This independence of biology assumption requires a belief in the existence of a psychological substrate that enables rules to causally influence one other and to cause behavior. The problem here is the complete lack of supporting evidence for any such causal substrate. This hypothetical psychological substrate seems to be no more real than humanellium; a mythical element that makes people human.

Mathematical Proof

A **twelfth** reason for preferring network models is that there is mathematical proof that networks constructed from three or more layers of processing nodes can, in principle, solve problems of any degree of complexity. No such mathematical proof has been provided for rule-based models.

Reasons Against Using Both Models

One might think that the reasonable compromise here is to use both models. There are at least two sound arguments against doing so. One argument for not using both models is the 12 reasons for not using rule-based models. Why should one wish to create so many limitations and problems? A second argument for not using both models is that to do so creates a form of the mind–body problem where rules represent mind and networks represent body. How can rules influence neural networks? How can neural networks interface with rules? Should we sometimes explain using rules and other times explain using networks? All of these problems disappear by focusing

[24] http://www.youtube.com/watch?v=seNkjYyG3gI&feature=related

exclusively on networks. Sloman (1996, p. 3) admitted the point I just made when he wrote that a dual model approach to cognitive psychology is fundamentally flawed: 'A psychologically plausible device that can integrate computations from associative networks and symbol-manipulating rules has proven elusive'.

Conclusions

The above-mentioned fatal flaws associated with rule-based models constitute sufficient reason not to pursue them further. Brains are constructed from real neural networks and therefore any psychological theory that is to be fully consistent with neuroscience must be some form of network theory. Psychological rules are metaphors; they are not real. There is no psychological substrate for rules to operate on. Hence, this formal schism should no longer divide most of us, and therefore this schism should no longer stand in the way of theoretical unification.

Introspection vs. Extraspection

This schism concerns the perspective from which science is conducted. Rychlak (1968) stated 'By perspective we mean here the standpoint from which the theoretical abstractions and relations are to be thought of, engaged in, or discussed' (p. 27). Introspection refers to taking the perspective of the object of study. For psychologists, that is the person being studied. Human science takes this perspective. Existentialism and qualitative studies are conducted from the introspective perspective of the person being studied. This perspective is also termed **subjective**[25] because it is the **subject's** perspective.

Extraspection refers to taking an observer's perspective. This perspective is termed **objective** because it distinguishes the **object** of study from the observer. Because it is possible to have multiple observers it is possible to compare observations. If the results are consistent across observers then they are considered to be true of the object of study and not merely the product of the observer; i.e., due to observer bias. Natural science has consistently taken the extraspective perspective.

Connectionist network models synthesize this schism because they can simultaneously take both an introspective and an extraspective perspective. The extraspective perspective is obvious, in that multiple observers can view the results of computer simulations used to implement network models. The introspective perspective occurs when the model is paused and

[25] Staats (1983) also addressed the subjective vs. objective schism.

investigators inquire of the model what concepts it has formed so far; i.e., how it sees and interprets stimuli and why it responds the way that it does. Here we have a model that we can ask introspective questions of. The answers we get will depend upon its nature, the network architecture it was given, and its nurture, which is to say its developmental history. Investigators can cause the network to report on its internal state(s) at any point during its development from 'birth', its origin, through 'adulthood', its fully trained state. Hence, this formal schism need no longer divide most of us, and therefore this schism need no longer stand in the way of theoretical unification.

Final vs. Efficient Causes

Psychologists, like philosophers, disagree about what constitutes cause. Rychlak (1968, pp. 120–3) reminded us that Aristotle[26] discerned four types of causes. M.S. Cohen[27] noted that Aristotle did not understand cause in the same way that we do today, as our contemporary views about cause were strongly influenced by David Hume (1711–1776). Aristotle's four causes are more appropriately referred to as four **explanations**. **Material cause** explains in terms of the substance, material, from which something is made; i.e., the properties in question are properties of the material from which the object is made. For example, copper conducts electricity because of its physical properties; i.e., availability of electrons. Cohen wrote: x is what y is [made] **out of.** **Formal cause** is the blueprint, recipe, or plan for making something that shows how the parts are combined to create the object being explained. Wertz (Personal communication, 27 April 2011) noted that formal causality includes mathematical, computational, models, and taxonomic systems. Mathematical explanations appeal to the form that an argument takes.[28] Explanations that are based on logic have a formal nature in that their truth depends directly upon the form that an argument takes. Cohen wrote: x is what it is **to be** y. **Efficient causes** refer to the necessary and sufficient conditions to bring about that which is to be explained. They concern the primary source of change, movement, or rest. They refer to the producer of events. Cohen wrote: x is what **produces** y. **Final causes** refer to the reasons why

[26] While tracing the history of ideas is always informative, it is discouraging when an author cites the work of ancient philosophers with the same relevance of modern authors. Doing so indicates that little if anything substantive has occurred in their field since ancient times.

[27] http://faculty.washington.edu/smcohen/320/4causes.htm

[28] I have long been fascinated by the fact that logic can conclusively establish the truth of a conclusion by examining the form that an argument takes without knowing anything about the specific content of the argument including its premises.

something exists; the purpose it serves. Cohen wrote: x is what y is **for**. Final causes are teleological in that they inspire one towards future goals, whereas efficient causes push one from the past.

Teleology[29] takes the position that final causes are crucial. The physical sciences dismissed teleology on the basis that: (a) the future does not exist until it becomes the present and therefore cannot influence the present; and (b) teleological arguments are circular and unscientific because they cannot be falsified. Nevertheless, Rychlak (1968, 1981a, 1981b) has consistently maintained that final causes are especially relevant to the study of people and therefore to clinical psychology.

Retrospection entails recalling past events. Introspection entails assessing present events. Prospection entails anticipating future events. Gilbert (2006), and Gilbert and Wilson (2006, 2007) defined prospection as 'the mental **simulation** of future possibilities' (Seligman et al., 2013, p. 120, bold emphasis added). All simulated brain states that prospect the future are temporally located in the present. Hence, prospection does not entail teleology. Rychlak did not mention or discuss prospection, but I expect that this is what he actually meant when he supported teleology.

Memories are activated **reconstructions**. **Prospections** are activated **simulations**. **Expectations** are prospections that are typically weighted in direct proportion to prior experience with such events. Consistent prior experience generates strong expectations that those events will repeat in the future. Sometimes events that have never occurred are simulated and the emotions that these simulations activate can act like, have the same impact and effect as, real events. People suffering from psychological disorders frequently exhibit unrealistic emotionally charged prospections. For example, persons with social phobias fear audience rejection despite the absence of any such prior experience. But they experience the negative emotions that would occur if ever those prospections happened. Simulated prospections can have the same effect as real events. It is common clinical practice for cognitive-behavior therapists to dispute these prospections by asking patients to systematically record their behavior and other people's reaction to it. Computers are now used to simulate fearful conditions as part of exposure therapy.

Kahneman's (2011b) view of prospection is that 'People make judgments and decisions by consulting their emotions. Do I like it? Do I hate it? How strongly do I feel about it' (p. 139). Haidt's (2001) article entitled '*The*

[29] http://en.wikipedia.org/wiki/Teleology

emotional dog and its rational tail'[30] reviews four sources of empirical evidence demonstrating that people initially make decisions based on emotions and cultural values, and subsequently seek reasons to justify these decisions. Evaluations of the mental simulations of possible future events called prospections can be expected to be as heavily biased by emotions and cultural values as are the economic decisions discussed by Kahneman (2011b) and the moral decisions discussed by Haidt (2001).

Sripada et al. (2013) contrast their cognitive view of prospection with the affective heuristic view of Kahneman (2011b). They maintained that Seligman et al. (2013) did not intend to pit cognition and emotion against one another as if it were possible for cognition and emotion to operate either independently or always cooperatively. Clinical psychologists will readily recognize that this idealized rational perspective characterizes few if any of their clients. The emotional conflicts and fears that bring people to therapy strongly influence how they think about themselves and other people. The mental simulations referred to in the previous paragraph activate subcortical networks that can generate strong emotions that potentiate the impact that some mental simulations have on behavior.

Teleology presumes free will.[31] This assumption is required to avoid the conclusion that our goals are the result of efficient rather than final causes. If our goals are determined by factors other than our completely free choice, if our goals are influenced in any way by inherited traits or life experience, then the view that we are drawn to our goals rather than shaped by our genetics and environment is an illusion. The massive empirical evidence reviewed in Chapter 3 concerning unconscious processing, and especially the evidence that brain changes precede conscious decision, seriously undercuts both free will and final causes. It seems that we are the **editor/monitor** of our thoughts rather than their **author/originator**. The temporal delay between brain activation and conscious decision is short but decisively sufficient to settle this matter.

In conclusion, people do set goals to which they aspire, but these goals are prospections that are grounded in prior experience and current context. Goals are computed based on possible futures but since these futures have not yet occurred, teleology per se is never operative. Prospections generate emotions. Together they jointly constrain behavior. Sometimes emotions are activated by other people in order to manipulate the choices people make, such as when politicians present fear-based messages to modify voting

[30] This creative title accurately conveys a crucial feature of human psychology.

[31] http://en.wikipedia.org/wiki/Free_will

behavior. In these cases some people generate goals that they would not otherwise have created, thereby demonstrating that their 'free will' is not free from external influences after all. Similarly, poorly paid police officers who have sworn to uphold the law are sometimes seduced by drug money. Drug addicts and alcoholics do not always freely choose their immediate goals which often revolve around obtaining more drugs or alcohol.

The final vs. efficient cause schism is a false dichotomy where choice seems to be required. A more productive solution is to reject this false dichotomy in favor of learning more about how genetic and environmental factors and unconscious and conscious processes interact to produce our cognitions, emotions, and behavior, including the goals that we set for ourselves. Hence, this formal schism need no longer divide most of us, and therefore this schism need no longer stand in the way of theoretical unification.

Experimental vs. Naturalistic Observation

Studies are said to have internal validity when they are sufficiently well controlled that one can identify causal factors. True experiments are also characterized by random assignment and manipulation. Random assignment is required to control for pre existing differences among participants in experimental and control groups. Manipulating one variable at a time while holding all others constant is required to separate cause from correlation. Psychologists who emphasize the importance of internal validity highlight the role of true experiments. These experiments are typically conducted in laboratory or artificial settings.

Studies are said to have external validity when they produce results that readily generalize to real-world settings. Selecting naturally occurring groups, such as groups formed by nature or accident due to real-world events, facilitates generalization. Psychologists who emphasize the importance of generalizability emphasize naturalistic studies. However, drawing conclusions from studies of naturally formed groups is tenuous at best. For example, the answers that centenarians give when asked how they lived to be 100 or more years old does not necessarily reveal variables that if manipulated in younger populations would cause them to live to become a centenarian.

Increasing internal validity typically decreases external validity and vice versa. Connectionist neural network models can have both high internal and high external validity. Connectionist models are internally valid because everything about them can be objectively defined and precisely manipulated as many times as is required to reach firm conclusions. Connectionist models are also externally valid to the extent that they incorporate properties of real neural networks. The Human Connectome Project aims to provide a wiring diagram of the major neural networks in the human brain.[32] Connectionist models that incorporate these findings will have greater external validity. Neural network models that are implemented in hardware use the same physical forces to drive electrons through transistors that nature uses to drive ions through neural membranes. This method increases the external validity of artificial neural network models.

In conclusion, network models avoid the necessity to favor internal validity over external validity. Whereas current network models implement relatively few neuroscience facts, their external validity can increase as neuroscience provides additional details. It is important to reiterate here that a complete list of neuroscience facts provides but half of a complete explanation. The remaining explanatory half is to show how psychology emerges from biology. One must show how these biological parts interact to produce cognition, affect, and behavior. Hence, this formal schism need no longer divide most of us, and therefore this schism should no longer stand in the way of theoretical unification.

Ideographic vs. Nomothetic

The ideographic orientation argues that psychology is about individuals and therefore should emphasize case studies. The nomothetic orientation argues that psychology is a science that seeks general laws that characterize groups of people. Read and Miller (2002) and Read et al. (2010) fully resolved this schism by combining both the ideographic and nomothetic approaches in their simulation of personality.

The fact that connectionist network models must be trained rather than programmed gives each of them a developmental history from 'birth' when the network is initialized, through 'childhood' where the network demonstrates partial competence, to 'adulthood' where the network reaches asymptotic performance. This feature provides an ideographic study. Connectionist network models can be used to simulate the study of groups of people by randomly, or otherwise, varying properties of the initial neural architecture (nature) and developmental history (nurture). Such research takes a nomothetic approach. Hence, this formal schism need no longer divide most of us, and therefore this schism need no longer stand in the way of theoretical unification.

[32] http://www.humanconnectomeproject.org/

Dialectical vs. Demonstrative

Rychlak (1981a) compared and contrasted dialectical[33] and demonstrative reasoning as follows:

> Thus, whereas demonstrative premises stated one and only one of two contradictories – "X is the case (and by implication Y is not)" – dialectical premises, said Aristotle, always depend upon the adversary's choice between the two contradictories – "Which do you take to be the case, X or Y? You say X? Fine, let us proceed"; but just as likely "You say Y? Fine, let us proceed." Thus, in dialectical arguments, rhetoric (the art of persuasion) always plays a part, because the direction the argument takes is arbitrary (p. 262).

Demonstrative reasoning entails formal logic. Demonstrative reasoning insists that only one of two contradictories can be true; it rejects contradictions. Dialectical reasoning is willing to sequentially, conditionally, entertain the truth of both contradictories. Rychlak (1968, 1981a) has argued that dialectical reasoning is highly characteristic of people because their thoughts, feelings, and behaviors are so frequently inconsistent or contradictory in part because they can see pros and cons, upsides and downsides of multiple premises.

The proposed Bio↔Psychology Network Theory resolves this schism by providing several ways to include both demonstrative and dialectic properties. The first resolution of this schism comes from understanding that the brain is composed of multiple neural networks. It is widely accepted that the seat of higher cognitive abilities, including thoughts, resides in the frontal cortex and in Broca's and Wernickes's areas in the left hemisphere that mediates language. In Chapter 5 we will learn that the brain also has subcortical neural networks that generate emotions. Sometimes the outputs of these neural networks are congruent and other times they are in conflict. In such cases each network differentially emphasizes one or another feature. It is quite possible for these networks to simultaneously process the two contradictories that Rychlak identified above.

The second resolution of this schism comes from the fact that neural networks can oscillate between two stable states. This happens with neural networks that simulate visual illusions, such as the Necker Cube and the Face/Vase illusions. In the case of the Necker Cube, sometimes a face of the cube is perceived to be in the foreground and other times in the background. In the Face/Vase illusion sometimes one sees two faces looking at each other and at other times just one vase. These states reflect the two contradictories that Rychlak identified above as characteristic of the dialectic.

[33] http://en.wikipedia.org/wiki/Dialectic

A third resolution of the schism comes from the fact that we have a left brain and a right brain. That these two brains think differently is clearly revealed by patients who have had a split-brain operation. In normal people, the left and right brains interact to produce a synthetic position.

A fourth resolution of this schism comes from the fact that we have a gut brain in addition to our skull brain. The brain in our skull generates what I call our **primary mind**. It gives rise to most of our thoughts and feelings. But we will learn in Chapter 3 that we also have another brain in our gut that generates what I call our **secondary mind**. It is the result of our enteric nervous system. It always processes unconsciously. The conscious result of enteric nervous system processing is mainly in the form of **feelings**. Sometimes these two networks are of the same mind and other times they can be of different minds that conflict with one another, thereby adding to the mix of thoughts and feelings that embody the two contradictories that Rychlak identified above.

Each of the multiple networks identified above can operate on demonstrative logic but arrive at different conclusions as a result of different patterns of excitation and inhibition existing among the processing nodes that comprise the different layers of the neural networks, thereby mediating our dialectical nature. In Rychlak's dialectic, demonstrative reasoning was used when reasoning from each of two contradictory premises. This means that the dialectic entails demonstrative reasoning. In no case was illogical reasoning considered to be acceptable. Rychlak's claim that Kantians accept contradiction because they endorse dialectical reasoning does not mean that Kantians reason illogically and that their arguments are riddled with contradictions. It just means that Kantians are willing to reason logically from each of two contradictory premises. Hence, there is no longer a need to choose between Lockean and Kantian theories as Rychlak suggests. The proposed Bio↔Psychology Network Theory provides a third possibility where both demonstrative and dialectical reasoning can naturally and fully exist without compromise or contradiction. Hence, this formal schism need no longer divide most of us, and therefore this schism need no longer stand in the way of theoretical unification.

I argue in Chapters 8–12 that theoretical unification facilitates psychotherapy integration. Here we have a good example of how this can occur. Psychodynamic theories/therapies are concerned with exploring and resolving dialectical conflicts between thoughts and feelings generated by our two minds, whereas cognitive-behavioral therapies seek to restructure cognitions generated primarily by our frontal cortex and language areas in the left hemisphere. The synthetic explanation provided above that characterizes the proposed Bio↔Psychology Network Theory and provides common ground for these two seemingly incommensurate/contradictory/opposing theoretical orientations. It shows that neither side is entirely correct or completely wrong. Cognitive-behavioral therapies have been shown to effectively treat a broad spectrum of problems. The synthetic orientation presented above provides a theoretical basis for examining, analyzing, and adjusting conflicting thoughts and emotions. Just because the processing done by the enteric nervous system is unconscious and therefore irrational does not mean that it is wrong. Gut feelings can often be right. For example, first impressions are based on too little data to be rational. Yet many of us know rather quickly if we are going to like someone or not, or if we find someone to be 'creepy'. 'Love at first sight' is also irrational, is clearly emotional, and can be valid. Therapies like Gendlin's focusing, discussed in Chapter 9, help people learn to recognize and clarify the results of their enteric network processing to better understand why they are conflicted. There is nothing here that would prevent a therapist from beginning in this way before restructuring the client's cognitions. The proposed Bio↔Psychology Network Theory provides a theoretical basis for such an eclectic practice.

CONCLUSIONS

Pessimists have consistently argued that theoretical unification is impossible. I believe that this was true before formal network models were introduced and provided a way forward. So-called impossibility proofs are difficult to construct and are easily disproven by a single positive instance which should caution those who are inclined to make them. Impossibility proofs particularly appeal to those who have tried and failed. That they have not made suitable progress is unfortunately offered as proof that no one can succeed. Placing a definitive upper limit on human creativity and ingenuity is a risky business, because young scientists love such challenges. The history of science indicates that what one generation finds to be impossible is sometimes not shared by the next generation. Human flight was once thought to be impossible, as was travel faster than 30 miles/hour. Much of modern progress would not have occurred if the younger generation fully accepted what the older generation claimed was impossible. So let us move forward now with regard to theoretical unification in psychology.

Levy and Anderson (2013) see our field becoming more unified. They opined that '... we believe that the field will evolve toward a theoretically integrative-based, evidence driven, cognitive behavioral-affective-motivational and relational approach. We believe this approach will incorporate biological, psychological, and social levels drawing on the collective wisdom offered in various orientations to be applied at multiple levels of the clinical encounter' (p. 215). The main point of this book is to bring this future into the present.

It is worth reiterating that theoretical unification is about consensus. Theoretical unification begins when a majority of psychologists adopt a common vocabulary and core concepts/phenomenon that have sufficient evidence to warrant acceptance. Theoretical unification is about common ground and shared perspective that enable the majority of psychologists to work together. This is the modest goal that I now pursue.

PART Two

A Proposed Solution

CHAPTER 3

Core Network Principles: The Explanatory Nucleus

Contents

Cognitive Neuroscience and Psychotherapy
http://dx.doi.org/10.1016/B978-0-12-420071-5.00003-X

This chapter begins the proposed solution promised in the previous two chapters. The proposed solution provides theoretical unification in the form of four core and eight corollary network principles. This theoretical unification enables psychotherapy integration of the following Big Five clinical orientations: (a) behavioral (applied behavior analysis); (b) cognitive; (c) cognitive-behavioral; (d) psychodynamic (emotion-focused therapy); and (e) pharmacologic. The proposed network orientation also transforms psychology into a mature science.

The **first goal** of this chapter is to present a neural network approach to psychological science in general, and clinical psychology in particular, that explains psychological phenomena in **physical** rather than **mental** terms based on four core and eight corollary network principles. The **second goal** of this chapter is to show how this network approach helps us understand how mind emerges from brain. This chapter discusses the first four network principles. They always occur together, which is why I refer to them as the **explanatory nucleus**. They enable the other eight network principles, which is why these additional network principles are referred to as corollary.

Network **Principle 1** concerns **unconscious processing**. The first subgoal here is to introduce a generic connectionist neural network model[1] for the purpose of defining basic terms. The second subgoal is to explain the **network cascade**; i.e., how **activation** spreads automatically and unconsciously across all layers of processing nodes via connection weights that simulate the synaptic properties of excitation and inhibition.

Network **Principle 2** explains how the neuroscience mechanism of **experience-dependent plasticity** (EDP), also known as neuroplasticity, physically modifies real neural networks and constitutes the biological basis of learning and memory. These modifications to the network cascade cause it to process differently the next time it is activated. We will learn that EDP

[1] Wikipedia provides a reasonably good introduction to connectionism at http://en.wikipedia.org/wiki/Connectionism. Dennis and McAuley described connectionist models of cognition (http://www.itee.uq.edu.au/~cogs2010/cmc/home.html). Stergiou and Siganos provided a comprehensive neural network tutorial along with a more detailed history of connectionism (http://www.doc.ic.ac.uk/~nd/surprise_96/journal/vol4/cs11/report.html). Medler posted a brief history of connectionism at http://neuron-ai.tuke.sk/NCS/VOL1/P3_html/vol1_3.html.

is the basic mechanism that mediates all normal and abnormal learning and memory, and therefore all psychological development across the lifespan including effects of psychological interventions.

Network **Principle 3** concerns the fact that the network cascade necessarily **transforms** stimulus microfeatures into latent constructs via a mechanism that is highly parallel to how factor analysis forms latent constructs. This principle explains how mind emerges from brain. The main objective here is to reveal how this transformation process can work.

Network **Principle 4** concerns the concepts of **activation** and **reactivation**. **Activation** occurs when a neuron fires; when a processing node turns on. It is a result of real or simulated **dendritic summation** and the associated **transfer function**. This function must be non-linear for the network to learn effectively. This necessity can be demonstrated by substituting a linear function, straight line, which substantially reduces what the network can learn. Transfer functions in PDP-CNN models are typically sigmoidal as they are in real neurons. The input to the transfer function is the sum of all activations emanating from upstream nodes. The output of the transfer function is either the probability that the node will activate; i.e., the probability that the neuron will fire, or the rate at which the neuron fires. The term **connectome** was defined by Seung (2012) as 'the totality of connections between the neurons in a nervous system' (p. xiii). More specifically, the term connectome refers to the pattern of excitation/inhibition that characterizes all synapses connecting all real or simulated neurons. Connectomes imply neural architecture in the same way that road maps imply the geographic architecture of cities and towns.

Reactivation refers to returning a network to a particular activation pattern/state. This is how memory works. Memory entails **redintegration**. Wikipedia[2] reports that 'redintegration refers to the restoration of the whole of something from a part of it'. Redintegration restores cognition, affect, and behavior to what it was at some point in the past. Complete redintegration returns the person/animal to the exact state that they were in when the memory first formed or when it was last activated when it is fully operative. Partial redintegration occurs more frequently instead. This view of memory is far more dynamic than retrieving bits of cognitive information. Our network Principle 6: Part-Whole Pattern Completion discussed in Chapter 4 provides additional details concerning how redintegration works. This

[2] http://en.wikipedia.org/wiki/Redintegration

principle is relevant to every psychological phenomenon and disorder that involves memory, which is essentially all of them.

These four intrinsic network properties always work together and do so simultaneously in parallel. Each processing cycle includes: (a) activation **cascades** that automatically, deterministically, and unconsciously spread across layers of neurons; (b) this network cascade necessarily **transforms** stimulus microfeatures into higher-order latent constructs, cognitions; and (c) this network cascade activates biological mechanisms that **physically modify** synaptic properties and neural architecture such as dendritic growth via experience-dependent plasticity mechanisms. Now the network processes differently than before. These network changes mediate learning, which entails memory formation. These network properties are presented as core principles of psychology because they are used to derive explanations for corollary principles that are then used to explain additional psychological phenomena. I refer to these core network principles as the **explanatory nucleus** because they are at the center of all explanations by the Bio↔Psychology Network Theory developed in this and the next chapter.

The **third goal** of this chapter is to replace our current **conscious-centric** orientation with an **unconscious-centric** one. Neuroscience and psychological science have definitively established that unconscious processing occurs. The ability to watch the human brain function using brain imaging technology has definitively established the reality of unconscious processing.[3] Eagleman (2011) provided book-length neuroscience evidence that supports unconscious processing. We will see that network processing entails an automatic mechanical cascade that is as unconscious as is the neural impulse along a neuron. Parsimony motivates one to assume as little as possible. It is more parsimonious to assume unconscious than conscious processing as a beginning point of theory construction.[4] We are not conscious of a great deal of the processing that the brain does to regulate heart rate, respiration, core temperature, blood sugar, walking, and many other functions. Why should we be more conscious of how it generates and guides our cognitions, emotions, and behaviors? I review evidence below showing that unconscious brain changes precede conscious decisions by about 200 milliseconds. We unconsciously process many psychological

[3] While I review psychological evidence that supports the reality of unconscious processing, the neuroscience/neuropsychological evidence for unconscious processing is truly definitive. There is no longer room for debate regarding the existence of unconscious processing.

[4] Assuming consciousness comes at the intellectual cost of never being able to explain it. One reasons *from* axioms, *not to* them. Any model that intends to explain how consciousness emerges from brain function cannot assume consciousness but must begin with an unconscious-centric orientation.

functions using automatic and deterministic processes. I specifically review cognitive heuristics that constitute defects in our ability to reason rationally. These heuristics demonstrate that we frequently reason automatically and with little if any awareness; i.e., unconsciously. Simon (1990) referred to heuristics as 'weak methods' (p. 9) suggesting that these methods are suboptimal. Newell and Simon (1972) used the word heuristic to describe a simple process that replaces a complex algorithm. Heuristics are commonly understood as automatic cognitive short cuts. Heuristics can also be understood as cognitive deficits/defects that constitute hard evidence of our inclination to process information automatically and unconsciously. The fact that cognitive heuristics were discovered only quite recently in the history of psychological science implies that psychologists were long unaware of them precisely because they operate unconsciously. We will learn that these automatic and unavoidable cognitive pitfalls are due to the proposed core and corollary principles. All of this evidence supports the unconscious-centric nature of our network orientation.

The **fourth goal** of this chapter is to explain learning and memory from a network perspective. Unlike computers, the brain does not separate processing from memory. Also unlike computers that remain unchanged by the processing they do, brains are physically modified by the processing they do through a biological mechanism known as **experience-dependent plasticity**. This process **physically sculpts** the brain during its development across the lifespan. Memories are learned and learning requires long-term memory. That the brain uses many of the same networks for processing as it does for memory makes learning and memory two facets of the same experience-dependent plasticity mechanism. It also means that learning necessarily modifies memory (see Tryon & McKay, 2009 for details).

The **fifth goal** of this chapter is to elaborate the transformation network principle and explain why transformation is an inherent property of functioning networks. The complexity and extent of the transformations appear to be directly proportional to the size and complexity of the network. This principle primarily explains how psychology emerges from biology.

In summary, input to a network architecture like that described below will be automatically, deterministically, and unconsciously processed by an **activation cascade** across its **connectome**. In sufficiently complex neural networks this **network cascade** will automatically and deterministically be **transformed** into latent constructs with cognitive properties. The network cascade activates experience-dependent plasticity mechanisms or their simulations that automatically and deterministically modify the connectome and associated neural architecture, thereby causing the network to process the next input differently. These are core network principles because they drive Piagetian-like assimilation–accommodation cycles that underlie all psychological processes and development across the lifespan. See the section on Piaget in Chapter 7 for further details. These neural network mechanisms are phylogenetically general in that they characterize all mammalian species. The vocabulary that accompanies these core principles is grounded in neuroscience, but pertains to psychology. This common vocabulary and core concept makes psychology consilient (Wilson, 1998) with biology and moves psychology towards becoming a mature science (Kuhn, 1962, 1970, 1996, 2012).[5] I begin by presenting a generic connectionist neural network model in order to define basic terms and concepts. Chapter 4 considers eight corollary network principles.

GENERIC CONNECTIONIST NEURAL NETWORK MODEL

The proposed Bio↔Psychology Network Theory developed in this and the next chapter begins with an understanding of the generic Parallel-Distributed Processing (PDP) Connectionist Neural Network (CNN) model. Some connectionist models implement more neuroscience facts than others. Investigators began with simple network architectures because they are easier to understand. Even the more biologically inspired network models are admittedly super-simplistic first approximations to real brains, even in simple life forms. To model a phenomenon is to simplify it to where it can be understood. All scientific models are necessarily incomplete to some degree and that makes them a simplification of the processes they aim to study. Practicality also requires simplification in order to actually construct models. Constructing a model that is as complicated and as difficult to study as the process being modeled is not a good starting point, because such models cannot be understood any better than what they are intended to be models of. Hence, complex models are not helpful as a starting point. The eventual goal of simulations is to have a model that fully incorporates all features of the phenomenon being modeled, but this is an end point and never a productive beginning point. A sure way to stifle scientific progress is to start with an unmanageably complex model.

[5] http://en.wikipedia.org/wiki/The_Structure_of_Scientific_Revolutions

An essential part of the model construction process is to select and implement crucial components of the phenomena under study. Parsimony typically motivates minimal implementation. Critics typically focus on these compromises as fatal flaws and reject all results based on such models. More moderate minds accept these limitations as necessary to begin systematic and progressive study. The objective is to gradually improve these models as more knowledge is acquired. Rejecting simple models outright forfeits this future.

All connectionist models share a common attribute in that they provide a disciplined and detailed way to discuss complex psychological and behavioral phenomena. We will discuss how these neural network models process cognition and affect resulting in simulated behavior, but like astrophysical models of supernova that do not actually explode and meteorological models that do not actually rain, these models do not actually think, feel, and behave.

The main purpose of this section is to introduce a generic PDP-CNN model in order to clarify basic terms and concepts. The central and essential insight upon which this book is based was provided in the two-volume seminal work by Rumelhart and McClelland (1986) and McClelland et al. (1986). They demonstrated that it is possible to effectively simulate psychological phenomena using brain-inspired PDP-CNNs. This extraordinary development integrates biology (neuroscience) and psychology in a fundamental way by providing both sciences with a common vocabulary and a shared set of basic concepts. This book aims to extend this integration by identifying core and corollary psychological principles that characterize PDP-CNN models. Connectionist models come in two basic types: local and parallel. We consider only parallel models because they better integrate biology and psychology.

Parallel Distributed Processing Connectionist Neural Network Models

Behavioral psychologists once theorized using a Stimulus → Response (S → R) model. Cognitive psychologists expanded this model to include how the organism processed and transformed stimulus information resulting in the Stimulus → Organism → Response (S → O → R) model where the O represents all cognitive and affective processing. Transformation is the defining feature of cognition. The O in the S → O → R model represents all of the transformations and cognitive processes that differentiate and distinguish cognitive from behavioral models and theory. Transformations

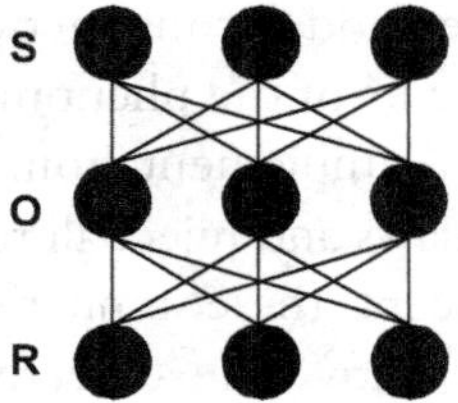

Figure 3.1 Illustration of a double generalization of the S → O → R model. The parallel generalization entails three S → O → R models. The distributed generalization entails connecting each S node to every O node and every O node to every R node.

are especially important cognitive processes because they enable one to generate explanations that go far beyond simple stimulus–response reflex-based explanations.

Figure 3.1 illustrates a generic form of a PDP-CNN model. It mainly serves to illustrate a basic form that these models can take and to provide a structure for describing basic terms and concepts. One can think of the S, O, and R elements/nodes as either artificial neurons, as I prefer, or more abstractly as psychological processing nodes. This generic network model is a double generalization of the classic S → O → R model. First, it has a **parallel** form; i.e., multiple copies of the S → O → R model enable, in this simplified case, three stimuli to be processed simultaneously. Second, it has a **distributed** form because all S-nodes connect to all O-nodes and all O-nodes connect to all R-nodes, thus enabling each stimulus to be processed by every O-node and to influence every R-node.[6] Thus, this model replaces the single **linear** S → O → R causal sequence with a **network/web** of **parallel** causal activations. Investigators have used this and related models to simulate a wide variety of psychological phenomena (e.g., Abbott, 2008; Arbib, 2002; McLeod et al., 1998; McClelland et al., 1986; O'Reilly & Munakata, 2000; Rumelhart & McClelland, 1986).

Stimulus or S-layer

Connectionist models require a way to represent basic stimulus features. One way to do this is to code for relevant stimulus components called microfeatures. For example, representing the perception of a cup of coffee may include the following stimulus microfeatures: type of container (e.g., paper cup, mug, or traditional cup); container size (e.g., large, medium, or small); amount of cream (e.g., none, some, more, a lot); amount of sugar

[6] Other more complex network architectures have been, and are being, studied.

0, 0, 1, 0, 0, 0, 1, 0, 1, 0, 1, 0, 0, 0, 1, 1, 1, 1, 1, 1, 1, 0, 0, 0, 1

Figure 3.2 Illustration of how perceiving (S-layer) and saying (R-layer) the letter 'A' results in turning 25 stimulus microfeatures on or off. The first block of five digits correspond to the off = 0, on = 1 status of the five pixels in the top row of an artificial retina. The remaining blocks of five digits describe the on–off status of the pixels in the remaining rows.

(e.g., none, some, more, a lot); and temperature (e.g., cold, hot, very hot). In this model, the number 1 represents the presence of a microfeature; 0 represents its absence. Hence, a string of 1s and 0s represents the presence/absence of a list of microfeatures that describe a particular stimulus.

A thermometer code can be used to code the amount or magnitude of a variable. For example, a 1–7 scale for the intensity or degree of some microfeature can be represented by seven S-elements where 0000000 indicates complete absence of intensity, 0000001 indicates very little, 0000111 indicates more, up to and including 1111111 that indicates the maximum amount of a particular microfeature.[7] Sixteen or 32 or more digits could be used if necessary.

A second way to represent stimulus microfeatures is to code what an artificial retina might see. For example, one can simulate the perception of the letter 'A' using the scheme illustrated in Figure 3.2, where each of five blocks (rows) of five microfeatures combine to represent the letter 'A' on an artificial retina. The first block of five digits (0, 0, 1, 0, 0) corresponds to the sequence of off, off, on, off, off where off = 0 = *white* and on = 1 = *black* pattern as found in the top row of Figure 3.2. The second through fifth blocks of digits code for the off–on pattern of the 'A' in rows two through five of Figure 3.2. Hence, a single string of 25 microfeatures below the boxes represents 'seeing' the letter 'A'.

Transformation or O-layer

The nodes in the O-layer in Figure 3.1 represent cognitions and emotions. For example, the O-nodes code for the transformations that generate latent constructs from stimulus microfeatures, just as they were said to do in the

[7] The 1s begin on the right, as that is how numbers expressed in base 2 format are constructed.

well-accepted S → O → R model. I describe this transformation process/mechanism in a separate section below as Principle 3.

Response or R-layer

Behaviors can be represented in at least the same two ways that stimuli can. One option is to code the presence of a behavior as 1 and its absence as 0. Representing the presence or absence of a single behavior such as a lever press in a Skinner box requires just a single R-node that is either on = bar is pressed = 1 or off = bar is not pressed = 0. If the Skinner box has two levers, the concurrent operant case, the animal must choose which lever to press. The corresponding model requires two R-nodes to represent responding on the two levers. Representing more complex behaviors requires more R-nodes. Another option is to use the matrix approach to represent behavior such as what letter the network might pronounce (see Figure 3.2 above).

Simulated Dendritic Summation

Notice that the processing nodes in the O- and R-layers receive inputs from all processing nodes in the preceding layer in our generic PDP-CNN model. This network architecture is intended to simulate dendritic summation, a neuroscience fact, in that the sum of all excitatory (positive connection weights) and inhibitory (negative connection weights) weights constitutes the **Net Input** to the receiving node. The probability that the receiving node will fire, become active, is a non-linear, usually sigmoidal, function of Net Input as illustrated in Figure 3.3. In real neural networks, neurons receive up to 10,000 inputs from other neurons. The sigmoidal function illustrated in Figure 3.3 is also called a **Transfer Function** because it determines if the summed inputs activate the receiving node or not. The

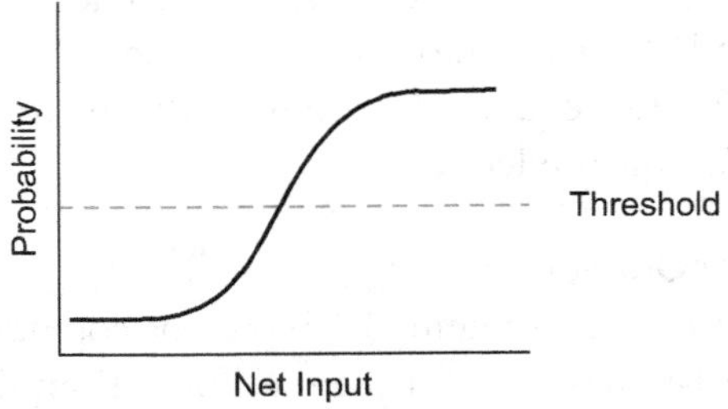

Figure 3.3 In some models the receiving node (neuron) is either off or on depending upon whether Net Input is below or above a threshold. In other models Net Input controls the probability that the receiving node (neuron) will become active (fire).

transfer function is sigmoidal in real neural networks and must also be so in artificial neural networks for them to function properly. This necessity can be demonstrated by substituting a linear function, straight line, which substantially reduces what the network can learn. This sigmoidal function is associated with logistic regression where the objective is to predict one of two different states. Here we have a fundamental connection with multivariate statistics.

Neural Architecture Variations (NAVs)

The generic connectionist model described above bears only a rudimentary resemblance to real neural networks found in the human brain. A slightly more realistic extension of this model is provided by Figure 3.4. Another style of neural architecture used by Li et al. (2005) that contains a binding area to integrate results from two other networks is presented as Figure 3.5. The crucial features are: (a) layers of simple processing nodes that are (b) highly interconnected. Sporns (2011) book entitled *Networks of the Brain* discussed how neural networks connect levels of organization in the brain and how brain structure enables brain function. Seung's (2012) book entitled *Connectome: How the Brain's Wiring Makes Us Who We Are* endeavors to relate neural architecture to psychology. Le Doux's (2002) book entitled *Synaptic Self: How Our Brain's Become Who We Are* documents the relevance of the synapse to psychology.

Size matters when it comes to the ability of artificial neural networks to do psychologically interesting things. The front page of *The New York Times* on November 24, 2012 carried an article entitled 'Learning Curve: No Longer Just a Human Trait' by John Markoff that contains the following quote 'The point about this approach is that it scales beautifully. Basically you just need to keep making it bigger and faster, and it will get better. There's no looking back now' (p. A3).

The term 'connectome' refers to all connections among all neurons in the brain. The **Human Connectome Project**[8] is currently mapping the structure of the major neural networks in the human brain and will provide much more realistic architectures for future network models. Connectomes are dynamic in that they are modified by what Seung (2012) refers to as the four Rs: 'reweighting, reconnection, rewiring, and regeneration' (p. xv). Behavior at any moment is determined by the connectome at that moment. Connectomes imply neural architecture in the same way that road maps

[8] http://www.humanconnectomeproject.org/

imply the geographic architecture of cities and towns. The geography of cities and towns is determined by the distances of the roads leading to and from them. Similarly, the physical structure of the brain is determined by the fibers connecting one neuron to another. Some neurons are connected to 10,000 other neurons and that suggests a great deal of complexity.

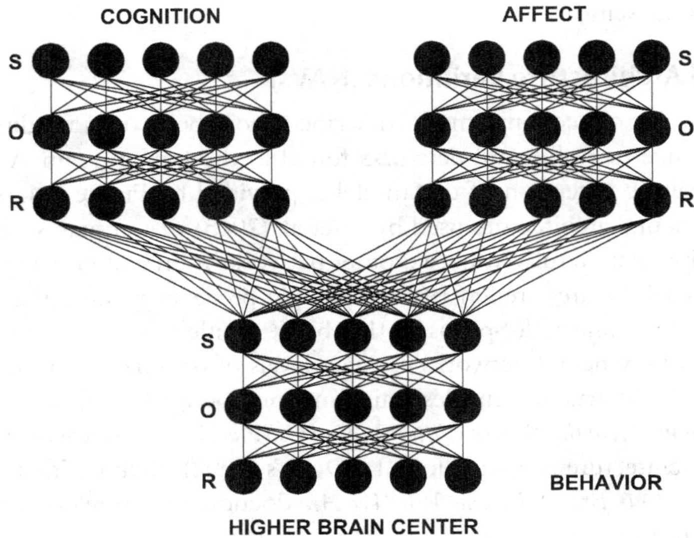

Figure 3.4 An example of the modular network of network architecture that better approximates the structures of real brains than does Figure 3.1.

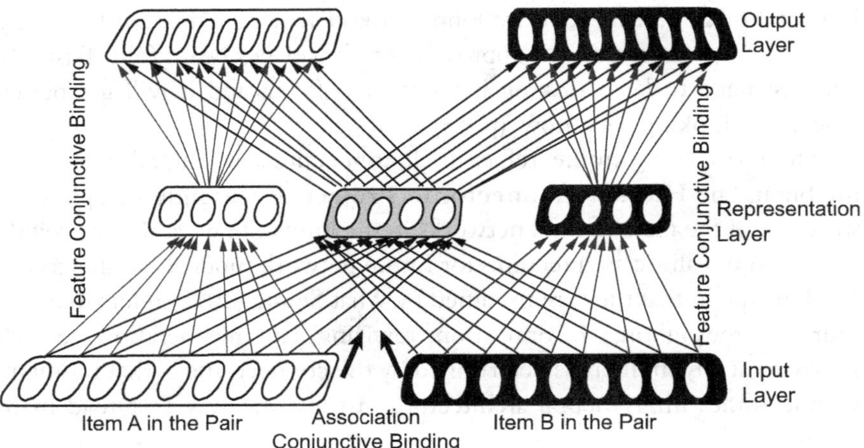

Figure 3.5 Artificial neural network used by Li et al. (2005) to find word pairs.

A major point of this section is that the capabilities of a neural network depend heavily upon its architecture. For example, the cerebellum has a specialized architecture that facilitates the massive specialized computation required to control motor movements such as hitting a ball with a bat. Another example is the visual system with its six layers found in the left and right lateral geniculate nucleus (LGN) that process information from the right and left eyes respectively.

One can also think of the brain as a **network of specialized networks**. The issue of the modularity of mind[9] has been hotly debated by psychologists, but neuroscience strongly suggests that the mind emerges from an interaction of multiple networks (Fox et al., 2005). The ACT-R-5.0 network proposed by Anderson et al. (2004) is modularized. Fair et al. (2009) noted that 'The mature human brain is both structurally and functionally specialized, such that discrete areas of the cerebral cortex perform distinct types of information processing' (p. 1). Experimental evidence concerning the interaction of multiple networks was reviewed by Rosenblum (2013) who showed that the visual, auditory, and somatosensory network systems interact to produce what we see, hear, and feel. It is common knowledge that smell influences taste. Rosenblum (2013) reviewed the McGurk effect[10] first reported by McGurk and MacDonald (1976) as follows. Participants watch a video clip of someone silently saying the syllable 'ga' while simultaneously listening to a speaker say 'ba'. This combination causes the participant to hear 'da' because the brain integrates vision and hearing. Rosenblum (2013) reported that this effect persists for him despite having studied this phenomenon for 25 years. Rosenblum (2013) also reported that an orange-flavored drink will have a cherry taste if tinted red. Moreover, a cherry-flavored drink will have an orange taste if tinted orange. Clinical evidence of brain modularity comes from patients with neurological disorders such as hemisphere neglect. See Oliver Sachs (1985) for additional evidence of brain modules.

Eagleman (2011, pp. 101–50) indicated that the brain can house different personalities. His example is Mel Gibson's anti-Semitic tirade while drunk on July 28, 2006 and his subsequent sober apology and repudiation of anti-Semitic beliefs and feelings. Eagleman stressed that neither of these aspects of Mel Gibson's personality is his true side, but rather both sides are equally real and genuine. In what Eagleman describes as *The Democracy of Mind* he explained that different neural networks activate conflicting tendencies but

[9] http://en.wikipedia.org/wiki/Modularity_of_mind

[10] http://en.wikipedia.org/wiki/McGurk_effect

like a jury or the voting public they express only a single position at any given time. Eagleman (2011, p. 133) described the brain as a team of rivals where each one has its own perspective but all work constructively together. He summarized his view with the Latin phrase **E Pluribus Unum** which translates to 'Out of many, one', 'From many, one', 'One from many' or 'Many uniting into one'. This was the motto suggested by a continental congressional committee appointed on July 4, 1776 to be part of the great seal of the United States of America. This phrase was used by Charles Thomson in 1782 when the final Great Seal was created. The central idea here was that America was one country populated by many different people. Eagleman (2011, pp. 133–40) used the phrase E pluribus unum to emphasize that our singular sense of self is the result of many interacting neural networks.

Using a political analogy Eagleman argued that the brain is essentially a two-party system: **reason** and **emotion**. He referenced the dual-processing theories that we discuss at length below in connection with unconscious processing. Eagleman used the trolley dilemma, also known as the trolley problem[11], to illustrate the conflicts that can occur between reason and emotion. For example, five workers are repairing a trolley track at the bottom of the hill. An out-of-control trolley is rapidly approaching them and will result in the certain death of all five workers if nothing is done. A bystander near a switch can divert the trolley down a different track where only a single worker will be killed. What should the bystander do? Most people vote for throwing the switch. Better to kill one person than five is the rational choice. Now consider that the bystander is on a bridge next to an obese person and sees that if he pushes the fat person off the bridge to his death, his body will throw the switch and the trolley will go down a track where no workers are. Most people refuse to push the person next to them to their death, killing one person, to save the five worker's lives. Emotion now overrules reason.

When Hans Berger discovered the electroencephalogram in 1929 he suggested that the brain was constantly active, with networks continually communicating with one another (Haas, 2003). This finding was subsequently minimized by fMRI investigators who assumed that the brain was at rest while participants lay in the scanner prior to receiving stimulation. Raichle et al. (2001) overturned this entrenched view with the discovery of what is now called the **Default Mode Network** (DMN).[12] The DMN is composed of the medial prefrontal cortex, the posterior cingulated cortex, and the parietal

[11] http://en.wikipedia.org/wiki/Trolley_problem
[12] http://en.wikipedia.org/wiki/Default_network

cortex. The prefrontal cortex is located behind the forehead and mediates what are known as our executive functions of planning, decision-making, and complex behaviors known as personality. The posterior cingulate is located underneath the top of the head and is partly responsible for awareness, episodic memory retrieval, and understanding other people. The parietal lobe is located just posterior to the central sulcus. It integrates sensory information including visual processing for 'where' (spatial vision) and 'how' (action vision). Further details are provided in the section below entitled '**Default Mode Network fMRI Studies**'. The important point here is that the DNM conclusively demonstrates that the brain consists of networks of networks that are constantly interacting with one another. These interactions are called 'stimulus-independent thoughts' (SITS) (Raichle & Snyder, 2007).

The **Human Connectome Project**[13] is currently mapping the structure of the more prominent neural networks in the human brain and will provide much more realistic architectures for future models.

PRINCIPLE 1: UNCONSCIOUS PROCESSING VIA THE NETWORK CASCADE

Activation in our generic PDP-CNN model begins in the top (S) layer automatically, deterministically, and unconsciously spreads across the middle (O) layer or layers to the response (R) layer. I refer to this process of **spreading activation** as the **network cascade**. The network cascade is a generalization of how neural impulses propagate along an axon. The network cascade consists of simultaneous neural impulses down the axons of many neurons over many synapses to many other neurons. These activations cascade across neural networks in an automatic, deterministic, and unconscious way. This network cascade is the causal physical basis of all Bio↔Psychology Network explanations. The subsequent sections below demonstrate that the neuroscience evidence for such processing is well beyond question at this point. We will see that Principle 1 is so strongly rooted in fact that no further empirical support is required.

Definition of Unconscious Processing

A good working definition of unconscious processing consists of two key elements: awareness and controllability. **Awareness** is the first element of our working definition of unconscious processing. Lack of awareness is the

[13] http://www.humanconnectomeproject.org/

hallmark of unconscious processing. **Attention** is a functionally equivalent term in that we are only fully aware of what we attend to and are largely unaware of what we do not attend to. Focusing our attention elsewhere renders us largely unaware of what we previously attended to. Awareness and attention pertain to the limits of consciousness. They are also the limits of our **introspectoscope**; the psychological tool that we use to probe our consciousness with. Cognitive and other brain processing that is not detectable by our introspectoscope is, by our definition, unconscious. Neuroimaging studies consistently reveal activation in parts of the brain to which our introspectoscope has no access. Processing by these brain areas can confidently and definitively be characterized as unconscious. Many brain imaging studies conclusively confirm that unconscious processing occurs. Eagleman (2011) reviewed much of this evidence at book length. Readers who have any residual uncertainty about the reality of unconscious processing after reading the following sections are encouraged to read his book.

Controllability is the second element of our working definition of unconscious processing. **Volition** is an equivalent alternative term because if we can voluntarily control and/or alter our perception, cognition, emotion, and/or behavior then we can also be said to be conscious of what we are doing. If we cannot completely control our perception, cognition, emotion, and/or behavior then we are to some extent unconscious of the processes that are involved. Disorders such as alien hand syndrome, where one hand may try to pick up a cookie while the other hand interferes with this action or where one hand buttons a shirt while the other hand unbuttons it, are examples of partial conscious control which means partial unconscious control (see Eagleman, 2011, pp. 131–2, 163–4). Relevant links are: http://en.wikipedia.org/wiki/Alien_hand_syndrome and http://science.howstuffworks.com/environmental/life/inside-the-mind/human-brain/alien-hand.htm. Video clips of this disorder can be seen at: http://www.youtube.com/watch?v=dIBBDuQrd-I and http://www.bbc.co.uk/news/uk-12225163.

Unconscious Processing

The role of unconscious processing has long separated psychodynamic psychologists from their cognitive-behavioral colleagues and constitutes a serious schism in psychology (Staats, 1983). In Chapter 9 I provide a brief history of unconscious processing that demonstrates that this topic was discussed for centuries before Freud 'discovered it'. Here I wish to describe and emphasize the central role that unconscious processing plays in PDP-CNN models, because this fact alone does much to theoretically unify psychodynamic thought with psychological science. **Un**conscious processing is a crucial central component of all psychodynamic theories, whereas conscious processing is the crucial central component of cognitive-behavioral theories. We shall now see that PDP-CNN models are consistent with both views and thereby provide a Hegelian synthesis of these seemingly oppositional positions.

PDP-CNN models are widely accepted as cognitive models yet a crucial central component of these models is that they process information unconsciously. Activation of the S-nodes spreads automatically, unconsciously, and deterministically to the O-nodes and again to the R-nodes through simulated synapses characterized by connection weights that quantify degrees of excitation or inhibition. As mentioned above, the automatic mechanical nature of this **network cascade** renders it an unconscious process. All of the psychological phenomena described below and in other chapters of this book, e.g., priming, part–whole pattern completion, etc., derive from, are the result of, this unconscious network cascade. The particular network architecture shown in Figure 3.1 allows activation from every S-node to spread to every O-node and on to every R-node if the transfer function illustrated in Figure 3.3 permits. This network cascade of activation occurs as automatically, deterministically, and unconsciously as neural conduction down an axon.

Figure 3.6 illustrates how the automatic mechanical network cascade works. The filled (black) circles represent active nodes whereas the open (white) circles represent inactive nodes. Positive numerical entries represent activation at excitatory synapses whereas negative numerical entries represent activation at inhibitory synapses. These simulated synaptic states are also known as connection weights because they connect pairs of processing nodes. Dendritic summation occurs by multiplying the on = 1 or off = 0 status of each sending node times the connection weight between that sending node and the receiving node. Since zero times anything is zero and one times any number equals that number, the simulated dendritic sum equals the sum of the connection weights emanating from, connecting all sending nodes to the receiving node. If the simulated dendritic (input) sum exceeds a threshold value, here zero, then the receiving node becomes active (fires). Otherwise it remains off or is turned off. For example, the left O-node receives activation of 0.1 from the left S-node, activation of –0.2 from the middle S-node, and activation of 0.4 from the right S-node for a total

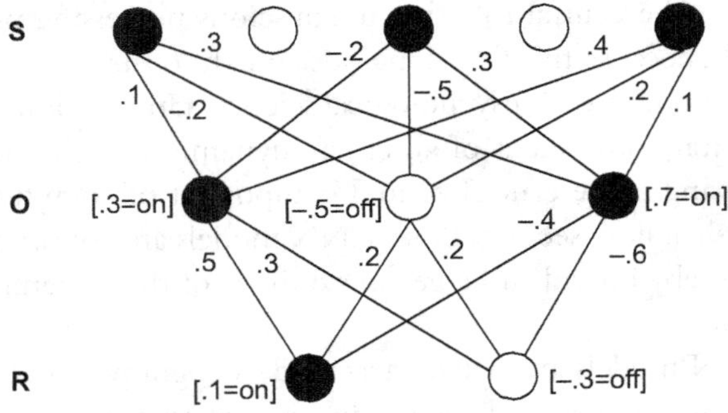

Figure 3.6 Illustration of how the automatic mechanical network cascade works. Filled (black) circles represent active nodes whereas open (white) circles represent inactive nodes. Positive numerical entries represent activation at excitatory synapses whereas negative numerical entries represent activation at inhibitory synapses. These simulated synaptic states are also known as connection weights because the simulated synapses connect pairs of processing nodes. Dendritic summation occurs by multiplying the on = 1 or off = 0 status of the sending node times the connection weight between the sending and receiving nodes. Since zero times anything is zero and one times a number equals that number, the simulated dendritic sum equals the sum of the connection weights from active nodes. If the simulated dendritic (input) sum exceeds a threshold value, here zero, then the receiving node becomes active (fires). Otherwise it remains off or is turned off.

activation of 0.3, which being greater than the threshold value of zero in this case activates the left O-node or keeps it active if it was on before.

The middle O-node receives activation of −0.2 from the left S-node, activation of −0.5 from the middle S-node, and activation of 0.2 from the right S-node for a total activation of −0.5, which being less than a threshold value of zero in this case deactivates, turns off, the middle O-node if it was on or keeps it off if it was already off. The right O-node receives activation of 0.3 from the left S-node, activation of 0.3 from the middle S-node, and activation of 0.1 from the right S-node for a total activation of 0.7, which being greater than a threshold value of zero in this case activates the right O-node or keeps it on if it was active before. Similar calculations turn on the left R-node and turn off the right R-node.

Empirical Evidence of Unconscious Processing

This section considers two major sources of scientific evidence that support the existence of unconscious processing. **Psychological science** is our first source; it provides **five** lines of evidence that support the reality of unconscious processing. We discuss these lines of evidence first because I am a psychologist and expect that most of my readers are either psychologists or students of psychology. **Neuroscience** is our second source. It provides **ten** lines of evidence that validate unconscious processing. The resulting **15** lines of evidence are collectively compelling in my view, and hopefully in your view as well. Readers who wish to reach a negative conclusion here will need to repudiate all 15 lines of evidence. Good luck with that.

Psychological Science

Hassin (2013) reviewed the available empirical literature and found that unconscious processing implements many of the same functions that have traditionally been thought to require conscious processing. These functions include: (a) cognitive control; (b) pursing goals and managing goal conflicts; (c) reasoning; and (d) decision-making. The author concluded '... that unconscious processes can perform the same fundamental, high-level functions that conscious processes can perform' (p. 195). In the remainder of this section I identify five lines of psychological cognitive science evidence regarding the reality of unconscious processing. These lines of evidence pertain to: (a) optical illusions; (b) heuristics, also known as cognitive illusions, derived from dual and triarchic processing theories; (c) Unconscious Thought Theory from social psychology; (d) implicit association testing; and (e) priming studies. It might seem as odd to you as to me that cognitive science has discovered so much evidence supporting unconscious processing that undercuts the conscious-centric orientation of their theories.

Optical Illusions

Optical illusions are discussed by every introductory psychology textbook that I have seen over the past 42 years. Our understanding of optical illusions prepares us to understand the cognitive illusions that we will encounter below. The visual system is understood to operate unconsciously. We see just fine without the need for conscious control. Light enters our eyes and makes its way to the visual cortex without any conscious participation on our part. Optical illusions reflect misperceptions, perceptual errors that derive from the functional properties of the neural networks that mediate our visual perception. These 'mistakes' would no doubt be avoided by engineers constructing an intelligent robot. The Internet provides many examples of optical illusions.[14] The 'stepping feet' illusion[15] is particularly instructive. Two colored (black and yellow) rectangles are perceived to pro-

14 http://www.michaelbach.de/ot/

15 http://www.michaelbach.de/ot/mot_feet_lin/index.html

ceed smoothly and horizontally, back and forth, across the screen at the same rate when viewed against a homogeneous gray background but are perceived to 'step' or shuffle when viewed against a background consisting of vertical black and white stripes. This **misperception** is caused by **properties** of the neural networks that **unconsciously** mediate our perceptions. It cannot be consciously controlled. The three emboldened words deserve further emphasis. First, the stepping illusion, like all optical illusions, is a **misperception**; a defective percept. It is not a good thing; something that an artificial life form would no doubt be designed not to do. It is what I call a man–machine difference. Second, illusions reflect peculiar **properties** of our neural networks that are hard-wired in us and therefore are unavoidable. We may be able to compensate for them, but we cannot avoid them. We compensate for myopia with glasses. We compensate for hearing loss with hearing aids. No amount of insight derived from education or experience can free us from optical illusions any more than insight can correct myopia or hearing loss. Insight cannot set us free from these neural network limitations. Third, the processes that generate optical illusions operate **unconsciously**. Kihlstrom (1987) and Kihlstrom et al. (1992) concur that PDP-CNN models of cognition have an unconscious-centric orientation.

Dual System Cognitive Models

Psychologists have long thought that the mind is composed of two systems: an **automatic** system and a **controlled** system that comprise what are known as dual processing theories of cognitive processing (Evans & Stanovich, 2013). Haidt (2001) referred to these two systems as: (a) the Intuitive System; and (b) the Reasoning System. These two systems differ respectively in the following ways: (a) fast and effortless vs. slow and effortful; (b) processing is unintentional and runs automatically vs. processing is intentional and controllable; (c) processing is inaccessible, only results enter awareness vs. processing is consciously accessible and viewable; (d) does not demand attentional resources vs. demands limited attentional resources; (e) parallel distributed processing vs. serial processing; (f) entails pattern matching, thought is metaphorical and holistic vs. symbol manipulation, thought is truth preserving and analytic; (g) common to all mammals vs. unique to humans over age 2 and perhaps some language-trained apes; (h) context dependent vs. context independent; and (i) depends upon the brain and body vs. platform independent. Evans and Stanovich (2013) stated 'A true dual-process theory that distinguishes two *types* of process will, by our definition, imply the engagement of distinct cognitive and neurological systems' (p. 226). Their list of defining features includes the following contrasts between intuitive and reflective processing: fast vs. slow; high capacity vs. limited capacity; parallel vs. serial processing; nonconscious vs. conscious; biased responses vs. normative responses; contextualized vs. abstract; automatic vs. controlled; associative vs. rule-based, experience-based decision-making vs. consequential decision-making; and independent of cognitive ability vs. correlated with cognitive ability.

Kahnemann (2011a) referred to his two systems by number as System 1 and System 2. He justified his decision to write about these two systems as fictitious characters engaged in a type of psychodrama because it was easier to do so and was more readily understood by the general and lay audience that he was writing for. Table 3.1 below summarizes some of the characteristics of Systems 1 and 2. Evans (2008) and Evans and Frankish (2009) reviewed the literature that gave rise to the terms System 1 and 2. Kahneman (2011b) has more to say about this history of dual-processing theories.

Most of the time, people process information using System 1, which operates associatively, unconsciously, automatically, and irrationally. Conversely, System 2 refers to logical, critical, step-by-step analytic thinking that people sometimes use when they are unemotional (calm), attentive (focused), and not under any time pressure to answer a question. Kahneman (2011a,b) described System 2 as effortful and tiresome to use and therefore people only use it when there is a compelling reason to do so. System 1 is so much easier to use because it relies on many cognitive short cuts called

Table 3.1 Characteristics of Dual-Processing Theories

Theorist	System 1	System 2
Schneider and Shiffrin (1977)	Automatic	Controlled
Sloman (1996)	Associative processing	Rule-based system
Evans (1984, 1989)	Heuristic processing	Analytic processing
Evans & Over (1996)	Tacit thought processes	Explicit thought processes
Reber (1993)	Implicit cognition	Explicit learning
Levinson (1995)	Interactional intelligence	Analytic intelligence
Epstein (1994)	Experiential system	Rational system
Pollock (1991)	Quick and inflexible modules	Intellection
Hammond (1996)	Intuitive cognition	Analytical cognition
Klein (1998)	Recognition-primed decisions	Rational choice strategy

heuristics which typically yield incorrect but approximate answers. Herbert (2010) discussed 20 heuristics in his book entitled *On Second Thought: Outsmarting Your Mind's Hard-wired Habits*.

Shah and Oppenheimer (2008) proposed that most heuristics simplify thought in the following five ways: (a) they examine fewer cues; (b) they reduce storage and retrieval processes; (c) they simplify cue weighting; (d) they integrate less information; and (e) they examine fewer alternatives. Winkielman et al. (2006) presented evidence to demonstrate that prototypes facilitate emotional and cognitive processing.

Automatic Unconscious System 1 Features Kahneman's (2011a) System 1 exhibits a long list of automatic unconscious processing features known as cognitive biases or heuristics. They are quick and dirty methods of getting an answer or coming to a conclusion without much reflection and rational thought. They clearly illustrate many different ways in which people jump to conclusions based on unconscious processing.

Cognitive science might seem to be the last place that one would expect to find evidence of unconscious processing, because cognitive science is mainly about conscious rational thought. This section contains two kinds of evidence that are consistent with unconscious processing. The first line of evidence concerns limitations of cognitive processing. Any processing that occurs outside these limits will, by definition, be unconscious. One of the earliest and best-documented empirical facts in cognitive psychology concerns the limit of cognitive processing known as Miller's (1956) magic number of 5 ± 2 that places a limit of 7 on the number of items that can normally be used in working memory. If any additional information is processed, it will be processed outside of conscious awareness; i.e., processed unconsciously.

The second line of evidence concerns cognitive heuristics; ways of thinking that we think we believe give us good answers but typically misinform us. Cognitive heuristics are traditionally considered to be nothing more than limitations of cognitive processing, but I submit that they also constitute evidence of unconscious processing because people are unaware that they are using them and they are unaware that such thinking is irrational. They are unaware, and therefore unconscious of, the fact that they are taking cognitive short cuts. It is mainly the lack of awareness that makes cognitive heuristics convincing evidence of unconscious processing.

Kahneman and Tversky (1979), Kahneman (2003a,b, 2011a,b) and Kahneman and Klein (2009) demonstrated several ways that normal people engage in non-rational, one might say irrational, processing. People unconsciously rely on heuristics; using intuition and guess-work to simplify and speed up decision-making. Kahneman (2011a) stated: 'The technical definition of *heuristic* is a simple procedure that helps find adequate, though often imperfect, answers to difficult questions. The word comes from the same root as *eureka*' (p. 98, italics in the original). This view that cognition is defective was not initially happily or readily accepted by cognitive psychologists because such a conclusion stands in the way of creating purely rational theories of human psychology and behavior. Kahneman and Tversky (1996) essentially settled this debate with their article entitled '*On the Reality of Cognitive Illusions*'. Their use of the term **cognitive illusion** is especially important, because like optical illusions that are widely acknowledged to be unconscious properties of our neural networks, Kahneman and Tversky consider cognitive illusions also to be unconscious properties of our neural networks.

As mentioned above in our discussion of dual process theories, Kahneman (2011a) distinguished between our cognitive System 1 which impulsively and unconsciously uses heuristics, and our rational cognitive System 2 that deliberately and effortfully uses logic. Unfortunately, System 1 governs most normal mental life, as Kahneman (2011a) noted when he wrote:

> A remarkable aspect of your mental life is that you are rarely stumped. True, you occasionally face a question such as 17 × 24 = ? to which no answer comes immediately to mind, but these dumbfounded moments are rare. The normal state of your mind is that you have intuitive feelings and opinions about almost everything that comes your way. You like or dislike people long before you know much about them; you trust or distrust strangers without knowing why; you feel that an enterprise is bound to succeed without analyzing it. Whether you state them or not, you often have answers to questions that you do not completely understand, relying on evidence that you can neither explain nor defend (p. 97).

Our brains evolved at a time when decision speed was crucial to survival. System 1 evolved to meet this need for speed. Our tendency to dependence upon cognitive heuristics is as hard-wired into our neural networks as are optical illusions; i.e., they both result from and behave in accordance with the core and corollary network principles reviewed in this chapter and the next one. Kahneman (2011a) referred to these heuristics as **cognitive illusions** to emphasize how unavoidable this form of unconscious processing is.

We now consider several cognitive heuristics that demonstrate unconscious processing, but in no special order. Relevant sources here are Kahneman and Tversky (1979), Kahneman (2003a,b), Kahneman and Klein (2009), and especially Kahneman (2011a,b).

Illusion of Validity The 'illusion of validity' refers to the fact that the results of cognitive heuristics appear as valid to our intuition as optical illusions do. Kahneman (2011b, Chapter 20, pp. 209–21) described this effect as the result of a strong parallel between visual processing and cognitive processing. Visual, optical, illusions have long been known to reflect unconscious processing by the human visual system that persist even after they are explained, as illustrated at the following web site http://www.visualillusion.net/. This persistence is evidence that they operate automatically and unconsciously.

Kahneman (2011b) maintained that we are subject to an illusion of validity because we tend to exaggerate our expectation of consistency and perceive the world as more regular and predictable than it actually is. He argued that memory mechanisms favor coherence and suppress inconsistent evidence, because consistent and familiar recollections speed decision-making. We can understand this as a consequence of the network coherence principle that we will discuss in Chapter 4. For example, objective evidence indicates that on average professional portfolio managers cannot consistently select stocks that outperform the market average. When given a spreadsheet summarizing investment outcomes of 25 wealth managers over eight years, Kahneman (2011b) computed the rank order correlations over managers for all possible year combinations resulting in $(8 \times 7)/2 = 28$ year-to-year correlations over the 25 wealth managers. If some wealth mangers were consistently better than others then these correlations would be positive. However, the average correlation was just $r = 0.01$, nearly zero, indicating that the year-end performance bonus system rewarded luck not skill. Yet these wealth managers did not question their ability to make valid decisions about complex financial matters even after being confronted with this evidence. They remained committed to their view of themselves as financial experts. Their inability to properly process the implications of objective statistical data is as unavoidable as is their tendency to perceive optical illusions because they both operate automatically and unconsciously. The problem here is that the natural and unconscious tendency of neural networks to seek consonance distorts cognitive processing in predictable ways that we will subsequently discuss as Principle 7.

Gärling et al. (2009) wrote an entire monograph on how psychological factors influence thinking about economics. They identified the following 'biases in financial decision making': (a) subjective value of money; (b) asymmetric risk attitudes; (c) reference point framing; and (d) loss aversion. They further identified the following 'cognitive biases': (a) overreaction to news; (b) disposition effect; (c) reactions to splits of stock shares; and (d) naïve risk diversification. They also discussed affective and social influences. All of this evidence testifies that irrational, emotional, and unconscious processing characterizes human cognition.

Experts typically feel that their judgments and intuitions are better predictors than are formulas. Meehl (1954, 1986) compared statistical versus clinical prediction and concluded that regression formulas consistently outperform expert judgment. Baseball scouts pride themselves regarding their knowledge of the game and their ability to pick players who will succeed in the major leagues. This includes scouts for the Oakland A's. The problem is that baseball is an unfair sport in that some franchises have much more money than others and therefore can successfully recruit the more talented players. The Oakland A's are among the poorest baseball franchises and therefore had to find another way to win games. Lewis (2003) wrote a book entitled *Moneyball: The Art of Winning an Unfair Game*[16] that chronicles efforts to use a heavily statistical approach in selecting affordable players that when combined were likely to win games. The book and resulting movie by the same name portrayed the enormous resistance that the owner faced from his scouts, who proclaimed that a statistical approach would fail miserably and that they could do much better. The fact that the Oakland A's had losing seasons when the scouts had their way provided motivation to try a new approach. To the great surprise of the scouts and coaches and over their formidable resistance, players selected by purely statistical methods provided, and continue to provide, the Oakland A's with winning teams on a shoestring budget compared to some other baseball franchises. Kahneman (2011b, p. 225) reported that experienced radiologists who evaluate chest X-rays as 'normal' or 'abnormal' contradict themselves 20% of the time when re-reviewing the same X-rays without knowing that they are doing so.

There are at least two reasons why statistical decisions are superior to human decisions. The first reason is that human judgments are less reliable than statistical judgments. Experts sometimes evaluate the same evidence differently, even when the same expert repeatedly evaluates the same evidence. Small details, context effects, can influence the decisions of experts thereby resulting in inconsistency. Unreliability always degrades validity. Of particular present interest is that experts are largely unaware of how unreliable their judgments are.

A second reason why experts often do less well than formulas concerns proper and consistent weighting of variables. Multiple regression formulas

[16] http://en.wikipedia.org/wiki/Moneyball

optimally weight variables relative to the training sample. Equal weights do remarkably well when prediction is tested on subsequent samples unless the training samples are both large and representative. Experts think that they can do a better job at weighting, but overall their meddling just reduces predictability. The lack of awareness that experts have regarding their cognitive limitations indicates that they are automatically and unconsciously substituting cognitive short cuts, heuristics, for rational processing. Stated otherwise, people believe that they are as rational as computers are except that they aren't and they are unaware of this fact.

Illusory Correlation

We are inclined to think that some things are correlated even when they are not; particularly when those things are expected to be related or stand out in a distinctive way. Illusory correlations stem from the fact that memory is better for confirmatory instances of co-occurrence than for contradictory outcomes. Consider the four observational elements that influence correlations illustrated in Table 3.2. Memory for Types A and D events typically exceed memory for Types C and B events resulting in the overestimation of the correlation between Events 1 and 2.

Consider the following example of illusory correlation. Redelmeier and Tversky (1996) collected judgments by 18 arthritis patients over 15 months to assess their claim that their condition was weather-related. The correlation with meteorological data over the same time period was near zero. Hamilton and Rose (1980) found that based on stereotypes, people over-estimated the co-occurrence of certain traits in members of particular groups. Hamilton and Gifford (1976) experimentally induced illusory correlations in participants by making selected attributes more distinctive, but not proportionally more representative, of one fictitious group versus another. These data indicate that people automatically and unconsciously draw unwarranted conclusions about correlations based on salience alone and remain unaware that they have done so.

The work of Chapman (1967) and Chapman and Chapman (1967) regarding illusory correlation has special relevance for psychological testing.

Table 3.2 Four Elements Required to Establish Correlation

		Event 2	
		Positive	Negative
Event 1	Positive	A	B
	Negative	C	D

Clinicians confidently conclude, and train students to conclude, that there is a correlation between eye size and paranoia on the projective Draw-A-Person test. These authors found no such correlation. They also found that college students could see this correlation in data presented to them when these features were completely uncorrelated. This cognitive heuristic is caused by the neural network property of preferring consonance and coherence over dissonance that we will discuss as Principle 7.

Invisible correlations are the opposite of illusory correlations. They refer to actual associations that are difficult for us to see, such as the relationship between smoking and cancer that took years of empirical research to demonstrate. The same can be said about climate change today. The actual relationships in question continue to reside outside of awareness for many people. There are none so blind as those who don't want to see.

Illusion of Understanding Bias Kahneman (2011b) devoted all of his Chapter 19 (pp. 199–208) and much of his Chapter 17 (pp. 175–184) to this bias, which is discussed here in two parts. **Regression towards the mean** is the first example of **illusory understanding** that we will discuss. I use the example that Kahneman (2011a, pp. 175–6) presented. Kahneman provided psychological training to flight instructors in the Israeli Air Force. After reviewing research on the benefits of rewarding success vs. punishing failure he was contradicted by a seasoned instructor as follows:

> On many occasions I have praised flight cadets for clean execution of some aerobatic maneuver. The next time they try the same maneuver they usually do worse. On the other hand, I have often screamed into a cadet's earphone for bad execution, and in general he does better on the next try. So please don't tell us that reward works and punishment does not, because the opposite is the case.

The problem here is that extremes are unstable and are typically followed by more representative, average, performance. This predictable result is known as **regression to the mean**.[17] Extremely positive responses are likely followed by less positive responses and that supports the illusion that praise does not work. Extremely negative responses are also likely followed by more positive responses and that supports the illusion that punishment works. The automatic misunderstanding of regression towards the mean constitutes a form of unconscious processing that unfortunately fosters an attitude that resists replicated research findings and promotes the continued use of suboptimal training methods based upon professional experience and opinion.

[17] http://en.wikipedia.org/wiki/Regression_toward_the_mean

The regression towards the mean illusion is an example of a more general **narrative fallacy** illusion of understanding. Kahneman (2011b, pp. 199–200) explained that this illusion consists of flawed stories based on past events that shape future expectations.

> Narrative fallacies arise inevitably from our continuous attempt to make sense of the world. The explanatory stories that people find compelling are simple; are concrete rather than abstract; assign a larger role to talent, stupidity, and intentions than to luck; and focus on a few striking events that happened rather than on the countless events that failed to happen (p. 199).

Narratives are judged largely on the basis of their coherence. Consistent stories are understood to be true by virtue of their consistency. **Halo biases** facilitate consistency by rendering narratives far more consistent than they might otherwise be. Halos can be negative as well as positive.

Narratives are also characterized by **hindsight bias** otherwise known as the **'I-knew-it-all-along'** bias or the **outcome bias**. Knowledge of outcomes modifies people's memory towards consistency. Their current narrative about their prior beliefs minimizes errors of commission and omission in ways that they are completely unaware of. An especially important feature of the hindsight bias is its ability to modify memory. Kahneman (2011b, p. 202) observed:

> A general limitation of the human mind is its imperfect ability to reconstruct past states of knowledge, or beliefs that have changed. Once you adopt a new view of the world (or any part of it), you immediately lose much of your ability to recall what you used to believe before your mind changed (p.202).

A major and defining feature of heuristics is that they characteristically substitute an easier-to-answer question for the more difficult posed question, but do so outside of awareness. Kahneman (2011b) noted that the hindsight bias substitutes a contemporary memory for a previous memory without the person's awareness.

> Asked to reconstruct their former beliefs, people retrieve their current ones instead – an instance of substitution – and many cannot believe that they ever felt differently (p. 202).

Kahneman (2011b, pp. 202–4) summarized a series of social psychological experiments conducted before and after major events including Richard Nixon's visit to China and Russia in 1972, the O.J. Simpson murder trial, the impeachment of President Bill Clinton, and the attack on the World Trade Center on 9/11/01 that clearly support the conclusion that the hindsight bias is robust and replicable. The lack of awareness associated with such cognitive processing qualifies it as unconscious processing.

Tryon and McKay (2009) provided a connectionist explanation for why new learning modifies memory based on the following two neuroscience facts. First, processing and memory storage are carried out on many of the same neural networks. This provides a physical basis for new learning to alter memory. Second, cognitive processing activates experience-dependent plasticity mechanisms that modify memories in ways that make them more consistent with the person's contemporary psychological state. Together these two network principles explain why people can feel as if 'I-knew-it-all-along' (p. 202), and why 'when asked to reconstruct their former beliefs, people retrieve their current ones instead' (p. 202). I emphasize here that this memory modification process is automatic and unconscious because it occurs outside of awareness.

Confirmation Bias Illusory correlation is also driven by confirmation bias; another defective heuristic that operates outside of awareness (Baron, 2000). Confirmation bias refers to our tendency to let subsequent information confirm our first impressions (Baron, 2000). Hence, the same subsequent information can confirm different points of view depending upon what our first impression was. Alternatively stated, we are preferentially sensitive to and cherry-pick facts that justify decisions we make and hypotheses that we favor, and are similarly insensitive to facts that either fail to support or contradict decisions we make and hypotheses that we favor. And the best part is that all of this continuously operates unconsciously; outside of our awareness. This heuristic has been called the **Positive Test Strategy** and is illustrated next.

Snyder and Cantor (1979) described a fictitious person named Jane. To one group Jane was described as an extravert; to another group Jane was described as an introvert. A couple of days later, half the participants were asked to evaluate Jane for an extraverted job of a real estate broker and half were asked to evaluate her for an introverted job of librarian. Evaluations for the real estate job contained more references to Jane's extraversion whereas evaluations for the introverted job contained more references to her introversion. This finding implies the use of a positive test strategy when trying to remember things about Jane. This cognitive heuristic is also caused by the neural network property of preferring consonance and coherence over dissonance that we will discuss as our Principle 7.

Representativeness Heuristic The more an exemplar represents its category, the more probable we think the event is. Thinking in terms of stereotypes is an example of the representative heuristic. Tversky and Kahneman (1974) described the representativeness heuristic as the cognitive bias towards thinking about the probability that A is associated with or caused B in terms of the degree to which A is representative of B; i.e., the degree to which A resembles B. The example Tversky and Kahneman (1974) gave is that of estimating the probability that a person is a librarian is dependent upon how similar, representative, the person is of the prototypical librarian mentioned above. People are unaware that they are unconsciously processing familiarity and representativeness as probability; i.e., they do it unconsciously. This cognitive bias derives from our neural network Principle 10 regarding prototype formation that we will discuss in the next chapter. Neural networks automatically and unconsciously extract prototypes and they influence cognitive decisions concerning probabilities based on representativeness.

This cognitive bias is **insensitive to the prior probability of outcomes** associated with base-rate frequencies. The example that Tversky and Kahneman (1974) gave is that the probability that a person is a librarian should depend upon the frequency of librarians in the local population. That there are many more farmers than librarians where this person lives should influence the probability estimate more than how representative the person seems to be of the librarian prototype. Prototypes form automatically and unconsciously. They unconsciously distort cognitions about probabilities.

The representativeness heuristic caused by the network property of prototype formation also biases people's cognitions about probability through **insensitivity to sample size**. Tversky and Kahneman (1974) informed participants that slightly more boys are born than girls and then asked whether the number of days on which more than 60% of births were boys was more frequent in a large than small hospital or was equally frequent in both hospitals. Most participants chose the equally frequent answer despite the fact that statistics are more stable in larger samples and therefore greater variability in the percentage of male births is to be expected in the smaller hospital.

The representativeness heuristic also distorts people's cognitions about the **sequence of chance events**. Tversky and Kahneman (1974) noted that people prefer to think that flipping a fair coin will likely result in a H–T–H–T–H–T sequence because this pattern is locally representative which is what they expect of a fair coin. That sequence seems more probable to them than the sequence H–H–H–T–T–T which contains a run of Hs followed by a run of Ts. Actual random sequences are rarely locally representative and can contain extended runs. Tversky and Kahneman

(1974) referred to the '**law of small numbers**' to characterize people's expectations, cognitions, that small samples are highly representative of the populations from which they were drawn. Clinical psychologists frequently make this cognitive mistake even after statistical training. We persist in automatically and unconsciously thinking in irrational ways. We do this unconsciously rather than on the basis of a conscious decision to think irrationally.

Availability Heuristic Tversky and Kahneman (1974) described the availability heuristic wherein the predicted frequency of an event is driven by how easily it can be brought to mind. More easily remembered events appear more frequent and probable to us than they are. For example, events that are repeated more often in the news are thought to occur more frequently in real life than they actually do because they are more easily recalled. **Repetition priming**, our network Principle 5 to be discussed in Chapter 4, makes it easier to recall repeated events and triggers the availability heuristic. For example, death by homicide is reported on TV news and in newspapers more frequently than is death by stomach cancer, which makes people think that death by homicide is more likely than death by stomach cancer even though it isn't. Deaths by shark attacks are over-estimated because they are so memorable when they occur. Memorable examples tend to get cited as confirming evidence even if they are not representative. Citing case histories as supportive evidence of a personality theory or psychotherapy is another example of this heuristic. The uniqueness, selectivity, and bias associated with such citations rarely enter the conversation. This tendency to confuse memory and probability occurs automatically and unconsciously.

An important corollary is that asking people to imagine a specific outcome makes it seem more likely even though it isn't. This effect is known as **imagination inflation** (Garry et al., 1996; Paddock et al., 1998). It also works automatically and unconsciously.

What you see is all there is (WYSIATI) Kahneman (2011b) observed: 'An essential design feature of the associative machine is that it represents only activated ideas' (p. 85). His reference to 'activated ideas' pertains to our Principle 4: Activation-Reactivation, to be discussed later in this chapter as core network principles.

Kahneman (2011b) further noted that System 1 excels at creating explanatory stories. 'The amount and quality of the data on which the story is based are largely irrelevant' (p. 85). 'System 1 operates as a machine for jumping to conclusions' (p. 85). For example, whereas a logical analysis directed by System 2 might ask what information would be needed to render a sound judgment about who to vote for President, System 1 renders a conclusion based on the ideas and perceptions that are currently activated such as the candidate's appearance. The tendency to think this way is unfortunately automatic and unconscious.

Blind Spot Bias We are much better at perceiving biases in other people than in ourselves (Pronin et al., 2004). We have a blind spot when it comes to examining our own thinking compared to thinking done by others.

Self-serving Bias This bias enables us to reach different conclusions when the same set of facts pertains to ourselves versus when they pertain to others (Bazerman et al., 1997). For example, the same set of facts might lead to a conclusion of guilty and therefore deserving of punishment when applied to others, but to a conclusion of not guilty if applied to ourselves or our children.

Anchoring Heuristic Tversky and Kahneman (1974) described the anchoring heuristic as a cognitive bias that occurs when people unconsciously rely too heavily on one piece of information when making a decision.[18] For example, information presented first tends to modify how we react to, can anchor, subsequent information more than we are aware of. Information presented first creates a background/context against which subsequent information is evaluated. This causes the background information to have more influence than if other information were presented first. For example, initially knowing the mileage of a used car before anything else may prejudice the customer's opinion more than if that was the last thing learned about the car. Extreme events can also anchor subsequent judgments. For example, knowing that one's grandfather lived to be 100 despite heavy smoking can result in underestimating the health risks of smoking.

Kahneman (2011b, p. 123) demonstrated that people's estimates can be biased, anchored, by providing them with a reference number. Consider the following example where participants were asked:

'Is the height of the tallest redwood more or less than 1200 feet?'

'What is your best guess about the height of the tallest redwood?'

[18] http://en.wikipedia.org/wiki/Anchoring_and_adjustment

Other participants were asked:

'Is the height of the tallest redwood more or less than 180 feet?'

'What is your best guess about the height of the tallest redwood?'

Participants gave higher estimates in the first case and lower estimates in the second case.

The anchoring effect is not unlike a visual after-effect in that it derives from the serial activation of neural networks. Activation of the first network provides a background context (anchor) against which activation of the second network is evaluated. For example, in psychophysics, first lifting light objects makes a test object seem heavier whereas lifting a series of heavy objects makes a test object seem lighter. Activation of the first network provides a frame of reference for evaluating subsequent stimuli. Helson (1948) presented a **general adaptation level theory** and supporting evidence. He extended the explanatory scope of this theory in his 1964 book entitled *Adaptation-Level Theory: An Experimental and Systematic Approach to Behavior.* The relevance of Helson's theory to the anchoring effect is provided by the following quote from the very first paragraph of Helson's 1948 *Psychology Review* article:

> The fact that all judgments are made with respect to a frame of reference was first postulated and experimentally demonstrated in psychophysical experiments and later extended to attitude-formation and social behavior generally. The terms standard, norm, value, **anchor**, and frame of reference are now as widely employed as conditioning, Gestalt, trial and error, past experience and association (p. 297; emphasis added).

In general, Gestalt effects may be understood as stemming from the part–whole pattern completion property of neural networks; our Principle 6.

Focusing Effect The focusing effect is a cognitive bias wherein people tend to focus on what is perceptually salient. People frequently think that they would be happier if they were richer because they focus on money as salient with regard to happiness, but empirical evidence does not support this view (cf. Kahneman et al., 2006). The focusing effect operates unconsciously and automatically. The priming property of neural networks, our Principle 5, can render certain features salient.

Superiority Illusion The illusion of superiority is the cognitive bias that causes people to overestimate their positive qualities and underestimate their negative qualities with the result that they see themselves as above average.[19] People consistently show this bias with regard to estimates of

[19] http://en.wikipedia.org/wiki/Illusory_superiority

their intelligence, driving ability, leadership, ethics, health, gambling, etc. This cognitive bias has also been called the superiority bias, above average effect, and Lake Wobegon effect after the novel by Garrison Keillor regarding a fictional town where all of the children are above average; a statistical impossibility since the average of a normal distribution is also its median above and below which half of the population lie. This is an example of the confirmatory bias discussed earlier that we traced to the neural network property of seeking consonance and coherence; avoiding dissonance. The superiority illusion operates automatically and unconsciously.

Substitution This cognitive bias refers to the heuristic of substituting an easier to answer question for a more difficult one. This substitution occurs reflexively, unconsciously, automatically, and appears to reduce the effort required in decision-making (cf. Shah & Oppenheimer, 2008). Substituting an easier to answer question for a more difficult one also speeds up decision-making; speed was often a critical survival factor in our evolution. It should therefore not be surprising that our neural networks have optimized around solution speed. Prototypes, our network Principle 10, are similarly important to cognitive psychology because they facilitate, i.e., speed up, processing. Prototypes function like stereotypes (e.g., Cin et al., 2009) in that they reduce complex issues to simple choices. All of this occurs automatically and unconsciously.

Kahneman (2003a,b) reported that people's intuition often incorrectly simplifies problems; i.e., substitutes a simpler problem for a more complex one and then solves the simpler problem as if it provided an answer to the more complex one without any awareness of doing so. For example, participants were presented with the following question: 'A bat and a ball together cost $1.10. The bat costs $1 more than the ball. How much does the ball cost?' A majority of participants simplified this problem into the bat cost one dollar and the ball cost ten cents. The correct answer requires the following reasoning:

$$bat + ball = 1.10 \qquad (1)$$

$$bat = ball + 1.00 \qquad (2)$$

Substituting equation 2 into equation 1 yields

$$(ball + 1.00) + ball = 1.10$$

$$2\ balls = 0.10$$

$$ball = 0.05$$

$$bat = 1.05$$

Check: The bat costs $1 more than the ball. Together they cost $1.10

It should be readily apparent that this correct form of reasoning is both complex and not particularly intuitive for most people. While participants with a high school education should be able to solve this problem, their intuition is that the solution is sufficiently obvious that mathematical reasoning is not required. The simpler and quicker heuristic is therefore substituted without any awareness of doing so. See Kahneman (2011b, p. 65) for two additional questions that have deceptively simple but incorrect answers. Together they constitute Shane Frederick's Cognitive Reflection Test.

Kahneman and Frederick (2002) identified **priming**, our network Principle 5, as a substitution mechanism. Reading recent reports on terrorism may alter judgments about the cost of travel insurance related to foreign travel. Activation of fear networks may prime judgments about the probability of death during foreign travel. Political campaigns are noted for using fear primes to alter voting preferences.

Base Rate Fallacy This cognitive defect, also known as **base rate neglect** or **base rate bias**, occurs when a conditional probability is evaluated without taking into account the prior probability of both components.[20] For example, to evaluate the probability of a hypothesis (H) being true given evidence (E), which can be written p(H | E), one must also know the p(H) and p(E) in addition to p(E | H) in order to satisfy Bayes Theorem which stated mathematically is:

$$p(H|E) = \frac{p(E|H)\,p(H)}{p(E)}$$

The complexity of this computation explains why people take a cognitive short cut, use a heuristic (cf. Fischhoff & Beyth-Marom, 1983), but the pertinent part here is that this short cut is taken unconsciously; without the person knowing that this is what they are doing.

Professional Applications Sunstein (2005) reported that the **attribution substitution** heuristic is widely used when making moral, political, and/or legal decisions. People substitute a prototypical case for an existing case and then substitute reasons given by noted authorities or other people for their own critical analysis.

Conclusions The following link lists approximately 50 automatic and unconscious cognitive biases, including those mentioned above, that render

[20] http://en.wikipedia.org/wiki/Base_rate_fallacy

cognitive decisions defective, distorted, biased, and just plain wrong.[21] The worst part is that we are almost always unaware of these unconscious processes. Automatic and unconscious memory defects, distortions, and biases further complicate our ability to reason effectively. A list of 45 common memory biases can be found at the following URL.[22] Together they form 95 ways in which people automatically and unconsciously process information without the slightest awareness of doing so.

There are two common themes or threads that run through the examples provided above. The first common theme is that we are typically unaware when we use these well-documented cognitive heuristics, which means that they often operate unconsciously. In fact there are so many of these biases that we cannot even keep them all in mind so as to consistently monitor if we are using them or not. Short-term memory is limited by Miller's magic number of 7 ± 2. The 95 biases reviewed or referenced above far exceed this capacity. So unless we keep a heuristic checklist in front of us at all times, and check it frequently, we may well unconsciously use one or more of them.

The second common theme is that cognitive and memory heuristics reflect functional properties of our neural networks just as optical illusions do. This explains why heuristics are reflexive and automatic. It also explains why education and insight into these heuristics cannot free us from them. We are left with recognizing and compensating for them. Recognition here means acceptance of unconscious processing as common and pervasive, given the approximately 100 ways in which it intrudes on our ability to think rationally.

Objections Some investigators remain unconvinced by the evidence presented above that dual processing theories are valid. They prefer to believe that people are of but one mind and that mind is rule-governed. For example, Kruglanski (2013) takes issue with Evans and Stanovich's (2013) support for dual-system theories. Kruglanski and Grigerenzer (2011) attempted to prove that rules exist by providing evidence concerning the validity of rule-based models to support their claim that cognition and behavior are rule-governed. Their argument takes the following form: (a) they assume and then conclude that rules govern behavior; (b) they developed rule-based models that predicted behavior rather well; and (c) present this accomplishment as proof that rules govern all forms of behavior.

21 http://en.wikipedia.org/wiki/List_of_cognitive_biases

22 http://en.wikipedia.org/wiki/List_of_memory_biases

This reasoning is unconvincing for at least three reasons. The **first** reason that their argument fails is because it assumes its conclusion. Kruglanski and Grigerenzer (2011) begin with a statement that all behavior is rule-governed, implying that only System 2 exists, and then conclude that all behavior is rule-guided by this system. The **second** reason that their argument fails is because it is illogical. They commit the logical error of **affirming the consequent**. In general, the form of such logical errors is, if p, then q, q, therefore p. A concrete example is informative. If it rains then the streets will be wet. The streets are wet. Therefore it has rained. Not necessarily. A hydrant may have been intentionally opened or accidentally ruptured. Alternatively, a street sweeper vehicle that applies water before cleaning might have passed by. In short, there is more than one possibility for why the streets are wet, so being wet does not necessarily prove that it must have rained. Let p equal the premise that people follow rules. Let q equal the observation that a single-process model explains behavior. The conclusion that q implies p constitutes the logical error of affirming the consequence, not proof that their premise is true. The **third** reason why their argument fails is that they confuse properties of their theoretical explanation with properties of people. **That they chose to understand behavior using rules does not prove that people follow those rules**. It only means that people's behavior is sufficiently regular that it can be described in terms of rules. Rules are a creation of the investigator; not a necessary property of the participants. This fatal flaw is general and pertains to all assertions that behavior can be explained on a rule-following basis.

Several problems arise when one thinks physically rather than mentally about rules. How are rules physically stored in the brain? Where are rules stored in the brain? How are rules accessed? How do the rules become behavior? By what mechanism is behavior generated from rules? Rule advocates side-step these questions by asserting that their discipline is not concerned with implementation. This enables them to construct theories that are physically implausible. But constructing theories that are incommensurate with neuroscience only serves to isolate this approach to cognitive science from the rest of science. Such isolation means that the rule-based approach to cognitive science can neither inform neuroscience nor be informed by neuroscience. The history of science does not bode well for such isolationist go-it-alone approaches.

On the other hand, connectionist theories are very plausible and entirely compatible with neuroscience. Connectionist models are based on networks of interconnected nodes as is the brain. All processing nodes, simulated neurons, receive multiple inputs that mimic dendritic summation. A sigmoidal transfer function determines if the summed inputs are sufficient for activation to continue as is the case with real neurons. All knowledge is contained within the connection weights, simulated synapses. Many PDP-CNN simulations have shown that learning and memory plus many psychological phenomena that entail learning and memory can emerge from these network models.

The reader is now faced with a choice between an illogical, physically unrealistic, computer-inspired rule-based approach versus a physically realistic, brain-inspired connectionist approach to understanding psychology and behavior. A decision in favor of connectionism should now be easy to reach. For those readers who remain unconvinced, I now consider additional evidence that further supports the dual processing model.

Unconscious Thought Theory (UTT)

Social psychologists have also found evidence of unconscious processing. They have empirically demonstrated that automatic unconscious processes causally influence social cognition (Bargh, 2006; Gawronski & Payne, 2010), including social cognition of close relationships such as transference and counter transference (Chen et al., 2007). It is difficult to underestimate the general importance of these findings because, as explained next, they imply that unconscious processing underlies all cognition. PDP-CNN models add the force of theory to this extensive empirical support.

The role of unconscious processing in social cognition has been formulated as Unconscious-Thought Theory (UTT: Bargh & Morsalla, 2008; Dijksterhuis & Nordgren, 2006). The supporting empirical literature regarding UTT demonstrates that unconscious processing is sometimes superior to conscious processing when people make complex decisions. For example, Dijksterhuis et al. (2006) presented evidence from four experiments that deliberation without attention can yield superior decisions regarding complex decisions such as which car or house to choose, and simple decisions such as which oven mittens to purchase. Dijksterhuis et al. (2009) presented evidence that unconscious thought, moderated by expertise, resulted in better judgments about which team would win a soccer match than did conscious thought. Eitam et al. (2008) presented evidence that non-conscious goals influenced implicit-learning. Kirsch and Lynn (1999) discussed the relevance of automaticity (automatic unconscious processing) to clinical psychology. Bargh and Ferguson (2000) presented evidence that automaticity influences higher mental processes. Bargh and Williams (2006) reviewed evidence that automaticity impacts social cognition. Nisbett and Wilson (1977) discussed unconscious processing by presenting evidence that people are sometimes unaware of important relevant stimuli, are sometimes unaware of responses they make, and/or are unaware of how certain stimuli influence their response. In short, they question whether true introspection occurs. Wilson and Schooler (1991) reported that asking students to analyze reasons for their preferences can cause them to focus on less relevant features that were ignored when giving their first impressions where unconscious processes undoubtedly played a larger role.

Social psychologists Gawronski and Payne (2010) provided 29 chapters of empirical evidence pertaining to the causal properties of unconscious cognition; far too many results to be summarized here. Custers and Aarts (2010) reported evidence that goals unconsciously activate behavior. They presented additional evidence that social situations and stimuli unconsciously activate goals. Shidlovski and Hassin (2011) concluded 'More generally, we suggest that the nature and intensity of experienced emotions are partly determined by people's nonconscious goals, and that this modulation of emotion is functional in nature; it serves to increase the probability of goal achievement' (p. 1381). Tamir et al., (2007) and Tamir (2009) support this instrumental view of emotions; i.e., that people can be unaware of the relationships between their emotions and their goals. Dijksterhuis and Aarts (2010) concluded their review of neuroscience, cognitive psychology, and social cognition with the view that goals can unconsciously guide actions. **Unconscious processing is now considered foundational and central to social cognition**.

Falk et al. (2012) reported that fMRI-assessed activation in the medial prefrontal cortex (mPFC) consistently predicted the rank order of effectiveness of three anti-smoking campaigns, whereas verbal report did not. These data indicate that unconscious processing in the medial prefrontal cortex was a better predictor of smoking cessation in 31 heavy smokers than was their conscious verbal report. Similar findings were seen by Falk et al. (2010, 2011). Terberg et al. (2012) demonstrated that sublingual administration of testosterone to 20 healthy young women unconsciously prolonged eye contact with images of angry faces.

The PDP-CNN explanation of priming provided below further demonstrates that one does not need consciousness to explain how this well-documented phenomena works. Nor is consciousness needed to explain many other psychological phenomena. This is more than my personal view, as illustrated by the following quote from Bargh (2006).

John Bargh has spent his research career studying the necessity of conscious intentions in social judgment, motivation, and behavior, and along the way has been as surprised as anyone else by how many complex psychological and behavioral phenomena operate just fine without them (2006, p. vii).

Implicit Association Testing

The term 'implicit' seems to be currently preferred over the term 'unconscious'; probably to distinguish and distance its authors from psychodynamic theory in order to avoid giving aid and comfort to the enemy. Hence, it is now fashionable to talk about implicit social cognition rather than unconscious social cognition. Payne and Gawronski (2010) wrote 'in every topic of study, implicit social cognition is concerned with automatic/implicit/unconscious processes underlying judgments and social behavior' (p. 1). We say that a psychological state is unconscious when people are unaware of being in that state. Implicit attitudes have been defined as 'the positive or negative thoughts, feelings, or actions towards objects which arise due to past experiences which one is either unaware of or which one cannot attribute to an identified previous experience'.[23] Payne and Gawronski (2010) provided a history of implicit social cognition with roots in selective attention research and implicit memory research. Greenwald and Banaji (1995) coined the term **implicit social cognition**. Admitting to and accepting unconscious processing requires methods for assessing such processing. In this section I consider several methods for doing so. Payne and Gawronski (2010) identified two major sources of methodology for measuring implicit cognition: (a) Implicit Attitude Test (IAT) – inspired methods (discussed here); and (b) priming-inspired methods (discussed in the next section). The most comprehensive single source regarding these methods is the *Handbook of Implicit Social Cognition: Measurement, Theory, and Application* edited by Gawronski and Payne (2010). Teige-Mocigemba et al. (2010) provided *A Practical Guide to Implicit Association Tests and Related Tasks.* An Implicit Attitude Test (IAT) on a variety of topics is freely available in 36 different languages at the following URL: https://implicit.harvard.edu/implicit/. One can either take a demonstration test or participate in ongoing research. Sekaquaptewa et al. (2010) provided *A Practical Guide to Paper-and-Pencil Implicit Measures of Attitudes.* De Houwer and Moors (2010) discussed similarities and differences among implicit measures. Zeigler-Hill and Jordan (2010) discussed implicit and explicit facets of self-esteem. Schnabel and Asendorpf (2010) extend this discussion

[23] http://en.wikipedia.org/wiki/Implicit_attitude

by reviewing new insights from implicit measures regarding the self-concept. Baldwin et al. (2010) considered the implicit measurements in close relationships.

Implicit Association Tests rest on the fact that it takes people longer to associate a negative concept with a positive word than it does to associate a negative concept with a negative word or a positive concept with a positive word. The robust empirical existence of this fact is evidence that unconscious processing exists.

Priming

The *APA Concise Dictionary of Psychology* (APA, 2009) defines priming in cognitive psychology as '... the effect in which recent experience of a stimulus facilitates or inhibits later processing of the same or similar stimulus' (p. 395). Kahneman (2011b) prefaced his partial review of the priming literature with sections entitled 'The Marvels of Priming' (pp. 52–4) and 'Primes That Guide Us' (pp. 55–8). He explained the anchoring heuristic in terms of suggestion which he further explained in terms of priming: 'The puzzle that defeated us is now solved, because the concept of suggestion is no longer obscure: suggestion is a priming effect, which selectively evokes compatible evidence' (p. 122). This statement is of great relevance to the proposed Bio↔Psychology Network Theory because it establishes an explanatory chain. The well-replicated empirically supported anchoring heuristic is explained by suggestion which is explained by priming which is explained by the **physical processes** of: (a) network cascade; and (b) experience-dependent plasticity mechanisms (see Principle 2 below). This is the longest explanatory chain that the Bio↔Psychology Network Theory presently has to offer. It also serves as a model of how all psychological explanations should be framed.

Eagleman (2011, pp. 64–6) also described priming effects. He reported that severely amnesic patients can be primed to fill in designated words despite denying that they ever saw these words. Seeing a picture of a person's face primes one to rate it as more attractive than if it was not previously shown. This is known as the '**mere exposure effect**'.[24] Your implicit memory of the prior exposure modifies your current judgment of its attractiveness. Commercials and political ads rely on the mere exposure effect to, sadly, reliably unconsciously influence consumer behavior and the voting practices of millions of citizens, which is why candidates with more

[24] http://en.wikipedia.org/wiki/Mere-exposure_effect

money to spend on mass-media advertising typically win elections. It also explains why citizens tend to believe whatever they have been repeatedly told, regardless of how inconsistent and contrary to facts the message is. Their cognitions are being manipulated unconsciously.

The priming literature is far too extensive to review here. It covers the following types of priming: repetition priming; semantic and lexical priming; conceptual priming; emotional priming; cultural priming; and idea-motor priming. These forms of priming are discussed in Chapter 4. Wentura and Degner (2010) provide *A Practical Guide to Sequential Priming and Related Tasks*. The consistent empirical support received by each of these types of priming cumulatively demonstrates the existence of unconscious processing.

Triarchic Cognitive Models

Chein and Schneider (2011) presented a triarchic theory of learning based on three neural network systems organized as a pyramid. The **Representation Network System** forms the base of this pyramid. It regulates visual, auditory, motor, gustatory, olfactory, somatosensory, autonomic processing, and multimodal associations. The **Cognitive Control Network System** constitutes the next layer. It mediates attention control and selection, action sequencing, reinforcements, and arousal. The **Metacognitive Network System** forms the top layer of this pyramid. It controls the general new behavioral routines, task sequencing/initiation, and performance monitoring. The authors argued that complex human learning entails a combination, interaction, of unconscious bottom-up and conscious top-down processing involving these three neural network systems.

Conclusion

The five areas of psychological evidence reviewed above make a strong case for unconscious processing. While reluctant readers may find fault with some of this research, I expect that no-one can overturn it all. If such a rare event were to occur, there would still be the ten areas of neuroscience research to which we now turn that further support the existence of unconscious processing.

Neuroscience

Eagleman (2011, p. 4) likened the relationship of people to their brain to that of a stowaway on a steamship that enabled him to cross the Atlantic Ocean. The passenger takes full credit for his journey without acknowledging the physical processes that operate the steamship. He argued that our brains run largely on autopilot and that conscious awareness has little access to the machinery that mediates our awareness (p. 5).

Default Mode Network fMRI Studies

Hans Berger discovered that the brain was constantly active in 1929, even during sleep, when he recorded the first electroencephalogram (EEG; Haas, 2003). Somehow this fact was minimized by fMRI investigators who considered that the brain was completely at rest during the **control** condition when participants lie quietly in an fMRI machine with eyes closed or eyes open fixed on a cross. Images taken under these conditions were considered to be just noise. The active **experimental** condition typically entailed the presentation of a stimulus; participation in a cognitive task. Only then was the brain expected to become active. There are two main approaches to analyzing the resulting data. The classic approach is to subtract the control image from the experimental image to see what brain networks were **activated**, turned on, by the stimulus or task. This approach assumes that all higher brain networks are quiet unless externally stimulated. No unconscious processing is thought to occur. Activity in lower brain structures responsible for autonomic functions such as respiration, heart rate, body temperature, blood pressure, and other autonomic functions is considered to be noise that is measured during the control condition. In short, this approach assumes a Pavlovian reflex perspective where the brain is passive until externally stimulated. This remains the dominant cognitive science research perspective.

The Default Mode Network (DMN) was discovered by Raichle et al. (2001). It was discovered by reversing the data subtraction procedure. The experimental image was subtracted from the control image to see what brain networks were **deactivated, turned off** when the brain attends to an external stimulus. This approach is based on the inverse perspective that the brain is always very busy doing its own thing while in the so-called 'resting' state, and interrupts itself when it needs to attend to an external stimulus or engage in a particular task.[25] These interactive neural networks constitute the Default Mode Network (DMN). Upwards of 90% of the energy consumed by the brain is used to support the DMN (Raichle & Snyder, 2007). The DMN continues to be active during sleep. DMN activity persists even during light anesthesia (Raichle, 2009). The supporting evidence for the DMN has now been sufficiently well replicated that it is a neuroscience fact.

[25] The fact that the EEG is active during sleep and only completely quiet upon brain death should have been sufficient evidence to conclude that the brain is always active and never passive.

The main point of interest for this section is that people are totally unaware of the massive amount of unconscious processing that is continuously done by the DMN. To mistake the activities of the DMN for rest demonstrates how far outside of consciousness it operates. No degree of introspection provides any access to the DMN. These findings alone provide sufficient reason to replace the contemporary conscious-centric approach to psychology with an unconscious-centric approach.

The research supporting the DMN also pertains to the question of whether all behavior is rule-governed, as alleged by the critics of dual-processing theories discussed above. Do these critics seriously believe that the DMN operates on the basis of rules? Would these be unconscious rules? It seems to me that the DMN conclusively demonstrates the existence of unconscious processing that is not rule-based and therefore single-process theories based on rule-following are false.

Split Brain Patients

The brain consists of left and right hemispheres. Neurologists Roger Sperry and Ronald Meyers began doing split brain operations to control intractable epilepsy in the 1950s. These operations sever the corpus callosum.[26] Roger Sperry was awarded the Nobel Prize in 1981 for his research concerning split brain operations. Many details of this line of research are provided by Reeves and Roberts (1995), by Gazzaniga (1970, 1972, 1998, 2005), and by Gazzaniga and LeDoux (1978). Patients who have had their corpus callosum severed seem to recover fully, in that they can return to their prior lifestyle without noticeable incident. However, experimentation reveals special deficits that conclusively demonstrate that people are literally of two minds and that only one of them can talk, which makes processing in the other hemisphere unconscious as illustrated in the following experiments.

By focusing on a point in space we establish a left and right visual field as illustrated in Figure 3.7. Objects placed in our left visual field are processed by our right hemisphere. Objects placed in our right visual field are processed by our left hemisphere. The motor fibers that control the left and right hands also cross in the spinal column. Hence, the left hemisphere controls the right hand and the right hemisphere controls the left hand.

The corpus callosum is a massive communication cable that connects the two hemispheres. We experience an integrated conscious experience only because the corpus callosum enables the two brain hemispheres to

[26] http://en.wikipedia.org/wiki/Corpus_callosotomy

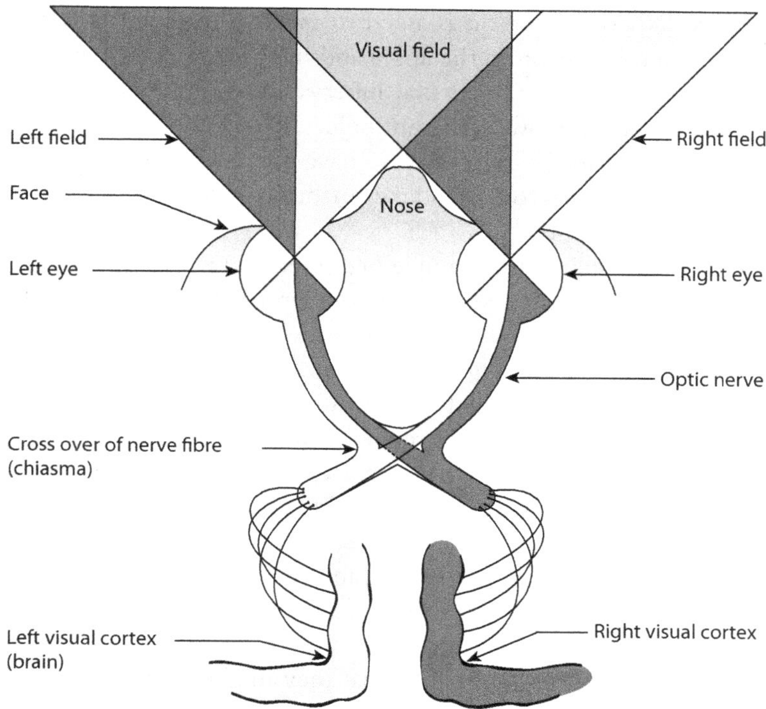

Figure 3.7 Illustration of visual fields. From http://www.thinkquwest.org The Oracle Education Foundation http://www.oraclefoundation.org www.oraclefoundation.org.

communicate with each other. Cutting the corpus callosum prohibits this communication and creates two independent brains, each living its own life completely unaware of the other; i.e., each brain operates unconsciously with respect to the other brain. Because language is located in the left hemisphere, it is the only brain that can talk; i.e., verbally answer questions. It generates confabulated explanations for motor behaviors generated by the right hemisphere. When the right brain makes a decision or choice, does something, the left brain automatically invents a story, rationale, regarding why that decision was made. These confabulations occur unconsciously; entirely outside of awareness. This tendency to unconsciously confabulate a supporting rationale raises serious concern about the validity of all self-reports.

Eagleman (2011, p. 124) described a situation where the word apple is flashed so as to be perceived only by the left hemisphere, while the word pencil is simultaneously flashed so as to be perceived only by the right hemisphere. When the person is asked to pick up the item they just saw, their right hand will pick up the apple and their left hand will pick up the pencil because the motor fibers that innervate the right hand cross in the spinal cord. Each brain saw a different object. Each brain is living a separate life. We are not normally aware that we have two brains that unconsciously communicate with each other and automatically provide us with a unified experience.

The following split brain example presented by Fields (2009, p. 219) also demonstrates the presence of unconscious processing. A viewer who has had their corpus callosum severed is asked to focus on the nose of a picture of a pirate wearing an earring in his left ear. This places the earring in the viewer's right visual field which is processed by their left hemisphere, the talking brain, and they correctly report seeing the earring. Switching the earring on the pirate to the right ear places the earring in the viewer's left visual field which is processed by their right hemisphere causing the person to deny seeing the earring. They do not 'consciously see' the earring because their right brain lacks a speech center and they do not have access to the speech center in their left brain because their corpus callosum has been severed. However, their left hand can reveal what their right brain perceived. Asked to draw with their left hand what they might have seen, the viewer draws the earring that they just denied seeing!

Gazzaniga and LeDoux (1978) presented a picture of a chicken's claw to the right visual field controlled by the left language-centered brain and a picture of snow to the left visual field of a split brain person. Then the man was presented with an array of images to both hemispheres and was asked to choose one. The man chose the image of a chicken to go with the claw and the image of a shovel to go with snow. When asked why he chose those images, the man replied that the chicken goes with the claw and the shovel is for cleaning out the chicken shed. His left hemisphere had created a coherent story based upon images available to it.

There are many other reports of peculiar behaviors by patients who have had their corpus callosum severed that could be cited here but should not be necessary to strongly support the conclusion that the right brain entails unconscious processing. Eagleman (2011, p. 137) stated that 'Fabrication of stories is one of the key businesses in which our brains engage'. The left brain confabulates to explain what the right brain does.

The following link is to a video of a split brain patient viewing images in their left and right visual fields (http://www.youtube.com/watch?v=ZMLzP1VCANo). This next link is to a *Scientific American* video of the same split brain person and demonstrates that split brain patients can simultaneously draw two different images presented to the left and right visual fields, whereas a person with an intact corpus callosum cannot (http://www.youtube.com/watch?v=lfGwsAdS9Dc). This video demonstrates how independent the left and right brains can become once the corpus callosum has been cut. We can safely conclude from these facts that conscious and unconscious processing can operate **side by side** in our left and right brains rather than **above and below** as implied by the classic Freudian model.

Anatomical Evidence

Fields (2009, p. 254) presented the following neuroanatomical evidence that unconscious processing occurs. The thalamus is a massive sensory switch box that connects to the cerebral cortex. Below it is the hypothalamus which is the master control center for regulating automatic, unconscious, functions such as heart rate, body temperature, blood sugar, etc. Underneath it, hanging like a cherry on a stem is the pituitary gland that secretes hormones into the bloodstream, thereby regulating our emotions and sexual behavior via our endocrine hormone system. Activations in these systems influence our thoughts, feelings, and behaviors but lie largely outside of our conscious awareness, which makes their processing unconscious.

Brain Damage Studies

We typically think that our hands are under our voluntary conscious control. The presence of unconscious processing is revealed in cases of alien hand disorder where one hand may button the person's shirt while the other hand unbuttons it. Patients with Anton-Babinsky syndrome[27] are cortically blind due to a stroke yet they report that they can see. Patients with Charles Bonnet syndrome[28] are also blind but can experience visual hallucinations.

Anosognosia[29] is the name given when patients are unaware of their disabilities resulting in what psychologists call poor insight. This condition characterizes 10–18% of cases of hemiplegia/hemiparesis after stroke, but can occur as a result of any type of neurological damage. Patients with multiple handicaps may be unaware of one handicap while conscious of the others. Some patients diagnosed with the Alzheimer's type of dementia claim that nothing is wrong with them. Eagleman (2011, p. 135) reported that supreme Court Justice William O. Douglas suffered a stroke on 31

[27] http://en.wikipedia.org/wiki/Anton%E2%80%93Babinski_syndrome

[28] http://en.wikipedia.org/wiki/Charles_Bonnet_syndrome

[29] http://en.wikipedia.org/wiki/Anosognosia

December 1974 that paralyzed his left side and confined him to a wheelchair. He claimed that reports of his paralysis were mistaken and invited reporters to join him for a hike. Instead, Douglas was dismissed from the bench.

Eagleman (2011, pp. 135–6) described two other interesting cases of anosognosia. A partially paralyzed patient was asked to put both hands on an imaginary steering wheel. The patient put one hand up. When asked if both hands were up on the wheel, the patient replied yes. When the same patient was asked to clap their hands they moved only one hand. When asked if they clapped, they said yes. When asked about the absence of sound, the patient replied that they did not feel like clapping. This response illustrates the way the brain confabulates excuses for what it cannot accomplish. Another brain-damaged patient could only close one eye. When asked if both eyes were closed, she said yes, but only one eye was closed. The request to close both eyes was repeated when she was in front of a mirror. She claimed that both eyes were closed. Then she was asked if she could see herself in the mirror. She said that she could. She could not explain why she could see herself when both eyes were closed. All of these neurological conditions demonstrate the presence of unconscious processing.

Emotion and Faces

Öhman (2002) presented evidence to support the view that the facial muscles of humans are genetically prepared to register emotions, and that human observers are genetically prepared to automatically and unconsciously react to viewing human faces by activating pertinent neural networks when viewing expressive faces. In particular viewing angry faces automatically and unconsciously activates the amygdale. Whalen et al. (1998) reviewed the empirical evidence in this regard. Morris et al. (1998) explained that this automatic activation could bypass the cortex via the superior colliculus of the midbrain and the right pulvinar of the thalamus.

Muscle Memory

Motor learning is a form of procedural memory where the ability to perform a specific motor task is consolidated through repetition to where it can be performed without conscious effort.[30] Riding a bike, skiing, playing a piano piece, and completing a gymnastic routine are examples. While a proficient typist is aware that their fingers are moving and what letters they are pressing, they are quite unaware of how this happens. Driving to a new destination initially requires conscious awareness. At first one may follow

[30] http://en.wikipedia.org/wiki/Muscle_memory

written directions or prompts from their navigation device. With practice, the driver becomes familiar with their route. Their complex driving behaviors become automatic because they are processed unconsciously.

A primary advantage of unconscious processing is speed. For example, a skilled tennis player or baseball player can react automatically faster to the sight and sound of the ball being struck than they can if they were to consciously process every move. This is especially the case when one realizes that their reaction entails a complex series of movements that must be coordinated.

A secondary advantage of unconscious processing is energy conservation (Eagleman, 2011, p. 62). Conscious processing requires more energy than unconscious processing. Experience-dependent plasticity, also known as neuroplasticity,[31] is the biological mechanism that modifies the nervous system to unconsciously process learned behaviors. I have more to say about this process of brain sculpting when I discuss learning and memory (see Principle 2 below).

Parasomnias

Parasomnias[32] are a category of dissociated sleep disorders characterized by unusual behaviors. They include somnambulism (sleepwalking), sleep terrors (nightmares), bruxism (teeth grinding), restless legs syndrome and periodic limb movements, sleep sex, and sleep-related eating disorders where people walk to the kitchen where they eat a variety of foods. Fugue state[33] is related to dissociative amnesia and involves complex motor acts that transport the person some distance away from where they went to sleep.[34] All of the complex behaviors that occur during parasomnias entail unconscious processing.

Medications

Ambien, also known as Zolpidem, is prescribed for people who have trouble sleeping. It has been known to produce complex unconsciously mediated behaviors. The following web site (http://www.ncbi.nlm.nih.gov/pubmedhealth/PMH0000928/) contains the warning: 'you should know that some people who took zolpidem got out of bed and drove their cars, prepared and ate food, had sex, made phone calls, were sleep-walking, or were

[31] http://en.wikipedia.org/wiki/Neuroplasticity

[32] http://en.wikipedia.org/wiki/Parasomnia

[33] http://en.wikipedia.org/wiki/Fugue_state

[34] http://medical-dictionary.thefreedictionary.com/Fugue+State

involved in other activities while not fully awake. After they woke up, these people were usually unable to remember what they had done. Call your doctor right away if you find out that you have been driving or doing anything else unusual while you were sleeping'. Similar effects have been reported for people who take Lunesta[35] and Intermezzo. The fact that people who take these medications sometimes perform complex behaviors without any memory for having done so demonstrates that cognitive processing can be done unconsciously.

Consciousness and Decision-Making

Normal experience suggests that we consciously make decisions; i.e., we are aware of the cognitive processing that we are doing that leads us to make a decision based on our 'free will' unless we are compelled by external circumstance to make a specific decision. Alternatively stated, we typically feel that our perceived self is in charge of the decisions that we make. The following link provides a general discussion of human agency (http://en.wikipedia.org/wiki/Inferring_self-agency). The following research questions whether we are in charge of the decisions that we make.

Eagleman (2011, pp. 6–7) likened the brain to national events and conscious awareness to a newspaper. Many daily events transpire in the lives of the more than 300 million U.S. citizens. Some of these events are reported in the newspaper but by then these events are largely underway or have already occurred. The mind is like this. Many specific events occur within it but only a few of them reach consciousness. But the mind is a peculiar type of newspaper in that it takes credit for what is printed in it. The mind takes credit for what it is aware of. The mind believes that it causes the decisions that it appears to make and credits itself with 'free will'. Eagleman (2011) provided other informative analogies that I do not mention here.

Libet (1985) reported research that analyzed average, over 40 trials, scalp-recorded readiness potentials (RP) regarding the conscious decision to flex the wrist. The 'time' at which participants made a conscious decision to flex their wrist was determined as follows. Participants observed a revolving dot on an oscilloscope and noted the 'clock time' that the dot was in when they decided to flex their wrist. The EEG data were analyzed for a RP prior to this time. Libet found that on average the RP occurred 200 milliseconds, one fifth of a second, before the appearance of a conscious will to press the button and the act of pressing the button. This research is discussed further at the following URL (http://en.wikipedia.org/wiki/Benjamin_Libet).

[35] http://www.lunesta.com/

Soon et al. (2008) demonstrated that brain activation in the prefrontal and parietal cortex occurred up to 10 seconds before the conscious decision to act entered awareness. Bode et al. (2011) replicated this study using ultrahigh-field 7-Tesla fMRI. They replicated the primary result that brain activation in the frontopolar cortex (FPC) preceded conscious awareness by up to 7 seconds. Sirigu et al. (2004) also reported that activity in the parietal cortex occurs prior to motor awareness.

Our ability to speak is closely associated with our consciousness and ability to decide. Wohlert (1993) reported EEG potentials at the cranial vertex (Cz) and over the left and right motor strips (C3′ and C4′) occurred in seven right-handed female participants before they performed a voluntary non-speech task (lip pursing), a speech-like task (lip rounding), and a single word production task. Carota et al. (2010) used magnetoencephalography to investigate the neurodynamics of the intention to speak. They found increased activation in the left and right parietal cortex before the participants became aware of their intention to speak. During this time they also observed increased activity in Broca's area which is crucial for inner speech. The authors concluded that coactivation of the parietal areas and Broca's area constitutes a cortical circuit. Related findings have been reported by: Libet (1985); Haggard and Eimer (1999); Haggard et al. (2002); and Brasil-Neto et al. (1992).

Wegner (2003) reviewed cognitive, social, and neuropsychological studies of apparent mental causation and concluded that the experience of conscious will frequently departs from actual causal processes. Haggard (2011) reviewed the literature on free will including a study by Fried et al. (2011) who recorded from indwelling electrodes placed in 12 patients with epilepsy and concluded: (a) that the pre-supplementary motor area, the anterior prefrontal cortex, and the parietal cortex underlay voluntary action; and (b) that these neural networks generate the conscious experience of intending to act.

Kounios et al. (2006) identified neural activity that preceded problem solution by sudden insight. They used EEG for temporal resolution and fMRI for spatial resolution. Together they identified heightened activation in the medial frontal cortex that mediates cognitive control, increased activation in temporal areas that mediate semantic processing, and increased activation in occipital areas that mediate visual attention. The important feature of these data for present purposes is that brain activity in the identified areas consistently preceeded, and consequently mediated if not outright presented the problem solution to consciousness as sudden insight.

Gelbard-Sagiv et al. (2008) demonstrated that neurons that were active at the time of memory formation reactivated 1,500 milliseconds **prior** to the verbal report of the memory. These investigators implanted electrodes into the hippocampus of 13 patients with pharmacologically intractable epilepsy prior to surgery. Participants viewed 48 5–10-second video clips of famous people, characters, and animals engaged in various activities and landmarks five to ten times in pseudorandom order. Participants then freely recalled what they had seen. Participants recalled an average of 83.2% (± 5% SEM) of the video clips. Electrical activity was recorded from 857 electrodes. Neurons that responded during viewing also responded during recall and did so 1,500 milliseconds prior to verbal report. The authors discounted the possibility that these results were due to epilepsy. This research strongly supports the proposed view that memory constitutes a reactivation, reconstitution, of our neural networks to the state they were in when the memory first formed.

An important implication of the research cited above is that brain activation precedes what appears to be our conscious voluntary decisions. **We are the editors, not the authors** of our thoughts. This includes our ability to reason. What appears to us to be a sequence of voluntary thoughts is in fact a series of thoughts that are preceded by a series of brain activations that we are unaware of. Once conscious, we seem to retain the ability to review, modify, and possibly reject each thought and/or decision depending upon how engaged our System 2 is (cf. Kahneman, 2011b). This view is consistent with an unconscious-centric orientation where causal processing begins with unconscious network cascades.

Biology and Morality

Moral judgment is the realm in which people feel most elevated above the animal kingdom and most in control of their mind as distinct and separate from their brain. Surely our ability to make moral decisions demonstrates our special status, because it is this faculty that is thought to determine our life in the 'next world'.

Young et al. (2010) performed an experiment to determine the role of the right temporoparietal junction (RTPJ) in moral judgment. They obtained moral judgments before and after administering transcranial magnetic stimulation (TMS) to the RTPJ. Their results showed that TMS reduced the importance that participants placed on beliefs and intentions, and increased the importance of whether the outcome was positive or negative. For example, adding what was thought to be a poison to someone's coffee when actually the substance was sugar was judged less immoral after TMS because no harm resulted despite the clear intention to kill. It seems that our moral assessments depend upon, are mediated by, our RTPJ and any disruption of its functioning compromises these moral assessments. This includes perpetrators and members of their jury. See related studies by Gobbini et al. (2007), Perner et al. (2006), Saxe and Kanwisher (2003) and Saxe and Powell (2006).

It is well known that alcohol impairs judgment, including moral judgment, in that people have been known to do things while intoxicated that they would not do when sober, though Steele and Southwick (1985) have shown that the effects of alcohol are mediated by expectations. People have many fewer expectations regarding how serotonin will influence their ability to make moral judgments. Crockett et al. (2010) cited seven studies showing that the serotonin system densely innervates the centromedial prefrontal cortex (vmPFC), insula, and amygdala, all of which are implicated in moral judgment and behavior. Davidson et al. (2000) and Krakowski (2003) reported that serotonin helps control violent impulses and down-regulate emotional reactions. Crockett et al. (2010) conducted an experiment where they compared the effects of a selective serotonin reuptake inhibitor (citalopram) with the effects of a selective noradrenaline reuptake inhibitor (atomoxetine) and placebo on moral judgments concerning three types of scenarios: (a) non-moral control scenarios; (b) emotionally salient personal scenarios; and (c) less emotionally salient impersonal scenarios. The results showed that serotonin made participants less tolerant of personal harm. Serotonin modified moral judgments by enhancing aversion to harming others.

The Homunculus Problem Clinical psychologists classically explained behavior in terms of Self, Id, Ego, and/or Super Ego. The Self, Ego, is frequently charged with making decisions that influence our thoughts, feelings, and behaviors. There are two problems here. The first problem is that giving a name to the mechanisms that generate decisions, be they self or ego, provides no mechanism information whatsoever. **Naming is not explaining**. The second problem here is that choice has been removed from the person to one of these theoretical **homunculi** without explaining what caused the homunculi to decide as they did. Identifying the self or ego as the source of decision-making appears to reify them; make them into actual things imbued with causal mechanisms that are neither identified nor explained. Relabeling the decision of the person as the decision of the homunculus has been substituted for explanation. It is truly amazing how many psychologists and lay people readily accept this explanatory maneuver as valid. The behavior of the homunculus is no more understandable or predictable than is the behavior of the person whose behavior is said to be explained by the actions of the homunculus. No uncertainty has been reduced. Therefore no information has been imparted and no explanation has been given (cf. Shannon, 1948).

Wegner (2003) offered a way forward. He raised the possibility that our impression that we consciously will our actions is an example of the classic 'third variable problem'. If A = intention and B = action then perhaps C causes both A and B, giving rise to the illusion that A causes B where C = unconscious brain processes generated by our neural networks. Wegner (2005) provided an extended discussion of 'voluntary control' from the perspective of 'the new unconscious'. Wegner (2003) reported clinical evidence that decisions arise unconsciously.[36] Further information is available from Wegner's home page.[37] A critical discussion of the problems of inferring self-agency can be found at the following site (http://en.wikipedia.org/wiki/Inferring_self-agency). All of this evidence raises concern over the extent to which we actually have free will.

General Importance

Several facets of general importance deserve emphasis with regard to the network cascade; our primary network principle. The **first** point to emphasize is that the network cascade is a neuroscience fact that here is the causal mechanism that causes all other network properties.

The **second** point to emphasize is that the network cascade helps us to understand the connection between neurotransmitters and the psychological and the behavioral functions that they mediate. Neurotransmitters that facilitate the transmission of activation across synapses up-regulate their neural networks. For example, too much thyroxin produces hyperthyroidism. Likewise, neurotransmitters that inhibit the transmission of activation across synapses down-regulate their neural networks. For example, too little thyroxin produces hypothyroidism. Neurotransmitters are to real neural networks what connection weights are to artificial neural networks. PDP-CNN models consistently and conclusively show the causal importance of connection weights to the normal and abnormal performance of artificial neural networks. Studying how the latent constructs and simulated behaviors that artificial neural networks generate are critically dependent upon

[36] http://www.wjh.harvard.edu/~wegner/conscwil.htm

[37] http://www.wjh.harvard.edu/~wegner/Home.html

connection weights provides a model that helps us to understand how real cognitions, emotions, and actual behaviors are critically dependent upon neurotransmitters.

Explaining Consciousness

Behaviorism forbade discussions of consciousness because such discussions lay well outside the scope of its science. Cognitive psychology presumed but did not attempt to explain consciousness. Having assumed consciousness, cognitive psychology precluded ever explaining it because **one reasons from axioms not to them**. The *APA Concise Dictionary of Psychology* (2009) defines an axiom as 'in logic and philosophy, a universally accepted proposition that is not capable of proof or disproof. Also called postulate' (p. 46). Hence, a major problematic limitation of assuming consciousness, agency, and free will means that one cannot ever predict or explain them or their relationship to behavior. Only by adopting an unconscious-centric perspective can psychology have any chance of explaining consciousness and decision-making.

Eagleman (2011, pp. 140–4) explained that consciousness exists to control and coordinate neural networks that unconsciously perform a wide variety of functions. Eagleman called these neural networks that operate outside of conscious awareness **zombie systems**. He asserted that consciousness comes online when events violate expectations generated by our **internal working models**. Eagleman argued that consciousness enables flexible intelligence because it allows for creative recombination of brain resources that in lower life forms would always take place in a fixed sequence. The ability to recombine brain resources is the essence of intelligence for Eagleman.

Explanations of consciousness are currently left to neuroscientists, even though consciousness provides the cornerstone of contemporary cognitive psychology. Will neuroscientists be able to explain consciousness to the satisfaction of psychologists? Do they have all of the theoretical concepts necessary for this task or are they missing something? I claim that they are missing something crucial to psychology. What is missing is an understanding of how psychology emerges from neural networks.

Network theories make no special claim to consciousness or to unconsciousness. The seemingly qualitative difference between consciousness and unconsciousness does not directly impact network principles. One might say that the conscious–unconscious distinction is a non-issue for network theories. Much of brain processing is clearly unconscious. Take vision for example. We do not have to think our way from sensation to perception. We look at something and perceive it. Many complex neural networks are involved but the process of seeing is transparent to us; it just happens automatically and unconsciously. Artificial neural network models of perception can therefore be characterized as involving unconscious processes.

Dijksterhuis and Nordgren (2006) proposed a theory of unconscious thought that differs from how conscious thought works in several ways. Their Unconscious-Thought Principle asserts that people sometimes think consciously and other times think unconsciously. The **UTT Capacity Principle** claims that whereas attention limits conscious processing to 7 plus or minus 2 bits of information, unconscious thought is not restricted by consciousness and can process about 11,200,000 bits of information per second, including some 10,000,000 bits per second by the visual system alone. Their Bottom-Up-Top-Down Principle maintains that whereas conscious thought works from the top Down directed by expectations and schemas (internal working models), unconscious thought works from the bottomup aschematically; i.e., absent schematic control. Unconscious thought therefore takes longer to integrate information than conscious thought does. The **UTT Weighting Principle** claims that unconscious thought naturally weights the relative importance of various attributes, whereas conscious thought frequently distorts these natural weights. The **UTT Rule Principle** claims that whereas conscious thought follows rules, unconscious thought does not but provides rough estimates instead.[38] The **UTT Convergence–Divergence Principle** claims that conscious thought is primarily convergent, whereas unconscious thought is primarily divergent in nature. The authors claim that unconscious thought can deliberate without benefit of attention. Their Figure 1 indicates that the quality of unconscious decisions remains constant as the complexity of the problem increases, whereas the quality of conscious decisions decreases as the complexity of the problem increases.

Why we are conscious at all and how consciousness comes about constitute a special field of connectionist inquiry. The journal *Neural Networks* devoted a special issue to consciousness in 1997 (Vol. 10, #7). Some of the authors and titles appearing in this issue were: Neural networks for consciousness by J. G. Taylor, Consciousness in neural networks? by E. T. Rolls, Consciousness and neural cognizers: A review of some recent

[38] I previously provided considerable evidence against the hypothesis that conscious thinking follows rules of any kind.

approaches by C. Browne et al. Learning, action, and consciousness: A hybrid approach toward modeling consciousness by R. Sun. Consciousness in a self-learning, memory-controlled, compound machine by R. A. Brown, and A neural global workspace model for conscious attention by J. Newman et al. The following figure provides a wagon wheel perspective on consciousness (Figures 3.8). Notice that the central hub of this diagram is labeled 'thalamus'. This is because a thalamic stroke obliterates consciousness, making the thalamus a critical neural network for consciousness. The next figure (Figure 3.9) illustrates a type of neural architecture thought to be pertinent to consciousness.

A major theoretical implication of the network theory of consciousness is that consciousness is an **emergent** property of a sufficiently complex and properly constructed neural network and not necessarily the exclusive province of humanity. Some animals appear to be conscious. At this writing Koko is a 38-year-old lowland gorilla who learned to speak American Sign

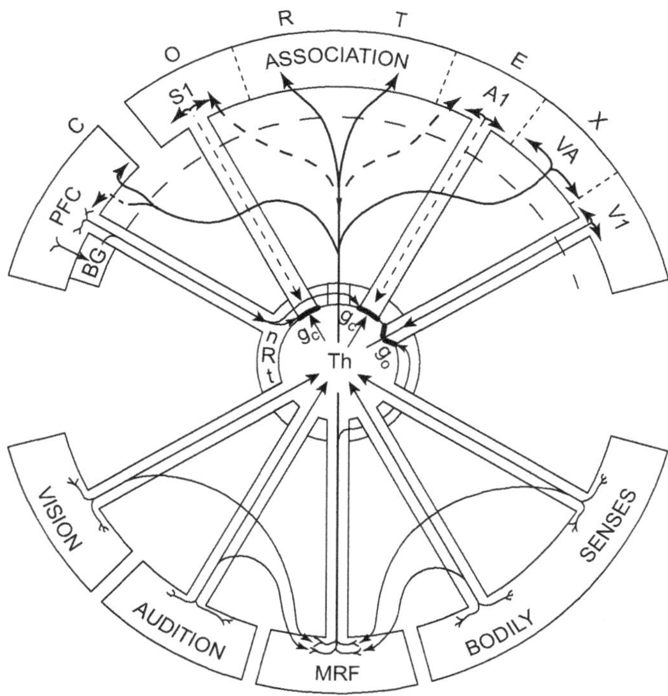

Figure 3.8 A wagon-wheel model of consciousness where the thalamic hub integrates inputs from the neural networks identified along the upper and lower rim.

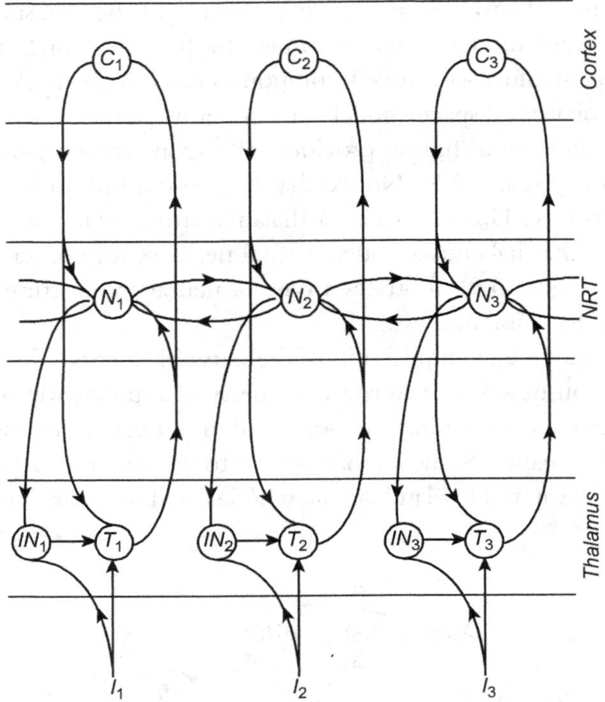

Figure 3.9 A special neural architecture thought to mediate consciousness.

Language when she was just a baby. She knows more than 1,000 signs and can understand some English. Koko has indicated that she intends to teach her babies sign language. Koko has developed new words on her own. For example, she calls a ring a 'finger-bracelet'. Koko is not unique. Another gorilla named Michael learned American Sign Language as well. Further details are available at Koko's web site www.koko.org.

Alex was an African gray parrot who had a vocabulary of 150 words,[39] He could identify 50 different objects, could identify quantities up to six, could recognize seven colors and five shapes, understood bigger vs. smaller, understood same vs. different, passed the Piagetian test of object permanence, and displayed surprise and anger.

A formal test of consciousness is the **Mirror Test**. A colored spot is attached to the forehead of the participant and then they are placed in front of a mirror. Participants that touch or otherwise orient to the spot are considered to be conscious of themselves. Humans older than 18 months

[39] http://en.wikipedia.org/wiki/Alex_(parrot)

pass the Mirror Test. So do chimps, orangutans, and gibbons, but not gorillas.[40] Bottle nose dolphins, pigeons, elephants, and magpies also pass the Mirror Test.

Explaining Unconsciousness – Sleep

Why do we sleep? Why are we unconscious when we sleep? Tononi and Cirelli (2013) reported evidence to support the view that sleep improves memory for what was learned during the previous waking period. Consciousness is turned off during sleep in order to prevent activation of experience-dependent plasticity mechanisms that drive the formation of new memories. That is, new memory formation is turned off so that existing memories can be further processed. This processing involves synaptic pruning; i.e., selective removal of synaptic connections that improve memory for what was learned during the previous period of wakefulness. Two lines of direct neuroscience evidence support this perspective that is fully compatible with the proposed Bio↔Psychology Network Theory. The number of synaptic spines in mice and fruitflies increases during wakening and **decreases** during the night. The number of AMPA receptors in adult rodents increases during wakening and **decreases** during the night. These decreases in synaptic spines and AMPA receptors constitute a pruning process. See Cirelli and Tononi (2008), Diekelmann and Born (2010), Vyazovskiy et al. (2011), and Bushey et al. (2011) for further details. No other theory that clinical psychologists rely on can explain why we need to sleep; i.e., what the function of sleep is.

Theoretical Reorientation

The evidence presented above collectively compels recognition that unconscious processing is real and requires formal acknowledgment. Bargh and Morsalla (2008) characterized contemporary cognitive psychology as **conscious-centric**. In this section I present reasons why, in addition to the massive empirical evidence presented above, psychological science requires an **unconscious-centric** orientation.

My first point is that an unconscious-centric orientation is able to explain much more than a conscious-centric orientation and therefore provides a much more general theoretical basis for psychological science. Contemporary cognitive psychology can explain only conscious cognitive phenomena but not consciousness itself. One argues from, not to, axioms.

[40] I don't know if Koko was ever given the Mirror Test.

Explanations of how consciousness arises therefore lie outside the explanatory scope of conscious-centric psychology. Cognitive psychology cannot explain unconscious phenomena.

Presuming consciousness creates pragmatic problems. It makes it difficult to determine where consciousness processing ends and unconscious processing begins. This problem has impeded research into unconscious processing from a conscious-centric perspective for many years (Erdelyi, 1992). Conscious-centric psychologists therefore either deny that unconscious processing exists or claim that it lies outside the relevant explanatory sphere of their science. Conversely, the unconscious-centric position need only show how consciousness emerges. The network perspective introduced here does not assume consciousness and therefore is not precluded from explaining it. Consequently, the unconscious-centric perspective constitutes a more fundamental position. Replacing our current conscious centric orientation with an unconscious-centric one constitutes a major paradigm shift (cf., Kuhn, 1962, 1970, 1996, 2012).

Unconscious processing is the cornerstone of essentially all variants of Freudian psychodynamic theory. Chapter 9 reveals that the concept of unconscious processing was not original to Freud. In fact, this idea was introduced by the Greek physician Galen (c. A.D. 130–200) over two thousand years ago, and was vigorously discussed in Europe since the 1600s. Arthur Koestler's introduction to Whyte's (1978) *The Unconscious Before Freud* stated:

> The general conception of unconscious mental process was *conceivable* (in post-Cartesian Europe) around 1700, *topical* around 1800, and *fashionable* around 1870–1880. It cannot be disputed that by 1870–1880 the general conception of the unconscious mind was a European commonplace and that many special applications of this general idea had been vigorously discussed for several decades.

Freud was writing about the unconscious in 1896. A scholar of his stature surely would have been aware of at least some of the extensive literature that he did not cite. Nevertheless, the evidence for unconscious processing is currently so extensive and robust that its existence seems finally to have been settled. Acceptance of unconscious processing by no means constitutes a full throated endorsement of psychoanalytic theory in its entirety. Rather, it recognizes that this part of psychodynamic theory is fully grounded in rigorous empirical research.

Conclusion

I trust that the five lines of psychological evidence and the ten lines of neuroscience evidence have convinced you that the brain really does engage in unconscious processing. The network cascade that constitutes our first and most basic network principle simulates how unconscious processing works. I trust that I have provided sufficient reason for you to accept my first network principle: unconscious processing via the network cascade.

PRINCIPLE 2: LEARNING AND MEMORY

Learning and memory are fundamental to all psychology. If infants could not learn and remember, they would not develop into the children, adolescents, and adults with which we are familiar. They would not acquire language or personality traits beyond temperament, nor would they show any recognizable form of psychological development. They also could not benefit from any psychological intervention. Psychologists would need to revise their textbooks beyond recognition if learning and memory did not exist. While an understanding of learning and memory may not be sufficient to explain all that people think and do, they must be part of any complete psychological explanation. Stated otherwise, a comprehensive explanation of psychological phenomena must include an account of how learning and memory work.

Psychologists have traditionally studied learning and memory as separate processes. The computer metaphor used by information processing and artificial intelligence investigators separates memory storage from the central processing unit justifies this separation. The processing that a computer does is independent of its memory. The rules that supposedly govern learning do not necessarily apply to memory formation and retrieval.

The parallel distributed processing connectionist neural network models that we are concerned with follow a brain metaphor where memory and processing are done by the same processing nodes. This changes everything because in such parallel processing learning necessarily modifies memory. Moreover, how one thinks about something is partially dependent upon what one remembers about it. How one thinks about something also modifies how one remembers it. This is a very dynamic model of learning and memory. The emotions activated by our subcortical neural networks (see Chapter 5) modify how we learn and remember. This view provides an integrated perspective missing from the traditional cognitive science perspective.

Psychologists once studied learning as a basic process (Bower & Hilgard, 1981). Psychologists largely abandoned this study when they adopted an information-processing orientation as part of the cognitive revolution (Bandura, 1978; Dember, 1974; Gardner, 1985; Mahoney, 1974, 1977;

Meichenbaum, 1977). In the interim, neuroscientists identified the biological mechanisms of learning and memory discussed below (Bear et al., 2007; Carlson, 2010; Hell & Ehlers, 2008; Kalat, 2009; Lisman & Hell, 2008; Squire et al., 2008). Multidisciplinary neuroscience research teams have made tremendous progress in identifying the mechanisms that mediate learning and memory by studying simple life forms such as *Aplysia*[41] and *Hermissenda*.[42] Conditioning methods activate experience-dependent plasticity mechanisms, also known as neuroplasticity mechanisms,[43] that modify neural networks. These modifications create memories and alter behavior in ways that are recognized as learning. This biological mechanism information explains previous unanswered basic science questions such as why reinforcers are reinforcing and how reinforcers modify behavior. Cognitive psychologists largely ignored operant conditioning because its simple R → S model ignored internal processing. The learning mechanisms discussed in this chapter provide a theoretical basis for operant conditioning (see also Tryon, 1993b). Donahoe (1997) agreed that a network perspective is needed when he wrote about the necessity of neural network simulations to the future of operant conditioning. These learning mechanisms also pertain to observational and other types of cognitive learning, including Piaget's assimilation/accommodation cycles that drive cognitive stages (Piaget & Inhelder, 1969). See the section on Piaget in Chapter 10 for further details. Carlson et al. (2010) defined learning in terms of memory; '*Learning* refers to the process by which experiences change our nervous system and hence our behavior. We refer to these changes as *memories*' (italics in the original) (p. 440). If you are forming memories, then you are learning.

Learning and memory represent two sides of the same coin. Gluck and Myers (1997) referred to computational neural network (CNN) models of learning and memory as providing '... the **conceptual glue** to bind together data from multiple levels of analysis' (p. 481, emphasis added) including 'cellular, physiological, anatomical, and behavioral levels' (p. 510).

Synaptic Modification: The First Experience-Dependent Plasticity Mechanism

Experience-dependent plasticity (EDP) refers to the ways that the brain changes in response to its interactions with the physical and social

[41] http://en.wikipedia.org/wiki/Aplysia

[42] http://en.wikipedia.org/wiki/Hermissenda_crassicornis

[43] http://en.wikipedia.org/wiki/Neuroplasticity

environment.[44] Unlike computers that remain unchanged by the processing they do, brains **are** changed by the processing they do (Martin et al., 2000). 'For the nervous system to translate experience into memory and behavior, lasting structural change at synapses must occur' (Shatz, 2009, p. 40).

An unavoidable consequence of the automatic unconscious CNN cascade is that it initiates **experience-dependent plasticity** mechanisms through the influx of calcium ions through N-methyl-D-asparate (NMDA) receptor channels when glutamate binds to α-amino-3-hydroxy-5-methyl-4-osoxazolepropioic acid (AMPA) receptors (Wilker & Kolassa, 2013). Long-term potentiation (LTP) and long-term depression (LTD) are among the better known EDP mechanisms. LTP enables incoming signals to produce a stronger response. Evidence exists for the following three LTP mechanisms: (a) presynaptic terminals may release more neurotransmitter; (b) the number of postsynaptic receptors may increase; and/or (c) present receptors may become more responsive to neurotransmitter (Lombroso & Ogren, 2008, 2009). Structural changes may also occur. Dendritic spines may increase in length (Bear et al., 2007) and/or other spines may grow at the same location (Lombroso & Ogren, 2008, 2009). Neurons that fire together wire together via EDP mechanisms.

Neurons that fire out of sequence strongly reduce the flow of calcium ions through NMDA receptors and create the LTD inhibitory state that includes opposite physical changes from those of LTP: (a) presynaptic terminals may release less neurotransmitter; (b) the number of postsynaptic receptors may decrease; and/or (c) present receptors may become less responsive to neurotransmitter. These and related dendritic spine modifications enable the brain to adapt to an ever-changing world throughout the lifespan, albeit in a gradually decreasing way. Together, these and other biological processes modify (up-regulate and down-regulate) and literally sculpt brain networks, thereby adapting them to their current physical and social environments. Experience-dependent plasticity enables lifespan development to occur. Extensive details about these and related EDP mechanisms are discussed by Bear et al. (2007), Carlson (2010), Hell and Ehlers (2008), Kalat (2009), Lisman and Hell (2008), and Squire et al. (2008). EDP mechanisms constitute the biological basis of all learning and memory; the two fundamental processes that enable all psychological phenomena to exist.

[44] I use the term experience-dependent plasticity in a more general sense in this book to include multiple ways in which environmental events, experience, influence either the construction or modification of our neural networks. This includes epigenetic tags, inheritance, and imprinting discussed later in this chapter.

Operant and respondent conditioning are two simple methods for activating EDP mechanisms that cause memories. Cognitive processes entail more complex methods for activating experience-dependent plasticity mechanisms. Theories of learning such as those summarized by Bower and Hilgard (1981, 1997) and Hergenhan and Olson (1993) are no longer needed or relevant now that we understand the basic biological mechanisms by which all learning occurs. I say all learning because the biology of learning and memory is phylogenetically general. Experience-dependent plasticity is to learning and memory what DNA is to genetics.

The EDP mechanisms that we are concerned with in this section are those that modify synaptic properties. They either increase or decrease excitation or inhibition and thereby up-regulate or down-regulate neural networks. Some synapses are added while others are cannibalized. Greene (2010) provided a basic introduction to how synaptic connections are added when new associations are learned and how synaptic connections are removed when those associations cease to exist. Behavior modification works because of, is caused by, synaptic modification in the brain and likely also in the enteric nervous system that lines the gut. EDP gives brains a dynamic and adaptive quality that computers currently lack. Because learning and memory occur within many of the same networks, learning modifies memory and memory changes can be used to track learning. Hence learning-based therapies necessarily modify memory and that memory modification can be used to validate the effects of learning-based therapies (Tryon & McKay, 2009).

Adding and deleting synapses sculpts the brain. When asked 'How did you create David?', Michangelo is reputed to have replied 'I got a block of marble and chipped away everything that wasn't David'. Oriental sculptors can carve magnificent works from ivory. Experience sculpts the brain in a similar manner. Brain synapses between the ages of 1 and 3 reach a maximum that is 50% greater than that of a young adult (Huttenlocher, 1979, 1990). Further growth spurts can occur during developing years. But the main process of sculpting away synapses that are not needed is the major mechanism behind all psychological development. Neurons that fire together wire together; i.e., are biologically reinforced. Synapses that do not regularly participate in neural circuits are cannibalized by EDP mechanisms that prune them. The result of this brain sculpting is an adult who is specialized to speak and act in ways that have adapted them to live in a particular physical and social environment. We refer to this process as psychological development.

Connectionist network models develop their capabilities through a training process that emulates the biological process of EDP mentioned in the previous paragraph. This training entails gradual modification of the strength of the weights associated with the connections among processing nodes. Setting connection weights to near zero simulates their deletion. Abbott (2008), McLeod et al. (1998), McClelland et al. (1986), O'Reilly and Munakata (2000), and Rumelhart and McClelland (1986) provide many examples of such models.

Epigenetics: A Second Experience-Dependent Plasticity Mechanism

Psychologists have long accepted the idea that nature and nurture interact to produce psychology and behavior in as integral a way as length and width interact to produce area. However, the biological mechanisms that enable these interactions have only recently been identified. Epigenetics refers to several biological mechanisms that enable the environment to regulate genetic expression.[45] The Human Epigenome Project (HEP) is an ongoing multisite research enterprise devoted to mapping the entire human epigenome.[46] The following ENCODE website contains a wealth of genetic and epigenetic information (http://www.nature.com/encode/#/threads).

Regulating genetic expression is crucial to adaptation and survival. Infants are born to parents who live in widely different environments, from equatorial forests to polar ice fields. Infants have and will always be born at different times throughout history when climatic, social, and technological demands vary widely. Neonates cannot anticipate or consciously prepare for the language(s) that they will need to learn. Adaptation to these variable and unknown demands requires flexible ways for the genome to be expressed. In the sections below we will see how this is done. We will also see how early mothering, diet, trauma, and exposure to toxins all regulate how our genes are expressed; i.e., whether they are activated or suppressed. We will further see that identical twins are only identical at birth. Experience physically modifies our genome across our entire lifespan, thus providing a second experience-dependent plasticity method.

Most readers are likely familiar with basic genetics but a brief review will enable us to better understand epigenetics and how it enables experiences such as early maternal care, diet, exercise, and trauma to modify the structure and/or function of our genome which controls how our

[45] http://en.wikipedia.org/wiki/Epigenetics

[46] http://www.epigenome.org

neural networks function. Much of the following regarding basic genetics comes from the following site (http://www.genetics.edu.au/factsheet).

Genetics Primer

We have 46 chromosomes consisting of 23 pairs where one partner comes from the mother and the other from the father. Our 24th pair is a sex chromosome; that is XX in females and XY in males. Each chromosome contains thousands of genes. Each **gene** consists of regions of DNA that can be expressed. These regions are called **exons**. The regions of DNA that were not thought to be expressed are called **introns**. Both regions are bounded by promoter amd termination sites. The term 'gene' traditionally refers to the exons. Introns have been called 'junk DNA' because at the time they were named no-one knew what this portion of our genome did. The prevailing view then was that genes only coded for proteins and if a DNA segment did not code for a protein then it must do nothing at all and therefore is junk left over from a time when it might have coded for some other protein. Research subsequently revealed that these regions contain instructions for how to assemble the coded proteins; i.e., they constitute the **genetic software** that controls the protein-coding genetic hardware. For example, HOX genes govern the basic body plan; i.e., where the eyes go, where the legs go, how many of each to build, etc., and are responsible for the tremendous diversity of life forms on earth. The following two short video clips illustrate more about HOX genes: http://en.wikipedia.org/wiki/Hox_gene, http://www.youtube.com/watch?v=gZtGrsr8DMY. The FOXO gene regulates about 100 'worker' genes that repair tissues of all types and has been strongly associated with longer healthy life in both laboratory specimens and people. The following video clip covers this story: http://www.pbs.org/wgbh/nova/body/can-we-slow-aging.html. Genes can be turned off by very short segments of RNA referred to as micro-RNA through a process described as RNA silencing. The following video clip discusses this research: http://www.youtube.com/watch?v=oANi7PRqalM&feature=fvsr.

Most genes are located in the cell nucleus, but approximately 20,000 genes are located in the cell mitochondria. They encode for many of the enzymes that make ATP (adenosine triphosphate), the body's energy system, work. Most of these genes are inherited from the mother.

Each chromosome consists of a long thin twisted strand of DNA (deoxyribonucleic acid) constructed like a ladder where the rungs are composed of base pairs using adenine (A) and thymine (T) or guanine (G) and cytosine (C). That is, the rungs in the DNA ladder are built from A–T or G–C pairs where the dash (–) indicates a hydrogen bond. The human genome contains approximately three billion of these base pairs. The ends of each chromosome are capped with telomeres, redundant DNA sequences, that mark, define, where each chromosome ends.

Gene expression begins with **transcription** as illustrated in the following video clip (http://www.youtube.com/watch?v=ztPkv7wc3yU&feature=related). This process creates a complementary RNA copy of the DNA sequence known as the template strand. It begins when RNA polymerase unwinds the twisted DNA ladder and breaks the hydrogen bonds between A and T and between G and C. Uracil (U) is substituted for thymine (T) during this process (don't ask me why). We now have messenger DNA (mDNA). **Translation** is the process of using the template strand to synthesize proteins. The following video clip illustrates this process (http://www.youtube.com/watch?v=-zb6r1MMTkc&feature=related). Every three letters of the mDNA sequence are called a **codon**. For example, AUG, AUC, AGU, ACU are all codons. With a few exceptions, each codon, base-pair triplet, codes for a distinct amino acid. Because there are four letters (A, U, G, C) in each of three positions, there are $4 \times 4 \times 4 = 4^3 = 64$ possible combinations, codons. Each codon codes for one of the 64 amino acids used to build proteins according to the RNA codon table which can be translated into the DNA codon table.[47] Start and stop codons sandwich the instructions for constructing each protein that is used to build our bodies, including our neural networks. The body planning, formerly considered junk, DNA also controls the construction of our neural networks; i.e., determines what networks we have and how they are wired together.

Jumping Genes

During the 1940s and 1950s Barbara McClintock[48] discovered that corn genes sometimes moved from place to place within the corn genome. She did her work on what are more formally known as **transposons**; also known as transposable elements.[49] Transposons are mobile genetic elements that use **cut and paste** mechanisms to move DNA elsewhere in the host's genome. Gage and Muotri (2012) reported jumping genes in other life forms, including humans. The jumping genes they studied are more

[47] http://en.wikipedia.org/wiki/DNA_codon_table
[48] http://en.wikipedia.org/wiki/Barbara_McClintock
[49] http://en.wikipedia.org/wiki/Transposable_element

formally known as retrotransposons.[50] They use copy and paste mechanisms to replicate their DNA elsewhere in the host's genome. Retrotransposons make up an astounding 50% of the human genome versus all protein coding DNA sequences ('real' genes) that constitute a mere 2% of the human genome. The retro part of the name comes from their mechanism of action. Retrotransposons, like the HIV retrovirus, use reverse transcription to build RNA and then DNA. Then, with the aid of a protein enzyme called endonuclease, the DNA chain is nicked at what appears to be a random point and that is where the DNA copy is inserted. These random genetic insertions have one of three general outcomes. (1) Mostly they don't matter because they are inserted in an inconsequential place. (2) Sometimes they are inserted where they distort the genetic expression of a valuable protein and thereby cause disease. (3) Occasionally they are inserted where they confer a selective advantage to the host. This combination of variation and selection constitutes evolution at work. Retrotransposons are sometimes inserted into a gene promoter region in which case they function as a genetic switch. That can have one of four general outcomes. A good or bad gene can be turned on or off.

The long interspersed element 1[51] appears to be especially important in the human genome. Unlike other mobile elements it appears to code for the machinery to duplicate itself and spread these copies elsewhere. It transcribes itself to a single strand of RNA. Then it moves from the cell nucleus to the cytoplasm where it serves as a DNA template. The molecular result then returns to the nucleus where endonuclease is used to open an insertion site in the host's DNA.

Genes jump only during cell division. This limits gene jumping to three general conditions. (1) Rapid cell division that occurs during all embryological stages. (2) Brain development that occurs throughout childhood. The frontal lobes are not fully myelinated until the mid-twenties. (3) Neurogenesis[52] that occurs during learning and memory formation, especially in the hippocampus, and in response to brain injury. This means that genes can relocate throughout the lifespan but with decreasing probability from gestation on. These facts carry major implications for behavior genetic studies of identical and fraternal twins. It is no longer tenable to assume that they share 100% and 50% of active genes respectively. Epigenetic mechanisms exacerbate this genetic diversity throughout the lifespan.

[50] http://en.wikipedia.org/wiki/Retrotransposon

[51] http://en.wikipedia.org/wiki/Retrotransposon

[52] http://en.wikipedia.org/wiki/Neurogenesis

Genetic Packaging and Expression

Nature solved the problem of putting the right genes in the right cells by placing all genes in every cell. Hence, every cell in the body contains the genetic information for creating every type of cell in the body. So how does each cell become specialized into a heart cell, a bone cell, an eye cell, a brain cell, etc.? The answer is to turn some genes on and the rest off so that only a small part of the genetic machinery works in a particular cell. This is primarily done using epigenetic switches. But to understand the mechanics of this process we must first understand how the DNA molecule that contains our genes is packaged so that it can fit within each cell, and how these genes can be accessed in order to become expressed.

Figure 3.10 is reproduced from Gonzáles-Pardo and Álvarez (2013). From this figure you can see how each chromosome is constructed. The process begins in the lower right-hand portion of the figure where DNA is coiled around histone spools. Each spool is created from four pairs of amino acids that can be visualized as two layers of four tennis balls. Imagine placing four tennis balls on a table so that they make a tight square and then gluing them together. Then make a second such cluster. Then place the second cluster on top of the first cluster and glue them together. Now we have a single histone spool model consisting of eight tennis balls. But the entire DNA strand cannot be coiled around a single spool. In fact, the DNA strand can only be wrapped 1.7 times around a single spool. Hence, many such spools are required, as illustrated in the two boxes at the bottom of Figure 3.10. More specifically, the DNA strand is wrapped 1.7 times around the first spool, 1.7 times around the second spool, etc., until the entire strand has been accommodated. This storage method results in a series of spools called a spool-based strand. The spool-based strand is much shorter than the original DNA strand, but is still very long.

The second packaging step is to twist and coil the string of spools into **nucleosomes** consisting of eight histones. The DNA plus the histone protein spools are collectively called **chromatin** and when twisted together form what we call **chromosomes**.[53] This packing method is illustrated in both of the following two video clips: http://www.youtube.com/watch?v=gbSIBhFwQ4s&noredirect=1 and http://www.yoanoso.com/watch?v=9kQpYdCnU14&feature=relmfu. These twisted packages are visible as chromatin when cells prepare to divide.

[53] http://en.wikipedia.org/wiki/Epigenetics

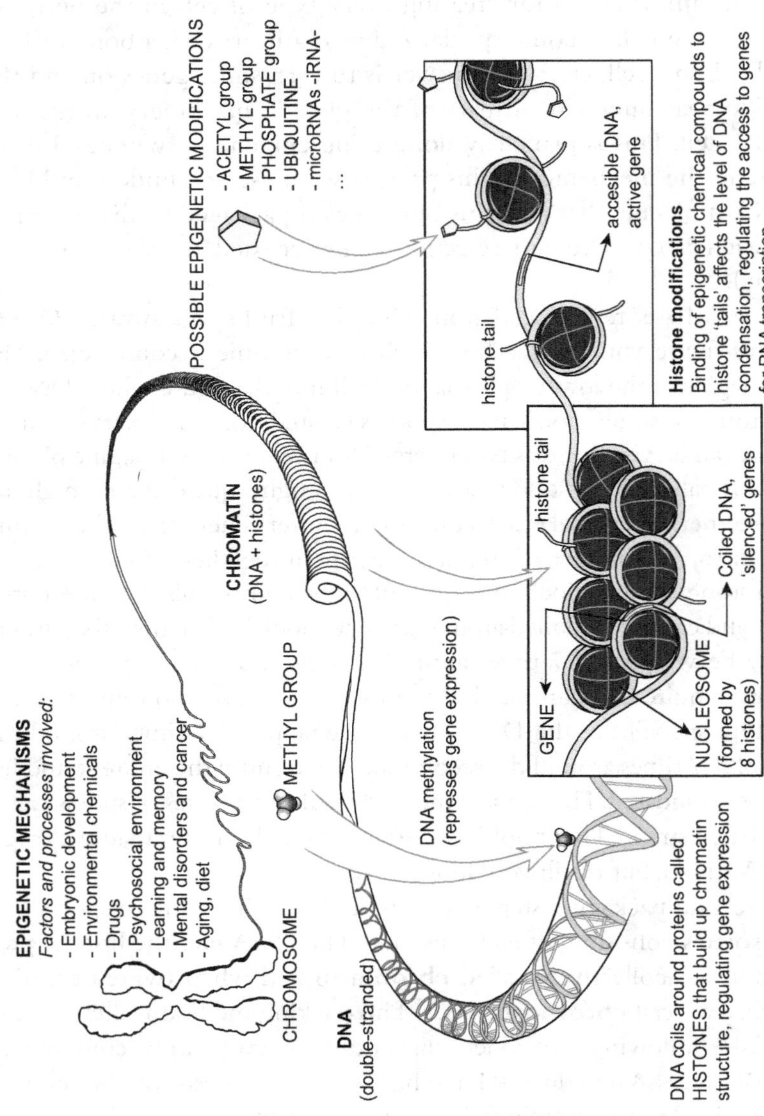

Figure 3.10 Illustration of how genes are packed within chromosomes.

Epigenetics Primer

Epigenetics entails several experience-dependent plasticity genetic mechanisms. The term 'epi' means over or above and is used because molecular 'tags' are attached either directly to the DNA molecule or to the histone tails around which the DNA is wrapped. We first consider how epigenetic tags are attached directly to the DNA molecule. Then we consider tags that are attached to the histone tails. The following three links provide additional information about the epigenetic system (http://www.genome.gov/27532724, http://learn.genetics.utah.edu/content/epigenetics/intro/, http://teach.genetics.utah.edu/content/epigenetics/).

DNA Methylation Tags

A methyl group consists of three hydrogen atoms surrounding one carbon atom, as illustrated in the top panel of Figure 3.11. Hence, methyl groups are symbolized as CH_3. Methyl groups can attach directly to DNA because they can form a chemical bond with cytosine to form 5-methylcytosine, as illustrated in Figure 3.11.

Methyl groups are strongly attached to cytosine in DNA regions called CpG islands. The 'p' indicates that C and G are connected by a phosphodiester bond. These connections are so strong they last as long as the DNA molecule does, which can be thousands of years in some cases.

Only accessible DNA is available for genetic expression. When DNA is tightly wrapped around the histone spools it is not accessible for genetic expression. Whether DNA is wrapped tightly or loosely is controlled by

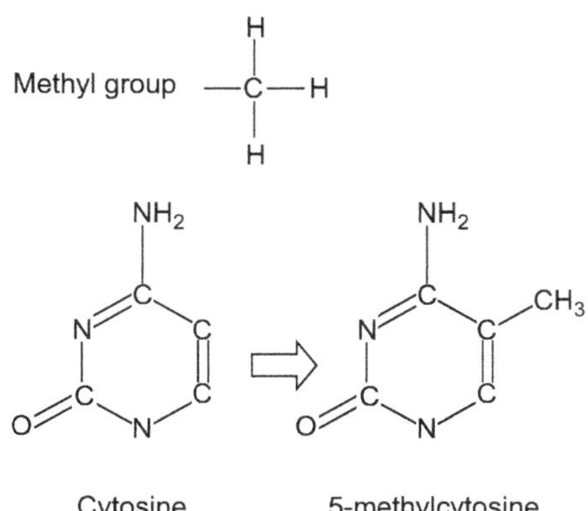

Figure 3.11 Chemical structure of a methyl tag and its attachment to cytosine. NH_2 is an amine group.

whether or not a methyl group is attached to histone's tail. I discuss this process of methylation below. Adding a methyl group tightly wraps DNA, thus turning genes off. Removing the methyl group loosens the wrapping and enables genes to be expressed if they are not otherwise deactivated.[54]

Histone Tail Tags

Histone tails have seven sites that can receive the following five epigenetic tags **acetyl group, a methyl group, a phosphate group, ubiquitine, or a microRNA** (see Figure 3.10). These tags modify the **transcription** process.[55] I limit coverage to the two most widely studied methods, methylation and acetylation, but the reader should keep in mind that there is much more to these epigenetic mechanisms than what I discuss here.

Methylation

Methylation, adding methyl groups, typically turns gene expression off by causing histones to twist in such a way as to tighten the DNA wrapped around them. This effectively turns associated genes off because the translation machinery is denied access to the tightly wrapped DNA segments. Removing methyl groups untwists the histones and thereby loosens the wrapped DNA, thereby allowing transcription access which enables the gene to be expressed.

Acetylation

The enzyme acetyltransferase (HAT) can attach an acetyl group (CH_3CO) to a histone tail by replacing a hydrogen atom with an acetyl group. This act provides a negative charge that neutralizes the positive histone charge and causes condensed chromatin to relax, thereby facilitating access to transcription mechanisms and gene expression; i.e., acetylation enables genes to be turned on. The enzyme deacetylase (HDAC) removes an acetyl group, thereby increasing the positive charge and tightening the relationship between the histones and the DNA and consequently turning genes off by denying access to transcription mechanisms.

Environmental Influences

While most genetic switches are turned on or off during embryonic development, we shall shortly see how experience can throw some of these switches as well, and do so throughout the person's lifespan. The

[54] http://en.wikipedia.org/wiki/DNA_methylation

[55] http://en.wikipedia.org/wiki/Histone_code

experience-dependent feature of epigenetic switches makes epigenetics very important to psychologists because epigenetic mechanisms are a second way that experience modifies the structure and function of our neural networks that govern our cognitions, emotions, and behavior.

Developmental psychologists and psychoanalysts have emphasized the importance of early experience on subsequent development. Cognitive scientists have criticized this view on the basis that the hippocampus, the brain structure that primarily mediates memory, is not fully developed before the age of three, which is why people cannot possibly remember what happened to them during infancy or any birth anxiety that they may have had. However, recent neuroscience evidence regarding epigenetic switches supports the psychodynamic claim that early experience is crucial to subsequent development. The following link documents that experiences during the first year of life can influence the rest of our lives,[56] even when no memories of these events form.

Maternal Care Weaver et al. (2006, 2007) and Zhang and Meaney (2010) provide an excellent review and discussion of experiments that demonstrate how early maternal care, especially tactile stimulation, in the first days and weeks of life turns genes that regulate how the newborn will respond to stress for the rest of its life on or off. This includes how they will parent their offspring. Females who have experienced good mothering in the form of considerable tactile stimulation become epigenetically disposed to be good mothers and sadly, females who have experienced little tactile stimulation as neonates are epigenetically disposed to provide little tactile stimulation to their offspring. These epigenetic mechanisms are an interesting form of 'inheritance'. I use quotes because we are discussing environmentally triggered epigenetic mechanisms of genetic expression rather than genetic mutation. I now provide additional details.

Licking and grooming (LG) is a major source of tactile stimulation for the neonatal rat. Rat mothers differ widely in the extent to which they lick and groom their offspring. Mothers who regularly lick and groom their pups are called high LG mothers. Mothers who rarely lick and groom their pups are called low LG mothers. Weaver et al. (2006) and Zhang and Meaney (2010) reviewed evidence showing that the offspring of high LG mothers show reduced fearfulness and more modest hypothalamic–pituitary–adrenal (HPA) axis responses to stress. This means that their response to stress is less severe. Zhang and Meaney (2010) cited studies showing that early tactile stimulation also regulates endocrine and cardiovascular function.

[56] http://www.economist.com/node/7941685

The hippocampus is involved in stress management as well as memory formation. Glucocorticoids (GCs) are a class of steroid hormones that bind to glucocorticoid receptors (GR). Attaching a methyl group to the genes that produce Nerve Growth Inducible Factor A (NGFI-A) decrease the ability to activate glucocorticoid receptor transcription throughout the lifespan (Zhang & Meaney, 2010), thereby reducing the number of GR receptors which result in elevated cortisol levels.

Cortisol is a GC hormone produced by the adrenal gland in response to stress. Cortisol increases blood sugar and helps the organism respond during stress. However, cortisol is toxic in large prolonged amounts, which is why it is also known as the *death hormone*. It is therefore best that cortisol decreases as soon as possible once the source of stress abates. This is important because excess cortisol can damage the hippocampus, thereby impairing learning and memory and consequently creating additional problems throughout the lifespan. Genes that inhibit GC synthesis are activated when GCs bind to glucocorticoid receptors in the hippocampus. More GC receptors means less cortisol which means a lesser stress response and more rapid recovery.

Rat pups are born with methyl tags on particular genes that regulate their response to stress. Methyl tags turn genes off. The genes in question here code for glucocorticoid receptors in the hippocampus. More methyl tags result in fewer glucocorticoid receptors causing more circulating cortisol causing a more extreme stress response and prolonged recovery from stress. Calm and caring mothering removes these methyl tags, resulting in pups that respond less severely to stress and recover faster from stress. Female pups who receive calm and caring mothering grow up to be calm and caring mothers themselves. Inattentive mothering adds methyl tags that cause their offspring to secrete more cortisol in response to stress, take longer to recover from stress, and grow up to become inattentive mothers (Zhang & Meaney 2010).

Weaver et al. (2006) have shown that the extent of maternal care during infancy determines the strength of this gene–environment regulatory system. Rats who receive more maternal care, more licking, have a stronger gene–environment regulatory system than rats who receive less maternal care, less licking. Rat pups that receive more maternal care during their first week of life calm down faster when a stressor terminates than rat pups who receive less maternal care during this time. They remain anxious and fearful for a longer time after the stressor is removed. Licking and grooming increases the production of a protein called NGFI-A which attracts two enzymes that are involved in epigenetic tagging; histone acetyltransferase which adds acetyl groups to proteins, and methylated DNA-binding protein-2 which removes methyl groups from DNA.

Child abuse creates epigenetic effects; i.e., throws genetic switches that influence adaptation later in life, including a predisposition to **suicide**. McGowan et al. (2008) demonstrated that the promotor region of ribosomal RNA (rRNA) in the brains of people who successfully committed suicide was hypermethylated which turned associated genes in the hippocampus off. People who commit suicide have less-active ribosomal RNA (rRNA) genes than people who die of other causes. In people who commit suicide, methyl levels are higher on rRNA genes in the hippocampus, which is important for learning and memory. More methyl tags means less rRNA production, which means fewer ribosomes, which means less protein production.

McGowan et al. (2009) reported that child abuse alters the hypothalamic–pituitary–adrenal (HPA) stress response and increases the risk of suicide. They found epigenetic differences in the brains of suicide victims with a history of childhood abuse compared to either suicide victims with no history of childhood abuse or controls. They concluded that their findings provide an epigenetic link between parental care and suicide risk. The epigenetic link between child abuse and suicide is discussed in the following video http://learn.genetics.utah.edu/content/epigenetics/brain/.

Compensatory Mothering Weder and Kaufman (2011) discussed evidence for the hypothesis that early experience with trauma produced irreversible effects; i.e., evidence in support of critical developmental periods. They reported research by Kaufman and Weder (2010) showing that the hypothalamic–pituitary–adrenal axis stress response can be normalized in rat pups that receive quality foster mothering after having received adverse early mothering.

Addictions Nestler (2011) used the term 'primed for addiction' (p. 80) to refer to epigenetic modifications associated with initial and subsequent administrations of cocaine. A single administration of cocaine has been shown to activate nearly 100 genes in the nucleus acumbens; the brain's reward center. These genes return to normal within a week if no further drug is administered. Repeated administrations of cocaine persistently overactivate some genes and underactivate others, thereby sensitizing the neural network to the drug for at least a month. The major problem faced by psychological treatments of drug addiction is how to provide experiences that deactivate the genes that cocaine turned on; i.e., how to turn these genetic switches off.

Social Defeat Pairing mild-mannered mice with aggressive mice for ten days subjects the mild-mannered mice to what is called chronic social defeat. This manipulation creates epigenetic modifications in approximately 2,000 genes in the nucleus acumbens. About 1,200 of these genes undergo histone methylation which forces DNA to wrap tightly and shut-down gene expression. Imipramine can reverse this process. Autopsies on people who were depressed at the time of death also show excessive histone methylation.

Nutrition It has been said that you are what you eat. Epigenetic research has shown that nutrition is another source of genetic switching. The Agouti gene gives rise to yellow coats, obesity, diabetes, and cancer in guinea pigs. Feeding pregnant mothers a diet rich in methyl donors turns the Agouti gene off. This results in brown coats, normal weight, and returns the risk of diabetes and cancer to normal levels. The following video clips illustrate these epigenetic effects http://www.pbs.org/wgbh/nova/genes/mice.html and http://learn.genetics.utah.edu/content/epigenetics/nutrition/.

Identical Twins A major epigenetic finding is that identical twins are genetically and epigenetically identical **only** at birth. They remain genetically identical for life, but become epigenetically different over time as their life experiences diverge. That is, their genome is differentially expressed across their lifespan. Environmental events throw genetic switches that cause differential genetic expression from then on, as illustrated in the following two video clips: http://www.pbs.org/wgbh/nova/sciencenow/3411/02.html and http://learn.genetics.utah.edu/content/epigenetics/twins/. These findings have enormous implications for psychology. The field of behavior genetics has depended heavily upon twin studies to demonstrate the genetic basis for many traits, behaviors, and disorders. Comparisons are typically made between pairs of identical twins, fraternal twins, and unrelated controls. While identical twins typically show a higher concordance rate for whatever is being examined, it has long been a mystery why these concordance rates are not 100% or close to 100% if the trait is genetically based. Investigators typically conclude that the environment is somehow involved, but no proximal causal mechanism has been provided. Now epigenetics provides answers. Turning some genetic switches on and others off differentially expresses the otherwise identical genome of identical twins, thereby explaining why one became schizophrenic, alcoholic, depressed, etc., while the other twin did not.

Innateness and Instinct

The concept of instinct has intrigued biologists and psychologists for a long time. Wikipedia provides a reasonably good introduction to this history.[57] Wilhelm Wundt discussed instincts in the 1870s. William McDougall[58] was another influential psychologist who emphasized the role of instincts as a factor that governs behavior. Seligman (1971) noted that people develop phobias regarding snakes, heights, and the dark more frequently than they do phobias about kittens, puppies, and butterflies. He attributed this to what he called biological preparedness. See Seligman (1970) and Seligman and Hager (1972) for further discussion of this and related issues.

Anne Anastasi[59] is noted, among other reasons, for her 1958 seminal *Psychology Review* article entitled 'Heredity, environment, and the question "how?",' where she sought mechanism information regarding how genetics interacts with the environment to produce psychology and behavior. Psychologists largely left this question to other disciplines to answer.

A favorite 'explanatory' activity of psychologists is to estimate proportions of variance associated with genetics and environment for normal traits such as intelligence, mechanical aptitude, and music ability, as well as disorders such as schizophrenia, alcoholism, and drug addiction. A major problem here is that such considerations are relatively pointless for at least two reasons. First, the **behavior = genetics × environment** equation is much like the **area = length × width** equation. Is area really more dependent upon the length of a rectangle than its width? Or is the area of a rectangle more dependent upon its width than its length? Advocates of length can always find long narrow rectangles to support their view whereas advocates of width can always find short wide rectangles to support their view. Clearly such debate is silly. The proportion of variance explained by genetics and environment suffers, is deficient, in the same way. Selecting participants from homogeneous environments will produce large heritability estimates (http://en.wikipedia.org/wiki/Heritability), whereas selecting participants from heterogeneous environments will produce small heritability estimates. Neither approach provides any mechanism information. Neither approach explains anything.

So how can instincts work? What is the biological basis of instincts? How can behavior be innate? What is going on here? Contemporary

[57] http://en.wikipedia.org/wiki/Instinct

[58] http://en.wikipedia.org/wiki/William_McDougall_(psychologist)

[59] http://en.wikipedia.org/wiki/Anne_Anastasi

psychologists more commonly speak of behavior genetics than of instincts.[60] It is understood today that psychology and behavior are the result of genetics interacting with the environment, but the mechanisms that implement these interactions are mostly unknown. Psychological theories simply assume that these mechanisms exist. I now present a connectionist perspective on how behaviors can be inherited; how they can be innate, and then I provide a few illustrations of this network mechanism.

Elman et al. (1999) considered the question of innateness from a connectionist perspective. The generic connectionist network model we have studied so far enables us to understand how genetics can result in specific behaviors. We previously saw that the network cascade (Principle 1) and the experience-dependent plasticity mechanism (Principle 2) interact to produce learning and memory. The normal development of artificial neural networks, and arguably many human neural networks, is through experience-dependent plasticity mechanisms that gradually produce the required levels of synaptic excitation or inhibition that enable 'adult' capabilities. A more direct route is for genetics to set the connection weights to the required 'adult' values in addition to constructing the necessary neural network. This would explain why spiders can spin webs as soon as they are hatched and in the absence of parental instruction. This is the position taken by the proposed Bio↔Psychology Network Theory. I now consider several examples with this new mechanism information in mind.

Activity Level

Activity level can be considered to be innate for the following reasons. Eaton and Saudino (1992) reviewed 14 studies showing that mothers can reliably and validly detect fetal activity beginning with the 28th week of gestation. Fetal activity appears to increase to a peak at around week 34 and then decrease through week 39. These prenatal activity differences constitute the first stable individual difference in behavior, and therefore constitute the first personality trait.

Robertson (1985) reported that cyclic motility is relatively stable after midgestation. Robertson (1987) measured movements in 41 fetuses from 1 to 7 times ($M = 3.5$, $SD = 1.7$) at postmenstrual ages ranging from 23 to 41 weeks. Motility measurements were taken again from 18–124 hours after birth ($M = 54$, $SD = 27$). Various between and within subject analyses were conducted. The most pertinent result for present purposes was the within

60 http://en.wikipedia.org/wiki/Behavioural_genetics

subject finding that cyclic movements during active sleep in the newborn are similar to fetal movements one month before birth. This direct connection between prenatal and postnatal activity supports the developmental continuity of activity level across the birth event.

Zuckerman (1991, pp. 7–8) reported that by age 9, activity level is among the temperament facets with the highest heritability ratios. Buss and Plomin (1984, pp. 118–14, Table 9.2) reported an identical twin activity correlation of 0.62 and a fraternal twin correlation of 0.13 based on 228 identical and 172 fraternal twins whose average age was 61 months. Their Table 9.4 presents mean identical/fraternal twin concordance rates for activity of 45/26, 88/59, 78/54, and 75/57. Their Table 9.6 reports MA/DZ twin correlations of 0.24/0.11 at 6 months, 0.33/0.28 at 12 months, 0.43/0.14 at 18 months, and 0.58/0.14 at 24 months in the same longitudinally studied subjects. Plomin (1990, p. 94) detailed findings from a Swedish study reporting a heritability coefficient for 59-year-old adults of 0.27 for activity level.

All of the above studies can be criticized because of their correlational methodology. It is always possible that a third uncontrolled variable is a common cause of both variables and therefore responsible for their correlation. Experimental studies avoid this pitfall by systematically manipulating the variable in question in the experimental group and holding it constant in the control group. The following research definitively establishes that the activity level is heritable. DeFries et al. (1970) published an initial description of this work. DeFries et al. (1978) published the results after 30 generations of selective breeding. They used an open-field test to measure activity level in 40 litters of mice. The most active male and female mice from each of ten randomly chosen litters were selected and mated at random. Their offspring comprised the first selected generation (S1) of a high-active line (H1). The least active male and female from the same ten litters were selected and mated at random to produce the first selected generation of a low-active line (L1). Two control groups were created from the remaining two sets of ten litters. A male and a female were randomly chosen and randomly mated from ten of the remaining 20 litters and their offspring produced the first generation of a control-1 line (C1). Likewise, a male and a female were randomly chosen and randomly mated from the remaining set of ten litters and their offspring produced the first generation of a control-2 line (C2). This process was repeated for 30 generations. The results were that the activity-level distributions of the H and L strains gradually and consistently diverged from each other and from both control groups until the activity distributions of these two genetic lines became distinct. The activity-level distributions for H30 and L30 did not overlap at all! The high- and low-active lines also diverged from both control groups whose activity level remained essentially the same and intermediate between the H and L strains over all 30 generations. These results conclusively demonstrate that activity level is heritable.

The evidence presented above establishes a strong biological basis for activity level. This evidence suggests that the neural network systems that mediate activity level have had their synapses preset to values that correspond to high, medium, or low activity levels. This is not an unreasonable function for genetics to provide. It is not qualitatively different than someone being born with an overactive or underactive thyroid. What is crucial here is that a network mechanism is being proposed that causes the activity-level differences that we call heritable. The stronger the weights are that characterize the connections among processing nodes in the generic network model presented as Figure 2.1, the stronger its output will be and vice versa.

Taming Foxes

The experimental taming of foxes is another instructive experimental example of behavior genetics. The following URL describes details of a breeding experiment conducted by Dmitri K. Belyaev over 40 generations.[61] Wild foxes were given a behavioral approach test to humans every month until sexual maturity at 7 months. Males and females with the highest tameness scores were allowed to breed. The relevant points here are: (a) that tameness increased over generations; (b) the foxes changed physiologically; i.e., their hypothalamic–pituitary–adrenal (HPA) axis became less active especially around people; and (c) their appearance changed; i.e., their ears became floppy and their coat hairs became curly and changed color.

I offer the following network explanation. The neural networks that constitute the HPA axis of the fox appear to have been modified via selective breeding. Although the structure of these networks likely remained relatively unchanged, the preset synaptic levels of excitation and inhibition could well have been genetically altered. Epigenetic changes may also be involved, because many such genetic switches are thrown during gestation. These and possibly other mechanisms may well have down-regulated the HPA axis in response to selective breeding.

[61] http://blogs.scientificamerican.com/guest-blog/2010/09/06/mans-new-best-friend-a-forgotten-russian-experiment-in-fox-domestication/

Glia: A Third Experience-Dependent Plasticity Mechanism

It may come as a surprise but the brain is mostly made up of glia; not neurons. Glia were once thought to be the glue that held neurons in place. A major problem with this view is that 80% of the brain would then be considered to be glue, because just 20% of the brain consists of neurons. Almost anyone would question the construction of a wall consisting of 20% bricks and 80% mortar. Obviously, glia must do more than fix the physical position of neurons within the skull, as was once thought. Fields (2009, p. 24) reported that glia outnumber neurons six to one on average with significant variations depending upon which part of the brain is in question. There are several varieties of glia. **Astrocytes** fill the spaces between brain neurons and blood vessels. They are the most numerous type of glia. Astrocytes regulate the chemical composition of this extracellular space. Their membranes contain receptors that absorb neurotransmitters from synaptic clefts and consequently regulate synaptic transmission that modifies neural network performance. Astrocytes also regulate the concentration of potassium ions that play a crucial role in neurotransmission.

Eroglu et al. (2008) discussed the role of glia in synaptic plasticity in their Section 5 (pp. 705–7). They pointed out that D-serine released by astrocytes is a major regulator of NMDA receptor function. Chapter 11 of this book reports animal and human studies demonstrating that d-cycloserine can facilitate therapeutic learning. NMDA receptors play an important role in hippocampal-mediated learning and memory. Therefore, glia are major regulators of experience-dependent synaptic plasticity. This mechanism is in addition to the LTP and LTD mechanisms discussed above. Eroglu et al. (2008) presented a gliocenric view of the synapse in their Figure 4 which I have repackaged into Table 3.3 below. The authors concluded their chapter by saying 'It is becoming increasingly clear that glia play a crucial and dynamic role at the synapse and influence functions that have long been thought to be strictly under neuronal control' (p. 707).

Whereas **Schwann cells** myelinate neurons outside of the brain and spinal cord, **oligodendrocytes** myelinate neurons inside the brain and spinal cord. They are especially numerous in the white matter which is mainly composed of myelinated fibers, as opposed to gray matter which is largely composed of cell bodies. More wraps of myelin result in faster transmission. Neurons that fire together wire together. Glia monitor neuron firing patterns during learning and add more myelin wrappings to

Table 3.3 A Gliocentric View of the Synapse

Synapse formation
Secrete synaptogenic factors
Developmental plasticity
Stabilize spines
Regulate critical period plasticity synaptic changes in the hypothalamus
Synapse function
Modulates presynaptic function
Modulates postsynaptic function
Responds to neuronal activity
Communicates with other glia
Synaptic plasticity
Modulates LTP via D-serine
Modifies synaptic scaling
Regulates homeostatic depression
Synapse elimination
Phagocytose axosomes (axon removal at developing synapses)
Strip degenerated synapses
Induce complement cascade
Synapse maintenance
Control ionic homeostasis
Secrete factors required for synaptic structure and function

speed up activations emanating from slower neurons to achieve synchrony. This is but one experience-dependent mechanism that glia use when participating in learning. Microglia are phagocytes that cannibalize invading organisms. They constitute the brain's immune system. Much more can be said about glia. I recommend reading *The Other Brain* by R. Douglas Fields (2009).

The biological mechanisms that we have discussed to this point provide a way to understand psychological processes such as learning and memory, and by extension all psychological phenomena that depend on learning and memory, in **physical** rather than **mental** terms, especially when considered in conjunction with the connectionist neural network framework discussed above. We now return to a more classic focus on conditioning which once was considered to constitute the entire field of learning, where we will learn that it too is caused by EDP mechanisms.

Conditioning

Psychologists have historically discussed conditioning as if it was learning, as if it provided mechanism information. This is not correct. Classical conditioning,[62] also known as respondent conditioning, constitutes a set of conditions under which new learning occurs, but these conditions do not explain why new learning occurs. Operant conditioning, also known as instrumental conditioning, also constitutes a set of conditions under which new learning occurs, but these conditions also do not explain why new learning occurs. The biological process known as experience-dependent plasticity explains why both forms of conditioning work as they do. Cognitive learning also depends upon experience-dependent plasticity mechanisms. Alternatively stated, conditioning is a behavioral result of experience-dependent plasticity mechanisms that drive learning and memory. Conditioning is but one of several manifestations of the learning/memory process. Classical conditioning was once considered to be a completely different form of learning than operant conditioning. This also is not true. They are both examples of experience-dependent plasticity; i.e., experience-dependent plasticity makes both of them possible and makes them work as they do.

The question of why reinforcers are reinforcing, why they strengthen behavior, why they increase the frequency, intensity, and/or duration of behavior cannot be answered from within a behavioral conditioning framework. Experience-dependent mechanisms are responsible for the neural network modifications that cause all operant and respondent conditioning phenomena. Alternatively stated, experience-dependent plasticity mechanisms constitute the biology behind learning and memory. In many ways it is accurate to say that behavior modification entails, is due to, and is caused by, synaptic modification.

Learning

In this section I integrate some of the information presented above with some new information, to show how the proposed Bio↔Psychology Network Theory enables us to understand how learning works. I do this with reference to a study by Tang et al. (1999). These investigators used genetic methods to create an experimental group of transgenetic mice that had an overabundance of NMDA receptors in their hippocampi which is well known to be a critical brain structure for learning and memory. More

[62] Classical conditioning was discovered by the Russian physiologist Ivan Pavlov while studying digestion in dogs when he was 65 years old. He noticed that his dogs began to salivate when they heard the trainer enter their building at feeding time. His work was translated into English by Anrep in 1927 with one huge mistake. The Russian word for condition**al** was mistranslated into the English word condition**ed**. Pavlov intended that we should understand conditioning as establishing a condition**al** relationship that could extinguish if the conditions were discontinued. Anrep then reported on many systematic studies performed by Pavlov.

particularly, the experimenters created mice whose NMDA receptors were mainly constructed from 2B subunits rather than alternative 2A subunits. (I explain why shortly.) Such events could happen naturally in the wild but have been specially created in the laboratory for reasons explained below.

Tang et al. (1999) compared the learning rates of the transgenetic mice to normal control mice on six behavioral tests: (a) a novel-object recognition task; (b) a retention test; (c) a contextual conditioning task; (d) a cued fear conditioning task; (e) a fear extinction task; and (f) a hidden-platform water maze test. The results were clear and conclusive. The transgenetic mice performed significantly better than controls on all six tests. See Jiao et al. (2008) for a similar study with parallel results.

Normally this is where discussion ends. We have seen that a high-tech genetic manipulation technology resulted in more intelligent behavior, but no way to explain how all of this could happen let alone why it actually happened. This sad but typical state of affairs is because we heretofore have not had mechanism information capable of explaining why there should be any relationship between the subunits that a neurotransmitter receptor is made of and ability to excel on six behavioral tests. We have had no mechanism information capable of explaining how psychology emerges from biology.

The proposed Bio↔Psychology Network Theory enables us to understand the relationships reported above as follows. The 2B subunits stay open longer than the 2A units do and therefore they make better coincidence detectors. Since neurons that fire together wire together, neural networks constructed from NMDA receptors composed of 2B subunits learn associations more quickly.[63] This explains why the transgenetic mice learned faster and performed better than the control mice. No other contemporary psychological theory explains the connection between NMDA receptor components and intelligent behavior as well or better than the Bio↔Psychology Network Theory does.

An alternative mechanism for enhancing synaptic plasticity involves the major histocompatibility complex class I (MHCI) which is a crucial component of our immune system. It was long thought that the MHCI was entirely blocked from entering the brain by the blood–brain barrier until Goddard et al. (2007) and Shatz (2009) discovered otherwise. They found MCHI mRNA in the developing visual system of cats. They created a special breed of knockout mice that lacked MHCI and discovered that this condition, along with a molecule designated as PirB, released the brakes regarding brain plasticity. Behavioral tests

[63] I remember this as B = better. It is noteworthy that the aging process replaces 2B subunits with 2A subunits and that is one reason why older people and animals learn more slowly than younger ones do.

in a water maze demonstrated that these MHCI knockout mice learned far quicker than did controls. Miller (2013) provides a review of this research. The problem here is that the mice had compromised immune systems.

Culture

Culture plays a central role in the proposed Bio↔Psychology Network Theory because it is proxy for many experiences that a person has throughout their lifespan. Culture activates EDP mechanisms that physically alter the neural networks that comprise our brain and enteric nervous system. Hence, our emphasis on **think physical, not mental** emphasizes rather than diminishes the role of culture.

Conclusions

Accreditation criteria established by the American Psychology Association require training in the biological bases of behavior. Achieving this objective requires understanding causal mechanisms. The proposed Bio↔Psychology Network Theory provides some of this mechanism information.

PRINCIPLE 3: TRANSFORMATION[64]

Introduction

Transformation is the hallmark of cognition. Transformation is what enables us to be more than S → R creatures. Thinking requires concepts. Concepts are defined by certain key stimulus features as indicated by a sign in the Bronx Zoo that reads 'If it has feathers it's a bird; if it doesn't it isn't'. We form concepts by processing stimulus microfeatures. For example, the stimulus microfeatures of wings, feathers, and beaks are positive indicators, defining features, of the concept 'bird'. Antlers are negative indicators of the concept 'bird'. If it has antlers it cannot be a bird. But how does the brain transform stimulus microfeatures into concepts? The following section provides my connectionist response.

Factor Analysis Analogy

I propose that connectionist neural networks transform stimulus microfeatures into concepts in roughly the same way that factor analysis transforms items into psychological constructs. I base this conjecture on the remarkable similarity between the neural architecture of our generic neural network model and the path diagram that describes simple factor analysis.

[64] An extended presentation of this transformation principle is available at http://www.fordham.edu/psychology/tryon.

Psychologists have used the well-accepted method of factor analysis to transform test items into psychological concepts since Spearman (1904) introduced this methodology over a century ago. Consider the following general intelligence example. If various verbal and mathematical tests are given to a sufficiently large sample of people and the scores on each test are correlated with the scores on every other test across all participants, it will be noticed that the correlations are all positive. This fact is curious as it contrasts with the null hypothesis that predicts that half of the correlations should be positive and the other half should be negative. So what is causing all of the correlations to be positive? The concept of general intelligence has been proposed as one answer. People do better or worse on all tests in direct proportion to their general intelligence.

Psychologists needed a way to quantify this phenomenon. They needed a way to move beyond the observed correlations among tests and/or test items to the underlying construct(s), such as general intelligence, that gives rise to them. Factor analysis provided a method for doing just that. The top half of Figure 3.12 illustrates a simple two-factor model derived from six tests, variables labeled V1–V6. Think of V1, V2, and V3 as verbal tests and V4, V5, and V6 as mathematical tests where F1 concerns the concept of verbal intelligence and F2 the concept of mathematical intelligence.[65] The lines connecting the two factors to the six measured variables carry numbers called factor loadings. These numbers can be understood as correlations between the underlying construct and each of its measured indicators when all variables have been standardized as Z-scores. The values of these loadings can range from −1 through 0 to +1 reflecting the degree to which the test is a positive or negative indicator of the latent construct, concept.

Two observations are crucial here. First, the computer identifies each factor by computing factor loadings that quantify the extent to which each indicator defines the positive and/or negative poles of the identified concept. In factor analytic terminology we would say that wings, feathers, and beaks load positively and antlers load negatively on the latent construct 'bird'. Second, humans only provide labels for the factors that the computer creates after reviewing the factor loadings that the computer calculated. Psychologists have willingly and comfortably labeled such computer-calculated constructs as intelligence, extraversion, and neuroticism, to name but a few core psychological concepts that have been widely and confidently used to explain behavior for over a century.

[65] A single factor solution was sought first and is generally symbolized as g for general intelligence.

The bottom half of Figure 3.12 illustrates a neural network with two layers of processing nodes and one layer of simulated synapses connecting them. The upper layer that previously represented tests now represents stimulus microfeatures. The lower layer continues to represent latent constructs. They are the O-nodes found in the middle layer of our generic neural network model. These O-nodes designate the factors that the neural network computes based on the stimulus microfeatures. The lines that connect the stimulus microfeatures to the factors carry the factor loadings mentioned above, but now they are called connection weights. They reflect the importance of each stimulus microfeature to the computed latent construct. These weights, factor loadings, characterize what the latent construct means. They define the positive and/or negative poles of the identified concept.

This factoring process is an automatic and unconscious result of the network cascade. The network cascade weights stimulus microfeatures and

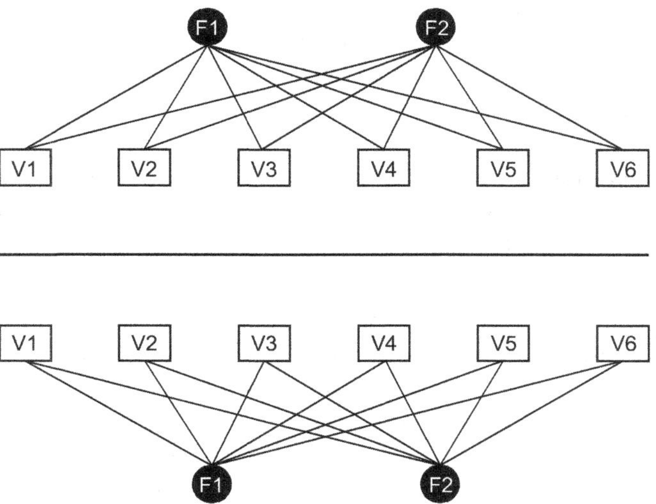

Figure 3.12 The top half of this figure illustrates a two factor (F1 & F2) model of responses to six psychological test items, variables (V1–V6). The computer calculates factor loadings, illustrated generically with lines that define the two latent constructs and show the importance of each item to each factor. The investigator names the constructs that the computer constructed. The figure in the bottom half of this diagram vertically inverts the two-factor diagram into a two-layer network model where the top row of six S nodes (V1–V6) now represent six stimulus microfeatures and the second row of two O nodes (F1 & F2) continue to represent two latent constructs that are transformations of the stimulus microfeatures. I became aware of the difference between **reflective** and **formative** models after press time. I amend the text discussion in a document posted at, http://www.fordham.edu/psychology/tryon.

Table 3.4 Centroid Factor Extraction Based on Loehlin's (1987) Description of Cyril Burt's (1917) Methods. Entries Consist of All Possible Pairwise Paths

Path a	Path b	Path c	Path d	Path e	Path f
aa	ba	ca	da	ea	fa
ab	bb	cb	db	eb	fb
ac	bc	cc	dc	ec	fc
ad	bd	cd	dd	ed	fd
ae	be	ce	de	ee	fe
af	bf	cf	df	ef	ff
aΣ	bΣ	cΣ	dΣ	eΣ	fΣ

thereby necessarily and unavoidably transforms them into latent constructs in the same way that factor loadings transform test items into factor scores. Some PDP-CNN models use principle components analysis (PCA) to form concepts as part of their training (e.g., McLeod et al., 1998; O'Reilly & Munakata, 2000).[66] The main point here is that as long as we accept factor analysis as computing legitimate latent psychological constructs we must also accept that PDP-CNNs also compute legitimate latent psychological constructs.

Further insight into how neural networks construct latent psychological constructs from stimulus microfeatures can be learned from Loehlin's (1987) description of Cyril Burt's (1917) centroid method of factor extraction. Table 3.4 presumes that the connection weights, path coefficients, lines in Figure 3.12 were labeled 'a' through 'f' respectively from left to right. Table entries consist of all possible pair wise paths. Equation 1 shows why the Path 'a' column equals aΣ, the sum associated the Path 'b' column equals bΣ, etc., through the sum of the Path 'f' column equals fΣ. Equation 2 shows that the sum of the sums equals the grand sum. Equation 3 redefines the grand sum to be its square root. Division yields values for the previously unknown path coefficients. Summation is the main operation here. Real neurons and PDP-CNN models are very good at dendritic summation. While it is less clear how real neural networks might accomplish square root extraction and division, simulated networks have no trouble doing so. The end result is the formation of legitimate latent psychological constructs using factor extraction methods that psychologists have accepted for more than a century. Application of these methods by artificial neural network models authorizes

[66] Connectionist models are part of mathematical psychology (Bower, 1994). PDP-CNN models are intimately related to multivariate statistics (White, 1989).

one to call the extracted factors **simulated constructs** or **simulated psychological factors** or **simulated psychological concepts**. In any case, the O-nodes compute a highly transformed version of the S-node microfeatures. This fact alone certifies connectionist models as cognitive models. The R-nodes compute second-order factors. Adding more processing levels in between the S- and R-nodes means that the R-nodes represent correspondingly higher-order factors; i.e., increasingly abstract concepts.

$$\text{Let } \Sigma = a + b + c + d + e + f \tag{1}$$

$$a\Sigma + b\Sigma + c\Sigma + d\Sigma + e\Sigma + f\Sigma = (a + b + c + d + e + f)\,\Sigma = \Sigma\Sigma. \tag{2}$$

$$\text{Redefining } \Sigma = \sqrt{\Sigma\Sigma} \tag{3}$$

$$\text{it follows that } a = \frac{a\Sigma}{\Sigma},\quad b = \frac{b\Sigma}{\Sigma},\quad c = \frac{c\Sigma}{\Sigma},\quad d = \frac{d\Sigma}{\Sigma},\quad e = \frac{e\Sigma}{\Sigma},\quad f = \frac{f\Sigma}{\Sigma}.$$

Oja (1982) presented a mathematical analysis of a variant of the Hebbian neuron that proves that such neurons extract the principle component, first Eigen vector, from their inputs. This mathematical proof provides strong support for our Network Principle 3: Transformation.

I now review the interpretation of the results of factor analyses that support the well-accepted Five Factor Model (FFM) of adult personality to further understand the relationship between factor analysis and how our network extracts, creates, latent constructs. Table 1 in Costa and McCrae (1995), reproduced here as Table 3.5, presents factor analytic results at the facet level for the five factor theory of personality. These authors draw attention to the bold-faced factor loadings. Facets N1–N6 load highest on the N factor. Facets E1–E6 load highest on the E factor. Facets O1–O6 load highest on the O factor. Facets A1–A6 load highest on the A factor. And Facets C1–C6 load highest on the C factor. These findings support the author's conclusions that adult personality, as measured by the NEO, is composed of five interpretable factors.

I now discuss these findings in terms of our network approach. Notice that Facets N1–N6 in Table 3.5 also load on, have connections with, all of the other factors (E, O, A, and C) as well. This means that the items comprising the N1 facet do not exclusively measure Factor N. Notice that the N2 facet also loads substantially on Factor A as well as Factor N. Table 3.5 assumes that all of the NEO items that measure each of the 30 facets completely and exclusively measure that facet. Nothing could be further from the truth. If we had a table showing the factor loadings on all 240

Table 3.5 Common and Specific Factor Loadings for NEO-PI-R Facet Scales

NEO-PI-R	Common Factor					
Facet Scale	**N**	**E**	**O**	**A**	**C**	**s**
N1: Anxiety	**.77**	−.04	−.01	.00	−.10	**.41**
N2: Angry Hostility	**.64**	−.12	.00	**−.45**	−.09	.34
N3: Depression	**.78**	−.17	.01	−.02	−.26	.33
N4: Self-Consciousness	**.67**	−.24	−.07	.07	−.21	.36
N5: Impulsiveness	**.49**	.20	.11	−.17	−.34	**.51**
N6: Vulnerability	**.68**	−.16	−.13	−.04	**−.40**	.33
E1: Warmth	−.09	**.72**	.14	.29	.15	.29
E2: Gregariousness	−.15	**.61**	.03	.01	.04	**.57**
E3: Assertiveness	−.30	**.45**	.15	−.30	−.38	**.46**
E4: Activity	−.05	**.47**	.18	−.17	**.44**	**.40**
E5: Excitement Seeking	.00	**.49**	.25	−.31	−.06	**.50**
E6: Positive Emotions	−.08	**.68**	.25	.15	.11	**.41**
O1: Fantasy	.19	.15	**.54**	−.14	−.28	**.56**
O2: Aesthetics	.08	.05	**.69**	.11	.08	**.51**
O3: Feelings	.35	.34	**.49**	−.01	.09	**.42**
O4: Actions	−.20	.22	**.51**	.02	.04	**.48**
O5: Ideas	−.17	−.02	**.69**	−.07	.15	**.51**
O6: Values	−.04	.12	**.42**	−.04	−.11	**.68**
A1: Trust	−.27	.33	.12	**.44**	.08	**.62**
A2: Straightforwardness	−.03	−.06	**−.08**	**.63**	.18	**.52**
A3: Altruism	**−.06**	**.46**	.02	**.57**	.26	.39
A4: Compliance	−.18	.00	**−.06**	**.69**	.01	.28
A5: Modesty	.12	−.18	−.07	**.50**	−.11	**.60**
A6: Tender-Mindedness	−.01	.18	.10	**.52**	.09	**.48**

Continued

Table 3.5 Common and Specific Factor Loadings for NEO-PI-R Facet Scales —cont'd

NEO-PI-R	Common Factor					
Facet Scale	**N**	**E**	**O**	**A**	**C**	**s**
C1: Competence	−.37	.22	.14	.09	**.60**	**.32**
C2: Order	−.02	.07	−.14	.03	**.59**	**.53**
C3: Dutifulness	−.21	.03	**−.02**	**.24**	**.63**	.34
C4: Achievement Striving	−.13	.19	.15	−.07	**.72**	.27
C5: Self-Descipline	−.33	.15	**.01**	.12	**.73**	.27
C6: Deliberation	−.31	−.16	−.11	**.22**	**.53**	**.49**

Note. These are varimax-rotated principal factors with iterated communalities. NEO-PI-R = Revised NEO personality Inventory; N = Neuroticism; E = Extraversion; O = Openness to Experience; A = Agreeableness; C = Conscientiousness; *s* = square root of the facet's specificity, which is estimated by coefficient alpha minus communality.

Data adapted from Costa, McCrea, and Dye (1991); $N = 1,539$. Loadings $\geq \pm .40$ are given in boldface.

NEO items we would see that each item loaded to some extent on all five factors and would have loaded on even more factors had Costa and McCrae chosen to extract them. Recasting these data in network terms would consist of an item (240 rows) by factor (5 columns) matrix where the cell entries are the factor loadings representing connection weights. The five factor interpretation given above effectively assumes that the off diagonal loadings are all zero. This is the equivalent of pruning, setting to zero, all connection weights that mediate all off diagonal factor–item connections. On the contrary, our network model retains all of these connections, which means that our network model captures the full complexity of all five extracted latent constructs. In general, PDP-CNNs extract as many factors as they have middle nodes. Part of the art of connectionist modeling is to determine the number of factors the model needs to extract to learn the assigned task or solve the stated problem.

I now provide another example that is intended to help understand how the factor analysis model enables us to understand how psychology emerges from biology. It is well known that testosterone drives libido in both men and women. Some of our neural network structures have receptors for testosterone. Taking either synthetic or bioidentical testosterone will bind to these receptors and more strongly activate associated synapses. This is the equivalent of augmenting selected factor loadings in our model. The nature of the latent constructs, concepts, formed by factor analytic methods is directly dependent upon their factor loadings. Selectively augmenting the factor loadings that define our libido explains why supplementing with testosterone increases sexual interest.

Cognition

Transformation is the hallmark of cognition. The ability of our generic network model to at least twice transform stimulus microfeatures qualitatively distinguishes PDP-CNN models from behavioral models and certifies them as cognitive models. PDP-CNN models therefore authorize discussions of Pavlovian conditioning in terms of expectations as Rescorla (1988) has done. It is noteworthy that the Rescorla-Wagner model of classical conditioning is mathematically equivalent to the Delta learning function used in connectionist models (Rescorla & Wagner, 1972).

I wish to emphasize an important difference between the way that psychologists use factor analysis and the way it is used in PDP-CNN models. Psychologists collect their entire data set and then perform a factor analysis on all of it. The computer calculates factor loadings and the investigator names the factors accordingly. The tendency is to treat the resulting factors as stable entities that estimate population parameters; an assumption that is heavily dependent upon sample size. Psychologists understand sampling error and recognize that different values for factor loadings will result if the factor analysis is performed on a different sample, and especially if it is performed on a much smaller data set. However, the new factor loadings are still assumed to estimate the same fixed population parameters.

PDP-CNN models take the perspective of a living system that begins with little or no data and continuously processes, factor analyzes, stimulus microfeature data as it becomes available. This means that the data set increases gradually. Computed factors change accordingly. Early on in development the factors extracted by PDP-CNN models can be expected to vary widely. They will stabilize with experience. This process makes PDP-CNN models inherently developmental. This process enables PDP-CNN models to explain psychological development.

That the factors that PDP-CNN models extract change incrementally might appear to contradict the Piagetian stage model, except that it doesn't. The following simulations demonstrate that gradual changes can produce the qualitative shifts that characterize developmental stages. Rumelhart and McClelland (1986) developed a CNN that learns to form past-tense English sentences. Although connection weights are modified incrementally by learning functions at every step, the network simulated three developmental stages that children go through in forming past-tense versions of verb stems. Sejnowski and Rosenberg (1986, 1987) created a PDP-CNN that taught itself to correctly pronounce English words through repeated exposure to 1024 words of child speech. When network phoneme output was played through a speech synthesizer called DECtalk, developmental stages were apparent. The network began by making babbling sounds. Then it distinguished vowels from consonants, learned word boundaries, generated pseudo words, and then spoke as young children often do. Finally, it produced reasonably adult speech. Kruschke (1992) described a PDP-CNN, called ALCOVE, that was designed to model the process of human category learning. ALCOVE demonstrated stage-like learning during a task designed to teach it a rule and an exception.

The network cascade necessarily results in transformation because activation traverses simulated synapses, connection weights, that function as factor loadings. Latent constructs (factors) are extracted with every network cascade because it is the process of traversing layers of synapses and the summation functions associated with every network cascade that extracts factors as per the numerical example presented above. This means that a factor or cognitive pulse is associated with every network cascade.

Simultaneous with the transformation that occurs as activation cascades across the network is activation of the experience-dependent plasticity process that modifies all connection weights to some degree and that changes how the network will transform stimulus microfeatures in future. These changes modify how the network 'thinks', 'feels', and 'behaves'. The network will transform differently because the connection weights have changed. If these weights did not change then the network would continue to transform in the same way. The network's behavior would vary as stimulus microfeatures varied, but no new learning would occur because the connection weights would remain unchanged. It is important not to confuse these stimulus-related variations with learning-related synaptic changes represented by connection weight changes. This dynamic interaction with the environment enables the network to adapt to its physical and social environment. Changing the network modifies the memories that it forms.

Emotion

Greenberg (2002, 2008, 2013) developed Emotion-Focused Therapy (EFT) as a method of modifying maladaptive emotions. Of the six principles that characterize EFT, the one that I address here is transformation. Greenberg emphasized the importance of emotions in transforming emotions. A corrective emotional experience is one where a more adaptive emotion is activated and replaces a maladaptive emotion. However, Greenberg offered no mechanism information for how this emotional transformation process works. A minor modification of our factor analytic explanation of transformation provides some of this missing mechanism information.

I previously defined stimulus microfeatures in Figure 3.12 entirely in cognitive terms; i.e., stimulus microfeatures V1–V6 were all considered to be cognitive. Now I partition these stimulus microfeatures into a cognitive group and an emotion group. For simplicity let V1, V2, and V3 be three cognitive microfeatures and V4, V5, and V6 be three emotion microfeatures. Other possibilities exist. We could let V1 be a cognitive microfeature and V2 be emotion microfeatures with the remaining nodes constituting two additional such pairs. At least four theoretical consequences follow from these partitions.

First, the F1 and F2 factors now consist of an integrated combination of cognitive and emotional microfeatures. The lines connecting the cognitive microfeatures to both factors simulate the synapses that mediate, carry, the cognitive influences. The lines connecting the emotional microfeatures to both factors simulate the synapses that mediate, carry, the emotional influences. Therefore, emotions and cognitions are inextricably integrated into both extracted latent constructs. This theoretical prediction is supported by Duncan and Barrett (2007) who reported empirical evidence that cognitions can function as emotions and emotions can function as cognitions. Efforts to emphasize cognition over emotion or emotion over cognition in this case are like emphasizing the importance of length over width or vice versa to area. Second, now we have a plausible proximal causal mechanism by which we can understand and explain how EFT procedures can transform emotions with emotions. Third, the same structure enables us to also understand and explain how EFT procedures can use emotions to transform cognitions. Fourth, the cognitive-emotion factors extracted by the middle nodes, the O-nodes, are what activate behaviors. We can therefore see that some behaviors may be more under cognitive control whereas other behaviors may be more under emotional control, depending upon the composition of the factors that characterize the middle layer.

Conclusion

Prominent differences between psychology and biology have long inspired the view that the mind differs from the brain. The question of how psychology emerges from biology has long been a mystery and a barrier to the theoretical unification of biology and psychology. The proposed understanding of how neural networks and their simulations transform stimulus microfeatures into latent constructs is a singularly important contribution of the proposed Bio↔Psychology Network Theory. These transformations are an automatic, unconscious, deterministic, necessary, and unavoidable consequence of the network cascade and a principal feature and key mechanism of the explanatory core.

PRINCIPLE 4: ACTIVATION AND REACTIVATION

The term **activation** refers to turning a processing node on or off. The term activation pattern refers to the on–off pattern of processing nodes that characterizes a network at any given instant in time. The term **reactivation** refers to a partial to complete return to a prior activation pattern. Reactivation is a memory-retrieval mechanism. Reactivation has been called **redintegration**.[67] It is a part–whole pattern completion (our Principle 6) process that restores thoughts, feelings, and behaviors to the original state that existed at the time memory formed.

The main reason for having a separate **reactivation principle** is to distinguish memory retrieval from ordinary processing. The following research authorizes this principle. Gelbard-Sagiv et al. (2008) demonstrated that neurons that were active at the time of memory formation **reactivated** 1,500 milliseconds prior to the verbal report of the memory. These investigators implanted electrodes into the hippocampi of 13 patients with pharmacologically intractable epilepsy prior to surgery. Participants viewed 48 5–10-second video clips of famous people, characters, and animals engaged in various activities and landmarks 5–10 times in pseudorandom order. Participants then freely recalled what they had seen. Participants recalled an average of 83.2% (± 5% SEM) of the video clips. Electrical activity was recorded from 857 electrodes. **Neurons that responded during viewing also responded during recall and did so 1,500 milliseconds prior to verbal report.** The authors discounted the possibility that these results were due to epilepsy.

Paz et al. (2010) reported data from single neurons from 13 patients with pharmacologically intractable epilepsy aged 18–54 years collected across 27 recording sessions where participants viewed 10–16 video clips lasting 5–10 seconds each in pseudorandom order. The neurons activated by viewing the video clips were **reactivated** during free recall.

Lehn et al. (2009) had 23 healthy females aged 23–29 years view a movie in Session 1 on Day 1 and recall scenes from this movie in Session 2 on Day 2. Hippocampal activity was monitored using fMRI. A total of 120 unique movie scene pictures were involved. The main result of interest here is that fMRI-assessed hippocampal **reactivation** was observed during free recall. These results support our reactivation principle.

Reactivation is an important network concept because: (a) it expands memory to be much more than cognitive recall. Memory now includes affect and behavior as well as cognition. (b) Reactivation makes remembering a much more active process than mere information retrieval as if from a file drawer. (c) Reactivation entails network mechanism information that explains how memory works. The organism is returned to the state it was in when memory was formed, or nearly so, by resetting relevant synapses to the level of excitation or inhibition that characterized them when the memory first formed or approximately so.

[67] http://en.wikipedia.org/wiki/Redintegration

The concept of **activation** is central to understanding networks because it is integral to the network cascade and transfer function that limits the extent to which the cascade propagates across the network. The network cascade is part of every processing cycle and drives the rest of the explanatory core and all corollary network principles. Activation is necessarily involved in learning and memory formation. Activation is what drives transformation.

The concept of reactivation entails **reconstitution**. A definition of reconstitute is: 'to constitute again or anew; *especially*: to restore to a former condition by adding water' (http://www.merriam-webster.com/dictionary/reconstitute) (emphasis in the original), as when one adds water to freeze-dried powdered milk to reconstitute it as a drink. **Memories entail reconstituted thoughts, feelings, and actions**. Network reactivation is a more accurate description than to say that we recall memories because reconstitution implies an active network process. Memory entails a **part–whole pattern completion process** discussed in Chapter 4 as Principle 6: Part–Whole Pattern Completion. Additional mechanism information is provided by the Bidirectional Memory Model (BAM) discussed in Chapter 4. **Prototypes** are memories, and therefore reactivations; i.e., they are network reconstitutions.

Activation is our preferred general term when we refer to a network processing. Reactivation is our preferred term when we speak of memory in any form because the relevant mechanisms entail returning the network to a prior state; to a prior activation pattern. For example, when we try to recall seeing someone from our past, our neural networks need to return to the activation state that they were in at the time when we actually saw this person. Imagination and vision use many of the same neural networks (Farah, 2000; Kosslyn & Thompson, 2000). Recollection entails revisualization and that requires reactivation of the visual pathways and relevant neural networks. This activation/reactivation principle specifies a fundamental aspect of what I refer to as neural network ontology.[68]

Reactivation is the complement of activation. Wikipedia defines complement as 'In many different fields, the **complement** of *X* is something that together with *X* makes a complete whole – something that supplies what *X* lacks' (http://en.wikipedia.org/wiki/Complement) (emphasis in the original). Reactivation is complementary to activation in the same way as memory is complementary to learning. One without the other is incomplete and non-functional. They must work together to produce a viable result.

[68] http://en.wikipedia.org/wiki/Ontology

Interaction

The four network principles that constitute the explanatory nucleus always work together in unison as part of every explanation, which is why I refer to them as an **explanatory nucleus**. The **network cascade** of **activations** received either from sensory systems or other neural networks is the basis of all psychology. These activations trigger experience-dependent mechanisms that modify connection weights, simulated synapses that enable **memories** to form and **learning** to occur. The process of traversing layers of connection weights, simulated synapses, automatically **transforms** stimulus microfeatures into latent constructs, concepts, where cognitive and emotional factors are fully integrated. **Reactivation** of networks reconstitutes neural states that we experience as memories for additional processing. Hence, these first four network properties necessarily always work together, which is why I refer to them as the explanatory core.

CONCLUSIONS

This chapter presented the explanatory nucleus. It characterizes every processing cycle and consists of the following four core network principles: (a) unconscious processing; (b) learning and memory; (c) transformation; and (d) activation/reactivation. The first principle transitions psychology from a conscious-centric to an unconscious-centric science. The second principle provides experience-dependent plasticity mechanism information regarding learning and memory; the two functions upon which all psychological phenomena depend. The factor analytic-like transformation mechanism explains how psychology can emerge from biology; how mind can emerge from brain. It is arguably the most important contribution made in this book. The activation/reactivation distinction formally separates experience from memory.

The next chapter considers eight corollary network principles. These principles derive from, are caused by, the four core network principles. They greatly expand the explanatory scope of the proposed Bio↔Psychology Network Theory.

Corollary Network Principles

Contents

Cognitive Neuroscience and Psychotherapy
http://dx.doi.org/10.1016/B978-0-12-420071-5.00004-1

Corollaries are true when what they are corollary to is true, as in mathematics where corollaries follow from theorems. The psychological principles presented in this chapter are true because they derive from the four core principles discussed in Chapter 3 which are intrinsic, essential, basic, built-in properties of connectionist networks. You may recall from Chapter 3 that Principle 1 concerns the automatic unconscious neural network cascade, Principle 2 refers to learning and memory that occur because of experience-dependent plasticity mechanisms that are triggered by the network cascade, and Principle 3 concerns the transformations that necessarily occur to varying degrees depending upon the complexity and architecture of the neural network. Principle 4 distinguishes between ongoing states of network activation and the deliberative or reflexive reactivation of a prior network state. Collectively these four core concepts constitute the explanatory nucleus, kernel, of the proposed Bio↔Psychology Network Theory.

I say that these four principles form an **explanatory nucleus** to emphasize that they always occur together; i.e., they work together indivisibly. Stated otherwise, transformation and experience-dependent learning and memory are immediate and necessary consequences of the network cascade which occurs unconsciously, automatically, mechanically, and deterministically. It is important to notice that this causal sequence contains a self-modifying element; namely that experience-dependent plasticity changes how the network processes over time. This feature enables neural networks, and connectionist models of them, to function adaptively and display psychological development. The explanatory nucleus gives rise to the corollary principles discussed next. I will endeavor to explain how the explanatory nucleus gives rise to each corollary principle. While I discuss eight such principles, there may be more. I am not claiming completeness here.

Figure 4.1 presents a visual summary of the psychological effects created by the unconscious cascade and its relationship to the corollary network principles. The long left arrow shows that the unconscious cascade causes transformations to occur that lead to conscious cognition and unconscious thought/processing, both of which produce expectations for good (placebo) or ill (nocebo). The long right arrow shows that the unconscious cascade produces learning and memory via experience-dependent plasticity and that networks seek consonance and coherence. Dissonance induction followed by reduction seems to be a common cause for why empirically supported treatments work. Networks naturally form prototypes. The left

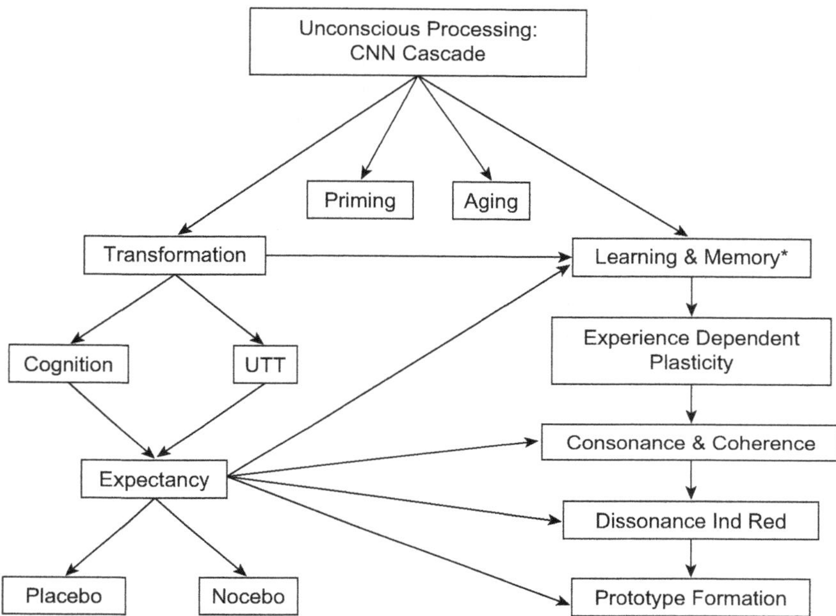

Figure 4.1 Illustration of the multiple effects caused by the unconscious cascade of network activations. UTT, Unconscious Thought Theory (see text). The * refers to the memory superposition principle. Not shown: Bottom-up processing flows from lower to higher network layers. Top-down processing flows in reverse from higher to lower network layers thereby creating feedback loops.

short arrow indicates that priming is readily explained by network processing in that subliminal processing modifies the pathways taken, thereby increasing the probability that they will be retaken. The short right arrow indicates that the effects of aging are effectively modeled by decreasing the slope of the transfer function.

Table 4.1 reviews and summarizes the four core principles that constitute the explanatory nucleus, the eight corollary principles, and provides examples of additional psychological phenomena that they can explain.

I do not attempt to complete the explanatory extension by exhaustively identifying every psychological phenomenon that can be explained using these core and corollary principles. My aim here is to illustrate that the explanatory scope is impressively diverse and sufficiently broad to make the proposed theory relevant to the majority of psychologists. This explanatory diversity also makes the proposed network approach at least a mid-level

Table 4.1 Core and Corollary Principles

- Explanatory nucleus consisting of four elemental network properties formulated as core psychological principles (they always work together simultaneously, automatically, and unconsciously).[a]
  - Network cascade
  - Experience-dependent plasticity (EDP) mediates learning and memory
  - Transformation
  - Activation/reactivation
- Emergent psychological phenomena formulated as corollary network properties/psychological principles
  - Priming (derives primarily from the network cascade and EDP core properties) and explains
    - Repetition priming
    - Semantic and lexical priming
    - Conceptual priming
    - Emotional priming
    - Cultural priming
    - Idea-motor priming
    - Active-self prime-to-behavior effects
    - Some aspects of social cognition
  - Part–whole pattern completion (derives primarily from repeated cascades as in the Bidirectional Associative Memory model, Tryon, 1999) and explains
    - Content-addressable memory
    - Mood-congruent recall
    - State-dependent memory
    - PTSD
    - False memories and confessions
    - Imagination inflation
    - Placebos
    - Nocebos
    - Auto association
    - Perception of gestalts
  - Consonance seeking (derives primarily from the gradient descent properties of the equations used to simulate EDP) and explains
    - Hot cognition
    - Attitude formation and change (as in the dissonance literature inspired by Heider & Festinger)
    - Stereotype usage
  - Dissonance induction/reduction explains
    - How and why all empirically supported treatments anxiety, depression, etc., work

Table 4.1 Core and Corollary Principles—cont'd

- Helps close our practice–theory gap by replacing manualized empirically supported treatments (ESTs) with empirically supported principles (ESPs)
- Helps reduce our clinical training problem by replacing over 150 ESTs with four core and eight corollary ESPs
- Helps reduce our post-doctoral training problem by replacing over 150 ESTs with four core and eight corollary ESPs

- Memory superposition (requires EDP to keep memories separate) and explains
  - Memory confusion for time, place, persons
- Prototype formation (transformation extracts averages) explains
  - Normal and abnormal schema formation
  - Self-concept
- Graceful degradation (derives from parallel distributed processing architecture and reduced slope for transfer function) explains
  - Normal cognitive aging effects
  - Resilience to traumatic brain injury
- Top-down vs. bottom-up processing (entails bidirectional network cascade) explains
  - How expectations facilitate perception
  - Interaction of emotion and cognition

[a]These three core network properties function in the same way as Piagetian assimilation/accommodation cycles do. See section on Piaget in Chapter 5 for further details.

theory and potentially a grand theory. The integration of psychology with neuroscience is a major achievement of its own. These corollary principles are roughly arranged in order of complexity.

PRINCIPLE 5: PRIMING

The *APA Concise Dictionary of Psychology* (APA, 2009) defines priming in cognitive psychology as '... the effect in which recent experience of a stimulus facilitates or inhibits later processing of the same or similar stimulus' (p. 395). Priming is a consequence of the Parallel Distributed Processing (PDP) Connectionist Neural Network (CNN) cascade and the experience-dependent plasticity (EDP) principle that enables learning and memory. Activation of stimulus microfeatures, S-nodes, cascades through the network via synapses simulated by connection weights. This process simultaneously activates EDP mechanisms that selectively modify, biologically reinforce, the synapses involved in the processing pathways taken. The modified synapses, connection weights, alter the latent constructs because the 'factor scores' associated with these latent constructs equal the sum of connection weights leading into each latent construct (factor).[1] Hence, the meaning of the latent constructs changes continuously and gradually with every processing cycle; i.e., with every network cascade. It is the interaction of the network cascade principle and the EDP mechanisms that explains how and why priming prepares preferential processing pathways through the network and consequently why priming produces cognitive effects.

Kahneman (2011b) prefaced his partial review of the priming literature with sections entitled 'The Marvels of Priming' (pp. 52–4) and 'Primes That Guide Us' (pp. 55–8). He explained the anchoring heuristic on the basis of suggestion which he further explained in terms of priming: 'The puzzle that defeated us is now solved, because the concept of suggestion is no longer obscure: suggestion is a priming effect, which selectively evokes compatible evidence' (p. 122).

It is difficult to overstate the importance of priming for psychological science and for clinical psychology. Priming comes in many forms, as we shall shortly see. Priming has such predictably strong effects that it is frequently used as a tool by experimental psychologists. A great many psychological phenomena can be described by priming. Hence, the ability of the Bio↔Psychology Network theory to explain priming substantially extends its explanatory scope.

Repetition Priming

The initial, often subliminal, stimulation automatically and unconsciously spreads, i.e., cascades, across the network (Principle 1). This processing alters the properties of the pathways taken via the experience-dependent plasticity process (Principle 2). The resulting changes biologically strengthen the connections crossed during the activation cascade, thereby increasing the likelihood that subsequent subliminal and/or supraliminal stimuli will follow this pathway through the network. Repetition priming can be demonstrated as follows. Have someone say the word 'boke' aloud rapidly with enthusiasm 15 times. Then ask them, 'What do we call the white portion of an egg?' Participants frequently respond by saying 'yolk' even

[1] The Weighted Sum Score method of computing factor scores entails multiplying the factor loading of each test item by its standardized scale score, Z-transformed value, and summing across test items. Stimulus microfeatures replace test items in our network application. The S-nodes that represent stimulus microfeatures are either on = 1 or off = 0. Because 0 times anything equals zero, and 1 times any value equals that value, the Weighted Sum Score becomes equal to the sum of the connection weights.

though that is the yellow portion of the egg. The network explanation of this phenomenon is that repeatedly saying the word 'boke' primes three of the four letters in the work 'yoke'; i.e., o, k, and e which facilitates saying yolk. Also, egg and yolk are common associates, which means that strong connections between these two words already exist.[2]

Wohldmann et al. (2007) noted that repetition priming can also be done mentally (i.e., without speaking aloud). Whereas the effects of priming are typically brief, Mitchell (2006) reported measurable consequences of repetition priming 17 years after completion of the initial experiment.

Semantic and Lexical Priming

The Deese-Roediger-McDermott (DRM: Deese, 1959; Roediger & McDermott, 1995) method of inducing **false memories** illustrates semantic priming. For example, Watson et al. (2005, p. 76) had participants pronounce the following words: '*bed, rest, awake, tired, dream, wake, snooze, blanket, doze, slumber, snore, nap, peace, yawn, drowsy*'. The investigators then asked participants to recall as many words as possible from the presented list. Predictably, a significant number of participants reported that the word 'sleep' was one of the presented words, except that it wasn't. This response occurred because the word 'sleep' was partially activated, primed, by each pronounced associate. The fact that false memories are so readily produced in the laboratory should serve to caution us all regarding their frequency in real life, and the everyday and clinical relevance of our priming principle.

Silberman et al. (2005) investigated semantic priming using a previously published artificial neural network model by Silberman et al. (2001). They episodically induced activation between two words that normally are not associated: cat and chair. This was done by overlapping activation that spread from the word cat to the word chair. Cat activates the associate dog because they are both pets. Table activates the associate chair because they are both furniture. Purposively associating dog with table episodically induced activation between cat and chair.

Conceptual Priming

Conceptual priming is a more general form of semantic priming that occurs when a word brings to mind more elaborated information via a rich associative network. For example, Voss and Paller (2006) reported that

[2] Some time ago I tried to recall the name of a character in the movie Ghost Busters. I recalled the character's name as Roy when it was Ray. My neural networks got the first and last letters correct.

seeing the face of a celebrity brought to mind, conceptually primed, preexisting biographical information about that person.

Emotional Priming

Emotional priming entails the repeated presentation of words that activate emotions. For example, Power et al. (1991) used sets of words to activate the following four basic emotions: (a) happiness, love, joy, pleasure; (b) sadness, grief, misery, depression; (c) anger, hate, jealousy, aggression; and (d) fear, panic, terror, anxiety.

Affective Priming

Lazarus (1982) articulated the generally accepted view that affect is generally considered to be post-cognitive; i.e., the result of cognition. But Zajonc (1980) marshaled evidence showing that '*preferences need no inferences*', meaning that emotions can be processed apart from and before cognition. Zajonc (1984) further advanced his argument by identifying anatomic structures capable of processing emotion independent of cognition. Priming entails a sequence of stimuli where the first stimulus influences the second. In affective priming the first stimulus activates an affect which then influences the participant's response to the following stimulus. Murphy and Zajonc (1993) published experimental evidence demonstrating the existence of affective priming. LeDoux (1986, 1994) hypothesized a dual route model of affective priming. The cortical route is thalamus → cortex → amygdale. The subcortical route is: thalamus → amygdale. Den Dulk et al. (2002) constructed a dual-route connectionist model of affective priming and concluded that a network with such an architecture could explain both fear conditioning and affective priming.

Cultural Priming

Cultural priming occurs when cultural symbols predispose a person to process subsequent stimuli differentially. For example, Hong et al. (2000) demonstrated that bicultural people responded differentially when primed with Chinese symbols than when primed with American symbols.

Idea-Motor Priming

James (1890/1950) and Carpenter (1893) identified an automatic link between thinking about an action and performing it. For example, Dijksterhuis and Bargh (2001) asked participants to imagine falling forward and noted that they exhibited unintended forward movements. Kahneman (2011b) cited a study by Barg where participants who were primed with associations about elderly persons walked slower while transitioning from one phase of the experiment to another; i.e., the 'Florida effect' (p. 53). Kahneman (2011b, p. 54) described other research conducted by Bargh and his colleagues where participants who were primed by walking at a slow rate of 30 steps per minute around a room for 5 minutes were quicker to respond to words associated with old age, such as forgetful, old, and lonely, than participants not so primed. Kahneman (2011b, p. 54) reported research based on holding a pencil in one's mouth so that the eraser and point took on a left–right or right–left orientation and forces one to smile versus holding a pencil in one's mouth with the eraser inside the mouth which forces one to frown. Persons physically primed to smile in this way rated cartoons as funnier than persons forced to frown. In another study half of the participants wearing head phones were instructed to nod their head up and down to see if that made a difference in sound quality, whereas other participants were instructed to move their head from side to side. This was done while listening to 'radio editorials'. Participants nodding up and down, primed for yes, agreed more with the editorials than participants moving their heads from side to side, primed for no. None of these participants was aware of the relationship between the priming activity and their psychological responses, indicating that priming took place unconsciously.

Kraft and Pressman (2012) acknowledged the work of James (1890/1950) and cited evidence that acting as though one feels a certain way will lead to feeling that way (see also Ben, 1972; Laird, 1974). They manipulated the facial expression of 170 participants by having them hold chopsticks in their mouths. The neutral group held the ends of two chopsticks between their teeth and maintained a natural expression. The standard-smile participants held the two chopsticks horizontally between their teeth and smiled. Participants in the Duchenne-smile group also held the two chopsticks horizontally between their teeth and were trained to activate the zygomaticus major and orbicularis oculi muscles around the eyes. The principal findings were that smiling subjects had lower heart rates during stress recovery than the neutral group did, with a slight advantage going to the Duchenne-smile group.

Active-Self Prime-to-Behavior Effects

The active-self refers to that portion of the associative network that constitutes self-knowledge and feelings. Wheeler et al. (2007) reviewed an extensive literature demonstrating the role that the self plays in generating and regulating behavior, including evidence that priming the active-self causes predictable behavior changes.

Social Cognition

A large portion of studies that provide empirical support for unconscious social cognition processing is based on priming methods (Gawronski & Payne, 2010). den Dulk et al. (2002) presented a connectionist dual-route model for affective priming. It is difficult to adequately summarize this article, which is why it should be read in its entirety.

Explaining the Anchoring Heuristic

The anchoring heuristic introduced in Chapter 3 is illustrated again here (Kahneman, 2011b, p. 123): First, anchor a person's mind with the following statement: 'Is the height of the tallest redwood more or less than 1200 feet?' Then pose the following question: 'What is your best guess about the height of the tallest redwood?' People will almost certainly give higher estimates than if you anchored their mind with the following statement: 'Is the height of the tallest redwood more or less than 180 feet?' So here we have a reliable psychological phenomenon that stands in need of explanation.

Kahneman (2011b) reported that he and his colleague Amos Tversky turned to suggestion as a plausible explanation for this phenomenon. The 1200-foot number suggested that redwood trees are extremely tall, and therefore also suggested that the correct answer is a value close to 1200 feet. Conversely, the 180-foot number suggested that a much lower number is correct. However, the deeper problem was to explain how and why suggestion works.

Then the authors learned about priming and Kahneman (2011b, p. 122) wrote: 'The puzzle that defeated us is now solved, because the concept of suggestion is no longer obscure: suggestion is a priming effect, which selectively evokes compatible evidence'. Our Principle 6 concerning Part–Whole Pattern Completion, discussed next, explains how and why compatible evidence is brought to mind. So we can now say that the anchoring heuristic is explained by suggestion, which in turn is explained by priming. Although this explanation appears to be adequate for Kahneman, other psychologists seeking an even deeper explanation can rightfully ask how priming works. The proposed Bio↔Psychology Network Theory provides this additional information.

PRINCIPLE 6: PART–WHOLE PATTERN COMPLETION

Introduction

The part–whole pattern completion principle refers to the well-replicated phenomenon that connectionist neural networks can **auto-associate** and thereby often generate a more complete or fully complete pattern from a partial stimulus through repeated processing. A more complete pattern is always generated and sometimes the complete pattern can be restored.

Part–whole pattern completion is another consequence of the network cascade and is known to psychologists by several other names. The general term, **content addressable memory**, refers to the fact that content of one kind can retrieve memory for related content; i.e., one fact can cause other facts to be recalled. For example, hearing the name of a city can cause one to recall additional details if they have ever been there. **Mood-congruent recall**, also known as **state-dependent memory**, is an alternative form of content-addressable memory that derives from the fact that emotions are encoded along with cognitions when memories form and consequently emotions constitute partial cues. People recall more positive events when happy than sad, and more negative events when sad than happy (cf., Blaney, 1986; Bower & Cohen, 1982; Isen, 1984; Matt et al., 1992; Teasdale & Fogarty, 1979; Williams et al., 1988). Memory retrieval is enhanced when retrieval mood matches the encoding mood (Eich & Macauley, 2006). Other examples of this principle come from perception, PTSD, forensics, false confessions, imagination inflation, placebos, and nocebos. All of these examples illustrate the part–whole pattern completion principle. Connectionist networks automatically process partial cues into more complete images, and/or memories, and/or stories by adding either correct or incorrect details to construct a more complete Gestalt. Network theorists refer to this process as **auto association**. Clinicians call this **confabulation** when done by brain-damaged patients.

This pattern completion principle is so powerful that Kurzweil (2012) featured it as a, if not the, primary mechanism that enables human thought in his book entitled *How to Create a Mind: The Secret of Human Thought Revealed*. Greene (2010) described the part–whole pattern completion principle without naming it as such when he discussed memory as a 'web of connections' (p. 27) and as a 'cascade of inferences' (p. 26) that constitute 'the foundations of comprehension' (p. 26). To comprehend meaning one must be able to place new experiences into the context created from past experiences. This entails pattern completion. That the act of feeling the shape of letters cut from sandpaper facilitates letter recognition is a practical application of the part–whole pattern completion principle where activation of tactile sense is connected to visual cues. Greene (2010) also reported that the hippocampus serves as a 'neural switchboard' (p. 25) that connects far-flung cortical regions that are as active when we imagine the future as when we remember the past. Hippocampal damage impairs comprehension and that impairs the ability to plan for the future, because remembered facts remain as disjointed bits of information rather than holistic concepts. Greene (2010) further noted that the part–whole pattern completion principle partially explains the false memories of eye-witnesses. For example, asking participants how fast a car was going when it smashed into another vehicle activates a crash scene Gestalt that is a composite prototype (see section on prototypes below) that includes details of all observed or vicariously experienced crashes through print and TV news media, etc. This Gestalt crash prototype includes details that may not have been present in the particular accident scene in question, but our witness is unaware of that fact and will swear that they saw some or all of the missing elements because the part–whole pattern completion principle reactivated those features in their memory of the event.

Emotions can also function as parts in an otherwise cognitive Gestalt. Sinaceur et al. (2005) demonstrated this in a study of the effects of the label 'mad cow disease' in France. They conducted a field study where individuals reduced their beef consumption after reading articles about mad cow disease, but not after reading articles about the same disease that used scientific names. Apparently, the term 'mad cow' was more effective in reactivating the visual image of a diseased cow and the implications of eating it than the scientific names did.

Perception

The part–whole pattern completion principle pertains to the ability of neural networks to construct a complete visual or auditory perception from partial information. **Perceptual completion** is the technical term that is more commonly used for pattern completion also known as **filling-in**.[3] Pessoa et al. (1998) provided a guide to perceptual completion for visual science. Lin and He (2012) reported that the visual system is intelligent because it can recover a coherent surface from an incomplete one. Perceptual completion plays a central causal role in the **Gestalt Laws** of Perceptual Organization (cf., Carlson et al., 2010, pp. 196–203). For example, the **law of closure** enables us to perceive shapes when all of the edges are not fully represented; people automatically and unconsciously fill them in. A classic example is the Kanizsa triangle illustrated in Figure 4.2. I refer to the apparent white triangle with the three black partially filled circles at its vertices. The resulting white triangle has no actual sides, no lines at all, but that does not prevent your visual system from seeing them; i.e., from

[3] http://en.wikipedia.org/wiki/Filling-in

Figure 4.2 Kanizsa triangle illustrating the Gestalt law of closure.

Figure 4.3 Panda illustrating the Gestalt law of closure. © *WWF. With permission from WWF.*

generating them. Another example of pattern completion is the black and white drawing of a panda where not all features are drawn in but the viewer fills them in when they recognize the entire figure as a panda (Figure 4.3).

Perception of the written word also entails pattern completion. Misspelled words can still be recognized as illustrated here.

> I cdnuolt blveiee that I cluod aulaclty uesdnatnrd what I was rdanieg. The phaonmneal pweor of the hmuan mnid aoccdrnig to rscheearch at Cmabrigde Uinervtisy, it deosn't mttaer in what oredr the ltteers in a word are, the olny imprmoatnt tihng is that the frist and lsat ltteer be in the rghit pclae. The rset can be a taotl mses and you can still raed it wouthit a porbelm. This is bcusea the huamn mnid deos not raed ervey lteter by istelf, bu*t the word as a wlohe. Amzanig hugh?* (p. 199).

PRINCIPLE 7: CONSONANCE AND DISSONANCE

Social Science

Heider (1958) noted and theorized that people seek consonance, also known as coherence (cf. Thagard, 1989, 2000, 2006). Festinger (1957, 1964) rephrased this motive as avoiding dissonance. These consistency theories have received extensive empirical support and constitute some of the most well-replicated findings that psychological science has to offer (cf., Abelson et al., 1968; Reed & Miller, 1998).

Connectionist network models also seek consonance. This network property derives from the mathematical properties of the learning functions used to simulate experience-dependent plasticity. This consonance-seeking property of PDP-CNN models has enabled them to accurately simulate the results of consonance experiments. That PDP-CNN models accurately do so reflects human behavior and validates the connectionist network theory that they were derived from. It also certifies these network models as important psychological research tools.

Consonance seeking derives from a combination of cognition and emotion. The study of how emotion constrains cognition has been called '**hot cognition**'. Taber and Lodge (2006) maintained that '**all reasoning is motivated**' (p. 756; emphasis added) and cited supporting literature. Kunda (1987) used the term '**motivated inference**' to refer to the self-serving interest that shapes cognitive processing. She reported the results of four studies demonstrating that people generate and evaluate causal theories in a self-serving manner. An important point here is that people's opinions can be primarily driven by emotional processing where rational processing is in the service of justifying emotionally arrived at positions. Logical inconsistency should not be expected in these cases because emotions are not logical. Rationalizations are provided to the extent that they are needed and can be different in different situations. These rationalizations can even be contradictory. Pointing out these inconsistencies is more likely to elicit an emotional response rather than an admission of illogical reasoning. One is unlikely to modify an emotionally held view with a reasoned argument. A former colleague of mine once referred to, and devalued, this form of cognition as 'bullshit and backfill'.

While people are not completely blinded by emotion, it seems clear that emotion distorts cognition in predictable ways. Consonance seeking is constrained in several ways. Kunda's (1990) seminal paper entitled *The Case for Motivated Reasoning* made the case for hot cognition as follows:

> There is considerable evidence that people are more likely to arrive at conclusions that they want to arrive at, but their ability to do so is constrained by their ability to construct seemingly reasonable justifications for these conclusions (p. 480).

> People do not seem to be at liberty to conclude whatever they want to conclude merely because they want to. Rather, I propose that people motivated to arrive at a particular conclusion attempt to be rational and to construct a

> justification of their desired conclusion that would persuade a dispassionate observer. They draw the desired conclusion only if they can muster up the evidence necessary to support it. In other words, they maintain an 'illusion of objectivity'... To this end, they search memory for those beliefs and rules that could support their desired conclusion. They may also creatively combine accessed knowledge to construct new beliefs that could logically support the desired conclusion. It is this process of memory search and belief construction that is biased by directional goals (pp. 482–3).

In the words of Simon and Garfunkle's song *The Boxer*, 'A man hears what he wants to hear and disregards the rest'. That people selectively attend to and 'cherry-pick' information from memory, archival sources, and their current environment to support previously arrived at emotionally held convictions while maintaining the illusion that they are being objective is very familiar to social and clinical psychologists. It is a primary reason why controlled research using standard research methods is required. This is the only way we can protect ourselves from this automatic unconscious psychological process. Network models formally recognize the ability of emotions to constrain, and sometimes seriously distort, cognition.

Kunda (1987) reported results of four studies demonstrating that people tend to generate evaluative causal theories in a self-serving manner. They tend to view their own attributes as predictive of positive outcomes. They are reluctant to believe theories that relate their attributes to negative outcomes. As a result, people tend to hold theories that are consistent with the belief that good things will happen to them but bad things will not. These self-serving cognitive biases are best explained as the result of motivational processes because they do not occur in the absence of such motivations.

Kunda and Thagard (1996) presented a parallel-constraint-satisfaction network theory of impression formation based on the assumptions that: (a) traits and behaviors constrain each other; and (b) emotions constrain cognition. Their connectionist model effectively simulated how stereotypes and traits modify behavior. Shultz and Lepper (1996) presented a connectionist network model that successfully simulated data from two major cognitive dissonance paradigms: insufficient justification and free choice. In several instances, the data from their model provided a better fit to the human data than did cognitive dissonance theory. Monroe and Read (2008) presented a general connectionist model of attitude structure and change based on constraint satisfaction. Empirical data supported their seven simulations.

Post-decision dissonance reduction is another well-documented social psychological phenomenon. People can be, and often are, conflicted prior to making a decision or purchase about what to do. There are almost always pros and cons regarding every decision one gets to make. However, dissonance is markedly reduced after making a decision. This phenomenon is called post-decision dissonance reduction. The TV shows House Hunters[4] and House Hunters International[5] clearly demonstrate post-decision dissonance reduction. The contestants in these shows are taken to see, inspect, and evaluate three homes from which they purchase one. The contestants specify what they like and don't like about each home before they purchase one of them. They frequently give fatal reasons for purchasing all three homes; they provide reasons why they could never live in any of the three houses they visited. Sometimes it is because the cost of the house is way over budget. Other times it is because the home is too far from work or the street is too noisy or the rooms are too small. Then the contestants make a decision, purchase one of the three properties, move in, and are interviewed 2 weeks to 6 months later. At that time the contestants say how happy they are in their new home. They point out its positive virtues and what they have done to decorate their place to make it their home. No mention is made of any fatal reason.

Thagard (1989, 2000, 2006) applied connectionist network models of coherence/constraint satisfaction to thoughts, actions, law, science, ethics, and everyday life in the form of a general theory of coherence that entails the satisfaction of multiple interacting constraints. The explanatory scope of the proposed Bio↔Psychology Network Theory is coextensive with the vast explanatory scope of Thagard's applications of coherence theory because Thagard's applications of consonance are but one of the 12 principles of the proposed Bio↔Psychology Network Theory.

Kahneman (2011b) discussed the role that coherence plays regarding our inborn tendency to see causes and intentions; a hardwired property of what he calls our System 1 which operates automatically and largely unconsciously. He summarized the following evidence published by Hassin et al. (2002). Participants were asked to read the following sentence along with many others: 'After spending a day exploring beautiful sights in the crowded streets of New York, Jane discovered that her wallet was missing' (p. 75). Participants were then given a surprise test in which the word 'pickpocket' was recalled more frequently than the word 'sights' despite the fact that only the second word was mentioned. There are several reasons why Jane's wallet could have gone missing. She could have left it in a restaurant or dropped it, but participants more frequently developed an explanation for the missing wallet that

[4] http://www.hgtv.com/house-hunters/show/index.html

[5] http://www.hgtv.com/hgtv56/videos/index.html

involved a thief. Coherence-based explanations are not necessarily correct. Here we find that our willingness to accept coherence as valid explanation is a fault, defect, or deficiency of our System 1 that we are largely unaware of, and consequently is a poor foundation upon which to construct a psychological science. Rychlak (1968, 1981a,b) contrasted procedural evidence which bases truth entirely on consistency.

Kahneman (2011b) summarized research by Heider and Simmel (1944) on the perception of apparent behavior. The following YouTube link shows a short scene that was shown to their participants. It involved a large triangle, a small triangle, and a circle moving in and around in a rectangle that has a doorway.[6] Participants explained these movements as a large triangle bullying a smaller triangle in the presence of a terrified circle. Attributing motives to inanimate objects and constructing a coherent story is what Kahneman (2011b) claims that our automatic System 1 is very good at.

A study by Leslie and Keeble (1987) on 6-month-old infants suggests that we are born being able to see **intentional causality** in the same way that we naturally see visual illusions and are subject to cognitive illusions. These tendencies are properties of our neural networks. It is noteworthy that people with Asperger's syndrome (AS) have difficulty or cannot see intentional causality; one might say that they are blind to it. It is also known that people with AS have dysfunctional mirror neuron systems, about which more will be said in connection with psychological mindedness and alexithymia in Chapter 9. But for now it is reasonable to suspect that perception of intentional causality is a property of our mirror neural network system.

Political Science

The social admonition to avoid discussing religion and politics is sound advice because these are topics that are highly infused with emotion. Political scientists have known for some time that people are not always rational when it comes to processing political information and voting. This section discusses studies that bear upon this claim.

Lord et al. (1979) demonstrated that people who hold strong opinions on complex social issues consider the evidence in a biased manner. They accept confirming evidence without question, but subject disconfirming evidence to harsh critical review. The authors presented additional information to two groups with opposing views about the death penalty. Each group used part of this information to strengthen their initial views. The

[6] http://www.youtube.com/watch?v=76p64j3H1Ng&feature=related

result was an increase in attitude polarization. Other investigators who have reported similar findings include Ditto and Lopez (1992), Huang and Price (2001), McGraw et al. (1996), Munro et al. (2002), and Sigelman and Sigelman (1984).

Lodge and Taber (2005) reported results from three hot cognition experiments based on the hypothesis that affectively charged constructs are automatically activated within a few milliseconds from exposure. They found that participants responded faster to affectively congruent than incongruent political stimuli. They found that such responses are proportional to the intensity with which attitudes are held. They concluded that emotionally controlled processing biases cognition.

Taber and Lodge (2006) began their article with the following quote from Ben Franklin 'So convenient a thing is it to be a rational creature, since it enables us to find or make a reason for everything one has a mind to' (p. 755). Then they proposed a motivated skepticism model to explain why citizens are biased information processors. They reported results from two studies concerning gun control. They found that attitudinally congruent arguments were evaluated as stronger than attitudinally incongruent arguments. They also found evidence of a confirmation bias where participants cherry-pick that part of new evidence that supports their prior beliefs. This bias strengthened their prior beliefs. Similar supportive evidence of hot cognition has been reported by Taber et al. (2001) and Morris et al. (2003).

Gains et al. (2007) stated that 40 years of research has documented the political ignorance of the American voter. Awareness of facts is not enough to determine how they will vote. Voters must make inferences such as whether or not a 1% increase in jobs shows that the incumbent's policies are working; something they cannot do. So they decide on emotional bases. Switching from a more difficult to an easier to answer issue such as the candidate's appearance is a well-known and common cognitive heuristic. These investigators addressed the question of whether partisanship influenced inferences. Using panel data collected during the Iraq war, the authors demonstrated that Democrats and Republicans used the same facts to reach quite different conclusions that were consistent with their prior beliefs, such as whether or not weapons of mass destruction existed, were moved, or were destroyed. It is a fundamental principle of social psychology that people favor in-groups over out-groups. Parks et al. (2013) discussed the willingness to accept suboptimal outcomes for one's in-group in order to achieve maximum advantage over out-groups as an example of emotionally based reasoning.

Kim et al. (2010) published a Bayesian computational model of political attitudes and beliefs. This learning model integrated cognitive and affective mechanisms. It was constructed using connectionist ACT-R (Adaptive Character of Thought-Rational) cognitive architecture (Anderson et al., 2004). Affective mechanisms were integrated with this cognitive model. The authors presented evidence that their computer model accurately simulated the attitudes of real people.

A recent review by Isbell (2012) summarized evidence showing 'How feelings drive political preferences and behavior'. The following material is heavily based on her article. She noted that reviews by Brader et al. (2011), Groenendyk (2011), and Isbell et al. (2006) demonstrated that emotions are fundamental determinants of political attitudes and actions. Isbell and Wyer (1999) and Ottati and Isbell (1996) have shown that affective experiences unrelated to politics can also influence how citizens view political candidates and how they evaluate risk and proposed policies.

Principle 5: Priming, discussed earlier in this chapter, is such a reliable, robust, and effective psychological principle that it can be used to manipulate independent variables in social psychological experiments. Isbell (2012) reviewed several studies where priming was used to activate the emotions of fear/anxiety and anger. These manipulations predictably altered the participant's perceptions and attitudes. For example, Lerner et al. (2003) and Nabi (2003) demonstrated that participants primed with anger perceived a lower risk of future terrorism than participants primed with fear. Anger-primed participants were less inclined to approve additional security measures than participants primed with fear. Participants primed with anger were more favorable to harsh penalties for drunk driving than participants primed with fear. MacKuen et al. (2011) reported that participants primed with anger tend to decrease attention to new information and rely on partisanship. Parker and Isbell (2010) reported that participants primed with fear are more open to new information compared to participants primed with anger. Valentino et al. (2008) found that worried citizens are more informed than angry citizens.

Other political science studies could have been reviewed here, but the results would be similar to those already presented. We can safely conclude that political opinions, like religious opinions, are heavily influenced by emotion. Reason is mainly used to justify emotionally held convictions. Reason and emotion cohere to achieve consonant beliefs. Disturbing this consonance produces dissonance, an aversive state, that will be reduced and consonance restored as soon as possible.

It is not always obvious when a discussion is emotionally based and when it is not. Discussions can begin with the appearance that both sides are open to evidence. Disputes over evidence constitute a red flag because evidence is often cherry-picked to support one's conclusions. Sometimes evidence is fabricated, such as a claim made during September 2013 that the Affordable Health Care Act was not working when it had not yet begun. Sometimes the core emotional issue is not immediately apparent, as when debate over the merits of affordable health care were in fact motivated by concerns over the role that government should play in the lives of people. For some the issue of affordable health care became the moral equivalent of abortion. Here we transition from an intellectual discussion to an emotional faith-based argument.

Personal Choice as Constraint Satisfaction

A limiting factor of all cognitive theories, including the Theory of Reasoned Action (TRA; Fishbein, & Ajzen, 1975; Ajzen, 1991; Fishbein, 2000), is that they do not provide mechanism information regarding how personal decisions are made or how decisions once made influence behavior. Decisions appear to be the product of 'free will', but that is not an acceptable scientific explanation. Orr et al. (2013) re-conceptualized intention formation and change in terms of a dynamic constraint satisfaction mechanism where prior beliefs interact with present social context to generate decisions. They provided a connectionist mechanism that makes personal decision-making understandable in natural science terms. This form of explanation has been recommended by Read et al. (1997). It has been used by Conrey and Smith (2007) and Monroe and Read (2008) to explain attitudes. Each element relevant to the decision process is represented by one or more processing nodes. If two nodes need to be active at the same time then their connection weight becomes positive. If one node needs to be active and another node needs to be inactive then their connection weight becomes negative. Connection weights of exactly zero probably never exist. Relevant features of a specific problem are represented by activating the nodes associated with these features. The system then seeks to satisfy all constraints as far as it possibly can using what are essentially multivariate statistical methods. The final solution constitutes the networks decision.[7] This approach to decision-making

[7] While multivariate statistics are completely rational, using them to maximize both rational and emotional constraints can result in irrational as well as rational behavior. This makes connectionist models good psychological models.

has proved successful in cognitive and social psychology (Read & Miller, 1998; Thomas & McClelland, 2008).

At least three conceptual advantages flow from this reconsideration. First, it re-conceptualizes intention as a dynamic rather than a static state that arises from a highly non-linear constraint satisfaction process involving internal and external factors. Intention formation results from the interaction of current social situations with past learning. Second, learning modifies the constraints. This means that intention formation is influenced by new learning. This new learning can derive from a social change, such as when a child moves from elementary to middle to high school to college to adult life. These and related factors enable the constraint satisfaction model to effectively model developmental processes. Third, the effects of the past constitute separate constraints from the effects of direct social influence.

PRINCIPLE 8: DISSONANCE INDUCTION AND REDUCTION

Principle 8 extends Principle 7. Artificial neural networks are trained, not programmed. These training methods help us understand how psychological interventions retrain real neural networks resulting in long-term benefits. I begin by describing how artificial neural networks are trained and retrained, and then describe how this generalizes to psychological interventions.

Artificial Neural Networks

Please recall the generic three-layer PDP-CNN model presented as Figure 3.1 in Chapter 3. The lines connecting processing nodes, artificial neurons, represent excitatory and inhibitory, positive and negative, connection weights that simulate artificial synapses. The activation level of each simulated synapse is set to a small random value to simulate the untrained 'newborn' state. Let's say that we want to teach the network to make a specific response to a particular stimulus. Training begins by presenting that stimulus to the network by turning on only those microfeatures, S-nodes, that characterize the stimulus. Computations such as those illustrated in Figure 3.6 will activate, turn on, some of the O-nodes and leave off, or turn off, other O-nodes. This process propagates to the R-nodes, turning some on and others off. The trainer then compares the on/off sequence across the R-nodes, where 1 = on and 0 = off, to see how close the network came to giving the correct response. The number of 1s that should be 0s and the number of 0s that should be 1s defines the **Hamming distance** between the computed and desired responses. Responding is completely correct when the Hamming distance is reduced to zero. Investigators frequently use the **back propagation**[8] algorithm to simulate experience-dependent plasticity mechanisms. This algorithm reduces Hamming distance by first changing connection weights between the R- and O-nodes and then between the O- and S-nodes; i.e., backwards relative to the normal processing flow. Mathematical properties of the back propagation algorithm ensure that the Hamming distance becomes smaller with each training trial, thereby systematically reducing the difference between the desired and computed response. One can also say that the computed response converges on the desired response as training continues. Training frequently succeeds but sometimes does not depending upon specific training features that lie beyond the scope of this section.

Retraining proceeds in the same way with the following exception. What are now considered to be the 'initial' connection weights are the 'final' connection weights from previous training. A new response is now required. The Hamming distance between the present and desired response code across the R-nodes constitutes the errors that will be back propagated. The resulting changes in the weights connecting processing nodes will reduce the Hamming distance over training trials until asymptotic performance is reached; until the network has done all that it can do to learn the new response.

Real Neural Networks

I will be brief here as I provide more details in Chapter 11 where I discuss the clinical applications of the corollary network principles presented. Clients come to therapy with previously established patterns of thinking and behaving. These features are mediated by their neural networks. Clients often ask for help in changing how they think and behave. Other times therapists recommend such changes. Dissonance is created when the client attempts to think and/or behave differently as requested by their therapist. This dissonance activates experience-dependent plasticity mechanisms that modify synaptic connections in ways that gradually ease this dissonance by increasing consonance. I suggest that this mechanism explains why the unified protocol described by Allen et al. (2008) and Barlow et al. (2011) for treating emotional disorders including anxiety and depression works (see Chapter 11). I further

[8] While the back propagation algorithm is not biologically plausible as far as we know, it is accepted because it models the systematic synaptic modifications made by real experience-dependent mechanisms. Models simulate rather than duplicate real events. For example, models of supernova do not actually explode.

suggest that it explains why all effective treatments work, regardless of the theoretical orientation from which they were developed.

PRINCIPLE 9: MEMORY SUPERPOSITION

Unlike computers that place memories in unique physical locations, people and PDP-CNN models store multiple memories in the same neural networks. Bechtel and Abrahamsen (1991, pp. 70–81) presented a simple numerical example to illustrate this process. I now review this example. Hebb (1949, p. 62) stated 'When the axon of cell A is near enough to excite a cell B and repeatedly or persistently takes part in firing it, some growth process or metabolic change takes place in one or both cells such that A's efficiency, as one of the cells firing B is increased' (Levine, 1991, p. 17.). This translates into Equation 4.1 where: Wij = synaptic strength between Neuron i and j, η = learning rate, Ni = activation level of Neuron i, and Nj = activation level of Neuron j. We will now form a paired associate memory between the first stimulus vector = 1, 1, −1, −1 and the first response vector = 1, −1, −1, 1 using the Hebbian learning rule where the learning rate η is set to 1/n where n = number of input units; i.e., η = ¼ = 0.25. Doing this results in the special case of one-trial learning[9] that simplifies this example because multiple processing cycles are avoided. Memories are formed by multiplying the row and column marginal entries times the learning rate. The results are in Table 4.2. Now we add a second memory where the second stimulus vector = 1, −1, −1, 1 is associated with the second response vector of 1, 1, −1, −1. Again we multiply the row and column marginal entries times the learning rate and add the resulting product to the existing cell entry. The results are in Table 4.3. Notice that some of the cell entries, simulated synaptic states, have grown more active, as indicated by the 0.5 entries whereas others have grown weaker, become more inhibited, as indicated by the 0 and −0.5 entries.

$$w_{ij}(t+1) = w_{ij}(t) + \eta N_i N_j \qquad 4.1$$

Now let's check to see if superimposing the second memory on top of the first memory destroyed the first memory, as would be the case with the von Neumann traditional computer model or if the first memory was preserved as is the case in neural network models. Table 4.4 illustrates the retrieval process. We present the first stimulus vector to the stimulus input nodes and compute as follows: Multiply the marginal row entries, the stimulus vector

[9] One ostensible criticism of connectionism is that they only learn in a gradual way. This example clearly contradicts this supposed limitation.

Table 4.2 Sample Formation of a Memory Formation where Stimulus Vector 1, 1, −1, −1 and Response Vector 1, −1, −1, 1 are Associated

Stimulus input units			Response output units			
			E	**F**	**G**	**H**
			1	**−1**	**−1**	**1**
	A	**1**	0.25	−0.25	−0.25	0.25
	B	**1**	0.25	−0.25	−0.25	0.25
	C	**−1**	−0.25	0.25	0.25	−0.25
	D	**−1**	−0.25	0.25	0.25	−0.25

Table 4.3 Sample Formation of a Second Memory Formation where Stimulus Vector 1, −1, −1, 1 and Second Response Vector 1, 1, −1, −1 are Associated within the Same Neural Networks. The Bidirectional Associative Memory (BAM) Model Discussed by Tryon (1999) Provides an Example of how Multiple Memories can be Stored in the Same Place and Correctly Retrieved Without Over-Writing One Another

Stimulus input units			Response output units			
			E	**F**	**G**	**H**
			1	**1**	**-1**	**-1**
	A	**1**	0.5	0	−0.5	0
	B	**−1**	0	−0.5	0	0.5
	C	**−1**	−0.5	0	0.5	0
	D	**1**	0	0.5	0	−0.5

Table 4.4 Recall Test to see if Memory for the First Association of Stimulus Vector 1, 1, −1, −1 can Accurately Recall the First Response Vector 1, −1, −1, 1

Stimulus input units			Response output units			
			E	**F**	**G**	**H**
	A	**1**	0.5	0	−0.5	0
	B	**1**	0	−0.5	0	0.5
	C	**−1**	−0.5	0	0.5	0
	D	**−1**	0	0.5	0	−0.5
Response output units E–H			**1**	**−1**	**−1**	**1**

values, by each of the four cells in the first column and add the resulting four products to get the first column result. This is what the network recalls for the first position of the response vector. Repeat this process with the second, third, and fourth columns to recall the remaining entries for the response vector. Notice that the first memory has been fully recalled without error. Alternatively stated, we used the same nodes to store both memories without destructively over-writing the first memory with the second one. Instead, we constructively superimposed the second memory on top of the first memory. This was done by creating a new pattern of synaptic activations that were consistent with both memories. This example provides remarkable insight into how the brain can possibly store multiple memories.

The number of memories that can be constructively stored is directly proportional to the number of nodes in the network, which for the brain is in the billions with trillions of synapses. The number of memories that can be constructively stored is also a function of how unrelated, different, they are. The two 'memories' stored in the above example are statistically orthogonal, independent, of each other. Such memories can be stored and retrieved with little, if any, interference. Memories blend and are less accurately recalled as they become related just as is the case with humans, which is another reason why connectionist models make such good psychological models. Principle 2 maintains that processing changes the network connections. It should be readily apparent that modifying the memory matrix values in Table 4.3 would necessarily return modified responses; i.e., would cause memory errors.

PRINCIPLE 10: PROTOTYPE FORMATION

Prototype formation is another important consequence of the PDP-CNN cascade and the transformation principle. The *APA Concise Dictionary of Psychology* (2009) defines a prototype as 'in the formation of concepts, the best or average exemplar of a category. For example, the prototypical bird is some kind of mental average of all the different kinds of birds of which a person has knowledge or with which a person has experience' (p. 402). Exemplars of a prototype are stimuli that possess some of the defining features of the prototype. Exemplars can vary from exhibiting just one defining feature up to exhibiting one less than all of the defining features.

Posner and Keele (1968) conducted one of the earliest experimental studies of psychological prototype formation. It remains especially informative. They began with four 'prototypical' stimuli: a triangle, the letters M and F, and a random dot pattern as illustrated in Figure 4.4. Then they created exemplars by distorting each prototype by a small, medium, or large amount. They showed participants only the exemplars. Participants had to categorize each exemplar as a triangle, M, F, or random dot pattern. Training continued until participants reached an accuracy criterion. Finally, participants were shown the prototypical stimuli. They responded faster and with fewer errors to the **never before seen** prototypes than they did to any of the training exemplars. This finding provides clear evidence of prototype formation.

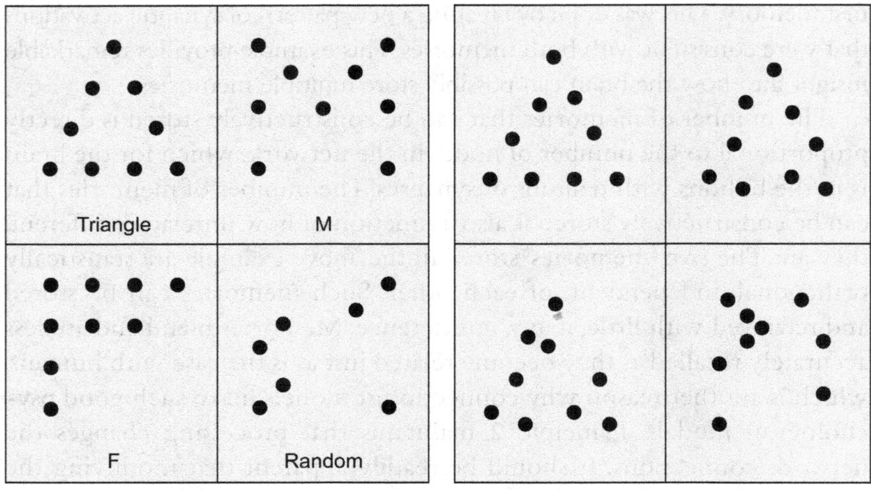

Figure 4.4 Prototypical and test stimuli used by Posner and Keel (1968).

PDP-CNN models form prototypes by extracting averages from repeated presentations of stimuli over time. Each stimulus represents the prototype plus deviations. The prototype gets biologically reinforced over trials by experience-dependent plasticity mechanisms, whereas the deviations vary and tend to cancel one another. This mechanism explains why a stronger response occurred to the never before presented prototypical stimulus than to any of the training stimuli.

Prototypes are important to cognitive psychology because they facilitate, speed up, processing. Winkielman et al. (2006) presented evidence to demonstrate that prototypes facilitate emotional and cognitive processing. Prototypes function like stereotypes (e.g., Cin et al., 2009).

PRINCIPLE 11: GRACEFUL DEGRADATION

Graceful degradation is a direct consequence of parallel distributed representation used in connectionist models. Unlike computers that store bits of information in only one specific location, parallel distributed processing (PDP) spreads representation across multiple physical sites. Hence, damage to a particular location results in a smaller performance decrement, if any, in a PDP network than in a computer network. PDP representation makes real biological networks resistant to trauma and the ravages of aging. It is particularly relevant to psychologists who work in rehabilitation settings.

PRINCIPLE 12: TOP-DOWN AND BOTTOM-UP PROCESSING

The brain consists of multiple interconnected neural networks. The human connectome project (http://www.humanconnectomeproject.org/) is a massive scientific effort to map the major neural networks in the human brain.

Bottom-Up Processing

Bottom-up processing occurs over connections that begin in the periphery, typically with sensory organs, and proceed 'up' through ever more complex ganglia to brain networks that are composed of layers of neurons where higher layers extract more abstract and complex information as per our factor analytic explanation (Principle 3) and combines information from sight, sound, touch, smell, and taste into holistic experience. We understand relatively little about the mechanisms that create a holistic impression of the massive and highly specific sensory information. In general we know that different neural network layers perform different functions, such as edge detection and position location in the visual system with greater integration occurring at higher brain centers. Visual illusions occur because of properties of our neural networks. As interesting as visual illusions are, the more psychologically interesting phenomenon derives from top-down processing and especially from the interaction of top-down and bottom-up processing.

Top-Down Processing

Top-down processing occurs over connections that begin in the higher brain centers, frequently frontal networks, and proceed 'down' in the form of expectations based on prior experience. Processing occurs simultaneously in both directions in order to speed conclusions; i.e., reduce response time. Fractions of a second can mean the difference between life and death in the natural world.

Internal Working Models

Eagleman (2011, pp. 48–51) described top-down processing as what **internal working models**[10] do. These models are built up from years of experience. They generate expectations. These expectations are combined

[10] Internal working models were hypothesized by psychoanalytic theorists in conjunction with their discussions of attachment (http://en.wikipedia.org/wiki/Attachment_theory). Cognitive psychologists refer to these cognitive models as schemas.

with sensory data that are processed from the bottom up. The result is sensory experience modulated by expectations generated by these internal working models. Eagleman (2011, p. 45) used the term **anchored perceptions** to refer to this phenomenon. One way to experimentally demonstrate the validity of this claim is to unanchor perception. Placing persons in pitch-dark solitary confinement is one way to do this. Another way is to put participants into a sensory deprivation chamber (http://en.wikipedia.org/wiki/Sensory_deprivation). While short-term sensory deprivation can be described as relaxing and conducive to meditation, long-term sessions can produce hallucinations.[11] Eagleman (2011, p. 45) reported that 10% of people who lose vision report visual hallucinations. Another example of unanchored perception comes from people suffering from Anton-Babinsky syndrome due to a stroke. They are cortically blind but claim they can see (http://en.wikipedia.org/wiki/Anton%E2%80%93Babinski_syndrome). Another example of unanchored perception concerns people suffering from lost vision due to Charles Bonnet syndrome (http://en.wikipedia.org/wiki/Charles_Bonnet_syndrome). They experience hallucinations. They may see flowers, birds, other people, and buildings that they know are not real. These experiences are known as **pseudohallucinations** (http://en.wikipedia.org/wiki/Pseudohallucination). The clinical importance of this understanding is that hallucinations are in a sense the normal expression of our internal working models. What makes them abnormal is when they are no longer adequately modulated, anchored, by sensory experience in people whose senses seem to be working just fine.

The thalamus is the anatomical site where the outputs from internal working models mix with sensory experience. The cortex sends expectations down to the thalamus which compares them with sensory information coming up to it. The thalamus reports discrepancies back to the cortex (Eagleman, 2011, p. 49). Consciousness is activated by these discrepancies and results in adjustments to the internal working model.

Prospection

Prospection refers to the process of generating, computing, what might possibly happen in the future. Seligman et al. (2013) stipulated that 'Prospection (Gilbert & Wilson, 2007), the representation of possible futures, is a ubiquitous feature of the human mind' (p. 119). Prospection entails a series of conditionals of the form 'If X, then Y'. Prospection is not teleology

[11] Long-term sensory deprivation can also produce bizarre thoughts, anxiety, and depression.

because these conditionals depend upon, are limited by, past experience. Hence, prospections are always prefactual in that they concern what might occur.

Prospection can lead to imagination inflation. Imagination inflation refers to the finding that imagining an event which never happened can increase confidence that it actually occurred (http://en.wikipedia.org/wiki/Imagination_inflation). Carroll (1978) initially reported that imagining a future event increased participants' confidence that the event would actually occur. Sherman et al. (1985) reported that easier-to-imagine outcomes produced greater imagination inflation. See Chapter 11 for additional details.

Prospections can be upward or downward. Upward prospections concern optimistic outcomes whereas downward prospections concern pessimistic outcomes. Prospections tend to generate appropriate emotion. Normal people generally generate more upward than downward prospections and therefore have a positive outlook. Depressed and anxious people tend to generate more downward than upward prospections and therefore have a negative outlook. Catastrophizing consists of extreme downward prospections. This process can work in reverse. Negative affect elicits downward prospections whereas positive affect elicits upward prospections.

Interaction

Frank et al. (2009) characterized the bottom-up processing system as automatic, intuitive, emotional, and implicit and the top-down system as controlled, deliberative, and explicit. They documented that both systems operate simultaneously and recommended computational models to better characterize how these two systems interact. This distinction is similar to the dual Systems 1 and 2 discussed earlier. This interaction principle emphasizes that the network cascade process simultaneously flows in opposite directions.

Salzman and Fusi (2010) presented evidence that the anatomical interconnections between the amygdala and the prefrontal cortex result in the simultaneous operation of these systems, thus seriously undercutting the CBT theoretical premise that cognition causes emotion and never the reverse. The ability of network models to inform psychologists regarding how cognition and emotion interact and reciprocally influence one another is a major contribution to the science and practice of psychology. The network perspective replaces simplistic either/or views on the generation of emotions with a more accurate and comprehensive understanding that is consistent with neuroscience evidence. I now further illustrate that networks interact.

Hearing/Listening

The real psychological magic concerns the interaction of top-down and bottom-up processing. For example, listening differs from hearing in that **hearing** is a bottom-up process that begins with the ear and ends in the brain whereas **listening** is a top-down process that begins in the brain. We best hear what we attend to. The top-down process of attention focuses, regulates, controls bottom-up processing in the form of what we hear. Consider conversations in a crowded room. We ignore the many other conversations in order to hear the one we are having.

Emotion

Psychologists have long debated whether emotions have their origins in perception (e.g., LeDoux, 2000; Phelps, 2006) or in cognition as Beck (1972), Ellis (1994) and others have argued. A network perspective renders this theoretical schism a false dichotomy. Ochsner et al. (2009) used fMRI to discover that emotion generation involves both top-down and bottom-up processes. Network processing flows simultaneously, in parallel, in both directions. Bottom-up processing begins in sensory organs, such as the eye and ear, and terminates in the visual and auditory cortices, among other places. Top-down processing begins in higher brain centers as expectations that influence perception constrained by attention. I have much more to say about emotion in Chapter 5.

Placebos and Nocebos

Placebos are expectations of benefit whereas nocebos are expectations of harm. Placebos and nocebos entail both bottom-up and top-down processing. The bottom-up unconscious cascade automatically generates the transformations that we experience as cognition and affect. Conscious top-down processing moderates bottom-up processing thereby enabling psychological interventions to augment or diminish placebo and/or nocebo effects. Hallucinations are pathological examples of how expectations change perception when they are no longer properly modulated by bottom-up processing.

Kirsch et al. (2008) reported that placebos are about 80% as effective as antidepressant medications are and 50% as effective as analgesic medications are. Kirsch and Sapirstein (1998) estimated that placebos were 75% as effective as antidepressive medications. They also reported a correlation of $r = 0.90$ between the placebo response and the drug response. Similar findings have been reported by Andrews (2001), Kahn et al. (2000), and Walsh et al.

(2002). These and other data demonstrate that placebos produce real observable effects. But how do they work? What mechanism information is involved? Some information is available at http://en.wikipedia.org/wiki/Placebo#Mechanism_of_the_effect. I now review standard explanations before presenting a preferred network explanation.

Expectation Explanation

Stewart-Williams and Podd (2004) reported that expectancy theory and classical conditioning are the two main 'mechanisms' thought to mediate the placebo effect. We have already seen that classical conditioning is the functional result of experience-dependent plasticity and not a causal mechanism. Expectations are putative cognitive mechanisms, but we learned in Chapter 1 that psychological mechanisms are metaphors. They are not real because there is no psychological substrate for them to operate upon. As a result Steward-Williams and Podd (2004) did not, because they could not, provide any mechanism information for how cognitive mechanisms generate placebo effects. Like all other psychological explanations we have encountered, or will encounter, cognitive theories are devoid of causal mechanism information despite appearing to offer such by using the word 'mechanism' in their title or text.

Neuroscience Explanation

Various biological explanations of the placebo effect have been provided. For example, Benedetti et al. (2005) identified neurobiological networks associated with the placebo effect but did not explain how those networks produced psychological effects. This is a general problem with all available biological explanations. **Identifying mediating structures does not explain how they work**. Benedetti et al. (2005) reported that release of endogenous opioids and modification of the neurotransmitter serotonin, along with effects on the pituitary and adrenal glands that mimic the analgesic effects of the drug Sumatriptan, are involved in placebo effects but again did not explain how these biological facts produced, explained, psychological effects. They used a 10% neurotransmitter activation criterion, as measured by a corresponding reduction in neurotransmitter binding potential, to identify placebo response in the rostral (pregenual) region of the anterior cingulate, left dorsolateral prefrontal cortex, right insular cortex, and the left nucleus accumbens, but again did not explain how these biological facts produced psychological effects.

Kong et al. (2006) used a creative sham acupuncture needle method to study placebo analgesia. They reported significantly greater pre-minus-post subjective pain rating decreases on the placebo-treated side compared with the control side. Functional magnetic resonance imaging revealed significant differences in the bilateral rostral anterior cingulate cortex, lateral prefrontal cortex, right anterior insula, supramarginal gyrus, and left inferior parietal lobule, but the authors again failed to explain how these biological facts produced psychological effects.

Mayberg et al. (2002) studied responses of hospitalized men with unipolar depression given either fluoxetine or placebo using PET imaging and reported that the placebo response was associated with metabolic increases in the prefrontal, anterior cingulate, premotor parietal, posterior insula, and posterior cingulate and metabolic decreases in the subgenual cingulate, parahippocampus, and thalamus. But again, the authors did not explain how these biological facts produced, explained, psychological effects.

Benedetti et al. (2007) described experimental evidence demonstrating that negative verbal suggestions, nocebos, can induce anticipatory anxiety concerning impending pain that can activate cholecystokinin (CCK), which facilitates pain transmission. They also reported that Parkinson's disease can be adversely affected by negative suggestions, but again did not explain how these biological facts produced psychological effects. Colloca and Benedetti (2007) provided a more general review of this material. Wagner et al. (2004) reported increased activity in the prefrontal cortex that mediates cognition and decreased activity in the thalamus, insula, and anterior cingulated cortex that mediate pain sensitivity. But again, neither author explained how these biological facts produce psychological effects.

These studies should be sufficient to make the point that identifying neural networks that mediate psychological phenomena does not constitute an explanation of **how** these networks produce psychological effects. Identifying the neural networks that mediate psychological phenomena does not constitute an explanation of how those psychological phenomena are created. Identifying the neural networks that mediate psychological phenomena is an important first step, but the crucial second step requires mechanism information that addresses how psychology emerges from biology and this requires some form of network theory. Connectionism is the best source of this information that is currently available.

Network Explanation

Missing mechanism information concerning how biology is transformed into psychology is provided by **Principle 3: Transformation** discussed in Chapter 3. Neural activation spreads across layers of neurons via synapses. This process was shown to strongly resemble factor analysis where augmenting the salience of some stimulus microfeatures and diminishing the salience of others gives rise to, generates, latent constructs that have been interpreted as psychological constructs since Spearman introduced this process over a century ago in 1904. The relevant mechanism information is provided in Chapter 3 and therefore will only be illustrated here. Stimulus microfeatures such as being in a doctor's office, seeing a physician wearing a white coat and receiving treatment of some kind are transformed into latent constructs, cognitions, and expectations, by roughly the same process that is involved in factor analysis. These activations cascade across layers of synapses and are transformed at each step into higher-order latent constructs of benefit in the case of placebos, and harm in the case of nocebos.

The factor analytic computational mechanism for understanding how the brain transforms stimuli into concepts is both simple and elegant. It directly addresses the otherwise difficult problem of how a layered network system can construct complex cognitive constructs. Complete acceptance of this process for the past hundred years has placed this explanation in full view for all to see, but it was not until connectionism proposed that cognition could be done with network models that an answer to how the brain forms cognitions could be understood.

Placebos are expectations of benefit whereas nocebos are expectations of harm. These expectations form because of suggestions that beneficial/harmful consequences will occur. Kahneman (2011b) noted that priming causes suggestion: 'The puzzle that defeated us is now solved, because the concept of suggestion is no long longer obscure: suggestion is a priming effect, which selectively evokes compatible evidence' (p. 122).

Hypnosis

I, like many people, once dismissed hypnosis as a carnival trick because there seemed to be no way to prove that the hypnotized person was not faking their responses. The desire to please and not embarrass oneself, especially in public, could account for what appeared to be increased pain tolerance and other purported hypnotic effects. A study by Raz et al. (2002) completely changed my mind. First, they replicated the well-known Stroop effect where participants take significantly longer to name the color of ink that words are printed in than to read the color word names. Cohen et al. (1990) provided a detailed network explanation regarding why this effect occurs. Then the participants were hypnotized and told that the words they would see were written in a foreign language that they did not understand. The result was that the Stroop effect disappeared!

Hypnosis can be understood to result from suggestion and, as we have previously seen, priming causes suggestion by selectively activating memory for supporting evidence (Kahneman, 2011b, p. 122). We now have a proximal causal mechanism information for hypnosis that is supported by empirical evidence.

NETWORK THEORY

My formal presentation of the Bio↔Psychology Network Theory is now complete. It consists of an explanatory core of four network principles and eight corollary network principles. The first four drive the remaining eight network principles. I consider all of these principles to be inherent properties of real neural networks that also characterize most if not all PDP-CNN models. I consider PDP-CNN models to be psychologically informative because the brain is constructed of interacting neural networks and therefore some form of network theory is ultimately required to explain how psychology emerges from biology; how mind emerges from brain. I do not claim completeness. Additional biological and psychological information regarding each of these principles will surely become available through future research. I fully expect that these details will elaborate rather than contradict any of the network principles that I have proposed. Additional network principles may exist that I have yet to discover. None of this should dampen our enthusiasm for what has been achieved to date.

CONCLUSIONS

This chapter discussed eight network principles that are corollary to the four network principles that constitute the explanatory nucleus. These corollary principles considerably expand the explanatory scope of the proposed Bio↔Psychology Network Theory. More corollary principles may be discovered in future, but these eight are sufficient to bear upon many psychological phenomena. This ends the formal presentation of the proposed Bio↔Psychology Network Theory. The next chapter provides a cognitive neuroscience perspective on emotion. This is followed by a chapter that discusses seminal connectionist models of psychopathology. It is followed by a chapter that evaluates the merits of the proposed Bio↔Psychology Network Theory.

Emotion

Contents

Mennin and Farach (2007) reported that 'Clinical psychology has historically underplayed the importance of emotions in conceptualizing and treating adult psychopathology' (p. 329). This is unfortunate given that emotion and cognition jointly determine behavior. A comprehensive psychological theory must be able to explain how cognition and emotion interact to produce behavior. This is the goal behind the American Psychological Association accreditation requirement that students in doctoral clinical psychology programs must receive training in the cognitive and affective bases of behavior. Most programs seem to meet this objective by requiring separate courses in cognition and emotion instead of a single course that considers the interaction of cognition and emotion as this book does. APA accreditation standards also require that students be educated regarding the biological bases of behavior. It would be best if training regarding how cognition and affect interact was integrated into training regarding the biological bases of behavior as this book does.

Cognitive Neuroscience and Psychotherapy
http://dx.doi.org/10.1016/B978-0-12-420071-5.00005-3

The failure to organize psychological science around principles has left psychologists providing interpretations rather than explanations (see Chapter 1). Psychologists who preferred similar interpretations formed schools and professional associations dedicated to perpetuating those interpretations. The psychodynamic perspective maintains that psychological disorders are caused by unconscious emotions and unacceptable cognitions that are automatically repressed. Unconscious processing is thought to generate symptoms that persist until psychoanalytic psychotherapy or psychoanalysis relieved these symptoms through insight into their nature and function; i.e., by making these unconscious processes conscious.

The cognitive-behavioral perspective simplified this complex view of psychopathology in two important ways. First, unconscious processing was denied by formally excluding it from consideration. One prominent remnant was Beck's concept of automatic thoughts that just seem to pop into one's mind. No explanation was given regarding what caused these thoughts or where they came from. Their presence was simply accepted and treatment was designed to dispute them. Second, genuine true emotions were said to require cognition. Because emotions were understood to be caused by cognitions, it followed that emotional disorders could be effectively and entirely treated by cognitive therapies. This cognitive perspective persisted for a couple of decades until evidence of the limited effectiveness of cognitive therapies for disorders of emotion regulation revealed that this perspective and therapeutic approach was flawed.

Contemporary understanding of emotional disorders is that they entail emotional dysregulation due to deficits in emotion regulation complicated by cognitive distortions (Barlow et al., 2011, p. 15). Newer therapies that emphasize emotional regulation, such as Dialectical Behavior Therapy (DBT), require a more comprehensive theoretical orientation that formally addresses (a) unconscious processing; (b) subcortical emotion generation; (c) cognitive processes; (d) behavioral principles; (e) neuroscience; and (f) pharmacologic findings. The proposed Bio↔Psychology Network Theory provides the required theoretical basis to integrate these perspectives. But first, let us consider the past so that we can build upon it and avoid making the same or similar mistakes.

HISTORICAL OVERVIEW

Plutchik (1980) identified four major approaches to the study of emotion. (a) Darwin (1872/1965) took an evolutionary approach where he applied principles of variation and selection to expressive behavior as well as anatomy, resulting in unlearned emotional expressions. (b) William James (1884; 1890) and Carl Lange (1834–1900) independently argued that a stimulus first activates the sensory cortex which then in some unspecified way activates somatic and motor responses that we feel and interpret as emotion. For example, we run and then experience fear. This theory altered the common-sense folk theory that emotions preceded feelings and behavior; we are afraid and then run. James did not explain how stimuli activated bodily responses. This is known as the James-Lange theory because Carl Lange, a European contemporary of James, provided a similar explanation. (c) Cannon (1929), a physiologist, presented five lines of evidence that essentially falsified James's behavior before emotion theory. (1) Severing the spinal cord and vagus nerves in dogs to block visceral feedback did not block emotional reactions. (2) Different emotions of fear, rage, fever, exposure to cold and asphyxia all produced similar physiological reactions such as increased heart rate, blood sugar, adrenaline, pupil size, and erection of body hair. (3) The viscera can be cut, torn, or crushed in unanesthetized humans without producing discomfort or emotions. (4) Emotional reactions occur more rapidly than viscera can provide feedback. (5) Inducing visceral changes does not produce emotional reactions. Cannon therefore provided a return to the common-sense view that emotions precede behavior. This view is now known as the Cannon-Bard theory because Philip Bard, a contemporary of Cannon's, proposed a similar view. (d) Freud (1895a/1936) described a theory of emotion in addition to presenting a theory of illness. He also suggested that the repression of strong emotions could give rise to illness.

Two additional schools of thought have been developed. (e) Behaviorists proposed theories of emotion. Watson (1919, 1924, 1929) understood emotion as an inherited holistic bodily reaction with emphasis on the visceral and glandular systems. Emotion for Watson was an unconditional stimulus. Skinner (1938, 1953, 1975) suggested that emotions predispose organisms to behave in characteristic ways. (f) Cognitive psychologists proposed other theories of emotion to which we now turn.

COGNITIVE PERSPECTIVE

Cognitive behavior therapies are among the most, if not the most, widely practiced empirically supported treatments that are currently available. They all share an informal cognitive theory that has assigned emotion to a subordinate role relative to cognition. Put succinctly, cognitions cause emotions. Hence, the way to change emotions is to alter cognitions. Blatt and Bers

(1993) correctly criticized this approach for being too cognitive. Barlow (1988) remarked that emotion is not much discussed in psychology, let alone clinical psychology, given its heavy cognitive emphasis. Barlow (2000) reported that research has since justified thinking about anxiety disorders from the perspective of emotion theory. Haynos and Fruzzetti (2011) criticized the now traditional CBT treatment of anorexia nervosa as neglecting emotions. They argued that emotion dysregulation is the underlying problem and that it should be addressed as directly as emotion dysregulation is treated in patients who have borderline personality disorder. Safer and Chen (2011) and Merwin (2011) agree with this view. Nevertheless, the cognitive perspective remains popular despite having been repeatedly falsified by the neuroscience evidence reviewed below. Such persistence demonstrates the resilience of theories in the presence of disconfirming evidence.

Schachter and Singer (1962)[1] and Schachter (1964) proposed that physiological arousal preceded cognitive attribution which then caused an emotional experience to occur. Alternately stated, emotion results from cognitively processing physiological arousal. In short, one had to interpret what their non-specific autonomic arousal meant to them psychologically. Plutchik (1980, pp. 36–8) and Reisenzein (1983) reported that empirical evidence does not support this view.

Zajonc (1980) provided several lines of evidence in support of his thesis that preferences (affect) need no inferences (cognition). First, he presented the following phenomenological argument: we have little control over our feelings. When activated, feelings can be very difficult to deactivate. While we may question our cognitions, we almost never question our feelings. Second, he presented behavioral data showing that repetitive subliminal exposure, too brief for conscious identification and processing, was sufficient to increase liking (Kunst-Wilson & Zajonc, 1980). The authors concluded that cognition was not necessary for affect. Third, an evolutionary argument was presented. Lower forms of life have emotions mediated by the limbic system. It seems unlikely that adding a cortex would obviate the role of the limbic system in generating affect. I find this argument to be compelling and sufficient to settle this matter.

Appraisal theories of emotion (Moors, 2010) addressed the subliminal processing criticism by maintaining that cognition could occur unconsciously. However, the other lines of negative evidence remain intact. Purely cognitive connectionist models have proliferated primarily, in my view,

[1] http://en.wikipedia.org/wiki/Two-factor_theory_of_emotion

because cognitions are easier to represent than are emotions. This fact also explains why we have so little understanding of how cognition influences emotion and how emotion influences cognition. A proposed solution to this problem is presented below.

Network theories maintain that emotions emerge from the associative/semantic networks that mediate emotional schemas (Moors, 2010). Network activation is considered to be a form of cognition. Lewis (2005) proposed a dynamic systems model of emotion that is a close cousin to the connectionist network models featured in this book. A review of neuropsychological research by Duncan and Barrett (2007) demonstrated that affect can function as cognition and cognition can function as affect, thus demonstrating that **the brain does not distinguish between cognition and affect**. It is difficult to overestimate the importance of this view. Storbeck and Clore (2007) indicated that cognition and affect are highly interdependent in ways that falsify the classic view that cognition and affect are processed differently. These views are highly consistent with and supportive of the proposed parallel processing perspective.

Levine and Leven (1992) considered a possible role for motivation and emotion in their network simulation of motivation, emotion, and goal direction. Hestenes (1992) considered emotion in the context of their network simulation of manic-depressive illness. Leven (1992) considered emotion as part of their network simulation of learned helplessness. Grossberg and Levine (1987) and Grossberg and Schmajuk (1987) considered affect in the context of classical conditioning in their network simulations. But none of these authors provided a specific method of encoding emotion in connectionist network models. One of the main objectives of this chapter is to present ways for representing emotions in connectionist simulations in order to make these models more comprehensive and realistic.

SUBCORTICAL BRAIN CENTERS

Jaak Panksepp[2] reviewed the large literature concerning the ability of subcortical structures to generate emotion in his 1998 book entitled *Affective Neuroscience: The Foundations of Human and Animal Emotions.* He updated this material in Panksepp (2005, 2008, 2011). He uses a method called Localized Electrical Stimulations of Specific Neural Systems (LESSNS) to

[2] http://www.bgsu.edu/departments/nmb/page26785.html

study emotions that are generated by subcortical neural networks. He also injects various drugs directly into the brain, thus bypassing the blood–brain barrier. Panksepp (2011) summarized his principle findings as follows:

> The relevant lines of evidence are as follows: 1) It is easy to elicit powerful unconditioned emotional responses using localized electrical stimulation of the brain (ESB); these effects are concentrated in ancient subcortical brain regions. Seven types of emotional arousals have been described; using a special capitalized nomenclature for such primary process emotional systems, they are SEEKING, RAGE, FEAR, LUST, CARE, PANIC/GRIEF and PLAY. 2) These brain circuits are situated in homologous subcortical brain regions in all vertebrates tested. Thus, if one activates FEAR arousal circuits in rats, cats or primates, all exhibit similar fear responses. 3) All primary-process emotional-instinctual urges, even ones as complex as social PLAY, remain intact after radical neo-decortication early in life; thus, the neocortex is not essential for the generation of primary-process emotionality. 4) Using diverse measures, one can demonstrate that animals like and dislike ESB of brain regions that evoke unconditioned instinctual emotional behaviors: Such ESBs can serve as 'rewards' and 'punishments' in diverse approach and escape/avoidance learning tasks. 5) Comparable ESB of human brains yield comparable affective experiences. Thus, robust evidence indicates that raw primary-process (i.e., instinctual, unconditioned) emotional behaviors and feelings emanate from homologous brain functions in all mammals (see Appendix S1), which are regulated by higher brain regions. Such findings suggest nested-hierarchies of BrainMind affective processing, with primal emotional functions being foundational for secondary-process learning and memory mechanisms, which interface with tertiary-process cognitive-thoughtful functions of the BrainMind (p.1).

Panksepp (2005) also concluded that emotional feelings are contained within the evolved emotional action apparatus of the extended trans-diencephalic, limbic subcortical emotional action systems of the brain and are shared homologously by all mammalian species.

Other findings also indicate that emotions have subcortical origins. For example social bonding is mediated by endogenous opioids (opium-like) and oxytocin that facilitate feelings of trust and social sensitivity. Opioids facilitate feelings of security, confidence, and dominance. Social bonding is naturally addictive. People with poor social bonds are consequently attracted to opiate drugs. Gregariousness to playfulness are mediated by endogenous opioids. The pleasure of touch is partly opioid-mediated. The power of companionate love is mediated by endogenous opioids and oxytocin. Separation distress is painful. LESSNS-induced separation distress can be reduced by injecting oxytocin or prolactin into brain ventricles. Early attachment failures predict depression. Opiates exert strong antidepressive effects. Figure 5 in Panksepp

(2011) lists the neurotransmitters that enable specified neural networks to produce particular emotions. These findings provide considerable understanding of emotional problems. Inadequate social bonds and secure early attachments diminish endogenous opioid release by social and tactile means, thus predisposing the person to depression and drug addiction.

People receiving LESSNS report emotional feelings that are commensurate with animal emotional behaviors elicited from homologous brain areas. Panksepp (2005) therefore considers the emotional experiences of animals to be a genuine form of consciousness that we humans share. I think that people with pets already know that their animal companions have genuine emotions.

LeDoux (1996) wrote a book for the general public entitled *The Emotional Brain: The Mysterious Underpinnings of Emotional Life.* He succinctly summarized the contents of this book as follows:

> *The Emotional Brain* provides an overview of my ideas about how emotions come from the brain. It is not meant as an all-encompassing survey of every aspect of how the brain produces emotions. It focuses on those issues that have interested me most, namely, issues about how the brain detects and responds to emotionally arousing stimuli, how emotional learning occurs and emotional memories are formed and **how our conscious emotional feelings emerge from unconscious processes** (p. 9, bold emphasis added).

Notice that LeDoux takes the position that conscious emotional feelings emerge from unconscious processes.

Eagleman's (2011) book entitled *Incognito: The Secret Lives of the Brain* presents neuroscience evidence that demonstrates that unconscious processes prominently influence how we think, feel, and behave. The gist of this book is entailed in the following quote:

> Brains are in the business of gathering information and steering behavior appropriately. It doesn't matter whether consciousness is involved in the decision making. And most of the time, it's not. Whether we're talking about dilated eyes, jealousy, attraction, the love of fatty foods, or the great idea you had last week, consciousness is the smallest player in the operations of the brain. Our brains run mostly on autopilot, and the conscious mind has little access to the giant and mysterious factory that runs below *it* (p. 5).

Plutchik (1980, pp. 50–67) reviewed several brain-based theories of emotion. Modern neuroscience has greatly improved our understanding of the biological mechanisms that mediate emotion. Kalat (2004, pp. 355–63) presented a more recent review of this literature. He identified the **limbic system** as a critical brain area for the regulation of affect (p. 361). The

amygdala plays an especially important role in fear. Bear et al. (2007) discussed brain mechanisms of emotion (pp. 563–83). They provided additional details regarding the limbic system and the **Papez circuit** which is thought to be critically important to the experience of emotion. They further clarified the meditational role played by the amygdale regarding learned fear. Animals can be taught to fear an auditory signal by pairing it with shock. The tone is processed by the auditory cortex and then by the basolateral nuclei of the amygdale. The central nucleus of the amygdale activates the hypothalamus, thus producing autonomic responses. It also activates the periaqueductal gray matter in the brain stem, thus producing a behavioral response. The amygdala also activates the cerebral cortex and that gives rise to our emotional experience.

The amygdala is also involved in aggression related to maintaining position in a social hierarchy. Lesioning the amygdala of a dominant monkey resulted in it losing its alpha, top male, status. Lesioning the amygdala of the next monkey to take over the alpha position in the colony social hierarchy also caused it to lose that position by becoming more submissive. I find this experimental design to be especially compelling.

Functional magnetic resonance imaging (fMRI) is an important tool for investigating the neuroscience of emotion. A fundamental question is whether emotions exist as basic categories or as dimensions. On the categorical side, Carroll Izard (2007) considered the nature of emotions, what activates them, and their functions as schemas. Barrett (2006) reviewed empirical evidence that is inconsistent with the existence of basic emotions that are determined by nature and explored the scientific implications of moving beyond a natural-kind view of emotion. Barrett and Wagner (2006) briefly summarized the fMRI evidence including meta-analytic reviews. They found some evidence that fear, sadness, and disgust demonstrated reasonable consistency and brain specificity, but noted complications. For example, the amygdala responds to reward as well as threat and therefore seems to compute affective significance in general. There is even less evidence for the dimensional position. The best support for the dimensional view comes from findings that many interactive brain centers seem to be involved in memory and therefore are probably also involved in emotion.

The sum total of the empirical evidence presented above completely contradicts cognitive theories that maintain that consciousness is required to have genuine emotions and/or that emotions essentially originate in the cortex. This evidence also seems to make moot the philosophical arguments that Ellis (1994) and others used to support this cognitive science perspective. This evidence fully supports the neural network perspective provided in this book.

MORE ABOUT UNCONSCIOUS EMOTION

Emotion has been connected with consciousness ever since William James defined it that way in 1884. Of course, defining emotion as part of consciousness does not make it so, even if such a definition might make the study of emotion more convenient. Assigning properties to things by definition is very risky because there is but one way to get it right and a nearly unlimited number of ways to get it wrong. Determining truth by definition is not how science is supposed to work. Inquiry should be left open rather than restricted by a preexisting axiomatic definition that protects conclusions from being falsified by empirical facts. We necessarily reason from definitions, axioms, and assumptions not to them. Hence, defining emotion as the result of conscious processes precludes accepting contrary findings even if they are correct. Evidence of unconscious emotions will consequently be dismissed on the basis that it is not emotional because it doesn't conform to the definition of emotion that requires the presence of consciousness to be considered real and valid. Saying that something is so does not actually make it so. Limiting inquiry by definition has little to recommend it. Granting axiomatic protection through definition constitutes faith-based science, which is a form of religion.

Clore (1994) incorrectly argued that consciousness is a necessary although not sufficient condition for an emotional state to exist. Freud (1950) also viewed emotion as a conscious experience, even though he believed that the causes of most, but not necessarily all, emotions were unconscious. This is a curious definitional mixture. For Freud, emotions begin unconsciously and thus one can say emotions have unconscious causes. This is correct, as Panksepp (2005, 2008, 2011) has shown that emotions originate in subcortical structures that are homologous in humans and animals. That emotions can end up in consciousness indicates that consciousness may modify emotions, but does not prove that consciousness generates them. Put otherwise, subcortical structures associated with emotions are the first not the last structures to activate when emotions occur.

The priming effects discussed in Chapter 3 clearly document that cognitive processing can occur automatically and outside of awareness. Winkielman and Berridge (2004) demonstrated that emotional processing can also occur automatically and therefore unconsciously. They demonstrated that unfelt emotions could be strong enough to alter behavior. Olds (1994) is a psychoanalyst who argued that connectionism provides a better conceptual model for psychoanalysis than the classic hydraulic model does. He pointed out that Freud based his writings on nineteenth and early twentieth century science, whereas connectionism is based on twenty-first century brain science and is therefore more relevant. Connectionism spares psychoanalysis from dualism with ego as homunculus. Of special relevance to this section is that connectionist models can be used to process information unconsciously as well as consciously. There is nothing special or qualitatively distinct about unconscious processing. Activation spreads across the network whether we are aware of it or not. The associative nature of networks lends renewed importance to the notion of free association to explore the properties of these networks. A major advantage of connectionism that Olds does not address is that its models can be constrained to where they make predictions that can be falsified, whereas some psychoanalytic propositions cannot be tested scientifically.

In Chapter 4 we reviewed extensive evidence that conclusively demonstrated the existence of unconscious processing. I especially emphasize the evidence presented in the previous section on Subcortical Brain Centers by Panksepp (2005, 2008, 2011). Direct brain stimulation of subcortical areas clearly demonstrates that activating these structures is sufficient to produce emotions in humans and animals. That anencephalic human infants who lack their entire cortex respond with positive facial expressions to sugar and with negative facial expressions of disgust to bitter substances (Steiner, 1973) clearly demonstrates that higher brain centers are not required for emotional expression. The unconscious-centric orientation of the proposed Bio↔Psychology Network Theory and its strong support for unconscious emotion processing constitutes a major source of agreement and synthesis with many psychodynamic theories. It is also consistent with Beck's position that automatic thoughts exist, and our generalization that automatic feelings also exist. Psychoanalysis and psychodynamic psychotherapy are concerned with how emotions influence cognitions. One might therefore say that psychoanalysis and psychodynamic psychotherapy are concerned with **motivated reasoning**. The unconscious-centric position taken by the proposed Bio↔Psychology Network Theory is fully compatible and consistent with psychodynamic theory that reasoning is always emotionally motivated to some degree. This view readily resonates with clinical psychologists and the general public, and it explains why psychodynamic theory remains appealing to the general population as well as book authors and movie producers.

EMOTION AND FACIAL EXPRESSIONS

It has long been understood that facial expressions are sensitive indicators of emotions. Woodworth (1938) developed what he considered to be a six-point **linear** rating scale for categorizing faces (see Table 5.1). Schlosberg (1952) used this scale to test pictures developed by Frois-Wittmann (1930). He noted that pictures whose sort modes fell into category 6 were sometimes classified as category 5 or 1. Schlosberg (1952) concluded 'This could only mean that the scale was **recurrent**, rather than linear' (p. 229, bold emphasis added), meaning that the six scale points formed a circle rather than a line. Schlosberg revealed that an unpublished honors thesis[3] by Miss Marjory L. Brown found evidence that the Ruckmick (1921) faces also formed a recurrent scale. A circular structure carries the following implications. A neutral point should lie at the center of the circle. Two dimensions should be sufficient in which to plot all faces because a circle is a two-dimensional object. Prior research conducted by Schlosberg (1941) indicated that the relevant two dimensions are Pleasantness (P)–Unpleasantness (U) and Attention (A)–Rejection (R). The first dimension needs no further clarification, but the second dimension does. Attention implies surprise. Rejection implies contempt and disgust. Each of the two dimensions was expressed as a difference score. The vertical dimension equaled P–U. The horizontal dimension equaled A–R. Each dimension was measured on a 9-point scale with Pleasantness and Attention each assigned a value of 9, and with Unpleasantness and Rejection each assigned a value of 1. These facts are illustrated in Figure 5.1.

Schlosberg (1952) conducted four experiments using the same methods. Participants first rated all 72 pictures regarding Pleasantness–Unpleasantness on a 9-point scale. Then they rated the same 72 pictures over again regarding Attention–Rejection on a 9-point scale. It appears that ratings were

Table 5.1 Woodworth's Six-Point Facial Rating System

Category	Facial Content
1	Love, happiness, mirth
2	Surprise
3	Fear, suffering
4	Anger, determination
5	Disgust
6	Contempt

From Woodworth, R. S. (1938). *Experimental psychology*. New York: Henry Holt.

[3] This shows the importance of undergraduate research to psychological science.

averaged across all pictures and then P–U and A–R differences were calculated for each picture and used to plot each picture in a circular space. The point 5,5 is the neutral midpoint and corresponds to the center of the circle. The results are presented in Figure 5.1. Picture 10 is circled to illustrate the plotting procedure. It had coordinates of P–U = 7 and A–R = 7. The circumference is divided into six equal parts. Woodworth's 6-point rating scale values are associated with each of the six sections as indicated in Figure 5.1. A line from the center of the circle through the plotted point that intersects the circle's circumference translates the plotted point into its corresponding Woodworth scale value. For example, the circled Picture 10 translated into

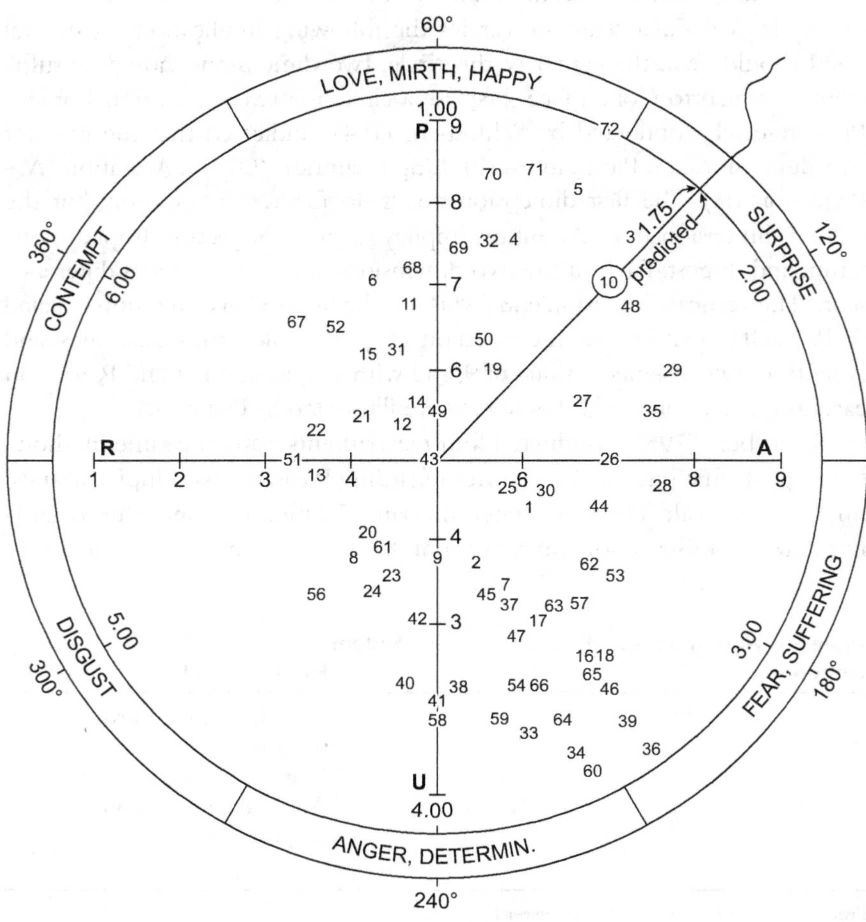

Figure 5.1 Picture 10 from Schlosberg (1952).

a Woodworth value of 1.75, which corresponded closely to its independently determined Woodworth value of 1.65. Schlosberg (1952) reported that the correlations between such ratings for all four experiments were 0.76, 0.94, 0.92, and 0.96. These data strongly indicate that Woodworth's 6-point scale is recurrent, circular, and not linear. Schlosberg (1954) added a third dimension that transformed his circle into a solid. This third dimension involved level of activation.

Öhman (2002) presented evidence to support the view that the facial muscles of humans are genetically prepared to register emotions and that human observers are genetically prepared to automatically and unconsciously react to viewing human faces by activating pertinent neural networks when viewing expressive faces. In particular, viewing angry faces automatically and unconsciously activates the amygdale. Whalen et al. (1998) reviewed the empirical evidence in this regard. Morris et al. (1998) explained that this automatic activation could bypass the cortex via the superior colliculus of the midbrain and the right pulvinar of the thalamus.

CIRCUMPLEX STRUCTURE

The circumplex[4] concept stemmed from early psychometric work by Guttman (1954) and work on personality theory by Leary (1957),[5] Block (1957), Becker and Krug (1964), and Wiggins (1973, 1979). Plutchik and Conte (1997) provide a comprehensive review of circumplex models of personality and emotions. They also related the circumplex model to clinical issues such as diagnosis and interpersonal problems; sometimes referred to as the interpersonal circumplex.

The primary psychometric properties of the circumplex are as follows. Two points that occupy the same position anywhere on the circumference of the circumplex (circle); i.e., that are separated by zero degrees, are perfectly positively correlated; i.e., $r = +1.0$. Two points near one another on the circumference of the circumplex are highly positively correlated. This positive correlation decreases as the points move further away from one another. Two points that are at right angles to one another on the circumplex; i.e., are separated by 90 degrees, are orthogonal, unrelated to one another. The correlation between two such points is $r = 0$. Two points on the circumference that are exactly opposite one another, are separated by

[4] http://en.wikipedia.org/wiki/Interpersonal_Circumplex

[5] Leary (1957) developed his personality measures based on the interpersonal theory of Sullivan (1953).

180 degrees, are perfectly negatively correlated; i.e., $r = -1.0$. This negative correlation decreases as the points move further away from one another.

There are a couple of different ways to obtain the x–y coordinates for a circumplex. One way entails the relationship between correlation and angles in the unit circle, as illustrated by Figure 5.2. This is called the unit circle because its radius x equals 1. Fixing the radius x at 1 establishes a relationship between the angle theta and the vertical projection from the point where x meets the circle down to the horizontal axis because the cosine of theta equals r/x. When theta equals zero, as it does when x is pointing east along the horizontal axis, r = x, r/x = 1 and the cosine of 1 correctly corresponds to an angle of zero degrees. Now imagine that the horizontal axis, diameter, is divided into 10 parts where 0 corresponds to the left end lying at the center of the circle and 1 lays at the right end of the horizontal axis where it meets the circle. To find the angle that corresponds to a correlation of say r = 0.7, we rotate x counterclockwise until the vertical line dropping down from where x meets the circle points to 0.7 on the horizontal axis. The cosine of this angle still equals r/x and now r = 0.7 and x = 1 so cos (θ) = 0.7. Using a calculator to compute the inverse of this cosine, we find that θ = 45.57 degrees. Therefore two items that correlate +0.70 must be placed 45.57 degrees apart from one another on the circumplex. Any point on the circle can be used as the reference point against which all other points are

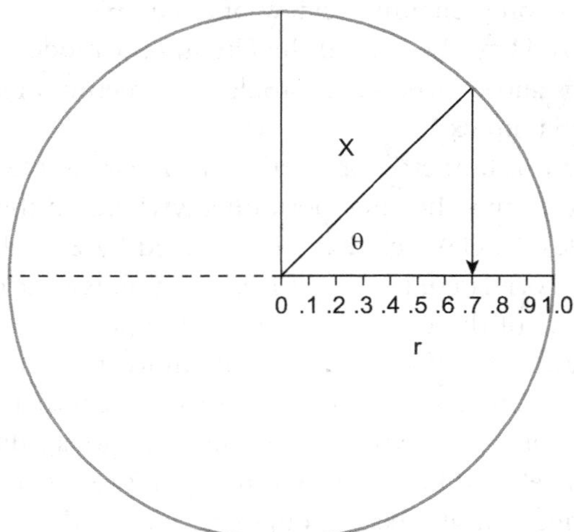

Figure 5.2 The unit circle has a radius where x = 1. The vertical projection down to the horizontal axis labeled r associates the angle theta with its corresponding correlation coefficient. In this case theta equals 45.57 degrees and cos(theta) = 0.7.

plotted. Items that are statistically independent of each other, i.e., are orthogonal, are separated by 90 degrees because the projection of x onto r is then at zero. The cosine of 90 degrees is also zero. To plot negative correlations one must extend the horizontal axis in Figure 5.2 from the middle to the left side of the figure as illustrated by the dotted line and mark it like a ruler with negative numbers starting from 0 at the center out to −1 where the dotted line meets the circle. To plot r = −0.4 rotate x past 90 degrees until the vertical line starting where x meets the circle points down to −0.4 which makes r = −0.4 and cos (θ) = r/x = −0.4 for which θ = 113.58 degrees. Hence, two items correlated r = −0.4 must be separated by 113.58 degrees on the circumplex. Two items that are perfectly negatively correlated at r = −1.0 lie on opposite sides of the circle and are separated by 180 degrees where x = r = 1 = cosine (180). Points separated by more than 180 degrees become less negatively related to one another until the x segment returns to zero when θ = 270 degrees. Further rotation results in a more positive association.

A second way to plot items on a circle is to factor analyze the intercorrelation matrix among stimuli, extract the first two factors, and use the corresponding factor loadings as x and y coordinates. Block (1957) used the semantic differential method developed by Osgood et al. (1957) to obtain correlation coefficients among 15 emotions by 40 male and 48 female college students. They factor analyzed these correlations and used loadings on the first two factors to plot stimuli on a circumplex. It is noteworthy that using Block's rotated factor loadings as coordinates, the graphed points populated the entire circumference of the circle.

BASIC EMOTIONS

Plutchik (2001) noted that as many as 90 different definitions of the word emotion have been provided. Plutchik (2003) presented 21 definitions of emotion (pp. 18–19). Even this number of definitions severely complicates the scientific study of emotion. One way that philosophers and investigators have coped with this situation is to concentrate on what might be called basic emotions.

Plutchik (1980, pp. 138–51) discussed the concept of basic emotions. Hindu philosophers identified eight basic emotions that they considered to characterize the natural state of mankind and are translated as: (1) sexual passion, love, or delight; (2) amusement, laughter, or humor; (3) sorrow; (4) anger; (5) fear or terror; (6) perseverance; (7) disgust; and (8) amazement (Plutchik, 2003, p. 60; Schweder & Hoidt, 2002).

Baruch Spinoza (1632–1677) identified three basic emotions: (1) joy; (2) sorrow; and (3) desire. All other emotions were considered to be combinations of these. Rene Descartes (1596–1650) identified the following six passions: (1) love; (2) hatred; (3) desire; (4) joy; (5) sadness; and (6) admiration. Thomas Hobbes (1588–1679) proposed the following seven simple passions: (1) appetite; (2) desire; (3) love; (4) aversion; (5) hate; (6) joy; and (7) grief. Darwin (1872/1965) proposed the following seven emotional clusters that could be found in both animals and humans: (1) low spirits, anxiety, grief, dejection, despair; (2) high spirits, joy, love, tender feelings, devotion; (3) reflection, meditation, ill-temper, sulkiness, determination; (4) hatred, anger; (5) disdain, contempt, disgust, guilt, pride, helplessness, patience, affirmation, negation; (6) surprise, astonishment, fear, horror; and (7) self-attention, shame, shyness, modesty, blushing.

Izard (1971) identified eight basic emotions as follows: (1) interest; (2) joy; (3) surprise; (4) distress; (5) disgust; (6) anger; (7) shame; and (8) fear. Cattell (1957, p. 112) factor analyzed emotional words and reported the following ten factors: (1) sex-lust; (2) fear; (3) loneliness; (4) pity, succorance; (5) curiosity; (6) pride; (7) sensuous, comfort; (8) despair; (9) sleepiness; and (10) anger. Plutchik (2003) reported that Etude identified the following 11 basic emotions: (1) fear; (2) anger; (3) sadness; (4) joy; (5) interest; (6) surprise; (7) distress; (8) shame; (9) shyness; (10) disgust; and (11) guilt. Notice that all lists include fear, anger, and sadness. Most lists also include joy, love, and surprise. There is no way to generate a definitive list of basic emotions. One must be guided by the utility of such decisions.

THE CIRCUMPLEX EMOTION COLOR WHEEL AND SOLID

McDougall (1921) observed an important similarity between colors and emotions. He noted that while we experience many different colors that can vary by small gradations, all of them can be created by blending primary colors in various ways. He hypothesized that emotions could be understood the same way; i.e., that the many emotions we experience can be created by combining basic emotions in various ways. A corollary implication of this hypothesis is that since colors can be organized into a circular wheel structure then perhaps emotions can also be organized in this way. Colors can be organized in the form of a wheel because our blue-yellow and red-green receptors and associated visual pathways and processing centers enable a two-dimensional representation in the form of a circumplex. Notice the similarity here to Schlosberg's (1941) use of the Pleasantness (P)–Unpleasantness (U) and Attention (A)–Rejection (R) dimensions, and his use of P–U and A–R as two dimensions for plotting his results.

Plutchik (1997) observed that the words used to describe **emotions** overlap substantially with the words used to describe **personality**. Emotions refer to **states** whereas personality refers to **traits**, yet words such as gloomy, resentful, and calm can refer to emotions or personality characteristics, which is why emotions can be represented the same way that personality items can. This is a strong theoretical reason for plotting personality traits as a circumplex. Plutchik and Conte (1997) reviewed much of this literature. The so-called Big Five personality factors have no theoretical basis. Their main claim is that investigators typically find five factors, although some find as few as three and others find as many as 16. No one has ever explained why there should be exactly five personality factors.

Conte and Plutchik (1981) reviewed literature showing that the majority of personality variance is carried by the first two factors, even though the five-factor model is favored today. Hence, the first two factors can be used to plot personality traits (Leary, 1957; Plutchik & Conte, 1997; Wiggins, 1979) as well as emotions. Plutchik (1997) provided an overview of efforts to construct a circumplex model of emotions.

Conte and Plutchik (1981) plotted emotions in a circumplex. They used three independent judges to select 223 trait terms from established lists and scaled them using two methods. Direct Similarity Scaling was the first method used. Six independent judges rated each of the 233 trait terms against each of three reference terms on an 11-point bipolar scale. The ratings could range from −5 through 0 to +5. A similarity rating of zero implied a correlation of zero. A similarity rating of +5 implied a correlation of r = +1.0 and a similarity rating of −5 implied a correlation of r = −1.0. Three reference words were taken from the work of Schaefer and Plutchik (1966). The three reference terms were taken to be approximately 120 degrees apart such that they formed an equilateral triangle relative to the circumplex. This maximized the differences among the three reference terms. Ratings were averaged and then transformed into angular placements using the cosine method described above.[6] The three reference terms were plotted as follows. One reference term was placed at zero degrees on the circumplex. The other two terms were placed at 120 degrees and 240 degrees to reconstruct the triangle noted in the work of Schaefer and Plutchik (1966). The standard deviation of the averaged angular position was taken as an index of

[6] Implied, but not stated, is that the average ratings were first transformed into correlations and then into angles based on their cosine equivalents.

consistency. A rating consistency analysis eliminated 52 terms, leaving 171 terms. This method guaranteed that stimuli would fall on a circle; i.e., would be equidistant from the center of the circumplex, but did not guarantee that the stimuli would populate the entire circumference of the circumplex. Figure 5.3 presents the results obtained by this Direct Similarity Scaling method. Notice that the circumference of the circle is almost fully populated; i.e., contains few gaps. Scaling was repeated on a sample of these trait items using three different reference terms. A correlation of $r = 0.98$ was reported between the angular placements for the two reference sets. It could be that these results were due to the scaling method used. To check on this

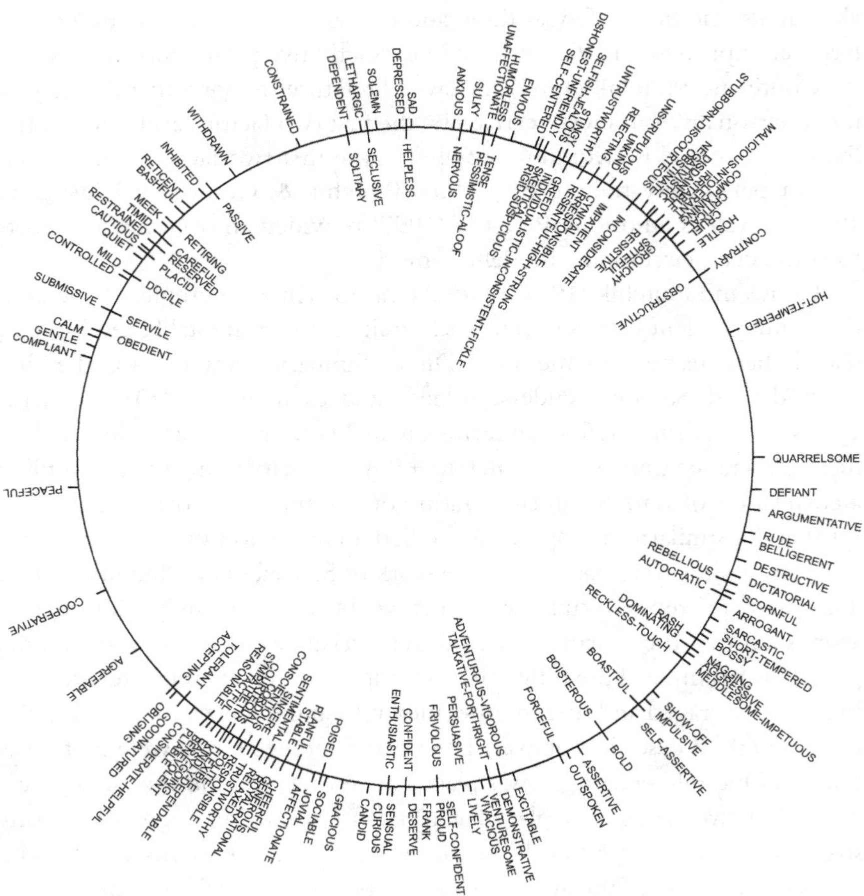

Figure 5.3 Angular placements of 171 personality trait terms derived from the method of direct similarity scaling.

possibility, the authors selected 40 of the 171 terms across all four quadrants that were most consistently rated and had ten new judges scale them on 30 seven-point semantic differential scales. A 40 × 40 intercorrelation matrix was computed and factor analyzed. The loadings on the first two factors were used as coordinates. This method did not guarantee either a circular shape or that plotted points would be equidistant from the center of the circumplex. The results of this second method are presented in Figure 5.4. Again, we notice that the 40 trait terms populate the entire circumference of the circumplex. We further notice that the points are mostly equidistant from the center of the circumplex. This is because the first two factors accounted for most of the variance. Put otherwise, circumplex models fit

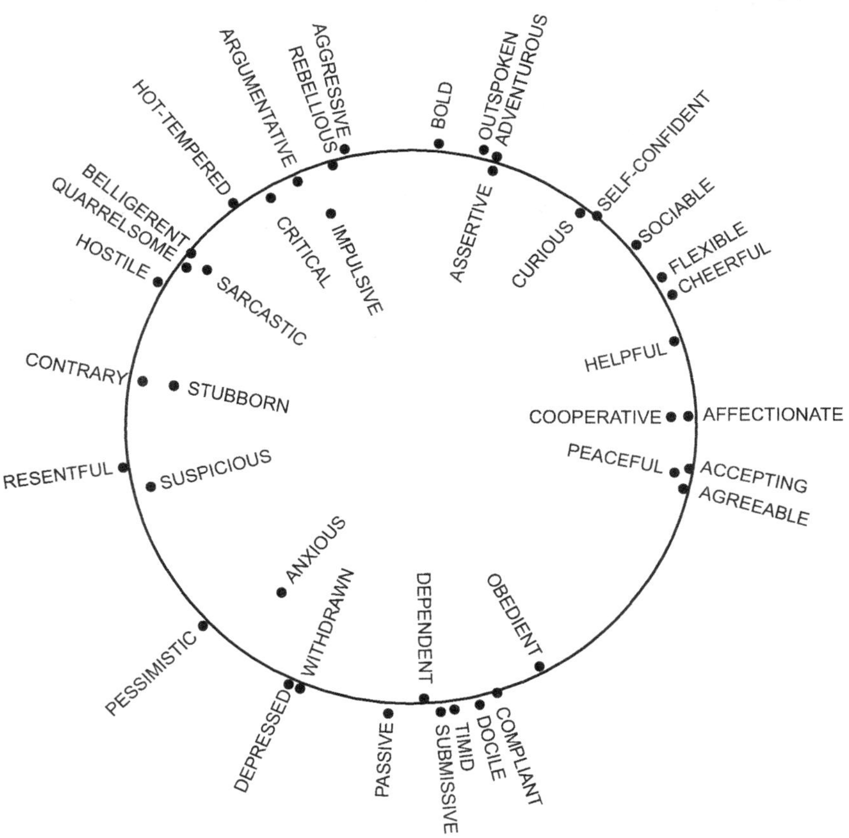

Figure 5.4 Angular placements of 40 personality terms using the semantic differential method.

correlation matrices that are mainly composed of two factors. The combination of circular distribution and nearly constant radii constitute convincing evidence that a circumplex model fits the data very well.

Fisher (1997) asked 141 college students to rate their moods on a five-point rating scale ranging from 0 (does not describe my mood) to 5 (definitely describes my mood) regarding 33 emotion words upon awakening and just before going to bed at night for 15 days. Only 17 of these words were taken from Plutchik's list of 171 personality traits. Averages were computed over the 30 ratings. Plutchik's (2003) Figure 4.2, reproduced here as Figure 5.5, compares the circular placement of these data compared to those published by Conte and Plutchik (1981). Notice that the stimuli are plotted in essentially the same positions around the circumplex. It is extraordinarily rare in psychology to find reports of replications, let alone results that are so well replicated.

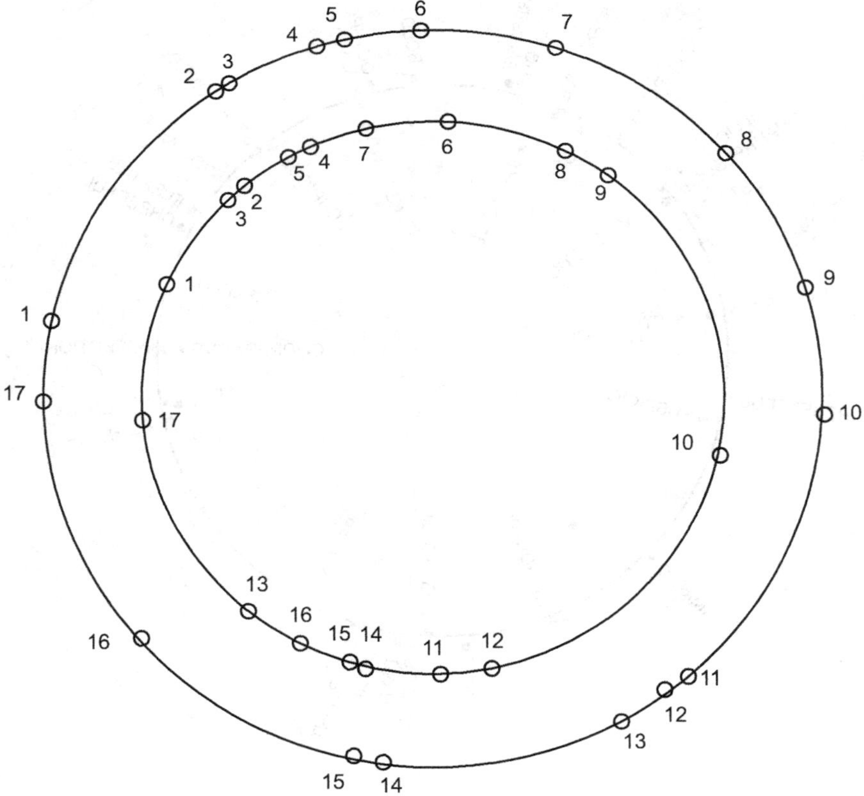

Figure 5.5 Replication of results by Conte and Plutchik (1981) by Fisher (1997).

Russell (1989) provided additional empirical support for the circumplex arrangement of emotion words. Plutchik (2003) presented additional evidence that the circumplex structure could be replicated for emotion words in Italian, French, Japanese, Finnish, and Cheke Holo/A'ara (spoken on the Solomon Islands).

Schlosberg (1954) proposed that the emotion-color wheel be given a third dimension of intensity to correspond with the emotional solid. Plutchik (1958) proposed a cone-shaped color-like model (see Figure 5.6) based on the following eight basic emotions arranged as four bipolar pairs: (a) joy vs. sadness; (b) anticipation vs. surprise; (c) anger vs. fear; and (d) disgust vs.

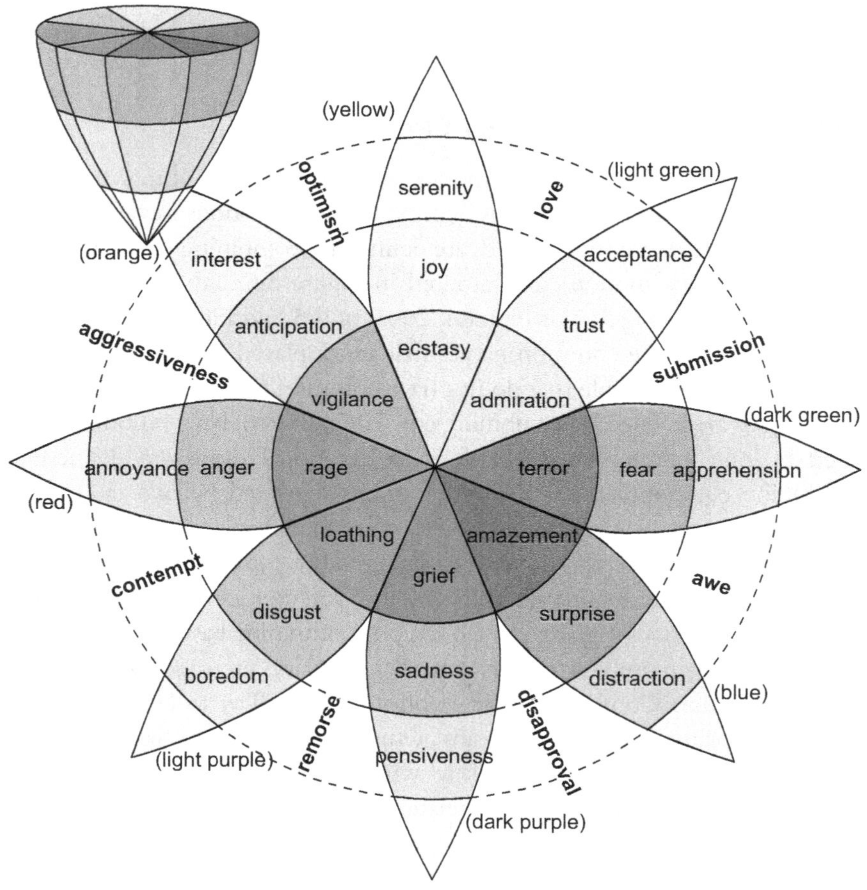

Figure 5.6 The emotion solid, reproduced with permission from Annette deFerrari. A color version of this figure is available at http://www.fordham.edu/psychology/tryon

trust. He added an intensity dimension as recommended by Schlosberg (1954). Emotional intensity constitutes the third dimension ranging from the top where emotions are intensely experienced, to the bottom where consciousness is lost, normally due to sleep.

It is especially important to note that six of the eight basic emotions identified above correspond to the six universal emotions identified in the worldwide facial expression research reported by Eckman (1999, p. 361). They are happiness (joy), fear, surprise, sadness, disgust, and anger. Trust and anticipation are the two additional emotions included in the emotion-color wheel that do not seem to have universal facial representations. A primary reason for their inclusion is that the perimeter of the circumplex would not be fully populated without them. I find this to be a compelling theory-based reason for their inclusion.

SECONDARY AND TERTIARY EMOTIONS

A major advantage of the color-emotion analogy is that one can synthesize a broad array of additional emotions by mixing basic emotions in various combinations. Primary emotional dyads are defined by combining equal quantities of adjacent basic emotions, as illustrated in Figure 5.6 and Table 5.2 below (reproduced from Fig 5-2 of Plutchik 2003, p. 105 and Figure 6 of Plutchik, 2001). They have the common names that are displayed on the figure. Other combinations are possible that do not have common names. Secondary emotional dyads are defined by combining equal quantities of basic emotions separated by one circumplex sector. Tertiary emotional dyads are defined by combining equal quantities of basic emotions separated by two circumplex sectors. Opposite emotions are defined by combining basic emotions separated by three circumplex sectors. Only four such unique combinations are possible. Combining basic emotions separated by four circumplex sectors equals tertiary emotional dyads with reversed notation. Combining basic emotions separated by five circumplex sectors equals secondary emotional dyads with reversed notation. Combining basic emotions separated by six circumplex sectors equals primary emotional dyads with reverse notation. Skipping seven circumplex sectors brings one back to where they started and thus does not result in a new combination. These relationships are illustrated in Table 5.2.

These combinations were created by combining equal amounts of the same intensity of basic emotions. Notice that the third dimension of the emotion cone is intensity where emotions represented in lower sections of the cone correspond to less intense emotions. All emotions go 'dark' at the bottom

Table 5.2 Eight Basic Emotions and their Combinations into Primary, Secondary, and Tertiary Emotional Dyads by Skipping One, Two, or Three Circumplex Sectors

Basic Emotions	Primary Emotional Dyad	Secondary Emotional Dyads	Tertiary Emotional Dyads
Joy	Joy + trust = love	Joy + fear	Joy + surprise
Trust	Trust + fear = submission	Trust + surprise	Trust + sadness
Fear	Fear + surprise = awe	Fear + sadness	Fear + disgust
Surprise	Surprise + sadness = disapproval	Surprise + disgust	Surprise + anger
Sadness	Sadness + disgust = remorse	Sadness + anger	Sadness + anticipation
Disgust	Disgust + anger = contempt	Disgust + anticipation	Disgust + joy
Anger	Anger + anticipation = aggressiveness	Anger + joy	Anger + trust
Anticipation	Anticipation + joy = optimism	Anticipation + trust	Anticipation + fear

which corresponds to the loss of consciousness, such as when one goes to sleep. Many more emotional combinations are possible if one combines different amounts (intensities) of basic emotions.

I therefore take the emotion-color analogy and the emotion wheel as an empirically supported fact that supports the principle that emotions can be combined like colors. A highly important and useful corollary of this principle is that a broad range of emotions can be represented in PDP-CNN models by combining eight basic emotions; a number that is not unreasonable from a cognitive neuroscience perspective.

ENCODING EMOTIONS IN CONNECTIONIST NETWORKS

Encoding Emotional Intensity

The emotion solid discussed above provides the key to encoding emotions in connectionist network simulations. It is worth remembering that connectionist simulations don't actually feel, any more than astrophysical simulations of super nova actually explode. In both cases, the simulations endeavor to capture essential features and relevant dynamics. For our code to be comprehensive, we need a way to select various amounts of at least two basic emotions. A 1-of-N code with N = 8 is a simple way to select one of the basic emotions. Starting anywhere on the emotional circumplex, the top layer of the emotional wheel, the code for each basic emotion would correspond to where, in a series of 8 digits, a 1 would appear. For example, the emotion in the first circumplex position could be coded 10000000. The emotion in the fourth position could be designated 00010000. The emotion in the last, eighth, position could be referenced as 00000001. Designating a second basic emotion entails using a second such 1-of-8 code. Hence, 16 stimulus microfeature input network nodes are required to designate a pair of basic emotions. A limitation of this method is that only one intensity level can be accommodated.

A thermometer code can be added to the emotion code to represent emotional intensity. The code 00000000 represents none of the emotion, the code 00000001 represents very little of the emotion. The code 00001111 represents half of the possible intensity of the emotion. The code 11111111 represents the maximum amount of the emotion. In short, intensity is represented in binary mathematical form using eight or more digits as required.

In the case where equal intensities of both emotions are mixed two 1-of-8 codes can represent the two emotions and a third 1-of-8 code would represent their equal intensities, resulting in 24 stimulus microfeature input network nodes. If two emotions of differing intensities are to be mixed then four 1-of-8 codes are required; one for each emotion and one for each intensity of that emotion. Hence, 32 microfeature input network nodes would be needed. There seems to be little reason to activate more than two emotions at any one time, but the above-mentioned approach is general and would accommodate representing a third or fourth basic emotion.

The above coding system provides limited protection against damage. This problem could be addressed by making multiple copies of the required codes. These copies could be concatenated end to end or they could be spatially distributed in some other way to minimize the effects of simulated trauma.

Coding Emotions in the BAM

The memory matrix of the Bidirectional Associative Memory (BAM) model discussed by Tryon (1999) and reviewed in Chapter 11 is composed of the outer matrix multiplication of the stimulus microfeatures associated with the two elements being associated in memory, but is illustrated below as Figure 5.7. Let's call them Elements A and B. Each of these elements has a set of cognitive nodes and a set of emotion nodes along with one or two sets of emotion intensity nodes, as described above, to enable mixing emotions of the same or different intensities. This approach results in a memory matrix composed of four quadrants. One quadrant associates the cognitive

		Element B	
		Cognitive Nodes	Emotion Nodes
Element A	Cognitive Nodes	Cognitive Cognitive	Cognitive Emotion
	Emotion Nodes	Emotion Cognitive	Emotion Emotion

Figure 5.7 Integrating cognitive and emotional features into memory matrices.

nodes of both memory elements. Another one quadrant associates the emotion nodes of both memory elements. The remaining two quadrants associate the cognitive nodes of Element A with the emotion nodes of Element B and the emotion nodes of Element A with the cognitive nodes of Element B. Cognition and emotion are fully mixed and intertwined in the resulting memory matrix. Memories are cognitive/emotional composites. Cognition and affect are encoded together; not separately. Hence, the part–whole pattern completion Principle 6 can return composite cognitive/emotional memories from either cognitive or emotional cues.

EMOTION AND ILLNESS

Can emotions may you sick? Cole et al. (2007) reported that social isolation increases the risk of all-cause mortality (Cacioppo & Hawkley, 2003; Seeman, 1996) and death from infectious, neoplastic, and cardiovascular disease (Caspi et al., 2006; Cohen et al., 1997; Cole et al., 2003; Kroenke et al., 2006). However, the biological mechanism responsible for this empirical effect was not known until Cole et al. (2007) further reported evidence that chronic loneliness impairs transcription of glucocorticoid response genes resulting in an elevated risk of inflammatory disease. They used DNA microarray analysis to identify 209 up- and down-regulating genes that were differentially expressed during immune activation, transcription control, and cell proliferation. These data are the first indication that genome-wide transcriptional activity is altered by chronic social isolation.

EMOTION AND BIRD SONG

Earp and Maney (2012) investigated the relationship between emotion and bird song on the basis that bird song plays an important role in mating and in territory protection; both behaviors known to be emotionally motivated. Although birds can be studied with fMRI while singing, the authors favored a more certain method of studying the underlying mechanisms of bird song that involve the immunolabeling of an early gene product Egr-1 in the reward pathway that is homologous with the mesolimbic reward system in humans. Bird song has different meanings during the breeding season for male and female white-throated sparrows (*Zonotrichia albicollis*) listening to conspecific male song. Males' song is positive for females who desire a mate and negative for males who are guarding their territories against intruders. All regions of the mesolimbic reward pathway in females with breeding-typical plasma levels of estradiol responded to male song. This finding mirrored those of humans listening to music depending upon sex and endocrine state.

In male birds the amygdale, but not the nucleus accumbens, became active in response to male bird song. This finding mirrored those of humans listening to unpleasant music. The authors concluded that birdsong and music activate the same neuroaffective mechanisms in humans as in birds. Since birds are not known for their cognitive abilities, it seems clear that the emotional responses of birds are generated by the identified subcortical neural networks. That humans possess homologous neural networks strongly suggests that emotion is also generated by subcortical networks in humans.

Krumhans (2002) discussed a general link between cognition and emotion that draws upon the work of Hevner (1936), who found that emotional responses to music can be represented as a circumplex. She also draws upon the work of Leonard Meyer (1956, 1967) who is a musicologist.

Conclusions

I suggest that the evidence reviewed in this chapter strongly supports the following conclusions. (a) There are eight basic emotions. They are: joy; trust; fear; surprise; sadness; disgust; anger; and anticipation. (b) They form a **recurrent** scale called a **circumplex**. (c) Pairs of basic emotions mix to produce primary emotional dyads such as love = joy + trust, secondary emotional dyads such as joy + fear, and tertiary emotional dyads such as joy + surprise. These facts enable connectionist network models to represent a broad range of emotions in a compact and efficient way. This enables more realistic simulations of the ways that cognitions and emotions interact to produce behaviors. (d) Emotions can make people sick.

We also know from our study of the Bidirectional Associative Memory (BAM) model that memories consist of integrated cognitive and emotional components that function as a composite Gestalt. Hence, partial emotions and/or cognitions can reactivate full cognitions, emotions, and behaviors; a process called **redintegration**.

Taken together, these developments substantially advance our understanding of emotions and how it is that they influence cognition and behavior. This information reinforces the unconscious-centric orientation that we took in Chapter 3. These developments provide a way forward towards psychotherapy integration because they provide common ground for clinicians who emphasize the importance of emotions, as well as for clinicians who emphasize the importance of cognitions, as well as clinicians who emphasize the importance of reinforcement history. Hence, cognitive, psychoanalytic, and behavioral (Applied Behavior Analysis) approaches to psychotherapy now have a common framework from which to operate.

CLINICAL APPLICATIONS

The contemporary understanding of emotional disorders that I spoke of in the beginning of this chapter is that they entail emotional dysregulation due to deficits in emotion regulation complicated by cognitive distortions. Newer therapies such as Dialectical Behavior Therapy emphasize the need to teach emotional regulation skills.

Emotional Regulation

Based on the work of Gross (1998, 1999), Liverant et al. (2008) defined emotion regulation as a 'heterogeneous set of processes, which involve changes in the experiential, behavioral, and physiological response systems that comprise emotion' (p. 1202). They distinguished between antecedent-focused response strategies that attempt to modify the production of emotion before it is generated and response-focused strategies that attempt to modify emotions after than have been generated. Emotion regulation is equally well known as **emotional dysregulation** given the clinical penchant for focusing on what is wrong. Gratz et al. (2006) provided the following functional definition of defined emotional dysregulation: '(a) lack of awareness, understanding, and acceptance of emotions; (b) lack of access to adaptive strategies for modulating the intensity and/or duration of emotional responses; (c) an unwillingness to experience emotional distress as part of pursuing desired goals; and (d) the inability to engage in goal-directed behaviors when experiencing distress (Gratz & Roemer, 2004; for a comparable conceptualization see Mennin, Heimberg, Turk, & Fresco, 2005)' (p. 850).

Emotional dysregulation is understood to be a central defining feature of **borderline personality disorder** (BPD; Gunderson, 2001; Linehan, 1993; Livesley et al., 1998; Skodol et al., 2002). Gratz et al. (2006) demonstrated that 17 participants diagnosed with BPD were significantly less willing to experience emotional distress in order to pursue goal-directed behaviors and were less able to pursue goal-directed behaviors than were control participants.

Emotional dysregulation is also recognized as a core issue for persons with **eating disorders**. Harrison et al. (2009) reported that women diagnosed with anorexia nervosa have a more difficult time regulating their emotions than normal control women do.

Mennin et al. (2005, 2009) maintain that **generalized anxiety disorder** (GAD) is characterized by the following four emotional regulation deficits. (a) People with GAD experience emotions more intensely than is normal. (b) People with GAD have difficulty identifying and describing their emotions. This deficit is called **alexithymia**. (c) People with GAD are prone to catastrophizing. (e) People with GAD have difficulty soothing their negative emotions. The *Handbook of Cognition and Emotion* by Robinson et al. (2013) and the second edition of the *Handbook of Emotion Regulation* by Gross (2013) provide many additional findings.

Normative Cases

I first discuss what can be considered as normative situations where emotion impacts cognition. In Chapter 4 Principle 7: Consonance and Dissonance we learned how emotion warps cognition. In this chapter we learned that emotions are unconsciously generated by subcortical structures. It therefore follows that unconscious emotions warp cognition. The fibers descending from the cortex to the amygdale are few, but the fibers ascending from the amygdale to the cortex are many. This anatomical fact further supports the ability of emotions to modify cognitions and to do so more effectively than cognitions can modify emotions. The normal process of emotions motivating us to cherry-pick among facts to support emotionally held positions discussed in Chapter 4 in connection with Principle 7: Consonance and

Dissonance is potentiated to a form of empirical blindness when faith-based beliefs are involved. Religious beliefs produce some of the strongest emotions that people can experience, even unto martyrdom. The extent to which faith-based beliefs trump scientific consensus is clearly evident in the WNET documentary entitled 'The Revisionaries' that aired on 28 January 2013. A preview of this show can be seen at http://www.pbs.org/independentlens/revisionaries/. J. D. McLeroy, D. D. S, known as Don McLeroy in the video, is a self-proclaimed Young Creationist[7] who believes that the world is just 6,000 years old and that humans once walked with dinosaurs, despite radiocarbon dating[8] evidence showing that the earth is 4.54 ± 0.05 billion years old.[9] When questioned about the age of the Earth, Don McLeroy replied '**I disagree with these experts. Someone has to stand up to them. Scientific consensus means nothing**' (minute 23:50 out of 55:24 in the full video). Don is welcome to disagree with a body of experts, but he goes well beyond disagreement when he substitutes his personal faith-based emotion-infused beliefs for scientific consensus at Texas School Board[10] Meetings where he helped dictate specific language to textbook publishers regarding what students will learn in school regarding evolution and social studies. By doing so he has imposed his religious beliefs on students beyond Texas as well.

To claim that scientific consensus means nothing is to categorically reject all possible evidence that such a consensus might be based on. Alternatively stated, no amount of evidence is now or ever will be sufficient to modify his faith-based conviction that the Bible is literally correct in every way, including the age of the Earth. This position is empirically blind in that it is independent of evidence. This makes so-called creation science not science at all because scientific hypotheses must be falsifiable. Creationists admit to no empirical fact that would falsify the Bible. Hence creationism is not a scientific hypothesis. Bible study is not biological science. This should end the debate over whether or not to teach creationism in biology classes but it has not yet done so, thereby revealing a consensus of other faith-based decisions.

Reasons to teach creationism took several forms in the video referred to above. One form of reasoning questioned the certainty with which evolutionary theory has been established by emphasizing that scientific theories

[7] http://en.wikipedia.org/wiki/Young_Earth_creationism

[8] http://en.wikipedia.org/wiki/Radiocarbon_dating

[9] http://en.wikipedia.org/wiki/Age_of_the_Earth

[10] The whole idea of creating a committee of ordinary citizens with little if any formal training to specify the exact wording of textbooks in science and history by voting on the inclusion and exclusion of specific words is an affront to science and scholarship.

are never completely proven because a new finding may emerge that falsifies the theory. Another form of reasoning questioned how life forms could have become so diverse. No mention of genetics and the mechanics of DNA were made. A third form of reasoning is emotion based. Don McLeroy claimed that he cannot understand why a particular woman who opposes the teaching of creationism is so fearful of Christian conservativism, implying that her opposition is purely emotional and consequently irrational. Don does not understand that he has **projected**[11] his own fear onto her, for if the Bible is proved wrong about the age of the Earth, then perhaps it is wrong in other ways as well, and that allows one to question everything in the Bible. This would dissolve the bedrock and emotional security of the life he has built including his role as Sunday School teacher where he endeavors to convince the children in his care of the complete correctness and literal truth of every word in the Bible. More than that, the Saturday February 2, 2013 edition of *The New York Times* printed the following quote from Paul Broun 'all that stuff I was taught about evolution and embryology and the Big Bang theory, all that is lies, straight from the pit of hell' and that evolution is one of those 'lies to try to keep me and all the folks who were taught that from understanding that they need a savior' (p. 16). Such emotionally charged convictions are sufficient for some parents to home school their children to protect them from perceived evil thought to emanate from the pit of hell by distorting scientific evidence as necessary in order to support their Christian faith.

Another illustration of emotionally held beliefs leading to empirical blindness comes from the good people at the Flat Earth Society.[12] The 'About the society link' reveals that 'The mission of the Flat Earth Society is to promote and initiate discussion of Flat Earth theory as well as archive Flat Earth literature'. Everyday experience for everyone on the planet is that the world is flat. The thought that people and trees at the equator are standing out at right angles and that people and trees in the southern hemisphere are standing on their heads is ridiculous. When I upend a glass of water the liquid spills out. So oceans in the northern hemisphere should slide to the equator and drop off while oceans in the southern hemisphere should simply fall away. These 'reasons' can be used to justify the view that the world is

[11] This and other examples demonstrate that projection is a legitimate psychological phenomenon. While projection is a **means** of avoiding unpleasant emotions such as the anxiety and uncertainty that would follow accepting that the Bible is not always correct it is not a **mechanism** because it does not provide a sequence of causal steps that is required of all true mechanisms.

[12] http://theflatearthsociety.org/cms/

flat. Those pictures of Earth as the big blue marble could have been photoshopped by the liberal media.

Clinical Cases

People who have built their psychological lives on strong emotionally held beliefs may not be willing to modify those beliefs even if maintaining them is difficult, problematic, or causes them psychological pain and has self-destructive consequences. The alternative psychological state associated with giving up a strongly held belief may produce more rather than less anxiety, as would seem to be the case with Don McLeroy. The same can be said for persons with low self-esteem. I am reminded of a statement attributed to Woody Allen that he would refuse to join any club that would have him as a member.

Clinical psychologists and psychiatrists mainly see patients for whom emotions have become problematic. Depression is said to be the common cold of psychiatry. Anxiety disorders are also common and are frequently comorbid with depression. Self-concept problems have an emotional core. Emotional dysregulation is a major consideration in borderline personality disorder (BPD), eating disorders (anorexia nervosa and bulimia), and non-suicidal self-injury (NSSI) patients. Psychologists need to address these issues, but should be aware that emotions derive from subcortical structures that are only minimally controlled by higher brain centers. It remains advisable to treat emotions cognitively because this is primarily the access that is available to clinicians, but unconscious processing can be expected to interfere with and limit the effects of CBT interventions. Research demonstrating the effectiveness and efficacy of emotion-focused therapy reveals that positive emotions can be used to modify negative emotions.

CONCLUSIONS

This chapter began with an overview of the literature regarding the existence of basic emotions. Strong empirical findings that Localized Electrical Stimulations of Specific Neural Systems (LESSNS) consistently produced emotions from subcortical brain centers in animals and homologous brain centers in humans convincingly demonstrated that emotions derive from primitive brain regions rather than from higher cortical centers as cognitive and cognitive-behavioral theorists have posited. Empirical evidence indicates that emotions form a recurrent circumplex scale. An emotion wheel and cone was described that is a direct analogy to the color wheel and cone. This approach enables the generation of primary, secondary, and tertiary emotional dyads by mixing basic emotions. This method enables many different emotions to be represented in artificial neural network models with the same clarity as cognitive variables are, and therefore should advance our understanding of how cognitive and affective variables interact to produce behavior. The next chapter discusses the need for simulations in software and/or hardware and reviews findings from selected connectionist simulations.

Simulating Psychological Phenomena and Disorders

Contents

Psychological theories have traditionally been formulated using just words. The author of a psychological theory typically just writes about it. This has been sufficient to communicate all that the reader needs to know about the theory. To this point I have described the proposed Bio↔Psychology Network Theory using words, but serious empirical research requires much greater precision. Network theories are simple in principle but complex in their elaboration. While it is possible to summarize their operations verbally and even specify the principles that govern their operation as I have done with the four core and eight corollary principles, it is not possible to make a falsifiable prediction without simulations. The quantitative methods used by connectionist modelers require one to stipulate all functional relationships

Cognitive Neuroscience and Psychotherapy
http://dx.doi.org/10.1016/B978-0-12-420071-5.00006-5

in mathematical terms; i.e., using equations. The great many complex sequential interactions that characterize the developmental history of these artificial neural network models require simulation using either software or hardware. These constraints are needed in order for the model to be sufficiently constrained that it can be falsified by data collected from real people. Without the possibility of falsification there can be no natural science. This necessity may disappoint and possibly upset those psychologists, and students of psychology, who had hoped that they could avoid mathematics and computers. I am sorry to disappoint those readers but simulations are unavoidable and are required to do original research in this area.

However, I quickly note that these math and computer skills are not needed by clinical psychologists in order for them to incorporate the results of connectionist simulations into their professional practice, any more than they need to know the physics associated with brain imaging to benefit from these studies. The main point of this chapter is to justify the need for simulating neural network models and to present some of their scientific results.

It is well beyond the scope of this chapter to survey and critically evaluate the 27 citations to connectionist simulations returned from PsychARTICLES or the 274 citations returned from PsychINFO on 29 August 2013 using the search terms 'connectionism' and 'simulation' in separate search fields. The 274 PsychINFO citations include books and book chapters pertaining to connectionist simulations. For example, van Overwalle (2007) published a book entitled *Social Connectionism: A Reader and Handbook for Simulations*. Dawson (2004) published a book entitled *Minds and Machines: Connectionism and Psychological Modeling*. O'Reilly and Munakata (2000) published a book entitled *Computational Explorations in Cognitive Neuroscience: Understanding the Mind by Simulating the Brain* based on freely available software previously called PDP++ now known as emergent.[1] Van Overwalle (2011) published a book chapter entitled *Cognitive Simulation as a Tool for Understanding Social Cognition and Neuroscience*. Segalowitz and Bernstein (1997) published a book chapter entitled *What Are Connectionist Simulations Good For?* Read and Monroe (2009) published a book chapter entitled *Using Connectionist Networks to Understand Social and Personality Psychology.* PsychINFO contains many more relevant sources.

Simulations provide additional benefits beyond falsifiability. Simulation requires the theorist to specify all necessary **assumptions** and **auxiliary hypotheses** for network processing to generate specific predictions. Physicists

[1] http://grey.colorado.edu/emergent/index.php/Main_Page

routinely use mathematical models to better understand properties of complex systems.[2] Psychometricians routinely use computer simulations to better understand the properties of complex statistical methods such as what happens to the probability of falsely claiming an effect when none is present or missing an effect that is present when assumptions underpinning the analytic method are violated. Studying the psychological properties of neural networks requires simulation to better understand how psychology emerges from biology.[3] Mark Gluck referred to computational modeling as providing the '**conceptual glue**' that binds psychology and neuroscience.[4] Perhaps the most significant conceptual feature of these simulations is that they enable us to understand psychology in **physical** rather than mental terms. This radical qualitative conceptual shift constitutes a paradigm shift (Kuhn, 1962, 1970, 1996, 2012).

NEW TOOLS AND METHODS

Neuroscience has already introduced new tools and methods into psychology. The tools that have received the most attention are brain-scanning instruments such as functional magnetic resonance imaging (fMRI). Psychology departments that are on the cutting edge of this technology have their own scanners, software for image processing, and associated radiological and statistical support staff. These new tools require new methods for conducting experiments and new statistical methods for analyzing data, some of which are highly controversial (cf. Vul et al., 2009). While these new tools and methods enable us to learn many new things about the neural basis of psychology and behavior they also have their limits. Perhaps the most serious limit is that they do not, because they cannot, advance our understanding of how the neural networks that they identify generate psychology and/or behavior. The question of how psychology emerges from brain neural networks cannot, in principle, be answered by brain-imaging methods. Brain-imaging technology was never intended to explain how mind emerges from brain. An entirely different technology is required to address the question of how mind emerges from brain. This technology consists of tools that enable PDP-CNN simulations of psychological phenomena.

[2] http://en.wikipedia.org/wiki/Mathematical_models_in_physics

[3] The large majority of connectionist simulations conducted to date have been concerned with the 'adult' properties of fully developed neural networks rather than with the details of how they got that way; i.e., how those abilities emerged. This contemporary focus of connectionist simulations should not distract us from the alternative use of these simulations to address the developmental questions concerning emergence.

[4] www.gluck.edu

Computational simulations provide mechanism information because they provide step-by-step causal details about how the network cascade selectively turns some processing nodes, simulated neurons, on and others off. Parallel Distributed Processing (PDP) Connectionist Neural Network (CNN) models **simulate** rather than **implement** real neural network **dynamics** in an effort to better understand how psychology emerges from biology. Mathematical equations are used to **simulate not implement** biological processes. Just as mathematical models of supernova do not actually explode and weather models to not actually rain, PDP-CNN models do not actually think, feel, and behave. Instead, these models simulate important functional relationships using mathematical equations. Software **simulations are not exact reproductions** of what they simulate because they entail mathematical equations. The following criticism of simulations fails to understand this point. When discussing Tryon's (2005) connectionist explanation of exposure therapy Carey (2011) noted that 'While this might be a model of how exposure *can* work, however, that does not necessarily mean that it is a model of how exposure *does* work' (p. 242, emphasis in the original). Even simulations that are implemented on neuromorphic chips (see below) are not exact reproductions of biological structures, despite the fact that the same forces that drive ions through transistors also drive ions across neural membranes because they are constructed from silicon rather than carbon. What is important is that simulations capture the most important functional relationships.

Simulations enable true experiments to be conducted. All variables are clearly defined. As much neuroscience information as possible can be incorporated to constrain these models. Initial events can be specified in detail. This includes implementing variations of neural architecture that can be 'normal' or damaged to simulate brain trauma. All events are manipulated by the experimenter. Learning histories can be completely specified and varied as desired, thereby enabling the study of developmental processes. Simulations provide the best methods for studying the process of **emergence** because it is possible to suspend network models at planned points throughout their development. Experiments can be exactly replicated by investigators. Firm conclusions about causal mechanisms can result. The 2013 Nobel Prize for chemistry was awarded to Michael Levitt, Martin Karplus, and Arieh Warshel for their work using computer simulations to study chemical reactions.

In addition to the misguided criticism noted above, simulations have been criticized as being too simplistic and unrepresentative of real living creatures, let alone humans, to be useful in any way. More complicated models are recommended. However, complex models introduce new issues of their own. One problem is how to create and implement very large neural networks. Computers, even massively parallel super computers, have their limits. The computational power of the human brain is so vast that even today's super computers that require large facilities and consume huge amounts of electricity can only simulate a small fraction of the processing capacity of the human brain. Hardware platforms allow for the construction of much larger but still limited networks.

Another problem arises from the successful construction of enormous network models. They can become too difficult to understand. It is not helpful to create a model that cannot be understood any better than the phenomenon it is supposed to simulate. Beginning with a model that is too complex to properly understand will inhibit rather than promote scientific progress. Geneticists continue to study fruit flies precisely because of the several practical advantages that they provide. Attempting to start with a complex model pretends that we have knowledge that we do not possess. Such self-puffery is not productive. Beginning with a simple model honestly reflects our current ignorance. Hence, one must begin with models that can be understood, but that represent core features of real neural systems.

Another basis of criticism is that the results of simulations are seen as little more than curve-fitting because they contain so many free parameters (Gigerenzer, 2009). This criticism focuses upon the end state of a connectionist model rather than on its development in response to experience. The main objective of connectionist simulations is to demonstrate that connectionist principles are sufficient to explain the emergence of a targeted psychological phenomenon. A successful simulation constitutes a **demonstration proof** that connectionist principles are sufficient to explain the emergence of the target phenomenon. Further comments and other criticisms are considered in Chapter 7.

Supportive comments can also be found. Mark Gluck commented on neural networks at the following link: http://www.youtube.com/watch?v=2Ei6wFJ9kCc&feature=channel. Geoffrey Hinton commented on the next generation of neural networks at the following link: http://www.youtube.com/watch?v=AyzOUbkUf3M. Computational neuroimaging is discussed at the following link: http://www.youtube.com/watch?v=znKNk8O39ik&feature=channel.

Software Simulations

The **Human Brain Project**[5] (Markram, 2012) aims to create a virtual brain simulator that will contain the world's neuroscience findings. If successful, this project will be much more than an archive. It will be to neuroscience what the Hubble telescope is to astronomy and what Fermilab's Tevatron and CERN's Large Hadron Collider are to physics; an indispensable tool for cutting edge research. This project currently consists of 80 universities around the world and has been awarded $1.3 billion to simulate the human brain.[6] This project is evidence of considerable interdisciplinary agreement regarding the need to assemble and synthesize the results of reductionistic neuroscience into a heavily neuroscience-constrained computerized brain simulator that can be used to study how psychology emerges from biology in order to provide currently missing proximal causal mechanism information. Markram's June 2012 *Scientific American* article described this project. Curiously, he made no mention of psychology or psychological science, leaving one to wonder why.

Researchers at IBM have used their Dawn Blue Gene/P supercomputer with its 147, 456 CPUs and 144 tera bytes of main memory to simulate a brain consisting of 1.617 billion neurons and 8.87 trillion synapses. This simulated brain has slightly more processing capacity than the brain of a cat, and just 4.5% that of a human brain. It runs from 100 to 1000 times slower than real brains do but provides an opportunity to conduct quantitative experiments on artificial neural networks. Related information is available at the following links: http://en.wikipedia.org/wiki/Blue_Brain_Project, http://arstechnica.com/science/news/2009/11/ibm-makes-supercomputer-significantly-smarter-than-cat.ars?utm_source=rss&utm_medium=rss&utm_campaign=rss, http://p9.hostingprod.com/@modha.org/blog/2009/11/post_3.html. Whereas simulations using computer software constitute the main method for constraining PDP-CNN models, hardware simulations enable larger networks to be studied more efficiently.

Hardware Simulations

In what may seem like an ironic turn of events, the size and energy problems faced by digital computers are being solved by analog devices. Because the forces that drive ions across transistors are the same as the forces that drive

[5] www.humanbrainproject.eu

[6] http://www.popsci.com/science/article/2013-02/how-simulate-human-brain-one-neuron-time-13-billion

electrons across cell membranes, it is possible to physically simulate neurons using transistors instead of simulating them on digital computers where each action requires thousands of transistors. The result is called a '**neuromorphic chip**' or '**neuromorphic electronic system**'. Carver Mead was the first person to develop a neuromorphic chip.[7] These devices differ fundamentally from standard computer chips that employ von Neumann computing, where a central processor is separated from data storage by a communications channel called a bus. von Neumann computing systems operate via step-by-step serial processing methods, whereas the neuromorphic chips use much faster parallel processing methods. Data storage and processing occur together in these devices as it does in the brain and that makes them more realistic. Kwabena Boahen at Stanford University builds silicon models to simulate brain functions that use a million times less electricity than a comparable computer. Kwabena Boahen described his work at the following link: http://www.youtube.com/watch?v=mC7Q-ix_0Po. The following link is to Boahen's lab: http://www.stanford.edu/group/brainsinsilicon/. Dharmendra S. Modha at IBM is developing neurosynaptic chips with funding from the Defense Advanced Research Projects Agency (DARPA).

Neuromorphic computing is surprisingly widespread, due in large part to funding from DARPA. The following Wikipedia entry is especially revealing in this regard: http://en.wikipedia.org/wiki/SyNAPSE. Related links are: http://www.darpa.mil/Our_Work/DSO/Programs/Systems_of_Neuromorphic_Adaptive_Plastic_Scalable_Electronics_(SYNAPSE).aspx, http://www.artificialbrains.com/darpa-synapse-program. Dharmendra Modha at IBM also contributes to the SyNAPSE program. SpiNNaker is another major neuromorphic chip development consortium. See contributions to this program by Steven Furber of the University of Manchester at the following links: http://www.artificialbrains.com/spinnaker, http://www.youtube.com/watch?v=NPeEXJqz6IE, http://www.eps.manchester.ac.uk/about-us/features/modelling-the-human-brain/. Karlheinz Meier of the University of Heidelberg[8] and Goicomo Indiveri of the University of Zurich[9] also contribute to neuromorphic computing. More information is available on the web using search terms such as 'neuromorphic chips', 'neuromorphic computing', etc. See also the following link: http://www.economist.com/news/science-and-technology/21582495-computers-will-help-people-understand-brains-better-and-understanding-brains.

[7] http://en.wikipedia.org/wiki/Carver_Mead

[8] http://www.uni-heidelberg.de/presse/news2013/pm20130128_hbp_en.html

[9] http://community.frontiersin.org/people/name/1395

SIMULATED PHENOMENA

What follows are selected simulations regarding topics basic to psychological science. They were chosen because I consider them to be seminal and therefore classic. I recognize that they do not fully represent the latest cutting edge simulations. I have included them because they illustrate and advance the network principles promoted in this book, and because I believe that readers will finding them interesting if not fascinating as I do.

I have emboldened the reference to the original source because I strongly recommend that you read the original reports rather than limit yourself to my brief summary of them. Please read for gist. This may mean skipping over many of the technical details that are mostly relevant to those who aim to do original research in this field. Please concentrate on the main findings.

Stroop Effect

J. R. Stroop (1935) reported that participants took longer to say the color of ink that the names of colors were written in than it did to read the color names. I begin with the Stroop effect because it is one of the most well-replicated phenomena that psychological science has to offer. This effect has been adapted to assess clinically relevant unconscious processing. See Chapter 9 for additional details.

Cohen et al. (1990) provided mechanism information regarding the unconscious processing that mediates the Stroop effect. The gist of this research is that the normal experience of reading has strengthened the synapses that mediate word reading more than the synapses that mediate color naming. Hence, it takes longer to name the colors of ink than to read the color names.

Language Acquisition

Sejnowski and Rosenberg (1986, 1987) created an artificial neural network called NETtalk that learned on its own to correctly pronounce English words by scanning transcriptions of informal speech of a child containing 1,024 words. When the network phoneme output was played through a commercially available speech synthesizer called DECtalk, several persuasive similarities with human speech were noted. First, the developmental speech acquisition sequence began with babbling sounds, then it distinguished between vowels and consonants, learned word boundaries, generated pseudo words, and finally produced intelligible speech. Learning followed a power law and the network generalized better as it learned more. It is especially noteworthy that all of these accomplishments emerged from a PDP-CNN model without the aid of pronunciation rules, lexical decisions, or rules of any kind. The following link is to the above-cited 1986 paper which is otherwise difficult to find: http://papers.cnl.salk.edu/PDFs/NETtalk_%20A%20Parallel%20Network%20That%20Learns%20to%20Read%20Aloud%201988-3562.pdf. The following link lets you hear samples of NETtalk speech taken during its babbling period, after it had learned from 10 000 training words, and how it generalized to reading new words: http://www.youtube.com/watch?v=gakJlr3GecE.

The take-home message here is that NETtalk constitutes a demonstration proof that connectionist principles are sufficient to explain how even relatively simple approximations to real neural networks can learn to perform the complex behavior of reading and pronouncing written English on their own without external training by humans.

Personality

The simulations by **Read and Miller (2002)**, and especially by **Read et al. (2010)** are, in my view, among the most important publications in personality theory in the history of psychology, because they are the first achievements that integrate two long-standing seemingly incompatible approaches to personality. I refer to the ideographic and nomothetic research traditions. The **ideographic** case study approach to personality began with clinical theorists like Freud, Jung, Adler, etc., who based their theories on the clients that they saw. This approach remains relevant today because it concerns how individuals think, feel, and behave, which is what practicing clinicians are mainly concerned with. Freud's clinical approach is called psychodynamic because it focuses on the active interaction of unconscious and conscious motives and how they determine thoughts, feelings, and behaviors. Clinicians treat individuals and consequently they prefer personality theories that explain why individuals think, feel, and behave as they do. Clinicians are especially interested in theories about the conflicts that their clients bring to therapy.

In Chapter 1 we learned that empirical evidence is far less persuasive than are theories that aid our understanding. Ideographic theories enable clinicians to understand their clients, and that is both the primary and a sufficient reason for them to prefer these theories as the basis of their clinical practice. Positive cases will always be encountered and they can serve as supporting evidence. Clinicians can use the same logic to justify their ideographic practices as Benjamin Rush, the founder of modern psychiatry[10]

[10] http://en.wikipedia.org/wiki/Benjamin_Rush

used to justify bloodletting to treat illnesses of all types, including mental illnesses. If the patient recovered, it was due to his treatment. If the patient died, their condition was deemed too severe to be saved by the treatment. This win–win logic precluded the possibility of failure/falsification and provided only positive evidence to continue treatment as usual. Followers of ideographic personality theories typically use such a cherry-picking evidential approach to justify their therapeutic approaches.

In contrast, the **nomothetic** trait-oriented approach to personality typically studies groups of individuals. The goal is to identify and quantify individual differences in an aggregate way. These investigators are mainly concerned with the structure of personality. A central question concerns the number of psychometric factors required to adequately classify and plot people in multidimensional space. Research psychologists frequently prefer this approach to personality theory because of its methodological rigor. Top-tier professional journals heavily favor nomothetic research. Personality tests such as the Minnesota Multiphasic Personality Inventory (MMPI) and the Personality Assessment Inventory (PAI) were developed on the basis of nomothetic research and were once commonly administered as part of clinical practice. Test reports about clients were typically written prior to beginning psychotherapy. While this information may have enabled the clinician to better understand their client, the type of therapy provided was largely the same depending upon the individual preference of the clinician; namely long-term dynamic psychotherapy.

The rise of behavior therapy made psychodiagnostic testing largely irrelevant. Behavioral assessment was preferred over psychodiagnostic testing. The fourth edition of the *Diagnostic and Statistical Manual* (DSM-IV) split psychiatric disorders into many groups, each with its own inclusion and exclusion criteria. Manualized treatments were developed for many diagnostic categories. Clinical psychologists mostly had little if any use for the results of nomothetic personality research because they provide little help in understanding individual clients, because nomothetic personality studies are generally about traits rather than motives. Traits are typically treated as stable qualities that therapy is unlikely to change, whereas motives are understood to be temporary and possibly in conflict with one another; something that therapy might help resolve.

Cognitive-behavioral therapies do not formally recognize or incorporate personality theory into their understanding of the etiology, diagnosis, or treatment of any disorder. Specialized tests to assess anxiety, depression, obsessions, and compulsions are sometimes used, but personality theory and testing per se are formally irrelevant to CBT. But clinicians know that all people are not created equal, and even if they were life experiences modify them to where they are quite different by the time they enter therapy. The mere fact that some people develop disorders that require treatment while other people do not is convincing evidence that individual differences exist.

Clinical interest in personality is slowly returning. This trend began when investigators focused on the fact that putatively distinct disorders shared negative emotion. Chorpita and Barlow (1998) specifically stipulated that anxiety is the product of the **behavioral inhibition system** (BIS) identified by Gray (1982, 1987) and Gray and McNaughton (2000). Chorpita and Barlow (1998) documented that anxiety, neuroticism, is also common to depression, thus explaining why clients with anxiety disorders are frequently found to also be depressed. The BIS controls sensitivity to punishment. Anxiety results when the possibility of punishment is not under personal control. Chorpita and Barlow (1998) documented this assertion by reviewing laboratory studies with animals before extending their discussion to locus of control in children and adult attributions. Bouton et al. (2001) cited evidence for a non-specific biological/genetic factor of neuroticism; and also referred to as negative affect and trait anxiety. They also identified non-specific psychological factors that include: (a) prior experience with control and mastery; and (b) prior experience with unpredictability. Barlow (2000) referred to anxiety as the shadow of intelligence, indicating that it takes intelligence to anticipate possible negative events. He documented the ascendance of emotion theory as a way to better understand anxiety disorders. It is against this background that David Barlow's James McKeen Cattell Fellow award lecture given at the twenty-fourth annual convention of the American Psychological Association about neuroticism reported by Jaffe (2012) is so newsworthy. Barlow reported covariation among anxiety, mood disorders, and neuroticism which he considers to be a temperament that entails strong negative emotional reactions to stress.

In particular, Barlow (2000) emphasized the role of the **behavioral inhibition system** mentioned above. Barlow et al. (2004) introduced a unified treatment for emotional disorders based upon a 'Negative Affect Syndrome' (p. 209) mediated by the behavioral inhibition system mentioned above (see also Barlow et al. (2011)). The **behavioral activation system** controls sensitivity to reward. It is the counterpart to the BIS. The BAS and the BIS are core components of the Read et al. (2010) simulation that integrates the ideographic and nomothetic approaches to understanding personality.

Labeling patients who present with strong negative emotional reactions to stress does not explain why they are this way despite the ready acceptance of many psychologists to engage in this form of explanation. Clinical psychologists and lay people want to know what makes some people this way. The section on **maternal care** in Chapter 2 provides epigenetic mechanism information that at least partly explains individual differences in response to stress. I briefly summarize some of this information here for the reader's convenience.

The hippocampus is involved in stress management as well as memory formation. Glucocorticoids (GCs) are a class of steroid hormones that bind to glucocorticoid receptors (GR). Cortisol is a GC hormone produced by the adrenal gland in response to stress. Short-term exposure to cortisol helps organisms cope with stress, but long-term exposure to cortisol is harmful. Glucocorticoid receptors take up cortisol. More glucocorticoid receptors mean quicker recovery from stress. Methyl tags inhibit the genetic mechanisms that produce these receptors, resulting in prolonged stress recovery. Calm and caring mothering removes these methyl tags resulting in rat pups that respond less severely to stress and recover faster from stress. Female pups who receive calm and caring mothering grow up to be calm and caring mothers themselves. Inattentive mothering adds methyl tags, causing their pups to secrete more cortisol in response to stress, take longer to recover from stress, and grow up to become inattentive mothers. These neuroscience mechanisms are also found in humans and that at least partly explains individual differences in neuroticism seen in clients and in their children.

The proposed Bio↔Psychology Network Theory uses such neuroscience mechanisms to think about personality, anxiety disorders, and mood disorders in physical rather than mental terms. This constitutes a paradigm shift because it is a qualitatively different approach to psychology. The **Read et al. (2010)** simulation is an unintended implementation of the Bio↔Psychology Network Theory. It is especially significant because it is a Hegelian synthesis of the ideographic and nomothetic approaches to personality. The Read et al. (2010) simulation does this by simulating contextualized interactions between the well-documented **behavioral approach system (BAS)** and **behavioral inhibition system (BIS)**. Traits and motives are modeled as sensitivities of these two systems. This approach simultaneously considers person–situation interactions from both perspectives. Moreover, this neural network model enables us to think about personality in **physical** rather than mental terms. That constitutes a qualitative shift in our thinking. It also integrates psychology with neuroscience.

Read et al. (2010) conducted eight personality simulations. Their first set of simulations demonstrated that their connectionist network model successfully learned relationships between different situations and the behaviors that are appropriate in those situations. They demonstrated that their model is not limited to learning to associate just a single behavior with a single situation, but demonstrated that any situation can be associated with several different behaviors. Conversely, they demonstrated that any behavior can be associated with several different situations. They represented situations in terms of their relevance to the actor's goals and motives. Thus, these simulations implement person–situation interactions in terms of the interaction between the motive systems (person) and the influence of situational features (situation) on those motive systems. The activation of motives in their model was a function of stable characteristics, such as the sensitivity of the relevant motivational system and the baseline activations of individual motives, as well as the activation that motives receive from situational features. The Read et al. (2010) model provides a mechanistic, computational model for thinking about how person characteristics interact with features of the situation; i.e., it provides much-needed mechanism information regarding how personalities and situations interact.

Their second set of simulations focused on the approach and avoidance goal layers, because they pertain to two major dimensions of personality: extraversion and neuroticism. These simulations demonstrated that individuals with a more sensitive approach system exhibited a broader pattern of approach-related or extraverted behavior, whereas individuals with a more sensitive avoidance system exhibited a broader pattern of avoidance-related or neurotic behaviors.

The following are some of the more important implications of the Read et al. (2010) simulations. They demonstrate how to bridge the gap between personality dynamics and dispositional approaches to personality based on constructs such as goals, motives, beliefs, and self-control. They emphasized how behavior changes over time and varies according to situations. Looking across individuals, one finds evidence of personality factors such as the Big Five. This structure is not seen for a single person, but is rather the result of the covariation among characteristics within a large sample of people. Read et al. (2010) demonstrated that personality traits are goal-based motivational structures. The clinical relevance of the Read et al. (2010) simulation is that it concerns motivations of individuals.

Social Psychology

Cognitive Dissonance

There have been several connectionist simulations of cognitive dissonance. They include but are not limited to Read and Miller (1994), Shultz et al. (1999), Spellman et al. (1993), Thagard (1989), and Van Overwalle and Jordan (2002). I do not feature these simulations because consonance seeking has been promoted to network Principle 7: Consonance and Dissonance. This principle is basic to connectionist models of attitude formation and change among other psychological phenomena.

Attitude Formation and Change

Attitude formation and change is a primary clinical task, as well as a major topic of social psychology research. Grounding clinical practice in psychological science requires incorporating what is known about attitude formation and change. **Monroe and Read (2008)** provided a general introduction to this topic and an explanation of the relevance of connectionist modeling. They extended connectionist reasoning to define attitudes as a form of constraint satisfaction. Their general model was aimed at theoretical unification rather than replication of one effect. The key idea here is that attitudes are linked together into a belief network, such that modifying one attitude requires adjustments in others. Conversely, attitude change in one area is resisted precisely because it requires attitude adjustment in other areas. The process of attitude formation and change is modeled as a dynamic network in accordance with the proposed core and corollary network principles.

Sterotypes

Stereotypes are a form of impression formation. **Kunda and Thagard (1996)** understand impression formation as a parallel constraint satisfaction problem, because the person needs to decipher and integrate perceived information into a network of preexisting knowledge concerning traits and behaviors. The authors presented a PDP-CNN model of stereotype formation.

Aging

Understanding the effects of age on cognitive performance is increasingly important for psychologists. PDP-CNN models provide a succinct way of understanding several cognitive effects of aging. In a remarkable series of simulations, **Li et al. (2001)** successfully modeled several important features of aging by changing a single network parameter that changes the slope of the transfer function. The transfer function was illustrated in Chapter 3 as

Figure 3.3. It relates the summed inputs into a single neuron to the probability of firing. A steeper slope means that small changes in summed inputs produce large changes in the probability of the neuron firing or the rate at which the neuron fires. A flatter slope means that the same input produces a smaller change in the probability of the neuron firing. Neural networks with flatter transfer functions require more processing cycles, take longer, to learn. Investigators effectively simulated the behavior of young, middle-aged, and old people by using three different slope levels. Networks with steeper transfer functions performed like younger people on several experimental tasks. Networks performed like older people as the slope of their transfer function decreased. Predictions from these models agree closely with data collected from real people of different ages. Another aspect of PDP-CNN models is that their parallel-distributed processing explains why their performance degrades gracefully, slowly, given network damage of various kinds just like people do during normal aging.

Li and Sikström (2002) used the same connectionist model to simulate additional data that compares well with actual data from human subjects. **Li et al. (2005)** extended the above-mentioned model to simulate age-related deficits in associative binding. These findings suggest that age-related impairment of associative binding explains some age-related psychological deficits.

PSYCHOLOGICAL DISORDERS

This section presents several clinically relevant connectionist models. Because of their complexity I only provide a brief introduction to each simulation where I highlight what I think are its most relevant points. Readers should consult the original articles for additional details, but remember to primarily read for gist. I begin with dyslexia because this simulation illustrates an especially convincing experimental design. Then I cover schizophrenia because it is such a serious mental disorder that is found worldwide. Next I discuss brain damage because head injuries and dementias are common, and because schizophrenia entails brain damage. I end with a simulation of the psychoanalytic case known as Lucy concerning hysteria.

Dyslexia

The **Hinton et al. (1993)** simulation of dyslexia illustrates an especially convincing experimental design. It begins by simulating normal reading behavior. Then the artificial neural network is damaged in specific ways that give rise to common clinical symptoms of surface and deep dyslexia. I find this type of evidence to be especially compelling because clinical symptoms emerge from damage done to the network, as is frequently the case in real life. To me such simulations clearly demonstrate that the underlying connectionist principles are valid, for how else could clinically specific features emerge given that they were not engineered into the model? The possibility of such emergence happening by chance seems to me to be exceptionally remote.

Early artificial intelligence models attempted to directly simulate aberrant behavior. Any success was clearly the work of the programmer. But here we have an entirely different situation in that normal behavior was simulated first, then the model was damaged, and then symptoms of surface and deep dyslexia emerged depending upon what part of the network was damaged. This sequence substantially increases one's confidence that the model is valid and accurately reflects the underlying mechanisms being modeled. This method closely parallels real life, where premorbid behavior is normal and symptoms of abnormal behavior occur after specific brain damage has occurred.

Schizophrenia

Simulations

Psychologists once attempted to distinguish patients with schizophrenia from patients with brain damage in order to identify an etiological role for psychology to play in this disorder. While occasional positive reports were published the preponderance of this research was negative. Patients with schizophrenia performed remarkably similar to brain-damaged patients on a wide variety of tasks. We see below that this is because schizophrenia results from brain damage.

The **Hoffman and Dobscha (1989)** simulation is based on evidence presented below demonstrating that the normal developmental sequence of cortical synaptic pruning does not end around age 18–20, but continues in those people who soon exhibit their first schizophrenic break. In short, the normal specializing process of brain sculpting continues too far and results in brain damage. The symptoms of schizophrenia are a direct consequence of this over-pruning. This simulation suggests that schizophrenia is an organic condition brought about by an abnormal extension of a normal developmental process that is under genetic control.

The **Hoffman and McGlashan (1993)** simulation extended the over-pruning hypothesis to see if it could account for hallucinations and delusions. They discovered that over-pruning produces what they called 'parasitic foci'; structures that gave rise to paranoid delusions; false memories for events that never occurred. This finding is especially important because we have not previously had any physical mechanism information capable of explaining how paranoid delusions could occur. **Hoffman and McGlashan (1997)** extended this work.

Synaptic Pruning Evidence

This section contains the neuroscience evidence upon which the above-mentioned simulations were based. **Huttenlocher (1979)** studied the brains of 21 normal humans ranging from newborn to age 90 years. Synaptic density of infants was high but increased and peaked between ages 1 to 2 years at a level that is approximately 50% greater than normal adult levels. Synaptic density declined from age 2 to 16 years along with a slight decrease in neuronal density. Synaptic density remained constant from age 16 to 72, but declined further from age 74 to 90.

Huttenlocher (1990) found that the number of synapses per cubic millimeter increased from gestation through birth and peaked at around 8 months of age. Synaptic density then steadily decreased through age 70. I quote the abstract to **Huttenlocher and Dabholkar (1997)** because it succinctly summarizes the main findings.

> The formation of synaptic contacts in human cerebral cortex was compared in two cortical regions: auditory cortex (Heschl's gyrus) and prefrontal cortex (middle frontal gyrus). Synapse formation in both cortical regions begins in the fetus, before conceptual age 27 weeks. Synaptic density increases more rapidly in auditory cortex, where the maximum is reached near postnatal age 3 months. Maximum synaptic density in middle frontal gyrus is not reached until after age 15 months. Synaptogenesis occurs concurrently with dendritic and axonal growth and with myelination of the subcortical white matter. A phase of net synapse elimination occurs late in childhood, earlier in auditory cortex, where it has ended by age 12 years, than in prefrontal cortex, where it extends to midadolescence. Synaptogenesis and synapse elimination in humans appear to be heterochronous in different cortical regions and, in that respect, appears to differ from the rhesus monkey, where they are concurrent. In other respects, including overproduction of synaptic contacts in infancy, persistence of high levels of synaptic density to late childhood or adolescence, the absolute values of maximum and adult synaptic density, and layer specific differences, findings in the human resemble those in rhesus monkeys (p. 167).

Glantz et al. (2007) tracked two synaptic marker proteins, presynaptic synaptophysin and postsynaptic density-95 in 42 subjects aged 18 weeks to 25 years. They found that synaptophysin levels increased slowly from birth until age 5 and then increased more rapidly to a peak at age 10. Synaptophysin then decreased until age 16 where adult levels were reached. PSD-95 levels increased postnatally to a stable plateau reached in early childhood, followed by a slight reduction through late adolescence and early adulthood.

The importance of these studies is that they confirm the fundamental brain-sculpting feature of the proposed Bio↔Psychology Network Theory. Neurons that fire together wire together and those that do not are removed. Learning customizes brain networks and this specialization uses fewer and fewer synapses. The observed rich array of synapses at birth, growth spurt during early childhood, and progressive decline with age and psychological development strongly supports the learning and memory mechanisms provided in this book.

Frontal Lobe Damage

Parks and Levine (1998) simulated normal and abnormal functioning on the Wisconsin Card Sorting Task (WCST) performance and on verbal fluency; two tests that reflect brain damage to the dorsolateral prefrontal cortex (DLPFC) and especially the left DLPFC in the case of verbal fluency. Their model is of Alzheimer's disease. Both are tests for cognitive flexibility. On the WCST, brain-damaged people can learn to sort as fast as normal people when color is relevant, but then they perseverate on color when the criterion turns to shape. There are several versions of the word fluency test. Participants can be asked to spontaneously generate as many words as possible beginning with the letters F, A, and S, or C, F, and L, or P, R, and W, disallowing proper names or repeating the same word with a different ending. These investigators were able to successfully model the perseveration that occurs with brain damage.

Hysteria

The **Lloyd (1994)** simulation is unusual in that it endeavors to explain symptoms of what was once called hysteria without explicitly simulating unconscious processes or ego defenses. However, we established in Chapter 3 that the network cascade always operates unconsciously.

Lucy was a governess and English tutor in the household of a widower who was a factory director. It seems that Lucy fell in love with this man after he expressed his gratitude over the care she provided for his children. Some months later a female guest violated Victorian standards by kissing the children on the mouth as she departed. The man took out his fury on Lucy because she did not protect the children from this insult. This was to be Lucy's first trauma, but her symptoms did not appear immediately. They occurred only after a second trauma several months later when another guest also kissed the children on the mouth, whereupon the man vented his fury on the guest but not on Lucy who recalled smelling cigar smoke during this incident. This was identified as the first moment of Lucy's hysterical conversion.

Several months later Lucy received a letter from her mother. While reading it she felt like quitting her job but was conflicted because she knew that she would miss her employer and the children. These conflicts traumatized her. Just then she became aware of the smell of burnt pudding. This was the second moment of hysterical conversion where the persistent smell of burnt pudding, a hallucination, began. This symptom, along with a chronic depression and an abnormally runny nose due to chronic rhinitis, caused her to seek treatment from Dr. Freud.

Freud discovered these events in reverse order. He first linked the pudding smell to the second trauma and then uncovered Lucy's love for her boss. Lucy's burnt pudding symptom began to fade, but then she reported a second symptom of hallucinating cigar smoke which then led to recovering memory for the first trauma. Several days later Lucy was reported to have made a full recovery. Just how and why her depression remitted and whether or not her runny nose improved was not reported.

Lloyd (1994) abstracted ten features of Lucy's case. Four agents were identified: (a) the boss (director); (b) the children; (c) the servants and other household members; and (d) the guests. One action, inappropriate kissing, was identified. Three clinical features were identified: (a) pain due to her rhinitis; (b) the smell of cigar smoke; and (c) the smell of burnt pudding. Two affects were identified: (a) love for the director and his children; and (b) generalized emotional distress. A separate processing node was used to represent each of the ten features. Each processing node was connected to all others. The most curious feature of this simulation for me is that it included only conscious components.

Phillips and Woody (1994) provided a brief commentary on the Lucynet model of hysteria presented above.

Olds (1994) was an Associate Clinical Professor at the Columbia College of Physicians and Surgeons and supervising analyst at the Columbia Center for Psychoanalytic Training and Research when he wrote '**Connectionism and Psychoanalysis**'. While not a simulation per se, this article articulates the relevance of connectionism to psychoanalysis better than any other article I have found.

CONCLUSIONS

Psychology has readily incorporated brain scanning as new tools for the study of psychological phenomena. These tools replace subjective introspective accounts with hard extraspective data, thereby advancing psychology as a natural science. A major limitation of this technology is that it does not, because it cannot, explain how the identified neural networks that mediate psychological phenomena actually generate psychology and behavior. Reductionism provides but half of a complete explanation. Synthetic emergent explanations are required to explain how mind emerges from brain; how psychology emerges from biology. Computer and hardware neural network simulations are the new tools that will enable psychological science to answer these fundamental questions.

Several criticisms of simulations were provided and rebutted. Successful simulations of the Stroop effect, language acquisition, personality, attitude formation and change, stereotypes, and aging were presented. Simulations of psychological disorders including dyslexia, schizophrenia, frontal lobe damage, and hysteria were presented. The next chapter provides a more comprehensive and critical evaluation of the proposed Bio↔Psychology Network Theory along with rebuttals. This next chapter concludes the first section of this book.

PART Three

Evaluation: Criticisms & Rebuttals

CHAPTER 7

Evaluation, Criticisms, and Rebuttals

Contents

Cognitive Neuroscience and Psychotherapy
http://dx.doi.org/10.1016/B978-0-12-420071-5.00007-7

I begin this chapter by considering the criteria that should be used when evaluating the proposed Bio↔Psychology Network Theory. Then I engage in a comparative analysis of this theory against a generalized version of cognitive theory and of psychodynamic theory using the identified criteria. Then I present 13 novel features and seven novel predictions derived from the proposed Bio↔Psychology Network Theory. Next I review criticisms of connectionism and provide rebuttals. Finally, I report that there is mathematical proof of the adequacy of the proposed network models, and conclude with comments concerning psychology as a unified science.

The proposed Bio↔Psychology Network Theory is not a new theory in the ordinary sense of needing to be tested to see if it can be empirically supported. Only its organization in terms of core and corollary network principles is new. Its content consists of the unanticipated, unarticulated, and unacknowledged implications of well-replicated psychological phenomena that can be explained by accepted neuroscience and connectionist mechanisms plus multivariate statistics.

CRITERIA FOR EVALUATING THEORIES

How shall we evaluate a psychological theory? This section sets forth a series of criteria for evaluating all psychological theories. The following section engages in a comparative evaluation of the proposed Bio↔Psychology Network Theory with a generalized form of cognitive theory upon which cognitive-behavior therapies are based, and a generalized form of psychodynamic theory upon which psychodynamic therapies are based.

Prediction

The goals of science are **prediction** and **explanation**. Quantitative predictions can be made statistically without any understanding of the causal mechanisms involved. One does not need to be able to explain anything in order to make predictions. Just measure the relevant variables and solve a multiple regression equation for the regression coefficients, beta weights, and begin predicting. No psychological understanding is required. The ability of psychological theories to predict can be assessed by comparing R^2 values associated with these multiple regressions.

None of the theories that clinical psychologists currently use make quantitative predictions of any kind. Some of the network simulations associated with the proposed Bio↔Psychology Network Theory reviewed in Chapter 6 make quantitative predictions that agree closely with data obtained from people. The ability of network models to make quantitative predictions via simulations based on first principles distinguishes them in a very positive way. A definitive advantage of neural network theories is that they can generate predictions that can be compared with human data.

Explanation

Explanation requires understanding. Advancing understanding is mainly why theories are highly valued. Psychological explanations are always functional because they lack causal mechanisms. They lack proximal causal mechanism information and therefore cannot actually explain how or why the functional relationships discovered by psychologists work as they do. What passes for explanation is based on structural equation models, path models, and regression models. These models **account** for variation but do not, because they cannot, **explain** this variation. These models do not explain variation because they do not inform us as to **why** or **how** the identified variables correlate as they do. Explanation requires **causal mechanism information**; i.e., a chain of necessary and/or sufficient conditions that bring about the effects to be explained. Statistical models do not provide this information because they were not developed to do so.

Proctor and Capaldi (2001) discussed the need to place facts into a theoretical context because, as is the case in courtrooms, the evidence does not speak for itself. A series of isolated facts may prove guilt beyond a reasonable doubt or not; the answer cannot be obtained from the facts alone. Someone needs to contextualize the facts. The prosecuting attorney creates a guilty meaning from the facts, whereas the defense attorney creates a not guilty meaning from the same facts. Similarly, scientific facts require placement into a causal context in order to create an explanation. Functional relationships need to be contextualized, situated, in a causal context to be fully understood.

There is considerable merit in being able to explain existing facts. Proctor and Capaldi (2001) reported that British geologists contextualized geologic facts in terms of plate tectonic theory well before American geologists did because they place a higher value on theory than Americans do. Oreskes (1999) noted that American geologists almost exclusively limited themselves to hypothesis testing and fact accumulation, which explains why they were behind the British when it came to explaining those facts. American psychological science seems similarly committed to finding facts rather than explaining them.

Explanatory Scope

Mini-theories have a narrow explanatory scope. They typically address one or a few phenomena of interest usually to a small group of investigators who have specialized in the same area. Scientists generally prefer theories with a larger explanatory scope. Ideally, we would like to have a single theory that explains everything of psychological interest, but that is an ideal that all existing theories fall short of so we should not require this of any particular theory. However, we prefer theories in direct proportion to their explanatory scope.

Supporting Evidence

Theories are conjectures until, and in direct proportion to, the empirical support that they receive. Disagreement exists regarding what constitutes evidence. Rychlak (1968, 1981a) discerned two types of evidence: procedural and validating. **Procedural evidence** only requires consistency. Theories are deemed supported if they are internally consistent. **Consistency** is accepted as sufficient evidence of **validity**. No further support is required for full acceptance from this perspective. Philosophical arguments and case formulations by therapists stimulate a sense of conviction through consistency that is accepted as proof. Freud made frequent use of procedural evidence according to Rychlak (1968, 1981a).

Validating evidence requires that a priori hypotheses be made and tested via observation. Consistency remains necessary but is no longer sufficient. Alternative consistent explanations are sought and when found research is required to decide among them. These epistemological requirements separate natural science from philosophy and theology.[1] Investigators who accept only validating evidence do not necessarily agree on what constitutes a sufficiently rigorous test. We saw in Chapter 4 regarding Principle 6 concerning consonance and dissonance that people set a low bar for confirming evidence and a high bar for disconfirming evidence relative to their preferred hypotheses.

[1] Human science (http://en.wikipedia.org/wiki/Human_science) is a branch of psychology that does not require validational evidence. Procedural evidence is fully acceptable.

Falsifiability

Scientific hypotheses must be falsifiable in order to be legitimate. Not all statements, conjectures, and/or predictions can be falsified by objective observation, and therefore not all statements, conjectures, and/or predictions constitute valid scientific hypotheses. Only legitimate scientific hypotheses can be properly tested because only legitimate scientific hypotheses can be falsified. Not all topics are amenable to natural scientific study.

Clinical Practice

Clinical psychologists, such as members of American Psychological Association Division 12, Society of Clinical Psychology, are a subset of all psychologists. They want a psychological theory that specifically addresses health care delivery which broadly entails: (a) etiology; (b) diagnosis; and (c) treatment of disorders specified by the *Diagnostic and Statistical Manual,* as well as other conditions not included there such as family and existential issues. While understandable, this is a somewhat unusual request. Members of Division 14, the Society for Industrial and Organizational Psychology, could demand to have a theory that specifically speaks to their concerns and professional issues. Members of Division 15, Educational Psychology, and members of Division 16, School Psychology, could likewise demand to have a theory that specifically addressed educational and school-related matters. I could continue with additional examples for each of the remaining 52 APA divisions, but trust that the reader now understands that the requirement for a comprehensive psychological theory to specifically address the professional issues of every one of the currently 56 APA divisions is an unreasonable requirement by any standard. What I am asking here is for the reader not to take an overly narrow view of psychological theory when rendering an evaluation. Stated otherwise, judging a theory exclusively on the basis that it meets all of the special needs and interests of any specific group constitutes an overly narrow and parochial perspective that fails to consider larger issues that pertain to psychological science as a whole. I ask that the proposed Bio↔Psychology Network Theory be evaluated against a broader context. Insofar as members of every APA division are applying principles of psychological science to specific areas and topics of interest, a comprehensive psychological theory should have a sufficiently broad explanatory scope to address their general concerns.

Novel Features

Science prefers theories that have novel features; i.e., features not found in other theories. This is because theories guide inquiry and novel features direct us to look for and at features that other theories do not focus our attention on. For example, being able to comment on, explain, consciousness is a novel feature because theories that psychologists commonly use do not address this topic; i.e., they assume consciousness exists and therefore make no effort to explain it. Connectionism is the only theoretical approach that endeavors to explain consciousness.

Novel Predictions

It should be sufficient for a theory to explain existing facts. The plate tectonics case mentioned above is evidence in support of this view. However, theories that make novel predictions are valued over those that do not because theory is supposed to direct and guide inquiry. Novel predictions direct investigators to look in new places and sometimes in new ways. Science therefore prefers theories that provide novel predictions.

Paradigm Shift

The penultimate criterion for evaluating theories is whether or not they provide/support a **qualitative** change in our understanding; what Kuhn (1962, 1970, 1996, 2012) described as a paradigm shift.[2] Theories that require a qualitative shift in our understanding are the theories that make the most impact on a science because such theories typically call for new methods, as well as new interpretations. Any theory that marshals evidence in support of a paradigm change makes a major contribution. We have already seen that the proposed Bio↔Psychology Network Theory is such a theory.

TYPES OF SUPPORTING EVIDENCE

There are two general types of logic that can be used to support theoretical analyses. The more persuasive argument concerns **common antecedents**, also known as **affirming the antecedent**, more formally known as **Modus Ponens**. The general form of this argument is If p, then q. p, therefore q. For example, Freud (1895) reported that every one of the 18 cases of hysteria that he saw were sexually molested as young children; i.e., before the age of the second dentition when they acquired their adult teeth. He concluded, and I believe correctly, that child sexual abuse is psychologically harmful.

The far less persuasive argument concerns **treatment response**, i.e., outcome evidence, because it commits the logical fallacy of **affirming the consequent**. The general form of this argument is If p then q, q, therefore p.

[2] http://en.wikipedia.org/wiki/The_Structure_of_Scientific_Revolutions

Although we generally credit the investigator's theory when their treatments work and when their hypotheses are supported, **investigators can be right for the wrong reasons**; they can make correct predictions regarding therapeutic outcomes for invalid reasons. Treatments can work for entirely different reasons than their authors believe. Alternatively stated, theorists can be completely wrong about the reasons why their therapies work. Proving causality is much more difficult than making predictions. The following sections document the problem of inferring causation from treatment results.

Systematic Desensitization

Multiple studies demonstrated that systematic desensitization is an effective treatment for phobias and other anxiety disorders. Wolpe (1958, 1969, 1995) explained these therapeutic results on the basis that deep muscle relaxation reciprocally inhibited anxiety. A detailed discussion of research that undercuts this clinical hypothesis is presented in Chapter 11. Some investigators claimed that systematic desensitization worked because of counterconditioning. Other investigators claimed habituation was the real cause. Still other investigators claimed that extinction was the real cause. Tryon (2005) falsified these and other explanations before providing a connectionist explanation that also fits the facts. In short, Wolpe's explanation of an effective treatment was wrong.

ADHD

Explanation of how medications work based on their clinical effects is also subject to error. Consider causal explanations of ADHD based on evidence that stimulant medications effectively treat symptoms of ADHD. There are many well-controlled double-blind intervention studies that have been conducted on large samples of children diagnosed with ADHD that clearly demonstrate that stimulant medication is effective (Greenhill & Ford, 2002). These effects have been used to infer causes of ADHD. A major problem with such inferences is that **all** children do better on stimulant medication, as do **all** adults. The benefits of stimulant medication for all children was clearly described in a front-page article in the October 9, 2012 edition of The New York Times by Alan Schwarz entitled *Attention Disorder or Not, Pills to Help in School* where children with poor academic performance and discipline problems in underfunded and inadequate schools are prescribed stimulant medication because the consistent result is that their attention and grades improve and they are more obedient with teachers and parents. One physician is cited as saying that he only gives these prescriptions to children with low grades, not to children who get As and Bs, to avoid the real and negative consequences of poor school performance. It is well known that students in professional schools such as law and medicine frequently use stimulant medication to improve their performance. The net result of stimulant medication helping normal children and adults as well as children with ADHD undercuts all causal inferences about psychopathology regarding ADHD. Put simply, ADHD is not caused by a lack of stimulants.

Depression

There is a large literature that supports the efficacy and effectiveness of psychotropic medications for depression (Nemeroff & Schatzberg, 2002). In Chapter 11 under the heading **Placebos Equal Antidepressive Medications** I discuss evidence that seriously questions inferences that are routinely made about the biochemical causes of depression. The first problem is that medications are not always superior to other treatments. Kirsch (2010) reviewed a meta-analysis of 38 clinical trials involving more than 3,000 depressed patients and found that the average improvement from drug was not better than psychotherapy, although both were better than placebo which was far better than no treatment.

Kirsch (2010) reported that the monoamine (serotonin, norepinephrine, and dopamine) hypothesis arose from uncontrolled clinical observations. He then presented evidence from controlled research that falsified this hypothesis. For example, selective serotonin reuptake inhibitors (SSRI) make serotonin more available in synapses and should be far more effective than norepinephrine dopamine reuptake inhibitors (NDRI), yet research shows a 60% recovery from depression with SSRI medications versus a 59% recovery rate with NDRI medications. Equivalent effectiveness of SSRI and NDRI medications falsifies the claim that serotonin deficiency is the cause of depression.

More telling is that selective serotonin reuptake **enhancer** (SSRE) medications are no more effective than selective serotonin reuptake **inhibitor** (SSRI) medications. SSRE medications decrease serotonin, whereas SSRI medications increase serotonin. Kirsch reported that SSRI medications resulted in 62% recovery, whereas SSRE medications resulted in 63% recovery from depression. The finding that they are equally clinically effective at treating depression indicates that serotonin is not directly causing depression. Then there are the 90 serotonin depletion studies in non-depressed participants that Kirsch (2010) cited. Chemically depleting the serotonin levels of non-depressed people did not make them depressed.

That these data are not isolated cherry-picked findings is supported by Mukherjee (2011) who cited Marcia Angell, a former *New England Journal of Medicine* editor as saying 'After decades of trying to prove [the chemical-imbalance theory], researchers have still come up empty-handed'. Kirsch (2010) also reported the stunning finding that a barbiturate sleeping aid and a synthetic thyroid medication relieve depression as well as antidepressive medications do. These facts seriously undercut all causal inferences about psychopathology based on evidence of clinical effectiveness of antidepressant medications.

Psychosis

There is substantial evidence that supports the efficacy and effectiveness of pharmacological treatments for schizophrenia (Bradford et al., 2002). The main putative mechanism of these medications is to suppress dopamine or serotonin activity.[3] Elevating dopamine or serotonin in normal people does not always make them schizophrenic. Hence, inferring the cause of psychosis from medication effects is untenable.

Medicine

Aspirin relieves pain. That fact does not inform us with regard to the mechanisms by which aspirin works. Evidence of clinical effectiveness is useful in treatment settings but carries little, if any, probative value regarding causal mechanisms. I now consider other types of supporting evidence.

Manipulation and Replication

True experiments require random assignment and manipulation. Investigators rely on **manipulation** and **replication** to separate causes from effects. Manipulation enables investigators to introduce a cause at a time of their choosing. This minimizes the possibility that some other 'real' cause was operative. Methodological replication entails reintroducing the putative cause in the same or different participants, depending upon the nature of the cause, to further minimize the possibility that some uncontrolled variables are at work.

Methodological replication is the acid test of science in that one must be able to replicate results, within and between laboratories, before confident conclusions can be drawn. This is why at least two investigators working in different laboratories must demonstrate positive outcomes before a treatment can be considered as empirically supported.

[3] http://en.wikipedia.org/wiki/Schizophrenia

One way that clinical outcome can confidently confirm clinical conjecture concerning the cause of a therapeutic response is through the use of **single-subject research designs**. For example, consider the ABAB research design where A represents baseline, and B represents intervention. If consistently high responding during baseline becomes consistently low during intervention, returns to being consistently high when intervention is suspended and baseline conditions are reinstated, and if responding returns to the previously observed consistently low levels during the second application of the intervention, then one can be confident that it was the intervention and not the therapeutic relationship or any other variable that was responsible for the observed behavioral changes. This is partly because the therapist chose the timing and duration of each ABAB phase. It would be very difficult for chance events to cause therapeutic effects to begin and end at exactly those times chosen by the therapist. Statistical analysis is unnecessary in these cases, but recent developments analyzing single-subject data with non-parametric methods have been developed (Levin et al., 2012). There are other single-subject research designs and all of them implement replication in some way. Unfortunately, not all clinical conditions can be studied using single-subject research designs. For example, one cannot give, remove, and then reinstate insight. Such things are not reversible and that precludes replication within a single subject.

Replication is not fool-proof. I now describe two situations in which investigators conducted highly controlled research, replicated findings, and then reached invalid conclusions based on their data.

A graduate student colleague of mine at Kent State University conducted a study of memory using rats. Rats prefer dark spaces. So he shocked these animals, thereby causing them to fear dark places. Then he decapitated the rats, extracted their brains, homogenized them in a blender, and used a centrifuge to spin off an extract that he hypothesized contained a molecular form of the fear memory called **photoscoben** as I recall. He injected this extract into the brains of naïve rats and put them in a maze with dark and light arms. The rats confirmed his hypothesis by avoiding the dark arm, preferring the light arm. It seemed like the brain extract transmitted the fear-of-the-dark memory to the naïve rats. He replicated this effect in multiple animals. So was his conclusion correct?

It turns out that the answer is 'No', because there was a confound that was responsible for the replicated results. He finally realized that rats urinated when shocked and that the urine of shocked rats could contain chemicals that other rats might detect. So he washed down his apparatus after shocking the experimental subjects to remove any urinary clues. He could no longer replicate his earlier results. The naïve rats injected with the brain extract consistently preferred the dark arm of the maze just like the control rats did. The take-home lesson here is that even well-replicated results should be cautiously interpreted, because some unknown factor may actually be the causal agent and the investigator's preferred explanation may be completely wrong. The other take-home message is that this graduate student was a bright astute investigator who took care to evaluate alternative explanations rather than stopping with the first positive result. His behavior serves as a model for us all.

My second example comes from my 1976 *American Psychologist* article entitled 'Models of Behavior Disorder' (Tryon, 1976b). I cited several studies that replicated the therapeutic finding that a procedure called flooding or implosion could reduce fear in animals. The procedure is as follows. A rat is shocked in a distinctive space shortly after a light is turned on. The rat escapes from that space as soon as the shock comes on, thereby terminating the shock and the light. Shock offset negatively reinforces running out of that area. The light becomes a discriminative stimulus that predicts shock onset. Hence, the animal learns to escape from that part of the apparatus as soon as the light comes on. The second part of the experiment concerns treatment. The **extinction** treatment, control condition, entails turning the light on but no longer administering the shock. The rat initially escapes as before, but gradually takes longer to leave and eventually learns that shock no longer follows light onset. The **flooding** treatment involves closing a door to the space thus preventing escape, turning the light on but not presenting the shock. As you can imagine, the trapped rat becomes frantic in their attempt to escape the expected shock. When no shock occurs, the rat eventually calms down. The door is then opened thereby allowing the rat to leave that area.

The main dependent variable is the latency to leave the area where shock was administered. The data seemed to clearly show that flooding was more effective at fear reduction than extinction was. When the animals who underwent flooding were put back into the shock compartment they took significantly longer to leave than did the animals that underwent extinction. These results are replicable. Were the investigators correct when they concluded that flooding was an effective method of fear reduction?

The answer is 'No' again. The flaw in this study was discovered by placing the animals in an adjacent chamber to the shock chamber. Food was placed inside the shock chamber where the rat could see and smell it. The experimenters measured the time it took for the animals to enter the former shock chamber to get the food. The extinguished rats readily and rapidly entered the enclosure with a short latency. The flooded animals reluctantly and hesitantly entered the enclosure. Flooding markedly reduced the rat's activity level in **all** situations. They were slow to leave the enclosure and were also slow to enter it. Such slowness is evidence of depression rather than therapeutic gain. Here we have a second example of how replicated results were used to support an incorrect explanation. Unfortunately, this study did not become nearly as well-known as did the flooding studies with the consequence that an untold number of patients were 'flooded' in the name of treatment.

The take-home lesson here again is that even well-replicated results should be cautiously interpreted when it comes to causal explanation, because some unknown factor or factors may actually be the causal agent and the investigator's preferred explanation may be completely wrong. Now that we have seen how causal inference can be so wrong even under laboratory conditions where relevant variables can be carefully controlled, we should be ever more wary of causal interpretations based on clinical evidence.

Necessary Condition Thesis

Freud justified the evidence he obtained from his clinical work and based his claim that he did not need to abide by the rigors of research methodology on what Grünbaum (1984) characterized as Freud's Necessary Condition Thesis, which is the conjunction of the following two causally necessary conditions:

> (1) only the psychoanalytic method of interpretation and treatment can yield or mediate to the patient correct insight into the unconscious pathogens of his psychoneurosis, and (2) the analysand's correct insight into the etiology of his affliction and into the unconscious dynamics of his character is, in turn, *causally necessary* for the therapeutic conquest of his neurosis. I shall refer to the conjunction of these two Freudian claims as his "Necessary Condition Thesis" or, for brevity, "NCT" pp. 139–40, (italics in the original).

In clinical practice the NCT works like a lock (patient's problem) and a set of keys (possible interpretations). Putting the wrong key into the lock does nothing. Only the one right key will turn the lock. That a particular key turned the lock is positive proof that it was the correct key. Outcome here is proof of cause. The interpretation that yields clinical benefit is taken as positive and definite proof of its validity even though it isn't. This reasoning is erroneously thought to guarantee certainty of conclusion and is seen to fully justify the validity of consulting room research, thus obviating the need for controlled scientific research because there seems to be no way to mistake the wrong key for the right one. No possibility of error is acknowledged here. Uncertainty about whether the key is the correct one or not is completely reduced when the key turns the lock or doesn't. Hence there is no perceived need for a control group or any other research method. The clinical consulting couch is mistakenly understood to be completely probative.

The fatal flaw in this reasoning is located in Freud's first assumption[4] that the psychoanalytic method is the **only** method that can produce therapeutic results. The efficacy and effectiveness of CBT and pharmacology, including placebos, reveals that the psychoanalytic method is not the only method that can produce therapeutic effects. Multiple keys can turn the lock. Hence, lock turning is no longer specifically or definitely probative, and cannot prove that the theory behind the method is correct. We are thus returned to the realm of uncertainty that constrains all reasonable persons. The need for controlled scientific research is firmly reestablished. The consulting room is not entirely probative and theories based on such evidence remain unvalidated.

Conclusion

The main message here is that evidence of clinical effectiveness is not definite positive proof of any specific causal explanation, because the clinical results could have been produced by any number of other causes other than the preferred explanation including placebo effects. Evidence of CBT efficacy and effectiveness does not prove that the associated cognitive theory is correct, nor does evidence of the efficacy and effectiveness of psychodynamic therapy prove that the associated psychodynamic theory is correct. Causal explanation is difficult and requires controlled investigation.

A COMPARATIVE EVALUATION

This section compares the proposed Bio↔Psychology Network Theory with a generalized form of cognitive theory that underlies cognitive-behavior therapies and a generalized form of psychodynamic theory that underlies psychodynamic therapies using the criteria for evaluating theories identified above. There is little more than a generalized abstract form of cognitive theory that underlies cognitive-behavioral therapies so my presentation here can be brief. However, there are many psychodynamic theories. I cannot comment on each one in detail. Nor can I do justice to any of them. I am therefore limited to commenting on general features that psychodynamic theories share.

[4] Fatal logical flaws are frequently found in assumptions, which is why one should be very very careful in what one assumes. Illusions and assumptions are two common routes to error.

Explanation

Cognitive Theory

The general cognitive theory that underlies all variations of cognitive-behavior therapy was presented by Judith Beck (2010), a leading CBT authority, in the section of her book entitled 'What is the theory underlying cognitive behavior therapy'. Her entire presentation was just one page long. It merely asserted that how people think influences how they feel and act. It did not explain how any of this works. No further details were provided regarding how cognitions influence each other, how cognitions cause emotions, and/or how cognitions and emotions cause behavior. All of this was assumed without explanation. This 'theory' serves only to justify clinical interventions that restructure cognitions.

Psychodynamic Theory

Psychodynamic theories are also functional theories, in that they claim that conscious and unconscious mental states influence each other and generate thoughts, feelings, and actions. No causal mechanism information is provided regarding how thoughts influence one another, how thoughts cause feelings, how feelings cause thoughts, or how thoughts and feelings cause behavior. No causal mechanism information is provided for how cognitions become unconscious or return to consciousness.

Bio↔Psychology Network Theory

Kazdin (2009, p. 276) evaluated the proposed Bio↔Psychology Network Theory as follows:

> The primary point I wished to make in the original article (Kazdin, 2008a) is that psychologists have no empirical or evidence-based explanation of how therapy achieves change or of the steps between what a therapist does and improvements in the patient. The model that Tryon presented might well be suited to the task, and perhaps because of its integrative nature and cognitive science underpinnings it should be moved to the front of the line in a long list of explanations of how therapy works (Lambert & Ogles, 2004).
>
> A model that explains is a superb beginning point. It is like a beautiful race horse right before the start of a race. Excitement and hope are present, and there are visions of bouquets and a trophy all crowded into a photo of the winner's circle. However, finishing the race, much less placing or winning, is another matter. A model all ready to go is roughly in the same place – we need to run the race and see the data.

Kazdin's reference to the beginning of a horse race equates the proposed Bio↔Psychology Network Theory with other new theories that await subsequent testing. He was unaware that the hybrid cognitive neuroscience explanation that I formulated in terms of four explanatory core and eight corollary network principles consists of well-documented psychological phenomena, widely accepted connectionist network and neuroscience mechanisms, and multivariate statistics, all of which are accepted without question. The race he refers to has been run over and over again a great many times and the resulting data have been available for a long time. Hence, the core and corollary Bio↔Psychology Network Theory principles are already fully supported and ready to use now with little fear that they will be falsified by subsequent research.

I mentioned above that functional explanations lack mechanism information. They can only assert that relationships exist, but cannot inform us as to why these relationships exist in the way that we find them. The proposed Bio↔Psychology Network Theory is unique in clinical psychology and psychological science generally, in that it was designed to provide mechanism information. This mechanism information is ready to be used to explain a wide variety of psychological phenomena.

Conclusion

The proposed Bio↔Psychology Network Theory approach is the clear and decisive winner here because of the mechanism information provided in Chapters 3 and 4. This theory was designed to provide missing mechanism information and therefore succeeds where other theories have failed.

Explanatory Scope

Cognitive Theory

The generalized cognitive theory that underlies all variants of CBT has a large explanatory scope, in that one can say that cognition influences affect and behavior regarding any topic. What is missing is a more nuanced explanation of each psychological topic that one claims falls within the explanatory scope of the cognitive theory underlying CBT. Whereas the Bio↔Psychology Network Theory has 12 principles that can be combined in specific ways to explain particular psychological phenomena, the generalized cognitive theory that underlies CBT has nothing comparable.

Psychodynamic Theory

The explanatory scope of psychodynamic theories is truly large. But it is also often vague and postdictive. While this is somewhat true of the other two theories, it seems to be more true of psychodynamic theory. In contrast, the Bio↔Psychology Network Theory was constructed from replicable psychological facts that have been predicted and observed so frequently as to no longer be seriously questioned.

Bio↔Psychology Network Theory

This theory has an enormous explanatory scope; much larger than I ever expected. The phenomena that can be explained by the four core network principles that constitute the explanatory nucleus and the eight corollary network principles cover a broad spectrum of basic psychological phenomenon.

Conclusion

The explanatory scope of Bio↔Psychology Network Theory is comparable to that of cognitive theory and psychodynamic theory.

Supporting Evidence

I now consider the degree to which several theoretical positions are supported by empirical evidence that meets natural science standards.

Cognitive Theory

The main, and perhaps only, support for cognitive therapy is the effectiveness and efficacy of CBT. We have seen that such evidence provides only weak support at best for the underlying theory. Therefore, the proper conclusion about the cognitive theory that underlies CBT is that it may or may not correctly explain why CBT works.

The following research suggests that CBT does not work for stated reasons. In a section entitled 'Mechanisms Underlying Psychotherapy Efficacy', Levy and Anderson (2013) reported that CBT does not seem to work for the hypothesized reasons. For example, Burns and Spangler (2001), Ilardi and Craighead (1994), Jacobson et al. (1996), and Tang and DeRubeis (1999) reported clinical improvements prior to cognitive changes and/or prior to implementation of cognitive-change strategies. Webb et al. (2010) failed to find the required association between adherence to CBT methods and treatment outcome. Of special relevance is that the cognitive theory underlying CBT predicts that cognitive change always precedes emotional and behavioral change. DeRubeis et al. (1990) tested and failed to support this causative sequence in their paper entitled '*How does cognitive therapy work? Cognitive change and symptom change in cognitive therapy and pharmacotherapy for depression*'. Levy and Anderson (2013) concluded their review of CBT mechanisms as follows: 'A host of studies have failed to find specific effects on specific, theory-driven mechanisms' (p. 215).

The Bio↔Psychology Network Theory makes a contrary prediction that cognition, affect, and behavior necessarily all change simultaneously in parallel; not in any serial sequence. This prediction is based on, derived from, the network cascade where activation spreads in parallel across multiple network layers. This transformative process (see Chapter 3 for details) simultaneously alters cognitions, emotions, and behaviors with every processing cycle. Hence, it is theoretically impossible for substantial or complete cognitive change to precede either emotional and/or behavioral change.

Psychodynamic Theory

Psychodynamic theory has long been supported by procedural evidence which is unacceptable by natural science standards. However, acceptable contemporary research has provided empirical support for psychodynamic therapies. Meta-analyses by Abbass et al. (2006), Anderson and Lambert (1995), Crits-Christoph (1992), de Maat et al. (2009), Leichsenring (2001, 2005), Leichsenring and Leibing (2003), Leichsenring et al. (2004) and Shedler (2010) have clearly demonstrated that psychodynamic therapies produce therapeutic effects that are greater than wait list controls, and sometimes equal to those produced by cognitive-behavior therapy. Group psychodynamic therapy has not fared nearly so well. Greene (2012) noted:

> Indeed, I have not found psychodynamic group psychotherapy documented as an evidence-based treatment either on any of the established data bases, …, or in recent treatment reviews (Gerber et al., 2011) and in meta-analyses (Burlingame et al., 2003) either because of insufficient rigor or lack of replication studies to date (p. 481).

Tryon and Tryon (2011) were concerned about efforts to attribute common factors exclusively to psychodynamic theory when in fact they pertain to all forms of psychotherapy. Again, we have a situation where therapeutic effects are used to support the theory that gave rise to them. Again I note that such reasoning is far from certain and provides little empirical support.

There are three major reasons to seriously question psychodynamic theory. The first reason to seriously question psychodynamic theory concerns Freud's retraction of his claim that actual sexual abuse causes mental illness and his replacement with an explanation based on the patient's **Oedipal fantasies** (Masson, 1984). The sad fact is that actual sexual abuse is a far more serious cause of psychological disorder than fantasy is. Ignoring the horror of child molestation and rape and recasting the resulting devastating psychological consequences as the result of the patient's own wishful fantasy is reason enough not to support a theory that has yet to formally retract the core explanatory role attributed to Oedipal fantasies. A corollary reason for rejection of psychodynamic theory is its over-dependence on fantasy as revealed by Masson (1984) who quoted from a letter that Anna Freud, Freud's daughter, wrote to him on September 10, 1981 wherein she said:

> Keeping up the seduction theory would mean to abandon the Oedipus complex, and with it the whole importance of phantasy life, conscious or unconscious phantasy. *In fact, I think there would have been no psychoanalysis afterwards* (p. 113, emphasis added).

Rejecting the key causative role of fantasy that Anna Freud understood constituted a central feature of the psychodynamic understanding of psychopathology seriously undercuts this theory.

The second reason to seriously question psychodynamic theory concerns the complete absence of empirical evidence of **symptom substitution**. Chapter 9 provides extensive documentation that psychodynamic theory requires symptom substitution in all cases where symptoms are removed and the underlying issues remain unaddressed and therefore unresolved. According to psychodynamic theory, these festering conflicts will predictably be expressed again in the form of more symptoms. That this prediction has not yet occurred despite the successful treatment of thousands of patients with behavioral and cognitive-behavioral therapies completely falsifies this crucial prediction of psychodynamic theory.

The third reason to seriously question psychodynamic theory is its reliance on the necessary condition thesis (NCT), discussed above, as a primary reason to believe the procedural clinical evidence generated by Freud and his many followers from their interactions with patients. This clinical experience may be suggestive, but it is definitely not probative. Psychodynamic theory must be rejected to the extent that it continues to act as if the NCT provides causal evidence.

Bio↔Psychology Network Theory

The Bio↔Psychology Network Theory was constructed from well-replicated psychological phenomena that could be explained using a combination of well-documented and already-accepted connectionist and neuroscience mechanisms. This theory construction approach confers two important properties: (a) first, because each Bio↔Psychology Network principle began with an already well-replicated psychological finding, it is most unlikely these principles will be falsified by subsequent research. (b) Second, because each Bio↔Psychology Network principle is based on already well-validated and widely accepted connectionist and neuroscience mechanisms, it is most unlikely that these mechanisms will be falsified by subsequent research. (c) Hence, the Bio↔Psychology Network Theory is already well supported by empirical evidence that meets natural science standards. Additional research is always needed and welcomed but is expected to further support, not falsify, the Bio↔Psychology Network Theory.

An alternative way to understand and appreciate the extent to which the Bio↔Psychology Network Theory is empirically supported is that it will remain valid until: (a) neuroscientists decide that neural impulses no longer traverse synapses and PDP-CNN models no longer simulate this process. (b) Neuroscientists reject experience-dependent plasticity principles as the basis of learning and memory. (c) Psychologists reject factor analysis as a legitimate way to generate latent constructs. (d) Reactivation is shown to have nothing to do with memory. (e) Psychologists falsify and reject priming as a valid psychological phenomenon. (e) Part–whole pattern completion no longer characterizes PDP-CNNs. (f) Psychologists falsify and reject the enormous amount of social psychological research showing that people seek consonance and avoid dissonance. (g) Psychologists falsify and reject prototype formation as a legitimate psychological phenomenon; and (h) psychologists falsify and reject all dual-processing theories. It is most unlikely that any, let alone all, of this will happen. The evidence requested by Kazdin (2009) is already in and has been in for quite some time. We can rest assured that the Bio↔Psychology Network Theory is and will remain very well empirically supported.

Conclusion

The Bio↔Psychology Network Theory has the strongest empirical support because it is based on well-replicated psychological findings and accepted connectionist neural network and neuroscience mechanisms.

Falsifiability

Cognitive Theory

DeRubeis et al. (1990) failed to confirm the mediation required by cognitive theory and consequently failed to support, i.e., falsified, CBT. Levy and Anderson (2013) cited several studies that have failed to support the theoretical mechanisms supporting CBT. I could not find supportive studies regarding the putative mechanisms underlying CBT. But we know that CBT works. It could be that CBT works for reasons other than what cognitive theory proposes. I suggest that our Network Principle 8 explains why CBT works.

Psychodynamic Theory

The most significant test of the psychodynamic theory of symptom formation and the primary rationale for psychodynamic therapy is the hard prediction that symptom substitution must necessarily occur when symptoms are directly treated and the underlying causal conflicts are not addressed and resolved. The consistent finding across hundreds if not thousands of studies is that symptom substitution does not occur. Hence, a major portion of psychodynamic theory has been convincingly falsified.

Bio↔Psychology Network Theory

This theory unequivocally predicts that cognitions, emotions, and behaviors change simultaneously because the network cascade entails parallel distributed processing. This is a novel and hard prediction that conflicts with the cognitive theory underlying CBT and all other theories that predict change in some serial order. Existing evidence has not yet established any specific sequence of change (DeRubeis et al., 1990; Levy & Anderson, 2013). This is the only type of evidence that can support the parallel processing claim of simultaneous change and hence no specific order.

The 12 principles that presently constitute Bio↔Psychology Network Theory entail well-replicated psychological facts and thoroughly established neuroscience mechanisms. While these facts and mechanisms are all potentially falsifiable, the amount of empirical support for them to date makes it most unlikely that subsequent research will falsify them.

Conclusion

The Bio↔Psychology Network Theory is both more supported by existing evidence and more resistant to subsequent falsification than is cognitive theory or psychodynamic theory.

Clinical Practice

Cognitive Theory

Cognitive theory provides a general rationale for assessing and modifying cognitions as a means of changing how people think, feel, and behave. No specific direction is provided by cognitive theory with regard to its application to any particular patient.

Psychodynamic Theory

Psychodynamic theory also provides a general understanding of and orientation to psychotherapy. Psychodynamic clinicians have written about doing psychotherapy from a psychodynamic perspective (e.g., Summers & Barber, 2010), but formally stated psychodynamic theory does not provide specific clinical guidance for any particular patient.

Bio↔Psychology Network Theory

The proposed network theory makes at least the five contributions to clinical practice that I presented in Chapter 1 under the heading 'Clinical Relevance'. I therefore will not repeat them again here. I wish to emphasize that this theoretical orientation returns clinical practice to a principled basis from a manualized basis.

Conclusion

The Bio↔Psychology Network Theory makes at least five specific contributions to psychotherapy. It also returns evidence-based clinical practice to a principled rather than a manualized basis.

Novel Features

Desirable theories are expected to have novel features. This section examines what is novel about the Bio↔Psychology Network Theory, cognitive theory, and psychodynamic theory.

Cognitive Theory

I am unaware of any novel features of cognitive theory as it is no longer novel to claim that cognitions influence emotions and behavior.

Psychodynamic Theory

Unconscious processing was once presented as a novel feature of psychodynamic theory, but the brief history of unconscious processing presented in Chapter 9 reveals that this was never actually the case. Freud simply avoided citing any of the many relevant authors who discussed unconscious processing well before he was born, in addition to contemporary scholars who discussed unconscious processing while Freud was 'discovering' it. Freud's emphasis on unconscious processing was not even original for psychology, in that William James had much to say about unconscious processing. However, it is fair to say that within clinical psychology circles, Freud's emphasis on unconscious processing was novel. Unfortunately, Freud prescribed cocaine for his clients and used it himself. He mistook the resulting dreams of sex and aggression for normal psychology rather than the result of cocaine. Hence, sex and aggression were over-represented in his theory. Because unconscious processing has been such a major defining feature of psychodynamic theory for so long it can no longer be considered to be novel.

Other possible novel features of Freudian thought once included the prediction that masturbation causes neuroses (Masson, 1984, p. 59), but novel predictions that prove wrong should discredit a theory; not support it.

Bio↔Psychology Network Theory

Every new theory is expected to be novel in some way in order to command attention. Novel predictions are especially valued. This section contains 13 novel features of the Bio↔Psychology Network Theory.

Novel Feature 1

The most novel feature of the proposed Bio↔Psychology Network Theory is that it provides mechanism information in **physical** rather than mental terms. This is what Freud attempted to do in his *Project for a Scientific Psychology*.

Novel Feature 2

A very novel feature of the proposed Bio↔Psychology Network Theory is that it is formulated in terms of four core principles that comprise an explanatory nucleus and eight corollary principles. No other contemporary psychological theory is formally constructed in this way.

Novel Feature 3

Unlike the clinical guidelines provided by Beutler and Castonguay (2006), the scientific principles presented as core and corollary network principles in this book have much greater explanatory power because they provide mechanism information.

Novel Feature 4

A novel to the point of being unique feature of the proposed network theory is that its general form has been mathematically proven to be able to solve problems of any degree of complexity. Mathematical support is a hallmark of a mature science. No other psychological theory has received such mathematical proof, let alone a psychological theory that has so much clinical relevance as the Bio↔Psychology Network Theory does.

Novel Feature 5

A novel feature of the proposed Bio↔Psychology Network Theory is that it uses a vocabulary that is common to psychology and neuroscience because this theory was developed to integrate psychology and neuroscience. Mischel (2009) maintained that a common vocabulary and tools are essential to the development of a cumulative science because they allow investigators to replicate and extend each other's work. Kuhn (1962, 1970, 1996, 2012) noted that a common vocabulary and set of basic concepts is required before a science can mature. I add that mature sciences replicate reports of findings before considering them to be facts that stand in need of explanation.

Novel Feature 6

The network theory presented in this book replaces the long-standing contemporary conscious-centric orientation of psychological theory with an unconscious-centric orientation. This is a novel, though not unprecedented, contribution and in some ways may be the most important contribution made by the proposed Bio↔Psychology Network Theory. Extensive documentation and discussion of this novel feature is presented in Chapters 3, 5, and 9.

Novel Feature 7

The network theory presented in this book provides a basis for the theoretical unification of psychological science.

Novel Feature 8

The network theory presented in this book provides a basis for psychotherapy integration. The 12 principles that form the Bio↔Psychology Network Theory are consistent with all of the Big Five clinical orientations: (a) behavioral (applied behavior analysis); (b) cognitive; (c) cognitive-behavioral; (d) psychodynamic (emotion-focused therapy); and (e) pharmacologic. This is because the provided mechanism information that advances our understanding of how cognition and affect interact to produce behavior also informs us regarding the nature and effective treatment of a wide range of psychological disorders; especially anxiety and depressive disorders. The proposed Bio↔Psychology Network Theory is fully consistent with Barlow's unified protocol (cf. Allen et al., 2008; Barlow et al., 2011).

Novel Feature 9

The network approach taken in this book was designed to meet both the spirit and letter of the American Psychological Association accreditation requirement that students should receive training in the cognitive and affective bases of behavior. While it seems satisfactory to the Committee on Accreditation for programs to provide separate courses in cognition and emotion, the spirit of this requirement concerns how cognition and affect reciprocally interact to produce behavior. No adequate theoretical orientation was available prior to the Bio↔Psychology Network Theory.

Novel Feature 10

The network approach taken in this book provides a novel explanation for how biofeedback works. Other explanations are critically considered and found to be less compelling than the proposed network explanation. See Chapter 10 for details.

Novel Feature 11

The ability of top-down processing to produce placebo and nocebo effects and the empirical fact that expectation of change ratings are highly correlated with positive therapeutic outcomes suggests that clinicians should first maximize client expectations before implementing their intended treatment.

Novel Feature 12

Therapy is best understood as retraining. This novel perspective derives from methods used to train and retrain artificial connectionist networks. We use this information to retrain biological neural networks. This information was presented as Network Principle 8: Dissonance Induction/Reduction.

Novel Feature 13

The Bio↔Psychology Network Theory explains why we need to sleep by explaining the function of sleep. Neurons that fire together wire together; i.e., their synapses are biologically reinforced. Connections among neurons that are not used are pruned during sleep. Sleep requires that experience-dependent plasticity mechanisms be turned off. This is why we are unconscious during sleep.

Conclusion

The Bio↔Psychology Network Theory has far more novel features than either cognitive theory or psychodynamic theory.

Novel Predictions

Desirable theories are expected to make novel predictions in addition to having novel features. This section examines the novel predictions made by Bio↔Psychology Network Theory, cognitive theory, and psychodynamic theory.

Cognitive Theory

The fact that cognitive theory has been around for so long means that none of its predictions are novel. I do not know of anyone who has recently made what might be considered to be a novel prediction using contemporary cognitive or cognitive behavioral theories.

Psychodynamic Theory

The fact that psychodynamic theory has been around for so long means that none of its predictions are novel. I do not know of anyone who has recently made what might be considered to be a novel prediction using contemporary psychodynamic theory.

Bio↔Psychology Network Theory

The proposed Bio↔Psychology Network Theory makes the following seven novel predictions.

Novel Prediction 1

Unlike computers that remain unchanged by the processing they do, neural networks are changed by the processing they do. This neuroscience fact is known as experience-dependent plasticity. We discussed this process at some length in Chapter 3, but for now it is sufficient to recall that processing modifies the connection weights, simulated synapses, and can even modify neural network architecture, simulated dendritic spines. Because the biological mechanisms of learning and memory modify synapses, because psychoactive substances activate synapses, and because connectionist models learn and remember by modifying connection weights, I predict that **just as biology unified around the concept of the cell, psychology will unify around the concept of the synapse. The connectome is to psychology what the genome is to biology**. I am supported in this regard by at least the following two authorities. First, I cite LeDoux (2002) whose book is entitled *Synaptic Self: How Our Brain's Become Who We Are.* He claims 'You are your synapses' (p. ix) and 'My notion of personality is pretty simple: it's that your "self", the essence of who you are, reflects patterns of interconnectivity between neurons in your brain' (p. 2). Second, I cite the following quote from the preface of Hell and Ehlers (2008) major 779-page work, entitled *Structural and Functional Organization of the Synapse.*

> Computationally, synapses play a central role in signal transmission and processing that represent evolution's solution to learning and memory. Nervous systems, including our own brains, possess an extraordinary capacity for

adaptation and memory because **the synapse, not the neuron, constitutes the basis unit for information storage** (bold emphasis added).

Novel Prediction 2

Carlson et al. (2010) defined learning in terms of memory, '*Learning* refers to the process by which experiences change our nervous system and hence our behavior. We refer to these changes as *memories*' (italics in the original) (p. 440). Learning and memory involve many of the same neural networks. It is a novel prediction that learning-based therapies such as CBT can be expected to automatically modify memory. See Tryon and McKay (2009) for additional details. Brian Pilicki's Fordham University doctoral dissertation is presently testing the validity of this prediction.

A novel corollary is that the memory matrices we previously discussed in Chapter 5 are composed of cognitive and affective elements that collectively can be graphically illustrated as a memory well; a structure that resembles an upside down Mexican sombrero is depicted in Figure 11.2. Modifying the cognitive and/or emotional components of these memory matrices modifies the structure of the associated memory well which alters how it functions. Here we have novel mechanism information for how CBT modifies memories.

Novel Prediction 3

Cognitive and cognitive-behavioral theories maintain that emotions are caused by cognitions. A novel prediction made by the proposed network theory is that the parallel processing network cascade principle on which it is based requires that thoughts, feelings, and behaviors change simultaneously; not sequentially. This hard novel prediction maintains that mediation effects do not actually exist, and that any evidence favoring mediation is due to artifact or some other non-substantive cause.

A corollary point is that in connectionist models such as the bidirectional association memory (BAM) model, cognition and affect are encoded together; not separately. Hence, there cannot be any serial processing between cognition and emotion. Either both cognition and memory change simultaneously or they don't.

A second corollary implication of the simultaneous change caused by parallel processing concerns the point of entry for clinicians. Behavior therapists first seek to change behaviors. Cognitive therapists seek to first change cognitions. Other therapists may seek to first change feelings. The proposed network position does not privilege any one point of entry over others. One can, in principle, obtain equal therapeutic effects starting from any one perspective.

It might well be easier or faster to begin with one point of entry or another for any given patient, but this is a pragmatic matter rather than a principled theoretical decision. It is largely a matter for therapists and clients to decide as part of establishing a working alliance. It is no longer a basis to develop and defend separate and competitive schools of psychotherapy.

Novel Prediction 4

Another novel prediction is that people have **automatic feelings** as well as automatic thoughts. This is because the network cascades that cause cognitions also cause feelings when pertinent neural networks are activated. The network cascade process occurs automatically, unconsciously, and deterministically. Hence, feelings can occur as automatically as thoughts.

Novel Prediction 5

Psychotherapists traditionally have understood client resistance in psychodynamic terms. A novel prediction of our theory is that some of the resistance that therapists encounter is actually post-decision dissonance reduction.

Novel Prediction 6

The proposed Bio↔Psychology Network Theory predicts that psychotherapists who maximize expectations of success will have more positive outcomes than clinicians who do not.

Novel Prediction 7

Nature appears to conserve neural networks. For example, the neural networks used for image generation (Farah, 2000), better known as imagination, largely overlap the neural networks used for vision (Kosslyn & Thompson, 2000). Vision is mainly a bottom-up process, whereas image generation is largely a top-down process. If the mirror neuron system is what mediates our ability to process and understand the thoughts and feelings of other people then it follows that the same network mediates our ability to understand our own thoughts and feelings. Hence, mirror neurons may mediate the social and cognitive deficits found in Asperger's syndrome. Future brain imaging research is needed to test this novel neuroscience hypothesis.

Conclusion

The Bio↔Psychology Network Theory makes many more novel predictions than do contemporary cognitive, cognitive-behavioral, or psychodynamic theories.

Paradigm Shift

It is a rare scientific theory that requires a paradigmatic shift in how phenomena are understood. The proposed Bio↔Psychology Network Theory is such a theory. The following realizations require paradigm shift: (a) psychological explanations are functional theories that lack real mechanism information because; (b) there is no psychological substrate for them to operate on. (c) Thinking in physical rather than mental terms requires some form of network theory in order to integrate psychology and neuroscience. (d) This conceptual shift is what the proposed Bio↔Psychology Network Theory provides.

ASSESSING THEORETICAL UNIFICATION

The purpose of this section is to assess the extent to which the proposed Bio↔Psychology Network Theory provides a basis for theoretical unification. Remember, theoretical unification is about **consensus**, not necessarily about being correct in every respect. Consensus here means acceptance of the proposed Bio↔Psychology Network Theory on the basis of what it can do for psychology. That reduces to reasons for and against adopting this perspective. But first I have a few words to say about how the search for mechanism information facilitates theoretical unification before assessing the reasons for and against adopting the proposed Bio↔Psychology Network Theory.

Search for Mechanisms Provides Synthetic Perspective

All previous attempts to achieve theoretical unification and/or psychotherapy integration have understandably been concerned with the **manifest content** of the theories in question. Beitman et al. (1989) provided a historical overview of the movement toward integrating the psychotherapies. Authors have repeatedly attempted to translate theoretical terms from one orientation into those of another, but important content always fails to translate. These consistent failures indicate that there is little reason to persist with trying to integrate the manifest content of diverse psychological theories.

The search for **mechanism information** provided an alternate route to theoretical unification in psychology for the following reasons: (a) contemporary psychological theories are functional theories and as such they cannot provide causal mechanism information. (b) This means that psychological theories don't have real mechanism information to offer, despite efforts to appear as though they do. (c) Thus, there are no conflicting positions regarding causal mechanisms that require resolution. (d) Hence, I start from a position of no-conflict which is a great advantage. (e) The proposed

Bio↔Psychology Network Theory explains psychological phenomena in **physical** rather than **mental** terms using neuroscience and connectionist mechanisms. (f) No other psychological theory does this. (g) Therefore, the only remaining question is whether individuals will endorse the proposed Bio↔Psychology Network Theory or not. I now consider the reasons for and against this decision.

Reasons for and Against Network Theory

This section is based on the assumption that residual differences remain regarding the philosophical issues that have so long divided us in the past into Lockeans, Kantians, and mixed Lockeans and Kantians. I now address the reasons for and against accepting the proposed Bio↔Psychology Network Theory stemming from each of these three perspectives.

Lockeans

Reasons for Bio↔Psychology Network Theory

Freud's (1895b) *Project for a Scientific Psychology* was intended to be a natural science explanation of psychological phenomena in physical terms for neurologists and neuroscientists. The proposed Bio↔Psychology Network Theory is what I believe Freud would have recommended had he been writing in 2014 instead of 1895. The approach that I offer is more fully integrated with neuroscience than any other contemporary psychological theory. This makes the proposed network approach especially relevant to clinical neuropsychologists. The ability to explain psychology in **physical** rather than **mental** terms is a long-sought Lockean objective. I therefore anticipate ready acceptance and endorsement by Lockeans.

APA accreditation standards require training in the biological bases of behavior. They also require training in the cognitive and affective bases of behavior. The proposed network theory integrates all three bases.

Reasons Against Bio↔Psychology Network Theory

The vocabulary associated with the proposed network approach is novel and perhaps strange to many psychologists who may prefer not to learn it. I have covered neuroscience facts that may be of little interest to some clinical psychologists despite my best efforts to demonstrate their relevance. It should be noted that one's daily professional activities may not require one to have or use full knowledge of all aspects of the network theory provided here. I did not include the technical details that are required to actually implement any of the network models discussed in this book because they were not needed to make my points. Clinical psychologists need only engage the Bio↔Psychology Network Theory conceptually, not technically.

Kantians

Reasons for Bio↔Psychology Network Theory

Emergence is the antithesis of reductionism. Emergence stresses the **transcendental** nature of what results when simple elements or basic mechanisms interact. The principle of emergence explains how mind can emerge from brain, and how people can **transcend** their biological nature and be what human science says that they can be. I should think that this view would be welcomed as good news by psychologists with an existential orientation.

Reasons Against Bio↔Psychology Network Theory

I can imagine that some readers may recoil from the proposed Bio↔Psychology Network Theory on the basis that it is too mechanical for their taste. This objection constitutes a rejection of the calls for mechanism information that served as the impetus for writing this book in the first place. Psychologists who do not wish to understand how and why psychological phenomena work as they do are welcome to return to the 1890s where the possibility of discovering such mechanisms seemed remote.

Mixed Lockeans and Kantians

Reasons for Bio↔Psychology Network Theory

The reasons given above for both Lockeans and Kantians should motivate mixed Lockeans and Kantians to endorse the proposed Bio↔Psychology Network Theory.

Reasons Against Bio↔Psychology Network Theory

The reasons given above for both Lockeans and Kantians should be reasons for mixed Lockeans and Kantians to be against the proposed Bio↔Psychology Network Theory.

Conclusion

The analysis presented above indicates to me that virtually all Lockeans and perhaps half or more Kantians should have a favorable view of the proposed Bio↔Psychology Network Theory. My analysis of the APA membership presented in Chapter 1 indicates that there are far more Lockeans than Kantians in psychology today. In sum, I expect a favorable supporting **consensus** among a clear and substantial working majority of psychologists.

Acceptance vs. Recognition

Acceptance is not the same as recognition. Acceptance is a personal **private** matter; recognition is a **public** matter. Both acceptance and recognition by a working majority of psychologists are needed in order for theoretical unification to occur. Whether or not **consensus** is reached is in your hands. **It begins with people like you** deciding whether or not you find enough common ground and merit in the proposed Bio↔Psychology Network Theory to use it to work together with your colleagues.

I recognize that universal acceptance by my readers is unlikely. Long ago I realized that it is not possible to please all of the people all of the time. However, I believe that I have provided a compelling case for adopting the proposed Bio↔Psychology Network Theory. I now anticipate reasons that readers may give for accepting or rejecting this new perspective and orientation.

Accept Themes

Acceptance of the proposed Bio↔Psychology Network Theory and the theoretical unification it provides can come in varying degrees. The best outcome for me is if I have completely succeeded in convincing you that I have met the reduced criteria that I set forth above for what constitutes theoretical unification such that you will both accept and recognize the proposed Bio↔Psychology Network Theory in your research and clinical work.

A more modest outcome consists of personal acceptance but not public recognition. While I may have privately convinced you regarding my proposal for theoretical unification, you may not be ready or willing to acknowledge this publically. This outcome is especially likely among graduate students who have yet to go on internship interviews. They will need to present themselves in a way that is both familiar and comfortable to the person who interviews them and to the committee members that decide who gets internships. They need to show that they are part of the clan that controls the internship site in question. A public identification with the proposed Bio↔Psychology Network Theory may not be beneficial here. I fully understand the need for discretion. Psychologists who have received their doctorates and require post-doctoral supervision may be in a similar situation. They may be privately convinced but find it awkward to say so publically because to do so might conflict with their mentor's theoretical orientation.

Psychologists who have completed all professional training and who are active in their professional organizations may also be reluctant to publically favor theoretical unification and psychotherapy integration because doing so might conflict with their duties and commitments to their professional organizations and the professional stature and reputation that these organizations have conferred upon them. I fully understand the need for professional organizations to compete with one another for dues-paying members and for leaders who will press for the special interests of their group including recruiting new members. Personal integrity is here pitted against professional aspiration and the desire for recognition by peers.

The private acceptance of the proposed Bio↔Psychology Network Theory is common to all of the accept themes reviewed above. It is an important first step towards meaningful theoretical unification. My experience of teaching Introductory Psychology, recently retitled Foundations of Psychology, has convinced me that undergraduate students are excited to learn that psychological science is more theoretically coherent than their textbooks suggest. Their views constitute the future of our profession.

Reject Themes

I now consider a variety of ways that one might resist accepting the proposed Bio↔Psychology Network Theory. The first four arguments have already been made by journal reviewers and editors that rejected manuscripts containing portions of this theory.

The first criticism is that the proposed Bio↔Psychology Network Theory offers too many new ideas. I plead guilty as charged. The second criticism is that the proposed Bio↔Psychology Network Theory is new and like all new theories awaits evidence of its validity. I reported above that the evidence supporting this theory has been accumulating for decades and in some cases more than half a century, and includes some of the most solid evidence that psychological science has to offer. Put otherwise, the evidential support for the proposed Bio↔Psychology Network Theory equals or exceeds that of any other theoretical orientation currently available.

A third criticism is that I have not sufficiently elaborated the relevant points for one to be able to sufficiently understand the proposed Bio↔Psychology Network Theory to form an opinion one way or another. I trust that this book-length presentation provides a sufficient introduction to the proposed Bio↔Psychology Network Theory to overcome this criticism.

A fourth criticism has been that the proposed Bio↔Psychology Network Theory is not sufficiently clinically relevant to be of interest to clinical psychologists. A portion of Chapter 1 and the entire second section of this book address this issue.

A fifth criticism is for the reader to claim that they did not understand anything that I said about the proposed Bio↔Psychology Network Theory and therefore nothing that I have said is of any significance to them. This is a wholesale rejection of the proposed Bio↔Psychology Network Theory without having to provide any specific reasons. This lays the entire blame for their rejection on me. The presumption here is that if I could ever manage to write clearly enough so that they could understand anything that I have said then they might be able to give me a reason why they have rejected the proposed Bio↔Psychology Network Theory. But until then they feel entirely comfortable continuing to practice psychology as they always have. I have written for the college sophomore and consequently find it difficult to believe that the reading and comprehension level of psychologists holding a doctorate is below this grade level. I therefore suspect that a more emotion-based reason motivates this response.

Reasons for Rejection

I now turn to other possible reasons that readers might have for rejecting the proposed Bio↔Psychology Network Theory. One possible criticism is to charge that the minimal criteria that I set for achieving theoretical unification placed the evidential bar too low to be meaningful or useful. Such criticism is compelling only if accompanied by reasons and supporting evidence, because otherwise it becomes a thinly veiled argument for continuing with our corrosive competitive separatist schools and camps. This position is a close cousin to the argument that making peace with the enemy equals surrender and defeat. Such an argument is unreasonable because it is based on emotion rather than reason.

A second possible reason for rejecting the proposed Bio↔Psychology Network Theory is that while the minimal criteria I have set for achieving theoretical unification are acceptable, I have failed to meet these criteria. This is a non-specific criticism in its present form because it does not specify the ways in which I have fallen short of meeting my objectives. This criticism merely asserts that I have failed without specifying how I have failed. What evidence did I not present that the critic holds to be so important? What more needs to be done? This argument is a close cousin to being found guilty without being informed of the charges.

A third reason for rejecting the proposed Bio↔Psychology Network Theory is that the reader may have rejected the minimal criteria I set for achieving theoretical unification in favor of more extreme criteria that I have not fulfilled. The net effect of this position is to obstruct the way towards the consensus required for theoretical unification by requiring an outcome that is essentially impossible to achieve. This view favors continuing with our corrosive competitive separatist schools and camps.

A fourth reason for rejecting the proposed Bio↔Psychology Network Theory is that the reader may agree **individually** with each and every one of the specific arguments and evidence that I used to construct the four core and eight corollary network principles that constitute the Bio↔Psychology Network Theory, but deny that **collectively** I have created a legitimate acceptable theory and consequently I have failed to achieve theoretical unification. Again I ask what is missing? What needs to be done to move beyond supporting all 12 principles to providing a suitable theory? The critic needs to be specific here for their criticism to be taken seriously.

A fifth reason for rejecting the proposed Bio↔Psychology Network Theory is that the reader may agree with each psychological phenomenon that I identify because of the massive empirical evidence that supports it but deny that it constitutes a network principle. My reply is that all of the psychological phenomena that I claim can be explained by connectionist network or neuroscience mechanisms, and that is what confers the status of principle upon them. Priming is an excellent example. Priming is so replicable and fully explained using experience-dependent plasticity mechanisms that it deserves the status of a psychological principle.

A sixth reason for rejecting the proposed Bio↔Psychology Network Theory is that you might be persuaded that I have constructed a basis for theoretical unification as defined by my minimal criteria, but do not wish to recognize or endorse it because one or two of your favorite positions were either not included or were expressly excluded. Some concepts are necessarily left behind when a science matures. Unreplicated findings are not trustworthy facts and therefore need not yet be explained let alone included within a unified theory. Hence, omitting such findings is not a valid criticism of the proposed Bio↔Psychology Network Theory. Or perhaps you just can't bring yourself to separate from your existing professional identity. I can sympathize with this conflict but there is nothing that I can do to help here beyond what I have already done.

A seventh reason for rejecting the proposed Bio↔Psychology Network Theory is that you may grant that I have unified psychology as a natural science, but have not adequately incorporated human science despite my emphasis on transformation as providing a crucial link. I have more to say about this under the heading Theoretical Unification below.

An eighth reason for rejecting the proposed Bio↔Psychology Network Theory might be that my approach is too mechanical. One might argue that people are not machines and that my emphasis on physical mechanisms is demeaning. My emphasis on mechanisms is a requirement of natural science explanation. It is also a response to the call for causal mechanisms which by definition are mechanical.

A ninth reason for rejecting the proposed Bio↔Psychology Network Theory is for a reader to claim that they continue to prefer the theoretical orientation that that had when they began to read this book. I only ask for what reasons? Have they imposed the same explanatory requirements on their preferred theoretical orientation as they have on mine? Have they set a high bar for me to pass and a low bar for their preferred theoretical orientation to pass? Specifically, what features of their preferred orientation do I not also offer? I would like to know. My email address is wtryon@fordham.edu.

A tenth reason for rejecting the proposed Bio↔Psychology Network Theory concerns personal motivations against the goal of theoretical unification that I addressed in Chapter 2 in a section entitled **Impediments Against Theoretical Unification**. There we discovered that the personality characteristics of some psychologists resist the very thought of theoretical unification. There is nothing that I can do about the personality characteristics of such resistant readers.

If you have not yet granted my claim of theoretical unification you might wish to reconsider doing so after reading the section below regarding the advantages that result from granting my claim of theoretical unification and reading Chapters 8–12 on psychotherapy integration. Put otherwise, any and all pragmatic advances towards psychotherapy integration constitute additional reasons for supporting the proposed Bio↔Psychology Network Theory. Chapters 8–12 aim to show how operating from this network perspective advances psychotherapy integration. That achievement alone may warrant acceptance of the proposed theory that enables this psychotherapy integration.

CRITICISMS AND REBUTTALS

Criticism can be constructive or destructive. Constructive criticism endeavors to improve on what already exists. It endeavors to improve a line of research or an explanation after having identified a deficiency of some sort. For example, a constructive criticism of connectionism might provide suggestions regarding more complete and/or more accurate mechanism information. Sadly, I could not find this type of criticism. Instead, I could only find destructive criticism.

Destructive criticism endeavors to tear down what already exists and terminate any further development of a line of inquiry. Focusing entirely on what a new position has not yet accomplished as evidence that it never will succeed is a common practice. A close cousin is claiming that the author has not adequately elaborated their points to warrant serious consideration and discussion of them. Further elaboration is always possible, but may not actually be necessary. Rejecting a 50-page manuscript as an inadequate **introduction** is an example of this practice. Such efforts impede and seem aimed to stop a line of inquiry.

With regard to connectionism, the focus of destructive criticism has been on what connectionism has not yet accomplished and why it cannot possibly succeed. The intent is to discourage all further study and inquiry. Rather than recognize what network models can do and have done, the emphasis here is on what is left to be done and how, in principle, failure is the only option. This perspective is revealed by titles such as, *Can connectionism save constructivism?* The thrust of this article is that connectionism cannot ever succeed (Marcus, 1998; reviewed below).

There are at least three major problems with destructive criticism. The first problem is that it is extremely difficult to prove what cannot be done. For example, one would need to know what all of the possible connectionist models are, and then show that none of them is satisfactory or could ever be made to be satisfactory. It is impossible to produce such a list. Hence, there is simply no way to certify that connectionism cannot ever succeed. The second problem with destructive criticism is that every new success is evidence against the prediction of certain failure. Predicting that nothing good can ever come from a line of inquiry is especially vulnerable to contradiction when a field is young and has not had much time to develop. Every well-established field was once young and was initially followed more out of promise of what it might provide than out of what it had already accomplished. The third problem with destructive criticism is that it is not constructive. It does nothing to provide a way forward. It is entirely pessimistic. All of the criticisms of connectionism that I could find are unfortunately of this type.

Some authors have criticized and rejected all efforts to integrate psychology and biology as a form of reductionism. We have previously discussed this matter and found that emergence constitutes an explanatory complement that provides at least half of what a complete explanation requires. Other authors have criticized PDP-CNN models as not falsifiable because they claim that they are little more than curve fitting with many free parameters (Gigerenzer, 2009). This may be true in some cases, but is not an inherent property of connectionist modeling. Some models are highly constrained by neuroscience facts and make specific numerical predictions that are readily falsifiable. This criticism also focuses on the end state of training. Psychologists typically collect all data and then analyze them. Connectionist models simulate growth and development as the result of sequential experiences. The aim here is to show that connectionist principles are sufficient to explain how psychological phenomena develop. Curve-fitting cannot provide competing explanations.

Most criticisms have addressed language acquisition where the connectionist simulations have been sternly dismissed by some critics in favor of an innatest position. I address these criticisms in the language acquisition section that follows after other sections on reductionism, emergence, falsifiability, simulations, catastrophic interference, and highly distributed vs. sparse coding that constitute additional lines of criticism.

Reductionism

I have addressed the question of reductionism at some length in Chapter 1, and so will just briefly review my main point here. Reductionism is the simpler of two possible relationships between psychology and biology. Reductionism seeks to break down psychological phenomena into constituent biological elements that constitute the mechanisms that mediate psychological phenomena. The feared result is that in this way neuroscience will completely explain all psychological phenomena and thereby replace psychology. The fatal flaw with this reasoning is that even a complete listing of the relevant parts of every biological mechanism cannot explain how those parts interact so that psychological phenomena emerge. What is missing is a synthetic explanation regarding how these biological parts interact to produce psychology. Reductionism entails **analysis**. It constitutes but half of a complete explanation. Emergence entails synthesis and constitutes the other half of a complete explanation. Psychology is about emergence and constitutes this other explanatory half. The proposed Bio↔Psychology Network Theory provides mechanism information needed to explain how psychology emerges from the biological mechanisms identified via reductionism. It is for this reason that psychology should welcome rather than fear reductionism. Psychology needs the mechanism information that reductionism provides as a **starting point** for its emergent explanation. Reductionism is a **starting** point for psychology; not an end point.

Whereas connectionist models are largely deterministic, they are clearly not reductionist because they emphasize the opposite process of **synthesis** that is fundamental to **emergence**. I believe that it is the deterministic nature of connectionist models that people frequently mistake for reductionism when they criticize connectionist models as reductionistic. Connectionism entails emergence which is the antithesis of reductionism.

Reductionism and emergence have a yin–yang[5] relationship that enables the proposed Bio↔Psychology Network Theory to integrate/unify psychology and neuroscience.

Emergence

Emergence concerns the more complex of two possible relationships between psychology and biology. The *APA Concise Dictionary of Psychology* (2009) defines *emergence* as 'the idea that complex phenomena (e.g., conscious experiences) are derived from arrangements of or interactions among component phenomena (e.g., brain processes) but exhibit characteristics not predictable from those component phenomena' (p. 163). For example, the physical properties of water differ qualitatively and dramatically from those of its gaseous constituent elements of hydrogen and oxygen gases. The emergent properties of water derive from its physical structure; i.e., how its atoms are interconnected.[6] PDP-CNN models presume that psychology emerges from the **connectome** which includes both the architecture of our neural networks and the degree of excitation or inhibition that characterize the synapses that connect neurons to one another. More specifically, the psychological and behavioral properties of real neural networks emerge from their genetic and epigenetic controlled architecture and the pattern of experience-dependent determined excitation and inhibition across all connections among processing nodes. These emergent network properties differ qualitatively from their constituent components as much as water differs from its constituent elements of hydrogen and oxygen. PDP-CNN models provide a unique opportunity to systematically empirically study the process of emergence because investigators have complete control over every facet of network development and can repeatedly pause the emergent process to learn more about it.

Emergence of Psychology from Biology

Functional magnetic resonance imaging (fMRI), and other brain-imaging technologies, enable investigators to observe and quantify brain activation occurring during psychological tasks. Cognitive neuroscientists have focused almost exclusively on identifying brain areas that mediate various

[5] http://en.wikipedia.org/wiki/Yin_and_yang

[6] The following URL provides detailed information about the physics and chemistry of water (http://en.wikipedia.org/wiki/Water_(molecule)#Physics_and_chemistry_of_water).

psychological functions.[7] These methods support biological rather than psychological explanations. Psychologists want to know how neural networks give rise to cognition. Our discussion of how the automatic CNN cascade transforms stimulus microfeatures into latent constructs and activates experience-dependent plasticity mechanisms that mediate learning and memory, which arguably for the basis of all psychology, conceptually integrates psychology and neuroscience.

I repeat the following story reported by Eagleman (2011, pp. 2-4) about the African tribesman who accused Arthur Alberts of stealing his tongue, because it provides an interesting perspective on our understanding of what it means for psychology to emerge from biology. Arthur taperecorded a villager and played his voice back to him. The native was shocked and concluded that Arthur has stolen his tongue for how else could he have possibly captured his voice so completely? After all, voice seems ephemeral and ineffable; it disappears into nothingness after spoken. How could Arthur's machine get hold of his voice except by stealing his tongue! This was no joke to the native and his tribe who wanted to kill Arthur for his terrible deed. Only by using a mirror could Arthur convince the native that he still possessed his tongue. Arthur was lucky that the native did not question the magic of the mirror to show him his tongue. This story may seem simple to us because we understand that Arthur's machine recorded the variations in sound waves that enabled the native's vocalizations to be heard. It did not actually record the native's voice nor did it steal his tongue. The qualitative distinction between a psychological experience such as hearing a voice and the physical basis for its occurrence, sound waves, is critical to the concept of emergence because it entails a type of transformation that is characteristic of emergence where the output differs qualitatively from the input. The physical basis of voice that was recorded is qualitatively different from the subjective experience of hearing a voice, but the sound waves provide the physical basis for hearing voice. Sound waves are the input and voice is the emergent output.

The relevance of this story for emergence is that the experience of hearing a person's voice when exposed to acoustic vibrations generated by the tape recorder can be understood as a form of emergence, in that the qualitative experience of a specific person's voice emerged from the sound waves. Stated differently, sound waves entered the ear and the experience of hearing the voice emerged as a psychological experience. The emergent experience of hearing one's voice is the result of an amazing synthesis. Nothing like reductionism is

[7] See www.humanconnectiomeproject.org for research aimed at constructing a map of the major brain connections.

involved. The central idea of emergence is that a synthetic product results from complex combinations of many simpler processes. Similarly, thoughts emerge from neural network cascades in a way that may well be similar to how factors emerge from factor analysis software as described in Chapter 3.

Falsifiability

At the highest level of abstraction, PDP-CNN models are not falsifiable. Gigerenzer (2009) correctly noted that neural network models can contain so many free parameters that they can fit any data. However, connectionist models can also be constrained by neuroscience facts and/or additional assumptions resulting in specific numerical predictions that render them falsifiable and therefore scientific (cf., Abbott, 2008). Put otherwise, not all PDP-CNN models are curve-fitting exercises.

Simulation

Parallel distributed processing connectionist neural network models develop their 'adult' properties through many complex interactions with a simulated environment. These causal sequences are sufficiently complex that they cannot be adequately characterized by verbal descriptions alone. These sequences must be simulated using digital computers or physical models[8] in order to determine the end result of many learning trials with sufficient precision to render the model falsifiable. Simulations can always be criticized for being artificial, incomplete, partial, and therefore inaccurate implementations of the phenomena that they represent. This is also true of every laboratory-based psychological study. Some compromises always get made when any phenomenon is rigorously studied. Some critics view these limitations as fatal and reject all controlled study including connectionist models. This, of course, leaves us nowhere to begin. More moderate minds recognize that modeling complex psychological phenomena requires some simplifying assumptions despite their limitations. The field of psychometrics has long recognized, and benefited from, computer simulations and mathematical models. Weather predictions are based on atmospheric models that are simplifications of real weather systems. Virtually every simulation used in science today is a simplification of the real phenomenon under study. Psychology should not be held to some impossible higher standard.

[8] I described the use of neuromorphic chips to simulate neural network models in the Hardware Simulation section of Chapter 1. Kwabena Boahen describes his silicone chip-based modeling work at the following link http://www.youtube.com/watch?v=mC7Q-ix_0Po. The following link is to Boahen's Lab http://www.stanford.edu/group/brainsinsilicon/.

It is important to realize that connectionist network simulations are mathematical representations of real neural networks. They are not living systems. Even the biologically inspired neuroscience-constrained neural network models are admittedly simplistic first approximations to real brains. In the same way that astrophysical models of supernova do not actually explode, and meteorological simulations do not actually rain, connectionist network models do not actually think, feel, and behave. Consequently, criticisms that connectionist models are artificial should not be seriously considered, because they misunderstand the nature and inherent limitations of all mathematical simulations. Moreover, the mechanism information that they provide is not to be confused with how nature actually implements the simulated processes and functions in real brains. All simulations are mathematical representations. They are constructed from equations rather than physical substances such as atoms, rain, or protoplasm. It is true that the back-propagation algorithm that is frequently used to adjust synaptic properties does not involve the same mechanisms that nature does, but that is because connectionist models mathematically simulate the functional effects of experience-dependent plasticity mechanisms, and do not duplicate them. One must accept that mechanism functionality can be simulated using mathematical methods. Simulations are not exact replications. Even the use of neuromorphic chips that depend upon the same ionic forces to move electrons through silicon as ions move across neural membranes are not exact replications of biological systems because they are constructed from silicon not carbon.

Connectionist simulations provide us with powerful new methods and tools. (a) They enable us to represent multiple complex functional relationships and constraints in clearly articulated ways that extend well beyond the ability of the written word to track. (b) They enable us to examine complex developmental sequences one step at a time to better see how experience-dependent phenomena emerge. (c) They enable precise control over initial conditions and developmental histories that may not be possible with living organisms. (d) They enable us to damage the network in very controlled ways that are presently technically impossible, impractical, and/or unethical in order to explore brain–behavior relationships. (e) They can facilitate theoretical integration. For example, Read et al. (2010) integrated personality dynamics and structure into a single model that agrees well with empirical findings.

Catastrophic Interference

A serious criticism of some connectionist models is that learning a second task can catastrophically interfere with prior learning. For example,

McCloskey and Cohen (1989) trained humans and a connectionist neural network (CNN) on two tasks concerning three separate lists of words: A, B, and C. The first task was to learn A–B paired associates; i.e., the first word on list A was to be memorized as associated with the first word on list B, etc. The second task was to learn A–C paired associates; i.e., the first word on list A was now to be memorized as associated with the first word on list C, etc. Memories formed during this second task were expected to conflict with memories formed during the first task. This was found to be the case with humans, but was dramatically worse for the CNN model. Performance by the CNN model was so much worse that the authors referred to the disturbance as *catastrophic interference*.

McClelland et al. (1995) interpreted catastrophic interference as evidence that the neocortex learns slowly but the hippocampus learns rapidly, which means that one type of CNN model will not suffice to explain and simulate both types of learning. The authors noted that **gradual interleaved learning** can mitigate such interference. This involves alternating A–B and A–C learning. Gradual interleaved learning allows the network to learn the required associations to perform both tasks. This solution does not address the core issue of why catastrophic interference occurs. The type of network architecture used was primarily responsible for observed catastrophic interference because it ensured that memories derived from the A–B task and the A–C task were stored in the same place; i.e., superimposed on one another. It is known with mathematical certainty that memory superposition works best when memories are orthogonal. Memories formed by the A–B and A–C tasks are clearly correlated by virtue of sharing stimulus words in list A. Therefore, interference can be expected with certainty. One solution to this problem is to use more biologically realistic neural network architectures such as sparse coding, discussed in the next section. Sparse coding solves the problem of catastrophic interference because different concepts are learned by different groups of neurons, thereby avoiding the conflict inherent in fully distributed architectures. This is a good example of how network models can be informed and constrained by experimental data.

Highly Distributed vs. Sparse Coding

Sparse coding uses separate clusters of nodes, simulated neurons, to learn different concepts; i.e., to form separate memories. The unresolved question is how sparse such coding needs to be in order to effectively simulate human behavior. Bowers (1983) argued against massively distributed coding and for sparse coding under the name 'grandmother cells', on the basis that a few neurons might be responsible for coding entire persons such as one's grandmother. More recently Quian Quiroga et al. (2013) discussed this issue and made several points. They reported that Jerry Lettvin of MIT estimated that as few as 18,000 neurons might be used to store individual memories. While 18,000 may seem like a lot of neurons, one must remember that the brain is estimated to contain 100 billion neurons making 100 trillion synapses. Dividing 100 billion by 18,000 equals 5,555,555, and that enables a lot of memory for persons and concepts. Stephen Wado was reported to place the upper bound at around 1,000,000 neurons per sparse group, resulting in memory for 100,000 people or concepts.

Quian Quiroga et al. (2013) presented evidence suggesting that grandmother cells are actually **concept cells**, in that they encode gist rather than specific details for concepts such as entire persons. Given the authors' estimate that a typical person remembers no more than 10,000 concepts, the brain easily has enough neurons to use somewhere between 18,000 and 1,000,000 neurons to code for each concept. Further sources of support for this claim include Quian Quiroga (2012), Quian Quiroga et al. (2007, 2008), and Suthana and Fried (2012).

Stephen Waydo (2008) developed a PDP-CNN for his doctoral dissertation entitled 'Explicit Object Representation by Sparse Neural Codes' that was based on the experimental work of Quian Quiroga et al. (2007), who recorded from single neurons in the human medial temporal lobe (MTL) where memory consolidation and cross-modal association occur. His PDP-CNN learned on its own, without supervision. It was able to distinguish the same people and/or objects even when presented in very different ways, just as people can. A summary of his findings is taken from Waydo et al. (2006, p. 10234):

> To animate this discussion with some numbers, consider 0.54% sparseness level. Assuming on the order of 109 neurons in both left and right human medial temporal lobes (Harding et al., 1998; Henze et al., 2000; Schumann et al., 2004), this corresponds to 5 million neurons being activated by a typical stimulus, whereas a sparseness of 0.23% implies activity in a bit more than 2 million neurons. Furthermore, if we assume that a typical adult recognizes between 10,000 and 30,000 discrete objects (Biederman, 1987), a 0.54% implies that each neuron fires in response to 50–150 distinct representations.

Waydo et al. (2006) noted that the above estimates of the number of neurons needed to represent a concept constitute an upper bound. The real value could be considerably smaller, but would still be a very large number. In conclusion, memories appear to be distributed over at least 18,000, probably hundreds of thousands, and possibly a few million neurons. While this is far short of exhaustive distribution, it contrasts sharply with the symbol manipulating computer metaphor-based positions where memories are located at single locations. Sparse distribution is still so massive that it supports distributed models. Hence, the experimental data that presumably contradicts connectionism actually support it.

Language Acquisition

Criticism of connectionism has been largely concentrated in the area of language acquisition. This area has been a test bed for the validity and future of connectionism. The criticism against connectionism with regard to language acquisition is that no current connectionist model completely explains everything about language and its acquisition. As mentioned earlier, this is a type of destructive criticism. Perfection is an unrealistically harsh standard against which to evaluate anything that people do. Such extreme criticism should be dismissed.

An apparent implication is that connectionist models are currently as good as they will ever get, and therefore present limitations constitute ultimate limitations that prove with certainty that connectionism is, and will always be, inadequate to the task of explaining anything useful about language acquisition. This implication is highly presumptuous and not to be taken seriously.

A second apparent implication is that only two explanations of language acquisition are possible. Either language is largely learned by the child in ways that are similar to how the child learns other things, or language learning is completely different; i.e., is entirely directed by a hypothetical innate language acquisition device (LAD). When combined with the extreme and highly presumptuous criticisms mentioned above we have the conclusion that connectionism's current inadequacies conclusively prove that language is innately acquired via a LAD.

Chomsky (1971, 1975, 1980, 1986)[9], Jerry Fodor[10], Steven Pinker[11], Fodor and Pylyshyn (1988), and Marcus (1998) explained language acquisition and qualitative developmental stages in terms of 'innate representation'.[12] They argued that infants are born with **cognitive modules**[13], specialized

[9] http://en.wikipedia.org/wiki/Noam_Chomsky
[10] http://en.wikipedia.org/wiki/Jerry_Fodor
[11] http://en.wikipedia.org/wiki/Steven_Pinker
[12] http://en.wikipedia.org/wiki/The_Language_Instinct
[13] http://en.wikipedia.org/wiki/Modularity_of_the_mind

genetically inherited psychological abilities, including an innate understanding of universal grammar[14] that enables them to learn language. They do not say what else these innate cognitive modules cause children to learn. The reference to **genetically inherited psychological abilities** suggests a broad spectrum of possibilities, including a general innate trait-based approach to personality. It is unclear if these authors are referring to the general behavior genetic model where genes and environmental factors interact or if they restrict their behavior genetic model to language acquisition. If only language is enabled by a genetically inherited cognitive module then proponents need to explain why this is so. If inherited cognitive modules cause many personality traits then language acquisition is less special than critics of connectionism imply.

Chomsky's Evidence

The following observations constitute the evidence that supports Chomsky's conclusions that language acquisition is innate: (1) children, even with an IQ of 50, acquire language. (2) Children learn language effortlessly. (3) Children learn language in a relatively short period of time. (4) Children learn language without formal instruction. (5) Language is complex. (6) Children learn language from a small unsystematic amount of data. (7) Children learn language with little imitation. (8) Children learn language with little reinforcement. (9) Children generate sentences that they have never heard adults say. From this evidence Chomsky concludes that: (a) infants are born with a language acquisition device (LAD), thus rendering language learning innate. (b) Exposure to language is all that a child needs to learn language. Exposure is critical, because children raised in isolation have language problems. The claim that exposure to language is all that is needed is primarily directed at Skinner (1957) and his account of verbal behavior, where reinforcement delivered by an adult speaker is required. Exposure to language is also all that connectionist models require for language development to occur. Hence, the language exposure feature does not distinguish the LAD from the connectionist perspective and thus it is not a criticism of connectionism.

Schoneberger (2000) documented that Chomsky's early work emphasized rules in the way that classic cognitive science does, but noted that he subsequently rejected rules thus departing from traditional cognitive science. This developmental change in Chomsky's work is important because

[14] http://en.wikipedia.org/wiki/Universal_grammar

it shows that he increasingly distanced himself from cognitive psychology. Perhaps this is one reason why Marcus (1998) criticized all of cognitive psychology by seriously questioning constructivism.

Piagetian Constructivism

Marcus (1998) expanded his criticism of connectionism to include Piaget and essentially all of cognitive psychology by tarring them with the same brush when he asked **if connectionism could save constructivism?** Marcus (1998) complained:

> Constructivism is the Piagetian notion that learning leads the child to develop new types of representations. For example, on the Piagetian view, a child is born without knowing that objects persist in time even when they are occluded; through a process of learning, the child comes to know that objects persist in time. **The trouble with this view has always been the lack of a concrete, computational account of how a learning mechanism could lead to such a qualitative change** (p. 153, emphasis added).

Marcus (1998) compared the constructivist position[15] of Piaget[16] with the nativist view that some knowledge is innate: 'This constructivist view contrasts with that of Spelke (1994) who proposes that abstract entities like *object*, *person*, and *place* are innate' (p. 154, italics in the original). Marcus (1998) both criticized connectionism for lacking mechanism information and contrasted connectionism with nativism, thereby implying that nativism does a better job of providing mechanism information regarding language acquisition than does connectionism. Marcus (1998) seems to have missed the fact that nativism provides no plausible proximal causal information of any kind! He vitiates nativism with this argument against connectionism.

The remainder of Marcus's (1998) article consists of criticisms of a book by Elman et al. (1999) entitled *Rethinking Innateness: A Connectionist Perspective on Development* in which the authors endeavored to show that connectionism can explain developmental stages. Marcus (1998) claimed to show that their arguments depend upon, assumed, innate representations. Marcus (1998) concluded that contemporary connectionism does not provide the necessary missing mechanism information to save constructionism. The merits of this portion of Marcus's argument are beside the main points of interest here which are: (a) the failure of one theory (connectionism) to provide plausible proximal causal mechanism information does not constitute valid mechanism information for any other theory (innateness); and (b)

[15] http://en.wikipedia.org/wiki/Constructivism_(learning_theory

[16] http://projects.coe.uga.edu/epltt/index.php?title=Piaget%27s_Constructivism

limitations of contemporary connectionism do not prove that connectionism can never provide satisfactory explanatory mechanism information.

The relevant comparative question that readers should be asking at this point is: 'who has more plausible mechanism information to offer; connectionism or nativism?' Connectionist models contain a great deal of mechanism information; nativism provides none! I grant that more connectionist mechanism information is needed, but the nativist approach appears to offer none and no way forward in this regard.

Humans vs. Cats

The Linguistics section of the Wikipedia entry for Noam Chomsky[17] aims to correct common misunderstandings about Chomsky's position. This entry, in part reads as follows:

> It is a popular misconception that Chomsky proved that language is entirely innate, and that he discovered a "universal grammar" (UG). In fact, Chomsky simply observed that while a human baby and a kitten are both capable of inductive reasoning, if they are exposed to exactly the same linguistic data, the human child will always acquire the ability to understand and produce language, while the kitten will never acquire either ability. Chomsky labeled whatever the relevant capacity the human has which the cat lacks the "language acquisition device" (LAD) and suggested that one of the tasks for linguistics should be to figure out what the LAD is and what constraints it puts on the range of possible human languages. The universal features that would result from these constraints are of*ten termed "universal grammar" or UG.*

This passage defines the LAD in terms of human vs. cat (infant vs. kitten) differences that explain why humans acquire language and cats don't. I now offer three alternative reasons why humans acquire language and cats don't.

One reason why humans acquire language and cats don't concerns the difference between the neural architecture of human and cat brains. Humans have special neural network coprocessors located in Broca's and Wernike's areas that are crucial for language processing; cats don't. The neural architecture of these networks makes them specialized language coprocessors. These neural networks are truly innate, in that they are present at birth. Excising them at birth would likely prevent language acquisition, because damaging them in adulthood is known to seriously impair language functioning. Cats don't have these neural networks, which is a compelling and sufficient reason to explain why they don't develop language. These neural network coprocessors only need to be exposed to language in order to undergo the

[17] http://en.wikipedia.org/wiki/Noam_Chomsky

same experience-dependent plasticity modifications that all of our neural networks undergo as we learn and remember. Connectionist models of these events can be understood as models of how Chomsky's LAD works. Connectionism is therefore, in principle, fully capable of explaining language acquisition. While Chomsky and his followers may take exception to this presentation, I remind readers that advocates of the innate LAD do not present an alternative, let alone a better, explanation of how the LAD works. They can only reiterate that the LAD is innate and that it is responsible for language acquisition, but cannot say anything about how it works.

The architecture of the neural networks associated with Broca's and Wernike's areas are essentially the same in humans the world over. These anatomical similarities likely explain linguistic generalities found in people around the world; i.e., all humans process language with the same neural networks. These structural similarities may even account for the linguistic similarities and regularities that Chomsky cites regarding why grammars have similar properties and why there seems to be a universal grammar.

A second reason why humans acquire language and cats don't is that cats lack the gene that enables their lips and tongues to form words. This difference alone is sufficient to explain why cats do not speak. Cats could have language and we would not know that because they can't speak nor can they write because they don't have fingers and an opposable thumb either.

A third reason why humans acquire language and cats don't is that the structure of the cat larynx is not suitable for speech. This difference alone is sufficient to explain why cats do not speak. Again, I note that cats could have language and we would not know that because they can't speak or write.

The above three differences between humans and cats are not exhaustive, but are certainly sufficient to explain why human infants acquire language and kittens don't when both are exposed to language. One does not need to advance a hypothetical innate LAD that neuroscience has no evidence of to explain why humans acquire language and cats don't. The Google define:word function returns the following definition for define:device: 'A **thing** made or adapted for a particular task, esp. a mechanism or electronic instrument' (emphasis added). There is no neuroscience evidence for such a **thing** as a separate and distinct LAD.

There are other differences between humans and cats that could be explained by referring to an innate device that demonstrate how ridiculous such explanatory efforts are. Consider the following three examples. Cats develop a tendency to follow and pounce on objects that move in front of them; infants and children do not. This difference could be explained by an innate pounce acquisition device (PAD). Cats develop an ability to jump much higher from a standing position relative to their body size than infants or children can. This developmental difference could be explained by an innate jump acquisition device (JAD). Cats develop the ability to right themselves when falling even when they are held upside down with all four of their legs pointing in the air; infants and children don't. This developmental difference could be explained by an innate righting acquisition device (RAD). These explanations are just as sensible, i.e., no more ridiculous, than explaining language acquisition with a LAD. It should be obvious to the reader that none of these so-called 'explanations' actually explains anything, because none of them provides any plausible proximal causal mechanism information. On the contrary, all three examples are about genetic differences that separate humans and cats and, yes, genes are innate. The problem here is reifying these genetic differences as a 'device' to explain a particular behavioral difference. One then needs as many devices as there are behavioral differences. Postulating these devices raises several needless questions including: (a) how do they work; (b) do they all work differently; and (c) do some of them work the same way?

The crucial question that readers should be asking right now is 'Who offers more proximal causal mechanism information; nativism or connectionism?' The facts are that nativism offers zero mechanism information and connectionism provides considerable mechanism information. This comparison should be sufficient to decide in favor of connectionism.

The claim that knowledge of universal grammar is innate and that children are born with a language acquisition device raises at least the following two questions. (a) How can knowledge of any kind be innate? (b) What causal mechanisms instantiate innate knowledge? Nativism is silent on both issues. Connectionism offers the following, and I find compelling, explanation. Consider the spider that weaves a web of a specific kind soon after hatching from an egg sack without any parental guidance or any example by any other spider. Knowing how to weave such a web is clearly innate. So how can the spider possibly do this? The spider has a primitive neural network with neurons that connect to one another via synapses. Its genetic code seems to have preset these synapses to the proper respective levels of excitation and inhibition to produce web weaving in addition to constructing the neural network itself. Hence, the spider's neural network has all of the functional properties of a trained 'adult' network upon hatching, and thus is able to weave a web on its own straight away. Higher life forms, especially humans, have a long developmental period where the environment, via experience-dependent plasticity mechanism, sculpts our neural networks and slowly modifies our synaptic settings so that we learn/remember what we need to know to function in our social and physical settings. The spider is hatched in its 'adult' state. This view also enables us to understand partial innateness; commonly known as biological preparedness (Seligman, 1971; Seligman & Hager, 1972).

Circular Logic

Another fact that discredits the hypothetical LAD is that it engages in circular reasoning. One cannot use evidence in two ways. One cannot first infer something from a body of evidence and then use what was inferred to explain the very body of evidence that gave rise to the inference. Consider the following example. One cannot cite unusual behavior as evidence of mental illness and then explain the unusual behavior as due to, caused by, mental illness. To infer the existence of the LAD based on the evidence for Chomsky's position that I presented above is OK. The problem starts when the LAD is used to explain the observations that were used to support the existence of the LAD. Such reasoning is circular and therefore illogical and unacceptable. It is not proof of anything other than the propensity of the proponent to reason illogically. The Greeks inferred that dryads[18] lived in trees based on observing that their limbs moved (Ebel, 1974). Then they explained the movement of tree limbs as caused by dryads. Such reasoning is unacceptable.

Connectionist Evidence

The abstract of a paper by Chalmers (1990) entitled 'Why Fodor and Pylyshyn Were Wrong: The Simplest Refutation' succinctly presents an important defense of connectionism:

> This paper offers both a theoretical and an experimental perspective on the relationship between connectionist and Classical (symbol-processing) models. Firstly, a serious flaw in Fodor and Pylyshyn's argument against connectionism is pointed out: if, in fact, a part of their argument is valid, then it establishes a conclusion quite different from that which they intend, a conclusion which is demonstrably false. The source of this flaw is traced to an underestimation of the differences between localist and distributed representation. It has been claimed that distributed representations cannot support systematic operations, or that if they can, then they will be mere implementations of traditional ideas. This paper presents experimental evidence against this conclusion: distributed representations can be used to support direct structure-sensitive operations, in a manner quite unlike the Classical approach. Finally, it is argued that even if Fodor and Pylyshyn's argument that connectionist models of compositionality must be mere implementations were correct, then this would still not be a serious argument against connectionism as a theory of mind (p. 340).

[18] http://en.wikipedia.org/wiki/Dryad, http://www.theoi.com/Nymphe/Dryades.html

A significant positive literature on how language acquisition might be learned is available. Of special importance is a paper by Sejnowski and Rosenberg (1986, 1987) concerning a connectionist model called NETtalk that learns to read and speak English on its own; i.e., without human training. NETtalk, like children, learns to babble before it learns to speak. NetTalk, like children, over-regularizes verbs as part of its language development. Are these similarities mere coincidences? How do proponents of nativism explain these facts? Hinton et al. (1993) developed a connectionist model that learned to read English sentences, but developed symptoms of surface and deep dyslexia when damaged. How do proponents of nativism explain how this happens? Alternatively, there are sensible and cogent connectionist explanations for these results. In short, the proposed Bio↔Psychology Network Theory provides far more mechanism information than nativism does.

The following two questions require answers by nativists if their view is to be preferred. First, why are children born with an excess of synapses if these structures are not involved with learning, including language acquisition? Second, why are children born with an excess of chemicals that facilitate making new neural connections, synapses, if they are not involved with learning, including language acquisition? Both of these features are innate in that they are present at birth. Forming new neural connections is consistent with nativism. Both features are integral to the connectionist position. We learned above that the neural networks found in Broca's and Wernike's areas are both present at birth and crucial for language acquisition. In general, connectionism is fully consistent with the gene x environment hypothesis. Connectionism is consistent with nativism in several significant ways.

Saffran et al. (1996) provided important empirical evidence regarding the sufficiency of experience-dependent learning mechanisms to account for language acquisition. They studied the ability of 24 8-month-old infants to detect word boundaries from a short sample of adult speech. Their clear and positive results led to the following conclusion by the authors:

> Our results raise the intriguing possibility that infants possess experience-dependent mechanisms that may be powerful enough to support not only word segmentation but also the acquisition of other aspects of language (p. 1928).

Conclusion

Connectionism has generated a fair amount of plausible mechanism information regarding language acquisition. Nativism, on the other hand, has provided none. The entire case for nativism consists of criticizing constructivism as an indirect way of criticizing connectionism. Marcus has essentially attacked all of contemporary cognitive psychology by criticizing constructivism. The expansiveness of his attack on cognitive psychology is an indication that his argument is flawed. I share Marcus's criticism that Piaget and most of contemporary cognitive psychology lacks plausible proximal causal mechanism information. But I do not share his extreme view that the child is therefore the passive recipient of an innate LAD that somehow does all the work of learning language. Readers might well ask how a position with no mechanism information gets to criticize a position that provides plausible mechanism information. Then there is the problem of circular reasoning associated with the LAD. Readers might well ask how peer review could overlook such issues and how illustrious careers could be based on such illogical and unscientific reasoning.

MATHEMATICAL PROOF

Minsky and Papert (1969) mathematically demonstrated the inadequacy of two-layered (S → R) networks to solve problems that require exclusive-or logic. Hornik et al. (1989, 1990) went much further in the opposite direction. They mathematically proved that three-layered (S → O → R) networks, such as the generic one introduced in Chapter 3, are universal approximators that can estimate any continuous non-linear input–output relationships to any desired degree of accuracy. This mathematical proof does not guarantee that any specific network model will work as planned, but only that some form of a three- or more layered network will work in principle. Their proof certifies that the generic network model introduced above is fully capable of even the most complex cognitive transformation; including those required to learn language. This degree of mathematical support is a major hallmark of a mature science and unique to connectionism.

Oja (1982) presented a mathematical analysis of a variant of the Hebbian neuron that proved that such neurons extract the principle component, first Eigen vector, from their inputs. This mathematical proof provides strong support for our Network Principle 3: Transformation.

THEORETICAL UNIFICATION

The question of whether or not psychology can be unified as a science reduces to the question of whether or not it is possible to find an orientation that a majority of psychologists can endorse. **Unification is more about psychologists than it is about psychology**. Psychology will become a unified science when most psychologists operate from a common perspective. Chemistry did not have to find a way to incorporate the perspectives of alchemists to become a mature unified science. There just became fewer and fewer alchemists and more and more chemists. So the bottom line here is about providing a theoretical perspective that most psychologists can endorse. This requires incorporating most of the 'must haves' of contemporary psychologists, but some things will inevitably be left out. Unreplicated facts and phenomena should be left behind because no theory should be expected to explain facts that cannot be trusted.

Presenting psychology as reflecting two fundamental orientations, human science and natural science, suggests that these approaches are equally represented today and that I have chosen to ignore half of what constitutes contemporary psychology. Teo (2012) reinforced this perspective with his claim that '... psychology is as much a **human science** as it is a **natural science'** (p. 807, bold in the original). While this statement may have once been true back in the day of Wilhelm Dilthey (1833–1911), it is no longer true when considered from the perspective that **psychology is what psychologists do.**[19] Statistics published by the American Psychological Association (APA) for the year 2011 conclusively demonstrate that psychology is not equal parts human and natural science. The APA is currently composed of 56 divisions. Assuming conservatively that all of the 480 members of Division 32, the Society for Humanistic Psychology[20], and all of the 379 members of Division 24, the Society for Theoretical and Philosophical Psychology, and 25% of the 1387 members of Divisions 1, the Society for General Psychology[21] strongly endorse human science yields an estimated total of 1,206 APA members that may prefer a human science approach to psychology. The total 2011 APA membership[22] was 71,247. Hence, 1,206/71,247 = 0.0169 or roughly 2% of psychologists may prefer a human science to a natural science approach to psychology. This fraction is negligible by almost any standard. Alternatively stated, my focus on natural science seems to accommodate the interests of approximately 98% of all psychologists. This figure may approach 100% for members of the American Psychological Society where natural science is by far the norm. The question of can psychology be unified theoretically has already been answered in the affirmative if one limits the test of unification to the binary choice of do you take a natural or human science approach to psychology. Further efforts are

[19] This view is related to the statement that intelligence is what intelligence tests measure.

[20] http://www.apa.org/about/division/div32-2011.aspx

[21] http://www.apa.org/about/division/div1-2011.aspx

[22] http://www.apa.org/about/archives/membership/index.aspx

needed to advance theoretical unification among the 98% of psychologists who currently endorse a natural science approach to psychology. I expect that a majority of the 98% of psychologists who take a natural science perspective will accept the proposed four core and eight corollary network principles.

Theoretical unification is not about being correct. People once uniformly thought that the Earth was flat, but they were wrong. People once uniformly thought that the Earth was the center of the universe, but they were wrong. People once thought that Newtonian physics was fully correct, but they were wrong or partly right depending upon one's perspective. **Popularity** does not necessarily confer **validity**, but **unification** is mainly about **popularity**.

Nevertheless, I believe that I offer advocates of human science a way forward through the emphasis I give to the principle of **emergence** which involves **transcendence**. The properties of water are qualitatively different from the properties of hydrogen and oxygen gases, yet the properties of water emerge from combining two molecules of hydrogen with one molecule of oxygen. One might say that the properties of water transcend those of hydrogen and oxygen. Similarly, one may wish to argue that human science studies the properties of people that transcend, emerge from, their biology.

This book is also a cognitive science text with a twist. Traditional cognitive science takes a highly insular approach to psychology in order to avoid the possibility of being reduced to biology in general and neuroscience in particular. This is accomplished by taking the position that there is no necessary relationship between psychology and biology; i.e., that there are an indefinite number of neurobiological implementations of every psychological state (cf. Fodor, 1968; Miller & Keller, 2000), and that biology cannot possibly inform psychology in any useful way. I believe that such an insular approach is no longer defensible. Instead, I take a much more consilient (see Wilson, 1998) approach that emphasizes: (a) psychology's need of **neuroscience** to provide important mechanism information; (b) acceptance of **reductionism** because it provides the first half of a complete explanation by identifying the biological structures that mediate psychological phenomena, a parts list; and (c) embracing **emergence** because it provides the second half of a complete explanation by showing how those structures function holistically to produce psychology; i.e., some assembly is always required!

MATURE SCIENCE

Kuhn (1962, 1970, 1996, 2012) stipulated that the hallmarks of a mature science are: (a) a common vocabulary; and (b) a common set of core explanatory principles. The vocabulary of the proposed Bio↔Psychology Network Theory is shared by neuroscience and psychology. The four core and eight corollary psychological principles provide a common and consistent way to address this broad range of topics. Together they have a large explanatory scope. I add two other characteristics of mature sciences: (a) they replicate facts before attempting to explain them; and (b) findings that have not been replicated to where they can be trusted are left behind when a science matures. I suggest that the proposed Bio↔Psychology Network Theory meets all of these requirements of a mature science. Its vocabulary is common to psychology and biology. Its four core and eight corollary principles explain how psychology emerges from biology. It is based upon well-replicated psychological principles. Here lies a way forward to maturity for psychological science for all those who wish to participate. Does that include **you**?

CONCLUSIONS

This chapter began by considering criteria for evaluating theories that included (a) prediction; (b) explanation; (c) explanatory scope; (d) supporting evidence; (e) falsifiability; (f) relevance to clinical practice; (g) novel features; (h) novel predictions; and (i) the ability to produce a paradigm shift; i.e., qualitatively redirect the field. A comparison of cognitive theory, a generalized form of psychodynamic theory, and the proposed Bio↔Psychology Network Theory finds in favor of the latter on almost all counts. Special emphasis is given to the 13 novel features, seven novel predictions made by the proposed Bio↔Psychology Network Theory and produce a paradigm shift.

Reasons for and against adopting the proposed Bio↔Psychology Network Theory based on residual allegiance to the Lockean, Kantian, and mixed Lockean and Kantian philosophical orientations was provided. Criticisms concerning the following issues were presented and answered: (a) reductionism; (b) emergence; (c) falsifiability; (d) simulation; (e) catastrophic interference; (f) highly distributed vs. sparse coding; and (g) language acquisition. Mathematical proof of the adequacy of the proposed network approach was presented. Accomplishment of theoretical unification was noted and a way to practice psychology as a mature science was provided. The next section of this book applies what has been learned in the first section to the task of psychotherapy integration where unification of the Big Five clinical orientations is provided.

SECTION 2

Psychotherapy Integration

Chapters 8 through 12 are concerned with psychotherapy integration that is enabled by the theoretical unification provided in Chapters 1–7. Chapter 8 discusses problems and issues facing psychotherapy integration. Chapter 9 applies what we learned about unconscious processing to psychotherapy integration. Chapter 10 applies what we learned about learning and memory to psychotherapy integration. Chapter 11 applies what we learned about network principles 3–12 to psychotherapy integration. Chapter 12 considers what psychotherapy integration looks like to the clinician based on the proposed Bio↔Psychology Network Theory.

Psychotherapy Integration: Problems and Issues

Contents

Cognitive Neuroscience and Psychotherapy
http://dx.doi.org/10.1016/B978-0-12-420071-5.00008-9

Psychotherapy began suddenly as a formal intervention with a discrete event that I call the Big Bang of Psychotherapy. I refer to Freud's (1905) (http://www.clarku.edu/research/archives/archives/FreudandJung.cfm) lectures[1] at Clark University where he presented a complete clinical package consisting of: (a) a **theory** of psychopathology; (b) a clinical **method** of treating all psychological disorders; and (c) supporting **evidence** in the form of case studies. News of this historic event spread rapidly across America to the west coast and back again to the east coast, and then across the Atlantic ocean to Europe and then to Asia. Freud's psychoanalytic theory and therapy were then known worldwide. All clinical psychologists who were trained over the next half century were largely trained in psychodynamic theory and therapy. Some doctoral programs continue to specialize in this form of clinical training. Other doctoral clinical programs include elements of psychodynamic theory and therapy as background. Programs that exclude psychodynamic theory and therapy likely do so in a reactionary way. These programs have also been influenced by Freudian thinking and therapy, but in an adversarial and rebellious way.

Freud did not limit his theory and treatment to just one type of psychopathology in one type of person. Nor did he accept variations on his theory or treatment. Instead, he presented a single school of personality and psychotherapy. Freud was a man of science who contributed evidence in support of Darwin's theory of evolution. He was also a physician. However, he presented his psychoanalytic theory and therapy more as a religion than as a science. Freud gathered together like-minded psychoanalysts. Trouble began when some of them began thinking for themselves. Alfred Adler was one such person. He was expelled from Freud's 'like-minded' group in 1911 for his divergent views. Wilhelm Stekel was expelled from Freud's 'like-minded' group soon after in 1912. Carl Jung also developed an unorthodox theory. These events set the scene for Freud to establish an inner circle[2] of his 'most trusted' psychoanalytic colleagues. This circle consisted of Ernest Jones, Sandor Ferenczi, Otto Rank, Hans Sachs, and Karl Abraham. Each

[1] See the section in Chapter 9 entitled 'More About Freud' for additional interesting facts.

[2] http://en.wikipedia.org/wiki/Inner_circle_(psychoanalysis)

one was given a gold ring to symbolize their marriage and pledge of fidelity to Freud. These actions better reflect a cult or religion than a natural science. Max Eitington was added to this central committee in 1919 and given a gold ring. Dissention fostered by Otto Rank and Sandor Ferenczi led to the dissolution of this secret committee in 1924. But then the committee was reconstituted, with Anna Freud replacing Otto Rank that same year. By now there were seven gold rings binding disciples to their master. Ernest Jones, Freud's biographer, seems to have been the last member to leave Freud's inner circle.

More 'heretics' soon followed and schools of psychoanalytic thought (Monroe, 1955) subsequently developed. Each alternative school sought to correct Freud's theory and/or therapy in some presumably crucial way that warranted forming a new single-minded school of psychotherapy that constituted the one true right way to treat all types of psychological disorders in all types of people. These differences among psychotherapies were minor in comparison to what they shared, and in comparison to what was to follow with the advent of behavior therapy. Most therapies were some variant of psychodynamic intervention in the 1940s and 1950s. One might say that this was a time of relative psychotherapy integration. Carl Rogers' (1946, 1951) client-centered therapy was the major alternative available to clinicians at this time.

PSYCHOTHERAPY PROLIFERATION

Psychotherapy was assumed to be effective because clinicians were unified in saying so. Questioning the effectiveness of psychotherapy was as unacceptable as questioning the effectiveness of prayer. Hence, there was little motivation to establish the efficacy or effectiveness[3] of psychotherapy. All of this changed when Eysenck (1952) published his first empirical literature review on psychotherapy outcome, where he concluded that psychotherapy was no more effective than spontaneous remission. Eysenck (1965) published a similar report.

Efforts to prove Eysenck wrong and restore the good name of psychotherapy began in earnest but in many different directions. Theoretical disunification precluded coordinated research. Theoretical disunification continues to be the driving force behind psychotherapy proliferation and

[3] Nathan and Gorman (2002) distinguished efficacy from effectiveness. *Efficacy* is concerned with replication of treatment effects that exceed appropriate control conditions. *Effectiveness* is concerned with practical results that can be obtained in clinical settings.

constitutes a major impediment to psychotherapy integration. Clinicians who think differently about psychopathology will almost certainly recommend different treatments. Only when clinicians operate from the same therapeutic orientation can one realistically expect an effective degree of psychotherapy integration. Variability among clinicians will always remain as it should given individual professional differences. But such extreme diversity and associated hostility and competitiveness as currently characterizes our field should dissipate given greater theoretical unification.

Psychotherapy research largely focused on outcome. There is good reason to first focus on treatment effects. If treatments are ineffective then there is no reason to inquire about their active ingredient(s), and no reason to seek mechanism information regarding how they work. But by 2001, Chambless and Ollendick estimated that there were approximately 150 empirically supported treatments (ESTs). Undoubtedly there are more ESTs today.[4] Aveline (2001) reported that upwards of 500 brand-name psychotherapies are presently available. Not all of them are empirically supported, but each one is based on some sort of informal theoretical rationale or conjecture. Clearly there cannot be more than 500 distinct and valid reasons why these treatments work.

The psychodynamic community was also hard at work demonstrating the efficacy and effectiveness of a variety of psychodynamic psychotherapies. Meta-analyses by Abbass et al. (2006), Anderson and Lambert (1995), Crits-Christoph (1992), de Maat et al. (2009), Leichsenring (2001, 2005), Leichsenring and Leibing (2003), and Leichsenring et al. (2004) demonstrated that psychodynamic therapies (PDTs) produce therapeutic effects that are greater than wait list controls, and sometimes equal to those produced by cognitive-behavior therapy (CBT). The International Society for Interpersonal Therapy[5] reported that there are currently over 250 empirical studies supporting the effectiveness and efficacy of interpersonal therapy (IPT).

It is notable that essentially all of this literature does not attempt to explain why or how these outcomes occur. No mechanism information is provided. The assumption seems to be that cognitive treatments work because cognitive theory is correct and that psychodynamic treatments work because psychodynamic theory is correct, but such conclusions are not logically warranted because they both commit the logical fallacy of affirming the consequent. Moreover, these two theories are contradictory.

[4] http://en.wikipedia.org/wiki/Evidence-based_practice

[5] http://interpersonalpsychotherapy.org/about-ipt/

OUR TRAINING PROBLEM

Pre-Doctoral Clinical Training Problems

The more than 150 ESTs, and over 500 psychotherapies, noted above have created a major pre-doctoral training problem. In how many of these ESTs or other therapies should students demonstrate clinical proficiency in prior to graduation? If not all interventions, then which ones should training directors require students to demonstrate clinical competence in? Should students also have to demonstrate proficiency in psychodynamic as well as cognitive ESTs? Is there a principled way to select which ESTs students should learn, or will available resources and/or faculty personal preferences dictate this choice? Few, if any, programs will have sufficient resources to train clinical competency in all ESTs. Few students would be willing to undergo the decade or more of graduate education that such training would require.

Post-Doctoral Clinical Training Problems

The more than 150 ESTs and over 500 psychotherapies noted above have also created a major post-doctoral training problem. Which ESTs should practicing clinicians learn and incorporate into their ongoing clinical practices that they were not trained in during graduate school? Who will train them? Where will they receive this training? Even if these matters are satisfactorily resolved, the major problem of acceptance remains.

Practicing clinicians have been, and continue to be, reluctant to learn and incorporate ESTs into their professional practice (Baker et al., 2009; Kendall & Beidas, 2007; McHugh & Barlow, 2010; Riley et al., 2007). Whereas clinical psychologists have agreed to abide by the ethics code that restricts their use of psychological tests to those with demonstrated reliability and validity, most clinicians are unwilling to restrict their use of psychological interventions to those that have even minimal evidence of efficacy or effectiveness. Instead, considerable professional opposition has arisen to thwart efforts to require the use of ESTs where applicable. This situation seems strange given that a primary motive for doing psychotherapy is to help people. I explore the reasons for and against ESTs next.

EMPIRICALLY SUPPORTED TREATMENT ISSUE

Mischel (2009) spoke of 'the widening gulf between clinical practice and scientific progress in psychology' (p. i) as part of his editorial introduction to the monograph by Baker et al. (2009) entitled *Current Status and Future Prospects of Clinical Psychology: Toward a Scientifically Principled Approach to Mental and Behavioral Health Care*. Lilienfeld et al. (2013) also documented resistance to empirically supported treatments by practitioners. If psychotherapists were drug manufacturers they would set the evidential bar for psychotherapy research as **low** as possible. Oddly, in an effort that seem designed to prohibit the use of ESTs, clinicians continue to set the evidential bar as **high** as possible without understanding that this is a call for prohibiting all forms of psychotherapy until acceptable evidence can be provided. This situation is clearly illustrated in the March issue of the journal *Psychotherapy*, where the history of psychotherapy research is discussed in the context of reprinting Eysenck's classic (1952) paper where he claimed that there is no convincing evidence that psychotherapy works and Strupp's (1963) reply that details the complexity of psychotherapy research without realizing that these arguments support the view that no form of psychotherapy should be allowed until all complexities of conducting psychotherapy outcome research have been fully resolved. On the contrary, Strupp's article seems to suggest that all forms of psychotherapy should be allowed regardless of the complexities of conducting psychotherapy outcome research. Such a permission first with evidence later if at all contrasts sharply with how health care is delivered in this country and elsewhere. I now consider reasons for resisting and dismissing ESTs.

Reasons Against ESTs

Lilienfeld et al. (2013) have identified the following six sources of resistance to using empirically supported treatments:

> (a) naïve realism, which can lead clinicians to conclude erroneously that client change is due to an intervention itself rather than to a host of competing explanations; (b) deep-seated misconceptions regarding human nature (e.g., mistaken beliefs regarding the causal primacy of early experiences) that can hinder the adoption of evidence-based treatments; (c) statistical misunderstandings regarding the application of group probabilities to individuals; (d) erroneous apportioning of the burden of proof on skeptics rather than proponents of untested therapies; (e) widespread mischaracterizations of what EBP[6] entails; and (f) pragmatic, educational, and attitudinal obstacles, such as the discomfort of many practitioners with evaluating the increasingly technical psychotherapy outcome literature (p. 883).

I now consider previously discussed sources of resistance.

[6] EBP stands for evidence-based practice

Comorbidity

An objective of EST research is to use diagnostically pure samples in order to strengthen conclusions about efficacy and effectiveness. Unfortunately, this scientific goal is compromised by diagnostic criteria that provide multiple options for reaching the same diagnosis. This means that groups intended to be 'diagnostically pure' can be, and likely have been, quite heterogeneous.

Clinicians see mainly comorbid patients; patients with more than one diagnosis. Strictly speaking, the results from ESTs based on single-diagnosis samples should not be generalized to comorbid samples. Hence, ESTs are seen to be of little or no use to practicing clinicians and are therefore resisted on this basis. The presumption here is that comorbidity completely negates the effectiveness of the treatments in question. No supporting empirical evidence for this claim is presented because none exists. It remains quite possible that comorbidity does not matter that much.

If comorbidity is a serious threat to ESTs then psychological interventions should be withheld from all comorbid patients until the requisite research has been conducted. Such insistence would put many professional psychologists out of business. Severe critics of EST research do not seem to understand that evidence of efficacy and effectiveness is needed to authorize providing psychotherapy to the public as a professional practice reimbursed by insurance companies. Setting a high evidential bar is not to their advantage.

Ethnicity

Psychotherapy research participants do not adequately represent the ethnic and cultural diversity of patients typically seen by clinicians. Results from existing EST research cannot therefore be confidently generalized across dimensions of diversity. Hence, ESTs are seen to have little or no practical value to clinicians and are therefore resisted. This view is premised on the assumption that cultural issues render majority and minority people so different that nothing we learn about majority people can be generalized in any way to minority people. While cultural factors are important, treating minority people as a separate species that bears no resemblance to majority people seems more offensive than legitimate, and is not an adequate basis to oppose ESTs. Should psychotherapy be withheld from all minority populations until the requisite research has been conducted to the satisfaction of all critics? I think not, but that is what insisting on a high evidential bar requires.

Diagnostic Diversity

ESTs have yet to be developed for every DSM diagnosis. If clinicians could only use ESTs then they could not treat all DSM disorders. They would have to curtail their clinical practice to those DSM diagnoses that had ESTs. This practice restriction is unworkable and made worse by the diagnostic purity and ethnicity issues just discussed. Clinicians would have to turn too many prospective clients away to stay in business. While this reasoning is used to avoid administering ESTs to any patients it can also be used to deprive patients whose diagnosis does not match any of those for whom ESTs have been developed of psychological services.

But could not one use ESTs for those clients who present with problems for which ESTs have been found effective? Does one have to either completely limit ones practice to ESTs or never use them at all? Is the fact that some DSM diagnoses don't have ESTs a valid reason for not learning any ESTs and refusing to use any of them in one's clinical practice? I think not.

Ease of Conducting Research

Not all theoretical orientations have ESTs because it is easier to conduct EST research for behavioral and cognitive treatments than it is for psychodynamic, family, and existential therapies. This is said to give behavioral and cognitive therapies an unfair advantage over more difficult-to-study therapies. Proponents of the more difficult-to-study therapies claim that it is unfair to expect the same level of scientific rigor from them as is expected of proponents of easier-to-study therapies. This is a peculiar argument. It is offered as a defense for not having conducted the required outcome studies. It is also offered as an excuse for never conducting such studies. However, this argument also indicates that psychodynamic, family, and existential therapies are not yet ready for commercial application and insurance reimbursement. Are these EST critics really trying to prohibit these forms of therapy?

This complexity argument suggests that evidential support is not needed for difficult-to-define therapies. This reasoning incentivizes psychologists to develop the most difficult and complex types of theories and treatments possible in order to be granted immunity from having to conduct research that demonstrates their efficacy and effectiveness of these treatments. But on what grounds could such immunity ever be granted? How, without research, could we ever know that research is not needed? Evidence that past psychotherapies have harmed up to half of all treated clients (Barlow, 2010; Bergin

1963, 1966; Franks & Mays, 1980; Mays & Franks, 1980, 1985) is sufficient to deny such a privileged status. Consumer protection demands evidence that consistently positive outcomes are possible.

Prohibiting Some Practices

Limiting the professional practice to ESTs would effectively 'outlaw' treatments based on some theoretical orientations. This perspective is resisted on the basis that it is ethically permissible to provide treatments that have no evidential basis because such treatments have always been available. Why should they not continue to be available? One answer to this question is that we now have sufficient evidence that psychotherapy can be harmful, as well as effective (Barlow, 2010; Bergin, 1963, 1966; Franks & Mays, 1980; Mays & Franks, 1980, 1985). Just because government does not regulate psychotherapies is no reason for professional organizations not to do so. Treatments without evidential basis could always be administered provided that the client signed an informed consent waiver.

Limiting treatments to ESTs would enable insurance companies to not reimburse undocumented therapies. Limiting treatments to ESTs might also make practitioners of unsupported interventions more vulnerable to law suits. One could always label these unsupported treatments as 'experimental' or 'untested' and let the consumer make a fully informed choice and sign an appropriate waiver.

That ESTs have not yet been developed from some orientations does not mean that they never will be. But requiring clinicians to use ESTs would impede their development from these orientations, as clinicians would not be allowed to practice based on them. Again, one could always label these unsupported treatments as 'experimental' or 'untested' and let the consumer make a fully informed choice and sign an appropriate waiver.

Limiting Professional Choice

Restricting treatments to ESTs limits professional choice. This alone is sufficient reason for some clinicians to exclude ESTs from their clinical practice. Professional ethics and legal statutes already restrict professional choice concerning therapies that involve sexual contact with clients. Moreover, professional choice is also limited when it comes to administering psychological tests. Professional ethics restrict psychological testing to the administration of reliable and valid psychological tests. We already accept considerable restriction of professional choice. Accepting additional restrictions would not set a precedent.

Overreliance on DSM

Restricting treatments to ESTs is said to increase our reliance on the DSM for diagnosis. This might discourage efforts to develop alternative diagnostic systems. APA long ago forfeited developing a diagnostic system. It is most unlikely that very many psychologists will be involved in developing an alternative diagnostic system any time soon.

Conclusions

In general, arguments against the use of ESTs are premised on the observation that EST research is flawed in one way or another. These flaws are used to justify **not** conducting better research or any outcome research at all. The comfortable and seemingly secure position from which EST critics operate seems to be that all unsupported forms of psychotherapy should continue because they have always flourished. These forms of therapy are presumed effective until proven otherwise, and since compelling research is too difficult to do no such research will be conducted thus enabling the presumption of effectiveness to continue indefinitely. Such a grandfather clause conflicts with the way modern health care is delivered.

Three crucial points are evident. First, professional training and state licensure seems understood to authorize administering almost any type of therapy to anyone. Having been trained in a therapeutic orientation seems to fully justify using it in their professional practice on the basis that they would never have been trained as they were unless those methods consistently produced positive outcomes. This is a very naïve self-serving view that is completely insensitive to the fact that some treatments may actually be harmful to some clients. It endeavors to transfer personal ethical responsibility to the training program. The need to demonstrate that interventions are at least not harmful is a major reason to support psychotherapy research and require that one's personal professional practice be based on vetted interventions.

Second, a corollary view is that individual practicing clinicians bear no responsibility for vetting the treatments that they use due to the presumption of effectiveness and the grandfather position identified above. Sometimes psychologists lose their license to practice, but that just means that they cannot call themselves a psychologist. They can continue administering treatments of their choice as a psychotherapist.

Third, a substantial body of research clearly demonstrates that psychotherapy can be effective, and therefore should be allowed and covered by insurance. This view suggests that clinicians might want to learn about these interventions so that they can better help their clients. Strong consistent opposition to EST demonstrates that this curative motive is insufficient to endorse ESTs.

Reasons for ESTs

Consumer Protection

The primary ethical directive that guides the professional practice of psychology and medicine is to do no harm. New drugs are first tested for safety, then efficacy. Unfortunately, new psychotherapies are naïvely assumed to be safe because they were designed to be effective. The same is true for new drugs. But not all psychological treatments are safe. While Eysenck (1952, 1965) questioned whether psychotherapy produced any positive effects, Bergin (1963, 1966) reported that approximately half of treated patients improved and **the other half got worse**. Franks and Mays (1980) and Mays and Franks (1980) attempted to defend psychotherapy against these charges, but Bergin (1980) demonstrated that psychotherapy could be harmful. Mays and Franks (1985) discussed the *Negative Outcome in Psychotherapy and What to do About it* at book length. Barlow (2010) provided a more recent discussion beginning with Bergin's (1966) deterioration effect, and concluded that psychological interventions can be harmful.

Psychotherapy is not that different from medications. While we are all familiar with the fact that medications have negative side effects, readers may not be aware that medications sometimes produce **paradoxical** reactions; effects opposite those intended.[7] For example, minor tranquilizers known as benzodiazepines sometimes paradoxically increase anxiety, agitation, and aggressiveness, and can lower inhibitions to a point where people become violent. Antidepressants can sometimes make people violent and suicidal. Psychotherapies intended to improve mental health can sometimes make people worse. Lilienfeld (2007b) provided a list of potentially harmful treatments that include: critical incident stress debriefing; scared straight interventions; facilitated communication; attachment therapies such as rebirthing; recovered-memory techniques; dissociative identity disorder oriented interventions; grief counseling for individuals with normal bereavement reactions; expressive-experiential therapies; boot camp interventions for children with conduct problems; and DARE programs. This long list means that a lot of harm is being done in the name of psychotherapy.

[7] http://en.wikipedia.org/wiki/Paradoxical_reaction

In sum, considerable empirical evidence indicates that one cannot simply assume that therapies are safe, let alone effective. There is a reasonable chance that a therapy may harm a substantial proportion of the people who receive it. Even when half of patients are harmed, many positive case studies remain. Advocates of the harmful therapy can selectively report these positive case studies as clinical evidence in support of a new treatment. Even clinicians who engage in reprehensible behaviors that end up in licensure revocation cite supportive case studies as part of their defense. A primary reason why psychotherapy research is needed is to prevent such case-study cherry-picking and get a good estimate of the proportion of patients who are harmed by the intervention, as well as a good estimate of the proportion of patients who are helped by the intervention. Ineffective treatments are better than harmful ones, in that they do not leave the patient worse off than before. But they waste valuable time and money invested by clients and third-party payers. Ineffective treatments provide clients with evidence against seeking further help from psychologists. Ineffective treatments guide patients away from effective treatments and thereby needlessly prolong suffering. One might consider this prolonged distress as doing harm, in which case it should be opposed on ethical grounds. Worse, clients who experience negative outcomes are likely to avoid future contact with psychologists.

Professional Ethics

The first and foremost ethical principle of professional psychology is to do no harm. As noted above, controlled evidence is required to determine the extent to which unintended harmful effects of new interventions occur. Evidence of efficacy and effectiveness is required in order to ensure the public safety.

Science Base

Clinical psychology is presented to society, and justified, as an applied science. Psychotherapy research is required to justify this presentation. Psychotherapy research has helped identify active ingredients known as common factors. We have a scientific obligation to investigate the mechanisms that enable psychotherapy to be effective. The proposed Bio↔Psychology Network Theory provides much of this missing mechanism information.

MOTIVES FOR PSYCHOTHERAPY

Lilienfeld et al. (2013) suggested that therapists who resist empirically supported treatments are like resistive clients in therapy. The peculiar arguments against ESTs reviewed above strongly suggest that the real underlying issue regarding their rejection by practicing clinicians has not yet been addressed. I suggest that a closer examination of the three motives for doing psychotherapy that Rychlak (1981a, pp. 171–91) identified is in order. The three motives are: **curative; ethical**; and **scholarly**.[8]

Curative Motive

Rychlak (1981a) identified the curative motive as follows:

> People come to doctors to be cured of illness. When the illness has to do with their "minds" (translated by the psychologist into behavior), then it is only natural that they analogize to physical illness and expect some kind of concrete assistance, manipulation, or prescription which might set matters straight. They come into therapy as "patients" in the true sense of that word, as passive recipients seeking help (p. 188).

The empirically supported treatment (EST) movement emphasizes the **curative motive**; the desire that psychotherapists have to help people feel and get better. The EST movement appears to assume that the curative motive is the primary, if not the only, motive that clinical psychologists have for engaging in psychotherapy. I primarily base this conclusion on the observation that virtually every justification and argument for using ESTs that I have encountered is based on evidence of their efficacy and/or effectiveness. Extensive evidence has demonstrated that arguments that appeal to the curative motive are, and will likely remain, ineffective (Baker et al., 2009; Kendall & Beidas, 2007; McHugh & Barlow, 2010; Riley et al., 2007).

Ethical Motive

Rychlak (1981a) identified the **ethical motive** as follows:

> There are undoubtedly many therapists who practice psychotherapy out of what can only be considered an ethical interest. Either they see in the nature of mental illness a reflection of the ethical injustices which they hope to rectify – or feel that the therapeutic benefits of the contact itself emanate from the "relationship", the coming together of two people in a certain way. Our prime example of the latter type of therapist is Carl Rogers, though keep in mind, we do not claim this is his only motive to the therapeutic contact (p. 182).

Division 29 (Psychotherapy) of the American Psychological Association has long competed with the EST movement on the basis of strong empirical evidence that the therapeutic relationship, working alliance, is a substantial

[8] Rychlak (1981b) reviewed the relevance of these motives to Adler, Bandura, Dollard and Miller, existentialists, Freud, Jung, Kelly, Rogers, Skinner, Stampfl, Sullivan, and Wolpe.

common factor that determines therapeutic effectiveness and efficacy. For example, Norcross (2011) edited a book entitled *Psychotherapy Relationships that Work: Evidence-Based Responsiveness*. Part I of this book reviews 'Evidence-Based Therapy Relationships'. Part II concerns 'Effective Elements of the Therapy Relationship: What Works in General'. Part III concerns 'Tailoring the therapy Relationship to the Individual Patient: What Works in Particular'. Part IV concerns 'Conclusions and Guidelines'.[9] It is noteworthy that the ethical motive is as focused and dependent upon outcome evidence as is the curative motive. The process of elimination directs us to consider the scholarly motive.

Scholarly Motive

Rychlak (1981a) identified the scholarly motive as follows:

> Students applying for graduate study in clinical psychology often give as their reason an untiring "interest in people." Taken at face value, this interest reflects our first motive to psychotherapy. We do psychotherapy to learn about people. Many clients who enter therapy do not think of themselves as necessarily maladjusted, and many more would so enter if they could financially afford it. They come to learn, to be educated, to be – *as we say – provided with insight* (p. 171).

Psychologists, and students studying to be psychologists, are curious people who intrinsically want to know about and understand why people think, feel, and act as they do. My experience with applicants to Fordham's doctoral clinical training program over 42 years is that they have uniformly expressed this curiosity. They also explain that they seek doctoral training because they believe that the additional understanding of people that doctoral training will give them will make them better therapists. They do not claim to have a burning desire to master structured diagnostic interviews and as many treatment manuals as possible.

When doctoral clinical psychology students interview for APA-approved internships they also commonly claim that they are interested in additional training to better understand their clients in order to be better therapists. These applicants are frequently asked to demonstrate their readiness for internship training by sharing how they have formulated one or more cases they have treated; i.e., how they have come to understand the person they treated and how their treatment relates to this understanding. The interviewer

[9] A major difference concerns the role of therapy manuals. Manuals are favored by the EST movement because they operationalize therapeutic procedures. Manuals are criticized by the relationship-oriented clinicians because they seem too rigid and they do not sufficiently emphasize the working alliance.

is probing their ability to understand people, typically in terms of the theoretical system that their graduate program is rooted in.

Fully fledged clinical psychologists characteristically see themselves as professionals who understand how and why people think, feel, and act as they do. They sometimes testify to these ends in court, or to the public via books, TV, the Internet or other mass media outlets. The definiteness with which psychologists dispense comments and advice is rarely constrained by the uncertainty that accompanies empirical research. The authority for their views comes from the theoretical basis of their clinical orientation. For example, a psychologist who commented on the Friday 14 December 2012 Sandy Hook Elementary School shooting in Newtown Connecticut explained the perpetrator's motive for shooting the children as a symbolic extension of killing the perpetrator's mother, who he also shot. How could the psychologist in question know this to be true? He didn't; but his statement did fit with what seems to be an undeclared psychodynamic theoretical orientation. He might have focused on the perpetrator's anger given that he shot some of his victims up to 11 times (New York Times, 17 December 2012, p. A 25). This example shows how influential one's theoretical orientation is.

Evidence is not Enough

Evidence of efficacy and effectiveness is the main rationale used to persuade clinicians to learn and incorporate ESTs into their professional practice. The considerable resistance against ESTs (Baker et al., 2009; Kendall & Beidas, 2007; McHugh & Barlow, 2010; Riley et al., 2007) shows that such evidence is not enough to change how people think and behave.

A stark example of how strong and consistent scientific evidence is sometimes not enough to change people's mind is exemplified by The Flat Earth Society web page (http://theflatearthsociety.org/cms/). At first I thought that this was some kind of a spoof until I read their mission statement at the following link: http://theflatearthsociety.org/cms/index.php?option=com_content&view=article&id=48&Itemid=65. It seems that their views are largely based on the Bible and are taken as a matter of faith. Moreover, personal experience and common sense seem to justify this position. When you look outside, the world does seem flat. Placing small figures of people on a globe has them standing at angles in the northern hemisphere everywhere except for the North Pole. These figures stand out horizontally when placed at the equator of a globe. These figures stand upside down everywhere in the southern hemisphere. Hence, common sense concludes that the world cannot be round but must be flat so that everyone can stand up straight, as we know from everyday experience that they do! Those photographs of Earth as a big blue marble that were allegedly taken from space could have been photo-shopped. Some people believe that the manned flight to the moon never happened; that it was all staged. Many citizens do not believe in climate change, despite massive empirical evidence that it is true. Evidence is clearly insufficient in these cases to modify how people think.

Some readers may differentiate psychologists from the lay public and dismiss the above example as unrepresentative of psychologists. I now provide a more professionally relevant example concerning the history of applied behavior analysis that demonstrates that psychologists are not different in this regard.

Applied Behavior Analysis History

The history of applied behavior analysis (ABA) clearly demonstrates that evidence is not even enough to preserve an already well-established empirically supported clinical practice. Skinner's experimental analysis of behavior (EAB) is a laboratory science based on controlled experimentation. ABA is a technology of behavior change based on this controlled scientific research that is sometimes referred to as behavior modification. The behavioral principles discovered by EAB and applied by ABA comprise some of the most empirically supported treatments that psychological science has ever developed. Alternatively stated, the empirical support for ABA is many times greater than for any EST. Behavior modification was once a widely accepted empirically supported clinical practice based on extensive research. But this widely practiced treatment method was largely marginalized by the cognitive revolution (Bandura, 1969, 1977, 1978; Dember, 1974; Gardner, 1985; Mahoney, 1974, 1977; Meichenbaum, 1977).

Why did this happen? The answer, I believe, lies with the explanatory limitations of behaviorism. The effectiveness of ABA treatments was explained by behavior theory, but these explanations omitted cognitive variables. Cognitive and cognitive-behavioral treatments were explained by cognitive theory. Cognitive theory explains much more than behavior theory does; i.e., it has a much greater explanatory scope. This explanatory advantage appears to have been sufficient for clinicians to largely abandon behavioral methods and their massive empirical basis in favor of new therapies that were only just beginning to be investigated. This new explanatory power trumped massive ABA outcome evidence. Put otherwise, widespread adoption of cognitive-based interventions did not wait until the evidential basis required supporting it. Cognitive-based interventions were initially adopted for explanatory reasons.

Curiously, Wolpe (1958) facilitated the cognitive revolution in clinical psychology when he offered a mechanism that could explain how systematic desensitization worked. He claimed that deep muscle relaxation reciprocally inhibited anxiety. Here was a physiological explanation of a clinical treatment derived from Wolpe's (1958) laboratory-based behavioral studies with dogs. Systematic desensitization quickly gained prominence in the clinical treatment of anxiety disorders. It was not long until cognitive factors were also said to inhibit anxiety. These cognitive-behavioral explanations led to new cognitive-behavioral and cognitive therapies.

Unintended Implication

The EST movement is not opposed to the scholarly motive in principle. There is nothing about EST research that limits or interferes with the scholarly motive per se. In fact, the CBTs that mainly constitute the ESTs are based on an informal cognitive theory that explains what people do and feel in terms of what they think. So where's the problem?

I believe that the main problem behind the opposition to ESTs by many clinical psychologists stems from an unintended implication of psychotherapy research that frustrates their scholarly motive for doing psychotherapy. Standardization is an important feature of quality control when conducting psychotherapy research. Establishing a reliable DSM diagnosis (American Psychiatric Association, 2000) is a crucial part of meeting inclusion and exclusion criteria for participating in a study. This is typically done using a structured clinical interview. Certifying that a particular form of treatment is consistently applied by all participating clinicians requires the development of a treatment manual to specify what is to be done during each session. Sessions are routinely videotaped and reviewed to determine how closely clinicians follow the manualized instructions for administering the intervention. Following the manual in every way is the goal. Positive research results provide empirical support for the combined procedure of administering a structured clinical interview, followed by administering the appropriate manualized treatment. Strictly speaking, clinicians who adopt ESTs should limit their practice to administering structured diagnostic interviews followed by manualized treatments in order to maximize generalizability from research to clinical practice.

This is an unappealing model of professional practice for many clinical psychologists. Research assistants are trained to do these things as graduate students. Masters level training is sufficient to certify such psychological technicians. So what is left for doctoral training and the professional practice of clinical psychology? I submit that these clinical psychologists are primarily invested in understanding their clients in terms of one or more theoretical orientations. These clinicians pride themselves on their ability to formulate what is wrong in terms of a theoretical orientation. For example, family therapists formulate problems in terms of family systems theory. These clinicians formulate a treatment plan based on their case formulation in order to address the particular needs of their client. The role of theory is so important to professional physicists that Arthur S. Eddington once wrote that 'No experiment should be believed until it has been confirmed by theory'.[10] The clinical psychology version of this quote might be 'No treatment should be believed until it has been confirmed by theory'.

Readers who doubt my claim that understanding is more important than evidence may wish to perform either or both of the following tests. The first test entails discussing with undergraduates why they have declared their major as psychology, or why they are thinking of doing so if that is the case. It is most unlikely that they will say that they look forward to learning how to administer structured diagnostic interviews and manualized treatments. It is more likely that they will say something about obtaining a better understanding of people. While they may also express a desire to help people, it will likely be through helping them to understand themselves better, rather than through the administration of a structured interview followed by manualized treatment. Most undergraduates that I have talked with about their choice of majors over the past 42 years are unaware of structured diagnostic interviews and manualized treatments either before or when they declare psychology as their major, so clearly these matters are not compelling factors in their decision to declare psychology as their major.

The second test is for instructors who teach graduate students in doctoral clinical psychology programs. They should ask their students the following two questions: (1) How many of you came to graduate school just to learn to administer structured interviews and manualized treatments? (2) How many of you came to graduate school to learn more about personality, psychopathology, and why effective treatments work? In my experience many more students endorse the second than the first option.

Theory–Evidence Knowledge Gap

A theory–evidence knowledge gap exists when a new theory is offered before supporting evidence is available, as is often the case with new

[10] http://home.nas.com/lopresti/manyq.htm

theories. A theory–evidence gap existed when CBTs were first introduced. A theory–evidence gap also exists when the degree of theoretical elaboration and discussion is much greater than the empirical literature regarding efficacy and effectiveness (Goldfried, 2012; Lazarus & Davison, 1971). Some contemporary psychological interventions have very little, if any, empirical support yet there are many clinicians who are eager and willing to incorporate these treatments into their professional practice. The popularity of the difficult-to-define therapies for which there is little if any empirical support demonstrates how the need to explain can completely override the need for empirical evidence.

Psychodynamic therapies are a good example of the theory–evidence knowledge gap. Many more pages of psychodynamic theory exist compared to pages of evidence from controlled research. All of the possibly harmful treatments identified by Lilienfeld (2007b) were accepted and practiced largely, if not exclusively, on the basis of some sort of psychological theory that explained why they should work. The absence of supportive evidence did and does little to hinder their appeal and use. These treatments include: critical incident stress debriefing; scared straight interventions; facilitated communication; attachment therapies such as rebirthing; recovered-memory techniques; dissociative identity disorder oriented interventions; grief counseling for individuals with normal bereavement reactions; expressive-experiential therapies; boot camp interventions for children with conduct problems; and DARE programs.

Interventions that have a theory–evidence knowledge gap tend to be based on difficult-to-study theories. The relative absence of controlled research does not dampen or diminish ready acceptance of interventions based on these theories by practicing psychologists. This shows just how unimportant evidence can be. A convincing theory can be accepted outright. It can be taught with authority, even in the total absence of controlled research, by cherry-picking supportive case studies. This clearly shows how important theory is compared to evidence. Theory almost always trumps evidence!

Freud is the defining quintessential classic example of the clinician as theoretician. He presented a series of five lectures at Clark University in 1909. They included: (a) a theoretical basis for the development of psychopathology; (b) a treatment for these disorders based on this theory; and (c) illustrative case studies. I say illustrative because case studies not based on single-subject research designs have no probative value. Positive case studies demonstrate that the treatment can have a beneficial effect; not that it typically does. The greatest value of case studies is to illustrate the application of a treatment method. Nevertheless, Freud's theory provided psychologists with a theoretical basis for understanding their clients' problems, including an understanding of how and why the recommended treatment should work. He presented case studies to illustrate his methods and to 'prove' that his treatment worked as explained. Because Freud's presentation was long on theory and short on evidence I characterize it as having a theory–evidence knowledge gap.

Two points deserve special emphasis. First, Freud's lecture series was a big hit and soon went viral. Tryon (2008a) characterized Freud's Clarke lectures as the '**big bang of psychotherapy**'. Freud's psychodynamic theory and psychoanalytic methods spread rapidly across the United States to California, then back to the east coast, across Europe, and finally around the globe because clinicians worldwide wanted this knowledge. Freud fulfilled the primary clinical need; a scholarly way to understand psychopathology and the basis for its treatment. Freud personified the clinician as theoretician. He spent much time thinking about, trying to make sense of, what his patients told him. Freud's voluminous correspondence and other writings testify to the importance and value he placed on theory and understanding.[11]

Second, it is especially pertinent for present purposes to note that a lack of hard evidence from controlled studies did not hinder broad immediate and largely complete acceptance of Freud's psychodynamic theory and psychoanalytic methods by clinical psychologists worldwide. Clinicians might have maintained that Freud's ideas, while interesting, had not yet been examined scientifically and that one must keep an open mind until a critical review of the evidence justifies reaching a positive or negative decision regarding whether or not to include psychodynamic treatment into their clinical practice. Not so, the understanding that Freud provided was immediately accepted and this achievement promoted him to international prominence well before any rigorous empirical support for his views was available. Acceptance of Freud's theory was so universal that at one point I venture to say that every clinical psychologist was analytically trained to some degree. Psychodynamic theory remains part of many contemporary clinical training programs; some even continue to specialize in it.

[11] It is important to note that Freud's 1909 lectures came at a time when no other theory of psychopathology and/or psychotherapy existed. He did not have to compete with a well-entrenched competitive theory. Freud filled a knowledge vacuum.

The role of evidence[12] was, and remains, fairly minor in clinical practice. For example, decisions to include or exclude psychodynamic thinking from one's clinical practice are still largely about theoretical issues rather than empirical evidence. It is axiomatic in science that a bad theory, even the worst kind of theory, cannot be displaced even by overwhelming negative evidence especially if the alternative is no theory at all no matter how consistent and compelling the negative evidence is. People will just not tolerate having no explanation at all. The ability of evidence to falsify a theoretical position is, in principle, supposedly decisive according to philosophers of science, but this is not so in psychology. In Chapter 9 we will see that the critical core psychoanalytic prediction of symptom substitution has been completely falsified without having even the slightest impact on psychoanalytic theory. One might say that this example demonstrates that evidence is largely irrelevant to clinical practices. Had symptom substitution been supported, behavior therapy and other symptom-oriented treatments would probably have been branded as a form of malpractice and possibly prohibited.

Two final observations are pertinent here. First, how many psychologists do you know who have completely abandoned their theoretical orientation on the basis of evidence? None is my answer. Second, our discussion of hot cognition in Chapter 4 demonstrated that people set a low bar for confirming evidence and a high bar for disconfirming evidence. Here we see how one's explanatory system distorts evidence-based discussions in favor of one's preferred theoretical orientation.

Evidence–Theory Knowledge Gap

That we have done a far better job at creating and documenting the efficacy and effectiveness of psychological interventions than we have at explaining why they work has created what I call the **evidence–theory knowledge gap**. Stated otherwise, the evidence–theory knowledge gap pertains to the difference between empirical evidence **that** our treatments work and a theoretical understanding of **why** they work. One very clear illustration of our evidence–theory knowledge gap is provided by Judith Beck (2010) in the second edition of her book entitled *Cognitive Behavior Therapy: Basics and Beyond*. The section of her book entitled 'What is the theory underlying cognitive behavior therapy' is just one page long. Her entire book, minus appendices and references is 360 pages long. So theory constitutes under 1/360 = 0.0028 or slightly less than 3/10s of one percent

[12] Clinicians still do not agree as to what constitutes persuasive evidence.

of the book. But wait, there's more, the entire text regarding theory on page 3 takes just two paragraphs, which is but 2/3s of the one page. The complete cognitive model is that dysfunctional thinking is common to all psychological disturbances. Here we have a one-sentence functional statement that strongly implies a causal connection between dysfunctional thinking and psychological disorders, with no mechanism information for how this happens. In sum, 99.7% of this book concerns practice and 0.3% concerns theory. Judith Beck is not the exception, but rather the rule. I take her work to be fully representative of empirically supported treatment publications generally.

It is rather embarrassing to find oneself in a position of not being able to adequately explain why empirically supported treatments work. Now that we have so much evidence that so many treatments work for so many disorders it seems time to ask how and why they work. Each of the more than 150 ESTs and up to 500 therapies is based on some sort of informal theoretical rationale. No one has yet provided a formal theoretical basis for why each of these interventions works to see if they all work for different reasons or if they share common active ingredients or perhaps share psychological principles. Surely there must be far fewer than 150 to 500 valid reasons for why these treatments work.

Clinicians who use empirically supported treatments may be **doing the right things for the wrong reasons. Psychological theory is to clinicians and researchers what insight is to clients**. But psychological science has been of little if any help in explaining why empirically supported treatments work. While it is possible for treatments derived from a flawed or even completely wrong theory to produce positive results, there is a much better chance that interventions will be effective and positive if they are based on a valid theory.

I suggest that the evidence–theory knowledge gap frustrates the scholarly motive for doing psychotherapy. ESTs do not come with a well-developed theoretical basis for understanding behavior disorder and an explanation, let alone mechanism information regarding how and why these interventions work. I believe that it is this absence of understanding that impedes the adoption of ESTs. The history of applied behavior analysis is evidence for the claim that the clinician's need to understand far outweighs evidence of efficacy and/or effectiveness.

Lest the reader still think that the scholarly motive is not more important, central, or essential to clinicians than is evidence of effectiveness, I now review neuroscience evidence that demonstrates just how important the need to explain is to human beings. People who have had their corpus callosum severed, the so-called split-brain operation, reveal that explanation is a brain property; something hard-wired into all people including clinical psychologists. When the left brain, the one that can speak because it mediates language, is asked about a behavior performed by the right brain, a confabulated answer is automatically generated by the left brain. People just don't report that they don't know, as one might expect of a good scientist when relevant data are unavailable. The brain doesn't suspend judgment. An answer is given based upon what else the brain knows, and for psychologists this is their theoretical grounding.

Consider another example. Psychologists typically interpret and report data that are not statistically significant as showing a trend; typically in the direction of their hypothesis instead of correctly concluding that their results are indeterminate (see Tryon, 2001 for additional details). In short, people almost always feel the need to provide some sort of explanation to justify why events occurred as observed. This is particularly true of clinical psychologists. Therefore, asking clinical psychologists, of all people, to suspend their inherent need to understand and explain while they follow some manual will be resisted if not refused outright. A major objective of this book is to address and satisfy this need to explain by providing a Bio↔Psychology Network Theory that integrates psychology and neuroscience in a way that informs clinical practice.

Conclusions

The need that therapists have to understand their clients in terms of psychological theory is the most important of the three motives for doing psychotherapy by far. This motive is sufficient to sustain clinicians even when they have little or no objective evidence that what they are doing actually helps people. The selective basis of memory will retain more positive outcomes and forget less positive ones, resulting in biased but supportive clinical evidence for their preferred therapy. Pointing out the lack of objective evidence will almost never cause them to alter their clinical practice. ESTs must therefore be supplemented with, integrated into, a theoretical system that helps clinicians to better understand their clients if ESTs are to be accepted and adopted. Put otherwise, ESTs will be accepted primarily because the associated theory facilitates understanding and clinical formulation, and secondarily because of evidence of efficacy and effectiveness. The proposed Bio↔Psychology Network Theory provides the required explanatory basis.

NEED FOR EMPIRICALLY SUPPORTED PRINCIPLES (ESPs)

To this point I have argued for ESTs. Now I will argue against them. The following five sections provide reasons why we should replace ESTs with empirically supported principles (ESPs).

Avoid Purple Hat Therapies

Most ESTs are comprised of multi-component packages. Current criteria for establishing ESTs unfortunately do not require: (a) demonstration of incremental validity of each treatment component; and/or (b) a principle-based explanation of how and why each of treatment component works. This means that one can add an inert component, such as requiring the client to wear a purple hat, to an already established EST like exposure therapy and claim to have a new treatment. The new treatment will pass all EST requirements because the established treatment already meets these criteria. The authors, however, can claim that the new treatment works because of the added element, e.g., wearing a purple hat during each session, without having to provide specific supporting evidence for this claim. Hence, Rosen and Davison (2003) argued for replacing ESTs with empirically supported principles (ESPs). Refocusing on ESPs avoids the 'purple hat' problem.

Prevent Needless Proliferation

In addition to preventing the development of new therapies by adding inert components, focusing on psychological principles will require that a truly new therapy be based on a new psychological principle. Variations of existing therapies would still be welcomed, as there may be multiple creative ways to implement the principles upon which established therapies are based. This requirement will incentivise clinicians to cooperate and cite one another rather than criticize existing approaches as they promote their 'new' therapy.

Identify Active Ingredients

Identification of ESPs will focus attention on the active ingredients of existing ESTs with an emphasis on common factors. The resulting focus should improve both basic and applied research into the development of improved therapeutics.

Simplify Clinical Training

Replacing ESTs with ESPs provides students and clinicians with conceptual, as well as therapeutic, tools that can be used to understand psychopathology and to formulate customized treatments for the particular individual seeking treatment. Pre- and post-doctoral training could focus on these principles, as they are certainly far fewer than the 150+ ESTs that are currently available. This approach is more manageable than attempting to train clinical competence in numerous specific ESTs. This approach also addresses the clinician's professional need to understand and treat their clients in a principled way.

Return Clinical Practice to a Principled Basis

There was a time when clinical psychology operated on a principled basis. I refer to the 1960s when treatments were based on principles of operant (instrumental) conditioning. Behavior therapy and behavior modification were two major clinical practices along with some classical conditioning therapies, such as the bell and pad method of treating enuresis.

Classical Conditioning Therapies

The classical conditioning basis of clinical practice likely began with Mowrer and Mowrer (1938), who introduced the still effective bell and pad method for treating enuresis. A small metal sensor is placed within a cotton bag and worn inside the child's pajamas. Presence of urine completes a circuit that activates a bell that wakes the child who then toilets himself. The bell constitutes the unconditional stimulus (US), waking the unconditional response (UR), bladder tension constitutes the conditional stimulus (CS), and waking to bladder tension constitutes the conditional response (CR). I expect that few clinicians, even clinicians specializing in children, are trained today in the bell and pad method of treating enuresis that Mowrer and Mowrer (1938) pioneered, even though its efficacy and effectiveness have been well established.

Stockhorst et al. (1993) explained why and how cancer patients receiving chemotherapy develop anticipatory nausea. The cytotoxic drug functions as the US producing nausea as the UR. Smells and tastes paired with chemotherapy function as CSs. The association of these smells and tastes with cytotoxic drugs produce a conditioned nausea response. This knowledge can be used clinically. Patients receiving chemotherapy can be advised to activate their taste buds with a distinctive substance that they won't mind giving up, such as a plum-flavored lollipop. This way only the taste of the plum flavor will get conditioned to the nausea instead of all of the desirable foods that they might otherwise eat prior to chemotherapy.

Behavior Therapy

Behavior therapy became widespread after Joseph Wolpe (1958) introduced a treatment that he developed in the laboratory with dogs. His systematic desensitization was based on the physiological principle of reciprocal inhibition. Eysenck (1964) claimed that 'Behaviour therapy may be defined as the attempt to alter human behaviour and emotion in a beneficial manner according to the laws of modern learning theory' (p. 1). Wolpe and Lazarus (1966) stated that behavior therapy entailed '... the application of experimentally established principles of learning' (p. 1). Wolpe (1969) defined behavior therapy as '...the use of experimentally established principles of learning for the purpose of changing unadaptive behavior' (p. vii). It turned out that these definitions of behavior therapy were mainly aspirational because learning theory, like the rest of psychological science, was in disarray at the time and only partially able to support clinical practice (cf., Tryon, 2000a, 2002c). Pointedly, Kazdin (1979) noted that there really was no modern learning theory upon which to base the broad array of therapeutic practices that clinical psychologists were using at the time. Successful animal models of psychopathology, such as the learned helplessness model of depression (Overmeier & Seligman, 1967; Seligman & Maier, 1967), generated much research but little by way of specific clinical application thereby demonstrating a double dissociation between theory and practice.

Cognitive-Behavior Therapy

The cognitive revolution (Bandura, 1969, 1977, 1978; Dember, 1974; Gardner, 1985; Mahoney, 1974, 1977; Meichenbaum, 1977) was supposed to enable clinical interventions to be based on principles of cognitive science. This new theoretical approach promised to significantly advance psychological theory to where it could provide a solid theoretical and research foundation upon which to construct new more effective therapies. Unfortunately, psychological theory has not yet developed as expected. Instead, practicing clinicians such as Ellis (1958, 1962, 1994), Beck (1964, 1967, 1970, 1972, 1976), Mahoney (1974, 1977), Meichembaum (1977), Linehan (1993) and others were forced to develop their cognitive therapies based on their **clinical practices** and/or their **personal lives**[13] because formal cognitive theory grounded in psychological science was, and remains, sufficiently disorganized not to be of much assistance.

[13] Marsha Linehan suffered from borderline personality disorder as a teenager and young woman, and was very critical of the then standard treatment she received. Her dialectical behavior therapy corrected many of these deficiencies (Carey, 2011).

It now seems somewhat ironic that Kazdin's (1979) criticism that behavior therapy was not based on modern learning theory as Eysenck (1964), Wolpe and Lazarus (1966), and Wolpe (1969) had claimed pertains equally well to contemporary cognitive-behavioral and cognitive therapies, in that they are also not based on modern learning theory or any other theory established by basic psychological science. We went from **not** having one kind of theory to **not** having another kind of theory.

Behavior Modification/Applied Behavior Analysis

Behavior modification, now better known as applied behavior analysis (ABA)[14] takes a principle-based approach to the treatment of socially important and clinically relevant behaviors. The *Journal of Applied Behavior Analysis*[15] publishes applied research based on basic research concerning principles of behavior that have been studied under laboratory conditions and published in the *Journal of the Experimental Analysis of Behavior.*[16] The operant conditioning basis of clinical practice was articulated by Keller and Schoenfeld (1950) in their book entitled *Principles of Psychology: A Systematic Text in the Science of Behavior.* This approach to clinical practice became known as behavior modification and applied behavior analysis. Martin and Pear's (2010) *Behavior Modification: What It Is And How To Do It* is an excellent contemporary textbook with many clinically relevant examples. While sometimes applied to individuals in clinic settings, this approach is primarily used in schools, inpatient institutions, and in group homes and settings, especially with developmentally disabled populations, but not in mainstream outpatient clinical practice.

PSYCHOTHERAPY INTEGRATION VIA THEORETICAL UNIFICATION

Clinicians who view people and their psychology in fundamentally different and incommensurate ways cannot be expected to agree on recommendations for clinical intervention. Genuine and effective psychotherapy integration requires theoretical unification. The proposed hybrid cognitive neuroscience Bio↔Psychology Network Theory consists of an explanatory core of four network principles and eight corollary principles that provide a theoretical basis for a comprehensive clinical practice where the decision

14 http://en.wikipedia.org/wiki/Applied_behavior_analysis
15 http://seab.envmed.rochester.edu/jaba/
16 http://seab.envmed.rochester.edu/jeab/

to intervene with behavioral, cognitive, and/or emotion-focused methods is made by a clinician in the context of treating a particular person rather than a basis for forming adversarial schools and camps. Behavioral problems are initially treated with behavior therapies. Cognitive problems are initially treated with cognitive therapies. Emotional problems are initially treated with emotion-focused therapies. Some combination of therapies is inevitably prescribed for every client. The theoretical basis for and authorization of this comprehensive clinical approach replaces what might formerly have been called eclecticism. Now under the guidance of a single theory clinicians can prescribe specialized treatments based on well-replicated psychological phenomena for which we have mechanism information.

CONCLUSIONS

Investigators were correct to obtain evidence of efficacy and effectiveness before attempting to explain why empirically supported treatments work. But with so many ESTs from the psychodynamic as well as cognitive clinical orientations, it is time to begin to ask why these treatments work. In short, we need to address our evidence–theory gap.

Reasons for and against ESTs were examined. One might think that clinicians are primarily motivated by the prospect of helping people. Remaining resistance on the part of most practicing clinicians against ESTs reveals that a stronger motive is operative. I proposed that the core problem is that ESTs, as currently presented, frustrate the scholarly motive for doing psychotherapy. A case for developing empirically supported principles (ESPs) was made. In response, the proposed Bio↔Psychology Network Theory was formulated in terms of four core and eight corollary network principles. Chapters 9, 10, and 11 discuss the clinical relevance and application of these principles. Chapter 12 provides a clinical perspective on psychotherapy integration.

Clinical Applications of Principle 1: Unconscious Processing

Contents

Cognitive Neuroscience and Psychotherapy
http://dx.doi.org/10.1016/B978-0-12-420071-5.00009-0

Chapters 3 and 4 presented the four core and eight corollary network principles that constitute the proposed Bio↔Psychology Network Theory. I characterize this theory as a **hybrid Bio↔Psychology cognitive neuroscience network learning theory** because it combines connectionist neural network principles and neuroscience facts with well-replicated psychological phenomena and multivariate statistics. This chapter discusses the clinical implications of the first network principle; unconscious processing. Chapter 10 discusses the clinical implications of the second network principle; learning and memory. Chapter 11 discusses the clinical implications of the remaining ten network principles. Chapter 12 puts all of this together into a description of what psychotherapy integration looks like to the practicing clinician who operates from the proposed network orientation.

I begin this chapter with a brief history of unconscious processing, before considering the clinical implications of accepting the required unconscious-centric orientation. I then consider unconscious processing in psychological treatments. I pay special attention to the issue of symptom substitution and methods of assessing unconscious processing. Then I discuss insight as psychological mindedness. Finally, I discuss the clinical relevance of the mirror and Gandhi neuron systems that unconsciously process so much that is of psychological interest.

A BRIEF HISTORY OF UNCONSCIOUS PROCESSING

The possibility of an unconscious mind can be traced back to Galen (c. A.D. 130–200), a Greek physician and founder of experimental physiology who recognized that we make unconscious inferences from perceptions (cf. Whyte, 1978, p. 78). The Roman philosopher Plotinus (c. 204–270) observed that we become aware of the process of thought only when we attend to it. He likened attention to a mirror that when properly positioned reflected unconscious processes. The Christian philosopher St. Augustine (354–430) likened the unconscious mind to a ghost that is experienced as a felt presence although invisible. St. Thomas Aquinas (1224–1274) developed a theory of mind that featured unconscious processing. The Swiss physician Paracelsus (1493–1541) recognized a role for the unconscious mind in the etiology of disease. Whyte (1978) noted that Descartes (1596–1650) believed that all unconsciousness was physiological and therefore did not recognize an unconscious mind as such. His emphasis on the conscious mind may be primarily responsible for our contemporary conscious-centric psychology.

Whyte's (1978) history of the unconscious before Freud begins in Europe around 1600 because issues of consciousness and self-consciousness were being discussed in Germany and England at that time. Spinoza (1632–1677) stressed the contributions that unconscious memory and motives make to human personality. Whyte (1978) reported that Leibniz (1646–1716) seems to have been the first European thinker to give clear expression to the idea of unconscious processing. He understood the mind as a marriage of conscious and unconscious processes. Tallis (2002) reported that Leibniz's *New Essays on Human Understanding*, published in 1765, speculated about inaccessible memories and considered actions taken without awareness. Hume (1711–1776) emphasized the role of unconscious factors in human behavior. Schopenhauer (1788–1860) made unconscious processing central to his views concerning human personality.

Although scientific psychology began as a study of consciousness via introspection, Wundt (1832–1920) emphasized the role of unconscious factors in decision-making. Whyte (1978) reported that in 1868 von Hartmann published a comprehensive survey of German philosophy and Western science entitled *Philosophy of the Unconscious.* Carpenter published his *Principles of Mental Physiology, With Their Applications to the Training and Discipline of the Mind, and the Study of its Morbid Conditions* in 1874. The prominent psychologist William James (1890) emphasized unconscious processing in his seminal work *The Principles of Psychology.* Myers (1893) published his work on subliminal consciousness. Kihlstrom (1984) noted that for William James and Wilhelm Wundt the field of psychology was almost entirely about unconscious processing, yet we almost exclusively acknowledge Freud in this regard and virtually never cite either William James or Wilhelm Wundt, the founder of experimental psychology in 1879.

Freud (1900/1938) introduced his first formulation of the unconscious in the form of the tripartite conscious, preconscious, and unconscious. Freud (1923/1962) introduced his second formulation of the unconscious when he connected the three levels of consciousness to his tripartite division of the mind: Ego; Id; and Super Ego (see Perry & Jean-Roch, 1984). Arthur Koestler's introduction to Whyte's (1978) *The Unconscious Before Freud* summarized part of the history reported above as follows:

> The general conception of unconscious mental process was *conceivable* (in post- Cartesian Europe) around 1700, *topical* around 1800, and *fashionable* around 1870–1880. It cannot be disputed that by 1870–1880 the general conception of the unconscious mind was a European commonplace and that many special applications of this general idea had been vigorously discussed for several decades.

Hence, unconscious processing was very well known and commonly discussed in Europe, Freud's homeland, well before Freud's 'discovery' of the unconscious mind. It is remarkable that scholars have given Freud so much credit for presenting the commonly discussed ideas of others as his original discovery. This includes Freud's now famous iceberg metaphor of the mind being 90% unconscious and 10% conscious. The following two paragraphs demonstrate Freud's motivation to take credit for the intellectual contributions of others.

Unlike Newton, who acknowledged that his contributions derived from his predecessors, Freud made no such attribution, fostering the widespread misimpression that he discovered unconscious processing and by this discovery delivered what he considered to be the third blow to humanity; that man was motivated by unconscious processes. The first blow to humanity was by Nicolaus Copernicus[1] who replaced the earth-centric view with a heliocentric one. The second blow to humanity was by Charles Darwin[2] who replaced divine creation with evolution by variation and natural selection.

[1] http://en.wikipedia.org/wiki/Nicolaus_Copernicus

[2] http://en.wikipedia.org/wiki/Charles_Darwin

Thus Freud nominated himself to sit by the historical scientific side of Copernicus and Darwin for discovering the unconscious mind, except that he didn't.

Freud's failure to credit his predecessors regarding the unconscious was not accidental. Evidence of this is provided by Wertz (1993) who noted, regarding Fritz Brentano (1838–1917), whose professorship at the University of Vienna began in 1874 that:

> He is remembered in the history of philosophy primarily for the ideas we have touched upon, and most of all for his tremendous influence on his students, such as Husserl, Stumpf, Meinong, Hildebrand, von Ehrenfels, and Freud, the only one who did not speak publicly of Brentano, let alone with the awe, reverence, and profound intellectual debt openly acknowledged by all the others (p. 106).

Wertz (1993, p. 107) further reported that in 1885 Freud wrote a letter to Martha Bernays, his fiancée, that he had destroyed all of his previous paper, notes and written communications with Brentano, in order to complicate his biographers' task.

Kihlstrom (1984) noted that behaviorism effectively ended inquiry into unconscious processing which was subsequently revived twice: once over subliminal perception (see New Look 0–3 below) and learning without awareness (Greenspoon, 1955), and again with the discovery of psychological deficits among patients who had undergone cerebral commissurotomy; the so-called 'split-brain' treatment for severe epilepsy (Gazzaniga, 1970, 1972, 2005; Gazzaniga & LeDoux, 1978; Segalowitz, 1983; Sperry, 1961, 1968; Springer & Deutsch, 1981). Sperry (1968) concluded:

> Observations like the foregoing lead us to favor the view that in the minor hemisphere we deal with a second conscious entity that is characteristically human and runs along in parallel with the more dominant stream of consciousness in the major hemisphere (p. 732).

Tallis (2002) observed that:

> Over the past fifty years the unconscious has made a comeback. Evolutionary theorists, neuroscientists, experimental psychologists, and those working in the field of artificial intelligence have all been forced to reconsider the concept of the unconscious. Gradually, individuals working in different disciplines, on different problems, but linked by a common goal of wishing to elucidate the properties of the mind, have been giving more and more emphasis to unconscious mental processes. Indeed, in the past half century the fortunes of the unconscious have been completely reversed. It is now almost impossible to construct a credible model of the mind without assuming that important functions will be performed outside of awareness (p. xi).

MORE ABOUT FREUD[3]

Sex and Aggression

One can argue that even if Freud did not discover unconscious processing, he at least discovered the prominent role played by sex and aggression in unconscious processing. Certainly the role of sex and aggression in conscious mental life was well known long before Freud. Emphasizing the roles of sex and aggression in unconscious mental life seemed like a valid original discovery. However, Freud began personally using cocaine around 1884. He praised its positive qualities and often prescribed it for his patients. What he did not realize is that cocaine creates vivid dreams dominated by sexual and aggressive themes. Naively, Freud generalized his and his patient's cocaine-fired dream findings to everyone, apparently unaware that he mistook a drug effect for normal psychology. While normal people sometimes dream about sex and aggression, these themes are almost certainly less prominent in the dreams of normal people than in people who habitually use cocaine. It seems that Freud substantially exaggerated these dream themes as a result of his and his patient's drug use.

False Claims of Cure

Freud claimed cures that he either recanted or that did not actually occur. Freud's first false claim of cure concerned the therapeutic effects of cocaine (Thornton, 1984, pp. 21–8). Cocaine was chemically isolated in 1860 and synthesized by Merck, Sharpe and Dohme. In 1884 Freud discovered a paper by Theodor Aschenbrandt, a German army surgeon, reporting his clinical experiences with cocaine. Freud also discovered a paper by W. H. Bentley in *The Therapeutic Gazette* of Detroit reporting the author's success in weaning opium and alcohol addicts using cocaine. This report was especially interesting to Freud because his colleague von Fleischl-Marxow was addicted to morphine as a result of taking it for chronic pain. Freud sent von Fleischl-Marxow some cocaine, began taking it himself, and sent some to his fiancée Martha. By 1885 von Fleischl-Marxow had successfully withdrawn from morphine but was seriously addicted to cocaine, taking up to a gram a day; a hundred times the dose Freud recommended for him to take. At some point von Fleischl-Marxow also began taking morphine. Knowing all of this Freud presented a paper on March 3, 1885 at the Physiological

[3] See section entitled Psychotherapy Integration: Problems and Issues in Chapter 8 for additional interesting facts.

Club and two days later at the Psychiatric Society claiming that von Fleischl-Marxow's case illustrated the rapid withdrawal from morphine under cocaine without subsequent addiction. This paper was then published on August 7, 1885 in the *Medicinisch-chirurgisches Centralblatt*. The prestigious journal *Lancet* subsequently abstracted this paper, thus giving it much wider circulation and credibility. During the next two years many reports about the addictive nature of cocaine were published in medical journals. Cocaine was considered to be the third scourge of humanity; alcohol and morphine being the first two. Freud endeavored to justify himself in a paper published in the *Wiener Medizinische Wochenschrift* in July 1887, where he largely blamed others for misrepresenting his views. Freud subsequently acknowledged that cocaine was addictive and discontinued his personal use of the drug by 1887.

Freud's second false claim of cure concerns the historic and pivotal case of Anna O (Thornton, 1994, pp. 36, 85, and Chapter VII on pp. 89–107) (see also http://en.wikipedia.org/wiki/The_Freudian_Fallacy). Anna O was a patient of his colleague Josef Breuer. Her case was widely acknowledged to be the first example of a 'cathartic cure' and a cornerstone of psychoanalysis. Carl Jung revealed in a 1925 seminar held in Zurich, Switzerland that Anna O was never cured in the way previously claimed. In 1953 Freud's biographer Ernest Jones identified Anna O as Bertha Pappenheim. Subsequent investigation revealed that Bertha was admitted to the Bellevue Sanatorium in the Swiss town of Keuzlingen. Medical records contradicted Josef Breuer's claim that Anna O's symptoms had been permanently removed by cathartic treatment. These medical records revealed that her previous symptoms continued unabated.

Child Sexual Abuse Recanted

Freud initially recognized child abuse as a common serious cause of neuroses based on his clients' revelations during psychoanalysis, but sadly he subsequently contradicted their testimonials and denied the reality of child abuse as psychologically destructive in favor of the view that his client's mental illness was caused by their own fantasies (Masson, 1984). See also http://en.wikipedia.org/wiki/The_Assault_on_Truth and http://en.wikipedia.org/wiki/Freud%27s_seduction_theory.

In 1860 Freud was aware of a book by Ambroise Auguste Tardieu (1818–1897) entitled *A Medico-Legal Study of Cruelty and Brutal Treatment Inflicted on Children*, as well as articles concerning sexual abuse of children by caretakers, often including parents. Masson (1984, p. 38), a former curator of the Freud

Archives (http://freudarchives.org/index.html), reported that Freud had three prominent books dealing with sexual assault against children in his personal library. In the same way that Freud did not cite previous works about unconscious processing by other investigators, he did not cite any of these works about the psychiatric consequences of early childhood sexual abuse, despite the fact that these sources would have supported his 1896 paper on *The Aetiology of Hysteria*.

Freud studied with Jean Martin Charcot (1825–1893), a renowned neurologist and hypnotist, at the Salpêtrière Hospital in Paris in 1885. Charcot argued that psychological trauma was the origin of the mental illness then known as hysteria. Charcot referred to this disorder as 'traumatic hysteria'.[4] These views were confirmed when Freud visited the Paris Morgue in 1885 where he witnessed first-hand the frequency and extent of childhood sexual abuse. It was during his time with Charcot that Freud's primary interest changed from neuropathology to psychopathology (Masson, 1984, p. 195).

Freud was well aware of how frequent and hidden child abuse was when he began analyzing cases of hysteria. After carefully studying 18 cases of hysteria in women Freud (1895a/1936) wrote and presented his first major paper entitled '**The Aetiology of Hysteria**'. Appendix B of Masson (1984) reproduces a translated version of this paper that was read before the Society for Psychiatry and Neurology in Vienna on April 21, 1896. Freud claimed that in every one of the 18 cases of hysteria that he examined the patient had experienced sexual abuse as a child. Freud argued:

> I therefore put forward the thesis that at the bottom of every case of hysteria there are *one or more occurrences of premature sexual experience*, occurrences which belong to the earliest years of childhood but which can be reproduced through the work of psych-analysis in spite of the intervening decades (p. 263; italics in the original).

> Sexual experiences in childhood consisting in stimulation of the genitals, coitus-like acts, and so on, must therefore be recognized, in the last analysis, as being the traumas which lead to a hysterical reaction to events at puberty and to the development of hysterical symptoms (p. 267).

These instances of sexual abuse typically occurred prior to the age of the second dentition; prior to the arrival of adult teeth. Masson (1984) reported that this 1896 paper presentation was Freud's first major public address to his peers. He did not expect the harsh negative reaction it received. Masson (1984, p. xviii) reported: 'Afterwards, he was urged never to publish it, lest

[4] http://en.wikipedia.org/wiki/Psychological_trauma

his reputation be damaged beyond repair'. But Freud considered his paper to be spot on. Mason (1984) reported that Freud expressed contempt for his colleagues. In a letter to Count Richard von Krafft-Ebing, the distinguished professor and head of the Department of Psychiatry at the University ofVienna, Freud wrote:'They can all go to hell' (Sie können mich alle gern haben). Freud knew that his patients had recalled their traumas 'with all the feelings that belonged to the original experiences' (p. 10). Freud subsequently published his paper despite the prospect of being ostracized professionally.

Freud then attended a debate about child sexual abuse while in Paris. Masson (1984, p. 50) reported that Ambroise Tardieu took the position that sexual traumas were real and created psychopathology. Alfred Fournier argued that reports of child sexual traumas were fantasies that had no psychological effects. Freud initially sided with Tardieu, but changed his position to that of Fournier with the exception that he argued that childhood sexual fantasies caused psychopathology.

The remainder of Masson's book documents how Freud recanted his original view that actual childhood sexual abuse caused hysteria. Freud completely reversed himself regarding the veracity of his patient's reports about their childhood sexual abuse. **Freud claimed that he made the mistake of believing his women patients**. Masson (1984, p. 107) reported that Freud's commitment to his former belief in real seduction, 'traumatic hysteria', ended abruptly on September 21, 1897, upon writing a letter to his colleague Wilheim Fliess. Freud claimed that in the past few months it had gradually dawned on him that the seductions reported by his women patients had never occurred. Masson (1984, pp. 108–10) reprinted Freud's entire letter. Masson (1984) quoted from a letter that Anna Freud, Freud's daughter, wrote to him on September 10, 1981 in response to Masson's view that Freud was wrong to give up the seduction hypothesis. She said:

> Keeping up the seduction theory would mean to abandon the Oedipus complex, and with it the whole importance of phantasy life, conscious or unconscious phantasy. In fact, I think there would have been no psychoanalysis afterwards (p. 113).

With the birth of psychoanalysis and its professional acceptance and recognition in the balance, it is not difficult to understand why Freud turned his back on his female patients and denied the validity of their sincere and strongly felt reports of early sexual trauma. Adding insult to injury, Freud revised and relegated their traumatic experiences to the realm of their own sexual fantasy; something they unconsciously desired and secretly brought upon themselves through their Oedipal complex. Unfortunately, the Oedipus complex continues to be taught as fact in introductory psychology textbooks and elsewhere[5] as if it were true rather than an aberration motivated to curry professional favor and fame at the cost of perpetuating a travesty upon abused women. A formal repudiation of this travesty is in order and remains awaited.

UNCONSCIOUS-CENTRIC ORIENTATION

To its credit, psychodynamic theory has long recognized and promoted unconscious processing. Cognitive-behavioral therapies (CBT) do not formally incorporate unconscious processing. None of the theoretical justifications for CBT acknowledge, let alone justify, any place for unconscious processing. The enormous weight of contemporary evidence in support of the existence of unconscious processing requires our acknowledgment and acceptance of it. Adopting an unconscious-centric perspective preserves the possibility of explaining consciousness which is prerequisite to psychology. I suggest that the greatest clinical contribution of Principle 1 is to replace our present conscious-centric orientation with an unconscious-centric one.

Neuroscience has rediscovered the reality of unconscious processing and has demonstrated that the iceberg analogy may well be correct, suggesting that 90% of brain processing is unconscious and automatic whereas but 10% is conscious; only System 2 is rational. The contemporary evidence for unconscious processing seems convincing beyond question. It is the time to rethink the theoretical and clinical implications of unconscious processing rather than reflexively accept all that has been previously said about it by psychodynamic clinicians, especially in light of the false and objectionable claims reviewed above. We shall see below that the psychodynamic understanding of psychopathology and symptom formation is fatally flawed. These findings alone provide sufficient reason to completely rethink how to incorporate unconscious processing into clinical practice and research.

A corollary implication of our shift from a conscious-centric to an unconscious-centric theoretical orientation is that it enables us, for the first time, to explain consciousness. It is logically impossible for contemporary conscious-centric psychology to explain consciousness, because **one reasons from axioms not to them**. One cannot explain what they assume as this entails illogical circular reasoning. Network models do not assume

[5] http://orinyc.org/Neurosis-Oedipal_Papiasvili.html

consciousness and therefore retain the possibility of explaining consciousness and rational processing. The automatic mechanical network cascade is the network extension of neural conduction down an axon on a macroscale. Activations spread across multiple neural layers under the supervision and control of glia. This includes our mirror and Gandhi neuron systems and the enteric nervous system in our gut that operates on many of the same neurotransmitters as our brain does. These network cascades are responsible for activating the experience-dependent plasticity mechanisms that enable memories to form and learning to occur, and for our brains to be physically sculpted and specialized and thereby adapted to our social and physical environment. These network cascades are also responsible for the transformations that underlie all of our cognitions and lifespan cognitive development. These network cascades are therefore the prime mover of all psychological development, both normal and abnormal, and all response to clinical intervention.

Replacing the conscious-centric orientation of psychological science and clinical practice with an unconscious-centric perspective is the first and perhaps the most profound and far-reaching clinical contribution made by Principle 1 to the professional practice of clinical psychology.

CLINICAL IMPLICATIONS OF UNCONSCIOUS PROCESSING

The network cascade that spreads as automatically and unconsciously across interconnected layers of processing nodes as conduction spreads down the axon of a neuron is an unconscious causal process that enables and drives all psychological phenomena. I now discuss four remarkable clinically relevant facts that derive from this network cascade: (a) processing is always parallel even when it appears to be serial; (b) processing begins unconsciously and may or may not become conscious; (c) the network cascade always transforms what it processes; and (d) processing activates experience-dependent plasticity mechanisms that modify the connections among processing nodes so that subsequent processing cycles function differently. I begin by considering the implications of simultaneous rather than serial processing.

Simultaneous Processing

Contemporary cognitive, behavioral, cognitive-behavioral, and psychodynamic theories are based on serial rather than parallel processing. They thereby privilege a single point of entry for clinical interventions. For example, cognitive therapists assume that cognitions cause emotions and behaviors. Cognitive therapists therefore intervene by changing cognitions which are then thought to change emotions and behaviors in some order. DeRubeis et al. (1990) attempted to demonstrate serial cognitive mediation but failed to do so effectively. Behaviorists assume that cognitions and emotions will change once behaviors are modified. Behavior therapists therefore intervene by changing behaviors. Emotion-focused therapists intervene by changing emotions in the hope that altered cognitions and behaviors will follow.

A major novel clinical implication of the proposed Bio↔Psychology Network Theory is the claim that the network cascade requires that thoughts, feelings, and behaviors **change simultaneously** rather than **sequentially** during treatment. The proposed network theory, therefore, does not privilege one point of entry over any other, given that parallel network cascade simultaneously impacts thoughts, feelings, and behaviors. For this reason, our network theory stands in opposition to all theories that prioritize a single or primary point of entry. This constitutes a novel prediction and a new perspective on clinical intervention.

Non-Rational Processing

Clinicians frequently encounter non-rational processing by their clients. The proposed network orientation recognizes the following sources of non-rational processing.

Emotion

Children learn what is good and bad long before they can fully understand reasons for holding such opinions. Children learn to value one religious perspective long before they understand theology. Children learn to value the family's political orientation long before they can understand their parent's reasons or think for themselves about relevant issues. When children acquire racial prejudices they do so long before they can understand what these views mean. Parents, peers, teachers, and clergy provide 'reasons' that harden these emotionally held views over time. People process information in ways that are consistent with these emotionally held positions. People resist thinking differently, in large measure because they have difficulty feeling differently about these matters.

In Chapter 3 we discussed the view presented by Taber and Lodge (2006) that '**all reasoning is motivated**' (p. 756; emphasis added) meaning **emotionally controlled**. This 'hot cognition' perspective testifies to the priority of emotion over reason. The proposed network orientation understands that discourse is likely to be processed emotionally more completely than rationally. We should therefore expect inconsistent and even contradictory arguments.

Resistance

Clinicians frequently comment that their clients exhibit resistance in therapy. Resistance is traditionally explained in terms of underlying unconscious conflicts between Id and Superego motives. I now consider two alternative sources of resistance.

Post-Decision Dissonance Reduction

The proposed network orientation predicts that resistance can also derive from **normal non-rational unconscious processing** mediated by subcortical neural networks that mediate one or more cognitive/memory heuristics. Although not specifically classified as a heuristic, **post-decision dissonance reduction** is a cognitive distortion that is driven by the neural network property of seeking consonance and avoiding dissonance; i.e., our Principle 7. The act of making a decision automatically entails a commitment to rationalize and defend it as the best possible decision now and in the future. All decisions carry some degree of post-decision dissonance reduction defense. Stated differently, people find it difficult to admit that they were wrong. Some people are especially stubborn in this regard. I return to the TV shows House Hunters[6] and House Hunters International[7] mentioned in Chapter 3, because they clearly demonstrate post-decision dissonance reduction. The contestants in these shows are taken to see and inspect three homes from which they purchase one. While the contestants are expected to specify what they like and don't like about each home, they frequently give fatal reasons for all three homes; reasons why they could never live in any one of them. Sometimes it is because the cost of the house is way over budget. Other times it is because the home is too far from work, the street is too noisy, or the rooms are too small. The contestants make a decision to purchase one of the homes, move in, and are interviewed at some later date ranging from 2 weeks to 6 months. At that time the contestants say how happy they are in their new home. They point out its positive virtues and what they have done to decorate their place. No mention is made of the fatal reasons. All is now positive without exception.

[6] http://www.hgtv.com/house-hunters/show/index.html
[7] http://www.hgtv.com/hgtv56/videos/index.html

Going forward it is wise to anticipate that each decision we make, and ask our clients to make, commits us and them to some degree of post-decision defense. For example, it may be better to primarily decide to get the best possible care and secondarily decide upon a specific health care provider than to decide that Dr. X is the best health care provider for me. This way one might be less defensive about switching health care providers should treatment not go as planned.

Prototype Formation

This alternative is discussed in Chapter 11 under clinical implications of Principle 10: Prototype Formation, but a few words are in order here. Prototypes form by averaging experience. Consider how one forms the prototype bird. Birds share common attributes. All have feathers, wings, beaks, legs, eyes, and all fly. Each bird presents the viewer with these elements that they constructively aggregate into an average concept of 'bird' called a prototype. Variations in wing span, beak structure, etc., are ignored. Our prototype for 'bird' is more like a sparrow than a condor, because most birds that we see look more like a sparrow than a condor.

The self-concept is also a prototype. It too is an experience-based average. Repeated success experiences lead to a positive self-concept, whereas repeated failures lead to a negative self-concept. The prototype-forming neural network mechanisms tend to discount or ignore facets of new experiences that differ markedly from the existing average. Their impact is diminished, if perceived at all. Therapists who endeavor to focus the client's attention on new experiences can therefore expect resistance based on how prototypes form. They can expect that the new information that they provide will be discounted in favor of the preexisting average self-concept. This is a normal process in that it is true of all people. However, as with all traits, I assume that this one is also normally distributed, which means that some people are more resistant than others. It may also be that some reinforcement histories exacerbate such resistance. Resistance is therefore not unique to neurotic or psychotic patients.

Pattern Completion

Our Principle 6: Part–Whole Pattern Completion constitutes a third source of resistance. We organize new information by fitting it into existing patterns called gestalts. This organizing principle is frequently referred to as a schema. For example, a comment made with neutral intent may be integrated into a pattern about the world being dangerous and consequently misinterpreted as an implied threat. Because gestalts function as reference points for appraising and understanding new information they are rarely questioned by their owners. The fact that schemas unconsciously organize new information into patterns means that we are unaware of how they are doing so, and this gives rise to the impression by therapists of unconsciously motivated resistance.

Ethics

Rogerson et al. (2011) reported that the **availability, representative, and anchoring heuristics** reviewed in Chapter 3 are among the non-rational processes that influence ethical decision-making. They found that people are generally unaware that these non-rational processes occur while they make ethical decisions. We are often not conscious of either the presence of these heuristics or how they modify our rational thought processes. These sources of irrational cognition can and are used by clients to resist therapeutic suggestions.

Clinical Reasoning

Kamphaus and Frick (2002, p. 349) noted that errors in clinical reasoning are driven by four cognitive heuristics: **the availability heuristic; the representative heuristic; the anchoring heuristic; and the confirmatory search strategy heuristic**. These heuristics are discussed in Chapter 3 as part of our confirmation bias. These sources of irrational cognition can characterize reasoning by therapists as well as clients. Therapists are people too, and consequently are subject to all of the unconscious biased cognitive heuristics that distort reasoning as clients are.

Hard Wired

Kahneman (2011b) commented directly on the parallel between **cognitive heuristics** and **optical illusions**. He noted that both persist even after a thorough explanation of each has been given, which means that insight does not free us from either optical illusions or cognitive heuristics. We saw in Chapter 3 that cognitive heuristics appear to be properties of our neural networks in the same way that optical illusions are. Hence, we need to treat them similarly. That is, we need to consciously compensate for them because insight as a result of education or personal therapy will not, because they cannot, free us from reflexively using cognitive heuristics any more than education about optical illusions can prevent us from routinely seeing them. However, we can compensate for most of these heuristics if and when we catch ourselves using them by taking steps to compensate for them, such as using research designs, statistics, and computers to more objectively and accurately process our experiences. A humorous example of compensation was provided by a scene from the 1992 movie *House Sitter* where Peter MacNicol tells Steve Martin, both acting parts as architects, that he cannot take Steve's brilliant idea to their boss Mosby. Peter reasons:

> If I take that in there and Moseby starts carrying on about how brilliant it is, I'm going to take the credit. What? Mm-hmm. You're my friend. Where're your ethics? [replied Steve Martin] My ethics are that I know this about myself…so I'm not going to take this in and screw you over.

A video clip of this scene can be viewed at http://www.metacafe.com/watch/an-PGNr2u4bthbJmm/housesitter_1992_gwen_helps_newton_with_promotion/.

Kahneman developed **reference class forecasting** to minimize the impact of cognitive heuristics on decision-making.[8] Neither clinicians nor their clients discipline their thinking in this way. That we reflexively use these heuristics makes it difficult to catch ourselves.

Therapists and Clients

Cognitive and cognitive-behavioral therapies presume that all therapists always reason rationally, but that clients do not always do so. The proposed network model makes it clear that we are all limited in how we typically reason, and that these limitations are a consequence of our neural networks. None of us are free from the approximately 100 previously reviewed cognitive heuristics that distort our thinking. Hence, an important clinical implication of Principle 1 is that the thinking of therapists and clients is frequently contaminated by non-rational processing, because we all use cognitive heuristics more than we care to admit. Causing every therapist to undergo therapy cannot cure them of these limitations, any more than therapy can cure them of optical illusions that are also mediated by our neural networks. The best that we can do is to compensate for these limitations by being aware of them as often as possible with the knowledge that we will likely miss some of them much of the time. Conclusions by clinicians should be tempered accordingly.

Automatic Feelings

An important clinical contribution of Principle 1 is that we have automatic feelings as well as automatic thoughts. Aaron Beck was psychodynamically

[8] http://en.wikipedia.org/wiki/Reference_class_forecasting

trained and therefore well-schooled in unconscious processing. His disillusion with and rejection of psychoanalytic methods did not include unconscious processing. He retained the idea that people have automatic thoughts that just pop into their head. Assessing and managing automatic thoughts became, and continue to be, central to all forms of cognitive-behavioral treatments.

CBT proponents have been taught that emotions are caused by cognitions. The supporting evidence consists of citations from ancient philosophers. The primary emphasis by rational emotive cognitive-behavior therapy (RECBT) that thoughts cause emotions implies that sensory pathways are first processed by higher cortical centers in the frontal lobes before being processed by lower brain regions such as the amygdale. Neurobiological facts clearly contradict this clinical lore. One brain structure that processes emotion, the amygdale, responds more rapidly than does the prefrontal cortex. The fibers that extend up from the amygdale to the prefrontal cortex are larger and more numerous than the fibers that extend down from the prefrontal cortex to the amygdale. This anatomical evidence shows that our neural networks process emotions more rapidly than they process cognitions, and that the influence of emotions on cognitions is more substantial than is the influence of the prefrontal cortex on the amygdale. These results require us to admit that we have automatic feelings as well as automatic thoughts. Both sets of automatic responses underlie social cognition including social cognition of close relationships (see Chen et al., 2007). Our Principle 7 regarding consonance and dissonance further demonstrates that emotion warps cognition by favoring emotionally congruent choices.

Gendlin's Focusing

The primary neural network across which activation cascades is the brain. The secondary neural network across which activation cascades is the **enteric nervous system** (ENS)[9] which is located in and controls our gastrointestinal system. Curiously, it operates on many of the same neurotransmitters as our brain does, which is the major reason why neuroleptic medications designed to alter psychological states by altering brain neurotransmitters have gastrointestinal side effects. The ENS is small relative to our brain. It is but one thousandth the size of our brain. The ENS is not actually small, in that it is composed of approximately 100 million neurons. The ENS seems to be involved in generating some of the automatic feelings mentioned in the previous section.

[9] http://en.wikipedia.org/wiki/Enteric_nervous_system

Eugene Gendlin[10] developed a psychotherapy that he called '**focusing**',[11] by which he meant **listening to oneself quietly with unconditional positive regard**. A 'felt sense' is expected to emerge as one quietly and patiently concentrates on how one feels in the moment. Gendlin collaborated with Carl Rogers. They jointly developed a manual for his mindfulness psychotherapy that taps unconscious processing. It sold over 400,000 copies. Gendlin was the first clinical psychologist to win the Distinguished Professional Psychologist of the Year award from Division (12), Clinical, of the American Psychological Association. Gendlin's focusing was intended to clarify feelings and connect them with behavior. That qualifies as insight. The ENS has neurological connections to the brain. Perhaps the 'felt sense' described by Gendlin is also related to the neurobiological activity in the limbic system described by Panksepp (1998, 2005, 2008, 2011).

Emotions Unconsciously Distort Cognition

Emotions are processed unconsciously as well as consciously. It is worth repeating the quote from Kunda's (1990) seminal paper entitled, 'The Case for Motivated Reasoning' that was presented in Chapter 4.

> There is considerable evidence that people are more likely to arrive at conclusions that they want to arrive at, but their ability to do so is constrained by their ability to construct seemingly reasonable justifications for these conclusions (p. 480). People do not seem to be at liberty to conclude whatever they want to conclude merely because they want to. Rather, I propose that people motivated to arrive at a particular conclusion attempt to be rational and to construct a justification of their desired conclusion that would persuade a dispassionate observer. They draw the desired conclusion only if they can muster up the evidence necessary to support it. In other words, they maintain an 'illusion of objectivity'... To this end, they search memory for those beliefs and rules that could support their desired conclusion. They may also creatively combine accessed knowledge to construct new beliefs that could logically support the desired conclusion. It is this process of memory search and belief construction that is biased by directional goals (pp. 482–3).

It is also worth repeating the following words of Simon and Garfunkle's song *The Boxer* previously presented in Chapter 4, 'A man hears what he wants to hear and disregards the rest'. A strong implication of unconscious processing is that people selectively attend to and 'cherry-pick' information from memory, archival sources, and their current environment to support previously arrived at emotionally held convictions, while maintaining the

[10] http://en.wikipedia.org/wiki/Eugene_Gendlin

[11] http://en.wikipedia.org/wiki/Focusing, http://www.focusing.org/gendlin/

illusion that they are being objective. All of this processing occurs automatically and unconsciously. We also encountered neuroscience and political science evidence of the fact that emotions bias cognitions.

That emotion warps cognition is a consistent theme within psychoanalytic theory. In Chapter 5 we learned that emotions are unconsciously generated by subcortical structures. It follows that these unconsciously generated emotions selectively favor emotionally congruent decisions, and that cognitive rationalizations are recruited to support them in order to achieve overall consistency. The neuroanatomical facts that descending fibers from the cortex to the amygdale are few and that ascending fibers are many, further supports the dominance of emotions over cognitions. Nevertheless, clinical intervention at the cognitive level has been shown to be effective. The point here is that clinicians need to recognize that unconsciously generated emotions in the form of automatic feelings and related automatic thoughts will interfere with and limit the extent to which CBT is effective. Hence, additional treatments may be needed to address these emotional distortions.

Another major clinical implication of these findings is that therapists as well as clients are equally open to these distortions. Presumably professional training has sensitized therapists to these unconscious motives, though no amount of personal therapy can free one from them any more than personal therapy can free one from optical illusions. We previously used the term cognitive illusion to emphasize the parallel with optical illusion. Network models formally recognize the ability of emotions to constrain, and sometimes grossly distort, cognition. Psychodynamic theorists have long recognized and emphasized that this is the case.

UNCONSCIOUS PROCESSING IN PSYCHOLOGICAL TREATMENTS

Psychological treatments can be rank ordered by how much unconscious processing they admit to. Cognitive therapy and rational emotive behavior therapy acknowledge the least amount of unconscious processing; i.e., are perhaps the most conscious-centric contemporary psychological interventions. They assume that cognitive biases cause all psychological distress and aim to help people think differently about themselves and other people. This was also the aim of Heinz Hartmann's (1939/1958) Ego psychology. Cognitive bias modification (CBM) is a relatively new CBT that makes therapeutic use of the dot-probe task, described below, and related methods. Hallion and Ruscio (2011) reported results of a meta-analysis regarding cognitive bias modification for the treatment of anxiety and depression. They reported that CBM produced a medium effect (g = 0.49) over 45 studies covering 2,591 participants that was stronger for interpretation biases (g = 0.81) than for attention biases (g = 0.29). CBM was found to have a small effect on anxiety and depression (g = 0.13).

Behavior theory says little about conscious or unconscious processing. Applied behavior analysis (ABA) applies principles of operant conditioning to the amelioration of behavior problems. These principles were developed in the laboratory on animals that presumably rely more on unconscious processing than humans do. Reinforcers strengthen behaviors, but people are unaware of the mediating neuroscience mechanisms. Thus, while arranging reinforcement contingencies is the result of conscious planning, the mechanism of behavior change remains outside of awareness. Exposure treatment seems to entail a fair amount of unconscious processing, because during the actual exposure trials the client mainly focuses their attention on what they are experiencing rather than on the change process. Exposure therapy is facilitated by d-cycloserine (DCS) that activates pharmacological mechanisms of which clients are completely unaware.

SYMPTOM SUBSTITUTION

Psychodynamic theory stipulates that psychopathology is caused by unconscious processes and that therapy is truly effective only when it addresses and resolves these matters. Psychodynamic theory maintains that direct symptom-oriented interventions cannot be effective because they do not address unconscious issues. Worse, direct symptom-oriented interventions are considered to be harmful because they further frustrate expression of unconscious conflicts. This understanding of psychopathology strongly predicts that direct symptom-oriented interventions will necessarily result in symptom substitution in all cases where significant unconscious conflicts are not treated and remain unresolved.

Some readers may believe that I have overstated matters and that psychodynamic theorists never really seriously believed that symptom substitution occurs and still do not. A variant of this position is to argue that psychodynamic theorists have been misunderstood. I therefore begin our examination of this issue with a trip down memory lane to review what the published record has to say about these matters. I quote extensively from authors to avoid the potential criticism that I have somehow misunderstood that psychoanalytic theory requires symptom substitution. Then I review the evidence concerning symptom substitution presented by Tryon (2008b).

Psychodynamic Theory

Grünbaum (1984) presented the theoretical basis for predicting symptom substitution as follows:

> A neurotic symptom is held to be a compromise formed in response to an unresolved conflict between a forbidden unconscious impulse and the ego's defense against it. The symptom is held to be sustained at any time given time by a coexisting, ongoing unconscious conflict, which – as claimed by NCT[12] – does not resolve itself without psychoanalytic intervention. Hence, if the repression of the unconscious wish is not lifted psychoanalytically, the underlying neurosis will persist, even if behavior therapy or hypnosis, for example extinguishes the particular symptom that only manifests the neurosis at the time. As long as the neurotic conflict does persist, the patient's psyche will call for the defensive service previously rendered by the banished symptom. Hence, typically and especially in severe cases, **the unresolved conflict ought to engender a *new* symptom**. And incidentally, this expectation qualifies as a "risky" prediction in Popper's sense, since such rival extant theories as behavior intervention disavow just that expectation (p. 162; italics is original, bold emphasis added).

Hand and Lamontagne (1976) stipulated that:

> In orthodox psychoanalysis, a symptom is regarded as a person's symbolic expression of an underlying conflict and as a defensive way of problem solving. **Removing this symbolic expression would thus result in a substitute symptom** or at worst lead to a breakdown of the defenseless patient (Bookbinder, 1962; Holland, 1967, p. 405; bold emphasis added).

Grossberg (1964) noted that:

> According to psychoanalytic formulations, maladaptive behavior is a derivative of the conflict between the contradictory impulses striving for discharge and defensive forces. This makes it impossible to discharge tension in the usual way, so tension accumulates, and the defensive system is overpowered by excitation, producing distorted discharges which are symptoms. It follows that treatment which leaves the central conflict unresolved will be unsuccessful, and **substitute symptoms are expected**. This issue is important not only because of the empirical question of the effectiveness of symptomatic treatment and patient welfare, but because it tests a hypothesis directly derived from psychoanalytic theory, thus bearing on the utility of this aspect of the theory (p. 83, bold emphasis added).

Yates (1958) noted that:

> The argument that symptomatic treatment is a waste of time has had as its strongest proponent the psychoanalytic school, which has insisted that symptoms are but the surface indicators of underlying conflicts, anxieties, etc. This

[12] NCT stands for necessary condition thesis.

> argument has been accepted by most "dynamic" psychologists, who concluded that **removing the symptom without also effectively treating the anxiety or conflict underlying it would lead to symptom substitution**. For example, even if tics could be treated directly and extinguished, the patient would quickly develop either new tics or some other form of symptomatic response. Even orthodox psychiatrists who have little patience with Freudian psychodynamics have accepted this point of view. Thus Kanner writes that "symptomatic therapy which does not care what the complaint is a 'symptom' of is rarely successful and leads to unwarranted pessimism" (p. 244) (p. 371, bold emphasis added).

Cahoon (1968) stated that:

> Traditional psychotherapeutic approaches are usually based upon "closed-energy" personality systems (Spiegel, 1967), within which the symptom may be conceived as a mechanism for the expression of psychic conflicts. **If the symptom should be suppressed or altered without modifying the antecedent conflict (the "underlying cause"), the formation of a new symptom is a likely occurrence** (p. 149, bold emphasis added).

Mikulas (1972) reported that:

> For many **the major issue against behavior therapy is that it might lead to symptom substitution.** If the person's behaviors are merely symptoms of a more basic underlying problem, then only treating the symptoms does not get at this basic cause. **If this basic problem is not treated then it will manifest itself in some other symptom: symptom substitution** (p. 90, bold emphasis added).

Kazdin (1982) observed that:

> In the 1950s and 1960s, symptom substitution was raised as a crucial issue that clearly delineated psychodynamic and behavior therapies (e.g., Eysenck, 1959; Ullmann & Krasner, 1965; Yates, 1958b). **Strong claims were made that symptom substitution would, according to psychodynamic conceptions of treatment, inevitably result from the treatment of overt behavioral problems** (pp. 349–50, bold emphasis added).

Psychologists are ethically bound to do no harm. That behavior therapy treated symptoms rather than the hypothesized underlying unconscious causes of behavioral and emotional disorders posed a clear and present danger that symptom removal would result in the substitution of a more serious problem, thereby harming the patient. Baker (1969) indicates that traditional psychiatry warned behavior therapists about symptom substitution, and that this consideration made many clinicians hesitant to use what then was a new form of therapy, because doing so might harm their clients and that would be unethical as well as unconscionable as follows:

> Traditional psychiatry (e.g., Freud, 1959) views maladjustive behavior as a sign that there is an underlying disorder, and **warns that even if a problem can be**

> **removed by a nondynamic therapy a relapse or another new problem will follow, since the basic causes have not been treated. This "symptom substitution" hypothesis is probably the principal theoretical reason why many clinicians hesitate to use behavior therapy** (p. 42, bold emphasis added).

Weitzman (1967) observed that:

> **In fact, analysts have tended to the belief that symptomatic treatment may be worse than no treatment at all, that is, that it may be dangerous** (p. 307, bold emphasis added).

Weitzman (1967) wrote:

> It has been pointed out, from both camps, that **analytic theory requires that symptom substitution or recurrence must attend a symptomatic treatment** which, by definition, does not affect the dynamic sources of the symptoms. The evidence is rather impressive that neither substitution nor recurrence typically follows treatment by systematic desensitization (p. 301, bold emphasis added).

Therapists who dared to use behavior therapies were bordering on malpractice, given the apparent dangerous risk to their clients due to the theoretical certainty of symptom substitution. Additional quotations could have been provided but presumably even skeptical readers will now admit that symptom substitution is no straw man, a distorted version of a misunderstood truth that can easily be defeated, but rather is an unavoidable hard prediction that reflects a core psychodynamic belief; i.e., it is a necessary and crucial prediction of psychodynamic theory that reflects their view of psychopathology, symptom formation, and the need for psychodynamic therapy.

Some skeptical readers may accept my quotations as characteristic of a time long past, but suggest that modern informed psychodynamic theorists no longer believe that unconscious conflicts cause symptoms in the way that psychodynamic theorists once did. Every field changes and some readers may feel that my characterization does not reflect modern times. The next section provides a way to demonstrate that concern over symptom substitution is alive and well today.

Case Conference Test

If all previous arguments have not convinced you that symptom substitution is an integral part of contemporary psychodynamic case formulation, then I invite you to consider conducting the following case conference test where a psychodynamic clinician presents a case.

Listen carefully the next time you participate in a case conference where a psychodynamic presentation is provided, and see if the following predicted sequence occurs or not. The case presentation will begin with a report of patient demographics followed by a description of one or more symptoms that justify an initial diagnostic impression. Establishing a working DSM diagnosis may be part of the case formulation. A personal and/or family history may follow. Then listen for a statement about underlying or core issues that have presumably given rise to the presenting complaint/symptoms as defenses that constitute the client's psychodynamics. The treatment recommendations that follow are sure to include short- or long-term intervention designed to address these underlying unconscious psychodynamic conflicts/issues. The causal relationship between the psychodynamic formulations and presenting symptoms should be crystal clear to everyone attending the case conference.

Now comes the crucial test. Raise your hand and recommend a direct symptomatic treatment be used instead of the proposed psychodynamic intervention. Then prepare yourself for a variety of negative comments and criticisms that will surely follow once your fellow psychologists recover from the shock created by your bold move. Prepare to be told that you are psychologically uninformed and clinically naïve. Prepare to receive concerns that bad things will happen to the client as a result of such misguided intervention. Their comments will clearly demonstrate that psychodynamic concern over symptom substitution remains genuine.

Empirical Evidence

Tryon (2008b) reviewed the available evidence regarding symptom substitution. The following discussion draws heavily on this article. His search covered literature published between 1973 and 2007; a span of 34 years. Other investigators who have looked for but not found any evidence include: Baker (1969); Kahn et al. (1968); Nolan et al. (1970); Ober (1968); and Paul (1968). Tryon (2008b) noted that this literature is small, uneven, and was published at irregular intervals. Little if any current discussion exists.

Nurnberger and Hingtgen (1973) reviewed the literature on systematic desensitization for phobias, behavioral treatment for nocturnal enuresis, stuttering and tics, as well as the modification of what they called 'bad habits'. They generously concluded that symptom substitution rarely occurs. This generosity included counting anxiety occurring 8 months after a successful behavior therapy. They conducted a 2.5-year follow-up of behavioral treatment for nocturnal enuresis and found no evidence of symptom substitution. Likewise, they found no evidence of symptom substitution in cases where stuttering was treated with a metronome.

Conversion disorders seem to be prime candidates for symptom substitution. Speed (1996) restored normal gait to five men and five women with conversion disorder symptoms. Seven to 36 months of follow-up revealed that while two patients returned to partial wheelchair usage, none of them developed a different disorder of any kind.

Fuchs (1980) treated 72 women complaining of vaginismus. They experienced pain during sexual intercourse. Presumably their pain was due to unconscious conflicts over having sexual relations. They reported that imaginal desensitization produced good results in 16 of 18 women. They reported good results in 53 of 54 women treated with in vivo desensitization. A 2- to 5-year follow-up study revealed no relapse or symptom substitution.

Psychodynamic theorists consistently maintained that enuresis was caused by unconscious conflicts (cf. Mowrer, 1950, p. 398). Hence, it is an especially informative disorder. Mowrer and Mowrer (1938) introduced a bell and pad method for treating enuresis on the basis that these children were heavy sleepers who failed to detect nocturnal bladder tension. The child wore a sensor in their pajamas. Urine closed a sensor circuit that woke the child who then relieved himself in the toilet. Bladder tension was the conditional stimulus (CS), the bell was the unconditional stimulus (UCS), waking to the bell was the unconditional response (UR), and waking to bladder tension was the target conditional response (CR).

A PubMed literature search using the string 'enuresis, behavior therapy, bell' returned 15 studies. While Nurnberger and Hingtgen (1973), cited above, included the Baker (1969) study, it is reviewed here in more detail because it was an especially thorough investigation. Baker (1969) assigned 30 enuretic children to three groups of ten. The conditioning group received 14 nights of the bell and pad treatment just described. A wake-up control group was fully wakened by parents at the same time every night. The third group was a wait-list control. Children in the conditioning and wake-up groups improved rapidly and to the same degree over the first 3 weeks. Children in the conditioning group continued to improve through week ten, whereas children in the wake-up group did not. Children in the wait list continued to wet 6 nights a week at the tenth week just as they had at the beginning of the study, as did the children in the other two groups before treatment began. No instances of symptom substitution occurred.

Wille (1994) used the bell and pad method to treat 29 children with primary nocturnal enuresis for 12 weeks in a double-blind study with

15 age- and sex-matched children as controls. No instances of symptom substitution were reported. These children were given psychological tests by Wille and Anveden (1995). No evidence of neurosis was found. No increase in psychopathology subsequent to treatment was reported.

Just two cases were found where the authors claimed to have evidence of symptom substitution. Henker (1979) reported the case of a 40-year-old man who weighted 290 lbs and stood 67 inches tall. He also had marital problems. He divorced, remarried, and moved to another city. His remarriage was against the advice of his friends and his church; religion was very important to him. His obesity treatment was successful in that his weight dropped to 170 lbs. However, 3 years later, he regained the lost weight and was again unhappy in his marital relationship. This is a case of **symptom return not substitution**, in that the same issues once again became problematic.

Perhaps the most absurd report of 'symptom substitution' was by Ottenbacher and Ottenbacher (1981) who reported the behavioral treatment of a 4-year-old child for thumb sucking. Thumb sucking was somehow classified as a symptom of an unspecified disorder and then subjected to behavioral treatment. The frequency of thumb sucking was reduced from an average of 40 times per week to 7 times per week during the first week of treatment, and then to zero during the second week of treatment. During this time the frequency of bed wetting increased from zero times per week before treatment to twice during the first week of treatment and then to every night during the second week of treatment. Behavioral treatment for thumb sucking was terminated. Bed wetting decreased to four nights and thumb sucking increased to five nights per week. The authors concluded that symptom substitution had occurred. The main problem with this report is that thumb sucking was never shown to be a symptom of a disorder. Thumb sucking is normal for young children. Sucking is the way infants obtain nutrition. Thumb sucking is also a method of self-soothing. It is not a symptom of a disease. Thwarting a natural behavior can, as this case demonstrates, result in bed wetting. This report seems more about the undesirable consequences of inadvisable treatment than about symptom substitution.

Blanchard and Hersen (1976) noted that some instances that might seem to demonstrate symptom substitution could arise as the result of secondary gains. Not being able to obtain reinforcement in an appropriate way may give rise to inappropriate behavior.

The stark negative contrast between the certain predicted expectation and clear warning that symptom substitution necessarily follows **every case** of symptom-oriented interventions and the total absence of supporting empirical evidence constitutes one of the most remarkable, if not the most remarkable, instances where a major theoretical prediction in clinical psychology has been so convincingly falsified. The fact that such a complete falsification has had little, if any, impact on psychodynamic theory is a remarkable testament to the willingness of psychologists to continue to support their favored theory regardless of how consistently negative the evidence is.

Reasons for Negative Results and Rebuttals

Had any evidence of symptom substitution been found, and especially if symptom substitution occurred with any regularity, then behavior therapists would have almost certainly been charged with malpractice. Any such evidence of symptom substitution would have been widely publicized with a notable 'I told you so' and 'cease and desist' tone, leaving behavior therapists even more vulnerable to charges of malpractice should they continue to knowingly and willingly put their clients at risk for exacerbated illnesses. But fortunately for behavior therapists, cognitive therapists, and cognitive-behavior therapists, symptom substitution does not occur. The predicted risks to patients are baseless in fact, though still required and predicted by contemporary psychodynamic theory.

While the absence of empirical support for symptom substitution has muted most contemporary claims of harm by behavior therapy from psychodynamic clinicians, the theoretical implications have also been uniformly ignored. One rarely hears about symptom substitution any more.[13] How come? One graduate student told me that his psychodynamic externship supervisor never discussed symptom substitution, implying that it is no longer a professionally relevant issue; i.e., not something that a supervisor should discuss with his students. I can understand why his supervisor avoided discussing empirical evidence that falsifies the psychodynamic understanding of psychopathology and symptom formation. This negative evidence also shows that psychodynamic treatment is not necessarily the preferred intervention. These are good reasons why psychodynamic supervisors should

[13] Psychoanalytic supervisors likely also do not also discuss penis envy, oral, anal, urethral, phallic, latency, and genital adult personality styles (Rychlak, 1981b, pp. 76–80) or castration, Oedipal and Electra complexes, because supportive empirical evidence is unavailable for these psychoanalytic concepts as well.

avoid discussing the negative evidence regarding symptom substitution. Instead, some authors have attempted to avoid the falsifying consequences of the negative empirical evidence regarding symptom substitution. I now consider their arguments.

Postdictive Theory

Weitzman (1967) aimed to avoid all negative consequences associated with the absence of empirical support for symptom substitution as follows:

> Rapaport (1959) has noted that psychoanalysis is, essentially, a postdictive system. It can rationalize events after their occurrence, but cannot predict these events. This assertion is, in part, based upon Freud's conception of the energetic relations between the system of the psychic economy (pp. 307–8).

The strong implication of this quote in an article about symptom substitution by a psychodynamic clinician is that the prediction of symptom substitution should never have been taken seriously, as prediction is beyond the bounds of what one can reasonably expect of psychodynamic theory due to its postdictive nature. This effectively dismisses the negative evidence against symptom substitution, but at a heavy cost. First, it creates an understanding of psychodynamic theory that contradicts the several quotations presented above that definitively predicted symptom substitution. Second, it claims that psychodynamic theory cannot make any predictions. If true, then no scientific hypotheses can ever be formulated and therefore psychoanalysis is not science. This is a heavy price to pay, but perhaps one worth paying given that the alternative is to reject the psychodynamic understanding of symptom formation and how psychopathology should be treated.

Inadequate Understanding

Another way that negative evidence of symptom substitution can be dismissed is to argue, as Weitzman (1967) and Cahoon (1968) have, that the prediction of symptom substitution is based on an inadequate understanding of psychoanalytic thought. I presented as many quotes as I did precisely to avoid this criticism, as one can always claim to have been misunderstood. But neither of these authors chose to correct this supposed misunderstanding by advancing arguments for why symptom substitution should not occur. It is insufficient to simply assert that one has been misunderstood. One needs to specify what the misunderstanding is and then clarify what was intended. Is there a psychodynamic position regarding symptom substitution that I have not presented that can be clearly presented? Or does the following quote from Joynt (1981, p. 108) pertain? 'Consciousess is like the

Trinity; if it is explained so that you understand it, it hasn't been explained correctly'. If symptom substitution is like consciousness or the Trinity then the problem of validation is insurmountable.

An alternate form of the misunderstanding argument offered by Weitzman (1967) is that there is a way to understand psychoanalysis that does not result in predicting symptom substitution and not all schools of psychoanalytic thought require one to believe in symptom substitution. Efforts to **causally isolate** underlying psychodynamic processes from symptom formation would, if successful, defend against the negative implications of no evidence for symptom substitution, but it would also be tragically devastating because it would make psychodynamic treatment of these underlying processes clinically irrelevant. If hypothesized underlying conflicts/issues are causally irrelevant to symptom formation then their treatment is also causally irrelevant. This equates to admitting that psychodynamic treatment can address underlying issues, but their resolution in no way can be expected to improve the problems that clients bring for treatment.

Demonstrating that underlying conditions exist may be interesting to the clinician who prefers to treat them, but this makes their treatment relevant to the clinician's interests rather than the client's benefit. Clients do not seek treatment to entertain clinicians. Hence, any psychodynamic theory that succeeds in avoiding the symptom substitution prediction by causally isolating itself and its hypothesized underlying psychodynamic processes from symptom formation automatically excludes itself from responsible clinical practice. It is **causal relevance that requires symptom substitution**. One cannot expect a result to disappear without removing its cause and psychodynamic causes require symptomatic expression which if suppressed or frustrated only makes matters worse. The corollary implication here is that psychodynamic theories **must** find a way to predict symptom substitution if they are to justify the treatment of hypothesized underlying conditions.

Methodological Problems

Kazdin (1982) argued that the question of symptom substitution is unscientific because of six methodological problems, and therefore this question was properly abandoned rather than answered.[14] Dismissing the question of symptom substitution as not a valid scientific question for methodological

[14] Kazdin seems to be a very unlikely apologist for psychodynamic theory. I do not understand why he would vigorously defend a theoretical position that he has spent most of his career working in opposition to.

reasons is an excellent defensive move, as it is far better to put this question out of reach than it is to face the theory construction consequences of consistent negative evidence. One can then maintain that perhaps someday the question will become tractable and then can be answered in a positive way, but that this day has not yet come and may not arrive in the foreseeable future given the difficulties involved. One can therefore comfortably continue indefinitely with their psychodynamic orientation. Montgomery and Crowder (1972) also raised some of these same methodological problems.

Tryon (2008b) rebutted Kazdin's (1982) six methodological reasons for concluding that the question of symptom substitution cannot be answered and must be abandoned. I now review these reasons. Kazdin's (1982) **first** problem was that symptoms of psychological disorders cannot be as clearly stated as can symptoms of medical disorders, and that without a clear definition of what constitutes a psychological symptom, one cannot determine if another symptom has been substituted. Tryon (2008b) replied that the *Diagnostic and Statistical Manuals* (DSM) specifically list psychiatric symptoms with sufficient clarity that they can be reliably assessed by two independent clinicians. These symptoms are sufficiently well understood that they are used to define a broad range of psychiatric disorders. Hence, Kazdin's first criticism is without merit and offers no defense against the negative evidence of symptom substitution.

Kazdin's (1982) **second** methodological problem can best be stated in question form: if a new problem presents after the first one is treated does it automatically and always constitute symptom substitution? This concern goes to the case where a second symptom arises. Symptom substitution cannot possibly occur unless a second symptom arises. Hence, in all cases where an initial symptom is treated and no second symptom arose, symptom substitution cannot possibly have occurred. Only in those cases where a second symptom emerges during therapy does the possibility of symptom substitiution arise. In these cases, cause must be demonstrated to establish symptom substitution. It is possible for a second symptom to be correlated with the first but not caused by it. Proving symptom substitution requires demonstrating that the second symptom is causally related to the first symptom. The burden of proof here is entirely on psychodynamic theory, because it is a core prediction of this theory.

Kazdin's (1982) **third** methodological problem is that the time course for symptom substitution is unclear. How soon must the new symptom appear after treatment of the first symptom? Must it appear immediately or can it be delayed for months or years? At what point can one conclude that a new symptom will not appear? Tryon (2008b) noted that the greatest concern and risk to behavior therapists is that the new symptom would emerge while the patient is undergoing behavior therapy and/or remains in the care of the behavior therapist and/or occurs sufficiently shortly thereafter behavior therapy concludes that a jury would likely hold the behavior therapist accountable for the client's exacerbated condition.

Kazdin's (1982) **fourth** methodological problem concerns the base rates of psychiatric problems. How are we to distinguish between the independent first occurrence of a second problem while the first problem is being treated from the case where direct intervention to treat the first problem causes symptom substitution and the presence of a second problem? Tryon (2008b) replied that this concern emerges only if a second symptom occurs and that does not seem to happen.

Kazdin's (1982) **fifth** methodological problem concerns comorbidity. How does one distinguish symptom substitution where the second symptom emerges after the first symptom has been successfully treated from the comorbid condition where both symptoms were present at intake but that the second problem only became noticeable after treating the first symptom? Tryon (2008b) noted that the negative empirical facts at issue here concerning symptom substitution pertain to symptom **absence**; not how to interpret symptom **presence**. What needs explained away is the **absence** of a new symptom after successful treatment of the target symptom(s).

Kazdin's (1982) **sixth** methodological problem is that demonstrating that symptom substitution does not occur under some conditions does not prove that it cannot occur under others. Tryon (2008b) noted that if psychodynamic theory is correct then symptom substitution must occur **every** time that a symptom-oriented treatment is applied to psychological conditions that are caused by unconscious conflicts, because symptom-oriented treatments, by definition, always fail to address the hypothesized underlying causal conditions. If symptoms are always an expression of an underlying problem then frustrating this expression by inhibiting or removing the symptom must always result in symptom substitution. Symptom substitution is a strong prediction of the psychoanalytic understanding of psychopathology and how symptoms form that has been consistently falsified by empirical evidence. This situation definitively falsifies the psychodynamic understanding of psychopathology and symptom formation.

Definitive Experiment

Another way to dismiss the negative evidence reported below is to say that the entire DSM approach is misguided, in that the behaviors it cites as part of inclusion and exclusion criteria do not constitute valid psychoanalytic symptoms. This approach divorces psychodynamic therapists from the psychiatric community which holds the copyright to the DSM series. But, for the moment, let's assume that DSM diagnostic criteria do not constitute genuine psychoanalytic symptoms. This means that all previous studies have yet to provide a valid test of the symptom substitution hypothesis, and therefore the question of whether symptom substitution exists remains open and yet to be investigated.

Tryon (2008b) recommended the following experiment to examine the symptom substitution hypothesis. Form two groups of patients with the same genuine psychoanalytic symptom by whatever assessment method is fully acceptable. Provide psychoanalytic treatment to one group and symptom-oriented behavior therapy to the other group. The group receiving psychoanalytic treatment should improve and retain this improvement, whereas the group treated with behavior therapy might seem to improve at first in that the treated symptom(s) might be reduced or even disappear, but then these participants should develop another genuine psychoanalytic symptom because their core issues were not addressed. The next step is to provide psychoanalytic therapy for these patients. They should get better and remain improved. In the case where behavior therapy did not produce any symptomatic improvement, symptom exacerbation or substitution is still predicted due to the frustration of unconscious expression created by direct symptom treatment. Until such evidence is provided the theoretical claim that unconscious conflicts cause symptoms remains without empirical basis; i.e., is unjustified. This evidence-based conclusion should be reflected in contemporary clinical training and practice.

Correlated Behaviors

But how can symptom substitution appear to occur? Behaviors can be correlated. Where one behavior or behavior problem is found, others may also be found for a variety of reasons, even causal reasons. This fact offers the possibility that modifying one behavior may change the frequency, intensity, and/or duration of other behaviors. Such a result does not in itself establish any of these behaviors as symptoms of an underlying disease or psychopathology. Hence, behavioral covariation is not the same as symptom substitution. Evidence of behavioral covariation is not proof of symptom substitution. Cause and effect must be established. Symptoms must be clearly linked to underlying disorders.

Conclusions

Sometimes, in fact most times, a cigar is just a cigar and not a phallic symbol. Most people who successfully quit smoking do so without first treating and curing their unconscious oral fixation complex. Likewise, there is no evidence that enuresis is a symptom of anything other than being a sound sleeper. Yet psychodynamic clinicians continue to insist that many behaviors are symptoms that are caused by underlying issues that must be addressed by psychodynamic therapy in order for long-term improvement to occur. Upon this view, direct symptomatic treatment only frustrates the unconscious expression of the underlying conflicts, and therefore cannot be helpful because these unconscious conflicts will only resurface in some other way thus causing symptom substitution. The claims that: (a) observable symptoms are a partial, and likely distorted, expression of unconscious conflicts and processes; and (b) that effective treatments must address these underlying issues in order to produce lasting positive results, continue to be taught and defended even though there is no evidence to support these claims.

Kazdin's (1982) claim that the symptom substitution hypothesis was and must be abandoned because it is not a scientific question has been shown to be without merit. The symptom substitution hypothesis is an empirically testable consequence of the psychodynamic theory of psychopathology. In fact, it may be the most crucial test of psychodynamic therapy.

I wish to emphasize that the positive evidence of unconscious processing presented earlier does not, should not, and cannot balance out or compensate for, the strong negative evidence that has falsified the psychodynamic theory of symptom formulation that is used to justify related interventions. While unconscious processing definitely occurs, it does not seem to play the role that psychodynamic theorists have claimed for it. It is time to rethink these issues. This includes rethinking the role of projective methods for assessing unconscious processing (Lilienfeld et al., 2000; Wood et al., 2001). I now consider alternative methods of assessing unconscious processing and treatments based on unconscious processing.

ASSESSING UNCONSCIOUS PROCESSING

Implicit Association

The term 'implicit' seems to be currently preferred over the term 'unconscious'; probably to distinguish and distance authors from psychodynamic theory. Hence, it is now fashionable to talk about implicit social cognition rather than unconscious social cognition. The equation of implicit, unconscious, and automatic is verified by Payne and Gawronski (2010), who wrote 'in every topic of study, implicit social cognition is concerned with automatic/implicit/unconscious processes underlying judgments and social behavior' (p. 1). We say that a psychological state is unconscious when people are unaware of being in that state. Implicit attitudes have been defined as 'the positive or negative thoughts, feelings, or actions towards objects which arise due to past experiences which one is either unaware of or which one cannot attribute to an identified previous experience'.[15]

Payne and Gawronski (2010) provided a history of implicit social cognition with roots in selective attention research and implicit memory research. Greenwald and Banaji (1995) coined the term implicit social cognition. Admitting to and accepting unconscious processing requires methods for assessing such processing. In this section I consider several methods for doing so. Payne and Gawronski (2010) identified two major sources of methodology for measuring implicit cognition: (a) implicit attitude test (IAT) – inspired methods; and (b) priming-inspired methods. The most comprehensive single source regarding these methods is the *Handbook of Implicit Social Cognition: Measurement, Theory, and Application* edited by Gawronski and Payne (2010). We have already considered priming as our first corollary principle designated as Principle 5 in Chapter 4. Wentura and Degner (2010) provided 'A Practical Guide to Sequential Priming and Related Tasks'. Teige-Mocigemba et al. (2010) provided 'A Practical Guide to Implicit Association Tests and Related Tasks'. Sekaquaptewa et al. (2010) provided 'A Practical Guide to Paper-and-Pencil Implicit Measures of Attitudes'. De Houwer and Moors (2010) discussed similarities and differences among implicit measures. Zeigler-Hill and Jordan (2010) discussed implicit and explicit facets of self-esteem. Schnabel and Asendorpf (2010) extend this discussion by reviewing new insights from implicit measures regarding the self-concept. Baldwin et al. (2010) considered implicit measurements in close relationships. Brunel et al. (2004) considered the validity and value of implicit consumer oriented measures of social cognition.

Implicit testing is used to assess unconscious attitudes. Many implicit attitude tests can be found at the following URLs: https://implicit.harvard.edu/implicit/demo/selectatest.htm and at https://implicit.harvard.edu/implicit/ where an implicit attitude test (IAT) is freely available in 36 different languages One can either take a demonstration test or participate in ongoing research. I now review how the implicit attitude test is scored to gain a better understanding of what this test is measuring. The main assumption is that cognitive schemas facilitate processing and therefore one will respond more quickly to stimuli for which they are schema consistent than schema inconsistent. Several

[15] http://en.wikipedia.org/wiki/Implicit_attitude

Implicit Attitude Scoring

- Preference: Yankees > Mets: RT on:
- Task 1: Left key = Yankees stimuli
- Right key = Mets stimuli
- Task 2: Left key = Stimuli representing Self
- Right key = Stimuli representing Others
- Task 3: Left key = Yankee or Self
- Right key = Mets or Others
- Task 4: Left key = Mets or Self
- Right key = Yankee or Others
- IAT Score = Task 3 – Task 4

Figure 9.1 Illustration of how perceiving the implicit attitude test works. Faster response to task 3 than 4 indicates a Yankee fan. Faster response to task 4 than 3 indicates a Mets fan.

sorting tasks are used and response time is measured. Let's take the example of determining if someone is unconsciously a Yankees or a Mets fan, as summarized in Figure 9.1. On the first sorting task the participant presses the left key when they see a Yankees stimulus and the right key when they see a Mets stimulus. On the second sorting task they press the left key when they see a stimulus pertaining to themselves and the right key when they see a stimulus pertaining to someone else. Now comes the joint sorting task. The third sorting task requires that the person press the left key if they see a Yankee stimulus or a stimulus about themselves, and press the right key if they see a Mets stimulus or a stimulus about other people. The final and fourth sorting task tests for the opposite combination. The participant presses the left key when they see a Mets stimulus or a stimulus pertaining to themselves, and presses the right key if they see a Yankee stimulus or stimulus pertaining to other people. The IAT score is the average response time on Task 3 – Task 4. Since faster means schema consistent, a negative difference indicates a Yankee fan and a positive difference indicates a Mets fan.

Gawronski et al. (2007) cited evidence against the following three assumptions upon which the IAT is based. First, that IAT measures unconscious attitudes that cannot otherwise be assessed with self-report measures. Second, that IAT measures are less susceptible to social desirability and other motivational distortions. Third, that IAT measures are stable because they are rooted in long-term socialization. The authors concluded their article with a statement of what these indirect measures can tell us. They claim that indirect measures reflect **activation of associations** in memory, whereas self-report measures reflect **validation processes** that evaluate the truth or falsity of these associations. Activated associations can continue to influence behavior even if they are considered to be inaccurate (Strack & Deutsch, 2004), and therefore indirect measures may help explain human behavior.

Carlston (2010) noted that the way that connectionist models represent memories as connections among processing nodes is well suited to understanding implicit social cognition. Ito (2010) reviewed neuroscience evidence supporting a network approach to implicit social cognition. Amodio and Mendoza (2010) discussed network models of implicit racial associations. Teachman et al. (2010) discussed clinical applications of implicit social cognition theories and methods. I now consider alternative methods for assessing unconscious processes.

Emotional Stroop (e-Stroop)

The standard Stroop Test (Stroop, 1935) consists of color words printed in different colors of ink. Initially, the time taken for participants to read all of the color names is measured. Then participants are asked to name the color of ink that each word is printed in. Typically it takes longer for participants to say the ink colors than it does to read the words. Cohen et al. (1990) provided a connectionist model whose information explains why this is so.

The emotional Stroop, also known as the e-Stroop test (Williams et al., 1996), uses target and control lists of words printed in various colors of ink. For example, the words on the target list would be anxiety-related if the study was about anxiety, or the words on the target list would be depression-related if the study was about depression. Neutral words that appear with the same frequency in the English language typically constitute the control list. The standard Stroop test is administered to control participants. They typically take longer to name the color of ink that the words are printed in than to read the names of the colors. Anxious persons show an exaggerated Stroop effect when the anxiety-related target list is used. Depressed persons show an exaggerated Stroop effect when the depression-related target list is used. Williams et al. (1996) have shown that the exaggerated Stroop effect can be used to assess a wide variety of psychopathology. The e-Stroop test is sufficiently sensitive that it can detect differences between neutral and emotionally charged words in normal college students. Teachman et al. (2010) reviewed more current clinical applications of the e-Stroop test.

Dot-Probe Task

The dot-probe task, also known as the visual-probe task, was developed by MacLeod et al. (1986). They presented participants with 288 vertically separated word pairs and the following instructions:

> In this experiment you are going to see words presented on the screen in pairs. One word will appear just above the center of the screen, and one just below. Please read the top word of each pair aloud as soon as it appears. Sometimes when the two words disappear a small dot will remain either in the area where the top word appeared or in the area where the bottom word appeared. When you see the dot, press this [hand-held] button as quickly as possible. Are there any questions? (p. 17).

Dots occurred on 96 trials. Half the time they replaced a high-threat word and half the time they replaced a low-threat word. Half the time the dot replaced a word in the up position and half the time the dot replaced the word in the down position. This resulted in 2 (up vs. down position) × 2 (high vs. low threat) × 2 (dot replaces high vs. low threat word) design that produces eight response time means and standard deviations. Quicker reaction time when the dot appears in the same position (up or down) as the threatening stimuli is taken as evidence that the person was already attending to that physical location and hence shows biased attention. Quicker reaction time to the dot when it occurs in the previous location that a threatening stimulus appeared in is interpreted as vigilance to threat. The authors reported the following three-way interaction for the anxious participants only:

> Probes in the upper area were detected more rapidly when preceded by a threat word in the upper (593 ms) rather than in the lower (652 ms) area; probes in the lower area were detected more rapidly when preceded by a threat word in the lower (663 ms) rather than in the upper (695 ms) area. As predicted, therefore, visual attention appeared to shift toward the threat term (p. 17).

Teachman et al. (2010) reviewed more current clinical applications of the dot-probe task.

Priming Tasks

Teachman et al. (2010) reviewed research demonstrating that depressed persons show larger subliminal and supraliminal priming effects when primed with depression-relevant words compared with neutral words on a lexical decision task. They also reviewed studies on affective priming where depressed persons, but not controls, responded faster to and endorsed more depression-related words as true of themselves after reading a brief emotional prime or a negative emotional prime.

INSIGHT AS PSYCHOLOGICAL MINDEDNESS

The topic of insight is relevant to unconscious processing, because from the psychodynamic perspective insight makes conscious what was previously unconscious. One might say that the primary objective of psychodynamic treatment is to increase insight. While the negative evidence on symptom substitution reviewed above justifies rejecting the psychodynamic explanation of symptom formation and treatments based upon this rationale, there is value to achieving insight when it is understood as psychological mindedness.

Psychological Mindedness Defined

Gough (1957/1975) identified psychological mindedness as being 'interested in, and responsive to, the inner needs, motives, and experiences of others' (p. 11). This entails their thoughts, feelings, and behaviors. Appelbaum (1973) noted that psychoanalysts used the term psychological mindedness in various ways. He sought to establish general agreement with the following definition: 'A person's ability to see relationships among thoughts, feelings, and actions, with the goal of learning the meanings and causes of his experiences and behaviour' (p. 36). Wolitzky and Reuben (1974) defined psychological mindedness '... as a tendency to understand or explain behavior in psychological terms, that is, to view behavior as expressing and communicating information about the needs, wishes, purposes, intentions, conflicts, defensive strategies, etc., of the person in question, oneself or another' (p. 26). Silver (1983) defined psychological mindedness as 'The patient's desire to learn the possible meanings and causes of his internal and external experiences as well as the patient's ability to look inwards to psychical factors rather than only outwards to environmental factors. ... [and] to potentially conceptualize the relationship between thoughts, feelings, and actions' (p. 516). Farber (1985) offered the following definition: 'Essentially, psychological-mindedness may be considered a trait or state that has at its core the disposition to reflect upon the meaning and motivation of behavior, thoughts, and feelings in oneself and others' (p. 170). Farber (1989) subsequently provided a slightly different definition of psychological mindedness as '... the disposition and ability to reflect on the meaning and motivation of behavior, thoughts, and feelings in oneself and others' (p. 210). McCallum and Piper (1990) defined psychological mindedness 'as the ability to identify dynamic (intrapsychic) components and to relate them to a person's difficulties' (p. 412), but they implied seeing relationships among thoughts, feelings, and behaviors. McCallum and Piper (1996) subsequently recognized that the term psychological mindedness has been used by psychologists of other theoretical orientations in a more general way that included '... insight, introspection, intraception, self-awareness, self-reflection, capacity for self-observation, private self-consciousness, and self-focused attention' (p. 48).

Hall (1992) defined psychological mindedness as an interest in and ability to be reflective of thoughts and feelings. Trudeau and Reich (1995) defined psychological mindedness as '... the awareness of one's and others' thoughts, feelings, and motives' (p. 699). Conte et al. (1996) defined psychological mindedness as 'an attribute of an individual that presupposes a degree of access to one's feelings, a willingness to try to understand oneself and others, a belief in the benefit of discussing one's problems, and interest in the meaning and motivation of one's own and others' thoughts, feelings, and behavior, and a capacity for change' (p. 258). Hatcher and Hatcher (1997) defined psychological mindedness very generally: 'Psychological mindedness is the capacity to achieve psychological understanding of oneself and others' (p. 66). Beitel et al. (2005a) noted that 'Psychological mindedness (PM), in its broadest sense, involves awareness and understanding of psychological processes, such as thoughts, feelings, and behaviors' (p. 740). Beitel et al. (2005b) reviewed a variety of definitions of psychological mindedness and summarized them using a three-dimensional table consisting of eight cells: 2 (Domain: Cognition, Affect) × 2 (Mode: Interest, Ability), × 2 (Stage: Awareness, Understanding). The Domain dimension refers to whether one is psychologically minded about thoughts or feelings. The Mode dimension refers to having an interest in versus and ability to be psychologically minded. The Stage dimension contrasts awareness of thoughts and feelings with an understanding of what drives cognition and affect. These authors concur that psychological mindedness entails understanding one's own thoughts, feelings, and behaviors as well as those of others. Grant (2001) suggested that 'Psychological mindedness is a form of metacognition: a predisposition to engage in acts of affective and intellectual inquiry into how and why oneself and/or others behave, think and feel in the way that they do' (p. 12).

Conte and Ratto (1997) expanded the definition of psychological mindedness to include self-observation and insight. Smith et al. (2009) also characterized psychological mindedness as involving 'insight, introspection, self-awareness, self-reflection and the capacity for self-observation' (p. 186). Nyklíček and Denollet (2009) commented that in addition to reflecting an attitude (interest in psychology), psychological mindedness also concerns the ability to achieve insight. McCallum and Piper (1990) also connected insight with psychological mindedness. Grant (2001) noted that self-observation and reflection enhance psychological mindedness which can lead to insight. Farber (1985) reported what he considered to be a general view among psychotherapists that psychological mindedness increases insight.

The link between psychological mindedness and psychoanalytic insight is made especially clear by the **Insight Scale** published in the appendix to a report by Johansson et al. (2010) concerning '**The mediating role of insight for long-term improvements in psychodynamic therapy**'. The positive features of their insight scale share many of the characteristics of psychological mindedness. In their view, treatments that promote psychological mindedness promote insight. Shill and Lumley (2002) similarly discussed psychological mindedness as a desirable therapeutic outcome. In sum, psychologically minded people can understand and discuss relationships among thoughts, feelings, and actions regarding themselves and others. They are said to have insight. What therapist does not want to help their clients better understand relationships between their own thoughts, feelings, and behaviors regarding themselves and other people? Insight is surely a common goal for all psychotherapies.

I provided so many definitions of psychological mindedness for two reasons. First, I wanted to ensure that readers understood that I was using a definition of psychological mindedness that is widely accepted. Otherwise, critics might have claimed that I was using a non-standard definition of psychological mindedness. Second, I wanted to clearly establish that psychological mindedness constitutes insight. This connection is important in that it clarifies what insight currently means.

Alexithymia

Sifneos (1967, 1973) described alexithymia as a personality disorder characterized by: (a) difficulty identifying and describing feelings, i.e., **feelings without words**; (b) a cognitive style characterized by concrete thinking; and (c) a reduced capacity to use images causing impoverished mental imagery.[16] Having feelings that one cannot describe in words is the antithesis of insight. No one can be said to have insight when they cannot describe how they feel. Taylor et al. (1989) explicitly contrasted psychological mindedness and alexithymia. They noted that '… the absence of psychological-mindedness is now usually subsumed under the broader construct of 'alexithymia', which evolved from observations of the cognitive/affective style of patients who were **unresponsive to insight psychotherapy**' (p. 732; bold emphasis added). Equating the absence of psychological mindedness with alexithymia defines psychological mindedness as insight. These authors created the **Toronto Alexithymia Scale** and used it to assess deficits in psychological mindedness and thereby identify who should not

[16] http://en.wikipedia.org/wiki/Alexithymia

participate in psychodynamic group therapy. It was important to exclude patients who are high in alexithymia from psychodynamic group therapy for two reasons. First, their disability restricts their participation in the group process. Second, their disability greatly reduces the likelihood that their insight will increase as a result of group therapy.

Bagby et al. (1994a,b) administered the Psychological Mindedness Scale (Conte et al. 1990) and the Toronto Alexithymia Scale (TAS-20; Bagby et al., 1994a,b) to 85 (28 male, 55 female) Canadian college students. They reported a statistically significant and substantial negative correlation between alexithymia and psychological mindedness ($r(83) = -0.68$, $p < 0.001$). Taylor and Taylor (1997) provided a review of the origin, development, and measurement of alexithymia. This body of evidence supports the conclusion that psychological mindedness and alexithymia form a theoretical bipolar construct symbolized here as PM/A.

Psychological Mindedness and Alexithymia (PM/A)

But are psychological mindedness and alexithymia different enough that they can be considered to be opposite poles of a single dimension; a bipolar construct? The observed negative correlation of ($r(83) = -0.68$, $p < 0.001$) is strong, but is it strong enough to justify claiming that psychological mindedness and alexithymia form a single bipolar construct? The short answer is yes it is. One reason for this conclusion is that this observed correlation is between imperfect measures of psychological mindedness and alexithymia. Measures are never 100% reliable, nor are they 100% valid. Therefore, one cannot expect a perfect negative correlation between measures of psychological mindedness and alexithymia. Equation (9.1) below is the standard psychometric way to correct for measurement unreliability. The reliability of psychological mindedness is estimated at 0.86 by coefficient alpha (Conte et al. 1990), and the reliability of the TAS is estimated at 0.81 by coefficient alpha and 0.77 by 3-week test–retest (Bagby et al., 1994a). Dividing –0.68 by the square root of 0.86×0.81 equals –0.81. Dividing –0.68 by the square root of 0.86×0.77 equals –0.83. Hence, after correcting for measurement unreliability we find that the relationship between psychological mindedness and alexithymia is on the order of –0.81 to –0.83. Tests are not perfectly valid either. If we had the data to correct the observed correlation for the lack of validity, remove their construct irrelevant variance, we might expect a similar increase of approximately 0.13 which would bring our correlations to approximately –0.94 to –0.96, which are sufficient to support the conclusion that PM/A constitutes a bipolar construct.

$$\hat{r}_{xy} = \frac{r_{xy}}{\sqrt{r_{xx} r_{yy}}} \tag{9.1}$$

The second issue concerns the differential conceptual scope of each pole of this construct. For example, Grant (2001) noted that alexithymia can be considered to be a narrower construct than psychological mindedness because it primarily focuses on emotion, whereas psychological mindedness considers thoughts, feelings, and actions. This concern is not compelling because alexithymia also concerns one's ability to connect their behavior to their feelings and thoughts. On balance, both poles of this construct seem to have a comparable conceptual breadth. This removes the final obstacle to accepting that psychological mindedness and alexithymia represent opposite poles of a single bipolar construct.

Psychological Mindedness as a Common Therapeutic Goal

It is widely recognized that all psychotherapies share common relationship factors (Norcross, 2011). This common ground reasonably extends to psychological mindedness as a common outcome goal for all clients. All therapists of every persuasion want their clients to better understand how their thoughts and feelings interact to create their behaviors, and how their thoughts, feelings, and behaviors influence their relationships with other people; especially their close relationships with significant others. Echoing Bordin (1979) who wrote: 'The terms of the therapeutic working alliance have their origin in psychoanalytic theory, but can be stated in forms generalizable to all psychotherapies' (p. 259), we can now confidently conclude that the terms of psychological mindedness can now also be stated in a form generalizable to all psychotherapies. While therapeutic approaches may differentially emphasize common factors (see Shedler, 2010), there can be no ownership of them (Tryon & Tryon, 2011). Hence, psychological mindedness is the province of all psychologists even though it has a psychodynamic origin.

Alexithymia as a Common Deficit

Accepting that psychological mindedness and alexithymia are opposite poles of a single bipolar construct and accepting psychological mindedness as a common goal of psychotherapy casts alexithymia as a common deficit. Alexithymia is here considered a deficit of psychological mindedness that all therapeutic modalities should seek to improve by their interventions. The following subsections present evidence that alexithymia is a common deficit that characterizes a variety of afflictions including personality disorders, eating disorders, non-suicidal self-injury (NSSI), major depressive disorder, generalized anxiety disorder, social anxiety disorder, and general adjustment.

Eating Disorders

It is well known that people with eating disorders tend to be high in alexithymia. For example, Laquatra and Clopton (1994) administered the TAS (Taylor et al., 1986) and the Eating Disorder Inventory (EDI; Garner & Olmstead, 1984) to 308 undergraduate women. They reported statistically significant correlations between each of the three TAS scores (Total, Inability to Identify Feelings, Inability to Communicate Feelings) and several EDI subscales. Other studies that support the relationship between alexithymia and eating disorders include: Bydlowski et al. (2005); Clyne and Blampied (2004); Cochrane et al., (1993); de Groot et al., (1995); De Berardis et al., (1995); Fairburn et al., (1995); Fassino et al., (2007); Pinaquy et al., (2003); McCarthy (1990); Polivy and Herman (2002); Schmidt et al., (1993); Taylor et al., (1996); van Strien and Ouwens (2007); and Zonnevylle-Bender et al., (2002, 2004).

Research has also shown that people with eating disorders are low on interoceptive awareness, defined as confusion and apprehension in recognizing emotional states (Garner, 1991). Greenberg (1999) reported that interoceptive awareness, as measured by the Eating Disorder Inventory 2 (EDI-2; Garner, 1991), is significantly impaired in persons with anorexia nervosa and bulimia compared to controls. There is considerable overlap between the constructs of interoceptive awareness and alexithymia (Bourke et al., 1985; Taylor et al., 1986). Persons high on alexithymia are low on interoceptive awareness (Bourke et al., 1985; Taylor et al., 1986). They have difficulty identifying and expressing emotion, show decreased daydreaming, and exhibit externally oriented thinking (Troop et al., 1995). Greenberg (1999) reported a strong correlation of $r(52) = 0.73, p < 0.001$ between the EDI-2 Interoceptive Awareness subscale scores and TAS-20 (Bagby et al., 1994a) total scores.

Personality Disorders

Borderline personality disorder (BPD) is characterized by affect dysregulation (Gratz et al., 2006; Jacob et al., 2011; Linehan, 1993). Marshall-Berenz et al. (2011) also reported emotional dysregulation as a core psychological process underlying BPD. Beblo et al. (2010) administered the Emotion

Regulation Scale (Gross & John, 2003) to 19 women diagnosed with BPD and 20 healthy controls. Persons with BPD reported significantly and substantially greater difficulty with emotional regulation than controls ($t(37) = 7.5$, $p < 0.001$). Rosenthal et al. (2008) conducted an extensive review of the clinical and empirical literature that documented emotional dysregulation as a core component of BPD.

Affect dysregulation also characterizes histrionic and narcissistic personality disorders, and therefore alexithymia is expected to be related to them as well. Having few if any words to describe emotions, alexithymia, makes affect regulation difficult if not impossible. In sum, people with various personality disorders are relatively high in alexithymia which is to say low in psychological mindedness, which makes increasing psychological mindedness a psychotherapeutic goal for all of them.

Autism

People who are on the autism spectrum are thought to have difficulty recognizing emotion from facial expressions. This disability has long been attributed to autism. Two ground breaking experiments by Cook et al. (2013) show that this problem is actually due to co-occurring alexithymia.

Non-Suicidal Self-Injury[17]

Favazza (1998) defined non-suicidal self-injury (NSSI) as '... the deliberate, direct destruction or alteration of body issue without conscious suicidal intent' (p. 260). People who engage in NSSI also seem to be alexithymic. Gross (1999) reviewed the origins of the concept of emotional regulation. Emotional dysregulation, especially the inability to control negative emotions, appears to be involved in the etiology of NSSI (Gratz & Roemer, 2008). Not having words to describe emotions, alexithymia, contributes to the emotional dysregulation that also characterizes this disorder. Polk and Liss (2007) reported that alexithymia helped discriminate individuals who injure themselves from those who do not. Evren and Evren (2005) reported that patients with a history of NSSI had significantly greater TAS-20 (Bagby et al., 1994a) scores ($t(134) = -2.07$, $p < 0.04$) than did patients without a history of NSSI. Paivio and McCulloch (2004) reviewed literature and presented new empirical evidence that childhood trauma leads to alexithymia, deficits in emotional regulation, and self-injury. Zlotnick et al. (1996) reported that the frequency of self-injury was positively and significantly

[17] Heather Schatten provided many of the references for this section. She was a doctoral student at Fordham University and worked with Dr. Peggy Andover when this chapter was written.

correlated with alexithymia (Taylor, 1984; $r(146) = 0.33, p < 0.001$), scores on the Dissociative Experiences Scale (Bernstein & Putnam, 1986; $r(146) = 0.39, p < 0.001$), and reported incidence of sexual abuse ($r(146) = 0.31, p < 0.001$). Gratz (2006) reported positive and significant correlations between self-harm (never vs. frequent) and maltreatment ($r(198) = 0.37, p < 0.01$), sexual abuse ($r(198) = 0.19, p < 0.01$), physical abuse ($r(198) = 0.26, p < 0.01$), emotional neglect ($r(198) = 0.27, p < 0.01$), and overprotection ($r(198) = 0.22, p < 0.01$).

Generalized Anxiety Disorder (GAD), Major Depressive Disorder (MDD), and Social Anxiety Disorder (SAD)

Mennin et al. (2007) reported two studies designed to elucidate the role of emotional dysregulation in GAD, MDD, and SAD; three highly comorbid anxiety and mood disorders. Their results indicated that poor understanding of emotions is related to the latent construct of emotional dysregulation. In Study 1, Mennin et al. (2005) reported significant differences in TAS scores regarding difficulty identifying and describing emotions in 538 undergraduates. In Study 2 they replicated these findings on 42 patients diagnosed with GAD at the Temple University Adult Anxiety Clinic. Turk et al. (2005) reported that 68 undergraduates diagnosed with GAD (60 women), and 105 undergraduates diagnosed with SAD (66 women) had more difficulty identifying and describing emotions than did 550 (369 women) undergraduate controls. Honkalampi et al. (2000) reported that alexithymia, as measured by the TAS-20, is strongly related to depression, as measured by the Beck Depression Inventory, in a Finnish sample of 2,083 people. Specifically, they reported that the prevalence of alexithymia among persons with BDI scores greater than 9 was 32.1% compared to just 4.3% in non-depressed controls ($p < 0.001$).

General Adjustment

Denollet and Nyklíček (2004) reported that psychological mindedness is important to behavioral medicine because it promotes general health and protects against psychopathology. Beitel et al. (2005a) reported a predicted substantial statistically significant correlation between scores on the Psychological Mindedness Scale (Conte et al., 1996) and scores on the Mindfulness Attention Awareness Scale (MAAS; Brown & Ryan, 2003) ($r(101) = 0.41, p < 0.0001$). Brown and Ryan (2003) noted that mindfulness '... is most commonly defined as the state of being attentive to and aware of what is taking place in the present' (p. 822), and argued that such open awareness facilitates self-determined choices as articulated by self-determination theory (Deci & Ryan, 1980, 1985; Ryan & Deci, 2000). Brown and Ryan (2003) reported substantial statistically significant predicted negative correlations between mindfulness scores and Beck Depression Inventory (Beckham & Leber, 1985) scores ($r(330) = -0.40, p < 0.0001$), Profile of Mood States (McNair et al., 1971) anxiety scores ($r(330) = -0.34, p < 0.0001$), and PANS negative affect scores ($r(330) = -0.41, p < 0.0001$). They also reported predicted positive correlations with Positive and Negative Affect Schedule (PANS; Watson et al., 1988) positive affect scores ($r(330) = 0.36, p < 0.0001$), and Rosenberg Self-Esteem (Rosenberg, 1965) scores ($r(330) = 0.44, p < 0.0001$). Trudeau and Reich (1995) reported that psychological well-being was positively and significantly correlated with mental well-being ($r(87) = 0.31, p < 0.01$).

Cecero et al. (2008) administered the Psychological Mindedness Scale (Conte et al., 1996) and the Young Schema Questionnaire-Short Form (Young, 1998) to 264 college students. They reported predicted significant negative correlations between psychological mindedness and mistrust/abuse ($r(262) = -0.27, p < 0.01$), defectiveness/shame ($r(262) = -0.36, p < 0.01$), social isolation ($r(262) = -0.24, p < 0.01$), emotional deprivation ($r(262) = -0.29, p < 0.01$), and Early Maladaptive Schemas (EMS) total scores ($r(262) = -0.32, p < 0.01$). These negative correlations show that alexithymia is associated with psychological disorder, suggesting the possibility that the conditions that produce EMS pathology also give rise to alexithymia. Or these findings show that EMS pathology gives rise to alexithymia, or that some third factor(s) gives rise to EMS pathology and alexithymia. One implication of these results is that treating alexithymia might reduce EMS pathology. Another implication is that treating EMS pathology might decrease alexithymia; i.e., increase psychological mindedness. Both of these clinical hypotheses deserve to be systematically studied.

Identifying and Tracking PM/A

It is important to know at intake where a client stands on the PM/A dimension in order to select the right combination of cognitive and behavioral interventions and to be able to track change along this dimension given the therapeutic goal of repairing the common deficit of alexithymia by enhancing psychological mindedness. Psychological mindedness can be directly assessed using the Psychological Mindedness Scale (PMS; Conte et al., 1990, 1996). It can also be indirectly assessed using the Toronto Alexithymia Scale (TAS-20; Bagby et al., 1994a). Each instrument is scored to assess one of two opposite poles of the PM/A continuum. While therapists typically assess deficits, they generally have positive therapeutic goals, which in this case consist of increasing psychological mindedness. This recommends administering and tracking changes in both scales. One way to combine the two scales is to: (a) compute a z-score for PMS; (b) compute a z-score for the reverse-scored TAS-20; and (c) average the two z-scores to determine a final position on the PM/A dimension.

Choosing the Best Cognitive/Behavioral Mix

Cognitive-behavioral therapies (CBT) include both cognitive and behavioral interventions by definition. But what is the correct mix for each patient? The wide variety of individual differences encountered by clinicians clearly indicates that one manualized approach is not optimal for all patients. But how can one determine the proper mix of cognitive and behavioral methods to use at the beginning, middle, and towards the end of therapy? No theoretical rationale or empirical evidence on this matter could be located. I now suggest the following approach. The more a client is located towards the alexithymia pole the more difficult it will likely be to cognitively modify the way they understand and relate to people. Such clients will probably benefit most from behavioral treatments. The more a client is located towards the PM pole, the more likely they will accept cognitive restructuring. Such clients will probably benefit from cognitive interventions.

Cognitive restructuring is a central theme for all cognitive-behavioral therapies. A primary objective of CBT is to discover and modify automatic thoughts that compromise emotional regulation and lead to maladaptive behaviors. For example, Linehan (1993) modified dialectical behavior therapy (DBT) to treat the maladaptive thoughts that compromise emotion dysregulation. Grabe et al. (2004) concluded that psychopathology is commonly characterized by 'difficulties in cognitively processing emotional perceptions' (p. 1299). Alexithymia entails difficulty in cognitively processing emotions. They noted that overcoming these deficits is a common goal of most psychotherapy. Grant (2001) remarked that psychological mindedness is entailed in directed behavioral change in both clinical and non-clinical domains. He argued that self-regulation depends in part on understanding the relationships among one's own thoughts, feelings, and behaviors as well as those of others; i.e., self-regulation depends upon psychological mindedness. Bateman and Fonagy (2004) defined cognitive therapies as mentalizing, by which they meant 'making sense of the actions of oneself and others on the basis of intentional mental states, such as desires, feelings, and beliefs'. (p. 36). Björgvinsson and Hart (2006) described how cognitive-behavioral therapy promotes mentalizing. Lewis (2006) argued that DBT particularly enhances mentalizing.

Recognition that alexithymia is a common deficit that characterizes personality disorders, eating disorders, non-suicidal self-injury (NSSI), major depressive disorder, generalized anxiety disorder, and social anxiety disorders warrants increasing its theoretical opposite, psychological mindedness, as an important therapeutic goal for patients who quality for these diagnoses and likely for other patients as well. DBT has such a therapeutic goal. Spek et al. (2008) have shown that alexithymia decreased as depression remitted in response to cognitive-behavior therapy in 201 participants (mean age = 54 years, SD = 4.4 years) diagnosed with subthreshold depression.

Relationship of PM/A to Asperger's Syndrome

Research has shown that persons with Asperger's syndrome (AS) have social skills difficulties that arise from a broader deficit in social cognition, independent of intellectual functioning (Baron-Cohen et al., 1985; Frith, 1989; Leslie & Frith, 1988). One aspect of social cognition that has been shown to be impaired in AS is 'theory of mind', which describes the ability to make inferences about the thoughts, feelings, and intentions of others, and then use this information to explain and predict behavior (Baron-Cohen, 1989). In addition to these deficits in interpersonal functioning, individuals with AS have shown decreased awareness of internal bodily feelings (Njiokiktjien et al., 2001). These deficits are strikingly similar to alexithymia. I therefore reasoned that persons with AS might also have alexithymia.

Then I discovered Tani et al. (2004) who administered the TAS-20 to 20 individuals diagnosed with AS, (30% female) and 10 healthy controls (30% female), and found significantly ($t(28) = 4.79$, $p < 0.0001$) higher TAS-20 scores for participants with AS ($M = 54.2$, $S = 12.4$) than for controls ($M = 34.5$, $S = 5.1$). This t-value corresponds to $r(28) = 0.67$. Schatten and Tryon (2014) replicated this finding. Hill et al. (2004) administered the 20-item Toronto Alexithymia Scale (TAS-20; Bagby et al., 1994a) to high-functioning participants with AS. They reported that these participants scored significantly higher on the TAS than did a normal adult control group. These results are important to clinical psychology, because they substantively extend the range of the range of disorders that share alexithymia as a common deficit.

Conclusions

The term 'psychological mindedness' was coined to describe good candidates for psychodynamic insight-oriented psychotherapy, because they had an interest in and some ability to examine and understand relationships among thoughts, feelings, and behaviors. Cognitive-behavioral therapies also help people understand relationships among their thoughts, feelings, and actions and those of others. This is especially true of interventions designed to facilitate emotional regulation such as DBT. The value of treating PM/A as a bipolar construct is that it links deficits (alexithymia) found in personality disorders, eating disorders, non-suicidal self-injury (NSSI), major depressive disorder, generalized anxiety disorder, social anxiety disorder, and general adjustment with a common therapeutic goal of increasing psychological mindedness and insight; a goal shared by virtually all psychotherapies. Understanding the connection between alexithymia and psychological mindedness is especially important for therapists who use dialectical behavior therapy (Linehan, 1993; Lynch et al., 2007) and/or other emotion regulation interventions (Aldao et al., 2010; Mennin, & Farach, 2007; Mennin & Fresco, 2009; Mennin et al., 2007) to treat patients with dysregulated emotions.

MIRROR NEURON SYSTEM

Two neural networks are known to mediate our ability to understand people. These neural networks may also mediate how we understand ourselves. I refer to the mirror and Gandhi neural systems. Mirror neurons are motor neurons that become active when a person makes a movement, such as picking up a peanut. Remarkably, the motor neurons in the premotor cortex are activated in every observer of this event. This provides direct brain-to-brain communication between the person who performs an action and all people who observe that action. We experience the activities of our mirror neuron system as **empathy** and **imitation**.[18] A 15-minute video discussing the discovery and nature of mirror neurons can be found at the following link http://cultureofempathy.com/References/Mirror-Neurons.htm.

When a child observes their parent tying their shoelaces, the motor neurons that fire in the parent's brain cause the premotor neurons in the child's brain to fire. This is a, and possibly the, mechanism by which motor skills are taught by imitation. Only by the adult actually moving the child's fingers could communication be more direct.

[18] http://en.wikipedia.org/wiki/Mirror_neuron

Mirror neurons explain why fans love to watch sports. Watching the quarterback pass the ball activates the mirror neurons in the fan; i.e., causes the same motor plan to be executed in the fan's premotor cortex as was activated in the quarterback's premotor cortex. Here we have a direct brain-to-brain connection between the quarterback and all of fans at the stadium and around the world who watch on TV. Having your premotor cortex activated in the same way as it is activated in major athletes explains why sports are so popular.

Mirror neurons also mediate feelings, as in 'I feel your pain'. Mirror neurons also reflect intentions, such as when you intend to drink from a cup versus just picking it up. These properties make the mirror neuron system crucially important to clinical psychology. I can't imagine that anyone can be an effective therapist without a healthy mirror neuron system.

Mirror neurons were initially discovered in the ventral premotor cortex and the anterior parietal regions of monkey brains (Di Pellegrino et al., 1992; Gallese et al., 1996; Rizzolatti et al., 1996), but have also been found in the pars opercularis of the inferior frontal gyrus, within Broca's area, and in the rostral posterior parietal cortex of the human brain (Iacoboni et al., 1999). Research has repeatedly documented mirror neuron system dysfunction in children with autism spectrum disorders including Asperger's syndrome (Dapretto et al., 2006; Hadjikhani et al., 2005; Martineau et al., 2008; Nishitani et al., 2004; Oberman et al., 2005; Theoret et al., 2005; Williams et al., 2006; Woods et al., 1999). I also expect that people high in alexithymia have compromised mirror neuron systems.

Nature appears to conserve neural networks. For example, the neural networks used for image generation (Farah, 2000), better known as imagination, largely overlap the neural networks used for vision (Kosslyn & Thompson, 2000). Vision is mainly a bottom-up process, whereas image generation is largely a top-down process. If the mirror neuron system is what mediates our ability to process and understand the thoughts and feelings of other people, then it follows that the same network mediates our ability to understand our own thoughts and feelings. Hence, mirror neurons may mediate the social cognitive deficits found in PM/A, as well as the social cognitive deficits found in Asperger's syndrome. Future brain imaging research is needed to test this novel neuroscience hypothesis regarding PM/A.

GANDHI NEURON SYSTEM

The Gandhi neuron system (GNS) is a subset of the mirror neuron system that also seems to be involved in our understanding of other people.[19]

[19] http://mettacenter.org/blog/gandhi-neurons-a-scientific-basis-for-interconnectivity/

Consider the following experiments. Ramachandran et al. (1995) used a vertical mirror to explore the effects of visually restoring a phantom arm limb in nine patients. The mirror was adjusted so that a reflection of the present hand appeared where the phantom hand should be. Movement by the patient of their present hand was experienced as movement in their phantom hand in seven of the nine patients. These sensations were not experienced when the patients closed their eyes, thereby establishing the crucial role of vision. The experimenter replaced the patient's present hand with their own hand. Movements made by the experimenter with their hand were also experienced in the phantom hand of six of nine patients, thereby further reinforcing the crucial role of vision. No such results were found with four control subjects. Five of nine patients suffered from painful hand-clenching spasms in the phantom limb. Instructions to open both hands immediately relieved this spasm in four of the five patients, but only in the eyes-open condition; no relief occurred in the eyes-closed condition. In sum, this study established a previously unknown role of vision in phantom limb phenomenon.

Ramachandran and Ramachandran (2008) clarified the role of vision with their report of the existence of a subset of mirror neurons that relate to touch. They wrote:

> fMR studies in humans have established that mirror neurons also exist for touch. If I touch a subject (A) his sensory touch neurons will obviously fire but remarkably a subset of these neurons will also fire when A watches ANOTHER subject B being touched in a corresponding location (p. 1233, emphasis in the original).

Based on results of control subjects in the previously reviewed study, these authors hypothesized the existence of inhibitory neurons that preserve our individual identity by inhibiting these touch mirror neurons in order that we can distinguish ourselves from others. The source of this inhibitory stimulation is hypothesized to be the touch site which is absent in the case where a phantom limb appears to be touched. These authors used the above-described mirror method to investigate what happens in situations where this inhibitory signal is not present. They hypothesized that the absence of such an inhibitory signal would allow direct mirror-neuron-mediated sensations of touch. Their participants were two phantom limb patients. The arm of a volunteer was placed in the above-described mirror apparatus so that it appeared where the patient's phantom arm would be. The experimenter touched and stroked the volunteer's arm. Both patients experienced the sensation of their phantom arm being touched and stroked, despite the lack of any physical contact with their body. Both patients reported that this illusion took a few seconds to activate.

Ramachandran and Ramachandran (2008) conducted a second experiment where a volunteer placed their arm with no hand 12–18 inches from the arms of each of the amputee patients. The experimenter then touched and rubbed the volunteer's arm. Both amputee patients reported similar feelings in their phantom limbs. This simulation was repeated eight times with each of the two amputee patients.

V. S. Ramachandran reported about half way through the following video segment taken from a lecture he gave at IBM[20] that anesthetizing the arm of a normal individual, and thereby preventing the hypothesized inhibitory signal preserving identity, enabled that person to feel the touch sensation associated with viewing another person being touched. More specifically, watching a person's hand get touched or rubbed caused the observer to feel touched or rubbed in the corresponding place on their anesthetized arm.

It has long been known that persons with autism or Asperger's syndrome have issues with touch; i.e., they exhibit touch sensitivity.[21] Most autistic persons do not like being touched at all.[22] Or, if they tolerate being touched, they require being touched in specific ways, such as either very lightly or firmly as in a tight hug. We also know that their mirror neuron system does not function normally. Some connection seems inevitable here, but its nature remains unclear at this time. The facts that people with AS also have touch issues and that they have mirror neuron deficits, and that Gandhi neurons are a subset of mirror neurons strongly suggests that people with AS also have Gandhi neuron deficits. All of these findings are completely compatible with the proposed Bio↔Psychology Network Theory.

MENTALIZING NEURON SYSTEM

The mirror neuron system appears to be one part of a three-part neural network system that mediates judgments of intentionality regarding one's self and others. A meta-analytic review of approximately 220 fMRI studies by Van Overwalle and Baetens (2009) confirmed the identity of the mirror neuron system consisting of the anterior intraparietal sulcus (aIPS), the premotor cortex (PMC), and the posterior superior temporal sulcus (pSTS). The mirror system is activated by observing body parts. For example, observing hand motion activates the anterior part of the intraparietal sulcus (aIPS), as well as

[20] http://www.youtube.com/watch?v=t0pwKzTRG5E

[21] http://asperger-syndrome-autism.blogspot.com/2005/10/is-your-child-touch-sensitive.html

[22] http://vickie-ewell.suite101.com/touch-sensitive-autistic-children-and-sensory-defensive-disorder-a337705

the premotor cortex (PMC). Observing hand, finger, feet, legs, and/or face movement activates the same areas as do self-generated movements; namely the anterior intraparietal sulcus (aIPS) and the premotor cortex (PMC). Observing whole-body movements activates the posterior part of the superior temporal sulcus (pSTS). Eye movement selectively activates the posterior part of the superior temporal sulcus (pSTS). Observing motor imitation activates the intraparietal sulcus (aIPS) and the premotor cortex (PMC).

Van Overwalle and Baetens (2009) also identified a mentalizing system consisting of the precuneus (PC), the temporoparietal junction (TPJ), and the medial prefrontal cortex (mPFC). The mentalizing system is activated when people attempt to infer intentionality in the absence of physical movements, such as when moral issues are discussed or geometric images are used to portray conflict such as when a large triangle appears to bully a small circle. Theory-of-Mind tasks typically activate the medial prefrontal cortex (mPFC) and the precuneus (PC). Judging the morality of norm-violating actions typically activates the TPJ, the medial prefrontal cortex (mPFC), and the precuneus (PC).

Denny et al. (2012) conducted a meta-analysis of 107 published neuroimaging studies to determine which brain regions are activated when people make judgments about others versus when they make judgments about themselves. These authors reported considerable overlap in activated neural networks including the ventromedial prefrontal cortex (vmPFC), the dorsal medial prefrontal cortex (dmPFC), the left temporoparietal junction (TPJ), and the posterior cingulate. These data support a distributed rather than localist account regarding judgments made about one's self and others.

Chiavarino et al. (2012) included the mirroring system but expanded the mentalizing system into a representational component and a conceptual component. They claimed that the mirroring system provided a behavior understanding, and that the representational and conceptual components of the mentalizing system interacted to enable us to understand intentions. They confirmed that the mirror system is activated by observing body movements, and that the temporoparietal junction (TPJ) is crucial to the representational component of the mentalizing system.

The frontal-insular cortex (FI), but especially the anterior cingulated cortex (ACC), mediate hunger, thirst, and pain, but more importantly for present purposes mediate our gut feelings for the pain and distress of others. These neural networks consist of spindle neurons,[23] also known as von

[23] http://en.wikipedia.org/wiki/Spindle_neuron

Economo neurons after Constantin von Economo (1876–1931) who described them in 1929. Wikipedia reports deficits in these neurons for persons with autism that may partially explain their blunted response to distress in other people.

FRONTOTEMPORAL DEMENTIA

Frontotemporal dementia (FTD)[24], also known as Pick's disease, results from a deterioration of the frontal and temporal lobes of the brain, including the anterior cingulated cortex, the frontal insula, the orbitofrontal cortex, and the temporal pole.[25] The psychological result is a lack of self-awareness and awareness of the feelings of emotions, along with emotional coldness, apathy, poor judgment, and a loss of inhibitions. Such people lose interest in how they are dressed and disregard social norms. They may also lose their ability to control their finances. This is the most common form of dementia in people under 60.

The point of this section is that mirror neurons are not the only neural networks that are involved in mediating social sensitivity. The above-mentioned neural networks also seem to play an important role.

OXYTOCIN

Oxytocin[26] mediates bonding between mother and offspring (Ross & Young, 2009). It also increases trust in humans (Kosfeld et al., 2005). Bartz et al. (2010) reported that oxytocin selectively improved empathetic accuracy in 27 healthy men. They used the autism spectrum quotient (AQ) self-report inventory developed by Baron-Cohen et al. (2001) to quantify social competence. Empathetic accuracy was measured by having the participants repeatedly rate how positive or negative they thought that the target person in five videos was on a 9-point scale. When participants were on placebo, empathetic accuracy systematically decreased as AQ scores increased. When participants were on oxytocin, empathetic accuracy remained constant as AQ scores increased. The net result was improvement in empathetic accuracy in direct proportion to AQ scores between 10 and 25, and a decrease in empathetic accuracy in direct proportion to AQ scores between 5 and 10.

24 http://en.wikipedia.org/wiki/Frontotemporal_dementia

25 http://en.wikipedia.org/wiki/Poles_of_cerebral_hemispheres

26 http://en.wikipedia.org/wiki/Oxytocin

CONCLUSIONS

This chapter discussed several clinical implications of proposed Principle 1 regarding unconscious processing. The prospect of unconscious processing was widely discussed long before Freud discovered it, which means that endorsing unconscious processing does not mean accepting all aspects of psychodynamic theory. Reasons for objecting to Freud's role for unconscious sexual fantasy were presented. The lack of evidence regarding symptom substitution falsifies the psychodynamic explanation of psychopathology and symptom formation. It also undercuts the primary rationale for psychodynamic therapy. However, insight formulated as psychological mindedness is a worthy treatment goal for psychotherapists of all persuasions.

The role of the mirror and Gandhi nervous systems was emphasized as the neurological basis of imitation and empathy. The roles of other neural networks that mediate frontotemporal dementia were also emphasized, as was the role of oxytocin.

The bottom line here is that there are several reasons why all psychotherapists should formally recognize the importance of unconscious processing. There are no longer good or sufficient reasons to ignore unconscious processing and to promote separate schools of therapy on that basis.

CHAPTER 10

Clinical Applications of Principle 2: Learning and Memory

Contents

Cognitive Neuroscience and Psychotherapy
http://dx.doi.org/10.1016/B978-0-12-420071-5.00010-7

This chapter discusses the clinical applications of Network Principle 2: Learning and Memory. I begin with an example of how thinking about psychological problems in physical rather than mental terms changes clinical practice. Next I distinguish emission from omission therapies. Then I distinguish learning from conditioning. This distinction enabled me to consider conditioning as cognition. Then I review an effort to create a psychological behaviorism that incorporates cognition among other psychological processes. I emphasize the need to think in physical rather than mental terms. I show that conditioning activates experience-dependent plasticity mechanisms that enable learning and memory modification. The main portion of this chapter reviews conditioning principles as empirically supported CBT principles. This is followed by a system of behavioral diagnosis that carries both causal and prescriptive information. Finally, I briefly discuss biofeedback and then consider implications for clinical practice, and end with a discussion of several theoretical issues.

THINK PHYSICAL NOT MENTAL

Jeffrey Schwartz is an excellent example of how the proposed Bio↔Psychology Network Theory translates into clinical practice. Volk (2013) provided an overview of the pioneering work of Jeffrey Schwartz and his physical approach to treating obsessive compulsive disorder (OCD). Schwartz initially conceptualized OCD in mental terms until he discovered with the aid of colleagues that the orbitofrontal cortex (OFC)[1] and caudate nucleus (CN)[2] were hyperactive in patients with OCD compared to controls. The OFC mediates decision-making and specializes in error detection. Hence, these structures become active when people doubt their decisions, such as occurs in the checking rituals common to OCD. Dr. Schwartz showed the PET scan images to his OCD patients to persuade them that their symptoms were the physical result of these brain circuits rather than their mental choice. Volk (2013) reported that his patients felt liberated by this information. They could finally dissociate their symptoms from their sense of self; i.e., they were not choosing to behave in this way; their symptoms were involuntary. Schwartz called this **relabeling** and **reattributing**. I emphasized the liberating effects of thinking about psychological problems in physical rather than mental terms in Chapter 1. Dr. Schwartz implemented exposure therapy, Network Principle 8, using mindfulness methods where patients were encouraged to tolerate the impulse to perform compulsions without doing so. He asked his patients to **refocus** on something else when their obsessions began to keep them from performing the related compulsions. He rescanned his patients after they improved clinically and found that activation of their OFC and CN had significantly subsided. Research by Baxter et al. (1987a,b, 1989, 1992, 1996), Brody et al. (1998), Saxena et al. (1998, 2009), and Schwartz (1998) supports this physical approach to understanding and treating OCD in particular, and psychological disorders in general. Del Casale et al. (2011) conducted a more recent literature review of functional imaging studies that have evaluated the physical changes produced by CBT for OCD. The authors reported on 143 studies covering 755 patients with OCD. Behavior therapy was shown to alter ten brain structures.

Linden (2006) reviewed literature demonstrating that psychotherapy results in brain changes that can be detected by non-invasive brain scans. Functional brain imaging is being used to document the brain changes produced by learning-based interventions. For example, Goldapple et al. (2004) conducted positron-emission tomography (PET) scans on 17 unmedicated patients diagnosed with major depression before and after 15–20 sessions of CBT that resulted in clinical improvement on the Hamilton Depression Rating Scale. These authors reported increased activation in the hippocampus and dorsal cingulate. These studies found decreased activation in the dorsal, ventral, and medial frontal cortex. In sum, they reported that CBT modulated activation in both limbic and cortical regions.

[1] http://en.wikipedia.org/wiki/Orbitofrontal

[2] http://en.wikipedia.org/wiki/Caudate_nucleus

EMISSION AND OMISSION TREATMENTS

Psychotherapies can be divided into two main groups; those that stress the emission of behavior and those that stress the omission of behavior. This distinction is directly parallel to the behavioral distinction made in Table 10.1. Emission treatments entail doing something, whereas omission treatments entail doing nothing, inhibiting the emission of behavior. For example, cognitive restructuring entails emitting behaviors because it is fundamentally about activating System 2 to control and mitigate the distress and life problems created by System 1. Ego psychology had the same focus (Tryon, 1986). Reason is applied to emotion-mediated thoughts and behaviors in an effort to create dissonance, so that it can be reduced in favor of reason as per Network Principle 8. Applied behavior analysis is also largely an emission-type intervention because it uses principles of operant conditioning to modify targeted behaviors. Chapter 11 provides relevant mechanism information as Network Principle 8.

Omission-type treatments require clients to withhold a response. This is the crucial component of exposure and response prevention (ERP). The therapist presents the phobic or other stimuli. The client is asked to not escape or to not engage in a compulsion. Their job is to omit behavior and tolerate the distress caused by the therapist. Notice the similarity here with acceptance and commitment therapy (ACT; Arch & Craske, 2008; Hayes et al., 2012). Notice also that the mindfulness therapy used by Dr. Schwartz in the section above asked his clients not to engage in their compulsions. Mindfulness therapies sometimes call for turning both Systems 1 and 2 down or off, and that entails a lot of not doing. The important point here is that the dissonance created by not responding activates the experience-dependent plasticity mechanisms that modify our neural networks in long-lasting ways that can be therapeutic, in accordance to Network Principle 8.

LEARNING VS. CONDITIONING

Most introductory psychology textbooks discuss operant and respondent conditioning as if they constituted the entire field of learning. Other textbooks confine conditioning to animal learning, and present human learning as distinctly different. No introductory psychology textbook that I have seen explains how all forms of learning derive from experience-dependent plasticity mechanisms, as shall be done here.

Pavlov (1960/1927) developed classical, also known as respondent, conditioning using a stimulus–response (S → R) model. Anrep (see Pavlov 1960/1927) seriously mistranslated Pavlov's word condition**al** into the word condition**ed**. Pavlov meant that meat powder **unconditionally** elicits salivation. The bell **conditionally** elicits salivation on the **condition** that it is associated with the **unconditional** stimulus of meat powder. These relationships extinguish in the absence of these **conditions**, which is why Pavlov claimed that these effects are **conditional**. This corrected view of classical conditioning is completely consistent with cognitive psychology because people are responsive to the conditions under which they live. The scientific problem here is that Pavlov did not provide any mechanism information to explain how and why conditional responses occur. The clinical problem here is that Anreps mistranslation made classical conditioning appear to be a brain reflex rather than a cognitive process. Consequently, cognitive psychologists largely dissociated themselves from classical conditioning.

Skinner (1938) took an entirely different approach to conditioning. Skinner reversed Pavlov's model. He proposed a response–stimulus (R → S) model where R referred to a behavior and S referred to physical and/or social consequences that follow this behavior. Skinner explained behavior in terms of ontogenetic evolution, evolution within one's lifetime, using the same principles of **variation** and **selection** that Darwin used to explain phylogenetic evolution. Positive consequences of behaviors increased the probability that the behavior in question would recur in future under similar circumstances. These consequences were called reinforcers because they strengthened behavior. They made behavior more likely to occur under similar circumstances. Those circumstances were termed discriminative stimuli and were symbolized as S^D. For example, if a feeder was operative only when a green light was illuminated, then the rat in the Skinner box would eventually learn to press the lever to get food only when the green light was illuminated. The green light became an S^D. The symbol S^Δ was used to refer to absence of an S^D; in this case when the green light was off. The scientific problem here is that Skinner did not provide any mechanism information to explain how and why variation and selection worked. Neither he nor his followers could explain why and how reinforcers modified behavior. Clinicians used these principles to create a therapeutic technology called applied behavior analysis (ABA). An extraordinary amount of supportive evidence demonstrates the efficacy and effectiveness of this technology. In an amazing disregard for evidence and an equally amazing demonstration of the importance of theory, clinicians largely abandoned this behavior change technology when the cognitive revolution occurred in psychology (Bandura, 1978; Dember, 1974; Gardner, 1985; Mahoney, 1974, 1977; Meichenbaum, 1977).

Neuroscience subsequently provided the missing mechanism information. Carlson et al. (2010, p. 440) stated: 'We now understand that "*Learning* refers to the process by which experiences change our nervous system and hence our behavior. We refer to these changes as *memories*"' (italics in the original). Chapter 3 reviewed three experience-dependent plasticity mechanisms: (a) synaptic plasticity; (b) epigenetics; and (c) glia. Together they provide much of the mechanism information that explains how and why operant and respondent conditioning principles work.

Bryck and Fisher (2012) discussed 'Training the brain: Practical applications of neural plasticity from the intersection of cognitive neuroscience, developmental psychology, and prevention science'. They began their article with a discussion of the developmental vulnerability that experience-dependent plasticity confers on the brain. They discussed the work of Levine (2005) who reviewed data published over half a century demonstrating that stressful rearing environments produce pathological brain changes in key regulatory systems. Converging evidence by Cicchetti et al. (2010) exists regarding maltreated children, and by Fisher et al. (2006) regarding foster children. On the positive side, Nithianantharajah and Hannan (2006), Sale et al. (2009), and van Praag et al. (2000) demonstrated that enriched environments can cause increased brain weight and size, increased dendritic branching and length, and increased synaptic size and density, along with behavioral improvements on long-term spatial memory tasks. Bryck and Fisher (2012) then reviewed studies demonstrating that cognitive training can improve executive functioning.

CONDITIONING AS COGNITION

Conditioning was misrepresented by Anrep's (1927; cited in Pavlov 1960) mistranslation of Pavlov as a brain reflex. Dogs could learn to salivate to a bell and rabbits could learn to blink their eye to a tone. Conditioning seemed to be something spinal or mediated at most by the brain stem. Thorndike introduced instrumental conditioning using a puzzle box where cats learned to operate a lever to escape confinement. This result seemed to show that cats were capable of thinking about a problem such as their confinement in the puzzle box and formulating a solution. Skinner studied pigeon behavior and emphasized choice. When placed in a Skinner box with one lever, the choice was to press or not to press. When placed in a Skinner box with two levers, the choice in this concurrent operant situation was to press the left lever, or not, or to press the right lever, or not, or to switch from the left to right lever, or vice versa. The matching law indicated that participants learned to press levers in direct proportion to the payoffs received. This finding also suggested that some level of thinking was going on. However, the limited cognition displayed made this body of research largely irrelevant to clinicians who preferred to discuss complex psycho-social topics with their clients in consulting rooms.

The cognitive revolution (Bandura, 1978; Dember, 1974; Gardner, 1985; Mahoney, 1974, 1977; Meichenbaum, 1977) promised, but did not produce, cognitive theories capable of explaining much more than behavior theory could. These theorists considered cognitive processes to be qualitatively different than all forms of conditioning, despite efforts by some investigators such as Rescorla (1987, 1988) who repeatedly emphasized that conditioning entails expectations. These events reveal just how blinding theory can be. Lacking a cognitive understanding of conditioning, decades of research documenting strong empirical support for conditioning principles and their effective clinical applications was ignored by leading clinical psychologists and not taught to their many students who now constitute several generations of professional psychologists.

The proposed Bio↔Psychology Network Theory understands that conditioning works because it modifies our neural networks via experience-dependent plasticity mechanisms, as does cognition. The proposed network orientation informs us that operant conditioning selects behaviors by modifying the network cascade via experience-dependent plasticity mechanisms that biologically reinforce particular processing pathways in accordance with our Principles 1 and 2. Stated alternatively, the consequences that function as reinforcers activate the experience-dependent plasticity mechanisms that biologically alter the network so as to increase the probability that the same or similar behavior will emerge under the same or similar circumstances. That Principle 3: Transformation is integral to the network cascade necessarily and unavoidably confers cognitive properties in direct proportion to the complexity of the neural networks involved. Consequently, operant and respondent conditioning are necessarily, inherently, cognitive in principle. Limitations of the neural networks of rats, pigeons, dogs, and other species constrain the cognitive level that can be demonstrated.

A major clinical implication of the conclusion that conditioning is cognitive is that clinicians can now comfortably include conditioning principles into their empirically supported cognitive-behavioral clinical practice. That clinical practices based on conditioning principles have received, and continue to receive, consistently strong empirical support warrants and certifies their inclusion into contemporary clinical practice.

PSYCHOLOGICAL BEHAVIORISM

Arthur Staats (1968, 1975, 2012) endeavored to make behaviorism into a general psychological theory by generalizing and expanding operant and respondent conditioning in various ways that he collectively called paradigmatic behaviorism. Tryon (1990) recommended that his efforts be called **psychological behaviorism**. This change was promptly implemented and continues today.[3] The following link provides references to 33 publications that present psychological behaviorism in detail (http://www2.hawaii.edu/~staats/chapters.htm). Figure 10.1 illustrates some of the central features of psychological behaviorism.

The three repertoires are a key feature of psychological behaviorism. Behavioral principles are presented as adequate explanations for how each of these repertoires develops. The three repertoires are functionally interconnected as illustrated in Figure 10.1. Unfortunately, mechanism information regarding how this all works is not provided. This is because behaviorism, like all psychological theories, provides functional explanations that stipulate relationships without providing any mechanism information for how and why these relationships work as they do. This is because there is no psychological substrate for so-called psychological mechanisms to work on. Hence, psychological behaviorism suffers from the same limitations as do all psychological theories when it comes to scientific explanation.

LEARNING ENTAILS MEMORY MODIFICATION

In this section we move well beyond conditioning and even conditioning as cognition. We discuss learning as memory formation, and the corollary point that new learning necessarily entails memory modification. This fact connects contemporary cognitive psychology with hermeneutic psychoanalysis (Shaffer, 1978).

[3] http://en.wikipedia.org/wiki/Psychological_behaviorism

Long-term learning requires memory. Carlson et al. (2010, p. 440) stated: 'We now understand that "*Learning* refers to the process by which experiences change our nervous system and hence our behavior. We refer to these changes as *memories*"' (italics in the original). Processing and memory are done by the same neural networks in PDP-CNN models. Hence, new learning requires new memories to be formed by the processing nodes that hold prior memories. Such memory superposition, our Network Principle 9, means that new learning often modifies existing memories. See Tryon and McKay (2009) for further details.

Whereas computers remain unchanged by the processing they do, biological and artificial neural networks are changed by the processing they do. These experience-dependent modifications entail synaptic plasticity; a phenomenon that is monitored and controlled by glia and involves epigenetic mechanisms that control genetic expression. It is these properties of real and artificial neural networks that enable them to learn from experience and adapt to an ever-changing environment. When these events occur in real neural networks they activate biological mechanisms that physically sculpt the brain. Brain sculpting continues across the lifespan, but at a reduced rate, and cumulatively results in what we call psychological development. These events also underlie and mediate the effects of every psychological intervention, including the memory modification that unavoidably accompanies new learning.

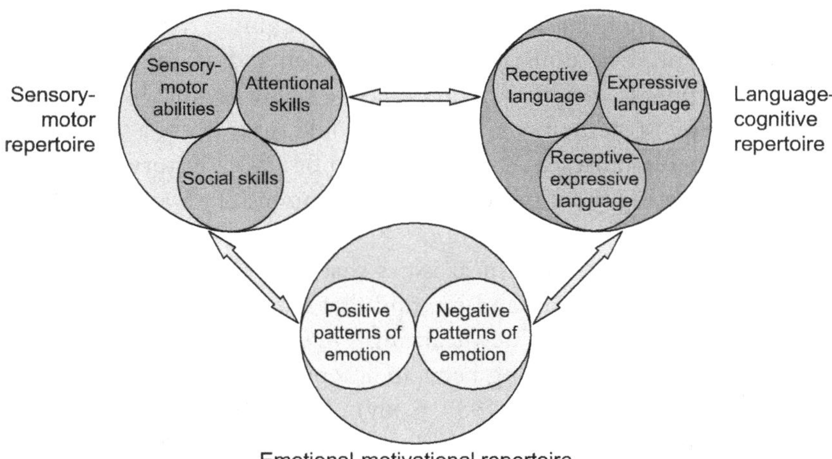

Figure 10.1 Schematic summary of psychological behaviorism.

Tryon and McKay (2009) claimed that learning-based interventions necessarily modify existing memories and that such memory modifications could be used as evidence of effective intervention. Research is currently underway to test this hypothesis with children suffering from OCD. It is expected that successful treatment will modify their memories such that they will be less able to recall the specific behaviors they used to ritualistically engage in prior to treatment. Alternatively stated, memory modification may be an unavoidable consequence of new learning.

Hermaneutic psychoanalysts took a more direct interest in memory modification. They targeted memories for modification and recommended memory modification as a therapeutic tool. Shaffer (1978) advanced the following three theses in his Yale lectures: (1) 'The first thesis is that a psychoanalysis consists of the construction of a personal past. It is not *the* personal past but *a* personal past. However convincing it may be, it remains a construction, merely a history of a certain kind' (p. 8). (2) 'At this point I want to move on to the second thesis, which is that a psychoanalysis consists of the construction of a present subjective world of a certain kind. Again, not *the* present world but *a* present world. Like the past, the psychoanalytic present is no more than one of a number of possible constructions' (p. 14). (3) 'My third thesis, which concerns the characteristic point of view taken of this distinctively Freudian past and present, is this: the psychoanalyst develops a view of the analysand's life history as action. The term *action* will be used in the sense that includes wishing, imagining, remembering, and other such mental acts along with physical acts in and on the environment' (p. 18) (all emphases original). The objective of successful therapy was to revise the patient's memories in ways that would make them less distressing. After all, their memories were considered to be just 'a history of a certain kind' (p. 8). Altering them to be a less distressing history was considered to be therapeutic.

There are a number of ethical issues that arise as a result of memory modification. On the one hand we find that memory modification is an unavoidable consequence of new learning. On the other hand we learn that memory modification has long been an accepted goal and tool of hermeneutic psychoanalysis. Loftus (1980, p. xiv) observed that, in principle, one could cure some psychological disorders if memory could be changed. For example, persons suffering from phobias could be helped if their fearful memories could be replaced with happy self-assured ones. She referred to this beneficent practice as that of a memory doctor.

Emotion-focused therapy (EFT; Angus & Greenberg, 2011; Greenberg, 2002, 2008; Pavio & Pascual-Leone, 2010) includes narrative construction and reconstruction (Angus & Greenberg, 2011, pp. 22–3) 'in which symbolized feelings, needs, self-experience, thoughts and aims are clarified and organized into a coherent story' (p. 22). 'Here, complex experiences, such as conflict or puzzling reactions, are organized into stories that are understandable and often new' (p. 22). 'Promoting reflection on emotional experience, as well as helping people make sense of their experience, promotes its assimilation into their ongoing self-narratives' (p. 23). EFT also includes 'Transformation of emotion and story outcomes' (p. 23) where the therapist helps the patient create 'new explicit meanings and story outcomes' (p. 23). Modifying life-story narratives is understood to cause emotional change. 'As such, emotional change, by definition, involves narrative change' (p. 24). EFT also includes 'identity reconstruction' (p. 24). 'A critical change process occurs when the client's most important personal stories and their emotional plotlines change. This final process involves different forms of identity transformation that result in the emergence of new self-narratives' (p. 24). 'Importantly, the integration of emotion processes and narrative structure facilitates the construction of a stored explanation of what happened, which can then be told to others and reflected on for further understanding and personal meaning construction. Therapy then is a process of clients coming to know and understand their own lived stories and articulating them as told stories – and in doing so changing their stories' (p. 25). 'The term autobiographical reasoning refers to this type of narrative meaning-making activity' (p. 25).

EFT clearly shares memory modification objectives with hermeneutic psychoanalysis, even though the lack of relevant citations by EFT authors suggests that they do not recognize this connection. These two therapeutic orientations differ from CBT, in that memory modification is inadvertent in CBT but a therapeutic goal in the other two approaches.

CONDITIONING AS EMPIRICALLY SUPPORTED CBT PRINCIPLES

The proposed Bio↔Psychological Network Theory of conditioning as methods for modifying expectations authorizes us to include empirically supported conditioning principles as part of a cognitive-behavior therapy (CBT) clinical practice. Conditioning principles are some of the most empirically supported findings that psychological science has to offer.

Clinicians who see themselves as applying psychological science in clinical settings should seriously consider including conditioning principles into their clinical practice if they are not already doing so.

Parents and teachers frequently refer children to psychologists because the target child is exhibiting a behavioral excess or deficit; i.e., too much or too little behavior. That is, the frequency, intensity, and/or duration are either excessive or insufficient. Parents and teachers want change. While they may also seek explanations, they mainly want change. Similarly, adults who seek psychologists frequently desire change. They often want to be less anxious, fearful, or depressed. Couples likewise seek a change in their relationship. The clinical relevance of conditioning is that operant and respondent procedures are general methods, recipes, to predictably modify behavior and the thoughts and feelings that go with new behavior.

Operant and respondent conditioning constitutes empirically supported psychological principles that were carelessly discarded during the cognitive revolution (Bandura, 1978; Dember, 1974; Gardner, 1985; Mahoney, 1974, 1977; Meichenbaum, 1977) by most clinical psychologists. Conditioning did not participate in the cognitive revolution, because no cognitive theory could explain why principles of operant and respondent conditioning worked. Influential clinicians such as Ellis, Beck, and Linehan created new clinical practices based on their personal and professional experiences rather than on empirically supported principles of psychological science. Clinical psychologists, and students of clinical psychology, eagerly followed these leaders never questioning what was left behind. Below I review some of the more fundamental principles that clinicians should know about.

It is ironic that neglect of learning by both psychological science and clinical practitioners has jointly exacerbated the previously identified evidence–theory knowledge gap. Psychologists once studied learning, but the cognitive revolution abandoned such inquiry and focused intellectual and financial resources on how people process information. Learning was subsequently assumed rather than investigated. This shift away from learning removed our professional identification with learning and aggravated the evidence–theory knowledge gap because it neglected to study the most basic process upon which therapists depend; how to get people to change the way they think, feel, and act. Hayes (2008) noted that 'Some previously foundational ideas (e.g., behavior therapists needed extensive training in the psychology of learning) began heading toward extinction' (p. 150). With regard to specific therapies, Hayes noted that '...the underlying principles became looser and less linked to behavioral science, resulting in theories that were harder to disprove. The original goal of empirically validated procedures was retained, but the original vision of a translational applied science linked to well-established basic principles weakened' (p. 151). These trends continue unabated today.

Taxonomy of Operant Conditioning

Operant conditioning comes in many forms. Table 10.1 presents a taxonomy of operant conditioning. This taxonomy was first proposed by Woods (1974) and was subsequently extended by Tryon (1976a, 1976b, 1996a). Behaviors, also referred to as **operants** because they operate on the physical and/or social environment, are composed of **distributions** of responses because there are many different ways of emitting the same behavior. Even the simple bar press can be done in different ways, e.g., with foot or nose, and/or with different degrees of force. Such variations naturally occur and can be selected for if one reinforces only bar presses having a specific topography or a specified force. Reinforcers are defined by their effects upon behavior. **Positive** reinforcers increase the frequency, intensity, and/or duration of behaviors when their onset or increase is contingent upon the emission of a response. **Negative** reinforcers also **increase** the frequency, intensity, and/or duration of behaviors when they offset or decrease contingent upon the emission of a response. The central idea here is that the term **reinforce always means to strengthen**; never to weaken. One can therefore strengthen behavior in one of two ways; either add something positive or remove something negative. One must independently identify stimuli as being positive or negative reinforcers prior to using Table 10.1. Many stimuli will not qualify as either positive or negative, but may serve as **discriminative stimuli** that signal when responding will be reinforced. One must identify a target response; hereafter referred to as the response being emitted or omitted. The concurrent operant condition entails two target responses. The explanatory nucleus of the network theory introduced in Chapter 3 provides the missing mechanism information regarding why reinforcers strengthen behavior. This is an important contribution because it answers one of the big questions that Skinner and his associates left to neuroscience during the cognitive revolution. Reinforcers are stimuli that activate one or more of the experience-dependent plasticity mechanisms that physically modify the neural network and alter synaptic function, thus modifying the network cascade that transforms stimulus microfeatures into cognitions and then into behaviors.

Table 10.1 Taxonomy of Operant Conditioning

		Consequent Event Unsignaled			Consequent Event Signaled		
		Onset or Increase	**No Change**	**Offset or Decrease**	**Onset or Increase**	**No Change**	**Offset or Decrease**
Response	Positive reinforcer	E^+ Reward[a] ↑[b]	E+ Extinction[c] ↓	E_+ Penalty ↓	sE^+ Signaled reward ↑	sE+ Extinction[c] ↓	sE_+ Signaled penalty ↓
emission	Negative reinforcer	E^- Punishment ↓	E– Extinction ↓	E_- Relief ↑	sE^- Signaled punishment ↓	sE– Extinction ↓	sE_- Signaled relief ↑
Response	Positive reinforcer	O^+ Omission reward ↓	O+ Extinction ↑	O_+ Omission penalty ↑	sO^+ Signaled omission reward ↓	sO+ Extinction ↑	sO_+ Signaled omission penalty ↑
omission	Negative reinforcer	O^- Omission punishment ↑	O– Extinction ↑	O_- Omission relief ↓	sO^- Signaled omission punishment ↑	sO– Extinction ↑	sO_- Signaled omission relief ↓

Note. Reprinted with permission from Tryon (1996); it extends the taxonomy by Woods (1974).
[a]The term conditioning should follow each entry.
[b]Upward arrows indicate behavioral increases; downward arrows indicate behavioral decreases.
[c]Extinction requires that all four entries in this column exist simultaneously.

The first thing to notice about Table 10.1 is that the top half of the table concerns how consequences can be provided contingent upon the **emission** of the target response, whereas the bottom half of the table concerns how consequences can be provided contingent upon the **omission** of the target response. This distinction presumes a time sampling approach where using either a fixed or variable interval schedule, one observes the target person and determines if the target behavior is present or absent. It is important to emphasize that animals and people can learn about response omission just as they can learn about response emission. Clinically, what does not happen, that should happen, frequently constitutes an important but unspoken consideration regarding both the diagnosis and treatment of behavior disorders.

The second thing to notice about Table 10.1 is that the right half of the table replicates the left half of the table, depending upon whether the consequence has been signaled or not. These signals are formally known as **discriminative stimuli**. Their importance to understanding and analyzing behavior is sufficient to justify occupying the entire right hand portion of the taxonomy.

We can now see that the taxonomy consists of four replications of the same 2 × 3 table. The two rows concern stimuli that function as either positive or negative reinforcers. The three columns concern whether these stimuli: (a) appear (onset) or increase; (b) remain unchanged; or (c) disappear (offset) or decrease. Shorthand symbols were constructed as follows: E represents response emission; O represents response omission. The + sign represents a positive reinforcer; the − sign represents a negative reinforcer. A superscript represents onset or increase. A subscript represents offset or decrease. A middle-script represents no change. An upward-pointing arrow indicates that the cell represents conditions that increase the frequency, intensity, and/or duration of the target behavior. A downward-pointing arrow indicates that the cell represents conditions that decrease the frequency, intensity, and/or duration of the target behavior.

Conditioning Principles

I now briefly review some of the more basic principles of behavior modification; also known as applied behavior analysis. This clinical practice applies empirically supported principles and findings from Skinner's experimental analysis of behavior in therapeutic ways as a form of cognitive-behavior therapy given that conditioning entails cognition and expectancies. The interested reader should consult the latest edition of Martin and Pear (2010) entitled *Behavior Modification: What It Is and How To Do It.* I especially like their 'Pitfalls' sections, where they show how ignorance or misuse of behavioral principles, typically by parents and teachers, shapes the undesirable behaviors that they complain about to clinicians. These sections help us better understand the etiological role played by these empirically supported principles. The two-volume *APA Handbook of Behavior Analysis* by Madden (2012) provides more comprehensive coverage. Volume 1 covers the logic, clinical utility, and methods of single-case research designs, in addition to an overview of the experimental analysis of behavior. Discussions of memory, attention, choice, behavioral neuroscience, and behavioral pharmacology are considered. Volume 2 includes chapters on a dozen behavior disorders.

Reinforcement

The word 'reinforce' means to make stronger. Both positive and negative reinforcers strengthen behavior; i.e., increase the probability of recurrence under similar circumstances. Reinforcement is an empirical concept. One determines if a stimulus is a reinforcer by presenting it contingent upon the presence (emission) of a behavior. If that increases in frequency (probability), then that stimulus is a **positive** reinforcer; otherwise it is not a reinforcer. Alternatively, one can remove, offset, a stimulus contingent upon the presence (emission) of a behavior. If that increases in frequency (probability), then the removed stimulus is a **negative** reinforcer; otherwise it is not a reinforcer. Such an empirical determination must be made for all stimuli before using the taxonomy of operant conditioning presented above.

The differential probability hypothesis, also known as Premack's principle,[4] is a relatively good guide to non-obvious reinforcers. This principle states that a more frequently engaged in behavior can reinforce a less frequently engaged in behavior. For example, with high probability a child comes home with homework. Premack's principle says that one can increase the frequency of the low probability behavior by requiring the child to engage in low probability behavior before being allowed to engage in high probability behavior. Hence, requiring homework before play will increase doing homework. Institutionalized patients frequently isolate themselves and infrequently attend social functions. I found that institutionalized patients will engage in social activities if they can have access to some place where they can be alone. While one might think that socializing has its own rewards, for some people socializing is not fun and solitude is worth

[4] http://en.wikipedia.org/wiki/Premack's_principle

working for. Simple observation can reveal what children and adults value, and thus what can be used as reinforcers.

Reinforcement Schedules

There are many ways to present, schedule, reinforcers. One way is to use **counters**. Reinforcing every behavior that occurs is called **continuous reinforcement** and is equivalent to setting the counter to 1. Reinforcement could be delivered after 2, 3, or more instances of the target behavior. Fixing the counter number at some such value results in a **fixed ratio** schedule. Letting the counter number vary around a specified mean and standard deviation results in a **variable ratio** schedule. Reinforcement can be scheduled with **timers**. Reinforcing the first instance of the target behavior after, say, a 60-second delay constitutes a **fixed interval 60-s** schedule. Letting the mean, and possibly standard deviation, of the intervals vary constitutes a **variable interval** schedule. Reinforcement can be scheduled with **speedometers**. These schedules are called differential reinforcement of low rate or of high rate. The same or different schedules can pertain to the two or more available responses, as is the case in the concurrent operant case. It might not be intuitively obvious that each of these reinforcement schedules causes different response patterns, but the experimental analysis of behavior has revealed otherwise. Ferster and Skinner (1957) published an entire textbook on the effects that reinforcement schedules have. The **matching law** shows that subjects match their behavior to the probability of receiving reward.[5]

Shaping

How do new behaviors get started? Where do new behaviors come from? Skinner suggested that the same principles that drive the origin of species drive the origin of new behaviors. These are the principles of **variation** and **selection**. Shaping by parents, teachers, and clinicians is done by identifying rudiments of the desired behavior and differentially reinforcing their appearance. Skinner shaped turning in a figure of eight pattern by pigeons as follows. First he trained the pigeon to associate a sound with availability of food in a hopper. Then Skinner waited for the pigeon to turn a little to one side before he presented the sound. After the pigeon reliably performed this behavior he waited until the pigeon turned a little more to that same side before he presented the sound. Little by little he shaped the entire figure of eight maneuver.

[5] http://en.wikipedia.org/wiki/Matching_law

Observational Learning

When a mother bear teaches her cubs how to find berries and how to fish, she simply finds berries and goes fishing. The cubs watch what she does and emulate her behavior. However, their initial attempts at foraging and fishing are inept and variable. Some forms of foraging and fishing (variation) work better for each cub than do others. The forms that work better are selected (reinforced) and are repeated with greater frequency (probability) than are the forms of these behaviors that are less effective. The result is that each cub effectively learns to fish and eat berries in a somewhat different way.

Extinction

Table 10.1 shows that the extinction procedure is unusual in that it requires that four conditions occur simultaneously, which partly explains why it is so difficult to implement in real-life clinical situations. One must ensure that there is no change in any positive or negative reinforcer contingent upon either response emission or omission. Only neutral stimuli can change and few stimuli are truly neutral. Extinction is easy to implement in the laboratory, as one need only deactivate the reward system, typically a feeder of some kind. Then no behavior or its absence delivers food. Insulating children from the effects of their behavior on the physical and/or social environment is not so easily accomplished.

Deprivation

Motivation is a key psychological variable. It has been said that one can lead a horse to water but cannot make it drink. This aphorism is not actually true. Depriving the horse of water for 24 or 48 hours prior to leading it to water dramatically increases the probability that it will drink! This is called an **establishing operation**. The following link (http://www.psychologicalscience.com/bmod/2010/09/establishing-operation-vs-discriminative-stimulus.html) states 'Establishing operations work by changing the reinforcement properties of a reinforcer. If a reinforcer is made to be more reinforcing, the consequence will be more desirable, which should have a greater effect on eliciting the target behavior. Establishing operations for reinforcers make us want something more that we might have'. Establishing operations are antecedents, in that they are applied before reinforcers are delivered.

Establishing operations are publically observable external manipulations. Motivations are hypothetical internal states. Hence, behaviorists prefer to discuss motivation in terms of establishing operations. Rats and pigeons, typical participants in behavioral experiments, are deprived of food, but not water, until their body weight drops to 80% of their free feeding weight before the study starts in order to ensure that contingent access to food will reinforce, strengthen, their behavior; i.e., they will be motivated to work for food. Satiation is another establishing operation that reduces the effectiveness of food reinforcers. For example, contingent access to food immediately upon finishing a large feast (e.g., thanksgiving or Christmas dinner) does not reinforce behavior.

Discriminative Stimuli

A stimulus that is sufficiently associated with the onset of a reinforcer, such that it predicts that a reinforcer will follow a response, becomes what is called a **discriminative stimulus** and is symbolized as S^D. Such stimuli discriminate between when a reinforcer is available from when it is not available. A stimulus that is predictably associated with the absence or unavailability of a reinforcer is also called a discriminative stimulus, but is symbolized as S^Δ to distinguish it.

Stimulus Control

Stimulus control is said to exist when an organism consistently behaves in some way in the presence of a discriminative stimulus. For example, people typically stop at red lights and go at green lights. This driving behavior is said to be under stimulus control. The following link (http://www.psychologicalscience.com/bmod/2010/09/establishing-operation-vs-discriminative-stimulus.html) states 'Discriminative stimuli work by telling us what behaviors will get reinforced or punished. In this way discriminative stimuli control our behavior and tell us what to do or how to act. When we reliably and predictably change our behavior in the presence of a discriminative stimulus we are said to be under stimulus control'. Discriminative stimuli are antecedents, in that they are typically established prior to conditioning studies unless the objective of the study is to establish a discrimination. Discriminative stimuli operate cognitively.

Generalization

Whereas discrimination entails discerning differences, generalization entails glossing over differences. 'Stimulus generalization occurs when behavior becomes more probable in the presence of one stimulus or situation as a result of having been reinforced in the presence of another stimulus or situation' (Martin & Pear, 1999, p. 145). This can occur due to physical similarity or due to conceptual learning. An example based on physical similarity is that pigeons that have been reinforced in the presence of a yellow light also respond in the presence of a green light. Pigeons have excellent color vision.

Response generalization '… occurs when a behavior becomes more probable in the presence of a stimulus or situation as a result of another behavior having been strengthened in the presence of that stimulus or situation' (Martin & Pear, 1999, p. 149). This can occur due to physical similarity or due to conceptual learning. For example, having learned a forehand stroke in tennis facilitates performing a forehand stroke in squash or racquetball.

Pitfalls

Natural laws, like gravity, hold whether or not people are aware of them, theoretically recognize them, or feel that they marginalize mankind in some philosophical or religious way. Conditioning principles are natural laws. Citizens and contemporary clinicians tend to be unaware or uninformed about conditioning principles and are therefore subject to their pitfalls.

One of the most clinically important parts of Martin and Pear's ***Behavior Modification: What It Is and How To Do It*** books is their pitfalls sections that occur throughout the book. These sections inform clinicians regarding possibly etiologies for behavior disorders. That is, behavioral principles can be unintentionally misused by parents, teachers, and significant others in ways that shape the very problems that are presented to clinicians to treat. Such information is clinically relevant because effective intervention means **identifying and discontinuing** those practices. Otherwise, those practices will compete with and undermine everything that the clinician tries to do therapeutically. The result will look like 'resistance' to the clinician, when in fact it is the unwitting anti-therapeutic use of empirically supported principles by well-meaning people who don't understand behavioral principles.

Another reason why these pitfall sections are important is because they alert the clinician to potential ways that therapy can get off track and have unintended negative consequences. That is, behavioral therapies that implement operant conditioning principles need to be correctly implemented by parents, teachers, and/or other care takers. These therapeutic techniques and procedures are new and often strange to parents, teachers, and/or other care takers. They therefore need training to effectively implement them. Because they frequently make mistakes and misapply the procedures early on in treatment, clinicians can expect either no or delayed positive results or even negative results. Almost always such results are traceable to misuse of behavioral principles due to some misunderstanding of them. I have consistently found that correctly implemented behavioral principles clearly show positive effects within two weeks. If a behavioral plan is not showing signs of effectiveness after two weeks, then it is time to try something else. What follows is a partial treatment of the pitfalls discussed by Martin and Pear in their book *Behavior Modification: What It Is and How To Do It.*

Pitfalls of Positive Reinforcement

Unintended social reinforcement by peers, parents, teachers, doctors, nurses, and others can strengthen undesirable behaviors to where they become clinical problems. This includes selective mutism, formerly known as elective mutism, and social isolation.

Pitfalls of Extinction

Common consequences of extinction include: (a) behavior becomes more intense; and (b) behavior becomes more variable. Behavior becomes more intense because people frequently think that they just need to push harder to make old behaviors work. The common observation of people banging on vending machines is a good example. Having put their money in and politely selected an item, the absence of that item being delivered sets the occasion for repressing the appropriate levers more vigorously and/or eventually pounding their fists against the vending machine. Extinction sets the occasion for what might be called 'emotional' behaviors. Asking for directions in a foreign country in a normal voice may not get the desired response. In such cases, people often repeat their request more loudly. The problem is not that the listener is hard of hearing but rather than they do not understand what has been asked of them. Parents may give their children a command. If ignored, parents may repeat the command in a louder voice. Again, the children are not hard of hearing; they are disobedient. Their behavior is not under what is technically known as 'stimulus control'. But there are procedures that effectively establish such control that clinicians can use; i.e., rewarding compliance and/or punishing non-compliance.

Behavior becomes more variable under extinction. This makes perfect sense. If an old behavior is no longer working as expected, then perhaps some variation of that behavior might be more effective. Remember, shaping occurs through variation and natural selection. Hence, the tendency to vary behavior seems to be innate in essentially every species. Variability can result in better or worse behaviors leading to short- and/or long-term positive or negative consequences. Experimentation with alternative behaviors need not work as clinicians plan.

Both increased intensity and variability are signs that extinction is effective. Stated otherwise, if one does not observe any increased intensity or variability then extinction is almost certainly not being implemented correctly. Clinicians need to advise their clients of this fact and prepare them with ways to effectively cope with the increased intensity and variability that extinction inevitably brings.

Pitfalls of Shaping

Maladaptive and/or harmful behaviors can be unwittingly shaped with positive reinforcement; usually attention. For example, bike riding can be shaped with parental social approval. Fast and risky bike riding can also be shaped by peer social approval.

Parents often expect children to behave 'normally' and may not be attentive to them when they do so. Children who have 'temper tantrums' will be noticed and attended to. Negative attention, even punishment, will not decrease these behaviors if good behaviors are not positively reinforced. This is frequently the case when parents complain that they have tried punishment and it does not work. True enough, punishment alone is often ineffective. Parents need to learn to combine discipline with positive reinforcement for desired behaviors.

Most people have witnessed children misbehaving in a checkout line. The child wants something on display. The parent, usually the mother, says no. The child repeats their request louder and more insistently. If the parent refuses again, the child can yell and scream. Now the parent is embarrassed and frequently gives in to quiet the child and complete their checkout, given that other customers are waiting in line and looking in a disapproving manner. If no further discipline occurs at home, one can expect that the child is likely to repeat this behavior the next time he or she goes shopping, and especially when shopping with the same parent.

Children learn to disrespect parents who say that they will impose limits and consequences on behavior but never do so or inconsistently do so. Children are keen observers of behavior. They develop expectations that guide future behavior. Parents who consistently fall into this and other pitfalls are unwittingly training their children to disregard what they say and value.

The noted psychologist Gerald Patterson once told about a situation where he inadvertently shaped bad behavior in his pet dog. He was in the habit of greeting his dog when he came home from work. Then came a time of preoccupation where he omitted this behavior, thereby unwittingly putting the dog on an extinction schedule. The dog's behavior increased in intensity and variability in an effort to be noticed and petted. It ended up that the dog jumped up and created a fuss when Patterson came home. Attending to his dog immediately upon returning home soon reshaped the dog's behavior back to normal. Many pet owners similarly shape undesirable pet behaviors and then complain that their pet has a problem, when actually it is the owner's behavior that needs modified.

Attention can lead to self-injurious behavior. Consider a developmentally disabled child who lives in an understaffed institution. Good behavior might often go unnoticed. But head banging will definitely be attended to.

Pitfalls of Intermittent Reinforcement

Extinction is typically used for undesirable behaviors. The inconsistent use of extinction can result in intermittent reinforcement of these behaviors. For example, parents may sometimes effectively ignore temper tantrums and other times give in. That effectively puts temper tantrums on an intermittent reinforcement schedule. This will result in more frequent and/or more extreme temper tantrums that will be even more resistant to extinction. One can readily see how parents can unwittingly strengthen undesirable behaviors to clinically significant levels.

Pitfalls of Schedules for Decreasing Behavior

There are several reinforcement schedules for decreasing behaviors. One schedule involves **differential reinforcement of low rates** (DRL). Reinforcement is delivered when the rate of behavior is at or less than a specified amount. For example, a child may receive a reinforcer if they 'talk out of turn' three times or less per half hour. **Differential reinforcement of zero** responding (DRZ) is an extreme form of DRL. **Differential reinforcement of other behavior** (DRO) generally entails reinforcing **incompatible** behaviors. Reward for gum chewing instead of donut eating or cigarette smoking are examples of DRO.

These reinforcement schedules are subject to many of the previously discussed pitfalls, but one possibility deserves special mention. Imagine a bright intellectually curious child who asks questions in class. The teacher may initially reward this behavior, thereby increasing its frequency. If this child is in a large class, the teacher may feel that they are calling on this child too much and unwittingly place him or her on a DRL schedule by calling on them less frequently. Underachievement by this student could be the unintended consequence.

Pitfalls of Stimulus Discrimination Training

A discriminative stimulus (S^D) is a stimulus that predicts reinforcement whereas other stimuli (S^Δ) do not predict reinforcement. Such stimuli are said to 'control' behavior because organisms behave differently in the presence of such S^D stimuli compared to their absence. For example, we stop at red lights and go when the light turns green. We obey traffic lights because they promote our safety.

Differential reinforcement is a procedure that brings about **stimulus control**. For example, parents that provide positive consequences for compliance with their directives and withhold access to positive reinforcers or administer aversive consequences for non-compliance with their directives will find that their children 'listen' to them which is how parents talk about children 'obeying' them.

Common examples of discrimination training pitfalls can be found in parent–child interactions. For example, a parent may ask a child to remove their books from the table so that the family can have dinner. The child ignores this request and continues what they are doing; perhaps watching TV. The parent asks the child a second time to remove their books from the table. Again the child ignores this request and continues with what they are doing. Sometimes a third or fourth request is made in a louder more threatening voice, but often to no avail. Finally, the emotionally distraught parent yells a final threat and then the child removes their books. Since no further consequences follow for the child's behavior, the child learns to wait for the final threat. In addition to experiencing these exchanges in my clinical practice, I witnessed a variation of this pitfall that took place at a community pool. An older sister told her younger brother that he should hurry up and change his clothes so that she could drive him home soon. He said that he would. But he took his very sweet time taking a shower and getting dressed. Throughout this time I could hear the sister threaten to drive home without him thus making him walk a modest distance. But she didn't. Instead, she begged and pleaded with him to hurry up, which he didn't. Finally, he was finished and met her outside the dressing room where she continued to scold him as they walked to the parking lot. He learned to ignore her demands because they were not correlated with any consequences.

Behavioral Diagnosis

Hickey (1998) questioned the utility and relevance of DSM-IV to behavior therapists.[6] I agree completely with Hickey but understand that no amount of criticism of the Diagnostic and Statistical Manual series (e.g., DSM-IV; APA, 1994) will make it any less popular, in the same way that no amount of criticism is sufficient to cause scientists to abandon a flawed theory; especially if it is the only alternative. One must put forward a preferred alternative. Wolpe (1958) proposed systematic desensitization as an alternative to psychoanalysis for treating anxiety disorders, in addition to criticizing psychodynamic therapy. This choice set the occasion for a major change in clinical practice by many psychologists. Similarly, behavior therapists must provide a better alternative to the DSM series in order to set the occasion for clinical change regarding diagnosis.

The National Institutes of Health (NIH) are moving away from the fifth edition of the *Diagnostic Manual of Mental Disorders* because it lacks mechanism information. This decision is consistent with the position taken in this book that psychological theories, including theories about psychopathology, are functional theories and the key defining feature of functional theories is that they lack mechanism information. The route to discovering real mechanism information, in my view, is to **think physical, not mental** about psychology and behavior. I have implemented this recommendation by focusing on well-replicated psychological phenomena that can be explained in network terms that involve neuroscience and connectionist mechanisms. This led to the formulation of the four core and eight corollary network principles that constitute the Bio↔Psychology Network Theory developed in previous chapters.

The conditioning principles used to construct the diagnostic system described in this section are reliable methods for activating the experience-dependent plasticity mechanisms that modify our neural networks so that we form memories and learn. Hence, the proposed system of behavioral diagnosis is a first approximation of the type of diagnostic system that NIH is looking for. The pitfalls sections show how we can learn our way into problems. Professional assistance is sometimes needed to learn our way out of these problems.

[6] I use the term behavior therapist in this chapter mostly out of respect for the historical fact that this is what clinicians whose customary clinical practice used behavioral diagnosis and customized conditioning treatments were called. My intention here is to show that conditioning entails cognition and consequently customized conditioning treatments can be included in contemporary clinical practice by all psychologists. Consequently, behavior therapists should be read as, understood to mean, clinical psychologists.

It seems axiomatic that sound treatment should be based on, derive from, accurate diagnosis. Some part of the clinical presentation by children and adults, but especially by children, involves behavioral excesses or deficits. Children's disorders can be classified as externalizing or internalizing, as can disorders for adults (Krueger, 1999; Krueger et al., 1998; Krueger & Markon, 2006). Professional help is sought to reduce the frequency, intensity, and/or duration of behaviors that occur too often, too intensely, and/or for too long. Professional help is also sought to increase the frequency, intensity, and/or duration of behaviors that do not occur often enough, do not occur with sufficient intensity, and/or do not occur for long enough.

Tryon (1976a) provided a behavioral alternative to DSM (DSM-IV; APA, 1994) that he subsequently revised and extended (Tryon, 1996). This system is based on Woods's (1974) taxonomy of instrumental conditioning. This taxonomy should be of special interest today, because conditioning principles are among the most empirically validated findings in psychology. This approach to behavioral diagnosis has two very important properties. First, diagnosis is based on etiological factors sufficient to explain the presence of behavioral excesses and/or deficits that constitute the behavior disorder. Second, behavioral diagnosis leads directly to prescriptive treatment for remediating the diagnosed problem. The DSM lacks both of these highly desired qualities and this is largely why it is so highly criticized. Clinical psychologists might try promoting this behavioral approach to diagnosis and see how many clinicians prefer an etiologically based and prescriptively oriented diagnostic system to the DSM.

Table 10.2 details the diagnostic relevance of an extended taxonomy of instrumental conditioning. Behavior disorders occur under at least four conditions: (a) the absence of contingencies that support positive behaviors (Type I); (b) the presence of contingencies that decrease positive behaviors (Type II); (c) the presence of contingencies that support negative behaviors (Type III); and (d) the absence of contingencies that decrease negative behaviors (Type IV). This taxonomy, and its shorthand notations, can be used to identify conditions sufficient to cause and/or maintain

Table 10.2 Four Diagnostic Types Based on Absence or Presence of Contingencies that Increase or Decrease Positive or Negative Behaviors

	Contingencies that Increase	**Contingencies that Decrease**
Positive behaviors	Absence of is Type I	Presence of is Type II
Negative behaviors	Presence of is Type III	Absence of is Type IV

Reprinted with permission from Tryon (1996).

the four broad classes of behavior disorders, excesses of emission or omission, categorized in Table 10.2. Behavioral diagnosis is prescriptive in that it: (a) calls for termination of contingencies that increase negative behaviors and/or decrease positive behaviors; and (b) calls for initiation of contingencies that increase positive and decrease negative behaviors. Reinforcement contingencies frequently occur in pairs. Table 10.3 reclassifies the entries in Table 10.1 into a 2 × 2 table on the basis of whether they accelerate or decelerate the emission or omission of behavior. Horizontal combinations produce non-contingent disorders. Vertical combinations produce approach–avoidance conflicts. Tryon (1976) described the various models of behavior disorder that can arise when certain pairs of operant conditions occur simultaneously, and they are considered next.

Non-Contingent Punishment Conditioning

Combinations across the second row have likely been the most studied pathological combination resulting in what has been called **learned helplessness**. Classic studies include Overmier and Seligman (1967) and Seligman and Maier (1967). Dogs were initially trained to escape shock by jumping over a low barrier. Then they were removed from the apparatus and placed into another apparatus where they were confined and given many trials of unsignaled uncontrollable shock; i.e., they were exposed to trials characterized by E^- and O^-. This combined simultaneous emission punishment conditioning and omission punishment conditioning made

Table 10.3 Taxonomy of Binary Contingencies

	Emission	Omission	Non-Contingent
Accelerate	↑ E^+ E_- sE^+ sE_-	↓ O^+ O_- sO^+ sO_-	A(E) • A(O) = A(E • O) = A = ↑[a]
Decelerate	↓ E_+ E^- E+ E- sE_+ sE^- sE+ sE-	↑ O_+ O^- O+ O- sO^+ sO_- sO+ sO-	D(E) • D(O) = D(E • O)= D = ↓
Approach–avoidance conflict	A(E) • D(E) = D(A • E) = DE = ↓[b]	A(E) • A(O) = A(E • O) = A = ↑	

Adapted from Tryon (1996).
[a]E O = 1 because they are inversely related. E = 1/O.
[b]AD = D because algebraically + (-) = -, which here means D.

shock non-contingent and consequently uncontrollable. Shock came on regardless of what the dogs did or did not do. The dogs were then returned to the first apparatus, but they no longer jumped to escape shock when the warning light came on. This result is consistent with the theoretical prediction presented in the right margin of the second row that has the downward-pointing arrow indicating that this combination decreases behavior.

Interestingly, the brain changes that occurred in these dogs were similar to those found in depressed people. Treatment with antidepressant medication was helpful. Administering antidepressant medication to the dogs prior to receiving uncontrollable shock diminished the effects of this stressful experience; i.e., reduced their learned helplessness.

Non-Contingent Penalty Conditioning

Table 10.3 shows that other binary combinations of conditions across the second row should also produce behavior disorder similar to learned helplessness. Consider the combination of emission penalty conditioning, E_{+}, and omission penalty conditioning, O_{+}, where something very positive is removed regardless of what the person does or does not do. Classic examples involve non-contingent maternal deprivation, including studies by Spitz (1946) and Harlow et al. (1970) where infant humans and monkeys, respectively, were separated from their mothers. These separations are non-coningent because nothing that the infant did or did not do caused the maternal deprivation to occur and nothing they could do or not do can bring mother back. Long-lasting psychological and behavioral consequences are well-known consequences of this combination of conditions (Lippmann et al., 2007; Moffett et al., 2007).

Non-Contingent Reward Conditioning

Combinations across the first row constitute uncontrollable reward conditioning. The combination of sE^{+} and sO^{+} constitute **classical conditioning** as illustrated in Figure 10.2 (cf. Tryon, 1976b, 1996). While non-contingent, this combination of conditions is theoretically associated with an upward-pointing arrow to increase behavior and that is what classical conditioning does. However, strange behaviors can result from these combinations. Skinner's (1948) classic demonstration of superstition in a pigeon is a good example. Opening the food hopper on a fixed interval 15-second schedule reinforced random behaviors that selected unusual stereotypic behaviors, such as standing on one leg or turning in circles. The analogy to human pageants, such as rain dances, is clearly evident.

Approach–Avoidance Conflict

Combinations down the left column have been shown to produce approach–avoidance conflicts. Accelerating the emission of behavior while simultaneously decelerating the emission of the same behavior puts the person into conflict. The downward-pointing arrow indicates that this combination of conditions decreases behavior which makes sense.

Neurotic Paradox

Mowrer (1948, 1950) observed that paradoxically, neurotic behavior is both self-defeating and self-perpetuating: '... the neurotic paradox lies in the fact that human behavior is sometimes indefinitely perpetuated despite the fact that it is seriously self-defeating' (Mowrer, 1950, p. 524). Our taxonomy indicates that emission punishment conditioning E^- should decrease behavior, in which case the self-defeating aspects of neurotic behavior should be self-limiting but clinical experience indicates otherwise. Mowrer focused on the not-learning from experience part of the paradox and argued that '... the neurotic is an individual *who has learned how not to learn*' (Mowrer, 1950, p. 526). However, Mowrer never explained what prevented new learning; i.e., he did not provide any mechanism information for how such a result might be caused.

Combining conditions down the right column of Table 10.3 is an alternative way of creating an approach–avoidance conflict that is predicted to increase or sustain behavior. Here we have two essential components of the neurotic paradox: (a) conflict and (b) increases or sustains behavior. Whereas the approach–avoidance conflict mentioned above concerns the **emission** of behavior, neurotic paradox approach–avoidance conflict concerns the **omission** of behavior. It appears that the essence of the neurotic paradox is that it consists of, one might say is driven by, an approach–avoidance conflict over not behaving in certain ways. This analysis is concerned with logical form that is content free in the same way that symbolic logic is content free, because it concerns the form rather than substance of arguments. Being content free implies that the conflict can be about anything or many things.

Diagonals

Combinations along the diagonals of Table 10.3 doubly strengthen or weaken behavior and are not intrinsically pathological. Such combinations can inadvertently strengthen undesirable behavior or weaken desirable behavior, or can be used therapeutically to strengthen desirable or weaken undesirable behavior.

Diagnosis

Table 10.3 complements Tables 10.2 and 10.1 in that all three tables can be used diagnostically. The clinician should first determine if any current conditions are supporting the problematic behaviors brought to their attention or are preventing the development of more desirable alternative behaviors. Clinicians who limit their diagnostic considerations to traditional DSM considerations are likely to miss such conditions. Tryon (1996a) discussed practical clinical methods for obtaining the necessary information to use the taxonomy to make behavioral diagnoses. These methods include interview, observation, and **home tape recording**. The use of technology to obtain behavioral samples (specimens) from natural environments is especially promising. The approach taken to behavioral diagnosis here is compatible with cognitive therapies, as well as with operant conditioning interventions. The main difference is that specific cognitions are substituted for target behaviors and for positive and negative consequences that increase (onset) or decrease (offset) contingently.

Activity Anorexia

Pierce and Epling (1994) and Epling and Pierce (1996) identified conditions that can induce male rats to quit eating and exercise excessively; running themselves to death! They documented strong similarities between activity anorexia and anorexia nervosa. Their basic experiment began with a baseline condition in which they measured the amount of food eaten per day by rats placed in a cage with an adjacent activity wheel that was locked so that it would not turn. The experimental phase began by unlocking the activity wheel and feeding the animals just once per day for a restricted time. This condition produced three remarkable effects. Food intake dropped to about one third of what it was during baseline during the next week. Wheel turns increased exponentially during the same week. Body weight decreased during the same week. The authors claimed that feeding these participants once per day simulated famine and set the occasion for migration to greener pastures. Access to the activity wheel enabled the participants to run. But because better food sources were not encountered, the rats continued running unto death in some cases.

Evaluative Conditioning

Evaluative conditioning concerns how we come to like or dislike something by way of associations. Advertising frequently uses classical conditioning to influence consumer behavior. Associating a movie star or star athlete with their product by having said person hold the product or talk favorably about the product while using it or wearing it is a frequently used method. A PubMed search for 'evaluative conditioning' on 8 September 2013 returned 180 citations indicating the presence of a substantial literature. Some evidence indicates that evaluative conditioning entails higher cortical processing than basic classical conditioning does, and that it is more long-lasting than simple classical conditioning. The proposed Bio↔Psychological Network Theory can handle all of this as it is both a cognitive and conditioning theory.

Tryon and Briones (1985) reviewed early research on what was then called semantic conditioning. They distinguished among the following types of semantic conditioning. **Primary semantic conditioning** provides meaning to emotionally neutral words. The closest study that could be found in the early literature was by Razran (1939), who conditioned a salivary response to the words 'style', 'urn', 'freeze', and 'surf', and demonstrated generalization to the homophones 'stile', 'earn', 'frieze', and 'serf'. Riess (1940, 1946), and Mednick (1957) replicated these findings using conditioned galvanic skin responses (GSR) rather than salivation. Razran (1949) extended this work to three-word sentences.

Primary semantic counter-conditioning aims to alter the evaluative meaning of existing words. Razran (1940) increased the positive valence of sociopolitical slogans such as 'America for Americans!' and 'Workers of the world unite!' by pairing these phrases with food, and decreased their positive valence by pairing them with putrid odors.

Higher-order semantic conditioning uses previously conditioned words as unconditioned stimuli to modify pleasant–unpleasant semantic differential ratings using classical conditioning. Staats and Staats (1957, 1958) published the original experiments. Staats et al. (1959), Blanford and Sampson (1964), and Tryon and Cicero (1989) replicated their methods and findings. Cicero and Tryon (1989) attempted to extend this research to the next level of higher-order conditioning, but were not successful. Staats (1968, 1975) and Staats et al. (1958) described these methods as **language conditioning** and extended this research. Lohr and Staats (1973) extended this work cross-culturally to Sino-Tibetan languages.

Higher-order semantic counter-conditioning entails the therapeutic use of language conditioning. Early (1968) increased social acceptance of social isolates compared to controls in fourth and fifth grade children by pairing their names with 14 positive words that the other children repeated out loud in class. Hekmat and Vanian (1971) used language conditioning to reduce fear in 15 snake-phobic participants, compared to 15 controls, by pairing the word 'snake' with 108 positive words. Hekmat

(1972) replicated this finding with fear of spiders and Hekmat (1973) replicated this result with fear of rats. Tryon and Briones (1985) extended this work to modifying the semantic differential ratings of premarital sexual behaviors in 303 unmarried Filipino women.

Conclusions

Those psychologists who believe that the DSM series has not and will not serve the needs of clinicians need to provide workable alternatives that are more useful. The system of behavioral diagnosis described above has three important properties: (a) it is theoretically consistent with the proposed Bio↔Psychological Network Theory; (b) it is etiologically based in that the taxonomy concerns conditions found sufficient for increasing and decreasing behaviour; and (c) behavioral diagnosis leads directly to intervention. The treatment approach implied by the above discussion of diagnosis is one where clinicians who are trained in behavioral principles customize treatments for specific target problems identified by individual clients rather than technicians who apply manualized treatment packages, with little or no variation, to all persons given a DSM diagnosis. I take this to be an additional advantage of the approach to behavioral diagnosis described above.

Classical (Respondent) Conditioning

Anrep (see Pavlov 1927/1960) seriously mistranslated the Russian word 'condition**al**' to the English word 'condition**ed**'. This small variation at the end of each word, 'al' to 'ed' produced a huge theoretical misunderstanding. Pavlov was arguably the first neuropsychologists in that he was interested in how the frontal lobes mediated behavior; i.e., how behavior was **conditional** on environmental stimuli. He began with uncondition**al** stimuli (UCS). These stimuli always produced a response; i.e., no special experiential history with these stimuli was needed for them to produce a response. He found that the UCS of meat powder consistently increased salivary flow, an uncondition**al** response, (UCR) in dogs. Pavlov's main contribution was to identify condition**al** stimuli (CS). These stimuli initially had no effect on the behavior labeled UCR, but came to have an effect on conditional being associated with, predicting, the UCS. For example, ringing a bell did not initially alter salivary flow. However, by presenting the CS a half second prior to the UCS Pavlov noted that, after a suitable learning history, presenting the CS (bell) alone increased salivary flow. Pavlov called the increased salivary flow upon hearing the bell a condition**al** response, because he learned that this response would disappear unless it was at least periodically reinforced. Pavlov demonstrated the conditional nature of this effect by repeatedly ringing the bell and observing that its effect on salivary flow gradually decreased to zero. He called this process extinction. Pavlov demonstrated that the dog did not fully forget the prior training experience by showing that the conditional effect could be restored with fewer learning trials than were required to initially establish the conditional response. The difference between the number of trials required to initially create the CR and those needed to reinstate it was referred to as the savings measure of memory/retention.

Tryon (1976b) demonstrated that classical conditioning is formally equivalent to programming two operant schedules. Woods (1974) presented line diagrams that defined various forms of operant conditioning. One of these two operant conditions is called signaled **emission** reward conditioning. It is illustrated by the solid lines in Figure 10.2. The solid line for a stimulus (S), known as a discriminative stimulus (S^D), precedes the response (R) that is exclusively followed by the onset of a positive reinforcing event (upward arrow associated with +). The other operant condition is signaled **omission** reward conditioning. It is identical to signaled emission reward conditioning except that the dotted line, indicating omission of response R, replaces the solid line representing its emission. In short, a stimulus is followed by a reinforcing event whether or not the subject responds. This is exactly what classical conditioning, also known as respondent conditioning, entails. That two forms of operant conditioning constitute one form of respondent conditioning when programmed simultaneously logically

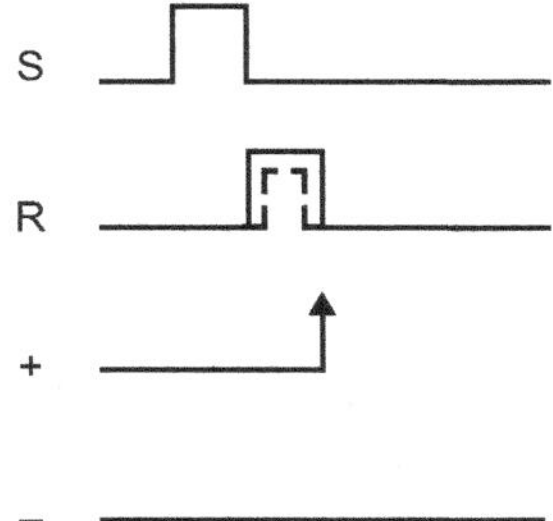

Figure 10.2 The superimposition of two figures taken from Woods (1974); signaled **emission** reward conditioning and signaled **omission** reward conditioning. (The solid line represents the presence of a response, and the dotted line represents the absence of a response. The + represents a consequence having positive reinforcing properties, and the – represents a consequence having negative reinforcing properties. Upward deflections indicate onset, and downward deflections indicate offset. The letter S represents stimulus, and R represents response.)

demonstrates that they entail the same type of learning; not two distinctly different forms of learning as was then thought. We now know that both types of conditioning occur because of experience-dependent plasticity; i.e., both forms of conditioning are caused by the same biological mechanisms.

Tryon (1995) noted that PDP-CNN models can explain many classical conditioning phenomena including: stimulus summation; blocking; unblocking; overshadowing; partial reinforcement effects; interstimulus effects; second order conditioning; conditioned inhibition; latent inhibition, extinction, reacquisition effects; backward conditioning; compound conditioning; discriminative stimulus effects; inverted-U in learning as a function of interstimulus interval; anticipatory conditioned responses; secondary reinforcement; attentional focusing by conditioned motivational feedback; superconditioning; and learned helplessness (Commons et al., 1991; Donegan et al., 1989; Gluck & Thompson, 1987; Grossberg & Levine, 1987; Grossberg & Schmajuk, 1987, 1989; Hawkins, 1989; Kehoe, 1988, 1989; Klopf, 1988; Sutton & Barto, 1981). See Burgos (2010), Donahoe and Packard-Dorsel (1997), Mignault & Marley (1997), Schmajuk (2010), and Tesauro (1990) for further details.

Classical Conditioning Treatments

The clinical relevance of classical conditioning principles is that they constitute some of our most effective clinical treatments. For example, the classical conditioning method for treating **enuresis** introduced by Mowrer and Mowrer (1938) is highly effective and as useful today as it was decades ago. The following link to a vendor of the required equipment indicates that the alarm method is currently the only cure for enuresis.[7]

Classical conditioning principles have been used to explain and treat nausea due to cancer treatment (Stockhorst et al., 1993). The basic problem with cancer treatments is that the person develops a taste aversion to whatever they ate prior to nausea-inducing chemotherapy. Given diet variation, chemotherapy can produce taste aversion to many foods, thereby causing the person to eat less when, if anything, they should be eating more. Moreover, eating healthy foods during chemotherapy creates taste aversion for them, resulting in a less-healthy diet subsequent to chemotherapy. The solution is to condition the taste aversion to a distinct taste that is already not preferred; say grape lollipops for instance. Consistently sucking on a grape lollipop before and during chemotherapy will condition taste aversion to it, leaving other foods alone.

[7] http://bedwettingstore.com/bedwetting-facts-treatments.html?&gclid=CKPDiteBu7QCFUWo4AodwTUARg

Hollands et al. (2011) used classical conditioning to increase the positive evaluation and choice of health foods. Participants were randomly assigned to either an evaluative conditioning (EC) or control group. Participants in the EC group saw pictures of energy-dense snack foods followed by images of potentially adverse consequences. Participants in the control group only saw images of snack foods. Conditioning resulted in more negative implicit attitudes towards energy-dense snack foods and a preference for fruit on a behavioral choice test compared to participants in the control condition.

Conditioned taste aversion has been successfully used to preserve wolves in the wild. Lacing a dead cow with nausea producing lithium will take cow meat off the wolf diet much more rapidly and certainly than hunting and/or trapping will.

Addictions

Tomie (1995) described classical conditioning research that is relevant to overcoming temptation, especially drug-related temptation. A condensed report of this research is provided by Kirsten Weir (2012).[8] The key insight provided by this research is that making the response manipulandum and the discriminative stimulus one and the same thing increases responding well above what it is when they are physically separated; i.e., when the discriminative stimulus is located on one wall and the response manipulandum is located on the opposite wall. Tomie (1995) refers to this as the cue and manipulandum (CAM) condition. Tomie described responding under CAM as 'excessive and compulsive' (p. 147).

Breland and Breland (1961, 1966) reported a related instance where raccoons were trained to pick up wooden coins and deposit them through a small slot into a metal box. This behavior was rewarded with a morsel of food. While training went well for a while, additional training resulted in the following misbehavior. The raccoons began to delay getting their reward by handling, chewing on, partially depositing and then retracting the coin, and in the end rarely deposited the coin to receive food. The raccoons became obsessed with the wooden coins. This misbehavior was not limited to raccoons. The Brelands discovered similar behaviors when training pigs, squirrels, monkeys, chickens, turkeys, otters, porpoises, and whales. This misbehavior is especially likely when a small object serves as a discriminative stimulus that signals reward and also serves as the response manipulandum. Contact with such a discriminative stimulus displaces using it as a response

[8] http://www.apa.org/monitor/2012/10/temptation.aspx

manipulandum to obtain a reward. Continued contact with the discriminative stimulus when such is not functional demonstrates that this contact is compulsive and therefore abnormal.

Tomie (1995) claimed that CAM-induced behaviors resembled human drug addiction, in that drug-taking implements induce drug-taking responses. Tomie cited 14 studies demonstrating physiological reactions to alcohol-related glassware parallel those to alcohol itself. Here the sight of alcohol-related glassware elicits a conditioned response that parallels the unconditioned response of actually consuming alcohol. Tomie then cited five studies demonstrating physiological responses to hypodermic syringes and needles that are parallel to physiological responses to opium. Then he also cited seven studies demonstrating physiological responses to cocaine-taking inplements such as tooters, sniffers, and vials as to cocaine itself. Here we have a conditioned response to the implements of drug taking that parallels the unconditioned response of actually taking drugs. The clear clinical application of these results is to avoid all of the conditioned stimuli.

Saunders and Robinson (2010) reported that some organisms are more succeptible to these conditioned cues than others. They conditioned rats to food and noted their conditioned response to food cues. Then they conditioned the same participants to cocaine. Participants who demonstrated stronger conditioning to the food cues also demonstrated stronger conditioning to the cocaine cues. Mahler and de Wit (2010) assessed cue-induced conditioning in 15 smokers after they abstained from smoking and again after they abstained from food. They reported that participants who had a stronger conditioned response to smoking also had a stronger conditioned response to food. This finding is supported by Weir (2012), who reported that obese people are more completely conditioned to food cues than are people of normal weight.

Chapter 11 discusses place conditioning which occurs when traumatic events are conditioned to the place in which they occurred. For example, a car accident tends to make the car an unsafe place. Being in the car tends to recall being in the accident.

BIOFEEDBACK

The technology of biofeedback has developed considerably over the past several decades. A PubMed search on 8 September 2013 for 'Biofeedback Therapy' returned 8,470 articles. Schwartz and Beatty (1977), Basmajian (1979), Olton and Noonberg (1980), Hatch et al. (1987), and Engel (2000) surveyed clinical applications of biofeedback. Montgomery's (2002) survey of clinical applications of electromyography, finger temperature, electrodermal, and electroencephalogram biofeedback is divided into several sections depending upon the degree of empirical support. His list of well-established biofeedback applications include: ADD/ADHD; anxiety disorders; asthma; chronic back pain; diabetes mellitus; essential hypertension; fecal and urinary incontinence, fibromyalgia; irritable bowel syndrome; motion sickness; muscle rehabilitation; Raynauds; and tension and migraine headaches. Montgomery's list of applications supported by multiple research studies includes Dyschezia (anismus), esophageal spasm, forearm and hand pain from repeated motion syndrome, hyperhydrosis, insomnia, nocturnal enuresis, specific seizure disorders, TMJ or MFP, and writer's cramp.

The vast majority of these publications bear on the effectiveness and efficacy of biofeedback as an intervention. However, the question remains why biofeedback work has remained largely unexamined and unanswered. The fact that biofeedback skills take time to acquire strongly implicates learning. Schwartz and Beatty (1977) presented three explanatory bases: control systems; operant conditioning; and cognition. Engel (2000) emphasized the role of operant conditioning. None of these explanations is satisfactory.

We now consider a connectionist explanation of biofeedback. The right-hand portion of Figure 10.3 presents a simple feed-forward connectionist network that represents the brain. It was derived from a parallel version of the classic stimulus–organism–response (S–O–R) model. The 'S' nodes represent that portion of the network responsible for perception. The single layer of 'O' nodes represents that portion of the network responsible for processing what is perceived. The single layer of 'R' nodes represents that

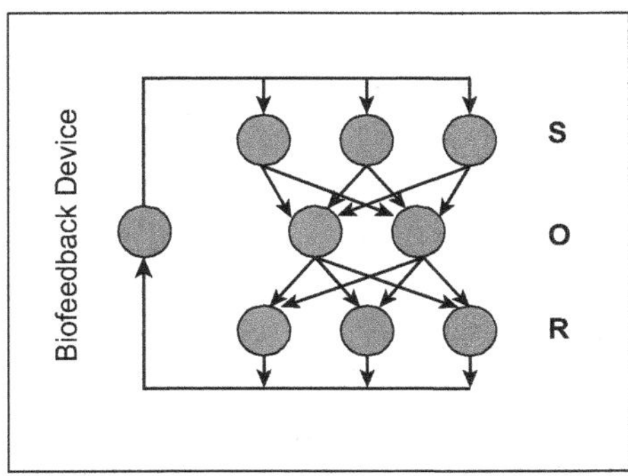

Figure 10.3 Connectionist model of biofeedback.

portion of the network responsible for activating those aspects of anatomy that enable behavior. The lines connecting the S, O, and R nodes represent synapses. Brain plasticity means that synaptic properties of excitation and inhibition change as a result of processing.

On the connectionist view, biofeedback alters normal network architecture by providing a temporary new connection between the output (R) and input (S) layers that transforms a feed-forward network into a recurrent network. The biofeedback device temporarily provides a new pathway by which experience can modify the long-term excitation and/or inhibition of synapses connecting the 'S' and 'O' neurons and the 'O' and 'R' neurons. This arrangement makes the biofeedback apparatus an integral part of the learning context. The biofeedback device also amplifies and thereby clarifies, makes more salient, the extent to which desired and actual physiological output differ. Since learning is driven by such discrepancy, procedures that amplify, quantify, and make it salient through visual and auditory display should facilitate learning. The neuroscience evidence that supports this explanation is both extensive and well accepted, as noted above.

The neural architecture diagrammed in Figure 10.3 is also consistent with the control systems theory in several ways. First, it entails the essential feedback loop. Second, the increases in synaptic weights implement the positive feedback aspect of control systems explanations, whereas the decreases in synaptic weights implement the negative feedback aspect of control systems explanations. Homeostatic control systems explanations can be formulated in connectionist terms. There appear to be no control systems explanations that cannot be formulated in connectionist terms. Hence, connectionism has an explanatory scope that is at least as large as that of control systems theory. An important advantage of the connectionist formulation over control systems theory is that software is currently available from a variety of vendors (cf. Tryon, 1995a) for simulating learning in these and related networks. The mathematical properties of networks and how they learn is receiving attention from mathematicians, biologists, computer scientists, and engineers, among others. Connectionism provides an active link to the work of these investigators.

The connectionist explanation provided above is also consistent with operant conditioning explanations in several important ways. First, and perhaps foremost, defining learning in terms of synaptic change, which can be independently measured thus avoiding the circular definitional problem of reinforcement. The concept of learning thereby acquires the more solid theoretical basis presumed by Engel (2000) and others.

Second, each simulated neuron in a PDP-CNN learns through association, which grounds this form of learning in biological science. Third, Black et al.'s (1977) operant explanation based on reinforcement for reducing a discrepancy between desired and actual behavior is how the connectionist Delta rule and back propagation of error procedures implement connectionist learning. It is important to note that the Delta-learning rule in connectionist networks is mathematically equivalent to the Rescorla–Wagner model of Pavlovian conditioning, which makes these two learning explanations the same.

Fourth, many conditioning phenomena have been successfully simulated using PDP-CNNs including: stimulus summation; blocking; unblocking; overshadowing; partial reinforcement effects; inter-stimulus interval effects; second order conditioning; conditioned inhibition; latent inhibition; extinction; reacquisition effects; backward conditioning; compound conditioning; discriminative stimulus effects; inverted-U in learning as a function of inter-stimulus interval; anticipatory conditioned responses; secondary reinforcement; attentional focusing by conditioned motivational feedback; superconditioning; and learned helplessness (Commons et al., 1991; Tryon, 1995a).

Fifth, Donahoe extensively articulated the compatibility between connectionism and conditioning (Donahoe, 1991, Donahoe & Palmer, 1989). Connectionism appears to explain all of the same phenomena that operant conditioning does. The explanatory extension of connectionism is therefore as large as that of operant conditioning. Connectionism completes operant explanations by providing proximal causal mechanisms for behavioral variation and selection.

IMPLICATIONS FOR CLINICAL PRACTICE

Learning as Professional Identity

If clients did not learn from their therapy sessions, then psychotherapy would not be effective. The only substantive differences among psychological interventions pertain to what should be taught and how best to teach what needs to be learned. '**Therapists, and the therapeutic approaches that currently divide us, differ only with regard to what is to be learned and how it is to be acquired**' (Tryon, 2010b, p. 10). These facts certify learning as a core component of professional practice and a core element of professional identity.

DiGuiseppe (2008) suggested '... that we explore what unites behavior therapy' (p. 155). I propose that our interest in learning and memory is what unites us and provides us with a solid and useful professional identity (Tryon,

2010b). Learning requires memory and memories are learned. Learning and memory are two facets of one major psychological mechanism. We can confidently conclude that all clinically effective empirically supported psychological interventions entail learning.

Neuroscience replaced our theories of learning (e.g., Bower & Hilgard, 1997) with detailed mechanism information regarding how experience-dependent plasticity (EDP) enables learning to occur and memories to form through the modification of synaptic architecture and function. Tryon (2012) and Tryon and McKay (2009) provided an overview of some of this mechanism information. Squire et al. (2008), Bear et al. (2007), and Carlson (2010) provided many more details. The *Journal of the American Academy of Child & Adolescent Psychiatry* informed child psychiatrists about the clinical implications of biological learning mechanisms (cf. Lombroso & Ogren, 2008, 2009). Operant and respondent[9] conditioning may have been the first two controlled methods that were used to systematically study the functional relationships between experience and behavior, but people learn in other ways as well, e.g., observational learning. Psychologists deferred to psychiatrists regarding diagnosis who then developed the *Diagnostic and Statistical Manual* (DSM) series that now dominates psychological research and clinical practice. Will psychologists now further defer to psychiatrists regarding learning and lose a second opportunity to lead our field?

Behavior therapy was once said to be based on modern learning therapy. Eysenck (1964) wrote, 'Behaviour therapy may be defined as the attempt to alter human behaviour and emotion in a beneficial manner according to the laws of modern learning theory' (p. 1). Wolpe and Lazarus (1966) wrote that behavior therapy entailed, '... the application of experimentally established principles of learning' (p. 1). Wolpe (1969) defined behavior therapy as '...the use of experimentally established principles of learning for the purpose of changing unadaptive behavior' (p. vii). It turned out that these definitions of behavior therapy were mainly aspirational because learning theory was in disarray at the time and only partially able to support clinical practice (cf., Tryon, 2000a, 2002c). Kazdin (1979) correctly pointed out that there was no modern learning theory that all, or even most, behavior therapists accepted so behavior therapy could not possibly be based on modern learning theory. The cognitive revolution (Bandura, 1978; Dember, 1974;

[9] Respondent conditioning is also known as classical conditioning for which Pavlov is generally credited. However, Pavlov was not a psychologist. He was a biologist who studied digestion until he was approximately 65 years of age. Only then did he concern himself with the influence of the frontal lobes on behavior. Pavlov is better characterized as a neuropsychologist than as a behaviorist.

Gardner, 1985; Mahoney, 1974, 1977; Meichenbaum, 1977) that swept psychology in general and behavior therapy in particular, during the 1970s promised to provide a better theoretical basis for generating new treatments than behaviorism did. Unfortunately, the cognitive revolution did not provide anything but informal theory. We have gone from not having a learning theory to not having a cognitive or cognitive-behavior theory. The proposed Bio↔Psychological Network Theory provides the missing theoretical support for behavioral and cognitive-behavioral practice that includes principles of operant and respondent conditioning. A primary implication of learning for the professional practice of clinical psychology is that it can return our identity as a professional whose practice is based on a truly modern learning theory, just as the founders of behavior therapy once proposed.

Interdisciplinary Teams

A second clinical implication of the learning/memory principle is that psychologists who practice in medical settings can now correctly claim to provide biological treatments. Learning-based treatments modify synaptic properties. Whereas pharmacologists promote short-term synaptic modifications through psychotropic medications, psychologists promote longer-term brain changes by learning-based therapies (DeRubeis et al., 2008). This behavioral medicine perspective may enhance appreciation of psychologists' work in medical settings as part of an interdisciplinary team.

Psychotropic Medications

A third clinical implication of the learning/memory principle is to enable psychologists to explain why neuroleptic drugs work, and therefore to explain to clients why they should continue to take these medications. Compounds that alter synaptic properties effectively: (a) alter connection weights among network processing nodes, neurons; that (b) change the network activation cascade processes that; (c) change how the network transforms stimulus microfeatures into latent constructs and that; (d) changes how people think, feel, and behave.

THEORETICAL ISSUES

We now consider several issues that concern learning and memory. Selectionism is Skinner's explanation of learning. It is also how PDP-CNN models implement learning. The necessity for neural network models continues this important discussion. The ability to explain both stability and change is crucial for all models of learning and memory. Finally, I show how the Bio↔Psychology Network Theory is fully consistent with Piaget's assimilation/accommodation cognitive engine.

Selectionism: Ontogenetic Evolution

You are probably familiar with Darwin's theory of phylogenetic evolution and its basis in variation and natural selection. You may also know that Darwin's theory was instantly controversial upon its publication in 1859. Sentiment at the time can be expressed as: let's hope that it is not true and if true, let's hope that it does not become widely known. Today one might add: let's keep it out of public education and home school our children if need be. What you may not know is that Darwin's theory was also firmly rejected by most of his scientific peers, biologists, because he could not explain the physical basis of variation and/or selection. Remember, this was before we understood anything about genetics. Darwin was said to have offered only a **functional** theory which was understood to be but a **partial** explanation because he lacked a proximal causal mechanistic explanation for: (a) how variation was instantiated; and (b) what exactly got selected. Tryon (1993b) reviewed some of this history. Bowler (1983), Catania (1978, 1987), Donahoe et al. (1993), and Mayr (1982) reported that Darwin's theory was marginalized for approximately 75 years. It was only after the introduction of population genetics, known as the modern synthesis, that Darwin's theory was fully acknowledged and accepted to where Darwin is now considered to be the father of modern biology and his theory the centerpiece of biological science. This history conclusively demonstrates the crucial role played by plausible proximal causal mechanism information in scientific theories.

This history lesson is relevant to clinical psychologists because it demonstrates how theory impacts professional identity. Very few biologists identified with Darwin when he first published his findings on evolution. Today, every biologist identifies with Darwin. Darwin was once ridiculed as a biologist. Today he is revered as a biologist. All of these changes in professional identity resulted because population genetics provided the missing mechanism regarding: (a) how variation was instantiated; and (b) what exactly got selected. I submit that the missing mechanism provided by the proposed Bio↔Psychological Network Theory can do for psychology what population genetics did for biology, and will dramatically change the professional identity of clinical psychologists. Specifically, I predict that B. F.

Skinner will be restored to a position of professional prominence because his ideas are very parallel to those of Darwin.

Skinner (1966, 1975, 1984a, 1984b) advanced an ontological evolutionary theory of behavior that was the functional equivalent of Darwin's phylogenetic theory of evolution. Skinner observed and reported experiments demonstrating behavioral variation and how it could be shaped via systematic selection. He used the term reinforcement to refer to behaviors whose probability could be increased by contingent consequences. In the same way that web feet appeared to be the result of divine creation because they worked so well for aquatic birds, but were really caused by variation and selection, Skinner argued in a parallel way. He claimed that many behaviors that appeared to be the result of free will and personal decision were actually the result of variation and selection. But he could not explain how this variation was instantiated, nor could he explain how selection worked. Most psychologists and nearly all clinical psychologists accordingly rejected Skinner's theory, methods, and findings.[10] These unknown processes constituted the proverbial 'black box' that Skinner left to the brain sciences to study and cognitive psychologists rejected in favor of functional cognitive theories that could not offer any real explanation because they could not provide any proximal causal mechanism information.

Rosenberg's commentary on Skinner's (1984b) article emphasized how crucial the missing theory was and is for the theory of ontogenetic evolution.

> Just as evolutionists have progressively found the required causal intermediaries between selection and evolution, so operant psychologists *must* find causal intermediaries between reinforcers and operants," and "Operant psychology *must* find a mechanism parallel to the physical factors on which fitness supervenes (pp. 495-6).

But Skinner and his followers insisted, as they continue to do today, on limiting their inquiry to functional explanations based on the experimental analysis of behavior, thereby forcing a clean break with cognitive psychologists. The cognitive revolution (see Bandura, 1969, 1977, 1978; Dember, 1974; Gardner, 1985), which began in the late 1960s, reduced the number of psychologists who do basic and/or applied research into the experimental analysis of behavior to a small and dwindling group of aging people who train very few students. Membership statistics from 2011 for Division 25 of

[10] Readers who question this claim should count the number of references to Skinner's work published in the last decade in journals where clinical psychologists publish. The virtual absence of these citations supports my claim.

the American Psychological Association, Behavior Analysis[11] show 625 members. That is but 625/71, 274 = 0.00877 or less than 1% of APA members. In effect, Skinner has been marginalized at least as much, if not more, than Darwin was during his 75 years of scientific exile.

My aim here is that the proposed Bio↔Psychology Network Theory will re-establish the importance of selectionist explanations for clinical psychologists, and in doing so will reposition B. F. Skinner as a relevant theoretician to all clinical psychologists. The next section continues this argument.

Necessity for Neural Networks

Skinner's marginalization continues because of reasons presented by Tryon (1993b) and more recently by Donahoe (1997) in his paper entitled 'The Necessity of Neural Networks'. Donahoe and I have somewhat different but converging reasons for this view. Necessity is a strong term, but one that I believe is warranted. It suggests that the scientific future of research concerning the experimental analysis of behavior requires inclusion of connectionist modeling. My view (Tryon, 1993b) is that Skinner's functional theory is scientifically inadequate, and has been rejected by most psychologists because it lacks mechanism information. The cognitive revolution provided cognitive explanations of clinically relevant behavior. These cognitive explanations did not include findings from the experimental analysis of behavior. Hence, clinicians, and most experimental psychologists, rejected Skinner's approach to psychology. The inability of Skinner to provide mechanism information capable of explaining how and why his empirically supported principles worked is responsible, in my view, for his scientific exile, because the lack of mechanism information was Darwin's problem and the reason for his scientific exile. Skinner did not have either a biological or a psychological explanation to offer, and therefore his functional explanation was abandoned in favor of a promised cognitive explanation that was never delivered. But psychologists will not be going back to the functional behavioral explanations that they have rejected.

The explanatory nucleus, our core Principles 1–4 presented in Chapter 3, provides the required plausible proximal causal mechanism information for understanding how behavioral variation and selection work. This information serves the same theory construction function for ontogenetic evolutionary theory that population genetics provided for

[11] http://www.apa.org/about/division/div25-2011.aspx

phylogenetic evolutionary theory. Principle 3: Transformation makes our network theory a cognitive theory. Hence, we have a cognitive explanation of operant conditioning that fully incorporates explanation by selection, thereby theoretically uniting operant conditioning with cognitive psychology. This is a major theoretical synthesis/advance and one that has key implications for clinical psychology. In particular, this mechanism information provides clinical psychologists with a modern learning theory upon which they can base rationale for their clinical interventions. John Donahoe (1998) is a radical behaviorist who has defended explanation by selection. He and his like-minded associate David Palmer favorably reviewed a seminal book on connectionism (Donahoe & Palmer, 1989) and have written about neural networks (Donahoe & Packard-Dorsel, 1997) and their necessity regarding the future of operant conditioning (Donahoe, 1997).

PDP-CNN models of operant conditioning have also been successfully developed and tested (Dragoi & Staddon, 1991; Grossberg, 1971; Nargeot et al., 1999a,b; Seung, 2003; Spencer et al., 1999). Applied behavior analysts continue to formulate clinical cases successfully and prescribe effective individualized treatments based on operant conditioning principles.

Donahoe (1997) focused on the explanatory parallel between Skinner's ontogenetic evolutionary explanations of behavior and Darwin's phylogenetic explanations of the origin of species. Donahoe (1997) argued that three elements, components, are needed to advance this parallel. (a) A functional selectionist principle is needed to modify behavior within the organism's lifespan. This already exists as the principle of reinforcement discussed above. (b) Biological mechanisms are needed to implement the functional changes referred to as reinforcement. They already are known to neuroscience as experience-dependent plasticity mechanisms that we reviewed in Chapter 3. (c) Quantitative techniques for tracing the cumulative effects of complex interactions of principles just mentioned in points (a) and (b) are needed. Donahoe firmly believes that neural network models can perform this crucial much needed role.

The proposed Bio↔Psychological Network Theory provides the required missing mechanism information in a way that is fully compatible with Skinner's selectionist position, is fully compatible with contemporary cognitive psychology, and is fully consistent with neuroscience. This consilient (cf. Wilson, 1998) achievement should bring operant conditioning technology back into the purview of cognitive behavior therapy as empirically supported principles of behavior change.

Stability vs. Change

A central scientific issue/problem for psychological science, developmental psychology, personality, learning theory, and therapeutic practices used by clinical psychologists is how to simultaneously explain **stability and change**. A theory that explains the stability of personality typically has trouble explaining developmental change, and in fact is likely to be falsified by evidence of change. Likewise, a theory that explains personality development typically cannot also explain personality stability, and in fact is likely to be falsified by evidence of stability. Our **Principle 1** explains **stability** in that if we take a snapshot of the network's **connectome** at a particular moment in time, which includes its structure, all interconnections, and their current weights, we can fully determine how it processes stimuli. The network's behavior is fully reproducible because you will get the same mathematical result every time you activate the same stimulus micro-feature nodes. Alternately stated, the structural stability of the network, the constancy of its architecture plus the stability of its excitatory and inhibitory connections, guarantees repeatable results. Here we can have complete stability, zero response variability regardless of how many trials are studied. No development is possible because no variation occurs.

Our **Principle 2** concerns, explains, **change**. Unlike computers that remain unchanged by the processing they do, real neural networks are changed by the processing that they do. These network modifications necessarily alter how the network processes stimulus activations. The resulting variability enables adaptation and development. Skinner (1989) correctly anticipated this fact when he wrote:

> We say the organism learns and stores rules. When, for example, a hungry rat presses a lever and receives food and the rate of pressing immediately increases, cognitive psychologists want to say that the rat has learned a rule. It now knows and can remember that "pressing the lever produces food." But "pressing the lever produces food" is our description of the contingencies we have built into the apparatus. We have no reason to suppose that the rat formulates and stores such a description. **The contingencies change the rat, which then survives as a changed rat** (p. 14, bold emphasis added).

In Chapter 3 we were quite specific about the ways in which the network changes because of experience-dependent plasticity mechanisms. Some of these changes are **structural**. Epigenetic tags that are attached or removed activate genetic mechanisms that add or remove dendritic spines and/or post-synaptic receptors. Other changes are **functional**. Epigenetic tags activate genetic mechanisms that synthesize, or inhibit the synthesis of, neurotransmitters that further activate or inhibit synaptic transmission. **Glial** mechanisms that modify functional network properties are also operative. Neurons that fire together wire together; are **biologically reinforced**. Circuits that are consistently not used are cannibalized to conserve energy; the brain version of'use it or lose it'. These biological mechanisms literally sculpt the brain in ways that cause it to adapt to the physical and social environment and therefore to develop across the lifespan. This adaptation process causes the brain to specialize in a particular language, culture, and personality style. In these ways the proposed Bio↔Psychological Network Theory fully explains both stability and change. This achievement strongly recommends that we professionally identify with this new theoretical perspective.

Piaget

Piaget (1983, 1985) is a major developmental psychologist that contemporary clinical psychologists essentially ignore. If clinical psychology is to be based on psychological science, then some way to incorporate Piaget into clinical psychology is important and crucial for clinical-child psychologists. I now show that the proposed Bio↔Psychology Network Theory incorporates Piaget's (1983, 1985) cognitive engine, driver of all cognitive development. It entails the reciprocal interaction of **assimilation/accommodation cycles**. Spitzer (1999) maintains that 'Almost by definition, assimilation and accommodation are present in any neural network model' (p. 196). Bechtel and Abrahamsen (1991) have succinctly described how connectionism might also provide a means to augment, reinterpret, or replace certain constructs in Piagetian theory (Piaget, 1952). Spitzer (1999) described matters as follows. '*Assimilation* means that an organism can only take in those parts of the environment that it somehow already knows. Every organism interprets the world according to its senses, perceptions, and cognitive structures' (p. 196, italics in the original). The architecture and connectome of a PDP-CNN model completely determine how it can process stimulus microfeatures. **Accommodation** refers to the real or simulated experience-dependent plasticity driven changes to the network; how the network is changed by the processing it does. Spitzer (1999, pp. 196–8) reviewed a neural network simulation of a Piagetian task where different-size weights are placed along a horizontal beam at various distances left and right of a fulcrum and children are asked which way the beam will tilt. The results replicated the stage-like behavior observed in children. This achievement grants us explanatory access to the rich history of empirical findings of Piagetian-based developmental psychology and that substantially expands the explanatory scope of the proposed Bio↔Psychology Network Theory.

Brain Sciences

Clinical psychology must embrace brain sciences if it is to be fully rooted in psychological science and to explain cognition, emotion, and behavior in physical rather than mental terms. Whereas some contemporary efforts are being made to incorporate brain sciences into psychology, Skinner off-loaded much of what constitutes cognitive psychology to neuroscience on the basis that they had the proper tools to study brain processes, as is illustrated by the following abstract from his 1986 *American Psychologist* article:

> Words referring to feelings and states of mind were first used to describe behavior or the situations in which behavior occurred. When concurrent bodily states began to be noticed and talked about, the same words were used to describe them. They became the vocabulary of philosophy and then of mentalistic or cognitive psychology. The evidence is to be found in etymology. In this article, examples are given of words that have come to describe the feelings or states of mind that accompany doing, sensing, wanting, waiting, thinking, and several other attributes of mind. The bodily states felt or introspectively observed and described in these ways are the subject of physiology, especially brain science (p. 13).

The remainder of Skinner's (1977) article is an exercise in explaining behavior without referencing any causal substrate in order to avoid cognitive terms and concepts. While artful, it seems to have left most psychologists wanting, as evidenced by the very few psychologists that currently identify with Skinner's approach. The proposed Bio↔Psychological Network Theory provides much of the missing mechanism information, and thereby reauthorizes clinical psychologists' interest in the empirically supported principles provided by Skinner's experimental analysis of behavior.

CONCLUSIONS

Learning is much more than conditioning. Conditioning is a form of cognition that activates experience-dependent plasticity mechanisms that modify neural networks such that they form memories and learn. Basic behavioral principles were reviewed. A taxonomy of operant conditioning was introduced as a way to guide behavioral diagnoses that pertain to etiology and provide therapeutic direction. A connectionist explanation of how and why biofeedback works was presented. Several theoretical issues were discussed that augment the need for clinical psychologists to think about cognition, emotion, and behavior in physical rather than mental terms. The next chapter discusses the clinical implications of the remaining network principles.

CHAPTER 11

Clinical Implications of Network Principles 3–12

Contents

Cognitive Neuroscience and Psychotherapy
http://dx.doi.org/10.1016/B978-0-12-420071-5.00011-9

This chapter discusses the clinical implications of Network Principles 3–12; they include: (3) Transformation; (4) Reactivation; (5) Priming; (6) Part–Whole Pattern Completion; (7) Consonance and Dissonance; (8) Dissonance Induction/Reduction; (9) Memory Superposition; (10) Prototype Formation; (11) Graceful Degradation; and (12) Top-Down vs. Bottom-Up Processing.

CLINICAL IMPLICATIONS OF PRINCIPLE 3: TRANSFORMATION

In Chapter 3 we learned that the neural network cascade necessarily transforms stimulus microfeatures into latent constructs, cognitions, via a process that is highly similar to factor analysis. The excitation and inhibition levels of real synapses, the positive and negative connection weights in simulated networks, function as factor loadings. Activation that passes over these connections is augmented or diminished accordingly. This process emphasizes the importance of some stimulus microfeatures and diminishes the importance of others, thereby forming a latent construct, concept, of the form that psychologists have accepted ever since Spearman (1904) introduced this procedure over a century ago. This mechanism, whereby mind emerges from brain, carries several clinical implications.

Learning-Based Interventions

Unlike computers that remain unchanged by the processing that they do, real and simulated neural networks are changed by the processing that they do. New learning modifies synaptic connections which mean that new learning modifies how transformations take place. Increasing activation at some synapses augments the importance of associated stimulus microfeatures in the transformed result. Decreasing activation at other synapses diminishes the importance of associated stimulus microfeatures in the transformed result. These altered transformations modify our thoughts and feelings that mediate our behaviors. They also modify our memories. Memory wells are composed of cognitive and affective components. Learning-based interventions alter their basins of attraction, thereby modifying what people recall. Because memories are superimposed upon one another new learning can modify many memories, including those that are only tangentially related to the objectives of the prescribed therapeutic new learning. The mechanics of memory formation and recall are discussed as part of Principle 6: Part–Whole Pattern Completion below.

The first implication of our transformation mechanism for clinical practice is that the small details, stimulus microfeatures, that client's notice are what get transformed into the constructs that modify and interact with their feelings to produce behavior. Therapists should therefore encourage their clients to pay more attention to positive details and less attention to negative details. Rehearsing and reminding themselves of the positive elements in their lives is recommended.

The second clinical implication of our transformation mechanism is that this transformative process is cumulative. It occurs during each processing cycle. Hence, cognitions, emotions, and behaviors can be expected to change gradually as well as simultaneously. This process can work negatively as well as positively. For example, rumination involves repetitive negative processing. Rumination is not problem-solving, although it resembles it. Rumination entails repetitive castigation that activates negative emotions. The cumulative result of rumination is that it exacerbates existing problems (Nolen-Hoeksema et al., 2008).

Professional Practice

Physicians are seen to treat biological problems with medications. Psychologists are seen to treat mental problems with psychotherapies. This sets up an adversarial relationship between physicians and psychologists. The transformation principle shows that psychologists are also producing biological changes by altering synaptic properties with learning-based interventions that activate experience-dependent brain plasticity mechanisms. The results of learning-based therapies can be seen with brain imaging. Whereas physicians prescribe medications that rather rapidly alter synaptic function, the learning-based interventions provided by psychologists take longer but produce more enduring outcomes (DeRubeis et al., 2008). These enduring outcomes are the product of long-term synaptic modifications that mediate and alter thoughts, feelings, and behaviors. This new common ground between medicine and psychology should authorize parity in terms of status, pay, and authority.

CLINICAL IMPLICATIONS OF PRINCIPLE 4: REACTIVATION

Principle 4: Reactivation[1] was introduced to focus upon a specialized form of activation that mediates memory. Reactivation pertains to the use of Principle 1: Unconscious processing via the network cascade to reset the connectome into the state it was in when memory first formed. These reactivations unavoidably and necessarily interact with other ongoing network cascades associated with processing contemporary stimulus microfeatures in ways that are both described and explained by **Network Principle 6: Part-Whole Pattern Completion**, discussed below. This means that the memory recall process is automatically modified by contemporary

[1] Redintegration is a related behavioral term (http://en.wikipedia.org/wiki/Redintegration).

processing, which explains how and why eye witness testimony can be contaminated by post- event information, as has been demonstrated in the section on 'False Memories' below. This dynamic process of reconstruction has disadvantages as well as advantages. The primary disadvantage of this process for clinicians is that it distorts patient reports of prior events, including medical ones, in ways that invalidate most items on structured interviews, as discussed by Malgady et al. (1992) and Rogler et al. (1992). The primary advantage of this process for clinicians is that it provides opportunities to therapeutically modify how the memory is reactivated in future.

Cognitive therapies depend upon the ability of post-event information to modify how memories are recalled as memory strongly influences how people think, feel, and behave. Dialectical behavior therapy (DBT) was developed by Linehan (1993) to treat persons with borderline personality disorder; especially their emotional dysregulation. Merwin (2011) considered anorexia nervosa and bulimia nervosa to be emotion dysregulation disorders and recommended that cognitive-behavioral interventions be expanded to address these issues. Mennin and Farach (2007) discussed how emotional regulation is being incorporated into treatments for adult psychopathology. Mennin and Fresco (2009) discussed emotion regulation as a framework for understanding and treating pathological anxiety. Mennin et al. (2005) presented preliminary evidence for an emotion dysregulation model of generalized anxiety disorder. Mennin et al. (2007) extended their emotion dysregulation model from anxiety to mood disorders. Emotion-focused therapy (see below) was developed to treat emotional dysregulation. Interventions that facilitate emotion regulation work because of Network Principles 4 and 6.

It is generally recognized that thoughts, feelings, and behaviors are causally interrelated, as indicated in Figure 11.1, if each side of the triangle is understood to entail a double-headed arrow indicating bidirectional causality. Behaviorists choose to intervene by modifying behavior on the basis that such treatment will also necessarily modify thoughts and feelings.

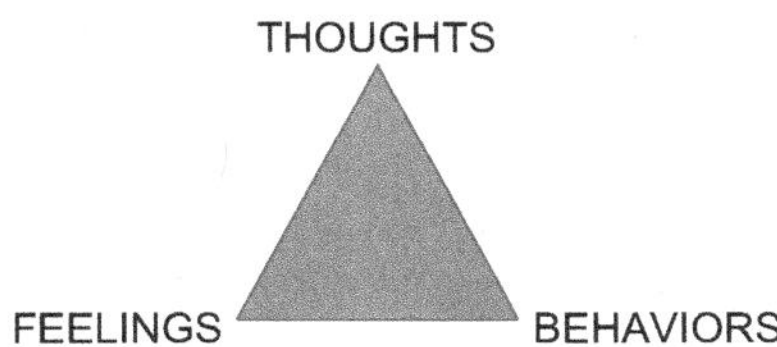

Figure 11.1 Bidirectional interaction among thoughts, feelings, and behaviors.

Cognitive and cognitive-behavioral therapists choose to intervene by modifying thoughts on the basis that such treatment will necessarily modify behaviors and feelings. Some psychodynamic therapists choose to intervene by modifying feelings on the basis that such treatment will necessarily modify thoughts and behaviors. It is this third clinical approach that I focus on in the next section. Traditionally, cognitive, behavioral, and psychodynamic theoretical perspectives have been seen as distinct, different, and even incommensurate and contradictory. The proposed network orientation understands these to be three clinical approaches/methods for producing new therapeutic learning, rather than the basis for establishing adversarial theoretical orientations.

Emotion-Focused Therapy

The main clinical reason for reactivating traumatic memories is so that they can be processed more adaptively before the memory is deactivated[2] because this additional processing necessarily modifies memory, which means that it will be recalled differently the next time that the memory is reactivated.[3] Greenberg (2002, 2008), Angus and Greenberg (2011), Paivio and Pascual-Leone (2010), and Pos et al. (2003) discussed emotion-focused approaches to therapy. Controlled research supports the efficacy of emotion-focused therapy (Ellison et al., 2009; Goldman et al., 2006a,b; Greenberg & Watson, 1998; Watson et al., 2003).

In Chapter 3 we emphasized the definition of learning provided by Carlson et al. (2010) who defined learning in terms of memory; '*Learning* refers to the process by which experiences change our nervous system and hence our behavior. We refer to these changes as *memories*' (italics in the original) (p. 440). If you are forming memories, then you are learning. Memories include emotions as well as cognitions, as we will better see when we discuss the bidirectional associative memory (BAM) model of post-traumatic stress disorder (PTSD) later in this chapter.

Emotion-focused therapy (EFT) is a way to modify the emotional component of memory. What follows is a brief overview of emotion-focused therapy. Greenberg (2002) did not cite the dual processing literature that we discussed in Chapter 2, but he acknowledged its content. The preface to his

[2] I chose the term activation to refer to memory retrieval in order to emphasize a network orientation. I also chose deactivation to refer to the point at which memory for an event ends for the same reason.

[3] I use the term reactivated instead of retrieved to emphasize that the connectome is being reset to a previous configuration.

book indicates that people are of two minds; one cognitive, the other emotional. Their cognitive system can become overly critical and dominated by negative beliefs assimilated from family, friends, and culture regarding what they should or ought to do. Their automatic emotional self sometimes requires professional emotion coaching in order to more effectively regulate and benefit from one's emotions. Emotional intelligence is central to this process. Greenberg's first chapter concerns emotions and emotional intelligence. His Exhibit 1.1 (p. 11) addresses how to use emotions intelligently. Included in his chapter are how emotions are understood as signals to oneself and to others. Emotions organize behavior for action. Emotions reflect the state of one's interpersonal relationships. Emotions send signals to other people. Emotion enhances learning. Emotional intelligence implies emotional regulation and selective expression. Emotional intelligence also concerns empathy; the ability to understand emotions in other people. Therapy is understood as emotional coaching. Greenberg's (2002) third chapter elaborates this position. His Chapter 4 details various steps involved in emotional coaching. The remainder of his book further elaborates how emotional coaching facilitates emotional awareness.

Greenberg (2008) wrote a chapter entitled 'The clinical application of emotion in psychotherapy'. He characterized EFT as follows:

> The objective of EFT is to access and restructure the habitual maladaptive emotional states that are seen as the source of the depression. This involves accessing feelings of shame-based worthlessness, anxious dependence, powerlessness, abandonment, and invalidation, and transforming these through accessing adaptive emotions (such as healthy grief and empowering anger), as well as reflecting on emotional experience to create new *meaning and develop new narratives* (p. 89).

Greenberg (2008) cited the following four studies as having demonstrated that a manualized form of EFT for depression was or was more effective than CBT, or a purely relational empathetic intervention, in relieving depression and also effective in preventing relapse; Greenberg and Watson (1998); Goldman et al. (2006a,b); and Watson et al. (2003). The remainder of Greenberg's (2008) chapter discusses ways that therapists can work with emotion to achieve therapeutic objectives.

The emphasis on 'reflecting on emotional experience to create new meaning and develop new narratives' (p. 89) mentioned above and the title of the book by Angus and Greenberg (2011) '*Working with Narrative in Emotion-Focused Therapy: Changing Stories, Healing Lives*' suggests a theoretical connection with hermeneutic psychoanalysis as discussed by Shaffer (1978). This connection is that both EFT and hermeneutic psychoanalysis seek to revise the client's personal narrative, the story that gives their life meaning, in a way that reduces their discomfort. Such **memory modification** is ethically acceptable because: (a) it relieves distress; and (b) people's recollection of past events is always inaccurate in various ways. The modified memory created by working with the person's narrative is likely to be as close to the truth on the positive side as the person's presenting narrative was on the negative side, in which case memory errors at the end of successful treatment are not more extreme than they were at the beginning of therapy; only their valence has changed.

Medications

Reprocessing or reactivated network states can be facilitated with medications. Memories change when they are reactivated.

Propranolol

The non-selective beta-blocker propranolol is used to treat hypertension because it moderates heart rate by dampening the nerve stimulation of adrenaline. Reactivating traumatic memories while taking propranolol should moderate the emotions associated with that memory. Hence, a less emotional memory should be restored and reactivated when next the traumatic incident is recalled. Hence, a progressive decrease in the emotionality of traumatic memories is expected. This is a form of desensitization. Pitman et al. (2002) employed just such a treatment. They randomized trauma victims to begin a 10-day course of double-blind 40 mg 4×/day propranolol ($n = 18$) versus placebo ($n = 23$) within 6 hours of the traumatic event followed by a 9-day taper period. Evaluations at 1 month post-trauma indicated that only 10% of patients in the propranolol group developed PTSD compared to 30% in the placebo group. Psychophysiological assessment (heart rate, skin conductance, EMG) revealed lower reactivity while listening to self-recorded trauma narratives at 3-month post-trauma.

Vaiva et al. (2003) reported results of 11 patients who received 40 mg or propranolol 3×/day for 7 days followed by an 8–12-day taper compared to eight patients who refused propranolol but agreed to participate in the study. Both groups were matched on demographics, exposure characteristics, physical injury severity, and peri-traumatic emotional responses. Two months after trauma, PTSD rates were 1 of 11 or 9% for patients taking propranolol and 3 of 8 = 38% for patients refusing the medication.

Stein et al. (2007) were only able to recruit 10% of qualifying patients study, where they randomly assigned patients to receive 14 days of the beta-blocker propranolol (n = 17), the anxiolytic anticonvulsant gabapentin (n = 14), or placebo (n = 17) within 48 hours of trauma. Propranolol was started at 20 mg 3×/day and increased over 2 days to 40 mg 3×/day. Gabapentin was started at 300 mg 3×/day and increased over 2 days to 400 mg 3×/day. Outcomes assessed at 1, 4, and 8 months post-injury did not reveal any significant differences among the three groups regarding the development of PTSD.

D-Cycloserine

The predominant model of fear conditioning suggests that habituation does not erase fear. Decrements in avoidance behavior occur because of new learning that inhibits the previously learned fear (Bouton, 1993). Newcomer and Krystal (2001) demonstrated that learning and memory depend heavily upon the glutamatergic NMDA receptor. D-cycloserine (DCS) is a partial agonist of the glycine binding site on NMDA receptors. Hence, DCS facilitates learning because it facilitates binding of glutamate to NMDA receptors. Research with animals has shown that NMDA antagonists inhibit extinction (Falls et al., 1992). Norberg et al. (2008) conducted a meta-analysis of the DCS literature on animals and humans published between June 1997 through September 2007. They concluded that DCS was effective at facilitating extinction in humans as well as in animals.

Animal Research

Barad et al. (2006) and Davis et al. (2006) reviewed the animal research and found that habituation to feared stimuli is enhanced when preceded by the administration of DCS. LeLong et al. (2001) demonstrated that DCS treatment facilitates learning. Ledgerwood et al. (2003) demonstrated that DCS treatment facilitates extinction of conditioned freezing in rats. Ledgerwood et al. (2004) subsequently replicated this effect and further demonstrated that DCS-treated animals are resistant to fear reinstatement. Ledgerwood et al. (2005) demonstrated that DCS treatment reduces untreated as well as treated fears; i.e., has a generalized effect. Parnas et al. (2005) demonstrated that repeated DCS treatment can interfere with extinction facilitation effects that fully recover after 28 days of no DCS treatment.

Human Research

Ressler et al. (2004) extended the animal studies to the treatment of acrophobia in humans. This study used a double-blind placebo controlled design for the administration of DCS to a group of 28 participants seeking treatment for acrophobia. Exposure treatment was administered using a virtual reality software package for fear of heights. DCS was administered 2–4 hours prior to participation in the exposure sessions, and administered in either 50 mg or 500 mg doses. There was no significant difference in improvement due to dosage. Treatment effects were found to be durable at 3-month follow-up. Furthermore, DCS did not have an effect on baseline anxiety. That is, in the absence of exposure treatment, DCS had no effect on anxiety.

Hofmann et al. (2006) reported that DCS is effective as an adjunct to exposure therapy for social anxiety disorder (SAD). Twenty-seven participants enrolled in the study, all with SAD and prominent public-speaking fear. Hofmann et al. used a double-blind design for administering DCS, in 50 mg doses. Treatment took place over five sessions, in either individual or group form. This study showed that participants taking DCS improved to a significantly greater extent than those who did not receive the medication. While both groups continued to improve at 1-month follow-up, the group who received DCS showed significantly greater improvement.

Guastella et al. (2007) reported DCS to be effective in the treatment of subclinical spider fear. This study used a double-blind design in the administration of 50 mg of DCS, compared to placebo. These investigators did not find a significant effect for DCS in alleviating fear in their participants following a single session of DCS plus exposure therapy for spiders. However, the authors noted that the effectiveness of DCS may not be obvious in nonclinical participants, or that a dose at that level (50 mg) may not be sufficient to activate their NMDA receptor sites.

Heresco-Levy et al. (2002) evaluated the efficacy of DCS in the treatment of post-traumatic stress disorder (PTSD) using a double-blind placebo controlled crossover design with 11 participants with a variety of traumatic reactions. DCS was administered at 25 mg twice daily. This is unlike more recent trials of DCS where the medication is taken only immediately preceding the active therapy, typically 1–2 hours prior to treatment. Participants were enrolled in therapy for 12 weeks. The authors found equivocal results for DCS and placebo. However, repeated administration of DCS has been found to have a limited benefit in facilitating learning and memory through the NMDA receptors (Davis et al., 2006). Therefore, any trial using DCS should rely on administration only prior to sessions of CBT, rather than as a standing dose. Tsai et al. (1999) reported cognitive enhancement in patients with Alzheimer's disease subsequent to short-term DCS treatment.

In summary, it appears that DCS holds promise for the treatment of anxiety disorders when administered just prior to sessions involving exposure-based interventions. Dosing of DCS is of critical importance given the sensitivity that accrues to this medication at the NMDA site. Dosing also must be at a sufficient level to activate the NMDA receptors during exposure.

CLINICAL IMPLICATIONS OF PRINCIPLE 5: PRIMING

Priming comes in several forms and therefore has multiple clinical applications. One of the more recent applications concerns a relatively new treatment called **cognitive bias modification** (CBM). This treatment primes patients with positive words and situations in order to help them respond in a more positive way to counteract the negative associations that they have developed. CBM presumes that children and adults naturally process information in a biased way and that these biases are exacerbated by certain experiences, thus sensitizing them to anxiety-inducing cues resulting in exaggerated responses and the need for clinical intervention in some cases. Repetition and semantic priming appear to be part of this etiology. Hallion and Ruscio (2011) conducted a meta-analysis of CBM across 45 studies ($n = 2{,}591$). They reported that CBM significantly reduced symptoms of anxiety but not depression.

Attention Bias

MacLeod et al. (1986), Mathews and MacLeod (1985), and Mogg and Bradley (1998) have shown that anxious people are automatically hyperattentive towards potentially threatening material. Watts et al. (1986) and Martin et al. (1992) have shown that this tendency slows color naming on the emotional Stroop test because attention to the threat word competes with attention to the color name. For example, Martin et al. (1992) reported that children fearful of spiders took longer to name the color of words such as 'creepy' and 'hairy' than to name the color of words such as 'table' and 'cars'. A meta-analytic review by Bar-Haim et al. (2007) supports these effects.

Vasey et al. (1995, 1996), Dalgleish et al. (2001), and Taghavi et al. (1999) reported evidence of biased attention in children using the dot-probe detection task described in Chapter 4. Attention biases prime the network in undesirable ways that clinicians need to address and correct as much as possible.

Interpretation Bias

Disproportionally interpreting ambiguous situations as threatening constitutes an interpretation bias. Barrett et al. (1996), Bögels and Zigterman

(2000), Chorpita et al. (1996), Dineen and Hadwin (2004), Hadwin et al. (1997), and Taghavi et al. (2000) provided evidence that higher levels of anxiety are associated with and likely cause interpretation bias. These interpretation biases prime the network in undesirable ways that clinicians need to address and correct as much as possible.

Reduced Evidence of Danger (RED) Bias

This bias is a variation on the interpretation bias mentioned above. Children read stories line by line. They are told that some of these stories have a good ending and others have a bad ending, and their task is to determine as rapidly as possible which ending each story has. Alternatively stated, children are to decide as soon as possible if the ending to a story is going to be scary or not. It is noteworthy that this assessment method is partly a projective test in that it taps the existing state of the child's network to complete a pattern. This test activates Network Principle 6 regarding part–whole pattern completion, discussed below and in Chapter 4.

Muris et al. (2000a,b,c, 2003a,b, 2007) have all shown that anxious children have RED bias. The clinical concern here is to minimize this bias. Because priming is a central etiological process, priming can also be used therapeutically.

Memory Bias

The tendency to selectively recall memories that are congruent with a current emotional state is called memory bias. Whereas Williams (2001) documented memory bias in adults, less research has been done with children. However, Daleiden (1998), Dalgleish et al. (2003), Moradi et al. (2000), and Watts and Weems (2006) have reported evidence of memory bias in children. Discussing how memory bias works may help normalize your client's symptoms and may help them cope better with this bias. Understanding memory bias is important for developing coping strategies.

Origins of Cognitive Distortions

Muris and Field (2008) identified two main sources of cognitive distortions: genetics and environmental factors. Genetics was the first source that they considered. They cited evidence by Eysenck (1967, 1992) that persons high on the heritable dimension of neuroticism are especially sensitive to threat information and are biased towards perceiving threat. Environmental factors were the second source that Muris and Field (2008) considered. Eley et al. (2003) reported that approximately 37% of the variance in child anxiety can be explained by non-shared environmental factors, and 18% can be explained by shared environmental factors, thereby documenting that the environment is a major contributor to childhood anxiety. Muris and Field (2010) discussed environmental factors in greater detail, including the role of children's books and the media.

Cognitive Bias Modification in Children

Lester and Field (2011) described a study that successfully modified children's interpretation bias about animal fear. Again I emphasize the relevance of the priming mechanism in this treatment.

Cognitive Bias Modification in Adults

Hertel and Mathews (2011) presented evidence that cognitive biases of attention, interpretation, and memory are not only associated with anxiety disorders, but appear to contribute to them. They discussed attention-training treatments designed to reduce attention bias and interpretation bias. They discussed procedures for changing memory designed to reduce memory bias. They also discussed connections with cognitive-behavior therapy.

Self-Disclosure

Getting clients to open up and disclose intimate personal details is a primary objective of clinical practice and a major source of client resistance. Priming can be used to foster self-disclosure. Grecco et al. (2013) used non-conscious priming to promote self-disclosure. They randomly assigned 50 volunteers to one of two conditions. One condition primed for self-disclosure; the other group primed against self-disclosure. Participants in the **disclosure** group were asked to unscramble 25 sentences favoring self-disclosure. They also provided ratings regarding how willing they were to talk about the content of each sentence to a stranger. Participants in the **non-disclosure** group were asked to unscramble 25 sentences discouraging self-disclosure. They also provided ratings regarding how willing they were to talk about the content of each sentence to a stranger. After priming, both groups wrote essays. The first essay was to describe the best thing that happened during the past month and how it made you feel. The second essay was to describe what you like the most about yourself. Participants in the disclosure group wrote significantly longer essays. Their essays also contained significantly more references to feelings. The general implication of this study is that clinicians can creatively prime for other behaviors that they wish to see in their clients.

Other Clinical Implications

Priming explains why repetition is important, both in treatment sessions and in homework. It also explains why subtle suggestions prepare clients for more direct interpretations or directives. We will see below that repetition can modify people's memories; a feature than can have either therapeutic or unfortunate consequences.

CLINICAL IMPLICATIONS OF PRINCIPLE 6: PART–WHOLE PATTERN COMPLETION

Part–whole pattern completion refers to the fact that a partial cue can, and often does, return a more complete memory (McClelland & Rumelhart, 1986; McLeod et al., 1998; O'Reilly & Munakata, 2000; Rumelhart & McClelland, 1986). The mechanics of this process can be visualized using Figure 11.2[4,5]. It provides a graphic representation of memory formation and recall that characterizes certain neural network models. As is the case with calculus and analytic geometry, some mathematical concepts can be illustrated graphically.

To understand this figure, think of its state before memory formation as a flat horizontal surface much like that of a trampoline. The act of memory **formation** warps this memory surface in the same way that putting a bowling ball does when placed in the middle of the trampoline. The memory corresponds to the bottom of the memory well; the point where the bowling ball would lie. Memory **recall** can be visualized as follows. Place a small marble anywhere on surface of Figure 11.2. If it rolls into the memory well and reaches the bottom, then the memory associated with these coordinates is recalled. Placing a marble almost anywhere on Figure 11.2, except perhaps at the outermost edge, will roll into the well. All of these starting positions that end up falling into the well define what is called the '**basin of attraction**' of the memory well. Stimuli associated with these loci are partial cues that will return the full memory. The process of memory recall is mathematically modeled as 'gradient descent' to the bottom of the well.

Readers should remember that this graphic is a **mathematical representation** of memory formation and recall. It is similar to how analytic geometry illustrates calculus facts. Such three-dimensional structures do not actually exist in the brain, but the mathematics that describes how some

[4] Memory wells have the same mathematical structure as gravity wells. Pitman and Orr (1990) referred to PTSD as 'The Black Hole of Trauma'.

[5] http://en.wikipedia.org/wiki/Gravity_well

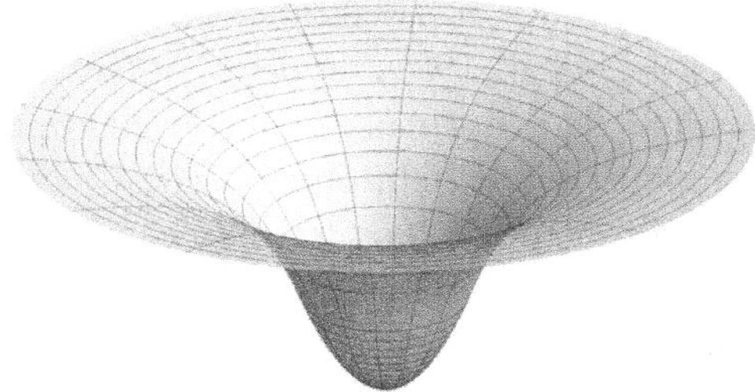

Figure 11.2 Image of a memory well. See text for explanation.

artificial networks operate can be visualized in this way and that makes their mechanics easier to understand.

Memories are constructed from cognitive and affective components. More intense cognitive and affective components result in more intense memories with broader basins of attraction and deeper wells. Alternatively stated, more strongly held cognitions, especially those that have strong emotional bases, create broad deep memory wells and therefore exert a strong influence on what is called the mind. Traumatic life experiences, as we shall see in the next section, can warp these memory wells to a pathological degree. Alternatively, psychological treatments designed to restructure cognitions and lessen emotions should shrink these memory wells to a more normal size, thereby restoring normal functioning. The formation of memory wells via experience and their modification as a result of psychological intervention is a general mechanism that informs clinical practice. The following sections discuss clinical implications of the part–whole pattern completion principle for PTSD, false memories, imagination inflation, and false confessions.

Post-Traumatic Stress Disorder

War, weather-related destruction by hurricanes, floods, typhoons, and tornados, automobile accidents, fire, and violent crime including rape, spousal and child abuse, can all create broad and deep memory wells. In some people, these memory wells are sufficiently broad and deep that they produce PTSD; the only DSM disorder with a known etiology. Treatments based on informal network theories of emotional processing and PTSD have been accepted for several decades. For example, Lang (1977, 1979, 1985) suggested that emotional images and related propositional constructs form a **visual-semantic network**. Foa and Kozak (1986) extended informal network theory to include emotional processing which results in gradual fear reduction (cf. Rachman, 1980). It has also been suggested that PTSD alters one's **fear structure** (Foa et al., 1989) rendering it larger, more intense, and more readily accessible than normal. A four-level **cognitive network**-based schema was proposed by Chemtob et al. (1988) and a five-stage network model was recommended by Creamer et al. (1992). Wilker and Kolassa's (2013) Figure 2 demonstrates that informal network models of PTSD are still being used despite the availability of formal models.

Dalgleish (1999) reviewed several cognitive theories of PTSD, but they all lack mechanism information. In general we prefer theories that provide more mechanism information than those that provide less mechanism information. Tryon's (1999) formal bidirectional associative memory (BAM) model provides more mechanism information than informal models do. In general, we prefer theories that have a larger explanatory scope because they can do everything and more than a theory with a more limited explanatory scope does; especially if the smaller explanatory scope lies totally within the larger explanatory scope. The Bio↔Psychological Network Theory introduced in Chapters 3 and 4 is a hybrid cognitive neuroscience theory that has a larger explanatory scope than any of the other cognitive theories reviewed by Dalgleish (1999).

Brewin and Holmes (2003) explained symptoms of PTSD using two memory systems. They stipulated that the '... automatic reactivation of situationally accessible knowledge' (p. 357) characterizes the amygdala-based situationally accessible memory (SAM) system. They referred to the cues that do so as 'reminders' (p. 357). While Brewin and Holmes (2003) did not use the term 'part–whole pattern completion' or its common synonyms, e.g., 'content-addressable memory' or 'state-dependent memory', their 'reminders'[6] work because of the part–whole pattern completion network principle. Brewin and Holmes (2003) also identified a hippocampal-based verbally accessible memory (VAM) system where one can deliberately retrieve memories (p. 356). This declarative memory also operates on the part–whole pattern completion principle (L. R. Squire, personal communication, May 12, 2010). For example, upon hearing that someone vacationed in New York City, one might recall aspects of his or her own visits to New York City. Tryon (1999) presented a bidirectional associative memory (BAM) model of this part–whole pattern completion process that meets all explanatory criteria identified by Jones and Barlow (1990) and Brewin et al.

[6] Creating a new term to refer to well-known content by other names impedes scholarship by suggesting originality where none exists.

(1996) and provides mechanism information for Brewin and Holmes's (2003) SAM and VAM systems.

Kosko (1987a, 1987b, 1988) formally introduced the bidirectional associative memory (BAM) model. Pittman and Orr (1990) suggested that such formal connectionist neural networks could help us understand PTSD. Li and Spiegel (1992) discussed neural network models of dissociative disorders, including PTSD. Tryon (1999) used the part–whole pattern completion property of the BAM to explain PTSD symptoms. The part–whole pattern completion principle enables people to reconstruct a more complete pattern from relatively few parts (McClelland & Rumelhart, 1986; McLeod et al., 1998; O'Reilly & Munakata, 2000; Rumelhart & McClelland, 1986). This phenomenon is also known as content addressable memory, because partial content can activate a more complete memory such as when someone mentions a vacation spot that you have visited and that returns memory of your vacation. Another name for this phenomenon is state-dependent memory, also called mood-congruent recall (cf. Blaney, 1986; Bower & Cohen, 1982; Isen, 1984; Matt et al., 1992; Teasdale & Fogarty, 1979; Williams et al., 1988). Happy people tend to recall happy memories whereas sad people tend to recall sad memories, because affect is part of the rich associative network that characterizes memory.

The BAM gets its name from the constructive memory generation process where memory cues are passed back and forth through a composite memory matrix. Each passage builds a more complete memory. This process is automatic, unavoidable, and continues until either a complete memory is constructed or memory recall becomes asymptotic; without further change. Affective and cognitive cues participate in this memory generation process.

Explanatory Criteria for PTSD

It is very unusual for one to be given a list of criteria for a complete explanation of anything in psychology or clinical psychology. However, Jones and Barlow (1990) and Brewin et al. (1996) produced similar lists of criteria for a complete explanation of PTSD. I now address each of these explanatory requirements and show that the bidirectional associative memory model satisfies all of them.

Normal vs. Abnormal Processing

Brewin et al. (1996) require that a comprehensive PTSD theory declare whether or not PTSD symptoms '...are themselves automatically indicative of an abnormal process' (p. 670). The BAM answer to this question is 'No'. PTSD occurs as the result of exaggerated but normal memory formation processes that result in oversized memory wells. I take the BAM as a useful model of normal memory formation mechanism information. Under normal circumstances it forms memory wells that are small versions of Figure 11.2 with relatively narrow basins of attraction and relatively shallow memory wells. Under traumatic circumstances, the BAM forms large versions of Figure 11.2 with relatively broad basins of attraction and relatively deep memory wells. Pitman and Orr (1990) reasoned by analogy that just as a black hole strongly warps space-time, so traumatic memories that spawn PTSD might severely warp memory by creating such large basins of attraction that PTSD can be accurately described as '**The Black Hole of Trauma**' (bold emphasis added). This is a much more dynamic and reactive process than are the classic symbol manipulating theories of memory that are based on a computer metaphor, where each bit of information is stored in just one small place whose physical size is inconsequential.

Trauma simultaneously modifies memory wells in two ways: (a) their basin of attraction becomes wider; and (b) the well becomes deeper. Trauma could possibly broaden the basis of attraction such that two or more memories merged to form a super basin of attraction. Consequently, stimuli that once would have recalled a normal memory by 'rolling' into its memory well may now flow to the global minimum of the super basin, thereby recalling a traumatic memory. Stated alternatively, the traumatic incident could warp the gradient of memory recall in such a broad way that previously innocuous stimuli may now recall memory for trauma. A normal memory formation mechanism has created an exaggerated memory. I conclude that PTSD exacerbates a normal memory process. Lacking mechanism information, answers to the process question posed by Brewin et al. (1996) by other authors means that their explanations are necessarily incomplete. They can only express an opinion on this subject, because they do not have mechanism information to support and justify their conclusions. Only by revealing the mechanics of how memories are formed can this question be adequately addressed and answered. Readers should therefore prefer the proposed Bio↔Psychology Network explanation on this basis alone.

Explain Clinical Symptoms

Both Jones and Barlow (1990) and Brewin et al. (1996) require that a comprehensive PTSD theory account for all diagnostic criteria. These authors cited the DSM-IV (APA, 1994) PTSD inclusion criteria that include: (a) persistently re-experiencing the traumatic event through memory; (b) persistent avoidance of stimuli associated with the trauma; (c) general emotional numbing; and (d) persistent symptoms of arousal. Each symptom is explained in the following sections.

Re-Experiencing Trauma Through Memory

Jones and Barlow (1990) specified that a comprehensive PTSD theory must explain why trauma is re-experienced through memory. The previously described super basin of attraction associated with traumatic memories provides the required mechanism information to explain why and how trauma is necessarily relived through memory. The increased breadth of the basin of attraction produced by traumatic memories incorporates stimuli relating to other memories. Whereas these stimuli once recalled normal memories they now return traumatic memories, because they now lie within the traumatic memories super basin of attraction. Explanations that lack mechanism information cannot firmly answer why trauma is re-experienced through memory. Only the proposed Bio↔Psychology Network Theory provides the required mechanism information.

Persistent Avoidance of Stimuli Associated with Trauma

DSM-IV requires that the patient avoid stimuli associated with trauma in order to be diagnosed with PTSD. The automatic part–whole pattern completion principle is sufficient to explain why persons with PTSD avoid all stimuli that could lead to recalling the traumatic memory. The Bio↔Psychology Network Theory and its associated bidirectional associative memory (BAM) model (cf. Tryon, 1998, 1999) is highly consistent with principles of operant and respondent conditioning (cf. Donahoe & Palmer, 1989), thereby authorizing the standard operant avoidance conditioning explanation to address this issue.

General Emotional Numbing

DSM-IV requires that a patient exhibit emotional numbing to be diagnosed with PTSD. The BAM enables us to understand emotional numbing as a direct consequence of, and corollary to, the memory recall process. Rumelhart et al. (1986) argued that we are only conscious of stable network configurations. This means that we are unaware of, and therefore are unable to control, the gradient descent process of memory recall. Like water running downhill, the locus of memory recall continues to descend into a traumatic super basin until it finds either a local minimum (possibly a normal memory) or a global minimum (traumatic memory). This property of memory recall is automatic and involuntary. The only way to avoid this uncontrollable slippery slope of memory recall (pattern completion) is to avoid all stimuli residing within the super basin of attraction. Because the person does not have this information, their best bet is to avoid stimuli of all kinds in the hope of avoiding traumatic memory recall. This means attempting to not think or feel anything that might initiate the pattern-completion process.

Mood regulates cognitive recall. State-dependent memory, also called mood-congruent recall, is an example of content addressable memory. People more readily recall positive events when happy and more readily recall negative events when sad (cf. Blaney, 1986; Bower & Cohen, 1982; Isen, 1984; Matt et al., 1992; Teasdale & Fogarty, 1979; Williams et al., 1988). The BAM model demonstrates content addressable memory for emotions as well as cognitions. Emotional numbing can be understood as an attempt to avoid unpleasant emotions that were stored in memory along with related cognitions. Emotional numbing can be understood as an attempt to prevent content addressable memory for emotions. This explanation is similar to the situationally accessible memories (SAMs) described by Brewin et al. (1996), but is based on mechanism information that they do not provide.

It is important to note that the psychodynamic concept of defense entails the concept of Ego repressing ID in the service of Superego. A similar view was provided by Creamer et al.'s (1992) extension of Lang (1977, 1985) and Foa et al.'s (1989) position that emotional numbing is a '... defense against the breakthrough...' of intrusive images (p. 452). This psychodynamic perspective differs markedly from the network view presented here. Emotional numbing is more accurately understood in the present context as an avoidance response, given the exaggeration of a normal memory formation and recall process. I understand that all avoidance responding can be construed as defensive in that it prevents the onset of aversive stimuli or the offset of positive stimuli. The main point here is that defensive avoidance is being effectively discussed in terms of part–whole pattern completion memory mechanisms instead of mentalistic terms Ego, Superego, Id, and repression.

Persistent Symptoms of Arousal

Such symptoms can be understood as a fear generated by accidentally encountering a cue that will trigger the uncontrollable automatic pattern-completion process resulting in the return of a full traumatic memory. The reality of this fear depends directly upon the frequency with which stimuli residing within the super basin of attraction associated with the traumatic memory are encountered. This depends upon the radius of the basin of attraction, in that larger-diameter basins of attraction will incorporate more stimuli and therefore a wider variety of stimuli which will make traumatic memory recall more frequent and therefore appear more persistent. The density of stimuli residing within the basin of attraction is also important, in that higher density means more stimuli which increase the probability of encountering one of them which raises the probability of traumatic memory recall and consequently appears more persistent.

Comorbidity

Brewin et al. (1996) also required that a comprehensive explanation of PTSD account for comorbidity. Fear that the part–whole pattern completion principle will return a traumatic memory explains the presence of anxiety. The helplessness caused by not being able to control the part–whole pattern completion network mechanism may be sufficient to explain the presence of depression. The tendency of patients to self-medicate either or both of these intense feelings is sufficient to explain the presence of substance abuse.

The requirement that a comprehensive PTSD theory explain comorbidity with other disorders assumes that specific reasons exist for why PTSD patients are comorbid that differ from the reasons why comorbidity exists for many DSM categories. Krueger et al. (1998) provided a general explanation for DSM comorbidity. They found evidence of a single factor underlying DSM-III-R diagnoses in a birth cohort at ages 18 and 21. Just as the intercorrelations among subtests of intelligence can be explained as the result of a single underlying factor called 'g' for general intelligence, comorbidity among DSM-III-R diagnoses can be explained as the result of a single underlying factor called 'P' for psychopathology. Persons higher in P will have greater severity and be more comorbid than persons lower in P. A better fitting structural equation model was obtained with two correlated factors: externalizing and internalizing disorders – the same factorial structure as is routinely found with children. Said otherwise, P is composed of correlated externalizing and internalizing factors. Hence, comorbidity can be viewed as a consequence of the multivariate structure of DSM entities. This means that there is nothing special about comorbidity for PTSD theories to explain. Nevertheless, I consider possible reasons for the specific comorbidities most frequently associated with PTSD in the following sections.

Generalized Anxiety Generalized anxiety disorder (GAD) shares similar dynamics with PTSD insofar as it too is understood to be a memory-based disorder that entails aversive emotions. There is no reason to expect that the memory mechanism that enables GAD differs from the memory mechanism that enables PTSD. The primary difference appears to be that GAD is mainly an emotional memory without the specific cognitive focus characteristic of phobias. This could occur because there are more emotional than cognitive cues for GAD than PTSD memories.

Depression Foa et al. (1992) reviewed the literature relating uncontroll ability and unpredictability to PTSD. This literature initially arose in connection with depression (cf. Peterson et al., 1993; Seligman, 1995). All of the reasons given by Foa et al. (1992) for why uncontrollability and unpredictability are relevant to PTSD can be cited as reasons why persons with PTSD are comorbid for depression. Their main point is that procedures used to induce experimental neuroses in general, and depression in particular, are traumatic. For example, Seligman and his colleagues typically administered many trials of uncontrollable and inescapable shock to induce helplessness and depression. The associated unpredictability and uncontrollability are likely to produce both anxiety and depression. Hence, these animal models pertain to PTSD as well as depression. Comorbidity of depression with PTSD is therefore explained on the basis of common causation via uncontrollable inescapable trauma that modifies memory in the ways described above.

Substance Abuse The BAM memory model of PTSD advocated here suggests two reasons why persons suffering from PTSD might abuse substances. On the basis that memories for traumatic events are less likely when in a positive than neutral or sad mood (state-dependent recall), it follows that persons with PTSD might try to artificially maintain a euphoric mood through substance abuse in order to prevent the pattern completion traumatic memory recall process from starting. Hence, alcohol, cocaine, and other mood elevators might well be abused. A second reason for persons suffering PTSD to engage in substance abuse would be to take drugs that interfered with memory recall. Excessive alcohol consumption, for example, impairs many aspects of cognition, including memory.

Individual Differences in Symptom Severity

Not everyone who is exposed to trauma develops PTSD. Jones and Barlow (1990) and Brewin et al. (1996) both require that a comprehensive PTSD theory must explain differences in symptom severity across persons. Ozer et al. (2003, 2008) investigated the following individual differences: (a) history of traumatic events; (b) prior psychological adjustment; (c) family history of psychopathology; (d) perceived threat to one's life during the traumatic event; (e) perceived social support following the traumatic event; (f) high levels of emotion during or after the traumatic event, peri-traumatic emotionality; and (g) dissociative experiences during or immediately after the traumatic event, peri-traumatic dissociation. These investigators reported that all of these individual differences were significantly related to PTSD, but that peri-traumatic dissociation was most strongly related (weighted $r = 0.35$). Dissociation exists on a continuum ranging from mild to severe. Tryon (1999) mistakenly attributed coping qualities to dissociation on the assumption that it might disrupt the formation of traumatic memory. Data presented by Ozer et al. (2003, 2008) contradicted this view and strongly suggested that extreme peri-traumatic dissociation marks the maximum possible psychological trauma that one can experience; the point where consciousness is disrupted. Stated otherwise, extreme peri-traumatic dissociation may function like a circuit breaker that disrupts consciousness when stress becomes intolerable. It may also mark a point of maximum adrenalization and consequently a point of maximum memory formation, thereby creating the deepest and widest memory wells that a particular individual can form. This perspective on peri-traumatic dissociation brings the BAM model in line with empirical evidence presented by Brewin and Holmes (2003) and by Ozer et al. (2003, 2008).

Brewin and Holmes (2003) reported that sometimes memory for traumatic events is clear and other times it is not. Their review showed that some studies found high levels of emotion associated with vivid memories of traumatic events, and other studies found only vague trauma memories. Brewin and Holmes did not explain why such disparate results occur. The formulation of peri-traumatic dissociation as a circuit breaker provides a possible explanation for contradictory findings. The process of memory formation may be corrupted at the point where consciousness is disrupted. Emotional microfeatures may become only partially integrated with cognitive microfeatures; that would explain why high levels of emotion do not always return traumatic memories. The relevant details of trauma memory formation may depend upon the complex chemical state of the brain at the time consciousness was disrupted; i.e., when memory formation 'crashed'. The psychological debris associated with such a serious memory crash may well determine how much anterior and retrograde amnesia occurs. The following three factors seem implicated in explaining variations in the severity of PTSD symptoms.

Factor 1 Variation in the frequency, intensity, duration, and/or controllability of the traumatic events should explain some portion of individual differences in symptom formation. PTSD symptom intensity is expected to vary in direct proportion to the frequency, intensity, and duration of these repeated traumatic events, such as the number and duration of military deployments in Iraq or Afghanistan. Herman (1992) and Terr (1991) distinguished between Type 1 traumas involving a single episode and Type 2 traumas involving repeated extreme stress. The super basin of attraction is hypothesized to broaden with more frequent trauma. Traumas differ with regard to intensity. More intense trauma is expected to result in broader and deeper traumatic memory wells and therefore produce more intense PTSD symptoms. Traumas vary in duration. Greater trauma duration is expected to broaden and deepen traumatic memory wells and therefore result in more intense PTSD symptoms. Helplessness, lack of controllability, during traumatic events varies. Lack of controllability appears to make aversive events more traumatic and thereby broaden and deepen memory wells. It is therefore expected that PTSD symptom severity is inversely proportional to the degree of controllability one has over important facets of the trauma. All four of these variables can be combined in varying degrees to explain the formation of mild to severe PTSD symptoms. Kolassa et al. (2010) provided clear evidence of a dose-dependent relationship between cumulative trauma, traumatic load, and the probability of life-time PTSD. Wilker and Kolassa (2013) reproduced this figure in their article. This evidence clearly supports this first factor. Wilker and Kolassa (2013) stipulated that careful trauma assessment is just as important as is correct PTSD diagnosis.

Factor 2 A second important factor underlying individual differences in symptom severity pertinent to our memory model is the effectiveness (completeness, quality, and duration) of memory formation and recall. Completeness refers to the proportion of details recalled. The pattern completion process is more complete for some people than others. Persons who correctly recall a greater proportion of details are hypothesized to have more severe PTSD symptoms than those who recall a lesser proportion of details. Quality of memory refers to memory fidelity. Persons who form high-fidelity memories and recall clear, distinct, and detailed memories in terms of sight, sound, feel, smell, and taste are hypothesized to develop more severe PTSD than are persons who form low-fidelity memories. This includes omitting entire dimensions as well as diminished fidelity. Duration refers to the temporal stability of memory. Memory fades with time faster for some people than others. Persons with more stable memories forget less over time and are expected to have more severe PTSD symptoms than are people with less stable memories. In short, the more realistic memory is for an individual, the more likely they are to develop PTSD in response to a traumatic event, and the more disturbed they are likely to be when re-experiencing trauma through memory. Wilker and Kolassa (2013) identified epigenetic modifications as partially responsible for individual differences in responsiveness to traumatic events and therefore in the development of PTSD.

Factor 3 A third factor is the efficiency of the pattern-completion memory retrieval process. I refer to the proportion of cognitive and/or emotional stimuli required to retrieve maximum memory understanding that the completeness and quality of memory varies as just discussed. People undoubtedly vary regarding the amount of partial information required to produce maximum recall. Some people may achieve maximum recall given only one or at most a few stimulus fragments. Other people may require more information. It is hypothesized that persons with efficient pattern-completion systems who obtain maximum recall on the basis of one or a few stimulus fragments will develop more severe PTSD than will persons with inefficient pattern-completion systems who require a larger proportion of cues to enable maximum recall.

Pattern-completion effectiveness and efficiency probably vary somewhat independently, are not perfectly correlated, thereby allowing us to talk about the interaction of these two abilities. We have assumed that memory cues are all equally effective; all equally salient. It is more likely that some stimuli are more salient than others. Some stimuli may be so salient that they are sufficient to trigger near complete recall, whereas other stimuli may be less salient.

Conditional Events David Dobbs (2012) reported on 'A New Focus on the "Post" in Post-Traumatic Stress' in the Tuesday December 25, 2012 issue of New York Times Science Times section. He reported on research conducted by Paul Plotsky, a neurobiologist at Emory University, who studied stress in rat pups by separating them from their mother for 15 or 180 minutes.[7] A 15-minute separation is normal because the mother needs to forage for food. Upon her return from a 15-minute separation the mother licks each pup, nurses them and sooths them with gentle ultrasonic warbles.

[7] http://psychiatry.emory.edu/faculty/plotsky_paul.html

All is well. The stress hormone levels in the pups are normal. Upon her return from a 180-minute separation she dashes about often stepping on her pups, emits panicky squeaks, and sometimes ignores them. The pups also squeal loudly. This trauma elevates stress hormones in the pups and makes them less able to cope with stress.

Dr. Plotsky discovered a confound in this research. The mothers and pups are reunited in the same cage from which the pups were 'kidnapped' by the experimenter. This could create a place conditioning effect.[8] When he reunited mother and pups in the anteroom of a new cage that was described as 'an eight-room condo', the mother moved her pups to a new room and then behaved as she did after a 15-minute separation. The pups showed few signs of stress. This separation procedure was repeated for eight consecutive days. Each time the mother and pups were taken from the 'kidnapping' cage and reunited in the same condo anteroom whereupon the mother took her pups to another room; often a new room.

This research demonstrates that place conditioning transforms the place in which the trauma occurred into a stressor. Reuniting the pups with their mother in the 'kidnapping' cage did not terminate stress for either the pups or the mother. The stress continued as long as they continued to live in that 'unsafe' place. This constant stress is likely what ultimately damages the animal's stress response.

The main clinical implication here is that place conditioning also constitutes a stressor in the lives of people. A person who continues to drive the same car that they had a traumatic automobile accident in will continue to be stressed by the place conditioning created by the accident. A person who was raped in their home will continue to be stressed by place conditioning as long as they continue living in that home. Natural variations in the severity and duration of place conditioning will likely determine individual differences in who develops PTSD and who does not. The epigenetic mechanisms identified by Wilker and Kolassa (2013) likely explain some of the individual differences regarding who develops PTSD.

A More Comprehensive Explanation

The proposed Bio↔Psychological Network Theory has at least three advantages over competing explanations of PTSD. First, it accounts for all of the published criteria for a complete explanation of PTSD. Second, it is a more

[8] http://psychology.wikia.com/wiki/Place_conditioning, http://en.wikipedia.org/wiki/Conditioned_place_preference

general theory than any of its competitors. Third, it provides mechanism information whereas none of its competitors do. An additional advantage of the BAM is that it is based on a theoretical orientation that has been shown to resolve several important theoretical schisms in psychology, as discussed in Chapter 2 and elsewhere (Tryon, 1993a, 1993b, 1995b, 1995c, 1995d).

Therapeutic Mechanism Information

Contemporary cognitive-behavioral interventions for PTSD implicate psychological and/or emotional processing as the basis for how therapeutic results are produced. These explanations lack specific mechanism information. The above discussion of memory wells and their construction from cognitive and affective components provides some of the missing mechanism information.

Loftus (1980, p. xiv) speculated that considerable psychological distress depends on memory including low self-esteem, anxiety, and worry. She argued that, in principle, one could cure these psychological disorders by replacing the offending memory base with a more positive and constructive one. This includes patients suffering from generalized anxiety disorder.

The role of memory in psychopathology is probably much broader than has traditionally been acknowledged. Attitudes, beliefs, expectations, and other similar cognitions are stored entities and therefore memories. While we may reason on the basis of our attitudes, beliefs, and expectations, memory forms the basis for such cognitive processing. It follows that this dependence on memory maximizes the relevance of the BAM to other DSM disorders.

False Memories

Clinicians rely on their clients to provide accurate reports about themselves and others, because their clients are either the only source of information they have or are the primary source of information they have regarding these matters. Psychologists have long known about the limitations of self-report, but routinely minimize or even dismiss these limitations when presenting 'clinical evidence' in support of a clinical claim about the client concerning their present, past, or future psychological state and/or behavior. Long ago Nisbett and Wilson (1977) reported that people unconsciously fill in memory blanks with plausible content as revealed by their title 'Telling more than we can know'. Schachter (1999) presented insights from psychology and neuroscience that he called the 'seven sins of memory'. Rogler, Malgady, and Tryon (1992) documented several common memory errors that raise serious questions about the validity of structured and unstructured interviews and diagnostic decisions based upon them. Network Principle 6 regarding part–whole pattern completion extends these clinical implications by providing mechanism information regarding how false memories are constructed. Experiments in forensic psychology have shown that leading questions and cues can cause people to fill in and report features that were not present originally, and to recall events that did not occur but that improve the suggested Gestalt (Loftus, 1996/1979, 2003; Brainerd & Reyna, 2005). Loftus and Pickrell (1995) induced a false memory in about 25% of children that they were once lost in a shopping mall when they were about 5 or 6 years old, an event that never occurred. Similarly, Heaps and Nash (2001) reported that about one third of children formed a false memory in which they believed that they nearly drowned but were rescued by a lifeguard. Porter et al. (1999) instilled a false memory in about half of the children they studied that they were the victim of a vicious animal attack. Principe et al. (2006) demonstrated that children who overheard an erroneous rumor from an adult conversation readily incorporated this event into recollections of their own experiences. In all these cases post-event cues are automatically and unconsciously incorporated into memory in ways that make the final result a good Gestalt; a consistent pattern.

Imagination Inflation

Imagination inflation refers to the ability of imagination to modify memory. There are several ways to produce imagination inflation. Imagination inflation can occur as a result of **counterfactual thinking** where people imagine events differently from how they actually occurred, including events that never occurred at all. **Upward** counterfactuals consist of alternative potential circumstances that are better than those that actually occurred and tend to elicit positive emotions, whereas **downward** counterfactuals consist of alternative potential circumstances that are worse than those that actually occurred and tend to elicit negative emotions (Garry & Polaschek, 2000). Normal people typically generally generate more upward than downward counterfactuals. Depressed and anxious people typically tend to generate more downward than upward counterfactuals. Catastrophizing consists primarily of downward counterfactual thinking. Negative affect automatically activates counterfactual thinking.

Imagining the past differently from what it was can change the way one remembers it (Garry & Polaschek, 2000). For example, Hyman and Pentland (1996) asked participants to imagine spilling punch all over the parents of the bride at a wedding or to merely think about doing so. Approximately one quarter of the participants who clearly imagined this event seemed to recall that it actually happened. Garry et al. (1996) reported that, when adults vividly imagined events that might have happened before they were ten years old, their confidence that these events actually occurred increased significantly. Paddock et al. (1998) replicated these results.

Prefactual events are events that have not yet occurred and may or may not actually occur at all. They are imaginary possibilities. Seligman et al. (2013) call them **prospections**. Gregory et al. (1982) reported evidence that rehearsing prefactual thoughts increased subjective confidence that the event would occur in future. Prefactuals also come in upward and downward forms that also elicit positive and negative emotions.

Imagination inflation occurs at least in part due to our Principle 6: Part–Whole Pattern Completion, because the imagined elements constitute parts that influence the whole Gestalt that constitutes the person's experience. Counterfactual details can complete a cognitive Gestalt in a way that is inconsistent with known facts. The dissonance that this creates is reduced by altering memory in ways that enable the post-event facts to make sense. Imagination inflation appears to be directly proportional to hypnotic suggestibility (Heaps & Nash, 1999) and dissociability (Paddock et al., 1998; Heaps & Nash, 1999); i.e., the tendency to confuse fact and fantasy.

False Confessions

Confession may be good for the soul, but it can be very damaging in forensic settings. Confessions are sought by police, prosecutors, and some psychologists who work for them, because of its evidential gold-standard status. The part–whole pattern completion principle can be used to convince suspects that they committed crimes of which they are innocent by presenting them with false, but incriminating, 'facts'. Continued questioning over many hours can induce people to change their reports until they constitute confessions (Kassin, 2005). Sometimes people are told that they can go home only after they confess. They do so on the false assumption that matters can be sorted out later. However, sometimes, remarkably, people who give false confessions actually recall engaging in the accused actions (Kassin & Gudjonsson, 2004).

Witnesses can be gradually led to a more certain and definite determination of the 'facts' in a case and become more certain of the identity of the persons they 'saw' at the scene of a crime by suggesting facts that are consistent with the suspect's guilt. To date (14 October 2013) there have been 311 DNA exonerations of suspects convicted by eye witness testimony.[9]

[9] http://www.innocenceproject.org/

Kassin (2012) discussed how false confessions produce a chain of confirmation biases that are especially difficult to overcome when the person on trial is truly innocent.

CLINICAL IMPLICATIONS OF PRINCIPLE 7: CONSONANCE AND DISSONANCE

A great deal of empirical research supports the principle that people seek cognitive consonance in the same way that perception follows the Gestalt laws of good form (prägnanz). Heider (1958) proposed that unbalanced attitudes motivate psychological and/or behavioral change in order to rebalance the person's perspective. Festinger (1957, 1964) rephrased consonance as dissonance, proposed that cognitive dissonance is aversive, and made various predictions regarding psychological and behavioral change for reducing dissonance that have been very well supported[10] (see Abelson et al., 1968 for 84 chapters of scientific support). Kunda (1990) reviewed extensive empirical support for the hypothesis that people endeavor to reach the conclusions that they want to reach to reduce dissonance[11] while attempting to appear rational and reasonable.

> There is considerable evidence that people are more likely to arrive at conclusions that they want to arrive at, but their ability to do so is constrained by their ability to construct seemingly reasonable justifications for these conclusions (p. 480).
>
> People do not seem to be at liberty to conclude whatever they want to conclude merely because they want to. Rather, I propose that people motivated to arrive at a particular conclusion attempt to be rational and to construct a justification of their desired conclusion that would persuade a dispassionate observer. They draw the desired conclusion only if they can muster up the evidence necessary to support it. In other words, they maintain an 'illusion of objectivity'... To this end, they search memory for those beliefs and rules that could support their desired conclusion. They may also creatively combine accessed knowledge to construct new beliefs that could logically support the desired conclusion. It is this process of memory search and belief construction that is biased by directional goals. (pp. 482–3).

Bastardi et al. (2011) reviewed research that supports Kunda's (1990) conclusions cited above. They also reported the results of a study showing that

[10] I continue to be amazed that Festinger was allowed to build an illustrious career by rephrasing Heider's consonance as dissonance. He and his students could have based all their impressive experiments on Heider's theory, but instead he took the toothbrush approach (see Chapters 1 and 9) and behaved as if he had discovered something entirely new.

[11] Readers should alternatively read 'reduce dissonance' as 'increase consonance'. People want to appear rational and that requires them to appear consistent, which here means consonant.

the interpretation of scientific evidence can also be biased by what is believed to be true beforehand.

That people selectively attend to and 'cherry-pick' information from memory, archival sources, and their current environment to support previously arrived at emotionally held convictions while maintaining the illusion that they are being objective is very familiar to social and clinical psychologists. Motivational interviewing uses this social psychological research foundation as a theoretical basis for explicitly using dissonance induction and reduction methods in the treatment of substance abuse and for health coaching (Miller & Rollnick, 2002; Tashiro & Mortensen, 2006).

Being able to construct a coherent story from a set of observations constitutes what Rychlak (1968, 1981a) described as **procedural evidence**; the basis of proof from the Kantian perspective. The evidence reviewed in Chapter 4 on apparent behavior by Heider and Simmel (1944) and by Leslie and Keeble (1987) strongly suggests that our tendency to accept procedural evidence as convincing is a System 1 defect directly analogous to our willingness to accept and be persuaded by visual and cognitive illusions. It is a normal but irrational human trait that Kahneman (2011b) suggested that we can become aware of so that we can compensate for it rather than succumb to it. This is as true for therapists as for clients. Alternatively stated, therapists can unwittingly act as irrationally as their clients. This is especially true when writing up reports of psychological testing where the ability to write a coherent report, one where the test results agree with one another, are consistent with each other, is frequently taken as solid clinical evidence. Caution should be exercised on the basis that coherence is not proof of causation, any more than correlation is and perhaps less so. Students are frequently warned against misinterpreting evidence of statistical correlation as proof of causation in statistics classes. Unfortunately, they are encouraged to interpret evidence of coherence among clinical facts as proof of causation in psychopathology and psychological testing classes.

In sum, the primary clinical implication of Network Principle 7 is that people naturally strive for consonance; to reduce dissonance. People tend towards self-consistency. This includes automatically and unconsciously detecting and minimizing discrepancies between thoughts and feelings, with the result that emotions can seriously warp cognitions. Emotions seem to have a greater effect. Cognitions appear to be warped to whatever degree is needed in order to become consistent with emotions. This process typically stays within normal bounds, but can become pathological when emotions become extreme.

CLINICAL IMPLICATIONS OF PRINCIPLE 8: DISSONANCE INDUCTION AND REDUCTION

The dissonance induction/reduction (DI/R) principle has the greatest direct relevance of all our 12 network principles to clinical practice, because it is the primary mechanism, active ingredient, that explains why all effective treatments work regardless of the theoretical orientation from which they originated.

Why Effective Treatments Work

Establishing a working alliance and engaging clients (G. S. Tryon, 2002) so that they return for subsequent sessions are clearly crucial, because without them there will be no opportunity to implement the treatments that induce and reduce dissonance that activate the experience-dependent plasticity mechanisms that modify and sculpt the brain so as to bring consonance to thoughts, feelings, and behaviors that are more beneficial than those that the client came to therapy with. Unfortunately, dissonance can also be reduced in counterproductive anti-therapeutic ways as clinicians who do motivational interviewing can attest (Miller & Rollnick, 2002; Tashiro & Mortensen, 2006). The healing art here is to manage both the dissonance induction and the dissonance reduction phases of therapy in a productive way.

Tryon (2005) discussed how Network Principle 8 explains why empirically supported treatments for anxiety work. Tryon and Misurell (2008) discussed how Principle 8 explains why empirically supported treatments for depression work. Principle 8 also explains why the unified protocol described by Allen et al. (2008) and Barlow et al. (2011) for treating a broad array of emotional disorders works. I submit that Principle 8 explains why all effective treatments work regardless of the theoretical orientation that gave rise to them. This means that the dissonance induction/reduction principle is a common active ingredient across all effective psychotherapies. Therefore this principle alone enables substantial theoretical unification and psychotherapy integration.

Clinicians are presently free to choose how they wish to implement the DI/R principle because there is no research that compares clinical methods for doing so. Undoubtedly, some methods will be found to be more effective at implementing this principle than others. Some methods of implementing this principle may work better for men than women, for older than younger clients, for minority and majority clients, and across all other dimensions of diversity. This research will be about clinical technique. Differences will concern clinical pragmatics rather than scientific principle, and therefore will not serve as a basis for isolating psychologists into competing schools and camps. The integrative principles of respect, flexibility, inclusion, interaction, attention to common factors, patient–treatment matching, stage–treatment matching, and empiricism discussed and promoted by Greben (2012) will naturally follow if and when clinicians unite around Principle 8.

Any list of clinical methods for implementing the DI/R principle that has been conditioned upon diversity dimensions will need to be adjusted depending upon the client's reaction to them. Clients who resist one method of implementing the DI/R principle may need to be treated with an alternative method of implementing the same principle. Additional details follow in the next two sections.

Mechanism Information and Psychotherapy Integration

Authors of new treatments tend also to provide a rationale for why it works, because treatments are based to some degree on the preexisting theory that the author of the treatment believes in. Clinicians who find the treatment interesting typically accept the provided explanation without question. When evidence of efficacy and effectiveness are provided belief in the associated explanation grows. Evidence of therapeutic effectiveness is commonly taken as proof that the associated theory is correct, but such conclusions may well be wrong. This reasoning is incorrect because it is illogical. It is illogical because treatments can work for reasons other than those provided by the theory that gave rise to the treatment in question. **It is quite possible for clinicians to do the right things for the wrong reasons**. Inferring theoretical validity from therapeutic efficacy and effectiveness commits the logical fallacy of affirming the consequent.[12] This fallacy has the following form:

1. If P, then Q
2. Q
3. Therefore, P.

The Wikipedia example of this fallacy is as follows:

1. If Bill Gates owns Fort Knox, then he is rich.
2. Bill Gates is rich.
3. Therefore, he owns Fort Knox.

[12] http://en.wikipedia.org/wiki/Affirming_the_consequent

In our case the logical error takes the following form:

1. If Theory X is correct then Treatment Y is effective.
2. Treatment Y works.
3. Therefore Theory X is correct.
4. Not necessarily!

It is entirely possible that treatments can work for very different reasons than the authors of the interventions believe. While science typically proceeds by affirming the consequent, doing so remains illogical despite the fact that it has often been useful to reason and proceed in this way. Below I illustrate this disconnect between theory and treatment by reviewing several explanations of why systematic desensitization and exposure therapy were thought to work. This material is a condensed summary of Tryon (2005). I begin by considering and rejecting six standard explanations for how systematic desensitization works, before proposing a network explanation that I believe does a better job. Then I extend this explanatory approach to the treatment of depression, thereby providing a common mechanism for treating anxiety and depression. I argue that proponents of existing treatments simply differ in the ways that they implement the relevant network principles.

Systematic Desensitization of Anxiety Disorders

We can effectively treat anxiety disorders but cannot explain why our ESTs work. Tryon (2005) reviewed the theoretical bases typically used to explain why **systematic desensitization and exposure therapy** work and found all of them defective. I briefly review each of them below.

Reciprocal Inhibition

Wolpe (1958, 1969, 1995) originated the treatment known as systematic desensitization. He explained its effectiveness using Sherrington's (1906/1961) physiological principle of reciprocal inhibition. Muscle relaxation was said to reciprocally inhibit anxiety. Consequently, patients were trained in deep muscle relaxation prior to undergoing systematic desensitization using Jacobson's (1938) methods, because this treatment entailed imagining fearful scenes while deeply relaxed. Wolpe's explanation seemed completely obvious and unquestionably correct when it was proposed. This explanation was widely accepted by investigators and clinicians alike. While a few studies have provided empirical support for the view that relaxation is a necessary component of systematic desensitization (Davison, 1968; Kass & Gilner, 1974) others have not (Miller & Nawas, 1970; Nawas et al., 1970). Agras et al. (1971), Cooke (1968), Craighead (1973), Crowder and Thornton (1970), Freeling and Shemberg

(1970), and Waters et al. (1972) reported that phobic anxiety is reduced whether or not relaxation training is used. It does not appear necessary to pair relaxation with imagery during desensitization (Aponte & Aponte, 1971). The crucial and telling experiment on this matter was conducted by Davison (1966). He used curare to temporarily paralyze all muscles in the body. Life support for his participants was provided by what then was called an Iron Lung that mechanically respirated each participant. The primary result was that participants could still feel anxiety! This result clearly falsified the hypothesis that muscle relaxation reciprocally inhibits anxiety, and therefore falsified Wolpe's (1958) explanation of how and why systematic desensitization works.

Additional negative evidence followed. Yates (1975) conducted a literature review and concluded 'Systematic desensitization is effective in reducing phobic anxiety, whether relaxation training is part of the program or not' (p. 156), and '… neither individualized hierarchies nor any special way of presenting the hierarchies are critical to the success of desensitization' (p. 158). Marks (1975) concluded that systematic desensitization is no more effective than graded exposure. This article gave rise to the term '**exposure therapy**'. Emmelkamp (1994) also concluded, based on a review of the empirical literature, exposure to phobic stimuli without avoidance is the essential ingredient in effective behavioral treatment for anxiety disorders.

Counterconditioning

The long-term benefits of systematic desensitization also required explanation. Wolpe (1958) used Guthrie's (1952) concept of counterconditioning to explain these long-term benefits (cf. Davison, 1968). The central idea here was that systematic desensitization replaced anxiety with relaxation. Davison (1968) maintained that counterconditioning was the long-term behavioral equivalent of the physiological process of reciprocal inhibition. This view was falsified by the finding that flooding (Miller, 2002) and implosive therapy (Levis, 2002) are effective and they are not thought to replace one emotional state with another, thus contradicting the counterconditioning hypothesis. Van Egeren (1971) and Van Egeren et al. (1971) reported little evidence in support of counterconditioning. Marks (1975) reviewed the empirical literature and concluded that systematic desensitization with relaxation is no more effective than graded exposure.

Habituation

Clinical psychologists frequently use the term habituation to explain anxiety decrements. This practice was begun by Harris (1943) who defined habituation as a 'response decrement due to repeated stimulation' (p. 385). Hence, the fact that clients become less anxious with multiple treatments implied that they habituated to anxiety cues. Lader and Mathews (1968) used the definition of habituation proposed by Harris (1943) to explain why systematic desensitization was effective. Lader and Mathews (1968) explained the effectiveness of systematic desensitization on the basis of this functional definition of habituation. However, habituation is rather more complex than that. Habituation is a non-associative form of learning. Thompson and Spencer (1966) identified nine conditions that must exist before one can claim habituation as an explanation. These criteria were expanded by Rankin et al. (2009). Wikipedia[13] describes the characteristics of habituation as follows:

- Repeated presentation of a stimulus will cause a decrease in reaction to the stimulus. This characteristic is consistent with the definition of habituation as a procedure, but to confirm habituation as a process additional characteristics must be demonstrated.
- Spontaneous recovery is observed. That is, a habituated response to a stimulus recovers (increases in magnitude) when a significant amount of time (hours, days, weeks) passes between stimulus presentations. After the initial 'recovery', responding returns to its habituated level with subsequent stimulus presentations.
- 'Potentiation of habituation' is observed when tests of spontaneous recovery are repeatedly made. In this phenomenon, the decrease in responding that follows spontaneous recovery becomes more rapid with each test of spontaneous recovery.
- An increase in the frequency of stimulus presentation (i.e., shorter inter-stimulus interval) will increase the rate of habituation and the 'size' of the response decrement.
- Within a specific sensory quality (e.g., hearing), weaker stimuli presentations will elicit stronger habituation.
- Continued exposure to the stimulus after the habituated response has plateaued (i.e., show no further decrement) may have additional effects on subsequent tests of behavior, such as delaying spontaneous recovery.
- Stimulus generalization and stimulus discrimination will be observed. Habituation to an original stimulus will also occur to other stimuli that are similar to the original stimulus (*stimulus generalization*). The more similar the new stimulus is to the original stimulus, the greater the habituation that will be observed. When a subject shows habituation to a new

[13] http://en.wikipedia.org/wiki/Habituation

stimulus that is similar to the original stimulus, but not to a stimulus that is different from the original stimulus, then the subject is showing *stimulus discrimination*. (For example, if one was habituated to the taste of lemon, their responding would increase significantly when presented with the taste of lime.) Stimulus discrimination can be used to rule out sensory adaptation and fatigue as an alternative explanation of the habituation process.

- A single introduction of a different stimulus late in the habituation procedure when responding to the eliciting stimulus has declined can cause an increase in the habituated response. This increase in responding is temporary and is called 'dishabituation' and always occurs to the original eliciting stimulus (not to the added stimulus). Researchers also use evidence of dishabituation to rule out sensory adaptation and fatigue as alternative explanations of the habituation process.
- Habituation of dishabituation can occur. The amount of dishabituation that occurs as a result of the introduction of a different stimulus can decrease after repeated presentation of the 'dishabituating' stimulus.
- Long-term habituation. The previous nine characteristics describe behavioral changes that occur during a habituation procedure in a single session or day. Some habituation procedures appear to result in a habituation process that last days or weeks. Habituation that persists over long durations of time (i.e., show little or no spontaneous recovery) is called long-term habituation in order to distinguish it from the short-term habituation identified by the nine characteristics listed above.

Four points listed above deserve special mention: (1) Lader and Mathews (1968) did not demonstrate that all of these conditions were met. (2) A decrease in response is not by itself sufficient to certify the presence of habituation. (3) Habituation is a **temporary** phenomenon and therefore cannot possibly explain the enduring long-term benefits of systematic desensitization. Van Egeren (1971) and Yates (1975, p. 165) both recognized the short-term nature of habituation. Hergenhahn and Olson (1993, pp. 4, 12) and Kalat (2003, pp. 383–4) noted that habituation generally entails a short-term response reduction given repeated stimulation. Systematic desensitization produces long-term response reduction. Therefore, systematic desensitization cannot be explained as habituation. Kandel (1991) reported that massed habituation can produce effects that last 3 weeks. This is known as long-term habituation. However, these effects do not last nearly as long as do the benefits of systematic desensitization, and therefore cannot possibly explain these benefits. The temporary nature of habituation should be widely known but apparently not among clinical psychologists. (4) Habituation can be disinhibited by additional stimulation. Hergenhahn and Olson (1993, p. 4) and Kandel (1991) have shown that sensitization can reverse habituation. Fortunately no such cancellation of the therapeutic effects of systematic desensitization has been reported. This fact alone is sufficient reason to conclude that systematic desensitization is not caused by habituation.

Extinction

Extinction produces a temporary increase in response strength followed by a gradual decrease in response strength. This gradual decrease gave rise to the hypothesis that the therapeutic effects of systematic desensitization were caused by extinction. For example, Waters et al. (1972) explained that the ability of systematic desensitization to treat phobias was based on extinction.

Extinction requires that a specific target response not be followed by reinforcement; i.e., the absence of onset or offset of stimuli with positive or negative reinforcing properties contingent upon either the emission or omission of a response. No specific 'response' is obvious during systematic desensitization. Hence, extinction cannot account for why systematic desensitization works.

Response decrement is explained in terms of the lack of reinforcement. Exposure or exposure plus non-avoidance are only partially consistent with an extinction explanation, because a complete extinction explanation needs to: (1) define the target behavior; (2) define the reinforcer; and (3) show that no onset or offset of the reinforcer occurred contingent upon either the emission or omission of the target behavior. The empirical literature on systematic desensitization does not strongly support the third criteria and only partially supports the other two. More importantly, extinction is a functional concept that lacks mechanism information. Behaviorism cannot explain why failure to reinforce a behavior causes its frequency to decrease. Extinction is a behavioral concept. Hence, extinction entails no mechanism information capable of explaining how or why systematic desensitization works. Wolpe (1995) criticized the extinction explanation on the basis that it lacked mechanism information and that it was falsified by his clinical experience; i.e., anxiety did not naturally extinguish. McGlynn et al. (1981) noted that '... exposure theory is not an explanation of therapeutic desensitization effects. Rather, it is simply a hypothesis concerning the necessary and sufficient procedural ingredients within the technique. The therapeutic effects of the exposure remain to be explained (e.g., as extinction, as counterconditioning, as habituation)' (p. 154). We have already seen that there is little supportive evidence for these explanations.

Two-Factor Model

Mowrer (1960) proposed that fear is acquired according to classical conditioning principles and is maintained by operant conditioning principle; i.e., escape and avoidance are reinforced by anxiety reduction. According to the two-factor model, fear is initially classically conditioned and then maintained by avoidant operant conditioning. McAllister and McAllister (1995) and McGlynn (2002) proposed that Mowrer's (1960) two-factor theory could explain why exposure therapy worked.

However, Menzies and Clarke (1995) reported that few phobic persons ever report a traumatic onset of their fears. Kheriaty et al. (1999) reported that over a quarter (28.6%) of their respondents had no memory for traumatic events. Seligman (1971) noted that people tend to develop fears regarding spiders, snakes, heights, and other evolutionary significant dangers more so than to rabbits and other soft furry creatures (see also Seligman & Hager, 1972) or to modern appliances and machines such as lawn mowers and chain saws that can be very dangerous.

Expectation (Placebo)

Borkovec (1973) identified nine studies supporting the view that expectancy influenced outcome and ten studies that did not. Yates (1975, p. 170) also reviewed the literature and found similarly mixed support for expectation as a valid explanation of systematic desensitization.

Placebo effects are quite powerful. I addressed both placebo and nocebo effects in Chapter 4 and this chapter. Wilkins (1973) reviewed the empirical literature regarding expectancy of therapeutic gain regarding systematic desensitization and concluded that the expectancy explanation of why systematic desensitization works is unsupported by empirical evidence.

Self-Efficacy

This explanation maintains that proceeding up a hierarchy induces self-efficacy and this increase in self-confidence explains why systematic desensitization is effective. Hierarchy construction is not necessary for systematic desensitization to work. Repeated exposure is both sufficient and necessary. Moreover, self-efficacy does not provide mechanism information to explain how fear reduction takes place. How does expectation of fear reduction actually reduce fear?

Cognitive Restructuring

Cognitive change is at best a corollary result; something that co-occurs with successful desensitization. Cognitive change cannot explain how or why systematic desensitization works, because no causal mechanism information is provided. How do cognitions cause other cognitions? How do cognitions cause emotions? How do cognitions cause behavior? How do cognitions cause anything? No mechanism information is available to answer any of these questions. Therefore, cognitive change cannot explain how or why systematic desensitization works.

DeRubeis et al. (1990) used Baron and Kenny's (1986) criteria for establishing mediation as the methodological basis for determining if changed cognitions mediated the effects of cognitive therapy. They were unable to satisfy all of Baron and Kenny's criteria for mediation and were therefore unable to clearly establish that systematic desensitization works because of cognitive mediation. Moreover, these authors did not provide any causal mechanism to explain how cognitive factors changed emotion and behavior despite their title 'How does cognitive therapy work?,' thereby failing to make their explanatory case.

Network Explanation

Informal network models by Chemtob et al. (1988), Creamer et al. (1992), Drobes and Lang (1995), Foa and Kozak (1986), Foa et al. (1989), Lang (1977, 1979, 1985), Rachman (1980, 1990), and Wilker and Kolassa (2013) lack the necessary details regarding their architecture and operating principles to explain how they perform any psychological functions. It is therefore not possible for them to explain how systematic desensitization works. Formal network theory, discussed below, has made progress regarding all of these issues and provides a basis for understanding how systematic desensitization and exposure therapy work.

Dismantling studies have shown that **exposure without avoidance** is the active therapeutic ingredient in systematic desensitization. I now use network mechanism information to explain how exposure therapy works. Connectionist networks are **trained**, not programmed. They cannot be programmed because that would require knowing how to set all of the connection weights among all of the processing nodes, and presently there is no way of knowing how to do this. The only solution is to let the network **settle** into the correct activation pattern through a learning process. Connectionist networks, like people, learn from their experiences. Connectionist networks can be taught by a trainer or patients can learn on their own. In either case, their 'adult' behavior is the result of a learning history as is the case for humans. The relevant network mechanism information concerning why exposure therapy and systematic desensitization work was presented in Chapter 3 as **Principle 8: Dissonance Induction/Reduction**.

Prior to treatment, fear stimulus microfeatures represented across the client's S-nodes activate cognitions and emotions represented across the O-nodes, which then activate avoidance behaviors represented across the R-nodes. Thus, the client avoids or escapes from the situation. Leaving the situation removes these stimuli which relieves the phobic cognitions and affect. This explains why anxiety disorders remain unchanged without treatment.

Effective treatment requires dissonance induction followed by reduction. The therapist induces dissonance by arranging for new responses to occur. This is done by exposing the client to relevant stimulus microfeatures associated with their anxiety while requiring an incompatible behavior. Activation of the stimulus microfeatures spreads across the first set of connection weights, simulated synapses, to the middle layer where cognitions and emotions are represented and then across the second layer of connection weights, simulated synapses, to the lower or response layer. The difference between the values computed by the network for the R-nodes and what the therapist has arranged for the R-nodes to be constitutes dissonance. This dissonance-inducing procedure is equivalent to 'clamping' the R-nodes to different values than the ones that the network computed prior to treatment. The number of 1s that should be 0s and the number of 0s that should be 1s defines the **Hamming distance**, between the computed and desired response. This measure of discrepancy is a measure of dissonance. A mathematical procedure is used to simulate the biological process of experience-dependent plasticity. For example, the **back propagation** algorithm is commonly used to reduce dissonance. It does this by first changing connection weights between the R- and O-nodes and then between the O- and S-nodes; i.e., backwards relative to the normal processing flow. Mathematical properties of the back propagation algorithm ensure that the Hamming distance becomes smaller with each training trial, thus reducing dissonance.

After repeated trials, processing has modified the connection weights such that the behavioral result computed by the network is more consistent with the desired behavior prescribed by the therapist than was the initial behavioral response. Alternatively stated, before treatment, the client processes one or more anxiety-related stimulus microfeatures into fearful thoughts, feelings, and avoidance responses. Dissonance results when a prescribed therapeutic response differs from the client's pre-treatment response. Continued exposure without avoidance enables experience-dependent plasticity mechanisms to modify synaptic properties to where processing is more consistent with the new behaviors, thus reducing dissonance and achieving therapeutic results.

The predictable post-treatment result is that the client thinks, feels, and behaves differently than they once did. Exposure treatment is a major component of the unified protocol described by Allen et al. (2008) and Barlow et al. (2011) for treating emotional disorders, including anxiety and depression. They justified their methods based on the following quote that also validates the connectionist explanation just provided:

> As noted by Izard (1971), data and hypotheses from emotion theory suggest that the most efficient and effective way to change emotions is by changing responses to them; thus, it is conceivable that the mechanism of change during an exposure is to prevent the action tendency associated with a particular emotional experience. Over the past several decades, research has focused on these action tendencies, and changing action tendencies has become an important treatment component for anxiety, as well as for other emotional disorders (Allen et al., 2008, p. 233).

Principle 8 emphasizes the need for clients to tolerate exposure to troublesome stimuli while engaging in prescribed new responses until their neural networks settle into a more consonant state.

The network processing information presented above provides a mechanism of change that constitutes a common active ingredient in all effective psychological interventions, regardless of the theoretical orientation that originated them. Therapists of various persuasions endeavor to get clients to think and behave differently though they go about it in various ways. For example, motivational interviewing explicitly uses dissonance induction and reduction therapeutically (Miller & Rollnick, 2002; Tashiro & Mortensen, 2006). Clinicians now have a common basis for constructive collaboration that may result in more effective interventions.

Depression

Tryon and Misurell (2008) extended the dissonance induction/reduction principle to the treatment of depression. The following three paragraphs show how this principle applies to three empirically supported methods of treating depression.

Operant Conditioning

People with depression tend to avoid opportunities to receive positive reinforcement (Zeiss et al., 1979).[14] The operant conditioning approach induces dissonance when therapists recommend and reinforce engaging in behaviors that are likely to be positively reinforced (Lewinsohn et al., 1979, 1985). Depressed people typically resist such recommendations on the basis that

[14] We usually associate avoidance with anxiety disorders, but it is also characteristic of depression.

they don't feel like engaging in these behaviors. Their aversion to engaging in recommended therapeutic behaviors reveals the presence of dissonance. However, compliance creates the conditions for experience-dependent brain plasticity to begin to modify thoughts and feelings in ways that are consonant with these new behaviors.

Cognitive-Behavioral Therapy

Cognitive restructuring increases dissonance as therapists challenge the evidential basis of their client's beliefs and expectations. Therapists also ask their clients to behave in new ways that are contrary to how they think they should behave. This dissonant state activates the experience-dependent plasticity process that physically alters synapses, such that the client thinks and feels more consistently with the new therapist-recommended ways of behaving.

Interpersonal Psychotherapy

Interpersonal psychotherapy for depression (Klerman et al., 1984; Weisman et al., 2000) induces dissonance when it focuses on grief, role disputes, role transition, and interpersonal deficits, and asks the client to adopt new roles and develop a new social identity. These efforts to increase social competency create dissonance that activates the experience-dependent brain plasticity mechanisms that change the way people think, feel, and behave.

Motivational Interviewing

Motivational interviewing (MI) is now an established evidence-based intervention. Miller and Rollnick (2002) provided a book-length description of motivational interviewing. The following URL contains several good sources including an 8-minute video covering the background and basics of MI (http://www.motivationalinterview.org/). In it one learns that MI arose as a part of the professional treatment of alcoholism instead of using recovered alcoholics as therapists. MI recognizes that people with substance abuse are ambivalent and conflicted about change. On the one hand they seek treatment because their substance abuse is causing problems, but on the other hand they continue to enjoy their substance of choice or use it to avoid uncomfortable cravings and withdrawal symptoms. Therapists traditionally take a change perspective in that their interventions are presented as a way to make change. The natural dialectic is for client's to take the other side and automatically, unconsciously, resist change. Therapists traditionally assume that people who abuse substances are overly defensive. This prompts therapists to try to breach perceived defenses via some form of confrontation. Challenging these clients to change only makes them angrier and more defensive, thus confirming the traditional therapist's assumption that their underlying problems are anger and defensiveness. The typical result is that these clients drop out of treatment unless therapy is court-ordered, which only fosters more anger and more resistance. Traditional therapists then typically conclude that their clients were not sufficiently motivated to change and thus are poor candidates for therapy. By contrast, MI therapists see their task as helping the individual develop their own reasons and methods for changing their behavior. Draycott and Dabbs (1998b) noted that MI grew out of William Miller's personal style of therapy (see Miller, 1983, 1996). Again we sadly see that an effective treatment was developed by a clinician as a result of their clinical practice, rather than as a reasoned extension of psychological science.

Draycott and Dabbs (1998a) observed that clinical psychology was not making full use of the then-available psychological research. These authors then reviewed the research on cognitive dissonance and concluded that it was relevant to clinical psychology. They reviewed the social psychological literature regarding ways to increase, maintain, and reduce dissonance. The final section of their article concerns the clinical applications of dissonance theory which they developed further in regard to MI in their subsequent article (Draycott & Dabbs, 1998b). One of the five clinical objectives of MI is to develop discrepancies between strongly held cognitions, beliefs, and their substance abuse behaviors in order to generate internal motivation for change. Another clinical objective is to help the person reduce this dissonance in a responsible way (cf. Tashiro & Mortensen, 2006).

Network Explanation

The same network explanation that was used to explain why empirically supported treatments of anxiety work could be repeated here to explain why empirically supported treatments for depression work. The common mechanism in both cases is that the therapist puts the client in a new and therefore dissonant position that the client is persuaded to tolerate by any possible means that are acceptable to the client and therapist until the biological mechanism of experience-dependent plasticity can modify the client's neural network to be more consonant with the new way of behaving and thinking that the therapist and client have agreed is desirable.

Psychodynamic Psychotherapies

A substantial and growing literature reports empirical support for a variety of psychodynamic psychotherapies. Meta-analyses by Abbass et al. (2006), Anderson and Lambert (1995), Crits-Christoph (1992), de Maat et al. (2009), Leichsenring (2001, 2005), Leichsenring and Leibing (2003), and Leichsenring et al. (2004) have demonstrated that psychodynamic therapies (PDTs) produce therapeutic effects that are greater than wait list controls, and sometimes equal to those produced by CBT. The International Society for Interpersonal Therapy[15] reported that there are currently over 250 empirical studies supporting the effectiveness and efficacy of interpersonal therapy (IPT). This literature concerns outcome, but does not endeavor to explain why these outcomes occur.

While we tend to accept the theoretical reasons provided by the authors of these treatments for why they are effective, we must also consider the possibility that like systematic desensitization, those reasons are incorrect. Clinicians can be right for the wrong reasons. The section in Chapter 9 on symptom substitution demonstrates that the psychodynamic theory regarding how and why 'symptoms' appear has been falsified. Hence, the effectiveness of these treatments cannot be offered as proof that the psychodynamic explanation for good outcomes is correct, because that would commit the logical error of affirming the consequent as noted above. On the contrary, there is every reason to believe that effective psychodynamic interventions work because they implement the dissonance induction/reduction principle which we have established as corollary to the explanatory nucleus that is composed of Network Principles 1–4.

Our synthesis of conscious cognitive and unconscious processing promotes psychotherapy integration. For example, the evidence supporting unconscious thought theory (UTT) and the evidence that goals are unconsciously chosen and automatically govern behavior support basic psychodynamic tenets. Additional evidence shows that affect can warp cognition so that people often conclude what they want to believe provides strong support for unconscious motivation. Olds (1994) and Westen and Gabbard (2002) discussed several contributions that connectionism makes to a psychodynamic understanding. Chen et al. (2007) discussed transference and counter-transference as an example of unconscious social-cognition of close relationships.[16] PDP-CNN models provide clinicians with ways to

[15] http://interpersonalpsychotherapy.org/about-ipt/

[16] Kihlstrom et al. (1992) noted that the cognitive unconscious is not as extreme as Freud conjectured.

understand how conscious and unconscious processing combines to produce behavior. Perhaps these models will help clinicians create new interventions that address the whole person.

Integration of Clinical and Experimental Psychology

It is ironic that the small part of psychological science known as the experimental analysis of behavior gave rise to the clinical practice known as applied behavior analysis, better known as behavior modification, while the large part of psychological science generated by the cognitive revolution provided little if any science base for clinical practice. Master clinicians have been left to develop therapies based on their personal and professional lives because the theoretical side of psychological science has not been very helpful.

The research relevant to System 1 summarized by Kahneman (2011b) provides a valuable explanatory link to several decades of work by experimental psychologists. The characteristics of his System 1 describe features of many clients that clinical psychologists see. I strongly recommend that clinical psychologists read Kahneman's (2011b) book with this in mind. For example, the cognitive distortions identified by Jeffrey Young[17] are System 1 activities and the early maladaptive schemas he has identified[18] appear to be products of System 1. I believe that it is fair to say that cognitive-behavior therapies, cognitive therapies, and ego psychology therapies (Tryon, 1986) can all be described as efforts to bring System 2 on line earlier and in a more focused way to control the craziness of System 1. Alternatively stated, everyone has both systems and this fact helps explain both the psychopathology of everyday life as well as people's ability to cope with it. However, some people's System 2 is particularly reticent and needs encouragement to become and stay active. CBT, CT, MI, and ego psychology therapies are essentially about how to do this. Therapists also have a System 1 and it can be both a source of clinical intuition, and an opportunity to seriously misjudge clients and say the wrong things. It may also be responsible for illusory evidence that clinicians sometimes cite to justify tests and treatments that either lack empirical support or have been contradicted by research evidence. Alternatively stated, clinicians need to take special care to see that their System 2 monitors and controls their own System 1 while they provide professional services.

It further seems to me that many psychodynamic theories and treatments endeavor to understand and modify System 1 properties; i.e., they

[17] http://www.cognitivetherapy.me.uk/cognitive_therapy.htm

[18] http://www.cognitivetherapy.me.uk/schema_therapy.htm

attempt to change how the person's System 1 operates. This objective is as misguided as is the task of attempting to preclude people from seeing visual illusions.

CLINICAL IMPLICATIONS OF PRINCIPLE 9: MEMORY SUPERPOSITION

Cognitive science has largely been based on the von Neumann computer model where a central processing unit (CPU) is separated from but connected to, a memory storage system by a data bus that transfers data to and from memory. In this model memory is static unless overwritten by explicit instructions issued by the CPU. Overwriting completely destroys the contents of the overwritten memory locations by replacing their binary content with new strings of 1s and 0s. One implication of this model is that memory remains unchanged by time as long as it is not overwritten. A second implication of this model is that since processing is carried out by a separate CPU, processing per se does not necessarily modify memory. For example, calculations done on your computer do not interfere with or change in any way the letters you have also written and stored on your computer. Memory and processing are completely separate processes on contemporary computers.

Principle 9 reflects the fact that in network models processing is done by the same nodes that are responsible for memory storage, and that multiple memories are stored on top of one another within the same network. Placing all memories in the same place that is used for processing predicts: (a) that memories will interfere with one another (see Rogler, Malgady, & Tryon 1992); and (b) that processing will modify memories (see Tryon & McKay, 2009). The parenthetically cited references report empirical evidence that supports each of these predictions in clinically important ways.

Evidence presented by Rogler et al. (1992) demonstrates that our '**retrospectoscope**' is flawed. We tend to confuse memories of events with similar elements. This flaw has serious and broad implications for psychometrics, and consequently for all areas of psychology that rely on testing methods that require retrospective client, teacher, parent, and clinician reports. This flaw is especially relevant to clinical psychology because it threatens the validity of memory-based diagnostic methods, which includes structured as well as unstructured interviews. This problem should caution clinicians against relying too heavily on client reports (cf., Nisbett & Wilson, 1977). Evidence presented by Tryon and McKay (2009) suggests that learning-based interventions necessarily modify memory, and that these modifications can be used to document the effectiveness of interventions.

CLINICAL IMPLICATIONS OF PRINCIPLE 10: PROTOTYPE FORMATION

Prototypes form by an averaging process where the redundant features constructively aggregate to form the core belief. This memory formation process likely involves unconscious as well as conscious processing. People can respond more rapidly to this constructed core prototype than to any particular training stimuli. Prototypes are clinically relevant because people extract them from their interpersonal relationships and respond to them more vigorously than to specific exemplars. Prototypes are a form of stereotype.

Prototype formation informs multicultural psychology. The averaging nature of prototype formation explains the well replicated **other-race effect**, also known as the **cross-race effect,**[19] by which individuals who have been raised around members of one race have difficulty distinguishing among members of another race. The prototype of 'children', 'adolescents', and 'adults' becomes less variable for people who are raised in a uniform racial environment compared to people who are raised in a diverse racial environment.

Prototypes as Internal Working Models that Activate Schemas

Psychodynamic theorists discuss the internal representations we have of other people as internal working models. These models are heavily dependent upon prototype formation. For example, repeated experience with mothers, fathers, men, women, authority figures, etc., results in the development of an average prototype for each category based on particular past experiences; i.e., developmental history. Cognitive theorists refer to these prototypes as schemas. I prefer the term prototype because the explanatory core presented in Chapter 4 explains how prototypes can form; i.e., provides missing mechanism information for this important clinical issue. Here we have another example of Hegelian synthesis between psychodynamic and cognitive theory that have long been considered to be polar opposites.

Eagleman (2011) noted that the thalamus is the neural network that compares the output from the neural networks that construct our internal working models against information coming in from the senses. Discrepancy drives conscious awareness and directs attention, thus providing feedback to the frontal lobes with resultant modification of our internal working model.

[19] http://en.wikipedia.org/wiki/Cross-race_effect

Prototype as Self-Concept

One's self-concept is a crucial prototype. The information processing section of Markus and Wurf's (1987) *Annual Review of Psychology* chapter summarized literature demonstrating that people process self-congruent information more rapidly than self-incongruent information. Psychologists working with clients with personality disorders have long recognized the importance of the self-concept prototype in particular, because it is quite difficult to change. PDP-CNN models contribute to psychology by providing a well-defined computationally specific context for studying the formation and modification of prototypes.

Generational Effects

We have long known that abused children are at risk of abusing their children, and that women who have children as teenagers frequently find that their daughters become pregnant as teenagers. But little mechanism information is available in this regard. Prototypes provide some of the missing mechanism information regarding how generational parenting effects occur. For example, children who are abused by their parents form a prototype of 'abusive adults' and 'abusive parents'. These prototypes guide the behavior of children as they grow up and become parents themselves. Our discussion of epigenetics in Chapter 3 provided mechanism information that supports this claim.

We noted above that prototypes are a memory process that creates an average aggregate based mainly on experience, but is also influenced by what one sees, reads, and hears. The average nature of prototypes means that they reflect central tendencies that function as core beliefs. Variations and exceptions are pruned away via cancellation. Test items provide an easy to understand example. According to classical test theory, each item measures the true score plus error. The total test score is a composite where the true scores aggregate constructively but the errors aggregate destructively, causing the measured score to approximate the true score with decreasing error. The strong implication here is that self-concepts develop in a parallel way. Consonant elements aggregate constructively and dissonant elements aggregate destructively. This creates difficulty for people with low self-esteem to accept evidence of higher self-esteem. Clients will automatically and unconsciously minimize dissonant evidence of high self-esteem and cherry-pick for consonant evidence of low self-esteem. Therapists will experience this process as client resistance.

Schemas are activated by circumstances. Prototypes are the memory structures that constitute schemas. Circumstances reactivate cognitions, emotions, and behaviors in accordance with Principle 4: Reactivation, discussed in Chapter 3. Hence, schemas involve averages compiled from birth and are modified each time that they are reactivated.

Maladaptive Schemas and Schema Therapy

Malformed schemas resulting from domestic violence and sex abuse understandably activate thoughts, feelings, and behaviors that differ from those of 'normal' people. The following link lists early maladaptive schemas (http://www.schematherapy.com/id73.htm) that are the basis of Jeffrey Young's schema-focused psychotherapy.[20]

Reactivation is the recommended term for referring to what happens when the network, connectome, is restored to the activation pattern that was present at the time that the memory was formed. Cognitions, emotions, and behaviors are returned to what they were at the time these memories were formed. Reactivation can be thought of as **reconstituted** thoughts, feelings, and actions; sort of like freeze-dried milk where adding water reconstitutes milk as a drink. Note that what we are discussing here is a result of the person's reinforcement history. Behaviorists had an important point here.

Averages are notoriously influenced by extreme values. One's prototype of dog typically includes four legs, a tail, barks, etc. But for someone who was bitten, even once, this traumatic experience modifies, seriously distorts, the previous average value that characterized the prototype. Moreover, there is no really effective way to delete, erase, this effect. Dogs do sometimes bite and the experience of having been bitten is not going to just go away.

Positive prototypes very likely provide psychological protection against life stress. In the same way that the negative prototypes that activate maladaptive schemas bias thoughts, feelings, and behaviors in neurotic ways, positive prototypes activate adaptive constructive schemas.

Prototypes as Memories

There is an inherent connection between prototypes and memory wells because prototypes are memories. Memory wells vary in both the depth and breadth of their basins of attraction. Normal and abnormal levels of both variables can be conceptualized. For example, a shallow prototype with a narrow basin of attraction will exert little influence on cognition, affect, and behavior. A deep prototype with a broad basin of attraction will exert a strong influence on cognition, affect, and behavior. As with all memory wells, retrieval cues that fall within the basin of attraction will activate

[20] http://en.wikipedia.org/wiki/Schema_Therapy; http://www.schematherapy.com/id201.htm

the prototype. This may be inconsequential in the case of positive prototypes, but could be clinically devastating in the case of a negative, emotionally laden, prototype.

An interesting feature of the averaging property of prototypes is the different way that congruent and incongruent information is treated. Congruent information is constructively aggregated and reinforces the prototype. Incongruent and/or unique information is frequently blunted or discarded. This automatic cherry-picking mechanism gives prototypes a self-fulfilling property that complicates therapeutic intervention. Prototypes influence what is learned from new experiences, including therapy sessions. Assuming that new experiences contain some facets that confirm existing prototypes and some facts that contradict them, the client is likely to be more influenced by the confirmatory than contradictory elements. This feature of prototype formation can create what clinicians experience as resistance. This resistance can be both cognitive and affective. This resistance is largely unconscious, because the prototype formation mechanism is unconscious. It stems from the explanatory nucleus described in Chapter 3.

Memory activation of prototypes and corresponding schemas is rapid and facilitates responding to social situations that would otherwise take way too much conscious cognitive computation. Prototypes help us efficiently and quickly understand where we are, who we are interacting with, and what we should be doing.

Asperger's Syndrome

Church et al. (2010) reported that children with high functioning autism don't form/use prototypes like control children do. They endorsed prototypes less often than expected and they appear to be less sensitive to difference between to-be-categorized items and the relevant prototype. This disability may negatively affect processing socially relevant cues such as facial expressions.[21]

CLINICAL IMPLICATIONS OF PRINCIPLE 11: GRACEFUL DEGRADATION

The main clinical implication of Principle 11 is that complex brain networks that mediate psychological processes are resistant to damage because they are distributed. Providing multiple processing pathways also offers the promise that compensatory processing can be found. This implication is especially important for psychologists who work in rehabilitation settings.

21 http://www.ncbi.nlm.nih.gov/pmc/articles/PMC3058590/

CLINICAL IMPLICATIONS OF PRINCIPLE 12: TOP-DOWN AND BOTTOM-UP PROCESSING

This section on top-down processing emphasizes the ability of higher brain centers, neural networks, to influence what we perceive, think, and do. It provides psychology with the ability to modify biology. Our previous descriptions of the network cascade have emphasized bottom-up processing where the network cascade begins with sensory systems. Real neural networks are interconnected by feedback systems that enable much more complicated processing. Figure 11.3 endeavors to illustrate that the network cascade typically travels in both directions, although by different routes.

Top-down processing refers to how higher brain centers influence experience that is being processed from the bottom-up. Expectations generated by internal working models by the prefrontal cortex can dramatically alter what is seen, heard, felt, smelled, and tasted. Our view and understanding of reality is synthesized as activation crosses multiple network layers where each layer adds something to the final Gestalt. Top-down processing attempts to rapidly reach decisions by categorizing bottom-up information as soon as possible, because response time is often critical to survival in the natural world. These jumps to a completed Gestalt speed cognition at the expense of sometimes being wrong, but at least they are fast. Many heuristics use speed cognitive processing. Readers are invited to review my discussion of heuristics in Chapter 3.

Placebos

Placebos refer to substances that should not have pharmacologic effects. Placebo is a negative term for positive psychological effects. Psychologists should have a positive rather than negative view of placebos. Placebo effects are real and positive; not false effects. Placebos provide clear evidence that

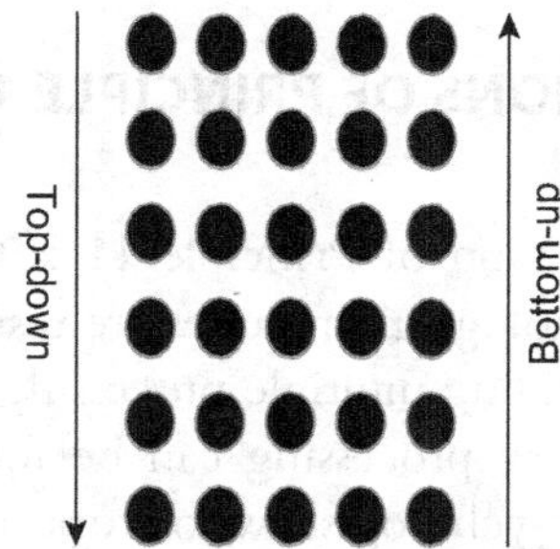

Figure 11.3 Diagram of top-down and bottom-up processing.

psychology is crucial to health and wellbeing. Our negative impression of placebos stems from the fact that the Food and Drug Administration (FDA) requires that pharmaceutical companies demonstrate that the effects of pharmacologic compounds to be sold as medicine demonstrate that they produce better therapeutic outcomes than placebos before being approved for sale. This translates to a requirement that medicines must be more effective than expectation of benefit which exert legitimate effects on their own.

Studies typically show that placebos produce substantial therapeutic benefits. I now draw heavily upon Irving Kirsch's (2010) book entitled *The Emperor's New Drugs* to document just how clinically effective placebos can be. I strongly recommend that readers of this book read Kirsch's (2010) book in its entirety. I have reorganized his evidence into two lines. The first line more directly comments upon the strength of placebos. The second line comments upon the illusion that antidepressive medications are more effective than placebos, which they are not. Viewing placebos as effective as antidepressive medications appropriately makes them seem stronger than people generally give them credit for.

Definitions

How do we know to call one substance an 'active Treatment' and another 'placebo'? The answer appears to turn on whether mechanism information is available. Active treatments carry accepted, not necessarily proven, mechanism information that explains how they work; placebos don't. Notice that I did not say scientifically validated mechanism information. We shall see next that the putative mechanism for why antidepressive drugs work is in fact wrong, but this does not matter when it comes to determining whether or not to consider these compounds medicines or placebos.

Kirsch (2010) reported that the monoamine (serotonin, norepinephrine, and dopamine) hypothesis arose from **uncontrolled** clinical observations. He then presented the following evidence from controlled research that has **falsified** this clinical speculation. Selective serotonin reuptake inhibitors (SSRI) should be far more effective in relieving depression than norepinephrine dopamine reuptake inhibitor (NDRI) medications if serotonin is specifically related to depression, but they are not. SSRI medications result in 60% recovery from depression whereas NDRI medications result in 59% recovery from depression. More telling is that selective serotonin reuptake **enhancer** (SSRE) medications that increase the rate of serotonin reuptake and therefore decrease available serotonin are as effective as selective serotonin reuptake **inhibitor** (SSRI) medications that decrease the rate of serotonin reuptake and therefore increase available serotonin. Kirsch reported that SSRE medications result in 63% recovery from depression, whereas SSRI medications result in 62% recovery from depression. The finding that SSRE and SSRI medications are equally clinically effective at treating depression indicates that serotonin is not directly causing depression. Kirsch (2010) reported that newer SSRIs were no more effective than older tricyclics. Then there are the 90 serotonin depletion studies in non-depressed participants. Chemically depleting their serotonin levels did not make them depressed. These data are not isolated cherry-picked findings. Mukherjee (2011) cited Marcia Angell, a former NEJM editor as saying 'After decades of trying to prove [the chemical-imbalance theory], researchers have still come up empty-handed'.

The absence of scientific support for the putative mechanism associated with SSRI medications as antidepressants means that they no longer have a plausible mechanism of action. That result should re-categorize them as placebos; i.e., compounds that have a demonstrable effect for reasons that we do not understand. But this has not and will not happen, because the Food and Drug Administration has categorized these compounds as medications and will not reclassify them as placebos. The lesson to be learned here is that even though one initially needs mechanism information for a substance to be classified as a medication and therefore an active treatment, the benefits of this classification remain even if the proposed mechanism is subsequently falsified.

Placebos are Effective

Direct Effects

Kirsch (2010, pp. 145–8) reported on the NIMH Treatment of Depression Collaborative Research Program Study. Patients rated expectancy of improvement on a 5-point scale. A rating of 1 indicated that 'I don't expect any improvement at all'. A rating of 5 indicated that 'I expect to feel completely better'. The main result of interest for us is that patient response to medication, psychotherapy, and placebo was directly proportional to their initial outcome expectation. That is, regardless of type of treatment, medication, psychotherapy, or placebo, patient response was directly proportional to their initial rating regarding their expectation of improvement. This remarkable finding suggests that clinicians should maximize their client's expectations of success before implementing whatever treatment they are going to use. I included this as a novel feature and prediction of the proposed Bio↔Psychology Network Theory in Chapter 7.

Expectations of improvement can have several facets. (1) The amount of change expected can be small, medium, or large. (2) The degree of confidence about the amount of expected change can be small, medium, or large. (3) The speed with which results are expected to occur can vary. Results can be expected immediately, gradually, or delayed. (4) The degree of patient involvement can vary. Patients can expect automatic effects, as in 'just take the pill', or patients can expect that they will need to work at recovery. Realistic expectations work best. Expectations need to be carefully considered as part of the therapeutic relationship, also known as the working alliance.

Placebos can be dosed. Patient's respond to placebo doses as they do to medication doses. One way to dose a placebo is to administer it multiple times per week. Another way to dose a placebo is to offer it in combination with another treatment. For example, sham acupuncture can be provided with and without 45 minutes of clinical interviewing. Medical clothing and accessories can also serve as placebos. The Tuesday April 3, 2012 New York Times, Science Times[22] carried an article reporting the following findings. Wearing a white coat that was said to belong to a doctor enhances attention, whereas attributing the same white coat to a painter does not. People are rated as warmer when they are holding a hot drink than when holding a cold drink. People who carry a heavy clip board feel more important than those who carry a lighter one.[23]

Side Effects

Placebo effects associated with active medicines arise partly from the side effects of active medications, because these side effects inform the patient that they have taken an active ingredient. The antidepressant Ement by Merck has very few side effects and is no better at relieving depression than placebos that have no side effects. Placebos that produce clear side effects are more effective than placebos that don't have noticeable side effects.

Single-blind studies are conducted to keep the patient from knowing whether or not they are receiving active medication. Double-blind studies take this logic one step further and, in principle, prevent both the physician and the patient from knowing who is receiving active medication. However, the side effects of medications break these blinds in both cases to both the patient and the treating physician. When patients experience side effects they believe that they are on active medications. When patients complain of

[22] http://www.nytimes.com/2012/04/03/science/clothes-and-self-perception.html

[23] Women who wear masculine fashion during a job interview are more likely to be hired than people who dress more casually. Unfortunately, this article provided no mechanism information.

these side effects to their doctors, then the physician also believes that they are on active medication. Kirsch (2010) reported that 80% of patients and 87% of doctors know who is getting active drugs based on side effects. Side effects generally emerge prior to therapeutic effects. Their presence helps patients believe that their medication is working.

While some people experience side effects while on placebo, the incidence of side effects on placebo is much less than when on active medication. The side effects of placebos are approximately half those of active medications. Nocebos are placebos that have negative side effects.

Placebos Equal Antidepressive Medications

Kirsch (2010) reported the stunning finding that a barbiturate sleeping aid and a synthetic thyroid medication relieve depression as well as antidepressive medications do. Part of the illusion that antidepressive medications are more effective than placebos stems from the review policies of government agencies responsible for certifying the effectiveness of these drugs. In his second chapter, Kirsch (2010, pp. 23–53) revealed what he calls 'The Dirty Little Secret' kept by these regulating agencies for promoting the illusion that antidepressive medications are more effective than placebos. He referred to actions taken by the Medical Products Agency (MPA) in Sweden and the Food and Drug Administration (FDA) in the United States. These institutions are aware that approximately 40% of antidepressant clinical trials are not published, primarily because they do not show that medications are significantly more effective than placebos. Data from some sites in multi-site studies are published whereas data from other sites are not. One published study consisted of just 27 cherry-picked patients out of a total sample of 245 patients. Pooled studies are the drug company's version of meta-analyses where specific studies are picked for pooling. Approximately 40% of studies are omitted. The same positive studies are published several times with different authors, thereby biasing meta-analyses that combine studies in a positive direction. The FDA is aware of and tolerates these practices because they claim that positive studies are statistically significant, as if that conferred some special status on them. This is an interpretative error that even students completing an introductory statistics course should not make.

Kirsch (2010) reviewed a meta-analysis of 38 clinical trials involving more than 3,000 depressed patients, and found that the average improvement from drug was not better than psychotherapy, but both were better than placebo which was far better than no treatment. He estimated that placebo resulted in 50% improvement whereas medication resulted in 75% improvement. FDA data indicate that 82% of the response to antidepressant medication is placebo as is 50% of the response to pain medication. Antidepressants produce an average improvement over placebo of only 1.8 points on the Hamilton Depression Scale which has a range of 51 points.

Kirsch (2010) reported the following questionable evaluation practice by the FDA. In what he calls 'The Assay Sashay' an 'active control arm' is added to the research design. This group receives an older already-approved medication against which the new medication will be judged. If the new drug is less effective or equally effective compared to placebo then the FDA checks to see how the previously approved drug fared. If it too was less or equally effective compared to placebo, then the entire trial is discarded as insensitive. Additional studies are performed as necessary until the desired positive evidence emerges.

Clinical practice differs from research in that physicians switch to a different medication if the patient is not improving, whereas research trials continue on the same medication regardless of outcome. Kirsch (2010, pp. 57–62) reported on what is known as the STAR*D Trial. Medication was changed if complete remission did not result by the fourth checkup. The results were 37% remission to the first drug, 19% more remission to the second drug, 6% more remission to the third drug, and 5% more remission to the fourth drug, resulting in a grand total of 67% remission. While this method seems to support the policy of finding the right drug for the right person, the further finding that 93% of participants either relapsed or dropped out during the first year demonstrates that such treatment is rather unacceptable and not very effective.

Kirsch (2010, pp. 59–62) described an alternate form of the STAR*D trial, cited as the 1957 Ipecac Study, that demonstrated how effective placebos can be. Ipecac is a drug that induces nausea and vomiting; effects that are clearly noticeable to every patient. I previously noted that patients interpret side effects as indications that the medication is working, and that more side effects make for a better placebo. Ipecac should therefore be a good placebo. The investigators first verified that Ipecac induced nausea and vomiting in all participants as an inclusion criterion. Then they began treating depressed patients with what the patients thought was an antidepressive medication but was instead Ipecac. Kirsch reported that just over 50% of patients responded to the first treatment. The non-responders were supposedly switched to a second medication, but actually were just continued on Ipecac. Kirsch reported that depression remitted in 17% more patients. Non-responders were supposedly switched to a third medication but, you guessed it, they were actually just continued on Ipecac. Kirsch reported that depression remitted in 20% more patients. This study continued through six such treatment segments, by which time depression had remitted in all patients.

The first conclusion from this study was that the placebo effect can kick in at any time. Ordinarily we expect the placebo effect to begin immediately, but the results reported above show that placebo effects can be delayed. The second conclusion was that clinicians can detect when a treatment works but cannot know why they work. Physicians have no way to study the mechanisms by which the medications that they prescribe work. They must rely on scientific studies. The interventions that clinicians provide can be effective when the underlying explanatory theory is completely wrong, as was the case for systematic desensitization reviewed above, and as appears to be the case for antidepressive medications. Case studies are useful for illustrating methods but worthless as probative evidence of associated theory regarding why observed changes occurred.

There is some evidence that drug effects are present in the most severely ill patients. The dose–response curve is flat across depression severity (mild, moderate, severe) but placebo effectiveness declines as severity of depression increases. This results in a drug effect for the most severely depressed patients. But only a 4-point Hamilton Depression Inventory change was found for severely depressed patients. However, the lack of smooth dose–response suggests that chemicals are not responsible.

Mechanism Information

Kirsch's (2010) Chapter 6 is entitled 'How Placebos Work'. It promised to provide mechanism information but did not do so. He emphasized the therapeutic relationship, which, while important, is not a mechanism. Feeling good in a room with a view was reported to speed hospital recovery, but this also is not a mechanism. He also discussed classical conditioning as a means of generating expectations. Expectations are not mechanisms, and while classical conditioning is a procedure for producing expectations it does not provide a causal sequence that explains why these procedures produce expectations.

It is important to note that it was an untested clinical hypothesis, conjecture, about a possible underlying mechanism that enabled physicians to ethically prescribe chemical compounds as 'antidepressant medications' in the first place. These chemical compounds were promoted to the status of active medications simply by proposing hypothetical mechanism information that explained why they should be effective. This mechanism information did not need to be scientifically evaluated and validated prior to promoting these substances to the privileged position of 'active medication' so that they could be ethically prescribed.

It is especially important to note that the lack of scientific support did not demote antidepressive medication to placebos status. This is because a government agency had already 'approved' these chemical compounds as 'medications'. There is no official procedure for declassifying and demoting an 'active medication' to the status of 'placebo' once controlled research has shown them to be no more effective than officially recognized placebos. The lessons to be learned here are: (a) provide probable mechanism information for your chemical compound; and (b) get your product approved by a government agency as an active medication. You need only provide evidence of effectiveness to get FDA approval. You do not need to validate the mechanism information that you provide. That is, you do not need to show that your product works for the stated reasons.

Now that the mechanism information for antidepressant medications has been falsified, do we reclassify antidepressant medications as placebos? The scientific answer should be 'yes', because we defined a placebo as a substance that has no credible mechanism of action. Presently, the serotonin hypothesis is little more than a cover story to sell pills. There is no longer a definitive mechanism that explains how they work. This remarkable result demonstrates the power and utility of asking for mechanism information. The clinical answer to our question must be 'no', because then antidepressant medications could not be ethically prescribed for the millions of people who take them and that would prevent these millions of people from benefiting from them.

Ethical Prescription of Placebos

It is presently unethical for physicians to prescribe a placebo. In this section I describe a way to remedy this situation so that placebos can be ethically prescribed. First, we need a compound. It could be a vitamin, herb, or some combination of both; something that does no harm, is not toxic, and may be beneficial. Then we must add an ingredient that will cause clearly noticeable side effects so that patients who take it will know that their medicine is working. Now we conduct as many double-blind studies against a placebo with minimal or preferably no side effects until we get the required statistically significant results. We can facilitate this process by providing reasons for excluding those patients who are minimally responsive to our 'medicine' so that effectively we end up analyzing data only from positive responders. The

FDA will now approve our product and physicians will be able to ethically prescribe it. Millions of patients will benefit and the pharmaceutical company that follows this advice will make hundreds of millions of dollars of profit. The lack of mechanism information or even negative evidence will not be a problem now or in the future, because the government will not recall our 'medicine' based on subsequent research findings. The fact that we began with a harmless or mildly positive substance protects us from recalls due to unexpected negative side effects, which of course should be minimized and under-reported to protect profits.[24]

In response to the positive evidence regarding the therapeutic power of placebos, the Harvard Medical School developed a new Program in Placebo Studies and the Therapeutic Encounter. The link to this program is as follows: http://programinplacebostudies.org/. Clinicians of all stripes need to know how to best use this information to maximize therapeutic responses in their patients.

Therapeutic Relationship as Placebo

Kaptchuk et al. (2008) dosed the doctor–patient relationship as follows. They treated 262 patients with irritable bowel syndrome with placebo acupuncture or wait list. The placebo group was divided into two groups. One group received a low doctor–patient dose consisting of placebo acupuncture without conversation. The other group received a high doctor–patient dose consisting of placebo acupuncture with **attention, active listening, and empathetic conversation**. These are crucial active ingredients to the therapeutic relationship that psychologists seek to establish with all of their patients.

The results were as follows. The wait list group experienced 28% improvement. The low doctor–patient dose group experienced 44% improvement. The high doctor–patient dose group experienced 62% improvement. Clearly attention, active listening, and empathetic conversation had a very positive effect. That these variables were studied in the context of a placebo experiment leads to the conclusion that the therapeutic alliance operates for the same reasons, and likely by the same brain mechanisms, by which placebos work. This in no way diminishes the importance of the working alliance. On the contrary, placebos are psychological effects that have the same valuable and powerful effects that the working alliance has. We need to positively value placebo effects as real and legitimate psychological effects caused by physical mechanisms.

[24] The primary obligation of all business is to maximize shareholder profit.

CONCLUSIONS

This chapter has reviewed clinical implications of Network Principles 3–12. Collectively these network principles provide a natural science base for clinical practice that is supported by controlled empirical studies. The next chapter takes a more integrative approach. It aims to show how the proposed Bio↔Psychological Network Theory results in psychotherapy integration.

CHAPTER 12

Psychotherapy Integration

Contents

Cognitive Neuroscience and Psychotherapy
http://dx.doi.org/10.1016/B978-0-12-420071-5.00012-0

Here is where I provide the sharpest focus currently available to me with regard to psychotherapy integration. In this chapter I aim to describe psychotherapy integration based on the network orientation authorized by the Bio↔Psychology Network Theory developed in previous chapters. But first I need to ask: How does one convincingly demonstrate psychotherapy integration? What must I do to show that I have actually integrated what I call the **Big Five clinical orientations** which are: (a) behavioral (applied behavior analysis); (b) cognitive; (c) cognitive-behavioral; (d) psychodynamic (emotion-focused); and (e) pharmacologic? The primary principle upon which I base my argument for psychotherapy integration is that **things equal to the same thing are equal to each other**. I therefore aim to demonstrate psychotherapy integration by showing how the proposed network orientation is fully consistent with each of the Big Five clinical orientations. This will make the proposed network perspective a Hegelian synthesis of the Big Five clinical orientations.

The secondary principle upon which I base my argument for psychotherapy integration is that clinical orientations are broader and more tolerant to exclusion than are the specific theories on which these orientations are based. For example, one can have a cognitive-behavioral orientation without endorsing every last claim made by every self-identified cognitive-behavioral theorist and/or therapist. One might not fully subscribe to everything that Ellis, Beck, Linehan, and others have said, and yet legitimately have a cognitive-behavioral clinical orientation. Similarly, one can have a psychodynamic orientation without subscribing to everything that every self-identified psychodynamic clinician or theorist has said. This distinction between theories and theoretical orientations enables me to limit my analysis to the conceptual 'must haves' of each clinical orientation. Some clinical constructs that have not been formally disclaimed are not included. I refer to Shedler's (2010, p. 98) complaint that 'Undergraduate textbooks too often equate psychoanalytic or psychodynamic therapies with some of the **more outlandish and inaccessible speculations** made by Sigmund Freud roughly a century ago, rarely presenting mainstream psychodynamic concepts as understood and practiced today' (bold emphasis added). Shedler did not specify these speculations, but one can guess that they include penis envy, oral, anal, urethral phallic, latency, and genital adult personality styles (Rychlak, 1981b, pp. 76–80), plus castration anxiety, and Oedipal and Electra complexes. The proposed network orientation does not incorporate these speculations.

I now present a brief history of psychotherapy integration and four standard approaches to psychotherapy integration to establish a context for our discussion before considering the compatibility of the proposed network orientation with each of the Big Five clinical orientations.

A BRIEF HISTORY OF PSYCHOTHERAPY INTEGRATION

This section is based heavily on the historical review provided in the first chapter of Stricker (2010). Psychotherapy integration could be said to have begun with a paper by French (1933) in which he noted the similarity of Pavlov's conditioned reflex and free association practiced in psychoanalysis; i.e., one idea reflexively actives another, etc. Rosenzweig (1936) coined the term **Dodo bird effect** to indicate that all psychotherapies were equally effective, because the active gradients consist of common factors shared by all psychotherapies. Alexander and French (1946) argued that emotional experience was common to all psychotherapies. They coined the term **corrective emotional experience**. Dollard and Miller (1950) translated psychoanalytic terms into learning theory as a way to show how similar both theoretical positions are. Frank (1961) argued that contemporary psychotherapies share much with ancient healing arts, including the cultivation of hope, social support, and culturally sanctioned healing rituals. Lazarus (1976, 1981) authorized clinicians to practice a multimodal form of behavior therapy that addresses seven aspects of treatment with his BASIC ID acronym: B = behavior; A = affect; S = sensation; I = imagery; C = cognition; I = interpersonal functioning; D = drugs/biology. Wachtel (1977) endeavored to integrate psychoanalysis and behavior therapy. Insight derived from psychoanalytic methods was said to result in behavior change, and behavior change produced by behavioral methods was said to result in insight. Wachtel's comments initiated contemporary interest in psychotherapy integration. Wachtel (1997) published a second edition of his book that included systems theory. Along with additional emphasis on common factors provided by Goldfried (1980) The Society for the Exploration of Psychotherapy Integration (SEPI)[1] was officially formed in 1983.

A transtheoretical approach to psychotherapy integration was published by Prochaska and DiClemente (2005). Linehan (1993) fostered psychotherapy integration when she developed dialectical behavior therapy (DBT) by combining Eastern philosophy and contemporary cognitive-behavior

[1] http://sepiweb.com

therapy. Heard and Linehan (2005) discussed applications of this form of integrative psychotherapy to patients diagnosed with borderline personality disorder. Major handbooks concerning psychotherapy integration have been published by Norcross and Goldfried (1992, 2005) and by Stricker and Gold (1993).

FOUR APPROACHES TO PSYCHOTHERAPY INTEGRATION

Stricker (2010) identified the following four general approaches to psychotherapy integration.

Common Factors

Stricker (2010, pp. 18–19) offered the following list of common factors: (a) therapeutic alliance; (b) exposure to prior difficulties plus a new corrective emotional experience; (c) expectation of positive outcome; (d) therapist characteristics of attention, empathy, and positive regard; (d) providing the client with a rationale for why treatment works; and (f) use of a culturally sanctioned healing procedure/ritual. See Grencavage and Norcross (1990) for additional details concerning common factors. Weinberger (1993, 1995) referenced common factors with the acronym REMA where R = relationships, **E = exposure**, M = mastery, and A = attribution. Of special interest to the proposed Bio↔Psychology Network Theory is that both Stricker and Weinberger agree that **exposure** is a common factor. The connectionist/experience-dependent plasticity mechanism explanation presented in this book as to why effective psychotherapies work features exposure as a necessary condition to activate the biological mechanisms that physically modify neural networks in therapeutic ways. Grencavage and Norcross (1990) provided additional details concerning common factors. The proposed Bio↔Psychology Network Theory is consistent with all of the common factors identified by Stricker (2010, pp. 18–19), by Weinberger (1993, 1995), and by Grencavage and Norcross (1990).

Of special interest to the proposed Bio↔Psychology Network Theory is that **exposure** is a common factor. Network **Principle 8: Dissonance Induction/Reduction** features exposure as a common method used by all effective therapies to activate the experience-dependent plasticity mechanisms that mediate therapeutic consonance and change.

The proposed Bio↔Psychology Network Theory introduces an additional common factor that has long escaped everyone's list; namely, **learning and memory**. Memory enables learning. If we could not form memories we could not learn, and that means we could not benefit from psychological interventions of any kind. A complete understanding of how psychotherapy works requires one to explain how people learn and form long-term memories. Psychotherapists have long assumed that people can learn and form memories, but have rarely discussed this matter formally. Shaffer (1978) discussed Hermaneutic psychoanalytic treatment as a form of memory modification, but did not provide any mechanism information regarding these effects. The proposed Bio↔Psychology Network Theory provides much of the missing mechanism information.

The pragmatics of delivering health care services requires clinicians to establish a therapeutic alliance, to generate a positive outcome expectation, to attend to the patient with empathy and positive regard, to provide some rationale for the treatment being administered, and to stay within culturally sanctioned limits. These are not scientific issues. The proposed Bio↔Psychology Network Theory is fully consistent with all of these pragmatic factors. It also provides an explanation of why and how placebo effects, better described as psychological effects, work. All of these factors demonstrate how compatible the proposed Bio↔Psychology Network Theory and these common factors are.

Technical Integration

Stricker (2010) defined technical integration as 'the use of techniques drawn from several different therapeutic approaches' (p. 22) and an 'approach to psychotherapy integration in which a combination of techniques are drawn from different therapeutic systems without regard for any specific theoretical approach' (p. 125). He warned that this approach is most easily confused with **eclecticism** which he defines as 'An approach in which the therapist chooses interventions because they work, without regard to theory or any other reason for using techniques other than efficacy' (p. 121). Stricker contrasted eclecticism with **syncretism** which he defined as 'combining techniques without any systematic rationale for doing so' (p. 125) 'other than the idiosyncratic preferences of the therapist' (p. 22). Stricker endeavored to resolve any confusion as follows: 'Where there is a systematic basis for the combination of techniques, technical integration is a valid and important approach to psychotherapy integration' (p. 22).

Assimilative Integration

Stricker (2010) defined assimilative integration as '... an approach in which a solid grounding in one theoretical position is accompanied by a willingness to incorporate techniques from other therapeutic approaches' (p. 26). Stricker noted that assimilative integration differs from technical integration by virtue of being primarily committed to a single theoretical orientation. This is the position that Stricker favors and illustrates in the remainder of his book.

Theoretical Integration

Stricker (2010) claimed that theoretical integration is the most difficult approach because it requires integrating disparate concepts based on fundamental incompatible world view differences. Messer and Winokur (1980, 1984) have written at length about the irreconcilable theoretical differences that separate psychoanalysis and behavior therapy. In short, Stricker's reference to this approach as constituting '... **an elusive holy grail**...' (p. 24, bold emphasis added) indicates that he considers this approach to be essentially impossible.

I show below that the network orientation supported by the proposed Bio↔Psychology Network Theory provides the required theoretical unification to integrate the Big Five clinical orientations. Theory enables us to explain. Theory guides research and practice, even when its presence is only informal and perhaps just intuitive. Psychologists who understand people differently should be expected to treat them differently in clinical settings. How could it be otherwise? The mechanism information provided by the four core network principles that constitute the explanatory nucleus and the eight corollary network principles that derive from them provides the required common conceptual core that enables clinicians to have a common understanding that naturally leads to psychotherapy integration. I therefore aim to show in this chapter how psychotherapy integration naturally follows from this theoretical unification.

UNIFYING THE BIG FIVE CLINICAL ORIENTATIONS

The purpose of this section is to explicitly show how the network orientation authorized by the Bio↔Psychology Network Theory is fully consistent with what I refer to as the Big Five clinical orientations. I aim to show that the proposed network orientation constitutes a Hegelian synthesis where each of the Big Five clinical orientations can be understood as a special consistent case of the network orientation. This network orientation consists of a hybrid cognitive neuroscience theory consisting of neuroscience and connectionist mechanisms, well-replicated psychological phenomenon, and multivariate statistics that provide mechanism information that is fully consistent with all of the Big Five clinical orientations.

Whereas some effort has been made to integrate psychodynamic and behavioral orientations (Wachtel, 1997), no effort, let alone significant progress, has been made toward integrating the manifest content of all five clinical orientations. Clinicians have always borrowed what they consider to be the best methods from other clinical orientations, despite concerns about eclectic practice mentioned above.

Common Absence of Causal Mechanism Information

In this section I draw attention to the absence of mechanism information as a novel basis for psychotherapy integration.

1. The first four clinical orientations are based on functional psychological theories which, by definition, lack causal mechanism information that can explain how and why the specified functional relationships occur as stated. This common absence of causal mechanism claims includes the absence of conflicting causal mechanism claims. This common absence takes us a long way towards psychotherapy integration, because the first four clinical orientations have not taken conflicting theoretical positions that then need to be resolved. That the mechanism information provided by the proposed Bio↔Psychology Network Theory is compatible with all of the Big Five clinical orientations (see below) effectively results in their integration by virtue of Hegelian synthesis, and on the basis that things equal to the same thing are equal to each other.
2. Rumelhart and McClelland (1986) and McClelland and Rumelhart (1986) demonstrated that a variety of psychological phenomena involving learning and memory could be simulated using artificial neural networks. Their work is generally referred to as connectionism. Connectionism is therefore a core feature of the proposed Bio↔Psychology Network Theory.
3. I realized that a modified form of connectionism provided a common basis for integrating all of the Big Five clinical orientations. Tryon (2012) combined connectionism, neuroscience, well-replicated psychological phenomenon, and multivariate statistics into a hybrid cognitive neuroscience Bio↔Psychology Network Theory.[2]

Integration with Behavior Therapy/Applied Behavior Analysis

The behavioral orientation is defined by its emphasis upon **learning**. Principle 2 (Learning and Memory) provides mechanism information that pertains to cognitive forms of learning as well as to operant and respondent

[2] The term Bio↔Psychology Network Theory had not yet occurred to me in 2012.

conditioning. Tryon (1995) reported that connectionist models can explain most major classical conditioning phenomena, including stimulus summation, blocking, unblocking, overshadowing, partial reinforcement effects, interstimulus effects, second order conditioning, conditioned inhibition, latent inhibition, extinction, reacquisition effects, backward conditioning, compound conditioning, discriminative stimulus effects, inverted-U in learning as a function of interstimulus interval, anticipatory conditioned responses, secondary reinforcement, attentional focusing by conditioned motivational feedback, super conditioning, and learned helplessness (Commons et al., 1991; Donegan et al., 1989; Gluck & Thompson, 1987; Grossberg & Levine, 1987; Grossberg & Schmajuk, 1987, 1989; Hawkins, 1989; Kehoe, 1988, 1989; Klopf, 1988; Sutton & Barto, 1981). See also Burgos (2010), Donahoe and Packard-Dorsel (1997), Mignault and Marley (1997), Schmajuk (2010), and Tesauro (1990) for further details. Connectionist models of operant conditioning have also been successfully developed and tested (Dragoi & Staddon, 1991; Grossberg, 1971; Nargeot et al., 1999a,b; Seung, 2003; Spencer et al., 1999). Hence, Principle 2 (Learning and Memory) is completely consistent, fully compatible, and supportive of the behavioral orientation and applied behavior analysis.

Carlson et al. (2010) defined learning in terms of **memory**; '*Learning* refers to the process by which experiences change our nervous system and hence our behavior. We refer to these changes as *memories*' (italics in the original) (p. 440). If you are forming memories, then you are learning. Operant and respondent conditioning are two simple methods for activating experience-dependent plasticity mechanisms that cause memories to form. Expectations consist of memories, in that they anticipate the future based on past events. Rescorla (1987, 1988) emphasized the role of expectations in conditioning.

Skinner (1981, 1984a, 1984b) patterned his functional theory of behavior after Darwin's functional theory of evolution. He proposed that behavioral variations exist and are selected by events that follow the emission or omission of behavior. Donahoe (1991) and Donahoe et al. (1993) emphasized the central role that selection plays in behavioral explanations. Connectionist models implement selection on a neural network basis when they simulate the biological fact that neurons that fire together wire together. See Tryon (1993b) and Chapters 3 and 4 for further details. Donahoe (1997) wrote about the necessity of neural network simulations to the future of operant conditioning. Reinforcement history is central to behavioral theory because it is a record of the effects of behavioral selection. Connectionist network models are trained, not programmed. Their training history is crucial to the selection of their 'adult' abilities.

The proposed Bio↔Psychology Network Theory constitutes a modern neuroscience-based learning theory that provides mechanism information to explain how and why operant and respondent conditioning phenomena occur. Therefore, the Bio↔Psychology Network Theory is fully consistent with the applied behavior analytic (behavioral) orientation, precisely because it provides a scientific biological basis for all behavioral principles. Hence, there is complete congruence between the Bio↔Psychology Network Theory and the behavioral orientation.

The behavioral orientation positively values determinism because it operates from a natural science perspective. The parallel distributed cascade of activation across the network is as deterministic as electrical propagation along an axon and drives all other network principles.

Redintegration (Principle 4: Activation and Reactivation) began as a behavioral concept referring to the restoration of behavior upon re-experiencing certain stimuli. This process is explained by Principle 6: Part–Whole Pattern Completion. Behaviorism has consistently stressed the impact that external stimuli have on psychology and behavior. Principle 12: Bottom-Up processing is completely consistent with the behavioral orientation.

Integration with the Cognitive Orientation

The proposed Bio↔Psychology Network Theory is a cognitive theory because it emphasizes how the organism transforms stimuli into concepts. **Principle 3: Transformation** provides a fundamental causal mechanism by which neural networks can generate cognitions. Transformation is the defining feature of cognition. It refers to all processes designated as 'O' in the classic Stimulus → Organism → Response (S → O → R) cognitive model. Cognition provides the ability to transform stimuli and thereby avoid explanation by S → R reflex.

Connectionism is widely recognized as a legitimate cognitive psychology that competes with traditional symbol-manipulating cognitive theories. Connectionist models of learning, memory, and language have consistently been accepted as cognitive models. Titles of connectionist books such as *Parallel Distributed Processing: Explorations in the Microstructure of Cognition, Vol. 1: Foundations* by Rumelhart, McClelland, and the PDP Research Group (1986), *Parallel Distributed Processing: Explorations in the Microstructure of Cognition*, Vol. 2: *Psychological and Biological Models* by McClelland, Rumelhart and the PDP Research Group (1986), and other books such as *Introduction to Connectionist Modelling of Cognitive Processes* by McLeod et al. (1998) definitively demonstrate that connectionist models are cognitive models.

Connectionism is accepted as a cognitive theory without question. The cognitive model described by Judith Beck (2011, p. 30) is completely consistent with the proposed Bio↔Psychology Network Theory, as is her emphasis on automatic thoughts and my extension to automatic feelings. The clinical guidelines that Beck (2011) provided in the remainder of her book are fully consistent with the proposed Bio↔Psychology Network Theory.

Further evidence that the network orientation is fully consistent with the cognitive orientation stems from the fact that cognitive phenomena can be explained by Bio↔Psychology Network Theory principles. For example, priming is such a robust cognitive phenomenon that it is commonly used in social-personality psychology to manipulate psychological states that serve as independent variables. The explanatory nucleus consisting of Principles 1 (Unconscious Processing via the Network Cascade), 2 (Learning and Memory), 3 (Transformation), and 4 (Activation and Reactivation) provide a mechanism for how priming works.

Heider's (1958) consonance and Festinger's (1957) dissonance clearly qualify as cognitive concepts and constitute our Principle 7: Consonance and Dissonance. Principle 8 (Dissonance Induction/Reduction) explains how empirically supported treatments for anxiety (Tryon, 2005) and depression (Tryon & Misurell, 2008) work, including how Barlow's unified protocol (Allen et al., 2008; Barlow et al., 2011) works. Prototype formation (Principle 10) has long been considered to be a cognitive process. Top-down processing (Principle 12) emphasizes internal working models and expectations, both of which are indisputably cognitive.

Principles 4 (Activation and Reactivation), 6 (Part–Whole Pattern Completion), and 9 (Memory Superposition) provide neuroscience-inspired memory mechanisms that are completely compatible with the cognitive orientation. Principle 4 (Activation and Reactivation) explains memory recall as reactivation of synapses to the state they were in when memory first formed. The active reconstructive nature of the Part–Whole Pattern Completion (Principle 6) process qualifies it as a cognitive process. Hence, there is complete congruence between the proposed Bio↔Psychology Network Theory and the cognitive orientation.

Integration with the Cognitive-Behavioral Orientation

Having established that the proposed Bio↔Psychology Network Theory is both a behavioral and a cognitive theory means that the recommended network orientation is fully consistent with the cognitive-behavioral orientation. Stated alternatively, given that connectionist models are completely consistent with both the behavioral and cognitive orientations, it follows directly that they also provide the cognitive-behavioral orientation with its conceptual 'must haves'.

Of special note is the strong relationship between the proposed Bio↔Psychology Network Theory and Barlow's Unified Protocol (Allen et al., 2008; Barlow et al., 2011) that is a common method for treating a wide variety of disorders, including anxiety and depression. Our Principle 8 presents a dissonance induction/reduction mechanism that explains why and how exposure therapy works. This principle can be communicated to clients to enhance their understanding of what they are expected to do for homework.

Integration with Motivational Interviewing

Motivational interviewing (MI; Miller & Rollnick, 2002; Tashiro & Mortensen, 2006) is a widely used cognitive-behavioral therapy that clearly features our Principle 8. Inducing dissonance to motivate clients and to manage dissonance reduction so that clients adopt more adaptive ways of thinking, feeling, and behaving rather than returning to substance abuse is a hallmark of motivational interviewing. This means that MI clinicians and CBT clinicians can refer to the same mechanism information when teaching their clients about the need to properly manage and reduce therapeutic dissonance.

Integration with the Psychodynamic Orientation

This section discusses four ways in which the proposed network orientation is consistent with, reflects, core elements of the psychodynamic orientation. I first discuss the compatibility of the proposed network principles with the psychodynamic orientation. Then I consider Shedler's analysis of what most characterizes the psychodynamic orientation to show how much of it is consistent with our network orientation.

Network Principles

Principle 1: Unconscious Processing

The psychodynamic orientation depends crucially upon unconscious processing. Without unconscious processing the psychodynamic orientation would not exist. The strong emphasis that the psychodynamic orientation places on unconscious processing has been a key barrier to psychotherapy integration, because cognitive and cognitive-behavioral therapies are entirely conscious-centric. The network orientation advocated here depends as crucially upon unconscious processing as does the psychodynamic orientation. These two clinical orientations are therefore completely congruent, identical, in this regard. Chapter 3 reviewed five sources of psychological evidence and ten sources of neuroscience evidence that require that psychological science takes an unconscious-centric orientation.

Principle 2: Learning and Memory

Core clinical features of psychodynamic theory emphasize the importance of early learning and associated memories. Our Principle 2 provides biological mechanism information that strongly supports this facet of psychodynamic theory. While episodic memory is poor or non-existent before age three due to inadequate hippocampal development, epigenetic research reviewed in Chapter 3 confirms that stressful experiences that occur even shortly after birth, such as maternal separation, can have lasting effects on the hypothalamic–pituitary–adrenal axis that regulates stress response into adult life. These data support psychodynamic claims regarding the importance of early experience. In short, the proposed network orientation places the same strong emphasis on early experience as does the psychodynamic orientation.

Freud (1895b) began to write a neuroscience book entitled *The Project for a Scientific Psychology* in which he explained psychology and behavior in physical terms. However, the limited neuroscience of his day precluded his writing more than three chapters (Centonze et al., 2004). Contemporary efforts are being made to restore a neuroscience base to psychodynamic theory. For example, Fotopoulou et al. (2012) edited a book entitled *Trends in Psychodynamic Neuroscience* that seeks a rapprochement between psychoanalysis and neuroscience based on recent technological and methodological innovations in neuroscience including computational neuroscience; a conceptual cousin to connectionism. Their approach is completely consistent with all 12 of our network principles.

Principle 4: Activation and Reactivation

This principle provides additional details regarding the reactivation of emotional memories that are fully compatible with the psychodynamic orientation. Principle 4 entails the reactivation of emotional memories in a way that is consistent with emotion-focused therapy (Angus & Greenberg, 2011; Greenberg, 2002; Paivio & Pascual-Leone, 2010). Principle 5 (Priming) explains how subliminal (unconscious) processing can predispose how supraliminal stimuli are consciously processed. Principle 6 (Part–Whole Pattern Completion) explains how a complete pattern can be reconstructed from some of its parts. This process is also consistent with psychodynamic theory.

Other Principles

Conflicts create dissonance. People seek ways of reducing dissonance; i.e., creating consonance. Sometimes this process is more heavily influenced by emotions than cognitions. Hence, Principles 7 (Consonance and Dissonance) and 8 (Dissonance Induction/Reduction) are consistent with the psychodynamic orientation. Principle 9 (Memory Superposition) addresses how multiple memories can be stored in the same neural network. Stacking memories together enables them to blend together in ways that are consistent with psychodynamic theory. The formation of prototypes regarding authority and parental figures is a long-standing psychodynamic theme. Principle 10 concerns prototype formation.

A major psychodynamic theme concerns interaction between the conscious and unconscious minds. This conceptual 'must have' is fully supported by Principle 12 (Top-Down, Bottom-Up Processing) in conjunction with Principle 1 (Unconscious Processing via the Network Cascade) that authorizes an unconscious-centric orientation to all of psychology. Top-Down processing (Principle 12) implements **internal working models**; a concept most frequently associated with attachment theory and consequently with psychodynamic theory.

The topic of insight is relevant to unconscious processing. One might say that the primary objective of psychodynamic treatment is to increase insight. Johansson et al. (2010) discussed their insight scale in terms consistent with psychological mindedness. In their view, treatments that promote psychological mindedness also promote insight. The psychologically minded person is one who understands how their thoughts and feelings interact to produce their behaviors. The psychologically minded person understands how their thoughts, feelings, and behaviors impact their relationships with other people; especially the close emotional relationships they have with significant others. See Chapter 9 for additional definitions of psychological mindedness that are similar to those provided here. Psychological mindedness is highly desirable and constitutes a legitimate goal of all forms of therapy. In sum, the 12 network principles provide the psychodynamic orientation with many of its conceptual 'must haves'.

Shedler's Analysis

Shedler (2010) claimed that psychodynamic therapists do more of the behaviors listed below than cognitive-behavioral therapists do. I now consider the seven features that Shedler (2010) claimed reliably distinguish psychodynamic therapy from all other therapies, with the aim of demonstrating compatibility with the proposed network orientation. Additional research is required to determine if all seven features are necessary to achieve therapeutic results.

1. Focus on Affect and Expression of Emotion

Shedler (2010) claimed that psychodynamic therapists help the patient express emotions, especially contradictory feelings and threatening feelings. The therapist helps clients identify feelings that they may not have initially recognized. This focus on emotional insight, in Shedler's view, stands in contrast to the cognitive focus of CBT. The emphasis that the proposed network orientation places on unconscious origins of emotions and other network principles reviewed above is fully consistent with the psychodynamic orientation. That empirically supported emotion-focused therapies are fully consistent with the proposed network orientation further establishes congruence between the proposed network and psychodynamic orientations.

2. Exploration of Avoidance

Shedler (2010) claimed that psychodynamic therapists help the patient to explore their attempts to avoid distressing thoughts and feelings; i.e., to explore their resistance and to acknowledge these feelings. The proposed network orientation is equally open to such efforts, and therefore is compatible with the psychodynamic orientation.

3. Identification of Recurring Themes and Patterns

Shedler (2010) claimed that psychodynamic therapists help the patient identify recurring themes and patterns regarding thoughts, feelings, relationships, and self-concept that the patient does not initially recognize. This is especially the case where painful themes are involved. The proposed network orientation is equally open to such efforts, and therefore is compatible with the psychodynamic orientation.

4. Discussion of Past Experience

Shedler (2010) claimed that psychodynamic therapists help the patient discover the developmental origin of the recurring themes and patterns just mentioned. This includes an analysis of early experiences and of attachment figures. While the proposed network orientation is equally open to such efforts, the question of whether evidence of incremental validity for empirically supported treatments that incorporate these practices can be found remains open.

5. Focus on Interpersonal Relations

Shedler (2010) claimed that psychodynamic therapists help the patient better understand their relationships with significant others and how these relationships bear upon their emotional needs. The proposed network orientation places a premium on psychological mindedness, insight, and is therefore fully compatible with this aspect of the psychodynamic orientation.

6. Focus on the Therapy Relationship

Shedler (2010) claimed that psychodynamic therapists help the patient use their relationship with the therapist to explore the repetitive themes identified above. While the proposed network orientation is equally open to such efforts, the question of whether evidence of incremental validity for empirically supported treatments that incorporate these practices can be found remains open.

7. Exploration of Fantasy Life

Shedler (2010) claimed that psychodynamic therapists encourage patients to speak freely about whatever is on their minds including desires, fears, fantasies, dreams, and daydreams, in order to better understand how the patient understands themself. The aim here is to produce clinical improvement that extends beyond symptom removal, and foster the positive presence of psychological capacities and resources and have more satisfying interpersonal relationships. While the proposed network orientation is equally open to such efforts, the question of whether evidence of incremental validity for empirically supported treatments that incorporate these practices can be found remains open.

Other Factors

Wachtel's (1977, 1997) identification of the cyclic influence of insight on behavior change and behavior change on insight is fully consistent with the proposed network orientation. The emphasis that Stricker (2010) placed on exposure as a common factor in all psychotherapies is fully consistent with the role of exposure in the proposed network orientation.

Shaffer (1978) emphasized the role of memory modification in Hermaneutic psychoanalysis. Tryon and McKay (2009) and our discussion in Chapter 3 demonstrated that new learning necessarily modifies memory to the point where memory modifications may be used to document the effects of psychotherapy. These findings further demonstrate congruence between the network and psychodynamic orientations.

Summers and Barber (2010, p. 10) provided a guide to evidence-based practice from a psychodynamic orientation. They recognized that dynamic therapy consists of a spectrum with psychoanalysis at one end and supportive psychotherapy at the other end. They presented six 'essential features of psychodynamic psychotherapy in current practice' (p. 12). They are: (a) 'use of exploratory, interpretative, and supportive interventions as appropriate'; (b) 'frequent sessions'; (c) 'emphasis on uncovering painful affects, understanding past painful experiences'; (d) 'goal is to facilitate emotional experience and increase understanding'; (e) 'focus on the therapeutic relationship, including attention to transference and countertransference'; and (f) 'use of a wide range of techniques, with variability in application by different practitioners'. All of these therapist behaviors are completely consistent with the proposed network orientation. Put otherwise, none of these clinical activities conflicts in any way with any of the dozen principles on which the proposed network orientation is based. Instead, they represent clinical decisions regarding how to proceed with clinical practice, and are subject to verification as part of empirically supported treatments.

Psychodynamic theories emphasize insight. The proposed network orientation understands insight as **psychological mindedness**. The psychologically minded person is one who is insightful with regard to how their thoughts, feelings, and actions interact and impact their relationships with other people; especially close emotional relationships. Psychological mindedness is very desirable and constitutes a legitimate goal of all forms of therapy. The value placed on insight as psychological mindedness makes the proposed network orientation consistent with the psychodynamic orientation.

Integration with Emotion-Focused Therapy

Behavior, cognition, and affect are causally interrelated. These relationships can be visualized by placing each word at the vertex of a triangle while understanding each side of the triangle as a double-headed arrow. Behavior therapy aims to modify behaviors with the expectation that modified behavior will change cognitions and affect. Cognitive therapy aims to modify cognitions with the expectation that altered thinking will modify behaviors and emotions. Emotion-focused therapy (EFT) aims to modify emotions with the expectation that altered emotions will modify cognitions and behaviors.

Greenberg (2013) stipulated that EFT is based on six principles. Three of these principles concern ways to expose clients to their emotions. Network Principle 3 concerns transformation and with slight modification presented below, explains how and why EFT works. Network Principle 8 regarding dissonance induction/reduction explains why all effective therapies work regardless of the clinical orientation that originated them.

EFT Principles

Greenberg (2013) stipulated that EFT is based on six principles. The following sections show that the proposed Bio↔Psychology Network Theory explains five of the six EFT principles.

Emotional awareness is the first EFT principle. It is achieved through self-observation, where clients keep a diary of the circumstances and consequences that bookend each instance of a maladaptive emotion targeted for therapy. This is much like the behavioral method of self-observation. This process is intended to make automatic feelings conscious. It consciously **exposes** the client to their emotions and in doing so helps them **accept** that they have these emotions. Some people tend to **avoid** and deny that they have strong feelings of hate, jealousy, etc., and try not to recognize them for cultural and religious reasons. **Avoidance** is what exposure exercises are designed to stop. **Acceptance** is a key ingredient in both EFT and acceptance and commitment therapy (ACT; Arch & Craske, 2008; Hayes et al., 2012). The intellectual acceptance that results from implementing this first EFT principle is therapeutic on its own, but is not sufficient for full gains to be made. The main point here is that this first EFT principle is fully consistent with the proposed network orientation.

Emotional expression is the second EFT principle. Having clients express strong negative maladaptive emotions in therapy helps them to emotionally accept these feelings. Expressing these emotions makes them real to the client, and consequently facilitates emotionally accepting them. Expressing maladaptive emotions constitutes in vivo emotional **exposure**. This EFT principle is fully consistent with the proposed network orientation.

Reflection on the intellectual and emotional insight gained through the first two EFT principles is the third EFT principle. It furthers acceptance and inhibits avoidance. Reflection helps integrate the fact that the client has these maladaptive emotions in their personal narrative. This EFT principle is fully consistent with the proposed network orientation.

Corrective emotional experiences are required to modify emotions and constitutes the fourth EFT principle. Only a more adaptive emotion can modify a maladaptive emotion according to EFT. Hence, therapy entails activating more adaptive emotions. This EFT principle is fully consistent with the proposed network orientation.

Emotional transformation is the fifth EFT principle. It entails a process that enables corrective emotional experiences to work. Our memory formation mechanisms and our Network Principle 3: Transformation provide mechanism information for how this core EFT principle can work. Figure 5.7 in Chapter 5 illustrates how memories are formed as composites of cognitive and emotional components. This authorizes us to interpret the first three microfeatures illustrated in the bottom panel of Figure 3.11 in Chapter 3 as cognitions and the second three microfeatures as emotions. In this case both factors illustrated in the bottom panel of Figure 3.11 are a composite of cognitive and emotional microfeatures. Hence, both the memory formation mechanism and the transformation mechanism necessarily cause cognitive and emotional microfeatures to interact and causally influence one another. This mechanism information explains how this fifth EFT principle works.

Regulation is the sixth EFT principle. It involves managing emotional intensity. None of the 12 network principles apply to it, because this is a clinical objective and not a scientific phenomenon that requires explanation. This shows that the network orientation has pertinent boundaries.

Integration with Other Psychotherapies

Our Principle 8 concerning dissonance induction/reduction was presented as a fundamental mechanism that explains why all effective psychotherapies work, regardless of the theoretical orientation that generated them. Such a common mechanism constitutes a common factor and that makes the proposed network orientation relevant to all psychotherapies, including interventions other than those associated with the Big Five clinical orientations. Identifying a single active ingredient for all effective treatments provides therapists of all persuasions with a common basis for constructively discussing their particular approaches to psychotherapy. Therapists can constructively discuss their techniques for implementing Principle 8 without divisive theoretical issues entering the conversation. Principle 8 provides important common ground on which therapists hopefully agree rather than argue about whose orientation is correct.

Integration with Pharmacology

The network orientation authorized by the Bio↔Psychology Network Theory is fully consistent with the pharmacologic orientation in two ways. The first way stems from the fact that PDP-CNN models use connection weights to simulate synapses. These weights connect simulated neurons with one another. Positive connection weights simulate synaptic excitation. Negative connection weights simulate synaptic inhibition. Psychotropic medications exert their effects through increasing or decreasing specific synaptic neurotransmitters that increase or decrease synaptic excitation or inhibition. This means that PDP-CNN models are highly consistent with the pharmacological orientation. The enteric nervous system lines the gut and runs on many of the same neurotransmitters as does the brain. This explains why psychotropic medications designed to alter the brain also affect the gut and can have gastroenterological side effects.

Connection weights are modified by learning equations that simulate experience-dependent plasticity mechanisms. Memories are simulated by modifying connection weights. Hell and Ehlers (2008) stated 'Computationally, synapses play a central role in signal transmission and processing that represent evolution's solution to learning and memory. Nervous systems, including our own brains, possess an extraordinary capacity for adaptation and memory because **the synapse, not the neuron, constitutes the basis unit for information storage**' (p. 779, bold emphasis added). This pharmacologic premise is fully consistent with PDP-CNN models.

The second way that the network orientation authorized by the proposed Bio↔Psychology Network Theory is fully consistent with the pharmacologic orientation is that Network Principle 3: Transformation provides a mechanism by which networks can generate latent constructs where connection weights, simulated synapses, function as factor loadings. Modifying these loadings necessarily changes the latent constructs generated by the network, thereby modifying simulated thoughts, feelings, and behaviors. It is noteworthy that medications such as D-cycloserine facilitate extinction of emotional memories because of their effects on NMDA synaptic receptors (Norberg et al., 2008).

Learning-based psychological interventions such as CBT produce physical brain changes. Linden (2006) reviewed literature demonstrating that psychotherapy results in brain changes that can be detected by non-invasive brain scans. Functional brain imaging is being used to document the brain changes produced by learning-based interventions. For example, Goldapple et al. (2004) conducted positron-emission tomography (PET) scans on 17 unmedicated patients diagnosed with major depression before and after 15–20 sessions of CBT that resulted in clinical improvement on the Hamilton Depression Rating Scale. These authors reported increased activation in the hippocampus and dorsal cingulate. These studies found decreased activation in the dorsal, ventral, and medial frontal cortex. In sum, they reported that CBT modulated activation in both limbic and cortical regions.

Baxter et al. (1992) conducted PET scans on patients with OCD before and after receiving either CBT or fluoxetine-hydrochloride. Their results demonstrated significant activation decreases in the head of the right caudate nucleus relative to that in the ipsilateral hemisphere. Del Casale et al. (2011) conducted a literature review of functional imaging studies that have evaluated the physical changes produced by CBT for OCD. The authors reported on 143 studies covering 755 patients with OCD. Behavior therapy was shown to alter ten brain structures.

Several other network principles demonstrate compatibility with the pharmacologic orientation. Principle 4 (Activation and Reactivation) stipulates that memory entails reactivating synapses across the connectome to the state they were in when the memory first formed. Priming (Principle 5) works because initial stimulus presentations biologically strengthen selected synapses that form a pathway through the neural network such that subsequent stimuli are predisposed to follow this processing pathway. The Part–Whole Pattern Completion (Principle 6) process works because neural networks naturally autoassociate. That is, their outputs become inputs resulting in improved outputs. This recursive process of simulated synaptic modification actively constructs more complete patterns from less complete ones.

The neural network training method expressed as Principle 8 (Dissonance Induction/Reduction) entails creating and maintaining dissonance by requiring that new behaviors be artificially maintained until experience-dependent plasticity processes can modify synaptic connections such that the network processes in ways that are more consonant with and supportive of the new behavior. This is a possible mechanism by which exposure therapy for anxiety (Tryon, 2005), depression (Tryon & Misurell, 2008), and the unified protocol (Allen et al., 2008) appear to work.

The third way that the network orientation authorized by the Bio↔Psychology Network Theory is fully consistent with the pharmacologic orientation is that both are based on neuroscience and associated biological mechanisms. The anatomical fact that the brain is composed of interconnected neural networks[3] means that some sort of network theory is required to integrate the pharmacologic orientation with the first four clinical orientations. The proposed Bio↔Psychology Network Theory provides the required network orientation.

Freud was a practicing neuroscientist prior to developing psychoanalysis. Freud (1895b) thought about psychology and behavior in physical terms, as does the Bio↔Psychology Network Theory, when he wrote his *Project for a Scientific Psychology*. Centonze et al. (2004) documented that Freud was aware of the work of Camillo Golgi, whose method of staining cells enabled visualization of single neurons for the first time in 1873, and the work of Ramon y Cajal who proved the existence of synapses that same year. Centonze et al. (2004) reported that Freud anticipated the now well-documented fact that memory is based on synaptic modification. Spitzer's (1999, p. 5) the Figure (reproduced on page xiii of this book) is of a neural network drawn by Freud in 1895 as part of his *Project for a Scientific Psychology*. However, neuroscience limitations circa 1895 precluded Freud from completing his book. I propose that the Bio↔Psychology Network Theory is the theory Freud would have written had he been writing in 2013 instead of 1895.

In sum, the proposed network orientation principles provide the pharmacologic orientation with all of its conceptual 'must haves' and more.

Conclusion

Clinical orientations are broader and more tolerant of exclusion than are the supporting theories. Things equal to the same thing are equal to each other. The proposed network orientation is consistent with the Big Five clinical orientations based on these two premises. It constitutes a Hegelian synthesis of all five clinical orientations.

CLINICAL PRACTICE

The above section demonstrated the conceptual congruence between our network orientation and the Big Five clinical orientations, but how does this translate into clinical practice? What does it mean to simultaneously adopt all of the Big Five clinical orientations? What does clinical practice look like from this composite network orientation? My answer is organized

[3] The Human Connectome Project has begun to map these neural networks (http://www.humanconnectomeproject.org/).

in terms of five primary ways that I expect that your professional practice will change if you adopt the proposed network orientation.

Professional Identity

You will think differently about yourself. Your primary professional identity will change. You will primarily identify with **principles** rather than **persons** such as august psychologists like Freud, Skinner, Rogers, Beck, Ellis, etc. Religions, philosophies, cults, and preparadigmatic sciences identify with people. Mature sciences identify with principles.

You will no longer primarily identify with any of the 'isms' such as behaviorism and cognitivism. Nor will you primarily identify with any one of the resulting Big Five clinical orientations: (a) behavioral (applied behavior analysis); (b) cognitive; (c) cognitive-behavioral; (d) psychodynamic (emotion-focused therapies); and (e) pharmacologic. This is because the proposed Bio↔Psychology Network Theory is fully consistent with all of them. Instead, you will see yourself as a professional whose healing arts are based on psychological science.

Think Physical not Mental

You will think about psychology and your client's problems in **physical** rather than **mental** terms. You will understand that psychotherapy entails brain change. The proposed Bio↔Psychology Network Theory fully integrates medicine and pharmacology into the clinical practice of psychology by explaining psychological phenomena and disorders in physical rather than mental terms. This facilitates participation in multidisciplinary teams; especially in medical settings. Your professional image will be more like that of your medical colleagues who will likely treat you with greater respect.

The proposed Bio↔Psychology Network Theory enables psychotherapists to explain many of their client's problems in physical rather than mental terms, thereby removing a major stigma associated with seeking psychological help. It will also increase your patient's tolerance of family members with psychological and/or behavioral disorders, as illustrated in Chapter 1. Being able to say that psychotherapy produces physical changes in the brains of our clients and that these physical changes are similar to those produced by medication but are more long lasting (DeRubeis et al., 2008) is a special benefit of adopting the proposed Bio↔Psychology Network Theory. The changes we create in the brains of our clients are physical and powerful. Psychotherapists should be proud and congratulate themselves regarding these accomplishments. This achievement puts psychotherapists on the same biological basis as physicians. Consequently they should receive the same level of respect as physicians enjoy.

The knowledge that therapy produces physical brain changes can be used to help clients better understand and accept the conditions needed to produce these changes. Network Principle 8 concerns dissonance induction and reduction. It was derived from methods for training artificial networks. These same methods can be used to retrain real neural networks. This principle was also derived from an enormous amount of social psychology research (see Abelson et al., 1968) requiring new behavior that is initially incompatible with what the neural network computes generates dissonance. This discomforting condition is what activates the experience-dependent plasticity mechanisms that will modify the client's neural network, and thereby change the ways that they think, feel, and act. These changes will reduce the dissonance induced by the therapist. This information can be shared with clients in order that they might better understand why their therapist intentionally made their life more difficult as they try to help them. The need to tolerate dissonance to achieve therapeutic goals is reminiscent of treatments provided by the noted psychiatrist Harry Stack Sullivan, who asked people to adopt a different persona as a part of their treatment. Behaving in new ways may initially seem odd and alien, but will become more familiar over time. Behavior therapists also ask their clients to behave differently, based on the expectation that cognitions and emotions will subsequently change and become more consonant with their new behavior. The mechanism information presented in this book supports these practices.

The proposed dissonance induction/reduction principle has important similarities with orthodonture, where discomfort is intentionally created by placing braces on teeth to put pressure on jaw bone. The pressure of tooth upon jaw bone causes the jaw bone at the tooth–jaw juncture to dissolve. The teeth move into the space created and new jaw bone grows behind the teeth that moved. The orthodontist intentionally creates pain knowing that it triggers the bone dissolving/regrowing mechanism that ultimately brings therapeutic results and comfort. The orthodontist repeats this procedure over time to physically straighten teeth and modify the jaw. Orthodonture is a gradual process, as is psychotherapy. Psychologists create dissonance through graded exposure and other methods, which must be tolerated, in order to produce the necessary neural network changes required to support new thoughts, feelings, and behavior. Repeated psychotherapeutic treatments are as necessary as are repeated visits to the orthodontist in order to achieve the desired physical changes.

Comprehensive Clinical Practice

Your clinical practice will become more comprehensive in at least the following ways.

Therapeutic Goals

The goals of therapy have traditionally been directed by one's chosen clinical orientation. Clinicians with a behavioral or cognitive-behavioral orientation primarily typically focus on symptom reduction/removal for several reasons. (a) Clients present with symptoms. (b) Diagnoses are arrived at using the Diagnostic and Statistical Manuals whose inclusion and exclusion criteria are symptom-oriented. (c) Manualized treatments have been constructed to describe how to modify symptoms. (d) Empirically supported treatments were developed based upon research evidence. Psychodynamic clinicians typically take a different view when developing therapeutic goals. They understand that many, most, or possibly all of the problems that client's bring to therapy are the result of deficient insight in the form of diminished **psychological mindedness**. The section entitled **Insight as Psychological Mindedness** in Chapter 9 provides many definitions of psychological mindedness. All of them stress awareness of how one's thoughts and feelings influence their behavior and how they interact with other people, especially in close personal relationships. If clients were more insightful, if they understood themselves better and understood the effects they have on other people better, then they might not have the problems that they currently present for treatment. Psychodynamic clinicians therefore see the goal of therapy as providing the necessary insight by increasing their client's psychological mindedness.

Your treatment goals will combine these therapeutic goals because the proposed Bio↔Psychology Network Theory is fully consistent with all of the Big Five clinical orientations. This includes goals of increasing psychological mindedness and improving emotion regulation, as is currently done in dialectic behavior therapy and emotion-focused therapy.

All Available Empirically Supported Treatments

Empirically supported treatments (ESTs) were once available only for the behavioral and cognitive-behavioral clinical orientations (CBT). ESTs are now available for other clinical orientations. Thoma et al. (2012) assessed the research design quality of 120 randomized controlled trials of CBT covering 10,423 patients, and 94 randomized controlled trials of psychodynamic therapy covering 7,200 patients. The mean and standard deviation of quality scores was 25.5 (SD = 9.13) for the CBT trials and 25.1 (SD = 9.04) for the psychodynamic trials. These highly similar means are not statistically or clinically different. Research quality was found to be inversely related to effect size, with better studies showing smaller effects (F (4,91) = 12.6, $p <$ 0.0001, Adjusted R^2 = 0.525) because they control for more sources of variation. Equity in research quality therefore means equity in effect size. In general, various treatments are equally effective when research design quality is controlled; i.e., is comparable.

Meta-analyses of applied clinical research by Abbass et al. (2006), Anderson and Lambert (1995), Crits-Christoph (1992), de Maat et al. (2009), Leichsenring (2001, 2005), Leichsenring and Leibing (2003), Leichsenring et al. (2004), and Shedler (2010) have demonstrated that psychodynamic therapies (PDTs) produce therapeutic effects that are greater than wait list controls, and sometimes equal to those produced by cognitive-behavior therapy (CBT).[4]

The International Society for Interpersonal Therapy reported that there are currently over 250 empirical studies supporting the effectiveness and efficacy of interpersonal therapy (IPT).[5] I do not cite evidence of effectiveness of CBT because it is so well established. Controlled research also supports emotion-focused therapy (Ellison et al., 2009; Goldman et al., 2006a, 2006b; Greenberg & Watson, 1998; Watson et al., 2003). This evidence suggests that the rigid clinical dogma that has divided clinicians into competing schools and camps on the basis that there is but one, and only one, effective way to help people is clearly false and should no longer be supported by responsible empirically informed clinicians.

Clinicians will now be expected to draw upon the full range of available ESTs as required by specific clinical cases. But how shall clinicians decide which treatment to begin with? Where is the required direction to come from? Treatment formulation before psychotherapy integration was much simpler. Permissible interventions were restricted by one's primary theoretical identification. This substantially reduced options for case formulation and therapeutic prescription unless one went off orientation such as Leahy (2009) did. I comment on his '**Confessions of a Cognitive Therapist**' below.

An enormous clinical literature published in the *Journal of Applied Behavior Analysis* and in books such as Martin and Pear's (2010) *Behavior Modification: What It Is and How To Do It* consistently demonstrate powerful clinical

[4] McKay (2011) cited important methodological issues that specifically pertain to Shedler's (2010) presentation and may well apply to other meta-analyses of psychodynamic therapy.

[5] http://interpersonalpsychotherapy.org/about-ipt/

effects associated with principles of operant conditioning. Chapter 10 authorizes these conditioning principles as cognitive-behavioral principles that are to be part of every clinician's comprehensive treatments. Fully integrating applied behavior analysis into your cognitive-behavioral clinical practice constitutes a major clinical change.

What now will provide the requisite clinical focus? I propose that clinicians be guided by the client's presenting problem(s). Behavior disorders should be first treated with behavior therapies, cognitive disorders should first be treated with cognitive therapies, and emotional disorders should first be treated with emotion-focused disorders. As a clinical psychologist I fully realize that these are highly interrelated matters and that clients present with multiple problems. Part of engaging the client and forming a working alliance with them is prioritizing what part of their presentation they want to start working on, and how they prefer to do that. The full range of therapeutic options should be reviewed. The question of whether to medicate or not can be informed by consultation if necessary. What additional empirically supported treatments are needed will be decided in part as a result of how successful the initial treatment is.

The question of what treatment selections and/or combinations of treatments work best for clients with particular combinations of presenting problems is best answered by clinical research. This is not a problem for basic psychological science to answer. The Bio↔Psychology Network Theory provides a solid science base that authorizes this work. Clinicians can be expected to disagree about these practical matters, but at least they will now be working from a common theoretical orientation and that should greatly facilitate achieving constructive results.

Medicine is presumably based on the hard sciences of physics, chemistry, and biology, yet we often encounter the term 'medical arts' in situations where clinical services are provided. Applying science in health care settings is always an art, because the relevant variables are always many, complex, and less well controlled compared to a science laboratory. Artistic issues concerning the application of science should not be confused with scientific uncertainty regarding causal mechanisms. Clinical doctrines concerning how best to proceed in a particular case need not preclude accepting fundamental principles of psychological science such as the 12 network principles introduced in this book.

Multiple Treatments

The network orientation derived from the Bio↔Psychology Network Theory developed in previous chapters provides a science base that supports comprehensive clinical practice where clinicians are authorized to use any combination of empirically supported treatments that offers the best chance of success. An important corollary to being open to all empirically supported treatments is that clinicians will expand their clinical practice to incorporate these treatments. This means that clinicians will no longer consistently operate from just their previously preferred choice among the Big Five clinical orientations. This effectively ends primarily identifying with one of those clinical orientations. This means that psychodynamic therapists must now consider doing behavioral diagnoses and prescribing behavioral interventions as part of their treatment plan, even though they continue to prioritize insight in the form of psychological mindedness. It means that psychodynamic clinicians will no longer worry about symptom substitution. It also means that behavioral, cognitive, and cognitive-behavioral clinicians will need to incorporate emotion-focused and interpersonal treatments into their clinical practice in an effort to increase psychological mindedness and emotional regulation. The popularity of dialectical behavior therapy and the general recognition of emotional dysregulation indicate that this is already happening. It further means that pharmacology should be incorporated either through consultation or through prescription privilege.

In all cases treatments should be limited to interventions with adequate empirical support, in the same way that clinicians limit their use of psychological tests to instruments with demonstrated reliability and validity. In short, clinical practice is expected to become systematically more comprehensive under the recommended network orientation.

Replace Eclecticism

Theories help us understand and explain, which is why our profession prefers theoretically guided research and practice. Eclecticism is currently discouraged, because no coherent formal theory exists that justifies or directs one to behave this way. Clinicians who practice from multiple, and possibly contradictory, theoretical perspectives are thought to put their clients at unnecessary risk, because contradictions in the underlying authorizing theoretical orientations strongly suggest that 'clinical mistakes' will eventually be made. It is therefore considered safer to practice from a single theoretical orientation. Yet most clinicians whom I have known over more than the past four decades recognize some merit in all available therapeutic approaches. All is fine when treatment goes as planned, but the eclectic clinician faces a problem when treatment does not go as planned. Should they continue with their current theoretical orientation or move to another one? If change is in order, then what clinical orientation should be adopted next? Eclectic clinicians presently lack a theoretical basis to support any choice that they make, which leaves these choices open to question.

Clinicians who identify with one primary theoretical orientation and supplement with others are sometimes shy about disclosing the extent to which they go 'off orientation' because they understand that to do so is sometimes considered giving aid and comfort to the enemy. Consider Leahy's (2009) '**Confessions of a Cognitive Therapist**' where he admitted that in addition to being a cognitive therapist, he also sometimes uses behavioral and existential methods depending upon the presenting clinical issues. The term 'confession' implies that wrong doing was hidden but is now revealed and forgiveness sought. Wrong doing is typically hidden in order to avoid punishment, which in his case might involve public criticism by other cognitive therapists for supporting competing orientations. He might also have expected problems publishing articles and getting grants, because of the dim view that reviewers typically take of different and competing theoretical orientations. The theoretical unification provided by this book should preclude all such apologies in future.

One partial exception to such secrecy is Arnold Lazarus (2005), who promoted what he called **technical eclecticism** (Lazarus, 2008). His **multimodal therapy**[6] (Lazarus, 2005) is based on his clinical experience that multiple treatments designed to address various facets of the patient's problem often produce the best clinical results. Clinicians need some way to understand why a comprehensive clinical practice that uses multiple methods is not only permissible, but is desirable and needed. The proposed Bio↔Psychology Network Theory provides psychotherapists with a sound basis for a comprehensive clinical practice, because this theory is consistent with all of the Big Five clinical orientations. The common theoretical ground provided by the proposed Bio↔Psychology Network removes the inconsistencies and contradictions associated with eclectic practice. The vocabulary provided by this theory is common to both psychology and neuroscience, and that facilitates conversations with physicians. This common ground was achieved in a selective way. Not all aspects of all five theoretical orientations have been included. Some aspects of cognitive-behavioral and psychodynamic orientations have been soundly criticized and rejected. Yet core considerations have been preserved. The net result is that the

[6] http://en.wikipedia.org/wiki/Multimodal_therapy

proposed Bio↔Psychology Network Theory supports a broader clinical practice than any other currently available theoretical orientation.

Empirically Supported Principles vs. Manuals

Another benefit of adopting the proposed Bio↔Psychology Network Theory is that it replaces the unmanageably large number of one-size-fits-all rigid therapy manuals that are too numerous to master, with a dozen psychological principles that identify active therapeutic ingredients. You will base your interventions on the four core and eight corollary principles introduced in Chapters 3 and 4 rather than on manuals. It is upon this psychological science base that professional clinical practice is constructed. The recognized factors that are common to all psychological treatments are fully accepted. Network Principle 8 regarding dissonance induction/reduction provides general guidance as to the necessary and sufficient conditions for therapeutic change. You will customize your interventions with your clients in the way described by Paul (1967) during the early days of behavior therapy. This returns clinical practice to a professionally managed principled basis. Greene (2012) cited the contemporary trend to replace manuals with principles as an important rapprochement between investigators and clinicians. It addresses what is probably the most frequently given reason for applicants seeking admission to Fordham's doctoral training program in clinical psychology, which is to better understand people so that they can become a more effective therapist.

Principle 8 regarding dissonance induction/reduction was derived from procedures used to train artificial neural networks, and is a good guide for modifying real neural networks. It is empirically supported by the 25 years of clinical research upon which Barlow's Unified Protocol is based (Allen et al., 2008; Barlow et al., 2011). The proposed Bio↔Psychology Network Theory helps us understand why Barlow's Unified Protocol works.

Absent effective theory, it was the right choice for clinicians to first find out what works in order to reduce, and perhaps eliminate, the negative effects of psychotherapy that seem to have afflicted approximately half of treated patients prior to the empirically supported treatment movement (Barlow, 2010; Bergin, 1963, 1966; Franks & Mays, 1980; Mays & Franks, 1980, 1985). Now, in light of many empirically supported treatments including Barlow's Unified Protocol (Allen et al., 2008; Barlow et al., 2011) we need to better understand why these treatments work. The proposed Bio↔Psychology Network Theory provides relevant mechanism information.

Conditioning as Cognition

The proposed Bio↔Psychology Network Theory authorizes principles of operant and respondent conditioning as cognitive-behavioral principles because they activate experience-dependent plasticity mechanisms that mediate our Principle 2: Learning and Memory. Conditioning principles are among the most well-documented phenomena that psychology has to offer. They have all been carefully studied under laboratory conditions prior to being used clinically. An extensive literature documents the therapeutic results that can be obtained with these principles. Unfortunately, the cognitive revolution largely dismissed them when behaviorism was discarded as an explanatory basis for most psychological research and clinical practice. The proposed Bio↔Psychology Network Theory is a cognitive theory that explains conditioning. It directs clinicians to incorporate operant and respondent conditioning principles into cognitive therapy. The proposed Bio↔Psychology Network Theory also directs clinicians to conduct a behavioral analysis in order to identify reinforcement contingencies that have either helped cause or maintain maladaptive thoughts, feelings, and behaviors. A method of behavioral diagnosis that prescribes specific interventions was presented in Chapter 10.

Ethical Considerations

With the realization that psychotherapists create real brain changes in our clients comes an important ethical consideration. Clinicians must carefully consider the consequences of making brain changes. Memory modification is an unavoidable consequence of effective learning-based treatments. Clients need to be informed that successful treatment will modify some of their memories.

We also have an ethical obligation to understand how and why the treatments we use work. The first ethical principle for clinical psychologists is to do no harm. Yet research has demonstrated that we sometimes do harm those that we treat. Mays and Franks (1985) discussed the *Negative Outcome in Psychotherapy and What To Do About It* at book length. They, along with others (Barlow, 2010; Bergin, 1963, 1966; Franks & Mays, 1980; Mays & Franks, 1980), revealed that as many as half of treated patients in the past have been harmed. Lilienfeld (2007) provided a list of potentially harmful treatments that include: critical incident stress debriefing; scared straight interventions; facilitated communication; attachment therapies such as rebirthing; recovered-memory techniques; dissociative identity disorder oriented interventions; grief counseling for individuals with normal bereavement reactions; expressive-experiential therapies; boot camp interventions for children with conduct problems; and DARE programs.

In sum, empirical evidence indicates that one cannot simply assume that therapies are safe, let alone effective, just because they were developed with the best of intentions to be helpful. There is a reasonable chance that a new therapy may harm a substantial proportion of the people who receive it. Even when half of patients are harmed, many positive case studies can be identified, thereby providing clinical evidence of benefit. A primary reason why controlled psychotherapy research is needed is to get a good estimate of the proportion of patients who are harmed[7] by the intervention, as well as to determine the proportion of patients who benefit from the intervention, in order to provide the consumer with a rational basis for selecting interventions.

We also have an ethical mandate to understand why our treatments work. While it is possible for treatments derived from a flawed or even completely wrong theory to produce positive results, there is a much better chance that interventions will be effective and positive if they are based on a valid theory. This provides an ethical reason to support the proposed Bio↔Psychology Network Theory.

CONCLUSIONS

Clinical psychologists can only be expected to treat people alike when they understand psychology in similar ways. The proposed Bio↔Psychology Network Theory provides the required theoretical unification of psychological science, because it is based on four core and eight corollary network principles that provide mechanism information that can explain a wide variety of psychological phenomena in addition to why our empirically supported treatments work. That these principles are based on well-replicated psychological phenomena that can be explained by accepted neuroscience and connectionist mechanisms plus multivariate statistics means that its evidential base is sufficiently solid that this new perspective can be used today. The demonstration that each of the Big Five clinical orientations is fully consistent with the proposed Bio↔Psychology Network Theory means that psychotherapy integration has been achieved. This achievement offers the potential for reconciliation among psychotherapy factions. Remember,

[7] Reporting the number of adverse outcomes should be required of all psychotherapy outcome research.

theoretical unification and psychotherapy integration begin with you and the decisions that you make regarding the proposed core and corollary principles presented here. The vocabulary and 12 network principles of the proposed Bio↔Psychology Network Theory are fully consistent with neuroscience. This achievement enables psychology to be practiced as a mature science.

Psychotherapy integration is a worthy goal because it means that students and professional psychologists no longer need to identify with one of the Big Five clinical orientations. Adopting the proposed **network orientation** equates to simultaneously adopting each and every one of the Big Five clinical orientations, based on the logic that things equal to the same thing are equal to each other. This simultaneous adoption means that clinicians will no longer primarily identify with any one of the Big Five clinical orientations. Instead, psychologists will identify themselves either as a **scientist** or as a **clinical science psychologist**. Clinicians are now authorized to construct a treatment plan based on any one or a combination of empirically supported treatments from what used to be competing psychotherapeutic orientations. This enables behavioral clinicians to address the larger insight, psychological mindedness, treatment goals that psychodynamic clinicians favor. It also motivates psychodynamic clinicians to address the symptom reduction/removal goals that behavioral clinicians favor. In short, all clinicians are expected to provide more comprehensive treatment from the proposed network orientation than they currently do from the one orientation that constitutes their current professional identification. I believe that this is good for all of us; do you?

REFERENCES

Abbass, A. A., Hancock, J. T., Henderson, J., & Kisely, S. (2006). Short-term psychodynamic psychotherapies for common mental disorders. *Cochrane Database of Systematic Reviews, 2006*(Issue 4). Art. No.: CD004687 http://dx.doi.org/10.1002/14651858.CD004687.pub3.

Abbott, L. F. (2008). Theoretical neuroscience rising. *Neuron, 60*, 489–495.

Abelson, R. P., Aronson, E., McGuire, W. J., Newcomb, T. M., Rosenberg, M. J., & Tannenbaum, P. H. (Eds.), (1968). *Theories of cognitive consistency: A sourcebook*. Chicago, IL: Rand McNally.

Agras, W. S., Leitenberg, H., Barlow, D. H., Curtis, N. A., Edwards, J., & Wright, D. (1971). Relaxation in systematic desensitization. *Archives of General Psychiatry, 25*, 511–514.

Ajzen, I. (1991). The theory of planned behavior. *Organizational Behavior and Human Decision Processes, 50*, 179–211.

Aldao, A., Nolen-Hoeksema, S., & Schweizer, S. (2010). Emotion-regulation strategies across psychopathology: A meta-analytic review. *Clinical Psychology Review, 30*, 217–237.

Alexander, F., & French, T. (1946). *Psychoanalytic therapy*. New York: Ronald Press.

Allen, L. B., McHugh, R. K., & Barlow, D. H. (2008). Emotional disorders: A unified protocol. In D. Barlow (Ed.), *Clinical handbook of psychological disorders: A step-by-step treatment manual* (4th ed.) (pp. 216–249). New York: Guilford.

Altschuler, E. L., Vankov, A., Hubbard, E. M., Roberts, E., Ramachandran, V. S., & Pineda, J. A. (2000, November). *Mu wave blocking by observer of movement and its possible use as a tool to study theory of other minds. Poster session presented at the 30th Annual Meeting of the Society for Neuroscience*. LA: New Orleans.

American Psychiatric Association. (1994). *Diagnostic and statistical manual of mental disorders* (4th ed.). Washington DC: American Psychiatric Association.

American Psychiatric Association. (2000). *Diagnostic and Statistical Manual of Mental Disorders* Text Revision (4th ed.). Washington, DC: American Psychiatric Association.

American Psychological Association. (2009). *APA concise dictionary of psychology*. Washington, DC: American Psychological Association.

Amodio, D. M., & Mendoza, S. A. (2010). Implicit intergroup bias: cognitive, affective, and motivational underpinnings. In B. Gawronski, & B. K. Payne (Eds.), *Handbook of implicit social cognition: Measurement, theory, and applications* (pp. 353–374). New York: Guilford.

Anastasi, A. (1958). Heredity, environment, and the question "how?" *Psychological Review, 65*, 197–208.

Anderson, E. M., & Lambert, M. J. (1995). Short-term dynamically oriented psychotherapy: A review and meta-analysis. *Clinical Psychological Review, 15*, 503–514.

Anderson, J. R. (1976). *Language, memory, and thought*. Hillsdale, N.J.: Erlbaum.

Anderson, J. R., & Bower, G. H. (1973). *Human associative memory*. Washington, DC: V. H. Winston.

Anderson, J. R., Bothell, D., Byrne, M. D., Douglass, S., Lebiere, C., & Qin, Y. (2004). An integrated theory of mind. *Psychological Review, 111*, 1036–1060.

Andrews, G. (2001). Placebo response in depression: Bane of research, boon to therapy. *British Journal of Psychiatry, 178*, 192–194.

Angus, L. E., & Greenberg, L. S. (2011). *Working with narrative in emotion-focused therapy: Changing stories, healing lives*. Washington, DC: American Psychological Association.

Aponte, J. F., & Aponte, C. E. (1971). Group preprogrammed systematic desensitization without the simultaneous presentation of aversive scenes with relaxation training. *Behavior Research and Therapy, 9*, 337–346.

Appelbaum, S. A. (1973). Psychological-mindedness: Word, concept and essence. *International Journal of Psychoanalysis, 54*, 35–46.
Apps, R., & Hawkes, R. (2009). Cerebellar cortical organization: A one-map hypothesis. *Nature Reviews Neuroscience, 10*, 670–681.
Arbib, M. A. (Ed.). (2002). *The handbook of brain theory and neural networks* (2nd ed.). Cambridge, MA: The MIT Press.
Arbuthnot, J. (1710). An argument for divine providence, taken from the constant regularity observ'd in the births of both sexes. *Philosophical Transactions of the Royal Society of London, 27*, 186–190.
Arch, J. J., & Craske, M. G. (2008). Acceptance and commitment therapy and cognitive behavioral therapy for anxiety disorders: Different treatments, similar mechanisms? *Clinical Psychology: Science & Practice, 5*, 263–279.
Aveline, M. (2001). Innovative contemporary psychotherapies. *Advances in Psychiatric Treatment, 7*, 241–242.
Ayllon, T., & Azrin, N. H. (1968). *The token economy: A motivational system for therapy and rehabilitation.* New York: Appleton-Century-Crofts.
Bagby, R. M., Parker, J. D. A., & Taylor, G. J. (1994a). The twenty-item Toronto alexithymia scale. I. Item selection and cross-validation of the factor structure. *Journal of Psychosomatic Research, 38*, 23–32.
Bagby, R. M., Taylor, G. J., & Parker, J. D. A. (1994b). The Twenty-Item Toronto Alexithymia Scale—II. Convergent, discriminant, and concurrent validity. *Journal of Psychosomatic Research, 38*, 33–40.
Bakan, D. (1966). The test of significance in psychological research. *Psychological Bulletin, 66*, 423–437.
Baker, B. L. (1969). Symptom treatment and symptom substitution in enuresis. *Journal of Abnormal Psychology, 74*, 42–49.
Baker, T. B., McFall, R. M., & Shoham, V. (2009). Current status and future prospects of clinical psychology: Toward a scientifically principled approach to mental and behavioral health care. *Psychological Science in the Public Interest, 9*, 67–103.
Baldwin, M. W., Lydon, J. E., McClure, M. J., & Etchison, S. (2010). Measuring implicit processes in close relationships. In B. Gawronski, & B. K. Payne (Eds.), *Handbook of implicit social cognition: Measurement, theory, and applications* (pp. 426–444). New York: Guilford.
Bandura, A. (1969). *Principles of behavior modification.* New York: Holt, Rinehart, & Winston.
Bandura, A. (1977). *Social learning theory.* Englewood Cliffs, NJ: Prentice-Hall.
Bandura, A. (1978). The self system in reciprocal determinism. *American Psychologist, 33*, 344–358.
Barad, M., Gean, P., & Lutz, B. (2006). The role of the amygdala in the extinction of conditioned fear. *Biological Psychiatry, 60*, 322–328.
Bargh, J. A. (2006). *Social psychology and the unconscious: The automaticity of higher mental processes.* Philadelphia: Psychology Press.
Bargh, J. A., & Ferguson, M. J. (2000). Beyond behaviorism: On the automaticity of higher mental processes. *Psychological Bulletin, 126*, 925–945.
Bargh, J. A., & Morsella, E. (2008). The unconscious mind. *Perspectives on Psychological Science, 3*, 73–79.
Bargh, J. A., & Williams, E. L. (2006). The automaticity of social life. *Current Directions in Psychological Science, 15*, 1–4.
Bar-Haim, Y., Lamy, D., Pergamin, L., Bakermans-Kranenburg, M. J., & van IJzendoorn, M. H. (2007). Threat-related attentional bias in anxious and nonanxious individuals: A meta-analytic study. *Psychological Bulletin, 133*, 1–24.
Barlow, D. H. (1988). *Anxiety and its disorders: The nature and treatment of anxiety and panic.* New York: Guilford.
Barlow, D. H. (1997). It's yet another empirical question: Commentary on "Can Contextualism Help?" *Behavior Therapy, 28*, 445–448.

Barlow, D. H. (2000). Unraveling the mysteries of anxiety and its disorders from the perspective of emotion theory. *American Psychologist, 55*, 1247–1263.

Barlow, D. H. (2010). Negative effects from psychological treatments: A perspective. *American Psychologist, 65*(1), 13–20.

Barlow, D. H., Allen, L. B., & Choate, M. L. (2004). Toward a unified treatment for emotional disorders. *Behavior Therapy, 35*, 205–230. http://dx.doi.org/10.1016/S0005-7894(04)80036-4.

Barlow, D. H., Farchione, T. J., Fairholme, C. P., Ellard, K. K., Boisseau, C. L., Allen, L. B., & Ehenreich-May, J. (2011). *The unified protocol for transdiagnostic treatment of emotional disorders: Therapist guide*. New York: Oxford University Press.

Baron, J. (2000). *Thinking and deciding* (3rd ed.). New York, NY: Cambridge University Press.

Baron, R. M., & Kenny, D. A. (1986). The moderator-mediator variable distinctions in social psychological research: Conceptual, strategic, and statistical considerations. *Journal of Personality and Social Psychology, 51*, 1173–1182.

Baron-Cohen, S. (1989). The autistic child's theory of mind: A case of specific developmental delay. *Journal of Child Psychology and Psychiatry and Allied Disciplines, 30*, 285–297. http://dx.doi.org/10.1111/j.1469-7610.1989.tb00241.x.

Baron-Cohen, S., Leslie, A., & Frith, U. (1985). Does the autistic child have a "theory of mind"? *Cognition, 21*, 37–46.

Baron-Cohen, S., Wheelwright, S., Skinner, R., Martin, J., & Clubley, E. (2001). The Autism-Spectrum Quotient (AQ): Evidence from Asperger syndrome/high-functioning autism, males and females, scientists and mathematicians. *Journal of Autism and Developmental Disorders, 31*, 5–17.

Barrett, L. F. (2006). Are emotions natural kinds? *Perspectives on Psychological Science, 1*, 28–58.

Barrett, L. F., & Wagner, T. D. (2006). The structure of emotion: Evidence from neuroimaging studies. *Current Directions in Psychological Science, 15*(2), 79–83.

Barrett, P. M., Rapee, R. M., Dadds, M. R., & Ryan, S. M. (1996). Family enhancement of cognitive style in anxious and aggressive children. *Journal of Abnormal Child Psychology, 24*, 187–203.

Bartlett, F. C. (1932). *Remembering*. Cambridge, England: Cambridge University Press.

Bartz, J. A., Zaki, J., Bolger, N., Hollander, Ludwig, N. N., Kolevzon, A., & Ochsner, K. N. (2010). Oxytocin selectively improves empathic accuracy. *Psychological Science, 21*(10), 1426–1428.

Basmajian, J. V. (Ed.) (1979). *Biofeedback: Principles and practice for clinicians*. Baltimore: Williams & Wilkins.

Bastardi, A., Uhlmann, E. L., & Ross, L. (2011). Wishful thinking: Belief, desire, and the motivated evaluation of scientific evidence. *Psychological Science, 22*, 731–732. http://dx.doi.org/10.1177/0956797611406447.

Bateman, A. W., & Fonagy, P. (2004). Mentalizing-based treatment of BPD. *Journal of Personality Disorders, 18*, 36–51. http://dx.doi.org/10.1037/a0014418.

Baxter, L. R., Jr., Thompson, J. M., Schwartz, J. M., Guze, B. H., Phelps, M. E., Mazziotta, J. C., Selin, C. E., & Moss, L. (1987). Trazodone treatment response in obsessive-compulsive disorder–correlated with shifts in glucose metabolism in the caudate nuclei. *Psychopathology, 20*(Suppl. 1), 114–122.

Baxter, L. R., Jr., Phelps, M. E., Mazziotta, J. C., Guze, B. H., Schwartz, J. M., & Selin, C. E. (1987). Local cerebral glucose metabolic rates in obsessive-compulsive disorder. A comparison with rates in unipolar depression and in normal controls. *Archives of General Psychiatry, 44*(3), 211–218. Erratum in Arch Gen Psychiatry 1987 Sep;44(9):800.

Baxter, L. R., Jr., Schwartz, J. M., Phelps, M. E., Mazziotta, J. C., Guze, B. H., Selin, C. E., Gerner, R. H., & Sumida, R. M. (1989). Reduction of prefrontal cortex glucose metabolism common to three types of depression. *Archives of General Psychiatry, 46*(3), 243–250.

Baxter, L. R., Jr., Schwartz, J. M., Bergman, K. S., Szuba, M. P., Guze, B. H., Mazziotta, J. C., Alazraki, A., Selin, C. E., Ferng, H. K., & Munford, P. (1992). Caudate glucose metabolic rate changes with both drug and behavior therapy for obsessive compulsive disorder. *Archives of General Psychiatry, 49*, 681–689.

Baxter, L. R., Jr., Saxena, S., Brody, A. L., Ackermann, R. F., Colgan, M., Schwartz, J. M., Allen-Martinez, Z., Fuster, J. M., & Phelps, M. E. (1996). Brain Mediation of Obsessive-Compulsive Disorder Symptoms: Evidence From Functional Brain Imaging Studies in the Human and Nonhuman Primate. *Seminars in Clinical Neuropsychiatry* (1), 32–47.

Bazerman, M. H., Morgan, K. P., & Lowenstein, G. (1997). Opinion: The impossibility of auditor independence. *Sloan Management Review, 38*, 89–94.

Bear, M. F., Connors, B.W., & Paradiso, M.A. (2007). *Neuroscience: Exploring the brain* (3rd ed.). Baltimore, MD: Lippincott, Williams & Wilkins.

Beblo, T., Pastuszak, A., Griepenstroh, J., Driessen, M., Schütz, A., Rentzsch, K., & Schlosser, N. (2010). Self-reported emotional dysregulation but no impairment of emotional intelligence in borderline personality disorder: An explorative study. *Journal of Nervous and Mental Disorders, 198*, 385–388. http://dx.doi.org/10.1097/NMD.0b013e3181da4b4f.

Bechtel, W., & Abrahamsen, A. (1991). *Connectionism and the mind: An introduction to parallel processing in networks*. Cambridge, MA: Blackwell.

Bechtel, W., & Abrahamsen, A. (2002). *Connectionism and the mind: An introduction to parallel processing in networks* (2nd ed.). Cambridge: Blackwell.

Beck, A. T. (1964). Thinking and depression: II. Theory and therapy. *Archives of General Psychiatry, 10*, 561–571.

Beck, A. T. (1967). *Depression: Causes and treatment*. Philadelphia: University of Pennsylvania Press.

Beck, A. T. (1970). Cognitive therapy: Nature and relation to behavior therapy. *Behavior Therapy, 1*, 184–200.

Beck, A. T. (1972). *Depression: Causes and treatment*. Philadelphia: University of Pennsylvania Press.

Beck, A. T. (1976). *Cognitive therapy and the emotional disorders*. New York: International Universities Press.

Beck, A. T. (2005). The current state of cognitive therapy: A 40-year retrospective. *Archives of General Psychiatry, 62*, 953–959. http://dx.doi.org/10.1001/archpsyc.62.9.953.

Beck, J. S. (2011). *Cognitive behavior therapy: Basics and beyond* (2nd ed.). New York: Guilford.

Becker, W. C., & Krug, R. S. (1964). A circumplex model for social behavior in children. *Child Development, 35*, 371–396.

Becker, S., Moscovitch, M., Behrmann, M., & Joordens, S. (1997). Long-term semantic priming: A computational account and empirical evidence. *Journal of Experimental Psychology: Learning, Memory, & Cognition, 23*, 1059–1082.

Beckham, E. E., & Leber, W. (Eds.). (1985). *Handbook of depression: Treatment, assessment, and research*. Homewood, IL: Dorsey.

Beitel, M., Ferrer, E., & Cecero, J. J. (2004). Psychological mindedness and cognitive style. *Journal of Clinical Psychology, 60*, 567–582. http://dx.doi.org/0.1002/jclp.10258.

Beitel, M., Ferrer, E., & Cecero, J. J. (2005). Psychological mindedness and awareness of self and others. *Journal of Clinical Psychology, 61*, 739–750. http://dx.doi.org/10.1002/jclp.20095.

Beitel, M., Blauvelt, K. S., Barry, D. T., & Cecero, J. J. (2005). The structure of psychological mindedness. *Poster presented at the American Psychoanalytic Association Winter Meeting*.

Beitman, B. D., Goldfried, M. R., & Norcross, J. C. (1989). The movement toward integrating the psychotherapies: An overview. *American Journal of Psychiatry, 146*, 138–147.

Ben, D. J. (1972). Self-perception theory. In L. Berkowitz (Ed.), *Advances in experimental social psychology Vol. 6*. (pp. 1–62). New York, NY: Academic Press.

Benedetti, F., Mayberg, H. S., Wagner, T. D., Stohler, C. S., & Zubieta, J. K. (2005). Neurobiological mechanisms of the placebo effect. *The Journal of Neuroscience, 25*(45), 10390–10402.

Benedetti, F., Lanotte, M., Lopiano, L., & Colloca, L. (2007). When words are painful: Unraveling the mechanisms of the nocebo effect. *Neuroscience, 147*, 260–271.

Bergin, A. E. (1963). The effects of psychotherapy: Negative results revisited. *Journal of Counseling Psychology, 10*, 244–250.

Bergin, A. E. (1966). Some implications of psychotherapy for therapeutic practice. *Journal of Abnormal Psychology*, *71*, 235–246.

Bergin, A. E. (1980). Negative effects revisited: A reply. *Professional Psychology*, *11*, 93–100.

Berkson, J. (1942). Tests of significance considered as evidence. *Journal of the American Statistical Association*, *37*, 325–335.

Berlin, I. (1953). *The hedgehog and the fox*. New York: Simon & Schuster.

Bernstein, E. M., & Putnam, F. W. (1986). Development, reliability, and validity of a dissociation scale. *Journal of Nervous and Mental Disease*, *174*, 727–735.

Beutler, L. E., & Castonguay, L. G. (2006). The task force on empirically based principles of therapeutic change. In L. G. Castonguay, & L. E. Beutler (Eds.), *Principles of therapeutic change that work* (pp. 3–10). New York: Oxford University Press.

Beutler, L. E., Blatt, S. J., Alimohamed, S., Levy, K. N., & Angtuaco, L. (2006). Participant factors in treating dysphoric disorders. In L. G. Castonguay, & L. E. Beutler (Eds.), *Principles of therapeutic change that work* (pp. 13–63). New York: Oxford University Press.

Beutler, L. E., Castonguay, L. G., & Follette, W. C. (2006). Integration of therapeutic factors in dysphoric disorders. In L. G. Castonguay, & L. E. Beutler (Eds.), *Principles of therapeutic change that work* (pp. 83–109). New York: Oxford University Press.

Biederman, I. (1987). Recognition-by-components: A theory of human image understanding. *Psychological Review*, *94*(2), 115–147.

Björgvinsson, T., & Hart, J. (2006). Cognitive behavioral therapy promotes mentalizing. In J. G. Allen, & P. Fonagy (Eds.), *Handbook of mentalization-based treatment* (pp. 157–170). Chichester, England: Wiley.

Bjornsson, A. S. (2013). Science and practice in clinical psychology doctoral training. *Clinical Psychology: Science and Practice*, *19*(4), 375–380.

Black, A. H., Cott, A., & Pavloski, C. R. (1977). The operant learning theory approach to biofeedback training. In G. Schwartz, & J. Beatty (Eds.), *Biofeedback: theory and research* (pp. 89–127). NY: Academic Press.

Blanchard, E. B., & Hersen, M. (1976). Behavioral treatment of hysterical neurosis: Symptom substitution and symptom return reconsidered. *Psychiatry*, *39*, 118–129.

Blaney, P. H. (1986). Affect and memory: A review. *Psychology Bulletin*, *99*, 229–246.

Blatt, S. J., & Bers, S. A. (1993). Commentary on "A cognitive perspective on self-representation in depression". In Z. V. Segal, & S. J. Blatt (Eds.), *The self in emotional distress: cognitive and psychodynamic perspectives* (pp. 131–170). NY: Guilford Press.

Block, J. (1957). Studies in the phenomenology of emotions. *Journal of Abnormal and Social Psychology*, *54*, 358–363.

Bode, S., He, A. H., Soon, C. S., Trampel, R., Turner, R., & Haynes, J. D. (2011). Tracking the unconscious generation of free decisions using ultra-high field fMRI. *PLoS ONE*, *6*(6), e21612. http://dx.doi.org/10.1371/journal.pone.0021612.

Bögels, S. M., & Zigterman, D. (2000). Dysfunctional cognitions in children with social phobia, separation anxiety disorder, and generalized anxiety disorder. *Journal of Abnormal Child Psychology*, *28*, 205–211.

Bordin, E. S. (1979). The generalizability of the psychoanalytic concept of the working alliance. Psychotherapy: Theory. *Research and Practice*, *16*, 252–260. http://dx.doi.org/10.1037/h0085885.

Borkovec, T. D. (1973). The role of expectancy and physiological feedback in fear research: A review with special reference to subject characteristics. *Behavior Therapy*, *4*, 491–505.

Bottjer, S. W., & Arnold, A. P. (1997). Developmental plasticity in neural circuits for a learned behavior. *Annual Review of Neuroscience*, *20*, 459–481.

Bourke, M. P., Taylor, G., & Crisp, A. H. (1985). Symbolic functioning in anorexia nervosa. *Journal of Psychiatric Research*, *19*, 273–278. http://dx.doi.org/10.1016/0022-3956(85)90028-7.

Bouton, M. E. (1993). Context, time, and memory retrieval in the interference paradigms of Pavlovian conditioning. *Psychological Bulletin*, *114*, 80–99.

Bouton, M. E., Mineka, S., & Barlow, D. H. (2001). A modern learning-theory perspective on the etiology of panic disorder. *Psychological Review, 108*, 4–32.

Bower, G. (1981). Mood and memory. *American Psychologist, 36*(2), 129–148.

Bower, G. H. (1994). A turning point in mathematical learning theory. *Psychological Review, 101*, 290–300.

Bower, G. H., & Cohen, P. R. (1982). Emotional influences in memory and thinking: Data and theory. In M. S. Clark, & S.T. Fiske (Eds.), *Affect and cognition* (pp. 241–331). Hillsdale, NJ: Erlbaum.

Bower, G. H., & Hilgard, E. R. (1981). *Theories of learning* (5th ed.). Englewood Cliffs, NJ: Prentice-Hall.

Bower, G. H., & Hilgard, E. R. (1997). *Theories of learning*. NY: Prentice Hall.

Bowers, K. S. (1983). On the biological plausibility of grandmother cells: Implications for neural network theories in psychology and neuroscience. *Psychological Review, 116*(1), 220–251. http://dx.doi.org/10.1037/a0014462.

Bowers, K. S., & Meichenbaum, D. (Eds.). (1984). *The unconscious reconsidered*. New York: Wiley.

Bowler, P. J. (1983). *The eclipse of Darwinism: Anti-Darwinian evolution theories in the decades around 1900*. Baltimore, MD: The Johns Hopkins University Press.

Boyden, E. S., Katoh, A., & Raymond, J. L. (2004). Cerebellum-dependent learning: The role of multiple plasticity mechanisms. *Annual Review of Neuroscience, 27*, 581–609.

Brader, T., Marcus, G. E., & Miller, K. L. (2011). Emotion and public opinion. In R.Y. Shapiro, & L. R. Jacobs (Eds.), *Oxford handbook of American public opinion and media* (pp. 384–401). New York: Oxford University Press.

Bradford, D., Stroup, S., & Liberman, J. (2002). Pharmacological treatments for schizophrenia. In P. E. Nathan, & J. M. Gorman (Eds.), *A guide to treatments that work* (2nd ed.). (pp. 169–199).

Brainerd, C. J., & Reyna, V. F. (2005). *Science of false memory*. NY: Oxford University Press.

Brasil-Neto, J. P., Pascual-Leone, A., Valls-Sole, J., Cohen, L. G., & Hallett, M. (1992). Focal transcranial magnetic stimulation and response bias in a forced-choice task. *Journal of Neurology, Neurosurgery, and Psychiatry, 55*, 964–966.

Bressler, S. L. (2002). Understanding cognition through large-scale cortical networks. *Current Directions in Psychological Science, 11*, 58–61.

Brewin, C. R., & Holmes, E. A. (2003). Psychological theories of posttraumatic stress disorder. *Clinical Psychology Review, 23*, 339–376.

Brewin, C. R., Dalgleish, T., & Joseph, S. (1996). A dual representation theory of Posttraumatic Stress Disorder. *Psychological Review, 103*, 670–686.

Brody, A. L., Saxena, S., Schwartz, J. M., Stoessel, P. W., Maidment, K., Phelps, M. E., & Baxter, L. R., Jr. (1998). FDG-PET predictors of response to behavioral therapy and pharmacotherapy in obsessive compulsive disorder. *Psychiatry Research, 84*(1), 1–6.

Brown, K. W., & Ryan, R. M. (2003). The benefits of being present: The role of mindfulness in psychological well-being. *Journal of Personality and Social Psychology, 84*, 822–848.

Brunel, F. F., Tietje, B. C., & Greenwald, A. G. (2004). Is the implicit association test a valid and valuable measure of consumer social cognition? *Journal of Consumer Psychology, 14*(4), 385–404.

Bruner, J. S., & Goodman, C. C. (1947). Value and need as organizing factors in perception. *Journal of Abnormal Social Psychology, 42*, 33–44.

Bruner, J. S., & Postman, L. (1947). Tension and tension-release as organizing factors in perception. *Journal of Personality, 15*, 300–308.

Bryck, R. L., & Fisher, P. A. (2012). Training the brain: Practical applications of neural plasticity from the intersection of cognitive neuroscience, developmental psychology, and prevention science. *American Psychologist, 67*(2), 87–100.

Burgos, J. E. (2010). The operant/respondent distinction: A computational neural-network analysis. In N. Schmajuk (Ed.), *Computational models of conditioning* (pp. 244–271). Cambridge: Cambridge University Press.

Burlingame, G. M., Fuhriman, A., & Mosier, J. (2003). The differential effectiveness of group therapy. A meta-analytic perspective. *Group Dynamics: Theory, Research, and Practice, 7*, 3–12.

Burns, D. D., & Spangler, D. L. (2001). Do changes in dysfunctional attitudes mediate changes in depression and anxiety in cognitive behavioral therapy? *Behavior Therapy, 32*(2), 337–369.

Burt, C. (1917). *The distributions and relations of educational abilities*. London: London County Council.

Bushey, D., Tononi, G., & Cirelli, C. (2011). Sleep and synaptic homeostasis: Structural evidence in Drosophila. *Science, 332*, 1576–1581.

Buss, A., & Plomin, R. (1984). *Temperament: Early developing personality traits*. Hillsdale, New Jersey: Lawrence Erlbaum.

Bydlowski, S., Corcos, M., Jeammet, P., Paterniti, S., Berthoz, S., Laurier, C., et al. (2005). Emotional-processing deficits in eating disorders. *International Journal of Eating Disorders, 37*, 321–329.

Cacioppo, J. T. (2007). Psychology is a hub science. *American Psychological Society Observer, 20*(8).

Cacioppo, J. T., & Hawkley, L. C. (2003). Social isolation and health, with an emphasis on underlying mechanisms. *Perspectives in Biology and Medicine, 46*(Suppl. 3), S39–S52.

Cahoon, D. D. (1968). Symptom substitution and the behavior therapies: A reappraisal. *Psychological Bulletin, 69*, 149–156.

Cameron, N. M., Shahrokh, D., Del Corpo, A., Dhir, S. K.; Szyf, M., Champagne, F. A., & Meaney, M. J. (2008). Epigenetic programming of phenotypic variations in reproductive strategies in the rat through maternal care. *Journal of Neuroendocrinology, 20*, 795–801.

Cannon, W. B. (1927). The James-Lange theory of emotions. Critical examinations and an alternative theory. *American Journal of Psychology, 39*, 106–124.

Cannon, W. B. (1929). *Bodily changes in pain, hunger, fear and rage*. New York: Appleton.

Carey, T. A. (2011). Exposure and reorganization: The what and how of effective psychotherapy. *Clinical Psychology Review, 31*(2), 236–248.

Carlson, K. A., & Russo, J. E. (2001). Biased interpretation of evidence by mock jurors. *Journal of Experimental Psychology: Applied*, 7, 91–103.

Carlson, N. R. (2010). *Physiology of behavior* (10th ed.). Boston, MA: Pearson.

Carlson, N. R., Miller, H., Heth, C. D., Donahoe, J. W., & Martin, G. N. (2010). *Psychology: The science of behavior* (7th ed.). Boston: Allyn & Bacon (p. 196).

Carlston, D. (2010). Models of implicit and explicit mental representation. In B. Gawronski, & B. K. Payne (Eds.), *Handbook of implicit social cognition: Measurement, theory, and applications* (pp. 38–61). New York: Guilford.

Carota, F., Posada, A., Harquel, S., Delpuech, C., Bertrand, O., & Sirigu, A. (2010). Neural dynamics of the intention to speak. *Cerebral Cortex, 20*(8), 1891–1897.

Carpenter, W. B. (1874). *Principles of mental physiology, with their applications to the training and discipline of the mind, and the study of its morbid conditions*. NY: D. Appleton and Company.

Carpenter, W. B. (1893). *Principles of mental physiology, with their applications to the training and discipline of the mind, and the study of its morbid conditions*. New York: D. Appleton and Company.

Carr, L., Iacoboni, M., Dubeau, M. C., Mazziotta, J. C., & Lenzi, G. L. (2003). Neural mechanisms of empathy in humans: A relay from neural systems for imitation to limbic areas. *Proceedings of the National Academy of Sciences of the United States of America (PNAS), 100*(9), 5497–5502.

Carroll, J. S. (1978). The effect of imagining an event on expectations for the event: An interpretation in terms of the availability heuristic. *Journal of Personality & Social Psychology, 36*, 1501–1511.

Carver, R. P. (1978). The case against statistical significance testing. *Harvard Educational Review, 48*, 378–399.

Carver, R. P. (1993). The case against statistical significance testing, revisited. *Journal of Experimental Education, 61*, 287–292.

Casey, M., & Tryon, W. W. (2001). Validating a double press method for computer administration of personality inventory items. *Psychological Assessment, 13*, 521–530.

Caspi, A., Harrington, H., Moffitt, T. E., Milne, B. J., & Poulton, R. (2006). Socially isolated children 20 years later: Risk of cardiovascular disease. *Archives of Pediatrics and Adolescent Medicine, 160*, 805–811.

Castonguay, L. G. (2011). Psychotherapy, psychopathology, research and practice: Pathways of connections and integration. *Psychotherapy Research, 21*(2), 125–140. http://dx.doi.org/10.1080/10503307.2011.563250.

Castonguay, L. G., & Beutler, L. E. (Eds.). (2006). *Principles of therapeutic change that work*. New York: Oxford University Press.

Catania, A. C. (1978). The psychology of learning: Some lessons from the Darwinian revolution. *Annals of the New York Academy of Sciences, 309*, 18–28.

Catania, A. C. (1987). Some Darwinian lessons for behavior analysis: A review of Bowler's The Eclipse of Darwinism. *Journal of the Experimental Analysis of Behavior, 47*, 249–257.

Cattell, R. B. (1957). *Personality and motivation: Structure and measurement*. New York: Harcourt Brace Jovanovich.

Cecero, J. J., Beitel, M., & Prout, T. (2008). Exploring the relationships among early maladaptive schemas, psychological mindedness, and self-reported college adjustment. Psychology and Psychotherapy: Theory. *Research and Practice, 81*, 105–118.

Centonze, D., Siracusano, A., Calabresi, P., & Bernardi, G. (2004). The Project for a Scientific Psychology (1895): A Freudian anticipation of LTP-memory connection theory. *Brain Research Reviews, 46*, 310–314.

Chabris, C. F., Herbert, B. M., Benjamin, D. J., Beauchamp, J., Cesarini, D., van der Loos, M., Johannesson, M., Magnusson, P. K. E., Lichtenstein, P., Atwwood, C. S., Freese, J., Hauser, T. S., Hauser, R. M., Christakis, N., & Laibson, D. (2012). Most reported genetic associations with general intelligence are probably false positives. *Psychological Science, 23*(11), 1314–1323.

Chalmers, D. (1990). Why Fodor and Pylyshyn Were Wrong: The Simplest Refutation. *Proceedings of the Twelfth Annual Conference of the Cognitive Science Society*, 340–347.

Chalmers, D. (2006). Strong and weak emergence. In P. Clayton, & P. Davies (Eds.), *The re-emergence of emergence: The emergentist hypothesis from science to religion* (pp. 244–254). Oxford, England: Oxford University Press.

Chambless, D. L., & Ollendick, T. H. (2001). Empirically supported psychological interventions: Controversies and evidence. *Annual Review of Psychology, 52*, 685–716.

Chapman, L. (1967). Illusory correlation in observational report. *Journal of Verbal Learning and Verbal Behavior, 6*(1), 151–155.

Chapman, L. J., & Chapman, J. P. (1967). Genesis of popular but erroneous psychodiagnostic observations. *Journal of Abnormal Psychology, 72*(3), 193–204.

Chartrand, T. L., & Bargh, J. A. (1999). The chameleon effect: The perception-behavior link and social interaction. *Journal of Personality and Social Psychology, 76*(6), 893–910.

Chein, J. M., & Schneider, W. (2011). The brain's learning and control architecture. *Current Directions in Psychological Science, 21*, 78–84.

Chemtob, C., Roitblat, H. L., Hamada, R. S., Carlson, J. G., & Twentyman, C. T. (1988). A cognitive action theory of post-traumatic stress disorder. *Journal of Anxiety Disorder, 2*, 253–275.

Chen, S., Fitzsimons, G. M., & Andersen, S. M. (2007). Automaticity in close relationships. In J. A. Bargh (Ed.), *Social psychology and the unconscious: The automaticity of higher mental processes* (pp. 133–172). Philadelphia: Psychology Press.

Chiavarino, C., Apperly, I. A., & Humphreys, G. W. (2010). Distinguishing intentions from desires: Contributions of the frontal and parietal lobes. *Cognition, 117*, 203–216. http://dx.doi.org/10.1016/j.cognition.2010.08.012.

Chomsky, N. (1971). *Syntactic structures*. The Hague: Mouton.

Chomsky, N. (1975). *Reflections on language*. New York: Parthenon Press.

Chomsky, N. (1980). *Rules and representations*. New York: Columbia University Press.

Chomsky, N. (1986). *Knowledge of language: Its nature, origin, and use*. New York: Praeger.

Chorpita, B. F., & Barlow, D. H. (1998). The development of anxiety: The role of control in the early environment. *Psychological Bulletin, 124*, 3–21.

Chorpita, B. F., Albano, A. M., & Barlow, D. H. (1996). Cognitive processing in children: Relationship to anxiety and family influences. *Journal of Clinical Child Psychology, 25*, 170–176.

Church, B. A., Krauss, M. S., Lopata, C., Toomey, J. A., Thomeer, M. L., Coutinho, M. V., Volker, M. A., & Mercade, E., III (2010). Atypical categorization in children with high functioning autism spectrum disorder. *Psychonomic Bulletin Review, 17*(6), 862–868.

Churchland, P. M. (1984). *Matter and consciousness*. Cambridge, MA: MIT Press.

Cicchetti, D., Rogosch, F. A., Gunnar, M. R., & Toth, S. L. (2010). The differential impacts of early physical and sexual abuse and internalizing problems on daytime cortisol rhythm in school-aged children. *Child Development, 81*, 252–269.

Cicero, S. D., & Tryon, W. W. (1989). Classical conditioning of meaning – II. A replication and triplet associative extension. *Journal of Behavior Therapy and Experimental Psychiatry, 20*, 192–202.

Cin, S. D., Worth, K. A., Gerrard, M., Gibbons, F. X., Stoolmiller, M., Wills, T. A., & Sargent, J. D. (2009). Watching and drinking: Expectancies, prototypes, and friends' alcohol use mediate the effect of exposure to alcohol use in movies on adolescent drinking. *Health Psychology, 28*, 473–483.

Cirelli, C., & Tononi, G. (2008). Is sleep essential? *PLOS Biology, 6*(8), 1605–1611.

Clore, G. L. (1994). Why emotions are never unconscious. In P. Ekman, & R. J. Davidson (Eds.), *The nature of emotion: Fundamental questions* (pp. 285–290). New York: Oxford University Press.

Clyne, C., & Blampied, N. M. (2004). Training in emotion regulation as a treatment for binge eating: A preliminary study. *Behaviour Change, 21*, 269–281.

Coan, J. A., Schaefer, H. S., & Davidson, R. J. (2006). Lending a hand: Social regulation of the neural response to threat. *Psychological Science, 17*, 1032–1039.

Cochin, S., Barthelemy, C., Lejeune, B., Roux, S., & Martineau, J. (1998). Perception of motion and EEG activity in human adults. *Electroencephalography and Clinical Neurophysiology, 107*(4), 287–295.

Cochrane, C. E., Brewerton, T. D., Wilson, D. B., & Hodges, E. L. (1993). Alexithymia in the eating disorders. *The International Journal of Eating Disorders, 14*, 219–222.

Cohen, H. L., & Filipczak, J. (1971). *A new learning environment: A case for learning*. Boston: Authors Cooperative, Inc.

Cohen, J. (1969). *Statistical power analysis for the social sciences*. San Diego, CA: Academic Press.

Cohen, J. (1988). *Statistical power analysis for the social sciences* (2nd ed.). Hillsdale, NJ: Erlbaum.

Cohen, J. (1992). Power primer. *Psychological Bulletin, 112*, 155–159.

Cohen, J. (1994). The earth is round ($p < .05$). *American Psychologist, 49*, 997–1003.

Cohen, J. D., Dunbar, K., & McClelland, J. L. (1990). On the control of automatic processes: A parallel distributed processing account of the Stroop effect. *Psychological Review, 97*, 332–361.

Cohen, S., Doyle, W. J., Skoner, D. P., Rabin, B. S., & Gwaltney, J. M. (1997). Social ties and susceptibility to the common cold. *Journal of the American Medical Association, 277*, 1940–1944.

Cole, S. W. (2009). Social regulation of human gene expression. *Current Directions in Psychological Science, 18*, 132–137.

Cole, S. W., Kemeny, M. E., Fahey, J. L., Zack, J. A., & Naliboff, B. D. (2003). Psychological risk factors for HIV pathogenesis: Mediation by the autonomic nervous system. *Biological Psychiatry*, *54*, 1444–1456.

Cole, S. W., Hawkley, L. C., Arevalo, J. M., Sung, C. Y., Rose, R. M., & Cacioppo, J. T. (2007). Social regulation of gene expression in human leukocytes. *Genome Biology*, *8*(9), R189.

Collins, A. M., & Loftus, E. F. (1975). A spreading-activation theory of semantic processing. *Psychological Review*, *82*, 407–428.

Collins, A. M., & Quillian, M. R. (1969). Retrieval time from semantic memory. *Journal of Verbal Learning and Verbal Behavior*, *8*, 240–247.

Colloca, L., & Benedetti, F. (2007). Nocebo hyperalgesia: How anxiety is turned into pain. *Current Opinion in Anaesthesiology*, *20*, 435–439.

Comer, R., & Gould, E. (2013). *Psychology around us* (2nd ed.). New York: Wiley.

Commons, M. L., Grossberg, S., & Staddon, J. E. R. (1991). *Neural network models of conditioning and action*. Hillsdale, NJ: Lawrence Earlbaum Associates.

Conrey, F. R., & Smith, E. R. (2007). Attitude representation: Attitudes as patterns in a distributed, connectionist representational system. *Social Cognition*, *25*, 718–735.

Conte, H. R., & Plutchik, R. (1981). A circumplex model for interpersonal traits. *Journal of Personality and Social Psychology*, *40*, 701–711.

Conte, H. R., & Ratto, R. (1997). Self-report measures of psychological mindedness. In M. McCallum, & W. E. Piper (Eds.), *Psychological mindedness: A contemporary understanding* (pp. 1–26). Mahwah, New Jersey: Erlbaum.

Conte, H. R., Ratto, R. R., & Karasu, T. B. (1996). The psychological mindedness scale: Factor structure and relationship to outcome of psychotherapy. *The Journal of Psychotherapy Practice and Research*, *5*, 250–259.

Conte, H. R., Plutchik, R., Jung, B. B., Picard, S., Karasu, T. B., & Lotterman, A. (1990). Psychological mindedness as a predictor of psychotherapy outcome: A preliminary report. *Comprehensive Psychiatry*, *1990*(31), 426–431.

Cook, R., Brewer, R., Shah, P., & Bird, G. (2013). Alexithymia, not autism, predicts poor recognition of emotional facial expressions. *Psychological Science*, *24*(5), 723–732.

Cooke, G. (1968). Evaluation of the efficacy of the components of reciprocal inhibition psychotherapy. *Journal of Abnormal Psychology*, *73*, 464–467.

Costa, P. T., Jr., & McCrae, R. R. (1995). Domains and facets: Hierarchical personality assessment using the Revised NEO personality inventory. *Journal of Personality Assessment*, *64*(1), 21–50.

Craighead, W. E. (1973). The role of muscular relaxation in systematic desensitization. In R. D. Rubin, J. P. Brady, & J. D. Henderson (Eds.). *Advances in Behavior Therapy: Vol. 4.* (pp. 177–197). New York: Academic Press.

Creamer, M., Burgess, P., & Pattison, P. (1992). Reaction to trauma: A cognitive processing model. *Journal of Abnormal Psychology*, *101*, 452–459.

Crits-Christoph, P. (1992). The efficacy of brief dynamic psychotherapy: A meta-analysis. *American Journal of Psychiatry*, *149*, 151–158.

Crockett, M. J., Clark, L., Hauser, M. D., & Robbins, T. W. (2010). Serotonin selectively influences moral judgment and behavior through effects on harm aversion. *Proceedings of the National Academy of Sciences of the United States of America (PNAS)*, *107*(40), 17433–17438.

Cronbach, L. J., & Meehl, P. E. (1955). Construct validity in psychological tests. *Psychological Bulletin*, *52*, 281–302. http://dx.doi.org/10.1037/h0040957.

Crowder, J. E., & Thornton, D. W. (1970). Effects of systematic desensitization, programmed fantasy and bibliotherapy on a specific fear. *Behavior Research and Therapy*, *8*, 35–41.

Cumming, G. (2008). Replication and p intervals: p values predict the future only vaguely, but confidence intervals do much better. *Perspectives on Psychological Science*, *3*(4), 286–300.

Custers, R., & Aarts, H. (2010). The unconscious will: How the pursuit of goals operates outside of conscious awareness. *Science*, *329*, *no*, *5987*, 47–50.

Daleiden, E. L. (1998). Childhood anxiety and memory functioning: A comparison of systemic and processing accounts. *Journal of Experimental Child Psychology*, *68*, 216–235.

Dalgleish, T. (1999). Cognitive theories of post-traumatic stress disorder. Post-traumatic stress disorders: Concepts and therapy. In W. Yule (Ed.), *Post-traumatic stress disorders: Concepts and therapy, Wiley series in clinical psychology* (pp. 193–220). New York, NY, US: John Wiley & Sons Ltd.

Dalgleish, T., Moradi, A. R., Taghavi, M. R., Neshat-Doost, H. T., & Yule, W. (2001). An experimental investigation of hypervigilance for threat in children and adolescents with posttraumatic stress disorder. *Psychological Medicine*, *31*, 541–547.

Dalgleish, T., Taghavi, R., Neshat-Doost, H., Moradi, A., Canterbury, R., & Yule, W. (2003). Patterns of processing bias for emotional information across clinical disorders: A comparison of attention, memory, and prospective cognition in children and adolescents with depression, generalized anxiety, and posttraumatic stress disorder. *Journal of Clinical Child and Adolescent Psychology*, *32*, 10–21.

Dapretto, M., Davies, M. S., Pfeifer, J. H., Scott, A. A., Sigman, M., Bookheimer, S. Y., & Iacoboni, M. (2006). Understanding emotions in others: Mirror neuron dysfunction in children with autism spectrum disorders. *Nature Neuroscience*, *9*, 28–30.

Darwin, C. (1859). *On the origin of the species by means of natural selection*. New York: D. Appleton.

Darwin, C. (1965). *The expression of emotions in man and animals*. London: Murray (Original work published 1872).

Davidson, R. J., Putnam, K. M., & Larson, C. L. (2000). Dysfunction in the neural circuitry of emotion regulation—a possible prelude to violence. *Science*, *289*, 591–594.

Davis, M., Ressler, K., Rothbaum, B. O., & Richardson, R. (2006). Effects of D-cycloserine on extinction: Translation from preclinical to clinical work. *Biological Psychiatry*, *60*, 369–375.

Davison, G. C. (1966). Anxiety under total curarization: Implications for the role of muscular relaxation in the desensitization of neurotic fears. *Journal of Nervous and Mental Disease*, *143*, 443–448.

Davison, G. C. (1968). Systematic desensitization as a counterconditioning process. *Journal of Abnormal Psychology*, *73*, 91.

Dawson, M. R. W. (2004). *Minds and machines: Connectionism and psychological modeling*. Malden MA: Malden Blackwell Publishing.

De Berardis, D., Carano, A., Gambi, F., Campanella, D., Giannetti, P., Ceci, A., Mancini, E., La Rovere, R., Cicconetti, A., Penna, L., Di Matteo, D., Scorrano, B., Cotellessa, C., Salerno, R. M., Serroni, N., & Ferro, F. M. (2007). Alexithymia and its relationships with body checking and body image in a non-clinical female sample. *Eating Behaviors*, *8*, 296–304.

De Berardis, D., D'Albenzio, A., Gambi, F., Sepede, G., Valchera, A., Conti, C. M., Fulcheri, M., Cavuto, M., Ortolani, C., Salerno, R. M., Serroni, N., & Ferro, F. M. (2009). Alexithymia and its relationships with dissociative experiences and internet addiction in a nonclinical sample. *Cyberpsychology & Behavior*, *12*(1), 67–69.

de Hamilton, C., Antonia, F., Brindley, R. M., & Frith, U. (2007). Imitation and action understanding in autistic spectrum disorders: How valid is the hypothesis of a deficit in the mirror neuron system? *Neuropsychologia*, *45*(8), 1859–1868.

de Groot, J. M., Rodin, G., & Olmsted, M. P. (1995). Alexithymia, depression, and treatment outcome on bulimia nervosa. *Comprehensive Psychiatry*, *36*, 53–60.

De Houwer, J., & Moors, A. (2010). Implicit measures: Similarities and differences. In B. Gawronski, & B. K. Payne (Eds.), *Handbook of implicit social cognition: Measurement, theory, and applications* (pp. 176–193). New York: Guilford.

de Maat, S., de Jonghe, F., Schoevers, R., & Dekker, J. (2009). The effectiveness of long-term psychoanalytic therapy: A systematic review of empirical studies. *Harvard Review of Psychiatry*, *17*, 1–23.

Deci, E. L., & Ryan, R. M. (1980). Self-determination theory: When mind mediates behavior. *The Journal of Mind and Behavior*, *1*, 33–43.

Deci, E. L., & Ryan, R. M. (1985). *Intrinsic motivation and self-determination in human behavior.* New York: Plenum Press.

Deese, J. (1959). On the prediction of occurrence of particular verbal intrusions in immediate recall. *Journal of Experimental Psychology, 58*, 17–22.

DeFries, J. C., Gervais, M. C., & Thomas, E. A. (1978). Response to 30 generations of selection for open-field activity in laboratory mice. *Behavior Genetics, 8*, 3–13.

DeFries, J. C., Wilson, J. R., & McClearn, G. E. (1970). Open-field behavior in mice: Selection response and situational generality. *Behavior Genetics, 1*, 195–211.

Del Casale, A., Kotzalidis, G. D., Rapinesi, C., Serata, D., Ambrosi, E., Simonetti, A., Pompili, M., Ferracuti, S., Tatarelli, R., & Girardi, P. (2011). Functional neuroimaging in obsessive-compulsive disorder. *Neuropsychobiology, 64*, 61–85.

Dember, W. N. (1974). Motivation and the cognitive revolution. *American Psychologist, 29*, 161–168.

den Dulk, P., Capalbo, M., & Phaf, R. H. (2002). A connectionist dual-route model for affective priming. *Cognitive Processing, 3-4*, 43–64.

Denissenko, M. F., Pao, A., Tang, M., & Pfeifer, G. P. (1996). Preferential formation of benzo[a] pyrene adducts at lung cancer mutational hotspots in P53. *Science, 274*, 430–432.

Dennett, D. C. (1995). *Darwin's dangerous idea.* New York, NY: Simon & Schuster.

Denny, B. T., Kober, H., Wager, T. D., & Ochsner, K. N. (2012). A meta-analysis of functional neuroimaging studies of self- and other judgments reveals a spatial gradient for mentalizing in the medial prefrontal cortex. *Journal of Cognitive Neuroscience, 24*(8), 1742–1752.

Denollet, J., & Nyklíček, I. (2004). Psychological mindedness: A new index to assess a major emotion-focused coping style? In I. Nyklíček, L. Temoshok, & A. J. J.M. Vingerhoets (Eds.), *Emotional expression and health: Advances in theory, assessment and clinical applications* (pp. 185–203). Hove, England: Brunner-Routledge.

DeRubeis, R. J., Evans, M. D., Hollon, S. D., Garvey, M. J., Grove, W. M., & Tuason, V. B. (1990). How does cognitive therapy work? Cognitive change and symptom change in cognitive therapy and pharmacotherapy for depression. *Journal of Consulting and Clinical Psychology, 58*, 862–869.

DeRubeis, R. J., Siegle, G. J., & Hollon, S. D. (2008). Cognitive therapy vs. medications for depression: Treatment outcomes and neural mechanisms. *Nature Reviews Neuroscience, 9*(10), 788–796.

Deutsch, R., & Strack, F. (2010). Building blocks of social behavior: Reflective and impulsive processes. In B. Gawronski, & B. K. Payne (Eds.), *Handbook of implicit social cognition: Measurement, theory, and applications* (pp. 62–79). New York: Guilford.

Di Pellegrino, G., Fadiga, L., Fogass,i, L., Gallese, V., & Rizzolatti, G. (1992). Understanding motor events: A neurophysiological study. *Experimental Brain Research, 91*, 176–180.

Diekelmann, S., & Born, J. (2010). The memory function of sleep. *Nature Reviews Neuroscience, 11*(2), 114–126.

DiGuiseppe, R. (2008). Surfing the waves of behavior therapy. *The Behavior Therapist, 31*, 154–155.

Dijksterhuis, A. (2004). Think different: The merits of unconscious thought in preference development and decision making. *Journal of Personality and Social Psychology, 87*, 586–598.

Dijksterhuis, A., & Aarts, H. (2010). Goals, attention, and (un)consciousness. *Annual Review of Psychology, 61*, 467–490.

Dijksterhuis, A., & Bargh, J. A. (2001). The perception-behavior expressway: Automatic effects of social perception on social behavior. In M. P. Zanna (Ed.), *Advances in experimental social psychology Vol. 33.* (pp. 1–40). San Diego, CA: Academic Press.

Dijksterhuis, A., & Nordgren, L. F. (2006). A theory of unconscious thought. *Perspectives on Psychological Science, 1*, 95–109.

Dijksterhuis, A., Bos, M. W., Nordgren, L. R., & van Baaren, R. B. (2006). On making the right choice: The deliberation-without-attention effect. *Science, 311*, 1005–1007.

Dijksterhuis, A., Boss, M. W., van der Leij, A., & van Baaren, R. B. (2009). Predicting soccer matches after unconscious and conscious thought as a function of expertise. *Psychological Science, 20*, 1381–1387.

Dineen, K. A., & Hadwin, J. A. (2004). Anxious and depressive symptoms and children's judgements of their own and others' interpretation of ambiguous social scenarios. *Journal of Anxiety Disorders, 18*, 499–513.

Ditto, P. H., & Lopez, D. F. (1992). Motivated skepticism: Use of differential decision criteria for preferred and nonpreferred conclusions. *Journal of Personality and Social Psychology, 63*, 568–584.

Dobbs, D. (2005). Fact or phrenology? *Scientific American Mind, 16*, 24–31.

Dobbs, D. (2012). *A New Focus on the 'Post" in Post-Traumatic Stress*. New York Times, Science Times. December 25, page D2.

Dollard, J., & Miller, N. E. (1950). *Personality and psychotherapy*. New York: McGraw-Hill.

Donahoe, J. W. (1991). The selectionist approach to verbal behavior: Potential contributions of neuropsychology and connectionism. In L. J. Hayes, & P. N. Chase (Eds.), *Dialogues on verbal behavior: The first international institute on verbal relations*. Reno: NV: Context Press.

Donahoe, J. W. (1997). The necessity of neural networks. In G. E. Stelmach & P. A. Vroon (Series Eds.) & J. W. Donahoe & V. P. Dorsel (Vol. Eds.), *Advances in Psychology: Vol. 121*, Neural-network models of cognition: Biobehavioral foundations (pp. 1–19). Amsterdam: Elsevier.

Donahoe, J. W. (1998). Positive reinforcement: The selection of behavior. In W. O'Donohue (Ed.), *Learning and behavior therapy* (pp. 169–187). Boston: Allyn and Bacon.

Donahoe, J. W., & Packard-Dorsel, V. P. (1997). Neural-network models of cognition: Biobehavioral foundations. In G. E. Stelmach, & P. A. Vroon (Eds.), *Advances in Psychology Vol. 121*. Amsterdam: Elsevier.

Donahoe, J. W., & Palmer, D. C. (1989). The interpretation of complex human behavior: Some reactions to parallel distributed processing, edited by J. L. McClelland, D. E. Rumelhart, and the PDP Research Group. *Journal of the Experimental Analysis of Behavior, 51*, 399–416.

Donahoe, J. W., & Palmer, D. C. (1994). *Learning and complex behavior* (pp. 18–27, 31–67). New York: Allyn and Bacon.

Donahoe, J. W., Burgos, J. E., & Palmer, D. C. (1993). A selectionist approach to reinforcement. *Journal of the Experimental Analysis of Behavior, 60*, 17–40.

Donegan, N. H., Gluck, M. A., & Thompson, R. F. (1989). Integrating behavioral and biological models of classical conditioning. *The Psychology of Learning and Motivation, 23*, 109–156. http://dx.doi.org/10.1016/j.neunet.2011.02.006.

Dragoi, V., & Staddon, J. E. R. (1991). The dynamics of operant conditioning. *Psychological Review, 106*, 20–61. http://dx.doi.org/10.1037/0033-295X.106.1.20.

Draycott, S., & Dabbs, A. (1998a). Cognitive dissonance 1: An overview of the literature and its integration into theory and practice in clinical psychology. *British Journal of Clinical Psychology, 37*, 341–353.

Draycott, S., & Dabbs, A. (1998b). Cognitive dissonance 2: A theoretical grounding of motivational interviewing. *British Journal of Clinical Psychology, 37*, 355–364.

Drobes, D. J., & Lang, P. J. (1995). Bioinformational theory and behavior therapy. In W. O'Donohue, & L. Krasner (Eds.), *Theories of behavior therapy: Exploring behavior change* (pp. 229–257). Washington, DC: American Psychological Association.

Duncan, S., & Barrett, L. F. (2007). Affect is a form of cognition: A neurobiological analysis. *Cognition and Emotion, 21*, 1184–1211.

Dunning, D. (1999). A new look: Motivated social cognition and the schematic representation of social concepts. *Psychological Inquiry, 10*, 1–11.

Eagleman, D. (2011). *Incognito: The secret lives of the brain*. New York: Vintage Books.

Earp, S. E., & Maney, D. L. (2012). Birdsong: Is it music to their ears? *Frontiers in Evolutionary Neuroscience, 4*(Article 14), 1–10.

Eaton, W. O., & Saudino, K. J. (1992). Prenatal activity level as a temperament dimension? Individual differences and developmental functions in fetal movement. *Infant Behavior and Development, 15*, 57–70.

Ebel, R. L. (1974). And still the dryads linger. *American Psychologist, 29*, 485–492.

Eckman. (1993). Facial expressions. In T. Dalgleish, & M. Power (Eds.), *Handbook of cognition and emotion* (pp. 301–320). New York: Wiley.

Eckman, P. (1999). Basic emotions. In T. Dalgleish, & M. Power (Eds.), *Handbook of Cognition and Emotion* (pp. 45–60). Sussex, U.K: John Wiley & Sons.

Eich, E., & Macauley, D. (2006). Fundamental factors in mood dependent memory. In J. P. Forgas (Ed.), *Feeling and thinking* (pp. 109–130). Cambridge, UK: Cambridge University Press.

Eitam, B., Hassin, R. R., & Schul, Y. (2008). Nonconscious goal pursuit in novel environments: The case of implicit learning. *Psychological Science, 19*, 261–267.

Eley, T. C., Bolton, D., O'Connor, T. G., Perrin, S., Smith, P., & Plomin, R. (2003). A twin study of anxiety-related behaviours in preschool children. *Journal of Child Psychology and Psychiatry, 44*, 945–960.

Ellenberger, H. F. (1970). *Discovery of the unconscious: The history and evolution of dynamic psychiatry*. New York: Basic Books. BF173.E6.

Ellis, A. (1958). *Sex without guilt*. New York: Lyle Stuart.

Ellis, A. (1962). *Reason and emotion in psychotherapy*. New York: Lyle Stuart.

Ellis, A. (1994). *Reason and emotion in psychotherapy; Revised and updated*. Secaucus, NJ: Carol.

Ellis, A., & Harper, R. A. (1961). *A guide to rational living*. Englewood Cliffs, NJ: Prentice Hall.

Ellison, J. A., Greenberg, L., Goldman, R., & Angus, L. (2009). Maintenance of gains at follow-up in experiential therapies for depression. *Journal of Consulting and Clinical Psychology*, 77, 103–112.

Elman, J. L., Bates, E. A., Johnson, M. H., Karmiloff-Smith, A., Parisi, D., & Plunkett, K. (1999). *Rethinking innateness: A connectionist perspective on development*. Cambridge, MA: The MIT Press.

Emmelkamp, P. M. G. (1994). Behavior therapy with adults. In A. E. Bergin, & S. L. Garfield (Eds.), *Handbook of psychotherapy and behavior change* (4th ed.) (pp. 379–427). New York: Wiley.

Engel, B. T. (2000). Visceral learning. In A. Baum, T. Revenson, & R. Singer (Eds.), *Handbook of health psychology* (pp. 85–94). Mahway, NJ: Erlbaum.

Epling, W. F., & Pierce, W. D. (Eds.). (1996). *Activity Anorexia: Theory, Research, and Treatment* (2nd ed.).

Epstein, S. (1994). Integration of the cognitive and psychodynamic unconscious. *American Psychologist, 49*, 709–724.

Erdelyi, M. H. (1974). A new look at the New Look: Perceptual defense and vigilance. *Psychological Review, 81*, 1–25.

Erdelyi, M. H. (1985). *Psychoanalysis: Freud's cognitive psychology*. New York: Freeman.

Erdelyi, M. H. (1990). Repression, reconstruction, and defense: History and integration of the psychoanalytic and experimental frameworks. In J. Singer (Ed.), *Repression and dissociation: Implications for personality, psychopathology, and health* (pp. 1–31). Chicago: Chicago University Press.

Erdelyi, M. H. (1992). Psychodynamics and the unconscious. *American Psychologist, 47*, 784–787.

Eroglu, C., Barres, B. A., & Stevens, B. (2008). Glia as active participants in the development and function of synapses. In J. W. Hell, & M. D. Ehlers (Eds.), *Structural and functional organization of the synapse* (pp. 683–714). New York: Springer Science + Business Media.

Evans, J. S. B. T. (1984). Heuristic and analytic processes in reasoning. *British Journal of Psychology, 75*, 451–468.

Evans, J., & St., B. T. (1989). *Biases in human reasoning: Causes and consequences*. London: Erlbaum.

Evans, J. B. T. (2008). Dual-processing accounts of reasoning, judgment, and social cognition. *Annual Review of Psychology, 59*, 255–278. http://dx.doi.org/10.1146/annurev.psych.59.103006.093629.

Evans, J. B. T., & Frankish, K. (Eds.). (2009). *In two minds: Dual processes and beyond*. New York: Oxford University Press.

Evans, J. B. T., & Stanovich, K. E. (2013). Dual-process theories of highter cognition: Advancing the debate. *Perspectives on Psychological Science, 8*(3), 223–241. http://dx.doi.org/10.1177/1745691612460685.

Evans, J., St., B. T., & Over, D. E. (1996). *Rationality and Reasoning*. Hove, UK: Psychology Press.

Evren, C., & Evren, B. (2005). Self-mutilation in substance-dependent patients and relationship with childhood abuse and neglect, alexithymia and temperament and character dimensions of personality. *Drug and Alcohol Dependence, 80*, 15–22.

Eysenck, H. J. (1952). The effects of psychotherapy: An evaluation. *Journal of Consulting Psychology, 16*, 319–324.

Eysenck, H. J. (1964). *Experiments in behaviour therapy: Readings in modern methods of treatment of mental disorders derived from learning theory*. New York: Macmillan.

Eysenck, H. J. (1965). The effects of psychotherapy. *International Journal of Psychiatry, 1*, 97–178.

Eysenck, H. J. (1967). *The biological basis of personality*. Springfield, IL: Thomas.

Eysenck, M. W. (1992). *Anxiety: The cognitive perspective*. Hove, UK: Lawrence Erlbaum Associates Ltd.

Fadiga, L., Fogassi, L., Pavesi, G., & Rizzolatti, G. (1995). Motor facilitation during action observation: A magnetic stimulation study. *Journal of Neurophysiology, 73*(6), 2608–2611.

Fair, D. A., Cohen, A. L., Power, J. D., Dosenbach, N. U. F., Church, J. A., Miezin, F. M., Schlaggar, B. L., & Petersen, S. E. (2009). Functional brain networks develop from a "local to distributed" organization. *PLoS Computational Biology, 5*(5), e1000381.

Fairburn, C. G., Norman, P. A., Welch, S. L., O'Connor, M. R., Doll, H. A., & Peveler, R. C. (1995). A prospective study of outcome in bulimia nervosa and the long-term effects of three psychological treatments. *Archives of General Psychiatry, 52*, 304–312.

Falk, E. B., Berkman, E. T., Mann, T., Harrison, B., & Lieberman, M. D. (2010). Predicting persuasion-induced behavior change from the brain. *Journal of Neuroscience, 30*, 8421–8424.

Falk, E. B., Berkman, E. T., Whalen, D., & Lieberman, M. D. (2011). Neural activity during health messaging predicts reductions in smoking above and beyond self-report. *Health Psychology, 30*, 177–185.

Falk, E. B., Berkman, E. T., & Lieberman, M. D. (2012). From neural responses to population behavior: Neural focus group predicts population-level media effects. *Psychological Science, 23*(5), 439–445.

Falls, W. A., Miserendino, M. J., & Davis, M. (1992). Extinction of fear-potentiated startle: Blockade by infusion of an NMDA antagonist into the amygdala. *Journal of Neuroscience, 12*, 854–863.

Fang, F. C., Steen, R. G., & Casadevall, A. (2012). Misconduct accounts for the majority of retracted scientific publications. *Proceedings of the National Academy of Sciences of the United States of America (PNAS), 109*(42), 16751–16752.

Fanselow, M. S., & Poulos, A. M. (2005). The neuroscience of mammalian associative learning. *Annual Review of Psychology, 56*, 207–234.

Farah, M. J. (2000). The neural bases of mental imagery. In M. S. Gazzaniga (Ed.), *The new cognitive neurosciences* (2nd ed.) (pp. 965–974). Cambridge, MA: The MIT Press.

Farber, B. A. (1985). The genesis, development, and implications of psychological-mindedness in psychotherapists. *Psychotherapy: Theory, Research, and Practice, 22*, 170–177.

Farber, B. A. (1989). Psychological-mindedness: Can there be too much of a good thing. *Psychotherapy, 26*, 210–217.

Fassino, S., Daga, G. A., Pierò, A., & Delsedime, N. (2007). Psychological factors affecting eating disorders. *Advances in Psychosomatic Medicine, 28*, 141–168.

Favazza, A. R. (1998). The coming of age of self-mutilation. *Journal of Nervous and Mental Disease, 186*, 259–268.

Fernald, R. D., & Maruska, K. P. (2012). Social information changes the brain. *Proceedings of the National Academy of Sciences of the United States of America, 109*, 17194–17199.

Ferrari, P. F., Gallese, V., Rizzolatti, G., & Fogassi, L. (2003). Mirror neurons responding to the observation of ingestive and communicative mouth actions in the monkey ventral premotor cortex. *The European Journal of Neuroscience, 17*(8), 1703–1714.

Ferster, C. B., & Skinner, B. F. (1957). *Schedules of reinforcement*. Englewood Cliffs, NJ: Prentice-Hall.

Festinger, L. (1957). *A theory of cognitive dissonance*. Stanford, CA: Stanford University Press.

Festinger, L. (1964). *Conflict, decision, and dissonance*. Stanford: CA: Stanford University Press.

Fields, R. D. (2009). *The other brain: From dementia to schizophrenia, how new discoveries about the brain are revolutionizing medicine and science*. New York: Simon & Schuster.

Fischhoff, B., & Beyth-Marom, R. (1983). Hypothesis evaluation from a Bayesian perspective. *Psychological Review, 90*, 239–260.

Fishbein, M. (2000). The role of theory in HIV prevention. *AIDS Care, 12*, 273–278.

Fishbein, M., & Ajzen, I. (1975). *Belief, attitude, intention and behaviour: An introduction to theory and research*. Reading, MA: Addison-Wesley.

Fisher, G. A. (1997). Theoretical and methodological elaborations of the circumplex model of personality traits and emotions. In R. Plutchik, & H. R. Conte (Eds.), *Circumplex models of personality and emotions* (pp. 245–269). Washington, DC: American Psychological Association.

Fisher, P. A., Gunnar, M. R., Dozier, M., Bruce, J., & Pears, K. C. (2006). Effects of a therapeutic intervention for foster children on behavior problems, caregiver attachments, and stress regulatory neural systems. In B. M. Lester, A. Masten, & B. McEwen (Eds.), *Annals of the New York Academy of Sciences Resilience in children: Vol. 1094*. (pp. 215–225).

Fisher, R. A. (1925). *Statistical methods for research workers*. London: Oliver & Boyd.

Foa, E. B., & Kozak, M. J. (1986). Emotional processing of fear: Exposure to corrective information. *Psychological Bulletin, 99*, 20–35.

Foa, E. B., & Kozak, M. J. (1997). Beyond the efficacy ceiling? Cognitive behavior therapy in search of theory. *Behavior Therapy, 28*, 601–611.

Foa, E. B., Steketee, G., & Rothbaum, B. O. (1989). Behavioral/cognitive conceptualization of post-traumatic stress disorder. *Behavior Therapy, 20*, 155–176.

Foa, E. B., Zinbarg, R., & Rothbaum, B. O. (1992). Uncontrollability and unpredictability in posttraumatic stress disorder: An animal model. *Psychological Bulletin, 112*, 218–238.

Fodor, J. A. (1968). *Psychological explanation*. New York: Random House.

Fodor, J. A. (1983). *The modularity of mind*. Cambridge, MA: MIT Press.

Fodor, J. A., & Pylyshyn, Z. W. (1988). Connectionism and cognitive architecture: A critical analysis. In S. Pinker, & J. Mehler (Eds.), *Connections and symbols* (pp. 3–71). Cambridge, MA: MIT Press/Bradford Books (Cognition Special Issue).

Fotopoulou, A., Pfaff, D., & Conway, M. A. (Eds.). (2012). *From the couch to the lab: Trends in psychodynamic neuroscience*. New York: Oxford University Press.

Fox, M. D., Synder, A. Z., Vincent, J. L., Corbetta, M., Van Essen, D. C., & Raichle, M. E. (2005). The human brain is intrinsically organized into dynamic anticorrelated functional networks. *PNAS, 102*(27), 9673–9678.

Frank, J. D. (1961). *Persuasion and healing: A comparative study of psychotherapy*. Baltimore, MD: Johns Hopkins University Press.

Frank, M. J., Cohen, M. X., & Sanfey, A. G. (2009). Multiple systems in decision making: A neurocomputational perspective. *Current Directions in Psychological Science, 18*, 73–77.

Franks, C. M., & Mays, D. T. (1980). Negative effects revisited: A rejoinder. *Professional Psychology, 11*, 101–105.

Freeling, N. W., & Shemberg, K. M. (1970). The alleviation of test anxiety by systematic desensitization. *Behavior Research and Therapy*, *8*, 293–299.

Freeman, J. B., & Ambady, N. (2011). A dynamic interactive theory of person construal. *Psychological Review*, *118*, 247–279.

French, T. M. (1933). Interrelations between psychoanalysis and the experimental work of Pavlov. *American Journal of Psychiatry*, *89*, 1165–1203.

Freud, S. (1895a). *Studies on hysteria*. Lepizig: Deuticke: First English translation by a. A. Brill. Nervous & Mental Disease Publications, 1936.

Freud, S. (1895b). *The Project for a Scientific Psychology*. Unpublished Manuscript.

Freud, S. (1938). The interpretation of dreams. In A. A. Brill (Ed.), *The basic writings of Sigmund Freud*. New York: Modern Library, Random House. (Originally published 1900).

Freud, S. (1950). In *Collected papers. J. Riviere, Trans Vol. 4*. London: Hogarth Press and Institute of Psychoanalysis.

Freud, S. (1962). *The ego and the id*. New York: Norton (Originally published 1923.).

Fried, I., Mukamel, R., & Kreiman, G. (2011). Internally generated preactivation of single neurons in human medial frontal cortex predicts volition. *Neuron*, *69*(3), 548–562.

Frith, U. (1989). *Autism: Explaining the enigma*. Oxford: Blackwell.

Frois-Wittmann, J. (1930). The judgment of facial expression. *Journal of Experimental Psychology*, *13*, 113–151.

Fuchs, K. (1980). Therapy of vaginismus by hypnotic desensitization. *American Journal of Obstetrics and Gynecology*, *137*, 1–7.

Gage, F. H., & Muotri, A. R. (2012). What makes each brain unique. *Scientific American*, *306*, 26–31 (March, #3).

Gains, B. J., Kuklinski, J. H., Qjuirk, P. J., Peyton, B., & Verkuilen, J. (2007). Same facts, different interpretations: Partisan motivation and opinion on Iraq. *The Journal of Politics*, *69*(4), 957–974.

Gallese, V., Fadiga, L., Fogassim, L., & Rizzolatti, G. (1996). Action recognition in the premotor cortex. *Brain*, *110*, 593–609.

Gallese, V., Eagle, M. N., & Migone, P. (2007). Intentional attunement: Mirror neurons and the underpinnings of interpersonal relations. *Journal of the American Psychoanalytic Association*, *55*, 131–176.

Gardner, H. (1985). *The mind's new science*. NY: Basic Books.

Gardner, H. (1992). Scientific psychology: Should we bury it or praise it? *New Ideas in Psychology*, *10*, 179–190.

Garner, D. M. (1991). *Eating Disorder Inventory-2 Professional Manual*. Psychological Assessment Resources, Inc.

Garner, D. M., & Olmsted, M. P. (1984). *Eating disorders inventory manual*. Odessa, FL: Psychological Assessment Resources, Inc.

Garry, M., & Polaschek, D. L. L. (2000). Imagination and memory. *Current Directions in Psychological Science*, *9*, 6–10.

Garry, M., Manning, C. G., Loftus, E. F., & Sherman, S. J. (1996). Imagination inflation: Imagining a childhood event inflates confidence that it occurred. *Psychonomic Bulletin and Review*, *3*, 208–214.

Gawronski, B., & Payne, B. K. (Eds.). (2010). *Handbook of implicit social cognition: Measurement, theory, and applications*. New York: Guilford.

Gawronski, B., LeBel, T. P., & Peters, K. R. (2007). What do implicit measures tell us? *Perspectives on Psychological Science*, *2*(2), 181–193.

Gazzaniga, M. (2005). Forty-five years of split-brain research and still going strong. *Nature Reviews: Neuroscience*, *6*, 653–659.

Gazzaniga, M. S. (1970). *The bisected brain*. New York: Appleton-Century-Crofts.

Gazzaniga, M. S. (1972). One brain-two minds? *American Scientist*, *60*, 311–317.

Gazzaniga, M. S. (1998). The split brain revisited. *Scientific American*, *279*(1), 35–39.

Gazzaniga, M. S., & LeDoux, J. E. (1978). *The integrated mind*. New York: Plenum.

Gelbard-Sagiv, H., Mukamel, R., Harel, M., Malach, R., & Fried, I. (2008). Internally generated reactivation of single neurons in human hippocampus during free recall. *Science, 322*(5898), 96–101.

Gendlin, E. T. (1996). *Focusing-oriented psychotherapy*. New York: Guilford Press.

Gerber, A. J., Kocsis, J. H., Milrod, B. L., Roose, S. P., Barber, J. P., Thase, M. E., & Leon, A. C. (2001). A quality-based review of randomized controlled trials of psychodynamic psychotherapy. *American Journal of Psychiatry, 168*, 19–28.

Gershon, M. D. (1981). The enteric nervous system. *Annual Review of Neuroscience, 4*, 227–272.

Gigerenzer, G. (1998). Surrogates for theories. *Theory & Psychology, 8*, 195–204.

Gigerenzer, G. (2009). Surrogates for theory. *Association for Psychological Science Observer, 22*, 21–23.

Gigerenzer, G. (2010). Personal reflections on theory and psychology. *Theory and Psychology, 20*(6), 733–743.

Gilbert, D. (2006). *Stumbling on happiness*. New York, NY: Knopf.

Gilbert, D., & Wilson, T. (2006). Miswanting: Some problems in the forecasting of future affective states. In S. Lichtenstein, & P. Slovic (Eds.), *The construction of preferences* (pp. 550–563). Cambridge, England: Cambridge University Press.

Gilbert, D., & Wilson, T. (2007). Prospection: Experiencing the future. *Science, 351*, 1351–1354.

Ginot, E. (2009). The empathetic power of enactments: The link between neuropsychological processes and an expanded definition of empathy. *Psychoanalytic Psychology, 26*, 290–309.

Glantz, L. A., Gilmore, J. H., Hamer, R. M., Lieberman, J. A., & Jarskog, L. F. (2007). Synaptophysin and PSD-95 in the human prefrontal cortex from mid-gestation into early adulthood. *Neuroscience, 149*, 582–591.

Gluck, M. A., & Myers, C. E. (1997). Psychobiological models of hippocampal function in learning and memory. *Annual Review of Psychology, 48*, 481–514.

Gluck, M. A., & Thompson, R. F. (1987). Modeling the neural substrates of associative learning and memory: A computational approach. *Psychological Review, 94*, 176–191.

Gobbini, M. I., Koralek, A. C., Bryan, R. E., Montgomery, K. J., & Haxby, J. V. (2007). Two takes on the social brain: A comparison of theory of mind tasks. *Journal of Cognitive Neuroscience, 19*, 1803–1814.

Goddard, C. A., Butts, D. A., & Shatz, C. J. (2007). Regulation of CNS synapses by neuronal MHC Class I. *Proceedings of the National Academy of Sciences of the United States of America (PNAS), 104*(16), 6828–6833.

Goldapple, K., Segal, Z., Garson, C., Lau, M., Bieling, P., Kennedy, S., & Mayberg, H. (2004). Modulation of cortical-limbic pathways in major depression: Treatment-specific effects of cognitive behavior therapy. *Archives of General Psychiatry, 61*, 34–41.

Goldfried, M. R. (1980). Toward the delineation of therapeutic change principles. *American Psychologist, 35*, 991–999.

Goldfried, M. R. (2012). More on closing the gap between research and practice. *Psychotherapy Bulletin, 47*(4), 2–4.

Goldfried, M. R., & Padawer, W. (1982). Current status and future directions in psychotherapy. In M. R. Goldfried (Ed.), *Converging themes in psychotherapy* (pp. 3–49). New York: Springer.

Goldman, R., Greenberg, L. S., & Angus, L. (2006a). The effects of adding emotion-focused interventions to the therapeutic relationship in the treatment of depression. *Psychotherapy Research, 16*, 537–549.

Goldman, R., Greenberg, L., & Angus, L. (2006b). The effects of specific emotion-focused interventions and the therapeutic relationship in the treatment of depression: A dismantling study. *Psychotherapy Research, 16*, 527–549.

González-Pardo, H., & Pérez Álvarez, M. (2013). Epigenetics and its implications for psychology. *Psicothema*, *25*(1), 3–12.

Gotlib, I. H., & McCann, C. D. (1984). Construct accessibility and depression: An examination of cognitive and affective factors. *Journal of Personality and Social Psychology*, *47*, 427–439.

Gough, H. (1957/1975). *California Psychological Inventory*. Palo Alto, CA: Consulting Psychologists Press.

Goyal, R. K., & Hirano, K. (1996). The enteric nervous system. *The New England Journal of Medicine*, *334*, 1106–1115.

Grabe, H. J., Spitzer, C., & Freyberger, H. J. (2004). Alexithymia and personality in relation to dimensions of psychopathology. *American Journal of Psychiatry*, *161*, 1299–1301. 9.

Grant, A. M. (2001). Rethinking psychological mindedness: Metacognition, self-reflection, and insight. *Behaviour Change*, *18*, 8–17.

Gratz, K. L. (2006). Risk factors for deliberate self-harm among female college students: The role and interaction of childhood maltreatment, emotional inexpressivity, and affect intensity/reactivity. *American Journal of Orthopsychiatry*, *76*, 238–250.

Gratz, K. L., & Roemer, L. (2008). The relationship between emotion dysregulation and deliberate self-harm among female undergraduates at an urban commuter university. *Cognitive Behaviour Therapy*, *37*, 14–25.

Gratz, K. L., Rosenthal, M. Z., Tull, M. T., Lejuez, C. W., & Gunderson, J. G. (2006). An experimental investigation of emotion dysregulation in borderline personality disorder. *Journal of Abnormal Psychology*, *115*, 850–855.

Gray, J. A. (1982). *The neuropsychology of anxiety: An enquiry into the functions of the septo-hippocampal system*. Oxford: Clarendon Press/Oxford University Press.

Gray, J. A. (1987). *The psychology of fear and stress* (2nd ed.). New York, NY: Cambridge University Press.

Gray, J. A., & McNaughton, N. (2000). *The neuropsychology of anxiety: An enquiry into the functions of the septo-hippocampal system* (2nd ed.). New York, NY: Oxford University Press.

Greben, D. (2012). The broad applicability of integrative principles. *Psychotherapy Bulletin*, *47*(4), 6–13.

Grecco, E., Robbins, S. J., Bartoli, E., & Wolff, E. F. (2013). Use of nonconscious priming to promote self-disclosure. *Clinical Psychological Science*, *1*(3), 311–315.

Green, C. D. (1992). Is unified positivism the answer to psychology's disunity? *American Psychologist*, *47*, 1057–1058.

Greenberg, L. S. (2002). *Emotion-focused therapy: Coaching clients to work through their feelings*. Washington, DC: American Psychological Association.

Greenberg, L. S. (2008). The clinical application of emotion in psychotherapy. In M. Lewis, J. M. Haviland-Jones, & L. F. Barrett (Eds.), *Handbook of emotions* (3rd ed.) (pp. 88–101). New York: Guilford.

Greenberg, L. (2013). Experimental rigor and clinical complexity. In D. Hermans, B. Rimé, & B. Mesquita (Eds.), *Changing emotions* (pp. 223–229). New York: Psychology Press.

Greenberg, L. S., & Watson, J. (1998). Experiential therapy of depression. Differential effects of client center relationship conditions and process experiential interventions. *Psychotherapy Research*, *8*, 210–224.

Greenberg, S. J. (1999). Alexithymia in an anorexic population: Prevalence and predictive variables. (interoceptive awareness). *Dissertation Abstracts International: Section B: The Sciences & Engineering*, *59*(11-B).

Greene, A. J. (2010). Making connections: The essence of memory is linking one thought to another. *Scientific American Mind*. July/August, 22–29.

Greene, L. R. (2012). Group therapist as social scientist, with special reference to the psychodynamically oriented psychotherapist. *American Psychologist*, *676*, 477–489. http://dx.doi.org/10.1037/a0029147.

Greenhill, L. I., & Ford, R. E. (2002). Childhood Attention-Deficit Hyperactivity Disorder: Pharmacological Treatments. In P. E. Nathan, & J. M. Gorman (Eds.), *A guide to treatments that work* (2nd ed.) (pp. 25–55).

Greenspoon, J. (1955). The reinforcing effect of two spoken sounds on the frequency of two responses. *American Journal of Psychology, 68*, 409–416.

Greenwald, A. G. (1988). Self-knowledge and self-deception. In J. S. Lockard, & D. L. Paulhus (Eds.), *Self-deception: An adaptive mechanism?* (pp. 113–131). Englewood Cliffs, NJ: Prentice Hall.

Greenwald, A. G. (1992). New Look 3: Unconscious cognition reclaimed. *American Psychologist, 47*, 766–779.

Greenwald, A. G., & Banaji, M. R. (1995). Implicit social cognition: Attitudes, self-esteem, and stereotypes. *Psychological Review, 102*, 4–27.

Gregory, W. L., Cialdini, R. B., & Carpenter, K. M. (1982). Self-relevant scenarios as mediators of likelihood estimates and compliance: Does imagining make it so? *Journal of Personality and Social Psychology, 43*, 89–99.

Grencavage, L. M., & Norcross, J. C. (1990). Where are the commonalities among the therapeutic common factors? *Professional Psychology: Research and Practice, 21*, 372–378.

Grieneisen, M. L., & Zhang, M. (2012). A comprehensive survey of retracted articles from the scholarly literature. *PLoS One*, 7(10), e44118.

Grill-Spector, K., & Kanwisher, N. (2005). Visual recognition: As soon as you know it is there, you know what it is. *Psychological Science, 16*(2), 152–160.

Groenendyk, E. (2011). Current emotion research in political science: How emotions help democracy overcome its collection action problem. *Emotion Review, 3*, 455–563.

Gross, J. J. (1998). Antecedent- and response-focused emotion regulation: Divergent consequences for experience, expression, and physiology. *Journal of Personality and Social Psychology, 74*, 224–237.

Gross, J. J. (1999). Emotion regulation: Past, present, future. *Cognition and Emotion, 13*, 551–573.

Gross, J. J. (2013). *Handbook of emotion regulation* (2nd ed.). New York: Guilford.

Gross, J. J., & John, O. P. (2003). Individual differences in two emotion regulation processes: Implications for affect, relationships and well-being. *Journal of Personality and Social Psychology, 85*, 348–362.

Grossberg, J. M. (1964). Behavior therapy: A review. *Psychological Bulletin, 62*, 73–88.

Grossberg, S. (1971). On the dynamics of operant conditioning. *Journal of Theoretical Biology, 33*, 225–255.

Grossberg, S., & Levine, D. S. (1987). Neural dynamics of attentionally modulated Pavlovian conditioning: Blocking, interstimulus interval, and secondary reinforcement. *Applied Optics, 26*, 5015–5030.

Grossberg, S., & Schmajuk, N. A. (1987). Neural dynamics of attentionally modulated Pavlovian conditioning: Conditioned reinforcement, inhibition, and opponent processing. *Psychobiology, 15*, 195–240.

Grossberg, S., & Schmajuk, N. A. (1989). Neural dynamics of adaptive timing and temporal discrimination during associative learning. *Neural Networks, 2*, 79–102.

Grossberg, S., & Stone, G. (1986). Neural dynamics of word recognition and recall: Attentional priming, learning, and resonance. *Psychological Review, 93*, 46–74.

Grove, W. M. (2005). Clinical versus statistical prediction: The contribution of Paul E. Meehl. *Journal of Clinical Psychology, 61*, 1233–1243.

Grünbaum, A. (1984). *The foundations of psychoanalysis: A philosophical critique*. Berkeley, CA: University of California Press.

Guastella, A. J., Dadds, M. R., Lovibond, P. F., Mitchell, P., & Richardson, R. (2007). A randomized controlled trial of the effect of D-cycloserine on exposure therapy for spider fear. *Journal of Psychiatric Research, 41*, 466–471.

Gunderson, J. G. (2001). *Borderline personality disorder: A clinical guide*. Washington, DC: American Psychiatric Publishing.

Guthrie, E. R. (1952). *The psychology of learning*. New York: Harper.

Guttman, L. A. (1954). A new approach to factor analysis. The radix. In P. F. Lazarsfeld (Ed.), *Mathematical thinking in the social sciences* (pp. 238–248). New York: Free Press.

Gärling, T., Kirchler, E., Lewis, A., & van Raaij, F. (2009). Psychology, financial decision making, and financial crises. *Psychological Science in the Public Interest, 10*(1), 1–47. http://dx.doi.org/10.1177/1529100610378437.

Haas, L. F. (2003). Hans Berger (1873–1941), Richard Caton (1842–1926), and electroencephalography. Journal of Neurology. *Neurosurgery & Psychiatry, 74*(1), 9.

Hadjikhani, N., Joseph, R. M., Snyder, J., & Tager-Flusberg, H. (2005). Anatomical differences in the mirror neuron system and social cognition network in autism. *Cerebral Cortex, 16*, 1276–1282.

Hadwin, J., Frost, S., French, C. C., & Richards, A. (1997). Cognitive processing and trait anxiety in typically developing children: Evidence for interpretation bias. *Journal of Abnormal Psychology, 106*, 486–490.

Haggard, P. (2011). Decision time for free will. *Neuron, 69*(3), 404–406.

Haggard, P., & Eimer, M. (1999). On the relation between brain potentials and conscious awareness. *Experimental Brain Research, 126*, 128–133.

Haggard, P., Clark, S., & Kalogeras, J. (2002). Voluntary action and conscious awareness. *Nature Neuroscience, 5*, 382–385.

Haidt, J. (2001). The emotional dog and its rational tail: A social intuitionist approach to moral judgment. *Psychological Review, 108*, 814–834.

Hall, C. S., & Lindzey, G. (1957). *Theories of personality*. New York: Wiley.

Hall, J. A. (1992). Psychological-mindedness: A conceptual model. *American Journal of Psychotherapy, 46*, 131–140.

Hallion, L. S., & Ruscio, A. (2011). A meta-analysis of the effect of cognitive bias modification on anxiety and depression. *Psychological Bulletin, 137*, 940–958.

Hamilton, A. F., Brindley, R. M., & Frith, U. (2007). Imitation and action understanding in autistic spectrum disorders: How valid is the hypothesis of a deficit in the mirror neuron system? *Neuropsychologia, 45*(8), 1859–1868.

Hamilton, D. L., & Rose, T. L. (1980). Illusory correlation and the maintenance of stereotypical beliefs. *Journal of Personality and Social Psychology, 39*, 832–845.

Hamilton, D. L., & Gifford, R. K. (1976). Illusory correlation in interpersonal perception: A cognitive basis of stereotypic judgments. *Journal of Experimental Social Psychology, 12*, 392–407.

Hammond, K. R. (1996). *Human judgment and social policy*. New York: Oxford University Press.

Hand, I., & Lamontagne, Y. (1976). The exacerbation of interpersonal problems after rapid phobia removal. *Psychotherapy Theory, Research and Practice, 13*, 405–411.

Harding, A., Halliday, G., & Kril, J. (1998). Variation in hippocampal neuron number with age and brain volume. *Cerebral Cortex, 8*, 710–718.

Hari, R., Forss, N., Avikainen, S., Kirveskari, E., Salenius, S., & Rizzolatti, G. (1998). Activation of human primary motor cortex during action observation: A neuromagnetic study. *Proceedings of the National Academy of Sciences of the United States of America (PNAS), 95*(25), 15061–15065.

Harlow, H. F., Suomi, S. J., & McMinney, W. T. (1970). Experimental production of depression in monkeys. *Mainly Monkeys, 1*, 6–12.

Harms, E. (1967). *Origins of modern psychiatry*. Springfield, IL: Thomas.

Harris, J. D. (1943). Habituatory response decrement in the intact organism. *Psychological Bulletin, 40*, 385–422.

Harrison, A., Sullivan, S., Tchanturia, K., & Treasure, J. (2009). Emotion recognition and regulation in Anorexia Nervosa. *Clinical Psychology and Psychotherapy, 16*, 348–356.

Hartmann, H. (1958). *Ego psychology and the problem of adaptation. (D. Rapaport Trans.)*. New York: International Universities Press (Original work published 1939).

Hassin, R. R. (2013). Yes it can: On the functional abilities of the human unconscious. *Perspectives on Psychological Science, 8*, 195–207.

Hassin, R. R., Bargh, J. A., & Uleman, J. S. (2002). Spontaneous causal inferences. *Journal of Experimental Social Psychology, 38*, 515–522.

Hatch, J. P., Fisher, J. G., & Rugh, J. D. (1987). *Biofeedback: Studies in clinical efficacy*. NY: Plenum Press.

Hatcher, R. L., & Hatcher, S. L. (1997). Assessing the psychological mindedness of children and adolescents. In M. McCallum, & W. E. Piper (Eds.), *Psychological mindedness: A contemporary understanding* (pp. 59–75). Mahwah, New Jersey: Lawrence Erlbaum.

Hawkins, R. D. (1989). A biologically realistic neural network model for higher-order features of classical conditioning. In R. G. M. Morris (Ed.), *Parallel distributed processing: Implications for psychology and neurobiology* (pp. 214–247). Oxford: Clarendon Press.

Hayes, S. C. (1998a). Understanding and treating the theoretical emaciation of behavior therapy. *The Behavior Therapist, 21*, 67–68. 87.

Hayes, S. C. (1998b). Resisting biologism. *The Behavior Therapist, 21*, 95–97.

Hayes, S. C. (2008). Avoiding the mistakes of the past. *The Behavior Therapist, 31*, 150–153.

Hayes, S. C., Strosahl, K. D., & Wilson, K. G. (2012). *Acceptance and commitment therapy: The process and practice of mindful change* (2nd ed.). New York: Guilford.

Haynos, A. F., & Fruzzetti, A. E. (2011). Anorexia Nervosa as a disorder of emotion dysregulation: Evidence and treatment implications. *Clinical Psychology: Science and Practice, 18*(3), 183–202.

Heaps, C. M., & Nash, M. R. (1999). Individual differences in imagination inflation. *Psychonomic Bulletin & Review, 6*, 313–318.

Heaps, C. M., & Nash, M. R. (2001). Comparing recollective experiences in true and false autobiographical memories. *Journal of Experimental Psychology: Learning, Memory, and Cognition, 27*, 920–930.

Heard, H. L., & Linehan, M. M. (2005). Integrative therapy for borderline personality disorder. In J. C. Norcross, & M. R. Goldfried (Eds.), *Handbook of psychotherapy integration* (2nd ed.) (pp. 299–320). New York: Oxford University Press.

Heatherington, L., Messer, S. B., Angus, L., Strauman, T. J., Friedlander, M. L., & Kolden, G. G. (2013). The narrowing of theoretical orientations in clinical psychology doctoral training. *Clinical Psychology: Science and Practice, 19*(4), 362–374.

Hebb, D. O. (1949). *The organization of behavior*. New York: John Wiley & Sons.

Heider, F. (1958). *The psychology of interpersonal relations*. NY: Wiley.

Heider, F., & Simmel, M. A. (1944). An experimental study of apparent behavior. *American Journal of Psychology, 13*, 243–259.

Hell, J. W., & Ehlers, M. D. (Eds.). (2008). *Structural and functional organization of the synapse*. New York: Springer Science + Business Media.

Helson, H. (1948). Adaptation-level as a basis for a quantitative theory of frames of reference. *Psychological Review, 55*(6), 297–313.

Helson, H. (1964). *Adaptation-level theory: An experimental and systematic approach to behavior*. New York: Harper & Row.

Hendricks, M. N. (2001). Focusing-oriented/experiential psychotherapy. In D. Cain, & J. Seeman (Eds.), *Humanistic Psychotherapy: Handbook of Research and Practice*. Washington: American Psychological Association.

Henker, F. O. (1979). Symptom substitution after obesity therapy. *Psychosomatics, 10*, 717–718.

Henriques, G. R. (2003). The tree of knowledge and the theoretical unification of psychology. *Review of General Psychology*, 7, 150–182.

Henriques, G. R. (2008). The problem of psychology and the integration of human knowledge: Contrasting Wilson's consilience with the tree of knowledge system. *Theory & Psychology, 18*, 731–755.

Henze, D. A., Borhegyi, Z., Csicsvari, J., Mamiya, A., Harris, K. D., & Buzsaki, G. (2000). Intracellular features predicted by extracellular recordings in the hippocampus in vivo. *Journal of Neurophysiology, 84*, 390–400.

Herbert, W. (2010). *On second thought: Outsmarting your mind's hard-wired habits.* New York: Random House.

Heresco-Levy, U., Kremer, I., Javitt, D. C., Goichman, R., Reshef, A., Blanaru, M., & Cohen, T. (2002). Pilot-controlled trial of D-cycloserine for the treatment of posttraumatic stress disorder. *International Journal of Neuropsychopharmacology, 5*, 301–307.

Hergenhan, B. R., & Olson, M. H. (1993). *An introduction to theories of learning* (4th ed.). Englewood Cliffs, NJ: Prentice Hall.

Herman, J. L. (1992). Complex PTSD: A syndrome in survivors of prolonged and repeated trauma. *Journal of Traumatic Stress, 5*, 377–391.

Hertel, P. T., & Mathews, A. (2011). Cognitive bias modification: Past, perspectives, current findings, and future applications. *Perspectives on Psychological Science, 6*, 521–536.

Hestenes, D. (1992). A neural network theory of manic-depressive illness. In D. S. Levine, & S. J. Leven (Eds.), *Motivation, emotion, and goal direction in neural networks* (pp. 209–257). Hillsdale, New Jersey: Lawrence Erlbaum Associates.

Hevner, K. (1936). Experimental studies of the elements of expression in music. *American Journal of Psychology, 48*, 246–268.

Hickey, P. (1998). DSM and behavior therapy. *The Behavior Therapist, 21*, 43–46.

Hill, E., Berthoz, S., & Frith, U. (2004). Brief report: Cognitive processing of own emotions in individuals with autistic spectrum disorders and in their relatives. *Journal of Autism and Developmental Disorders, 34*, 229–235.

Hinton, G. E., & Anderson, J. A. (1981). *Parallel Models of Associative Memory.* Hillsdale, NJ: Lawrence Erlbaum Associates.

Hinton, G. E., Plaut, D. C., & Shallice, T. (1993). Simulating brain damage. *Scientific American, 269*, 76–82.

Hoffman, R. E., & Dobscha, S. K. (1989). Cortical pruning and the development of schizophrenia: A computer model. *Schizophrenia Bulletin, 15*, 477–490.

Hoffman, R. E., & McGlashan, T. H. (1993). Parallel distributed processing and the emergence of schizophrenic symptoms. *Schizophrenia Bulletin, 19*, 119–139.

Hoffman, R. E., & McGlashan, T. H. (1997). Synaptic elimination, neurodevelopment, and the mechanism of hallucinated "voices" in schizophrenia. *American Journal of Psychiatry, 154*, 1683–1689.

Hofmann, S. A., Meuret, A. E., Smits, J. A. J., Simon, N. M., Pollack, M. H., Eisenmenger, K., Shiekh, M., & Otto, M.W. (2006). Augmentation of exposure therapy with d-cycloserine for social anxiety disorder. *Archives of General Psychiatry, 63*, 298–304.

Hofmann, W., & Wilson, T. D. (2010). Consciousness, introspection, and the adaptive unconscious. In B. Gawronski, & B. K. Payne (Eds.), *Handbook of implicit social cognition: Measurement, theory, and applications* (pp. 197–215). New York: Guilford.

Hollands, G. J., Prestwich, A., & Marteau, T. M. (2011). Using aversive images to enhance healthy food choices and implicit attitudes: An experimental test of evaluative conditioning. *Health Psychology, 30*, 195–203.

Hong, Y.-Y., Morris, M. W., Chiu, C.-Y., & Benet-Martinez, V. (2000). Multicultural minds: A dynamic constructivist approach to culture and cognition. *American Psychologist, 55*, 709–720.

Honkalampi, K., Hintikka, J., Tanskanen, A., Lehtonen, J., & Hiinamäki (2000). Depression is strongly associated with alexithymia in the general population. *Journal of Psychosomatic Research, 48*, 99–104.

Hornik, K., Stinchcombe, M., & White, H. (1989). Multilayer feed-forward networks are universal approximators. *Neural Networks, 2*, 359–366.

Hornik, K., Stinchcombe, M., & White, H. (1990). Universal approximation of an unknown mapping and its derivatives using multilayer feedforward networks. *Neural Networks, 3*, 551–560.

Huang, L. N., & Price, V. (2001). Motivations, goals, information search, and memory about political candidates. *Political Psychology, 22*, 665–692.

Hull, C. L. (1943). *Principles of behavior.* New York: Appleton-Century-Crofts.

Hunter, J. E., & Schmidt, F. L. (1990). *Methods of meta-analysis: Correcting error and bias in research findings.* Newbury Park: CA: Sage Publications.

Huttenlocher, P. R. (1979). Synaptic density in human frontal cortex: Developmental changes and effects of aging. *Brain Research, 163*, 195–205.

Huttenlocher, P. R. (1990). Neuromorphic study of human cerebral cortex development. *Neuropsychologia, 28*(6), 517–527.

Huttenlocher, P. R., & Dabholkar, A. S. (1997). Regional differences in synaptogenesis in Human Cerebral Cortex. *The Journal of Comparative Neurology, 387*, 167–178.

Hyman, I. E., & Pentland, J. (1996). The role of mental imagery in the creation of false childhood memories. *Journal of Memory and Language, 35*, 101–117.

Iacoboni, M. (2005). Neural mechanisms of imitation. *Current Opinion in Neurobiology, 15*(6), 632–637.

Iacoboni, M., & Dapretto, M. (2006). The mirror neuron system and the consequences of its dysfunction. *Nature Reviews. Neuroscience*, 7(12), 942–951.

Iacoboni, M., Woods, R. P., Brass, M., Bekkering, H., Mazziotta, J. C., & Rizzolatti, G. (1999). Cortical mechanisms of human imitation. *Science, 286*, 2526–2528. http://dx.doi.org/10.1126/science.286.5449.2526.

Iacoboni, M., Lieberman, M. D., Knowlton, B. J., Molnar-Szakacs, I., Moritz, M., Throop, C. J., & Fiske, A. P. (2004). Medial prefrontal and parietal activation while watching social interactions compared to a resting baseline. *NeuroImage, 21*, 1167–1173.

Iacoboni, M., Molnar-Szakacs, I., Gallese, V., Buccino, G., Mazziotta, J. C., & Rizzolatti, G. (2005). Grasping the intentions of others with one's own mirror neuron system. *PLoS Biology, 3*(3), e79.

Ilardi, S. S. (2002a). The cognitive neuroscience perspective: A brief primer for clinical psychologists. *The Behavior Therapist, 29*, 49–52.

Ilardi, S. S. (2002b). The cognitive neuroscience framework and its implications for behavior therapy: Clarifying some important misconceptions. *The Behavior Therapist, 29*, 87–90.

Ilardi, S. S., & Craighead, W. E. (1994). The role of nonspecific factors in cognitive-behavioral therapy for depression. *Clinical Psychology: Science and Practice, 1*(2), 138–155.

Insel, T., Cuthbert, B., Garvey, M., Heinssen, R., Pine, D. S., Quinn, K., & Sanislow, C. (2010). Research domain criteria (RDoC): Toward a new classification framework for research on mental disorders. *American Journal of Psychiatry, 167*(7), 748–750.

Isbell, L. M. (2012). The emotional citizen: How feelings drive political preferences and behavior. *American Psychological Association Observer, 25*(8), 13–16.

Isbell, L. M., & Wyer, R. S. (1999). Correcting for mood-induced bias in the evaluation of political candidates: The roles of intrinsic and extrinsic motivation. *Personality and Social Psychology Bulletin, 25*, 237–249.

Isbell, L. M., Ottati, V. C., & Burns, K. C. (2006). Affect and politics: Effects on judgment processing and information seeking. In D. P. Redlawsk (Ed.), *Feeling politics: Emotion in political information processing* (pp. 57–86). New York: Palgrave Macmillan.

Isen, A. M. (1984). Affect, cognition, and social behavior. In R. S. Wyer, & T. R. Srull (Eds.), *Handbook of social cognition* (Vol. 3). (pp. 179–236). Hillsdale, NJ: Erlbaum.

Ito, M. (1984). *The cerebellum and neural control*. New York: Raven Press.

Ito, T. A. (2010). Implicit social cognition: Insights from social neuroscience. In B. Gawronski, & B. K. Payne (Eds.), *Handbook of implicit social cognition: Measurement, theory, and applications* (pp. 80–92). New York: Guilford.

Izard, C. E. (1971). *The face of emotion*. New York: Appleton-Century-Crofts.

Izard, C. E. (2007). Basic emotions, natural kinds, emotion schemas, and a new paradigm. *Perspectives on Psychological Science, 2*(3), 260–280.

Jacob, G. A., Arendt, J., Kolley, L., Scheel, C. N., Bader, K., Lieb, K., Arntz, A., & Tüscher, O. (2011). Comparison of different strategies to decrease negative affect and increase positive affect in women with borderline personality disorder. *Behaviour Research and Therapy, 49*, 68–73.

Jacobson, E. (1938). *Progressive relaxation*. Chicago: University of Chicago Press.

Jacobson, N. S., Dobson, K. S., Truax, P. A., Addis, M. E., Koerner, K., Gollan, J. K., Gortner, E., & Prince, S. E. (1996). A component analysis of cognitive-behavioral treatments for depression. *Journal of Consulting and Clinical Psychology*, *64*, 295–304.

Jaffe, E. (2012). Inside the neurotic mind: A brief look at the past, present, and future of negative affect. *American Psychological Association Observer*, *25*(10), 17–18.

James, W. (1884). What is emotion? *Mind*, *19*, 188–205.

James, W. (1890). *The principles of psychology*. (Vol. 1 & 2)New York: Henry Holt & Co.

James, W. (1950). *The principles of psychology*. Oxford, UK: Dover (Original work published 1890).

James, W. (1975). *The meaning of truth*. Cambridge, MA: Harvard University Press (Original work published 1909).

James, W. (1979). *The will to believe*. Cambridge, MA: Harvard University Press (Original work published 1897).

Jiao, J., Nakajima, A., Janssen, W. G. M., Bindokas, V., Xiong, X. L., Morrison, J. H., Brorson, J. R., & Tang, Y. P. (2008). Expression of NR2B in cerebellar granule cells specifically facilitates effect of motor training on motor learning. *PLoS ONE*, e-1684. 1–11.

Johansson, P., Høglend, P., Ulberg, R., Amlo, S., Marble, A., Bøgwald, K. P., Sorbye, Ø., Sjaastad, M. C., & Heyerdahl, O. (2010). The mediating role of insight for long-term improvements in psychodynamic therapy. *Journal of Consulting and Clinical Psychology*, *78*, 438–448.

Jones, E. (1961). *The life and work of Sigmund Freud*. Garden City, NY: Doubleday.

Jones, J. C., & Barlow, D. H. (1990). The etiology of post-traumatic stress disorder. *Clinical Psychology Review*, *10*, 299–328.

Jonides, J., Schumacher, E. H., Smith, E. E., Lauber, E. J., Awh, E., Minoshima, S., & Koeppe, R. A. (1997). Verbal working memory load affects regional brain activation as measured by PET. *Journal of Cognitive Neuroscience*, *9*, 462–475.

Joynt, R. J. (1981). Are two heads better than one? *Behavioral and Brain Sciences*, *4*, 108–109.

Kahn, M., Baker, B. L., & Weiss, J. M. (1968). Treatment of insomnia by relaxation training. *Journal of Abnormal Psychology*, *73*, 556–558.

Kahneman, D., & Frederick, S. (2002). Representativeness Revisited: Attribute Substitution in Intuitive Judgment. In Thomas Gilovich, Dale Griffin, & Daniel Kahneman (Eds.), *Heuristics and Biases: The Psychology of Intuitive Judgment* (pp. 49–81). Cambridge: Cambridge University Press.

Kahneman, D. (1973). *Attention and effort*. Englewood Cliffs, NJ: Prentice- Hall.

Kahneman, D. (2003a). A perspective on judgment and choice: Mapping bounded rationality. *American Psychologist*, *58*, 697–720.

Kahneman, D. (2003b). Maps of bounded rationality: Psychology for behavioral economics. *American Economic Review*, *93*(5), 1449–1475.

Kahneman, D. (2011a). *The surety of fools*. The New York Times Magazine. October 23, pp. 30–33, 62.

Kahneman, D. (2011b). *Thinking, fast and slow*. New York: Farrar, Straus, and Giroux.

Kahneman, D., & Tversky (1979). Prospect theory: An analysis of decisions under risk. *Econometrica*, *47*, 263–291.

Kahneman, D., & Tversky (1984). Choices, values, and frames. *American Psychologist*, *39*, 341–350.

Kahneman, D., & Klein, G. (2009). Conditions for intuitive expertise. *American Psychologist*, *64*, 515–526.

Kahneman, D., & Tversky, A. (1996). On the reality of cognitive illusions. *Psychological Review*, *103*. 582–291.

Kahneman, D., Krueger, A. B., Schkade, D., Schwarz, N., & Stone, A. A. (2006). Would you be happier if you were richer? A focusing illusion. *Science*, *312*(5782), 1908–1910.

Kalat, J. W. (2001). *Biological psychology* (7th ed.). Australia: Wadsworth.

Kalat, J. W. (2003). *Biological psychology* (8th ed.). Australia: Wadsworth.

Kalat, J. W. (2004). *Biological psychology*. Belmont, CA: Wadsworth/Thompson.
Kalat, J. W. (2007). *Biological Psychology (with CD-ROM and infoTrac)* (9th ed.). Belmont, CA: Thompson/Wadsworth.
Kalat, J. W. (2009). *Biological psychology* (10th ed.). Belmont, CA: Wadsworth/Thompson.
Kamphaus, R. W., & Frick, P. J. (2002). *Clinical assessment of child and adolescent personality and behavior* (2nd ed.). Boston: Allyn & Bacon.
Kandel, E. R. (1991). Cellular mechanisms of learning and the biological basis of individuality. In E. R. Kandel, J. H. Schwartz, & T. M. Jessell (Eds.), *Principles of neural science* (pp. 1009–1031). Norwalk, CT: Appleton & Lange.
Kaplan, J. T., & Iacoboni, M. (2006). Getting a grip on other minds: Mirror neurons, intention understanding, and cognitive empathy. *Social Neuroscience, 1*, 175–183.
Kaptchuk, T. J., Kelley, J. M., Conboy, L. A., Davis, R. B., Kerr, C. E., Jacobson, E. E., Kirsch, I., Schyner, R. N., Nam, B. H., Nguyen, L. T., Park, M., Rivers, A. L., McManus, C., Kokkotou, E., Drossman, D. A., Goldman, P., & Lemboy, A. J. (2008). Components of placebo effect: Randomised controlled trial in patients with irritable bowel syndrome. *British Medical Journal, 336*(7651), 999–1003.
Kass, W., & Gilner, F. H. (1974). Drive level, incentive conditions and systematic desensitization. *Behavior Research and Therapy, 12*, 99–106.
Kassin, S. (2005). On the psychology of confessions: Does innocence put innocents at risk? *American Psychologist, 60*, 215–228.
Kassin, S. M. (2012). Why confessions trump innocence. *American Psychologist, 67*(6), 431–445.
Kassin, S. M., & Gudjonsson, G. H. (2004). The psychology of confessions: A review of the literature and issues. *Psychological Science in the Public Interest, 5*, 33–67.
Kaufman, J., & Weder, N. (2011). Neurobiology of early life stress: Evolving concepts. In A. Martin, L. S. Scahill, & C. Kratochvil (Eds.), *Pediatric psychopharmacology: Principles and Practice* (2nd ed.) (pp. 112–123). New York: Oxford University Press.
Kazdin, A. E. (1977). *The token economy: A review and evaluation.* New York: Plenum Press.
Kazdin, A. E. (1978). *History of behavior modification: Experimental foundations of contemporary research.* Baltimore, MD: University Park Press.
Kazdin, A. E. (1979). Fictions, factions, and functions of behavior therapy. *Behavior Therapy, 10*, 629–654.
Kazdin, A. E. (1982). Symptom substitution, generalization, and response covariation: Implications for psychotherapy outcome. *Psychological Bulletin, 91*, 349–365.
Kazdin, A. E. (2007). Mediators and mechanism of change in psychotherapy research. *Annual Review of Clinical Psychology, 3*, 1–27.
Kazdin, A. E. (2008). Evidence-based treatment and practice: New opportunities to bridge clinical research and practice, enhance the knowledge base, and improve patient care. *American Psychologist, 63*, 146–159.
Kazdin, A. E. (2009). Bridging science and practice to improve patient care. *American Psychologist, 64*, 276–279.
Kehoe, E. J. (1988). A layered network model of associative learning: Learning to learn and configuration. *Psychological Review, 95*, 411–433.
Kehoe, E. J. (1989). Connectionist models of conditioning: A tutorial. *Journal of the Experimental Analysis of Behavior, 52*, 427–440.
Keller, F. S., & Schoenfeld, W. N. (1950). *Principles of Psychology: A systematic text in the science of behavior.* New York: Appleton-Century-Crofts.
Kendall, P. C., & Beidas, R. S. (2007). Smoothing the trail for dissemination of evidence-based practices for youth: Flexibility within fidelity. *Professional Psychology: Research and Practice, 38*, 13–20.
Khan, A., Warner, H. A., & Brown, W. A. (2000). Symptom reduction and suicide risk in patients treated with placebo in antidepressant clinical trials: an analysis of the Food and Drug Administration database. *Archives of General Psychiatry, 57*, 311–317.

Kheriaty, E., Kleinknecht, R. A., & Hyman, I. E., Jr. (1999). Recall and validation of phobia origins as a function of a structured interview versus the Phobia Origins Questionnaire. *Behavior Modification, 23*, 61–78.

Kihlstrom, J. F., Barnhardt, T. M., & Tataryn, D. J. (1992). The psychological unconscious: Found, lost, and regained. *American Psychologist, 47*(6), 788–791.

Kihlstrom, J. F. (1984). Conscious, subconscious, unconscious: A cognitive perspective. In K. S. Bowers, & D. Meichenbaum (Eds.), *The unconscious reconsidered* (pp. 149–211). New York: Wiley.

Kihlstrom, J. F. (1987). The cognitive unconscious. *Science, 237*, 1445–1452.

Kihlstrom, J. F., Barnhardt, T. M., & Tataryn, D. J. (1992). The psychological unconscious: Found, lost, and regained. *American Psychologist, 47*(6), 788–791.

Kim, S.-Y., Taber, C. S., & Lodge, M. (2010). A computational model of the citizen as motivated reasoned: Modeling the dynamics of the 2000 presidential election. *Political Behavior, 32*, 1–28.

Kirsch.2010). *The Emperor's New Drugs.* NY: Basic Books.

Kirsch, I., & Lynn, S. J. (1999). Automaticity in clinical psychology. *American Psychologist, 54*, 504–515.

Kirsch, I., & Sapirstein, G. (1998). *Listening to Prozac but hearing placebo: A meta-analysis of antidepressant medication.* Prevention and treatment, Vol. I, article 0002a, posted June 26, 1998, available at. http://journals.apa.org/prevention/volume1/pre0010002a.html.

Kirsch, I., Deacon, B. J., Huedo-Medina, T. B. H., Scoboria, A., Moore, T. J., & Johnson, B. T. (2008). Initial severity and antidepressant benefits: A meta-analysis of data submitted to the Food and Drug Administration. *PLoS Medicine, 5*, 260–268.

Klempan, T. A., Ernst, C., Deleva, V., Labonte, B., & Turecki, G. (2009). Characterization of QKI gene expression, genetics, and epigenetics in suicide victims with major depressive disorder. *Biological Psychiatry, 66*, 824–831.

Klerman, G., Weissman, M., Rounseville, B., & Chevron, E. (1984). *Interpersonal psychotherapy of depression.* New York: Basic Books.

Klopf, A. H. (1988). A neuronal model of classical conditioning. *Psychobiology, 16*, 85–125.

Koch, C. (2011). Probing the unconscious mind. *Scientific American, 22*(5), 20–21.

Koch, S. (1981). The nature and limits of psychological knowledge: Lessons of a quarter century qua science. *American Psychologist, 36*, 257–269.

Kohlberg, L. (1963). The development of children's orientation toward a moral order: I. Sequence in the development of moral thought. *Vita Humana, 6*(1-2), 11–33.

Kohlberg, L. (2008). The development of children's orientations toward a moral order: I. Sequence in the development of moral thought. *Human Development, 51*(1), 8–20.

Kohler, E., Keysers, C., Umilta, M. A., Fogassi, L., Gallese, V., & Rizzolatti, G. (2002). Hearing sounds, understanding actions: Action representation in mirror neurons. *Science, 297*, 486–488.

Kolassa, I. T., Ertl, V., Eckart, C., Glöckner, F., Kolassa, S., Papassotiropoulos, A., de Quervain, D. J., & Elbert, T. (2010). Association study of trauma load and SLC6A4 promoter polymorphism in posttraumatic stress disorder: Evidence from survivors of the Rwandan genocide. *Journal of Clinical Psychiatry, 71*(5), 543–547.

Kolb, B., & Whishaw, I. Q. (1998). Brain placticity and behavior. *Annual Review of Psychology, 49*, 43–64.

Kong, J., Gollub, R. L., Rosman, I. S., Webb, J. M., Vangel, M. G., Kirsch, I., & Kaptchuk, T. J. (2006). Brain activity associated with expectancy-enhanced placebo analgesia as measured by functional magnetic resonance imaging. *The Journal of Neuroscience, 26*(2), 381–388.

Kopelowicz, A., Lieberman, R. P., & Zarate, R. (2003). Psychosocial treatments for schizophrenia. In P. E. Nathan, & J. M. Gorman (Eds.), *A guide to treatments that work* (2nd ed.) (pp. 157–168). New York: Oxford University Press.

Kosfeld, M., Heinrichs, M., Zak, P. J., Fischbacher, U., & Fehr, E. (2005). Oxytocin increases trust in humans. *Nature, 435*(7042), 673–676.

Koski, L., Iacoboni, M., Dubeau, M. C., Woods, R. P., & Mazziotta, J. C. (2003). Modulation of cortical activity during different imitative behaviors. *Journal of Neurophysiology, 89*(1), 460–471.

Kosko, B. (1987a). Adaptive bidirectional associative memories. *Applied Optics, 26*, 4947–4960.

Kosko, B. (1987b). Constructing an associative memory. *Byte, 12*, 137–144.

Kosko, B. (1988). Bi-directional associative memories. IEEE Transactions on Systems. *Man and Cybernetics, 18*, 49–60.

Kosslyn, S. M., & Thompson, W. L. (2000). Shared mechanisms in visual imagery and visual perception: Insights from cognitive neuroscience. In M. S. Gazzaniga (Ed.), *The new cognitive neurosciences* (2nd ed.) (pp. 975–985). Cambridge, MA: The MIT Press.

Kounios, J., Frymiare, J. L., Bowden, E. M., Fleck, J. I., Subramaniam, K., Parrish, T. B., & Jung-Beeman, M. (2006). The prepared mind: Neural activity prior to problem presentation predicts subsequent solution by sudden insight. *Psychological Science, 17*, 882–890.

Kraft, T. L., & Pressman, S. D. (2012). Grin and bear it: The influence of manipulated facial expression on the stress response. *Psychological Science, 23*(11), 1372–1378.

Krain, A. L., Wilson, A. M., Arbuckle, R., Castellanos, F. X., & Milham, M. P. (2006). Distinct neural mechanisms of risk and ambiguity: A meta-analysis of decision-making. *NeuroImage, 32*, 477–484.

Krakowski, M. (2003). Violence and serotonin: Influence of impulse control, affect regulation, and social functioning. *Journal of Neuropsychiatry and Clinical Neurosciences, 15*, 294–305.

Krasne, F. (2002). Neural analysis of learning in simple systems. In H. Pashler, & R. Gallistel (Eds.), *Stevens' handbook of experimental psychology* (3rd ed.) *Learning, Motivation, and Emotion; Vol. 3.* (pp. 131–200). New York: Wiley.

Krasne, F. B., & Glanzman, D. L. (1995). What we can learn from invertebrate learning. *Annual Review of Psychology, 46*, 585–624.

Kroenke, C. H., Kubzansky, L. D., Schernhammer, E. S., Holmes, M. D., & Kawachi, I. (2006). Social networks, social support, and survival after breast cancer diagnosis. *Journal of Clinical Oncology, 24*, 1105–1111.

Krueger, R. F. (1999). The structure of common mental disorders. *Archives of General Psychiatry, 56*, 921–926.

Krueger, R. F., & Markon, K. E. (2006). Reinterpreting comorbidity: A model-based approach to understanding and classifying psychopathology. *Annual Review of Clinical Psychology, 2*, 111–133.

Krueger, R. F., Caspi, A., Moffitt, T. E., & Silva, P. A. (1998). The structure and stability of common mental disorders (DSM-III-R): A longitudinal-epidemiological study. *Journal of Abnormal Psychology, 107*, 216–227.

Kruglanski, A. W. (2001). That "Vision Thing": The state of theory in social and personality psychology at the edge of the new millennium. *Journal of Personality and Social Psychology, 80*(6), 871–875.

Kruglanski, A. W. (2013). Only one? The default interventionist perspective as a unimodel – commentary on Evans & Stanovich (2013). *Perspectives on Psychological Science, 8*(3), 242–247.

Kruglanski, A. W., & Gigerenzer, G. (2011). Intuitive and deliberate judgments are based on common principles. *Psychological Review, 118*(1), 97–109.

Krumhans, C. L. (2002). Music: A link between cognition and emotion. *Current Directions in Psychological Science, 11*(2), 25–50.

Kruschke, J. K. (1992). ALCOVE: An exemplar-based connectionist model of category learning. *Psychological Review, 99*, 22–44.

Kuhn, T. S. (1962). *The Structure of Scientific Revolutions* (1st. ed.). Chicago: Univ. of Chicago Press.

Kuhn, T. S. (1970). *The Structure of Scientific Revolutions. Enlarged* (2nd. ed.). Chicago: Univ. of Chicago Press.
Kuhn, T. S. (1996). *The Structure of Scientific Revolutions* (3rd. ed.). Chicago: Univ. of Chicago Press.
Kuhn, T. S. (2012). *The Structure of Scientific Revolutions. 50th anniversary* (4th. ed.). Chicago: Univ. of Chicago Press.
Kukla, A. (1992). Unification as a goal for psychology. *American Psychologist, 47*, 1054–1055.
Kunda, Z. (1987). Motivated inference: Self-serving generation and evaluation of causal theories. *Journal of Personality and Social Psychology, 53*, 636–647.
Kunda, Z. (1990). The case for motivated reasoning. *Psychological Bulletin, 108*, 480–498.
Kunda, Z., & Sinclair, L. (1999). Motivated reasoning with stereotypes: Activation, application, and inhibition. *Psychological Inquiry, 10*, 12–22.
Kunda, Z., & Thagard, P. (1996). Forming impressions from stereotypes, traits, and behaviors: a parallel-constraint-satisfaction theory. *Psychological Review, 103*, 284–308.
Kunst-Wilson, W. R., & Zajonc, R. B. (1980). Affect discrimination of stimuli that cannot be recognized. *Science, 207*, 557–558.
Kurzweil, R. (2012). *How to create a mind: The secret of human thought revealed*. New York, NY: Viking.
Lader, M. H., & Mathews, A. M. (1968). A physiological model of phobic anxiety and desensitization. *Behaviour Research and Therapy, 6*, 411–421.
Laird, J. D. (1974). Self-attribution of emotion: The effects of expressive behavior on the quality of emotional experience. *Journal of Personality and Social Psychology, 29*, 475–486.
Lambert, M. J., & Ogles, B. M. (2004). The efficacy and effectiveness of psychotherapy. In M. J. Lambert (Ed.), *Bergin and Garfield's handbook of psychotherapy and behavior change* (5th ed.) (pp. 139–193). New York: Wiley.
Lang, P. J. (1977). Imagery in therapy: An information processing analysis of fear. *Behavior Therapy, 8*, 862–886.
Lang, P. J. (1979). A bio-information theory of emotional imagery. *Psychophysiology, 16*, 495–512.
Lang, P. J. (1985). The cognitive psychophysiology of emotion: Fear and anxiety. In A. H. Turner, & J. Maser (Eds.), *Anxiety and the anxiety disorders* (pp. 131–170). Hillsdale, NJ: Lawrence Erlbaum Associates.
Lang, P. J. (1994). The motivational organization of emotions. In S. van Goozen, N. E. van de Poll, & J. A. Sergent (Eds.), *Emotions: Essays on emotion theory*. Hillsdale, NJ: Lawrence Erlbaum.
Laquatra, T. A., & Clopton, J. R. (1994). Characteristics of alexithymia and eating disorders in college women. *Addictive Behaviors, 19*, 373–380.
Lavond, D. J., Kim, J. J., & Thompson, R. F. (1993). Mammalian brain substrates of aversive classical conditioning. *Annual Review of Psychology, 44*, 317–342.
Lazarus, A. A. (1976). *Multimodal behavior therapy*. New York: Springer.
Lazarus, A. A. (1981). *The practice of multimodal therapy*. New York: McGraw Hill.
Lazarus, A. A. (2005). Multimodal Therapy. In J. C. Norcross, & M. R. Goldfried (Eds.), *Handbook of Psychotherapy Integration* (pp. 105–120). New York: Oxford.
Lazarus, A. A. (2008). Technical eclecticism and multimodal therapy. In J. L. Lebow (Ed.), *Twenty-First Century Psychotherapies* (pp. 424–452). Hoboken, NJ: Wiley.
Lazarus, A. A., & Davison, G. C. (1971). Clinical innovation in research and practice. In A. E. Bergin, & S. L. Garfield (Eds.), *Handbook of psychotherapy and behavior change* (pp. 196–213). New York: Wiley.
Lazarus, R. S. (1982). Thoughts on the relations between emotion and cognition. *American Psychologist, 37*, 1019–1024.
Leahy, R. L. (2009). The confessions of a cognitive therapist. *The Behavior Therapist, 32*(1), 3.
Leary, T. (1957). *Interpersonal diagnosis of personality: A functional theory and methodology for personality evaluation*. New York: Ronald Press.

Ledgerwood, L., Richardson, R., & Cranney, J. (2003). Effects of D-Cycloserine on extinction of conditioned freezing. *Behavioral Neuroscience, 117*, 341–349.

Ledgerwood, L., Richardson, R., & Cranney, J. (2004). D-Cycloserine and the facilitation of extinction of conditioned fear: Consequences for reinstatement. *Behavioral Neuroscience, 118*, 505–513.

Ledgerwood, L., Richardson, R., & Cranney, J. (2005). D-Cycloserine facilitates extinction of learned fear: Effects on reacquisition and generalized extinction. *Biological Psychiatry, 57*, 841–847.

LeDoux, J. E. (1986). Sensory systems and emotion: A model of affective processing. *Integrative Psychiatry, 4*, 237–248.

LeDoux, J. E. (1994). Emotional processing, but not emotions, can occur unconsciously. In P. Ekman, & R. J. Davidson (Eds.), *The nature of emotion* (pp. 291–292). Oxford, UK: Oxford University Press.

LeDoux, J. E. (1996). *The emotional brain: The mysterious underpinnings of emotional life*. New York: Simon & Schuster.

LeDoux, J. E. (2000). Emotion circuits in the brain. *Annual Review of Neuroscience, 23*, 155–184.

LeDoux, J. E. (2002). *Synaptic self*. New York: Penguin Books.

Lehn, H., Steffenach, H.-A., van Strien, N. M., Veltman, D. J., Witter, M. P., & Haberg, A. K. (2009). A specific role of the human hippocampus in recall of temporal sequences. *The Journal of Neuroscience, 29*(11), 3475–3484.

Leibniz, G. W. (1981). *New essays on human understanding*. In Remnant, & J. Bennett Trans. (Eds.). Cambridge, England: Cambridge University Press (Original works written ca. 1704).

Leichsenring, F. (2001). Comparative effects of short-term psychodynamic psychotherapy and cognitive-behavioral therapy in depression: A meta-analytic approach. *Clinical Psychology Review, 21*, 401–419.

Leichsenring, F. (2005). Are psychodynamic and psychoanalytic therapies effective: A review of empirical data. *International Journal of Psychoanalysis, 86*, 841–868.

Leichsenring, F., & Leibing, E. (2003). The effectiveness of psychodynamic therapy and cognitive behavior therapy in the treatment of personality disorders: A meta-analysis. *American Journal of Psychiatry, 160*, 1223–1232.

Leichsenring, F., Rabung, S., & Leibing, E. (2004). The efficacy of short-term psychodynamic psychotherapy in specific psychiatric disorders: A meta-analysis. *Archives of General Psychiatry, 61*, 1208–1216.

LeLong, V., Dauphin, F., & Boulouard, M. (2001). RS 67333 and D-cycloserine accelerate learning acquisition in the rat. *Neuropharmacology, 41*, 517–522.

Meyer, Leonard B. (1967). *Music, the Arts, and Ideas*. Chicago, IL: University of Chicago Press.

Lerner, J. S., Gonzalez, R. M., Small, D. A., & Fischhoff, B. (2003). Effects of fear and anger on perceived risks of terrorism: A national field experiment. *Psychological Science, 14*(2), 144–150.

Leslie, A., & Frith, U. (1988). Autistic children's understanding of seeing, knowing and believing. *British Journal of Developmental Psychology, 6*, 315–324.

Leslie, A. M., & Keeble, S. (1987). Do six-month-old infants perceive causality? *Cognition, 25*, 265–288.

Lester, K. J., & Field, A. P. (2011). Experimental modification of interpretation bias about animal fear in young children: Effects on cognition, avoidance behavior, anxiety vulnerability, and physiological responding. *Journal of Clinical Child & Adolescent Psychology, 40*, 864–877.

Leven, S. J. (1992). Learned helplessness, memory, and the dynamics of hope. In D. S. Levine, & S. J. Leven (Eds.), *Motivation, emotion, and goal direction in neural networks* (pp. 259–299). Hillsdale, New Jersey: Lawrence Erlbaum Associates.

Levin, J. R., Ferron, J. M., & Kratochwill, T. R. (2012). Nonparametric statistical tests for single-case systematic and randomized ABAB…AB and alternating treatment intervention designs: New developments, new directions. *School Psychology, 50*, 599–624.

Levine, D. S. (1991). *Introduction to neural and cognitive modeling*. Hillsdale, NJ: Lawrence Earlbaum Associates.

Levine, D. S., & Leven, S. J. (Eds.). (1992). *Motivation, emotion, and goal direction in neural networks* (Part II: pp. 169–365). Hillsdale, New Jersey: Lawrence Erlbaum Associates.

Levine, S. (2005). Stress: An historical perspective. In T. Steckler, N. H. Kalin, & J. M. H. M Reul (Eds.), *Handbook on stress and the brain* (pp. 3–23). Amsterdam, the Netherlands: Elsevier Science.

Levinson, S. C. (1995). Interactional biases in human thinking. In E. Goody (Ed.), *Social intelligence and interaction* (pp. 221–260). Cambridge: Cambridge University Press.

Levis, D. J. (2002). Implosive therapy. In M. Hersen, & W. Sledge (Eds.). *Encyclopedia of Psychotherapy: vol. 2.* (pp. 1–6). New York: Elsevier Science.

Levy, K. N., & Anderson, T. (2013). Is clinical psychology doctoral training becoming less intellectual diverse? And if so, what can be done? *Clinical Psychology: Science and Practice, 20*, 211–220.

Lewinsohn, P. M., Hoberman, H. M., Teri, L., & Hautzinger, M. (1985). An integrated theory of depression. In S. Reiss, & R. Bootzin (Eds.), *Theoretical issues in behavior therapy* (pp. 331–359). New York: Academic Press.

Lewinsohn, P. M., Youngren, M. A., & Grosscup, S. J. (1979). Reinforcement and depression. In R. A. Dupue (Ed.), *The psychobiology of depressive disorders: Implications for the effects of stress* (pp. 291–316). New York: Academic Press.

Lewis, L. (2006). Enhancing mentalizing capacity through dialectical behavior therapy skills training and positive psychology. In J. G. Allen, & P. Fonagy (Eds.), *Handbook of mentalization-based treatment* (pp. 171–182). New York: Wiley.

Lewis, M. (2003). *Moneyball: The art of winning an unfair game*. New York: W. W. Norton.

Lewis, M. D. (2005). Bridging emotion theory and neurobiology through dynamic system modeling. *Behavioral and Brain Sciences, 28*, 169–194.

Li, D., & Spiegel, D. (1992). A neural network model of dissociative disorders. *Psychiatric Annals, 22*, 144–147.

Li, S.-C., & Sikström, S. (2002). Integrative neurocomputational perspective on cognitive aging, neuromodulation, and representation. *Neuroscience and Biobehavioral Reviews, 26*, 795–808.

Li, S.-C., Lindenberger, U., & Sikström, S. (2001). Aging cognition: From neuromodulation to representation. *Trends in Cognitive Sciences, 5*, 479–486.

Li, S.-C., Naveh-Benjamin, M., & Lindenberger (2005). Aging neuromodulation impairs associative binding: A neurocomputational account. *Psychological Science, 16*, 445–450.

Libet, B. (1985). Unconscious cerebral initiative and the role of conscious will in voluntary action. *The Behavioral and Brain Sciences, 8*, 529–566.

Lieberman, M. D., Berkman, E. T., & Wager, T. D. (2009). Correlations in social neuroscience aren't voodoo: Commentary on Vul et al. (2009). *Perspectives on Psychological Science, 4*, 299–307.

Lilienfeld, S. O. (2007a). Cognitive neuroscience and depression: Legitimate versus illegitimate reductionism and five challenges. *Cognitive Therapy and Research, 31*, 263–272.

Lilienfeld, S. O. (2007b). Psychological treatments that cause harm. *Perspectives on Psychological Science, 2*, 53–70.

Lilienfeld, S. O. (2012). Public skepticism of psychology: Why many people perceive the study of human behavior as unscientific. *American Psychologist, 67*, 111–129.

Lilienfeld, S. O., Wood, J. M., & Garb, H. N. (2000). The scientific status of projective techniques. *Psychological Science in the Public Interest, 1*, 27–66.

Lilienfeld, S. O., Lynn, S. J., & Lohr, J. M. (Eds.). (2003). *Science and pseudoscience in clinical psychology*. New York, NY: The Guilford Press.

Lilienfeld, S. O., Ritschel, L. A., Lynn, S. J., Cauin, R. L., & Latzman, R. D. (2013). Why many clinical psychologists are resistant to evidence-based practice: Root causes and constructive remedies. *Clinical Psychology Review, 33*(7), 833–900.

Lin, Z., & He, S. (2012). Emergent filling in induced by motion integration reveals a high-level mechanism in filling in. *Psychological Science, 23*(12), 1534–1541.

Linden, D. E. J. (2006). How psychotherapy changes the brain – the contribution of functional neuroimaging. *Molecular Psychiatry, 11*, 528–538.

Linehan, M. M. (1993). *Cognitive-behavioral treatment of borderline personality disorder.* New York: Guilford Press.

Lippmann, M., Bress, A., Nemeroff, C. B., Plotsky, P. M., & Mongeggia, L. M. (2007). Long-term behavioural and molecular alterations associated with maternal separation in rats. *European Journal of Neuroscience, 25*(10), 3091–3098.

Lisman, J. E., & Hell, J. W. (2008). Long-term potentiation. In J. W. Hell, & M. D. Ehlers (Eds.), *Structural and functional organization of the synapse* (pp. 501–534). New York: Springer.

Liverant, G. I., Brown, T. A., Barlow, D. H., & Roemer (2008). Emotion regulation in unipolar depression: The effects of acceptance and suppression of subjective emotional experience on the intensity and duration of sadness and negative affect. *Behaviour Research and Therapy, 46*, 1201–1209.

Livesley, W. J., Jang, K. L., & Vernon, P. A. (1998). Phenotypic and genetic structure of traits delineating personality disorder. *Archives of General Psychiatry, 55*, 941–948.

Lloyd, D. (1994). Connectionist hysteria: Reducing a Freudian case study to a network model. *Philosophy, Psychiatry, & Psychology, 1*(2), 69–88.

Lodge, M., & Taber, C. S. (2005). The automaticity of affect for political leaders, groups, and issues: An experimental test of the hot cognition hypothesis. *Political Psychology, 24*(3), 727–745.

Loehlin, J. C. (1987). *Latent variable models: An introduction to factor, path, and structural analysis.* Hillsdale, NJ: Lawrence Erlbaum.

Loftus, E. F. (1980). *Memory: Surprising new insights into how we remember and why we forget.* Reading, MA: Addison-Wesley.

Loftus, E. (1996). *Eyewitness testimony*. Cambridge, MA: Harvard University Press (Original work published 1979).

Loftus, E. (2003). Make-believe memories. *American Psychologist, 58*, 867–873.

Loftus, E. F., & Klinger, M. R. (1992). Is the unconscious smart or dumb? *American Psychologist, 47*, 761–765.

Loftus, E., & Pickerell, J. E. (1995). The formation of false memories. *Psychiatric Annals, 25*, 720–725.

Lohr, J. M., & Staats, A. W. (1973). Attitude conditioning in Sino-Tibetan languages. *Journal of Personality and Social Psychology, 26*, 196–200.

Lombroso, P., & Ogren, M. (2008). Learning and memory, Part I: Brain regions involved in two types of learning and memory. *Journal of the American Academy of Child & Adolescent Psychiatry*, 47, 1219–1223.

Lombroso, P., & Ogren, M. (2009). Learning and memory, Part II: Molecular mechanisms of synaptic plasticity. *Journal of the American Academy of Child & Adolescent Psychiatry, 48*, 5–9.

Lord, C. G., Ross, L., & Lepper, M. R. (1979). Biased assimilation and attitude polarization: The effects of prior theories on subsequently considered evidence. *Journal of Personality and Social Psychology, 37*, 2098–2109.

Lothane, Z. (2006). Freud's 1895 project: From mind to brain and back again. *Annals of the New York Academy of Sciences, 843*(1), 43–65.

Lynch, G. (2000). Memory consolidation and long-term potentiation. In M. S. Gazzaniga (Ed.), *The new cognitive neurosciences* (2nd ed.) (pp. 139–157). Cambridge, MA: The MIT Press.

Lynch, T. R., Trost, W. T., Salsman, N., & Linehan, M. M. (2007). Dialectical behavior therapy for borderline personality disorder. *Annual Review of Clinical Psychology, 3*, 181–205.

Lynn, R. (1967). *Attention, arousal, and the orientation reaction.* Oxford, England: Pergamon Press.

Lyubomirsky, S., & Tkach, C. (2004). The consequences of dysphoric rumination. In C. Papageorgiou, & A. Wells (Eds.), *Depressive rumination: Nature, theory and treatment* (pp. 21–41). New York: Wiley.

MacLeod, C., Mathews, A. M., & Tata, P. (1986). Attentional bias in emotional disorders. *Journal of Abnormal Psychology, 95*, 15–20.

Madden, G. J. (Ed.). (2012). *APA Handbook of Behavior Analysis*. Washington, DC: American Psychological Association.

Mahler, S.V., & de Wit, H. (2010). Cue-reactors: Individual differences in cue-induced craving after food or smoking abstinence. *PLoS ONE, 5*(11), e15475.

Mahoney, M. J. (1974). *Cognition and behavior modification*. Cambridge, MA: Ballinger Publishing Co.

Mahoney, M. J. (1977). Reflections on the cognitive-learning trend in psychotherapy. *American Psychologist, 32*, 5–13.

Makel, M. C., Plucker, J. A., & Hegarty, B. (2012). Replications in psychology research: How often do they really occur? *Perspectives on Psychological Science*, 7, 537–542.

Malgady, R., Rogler, L. H., & Tryon, W. W. (1992). Issues of validity in the Diagnostic Interview Schedule. *Journal of Psychiatric Research, 26*, 59–67.

Malone, J. C. (1990). *Theories of learning: A historical approach*. Belmont, CA: Wadsworth.

Marcus, G. E. (1998). Can connectionism save constructivism? *Cognition, 66*, 153–182.

Markram, H. (2012, June). The human brain project. *Scientific American, 306*(6), 50–55.

Marks, I. (1975). Behavioral treatments of phobic and obsessive compulsive disorders: A critical appraisal. In M. Hersen, R. M. Eisler, & P. M. Miller (Eds.), *Progress in Behavior Modification* (vol. 1). New York: Academic Press.

Marks, I. M. (1969). *Fears and phobias*. New York: Academic Press.

Markus, H., & Wurf, E. (1987). The dynamic self-concept: A social psychological perspective. *Annual Review of Psychology, 38*, 299–337.

Marshall-Berenz, E. C., Morrison, J. A., Schumacher, J. A., & Coffey, S. F. (2011). Affect intensity and lability: The role of posttraumatic stress disorder symptoms in borderline personality disorder. *Depression and Anxiety, 28*, 393–399.

Martin, G. L., & Pear, J. (2010). *Behavior modification: What it is and how to do it* (9th ed.). Upper Saddle River, NJ: Pearson/ Prentice Hall.

Martin, M., Horder, P., & Jones, G.V. (1992). Integral bias in naming of phobia-related words. *Cognition and Emotion, 6*, 479–486.

Martin, K. C., Bartsch, D., Bailey, C. H., & Kandel, E. R. (2000a). Molecular mechanisms underlying learning-related long-lasting synaptic plasticity. In M. S. Gazzaniga (Ed.), *The new cognitive neurosciences* (2nd ed.) (pp. 121–137). Cambridge, MA: The MIT Press.

Martin, S. J., Grimwood, P. D., & Morris, R. G. M. (2000b). Synaptic plasticity and memory: An evaluation of the hypothesis. *Annual Review of Psychology, 23*, 649–711.

Martineau, J., Cochin, S., Magne, R., & Barthelemy, C. (2008). Impaired cortical activation in autistic children: Is the mirror neuron system involved? *International Journal of Psychophysiology: Official Journal of the International Organization of Psychophysiology, 68*, 35–40.

Martinez, J. L., Jr., & Derrick, B. E. (1996). Long-term potentiation and learning. *Annual Review of Psychology, 47*, 173–203.

Martínez-García, M., Rolls, E. T., Gustavo, D., & Romo, R. (2011). Neural and computational mechanisms of postponed decisions. *Proceedings of the National Academy of Sciences of the United States of America (PNAS), 108*(28), 11626–11631. July 12.

Masson, J. M. (1984). *The assault on truth: Freud's suppression of the seduction theory*. New York: Farrar, Straus & Giroux.

Matelli, M., Luppino, G., & Rizzolatti, G. (1985). Patterns of cytochrome oxidase activity in the frontal agranular cortex of the macaque monkey. *Behavioural Brain Research, 18*(2), 125–136.

Mathews, A., & Mackintosh, B. (2000). Induced emotional interpretation bias and anxiety. *Journal of Abnormal Psychology, 109*, 602–615.

Mathews, A., & MacLeod, C. (1985). Selective processing of threat cues in anxiety states. *Behaviour Research and Therapy*, *23*, 563–569.

Matt, G. E., Vazquez, C., & Campbell, W. K. (1992). Mood-congruent recall of affectively toned stimuli: A meta-analytic review. *Clinical Psychology Review*, *12*, 227–255.

Matzel, L. D. (2002). Learning Mutants. In Harold E. Pashler (Ed.), *Steven's Handbook of Experimental Psychology* (pp. 201–238). New York: John Wiley and Sons.

Mayberg, H. S., Silva, J. A., Brannan, S. K., Tekell, J. L., Mahurin, R. K., McGinnis, S., & Jerabek, P. A. (2002). The functional neuroanatomy of the placebo effect. *American Journal of Psychiatry*, *159*, 728–737.

Mayr, E. (1982). *The growth of biological thought: Diversity, evolution, and inheritance*. Cambridge, MA: Harvard University Press.

Mays, D. T., & Franks, C. M. (1980). Getting worse: Psychotherapy or no treatment – The jury should still be out. *Professional Psychology*, *11*, 78–92.

Mays, D. T., & Franks, C. M. (Eds.). (1985). *Negative outcome in psychotherapy and what to do about it*. New York: Springer.

McAllister, W. R., & McAllister, D. E. (1995). Two-factor fear theory: Implications for understanding anxiety-based clinical phenomena. In W. O'Donohue, & L. Krasner (Eds.), *Theories of behavior therapy: Exploring behavior change* (pp. 145–171). Washington, DC: American Psychological Association.

McCallum, M., & Piper, W. E. (1990). The psychological mindedness assessment procedure. *Psychological Assessment*, *2*, 412–418.

McCallum, M., & Piper, W. E. (1996). Psychological mindedness. *Psychiatry*, *59*, 48–64.

McCarthy, M. (1990). The thin ideal, depression and eating disorders in women. *Behaviour Research and Therapy*, *28*, 205–215.

McClelland, J. L. (2010). Emergence in cognitive science. *Topics in Cognitive Science*, *2*, 751–770.

McClelland, J. L., Rumelhart, D. E., & the PDP Research Group (1986). *Parallel distributed processing: Explorations in the microstructure of cognition. Psychological and biological models* . (Vol. 2) Cambridge, MA: MIT Press.

McClelland, J. L., McNaughton, B. L., & O'Reilly, R. C. (1995). Why there are complementary learning systems in the hippocampus and neocortex: Insights from the successes and failures of connectionist models of learning and memory. *Psychological Review*, *102*(3), 419–457.

McCloskey, M., & Cohen, N. J. (1989). Catastrophic interference in connectionist networks: The sequential learning problem. In G. H. Bower (Ed.). *The psychology of learning and motivation: Vol. 24*. (pp. 109–165). New York: Academic Press.

McCutchen, B. (2006). *Learning without learning: The events of childhood may have an impact on the brain, even if no conventional memory is formed*. Posted 09/21/2006 at from the 09/21/2006 print edition of The Economist. http://www.economist.com/node/7941685.

McDougall, W. (1921). *An introduction to social psychology*. Boston: Luce.

McGlynn, F. D. (2002). Systematic desensitization. In M. Hersen, & W. Sledge (Eds.), *Encyclopedia of psychotherapy* (Vol. 2. pp. 755–764). New York: Elsevier Science.

McGlynn, F. D., Mealiea, W. L., Jr., & Landau, D. L. (1981). The current status of systematic desensitization. *Clinical Psychology Review*, *1*, 149–179.

McGowan, P. O., Sasaki, A., Huang, T. C., Unterberger, A., Suderman, M., Ernst, C., Meaney, M. J., Turecki, G., & Szyf, M. (2008). Promoter-wide hypermethylation of the ribosomal RNA gene promoter in the suicide brain. *PLoS One*, *3*(5), e2085. May 7.

McGowan, P. O., Sasaki, A., D'Alessio, A. C., Dymov, S., Labonte, B., Szyf, M., Turecki, G., & Meaney, M. J. (2009). Epigenetic regulation of the glucocorticoid receptor in human brain associates with childhood abuse. *National Neuroscience*, *12*, 342–348.

McGraw, K., Fischle, M., Stenner, K., & Lodge, M. (1996). What's in a word? Bias in trait descriptions of political leaders. *Political Behavior*, *18*, 263–287.

McGurk, H., & MacDonald, J. (1976). Hearing lips and seeing voices. *Nature, 264*(5588), 746–748.

McHugh, R. K., & Barlow, D. H. (2010). The dissemination and implementation of evidence-based psychological treatments. *American Psychologist, 65*, 73–84.

McKay, D. (2011). Methods and mechanisms in the efficacy of psychodynamic psychotherapy. *American Psychologist, 66*(2), 147–148.

McKuen, M., Wokak, J., Keele, L., & Marcus, G. E. (2011). Civic engagements: Resolute partisanship or reflective deliberation. *American Journal of Political Science, 54*, 44–458.

McLaughlin, K. A., Borkovec, T. D., & Sibrava, N. J. (2007). The effects of worry and rumination on affect states and cognitive anxiety. *Behavior Therapy, 38*, 23–38.

McLeod, P., Plunkett, K., & Rolls, E. T. (1998). *Introduction to connectionist modelling of cognitive processes*. Oxford: Oxford University Press.

McNair, D. M., Lorr, M., & Droppleman, L. F. (1971). *Profile of mood states*. San Diego, CA: Educational and Industrial Testing Service.

McNally, R. J. (1992). Disunity in psychology: Chaos or speciation? *American Psychologist, 47*, 1054.

Meaney, M. J., & Ferguson-Smith, A. C. (2010). Epigenetic regulation of the neural transcriptome: The meaning of the marks. *Nature Neuroscience, 13*, 1313–1318.

Mednick, M. (1957). Mediated generalization and the incubation effect as a function of manifest anxiety. *Journal of Abnormal and Social Psychology, 55*, 315–321.

Meehl, P. E. (1954). *Clinical versus statistical prediction: A theoretical analysis and a review of the evidence*. Minneapolis: University of Minnesota.

Meehl, P. E. (1986). Causes and effects of my disturbing little book. *Journal of Personality Assessment, 50*, 370–375.

Meehl, P. E. (1992). Theoretical risks and tabular asterisks: Sir Karl, Sir Ronald, and the soft progress of slow psychology. In R. B. Miller (Ed.), *The restoration of dialogue* (pp. 523–555). Washington, DC: American Psychological Association (Original work published 1978).

Meehl, P. E., & Sellars, W. (1956). The concept of emergence. In H. Feigl, & M. Scriven (Eds.), *Minnesota studies in the philosophy of science The foundations of science and the concepts of psychology and psychoanalysis: Vol. 1*. (pp. 239–252). Minneapolis: University of Minnesota Press.

Meichenbaum, D. (1977). *Cognitive-behavior modification: An integrative approach*. New York: Plenum Press.

Mennin, D. S., & Farach, F. J. (2007). Emotion and evolving treatments for adult psychopathology. *Clinical Psychology: Science and Practice, 14*, 329–352.

Mennin, D. S., & Fresco, D. M. (2009). Emotion regulation as a framework for understanding and treating anxiety pathology. In A. M. Kring, & D. M. Sloan (Eds.), *Emotion regulation in psychopathology*. New York: Guilford Press.

Mennin, D. S., Heimberg, R. G., Turk, C. L., & Fresco, D. M. (2005). Preliminary evidence for an emotion dysregulation model of generalized anxiety disorder. *Behaviour Research and Therapy, 43*, 1281–1310.

Mennin, D. S., Holoway, R. M., Fresco, D. M., Moore, M. T., & Heimberg, R. G. (2007). Delineating components of emotion and its dysregulation in anxiety and mood psychopathology. *Behavior Therapy, 38*, 284–302.

Mennin, D. S., McLaughlin, K. A., & Flanagan, T. J. (2009). Emotion regulation deficits in generalized anxiety disorder, social anxiety disorder, and their co-occurrence. *Journal of Anxiety Disorders, 23*, 866–871.

Menzies, R. G., & Clarke, J. C. (1995). The etiology of phobias: A nonassociative account. *Clinical Psychology Review, 15*, 23–48.

Merikle, P. M. (1992). Perception without awareness: Critical issues. *American Psychologist, 47*, 792–795.

Merton, R. K. (1957). *Social theory and social structure* (Rev. ed.). Glencoe, IL: Free Press.

Merwin, R. M. (2011). Anorexia Nervosa as a disorder of emotion regulation: Theory, evidence, and treatment implications. *Clinical Psychology: Science and Practice, 18*(3), 329–352.

Messer, S. B., & Winokur, M. (1980). Some limits to the integration of psychoanalytic and behavior therapy. *American Psychologist, 35*, 818–827.

Messer, S. B., & Winokur, M. (1984). Ways of knowing and visions of reality in psychoanalytic therapy and behavior therapy. In H. Arkowitz, & S. Messer (Eds.), *Psychoanalytic therapy and behavioral therapy: Is integration possible?* (pp. 63–100). New York: Plenum.

Meyer, L. B. (1956). *Emotion and meaning in music*. Chicago: University of Chicago Press.

Meyer, L. B. (1967). *Music, the arts, and ideas*. Chicago: University of Chicago Press.

Michotte, A. (1945/1963). *The perception of causality*. Andover, MA: Methuen.

Mignault, A., & Marley, A. J. (1997). A real-time neuronal model of classical conditioning. *Adaptive Behavior, 6*, 3–61. http://dx.doi.org/10.1177/105971239700600102.

Mikulas, W. L. (1972). Criticisms of behavior therapy. *The Canadian Psychologist, 13*, 83–104.

Miller, C. (2002). Flooding. In M. Hersen, & W. Sledge (Eds.), *Encyclopedia of Psychotherapy* (vol. 1. (pp. 809–813). New York: Elsevier Science.

Miller, G. A. (1956). The magical number seven, plus or minus two: some limits on our capacity for processing information. *Psychological Review, 63*(2), 81–97.

Miller, G. A. (2010). Mistreating psychology in the decades of the brain. *Perspectives on Psychological Science, 5*, 716–743.

Miller, G. A., & Keller, J. (2000). Psychology and neuroscience: Making peace. *Current Directions in Psychological Science, 9*, 212–215.

Miller, H. R., & Nawas, M. M. (1970). Control of aversive stimulus termination in systematic desensitization. *Behavior Research and Therapy, 8*, 57–61.

Miller, K. (2013). Brain benders. *Discover*, October, 30–37.

Miller, W. (1983). Motivational Interviewing with problem drinkers. *Behavioural Psychotherapy, 11*, 147–172.

Miller, W. (1996). Motivational interviewing: Research, practice and puzzles. *Addictive Behaviors, 21*, 835–842.

Miller, W. R., & Rollnick, S. (2002). *Motivational interviewing: preparing people for change*. New York: Guilford.

Minsky, M. L., & Papert, S. A. (1969). *Perceptrons*. Cambridge, MA: MIT Press.

Mischel, W. (2008). The toothbrush problem. *Association for Psychological Science Observer, 21*, 11.

Mischel, W. (2009). Editorial: Connecting clinical practice to scientific progress. *Psychological Science in the Public Interest, 9*(2), i-ii.

Mitchell, D. B. (2006). Nonconscious priming after 17 years. *Psychological Science, 17*, 925–929.

Moffett, M. C., Vicentic, A., Kozel, M., Plotsky, P., Francis, D. D., & Kuhar, M. J. (2007). Maternal separation alters drug intake patterns in adulthood in rats. *Biochemical Pharmacology, 73*(3), 321–330.

Mogg, K., & Bradley, B. P. (1998). A cognitive-motivational analysis of anxiety. *Behaviour Research and Therapy, 36*, 809–848.

Monroe, B. M., & Read, S. J. (2008). A general connectionist model of attitude structure and change: The ACS (attitudes as constraint satisfaction) model. *Psychological Review, 115*, 733–759.

Monroe, R. L. (1955). *Schools of psychoanalytic thought*. New York: Holt, Rinehart, & Winston.

Monshouwer, K., Have, M., van Poppel, M., Kemper, H., & Vollegergh, W. (2012). Possible mechanisms explaining the association between physical activity and mental health: Findings from the 2001 Dutch Health Behaviour in School-Aged Children Survey. *Clinical Psychological Science, 1*(1), 1–8.

Montgomery, D. D. (2002). Biofeedback. In M. Hersen, & W. Sledge (Eds.), *Encyclopedia of psychotherapy* (pp. 331–344). New York: Academic Press.

Montgomery, G. T., & Crowder, J. E. (1972). The symptom substitution hypothesis and the evidence. *Psychotherapy: Theory, Research and Practice, 9*, 98–102.

Moors, A. (2010). Theories of emotion causation: A review. In J. DeHouwer, & D. Hermans (Eds.), *Cognition and emotion: Reviews of current research and theories* (pp. 1–37). New York: Psychology Press.

Moradi, A. R., Taghavi, M. R., Neshat-Doost, H. T., Yule, W., & Dalgleish, T. (2000). Memory bias for emotional information in children and adolescents with posttraumatic stress disorder: A preliminary study. *Journal of Anxiety Disorders, 14*, 521–534.

Morris, J. P., Squires, N. K., Taber, C. S., & Lodge, M. (2003). The automatic activation of political attitudes: A psychophysiological examination of the hot cognition hypothesis. *Political Psychology, 24*(4), 727–745.

Morris, J. S., Öhman, A., & Dolan, R. J. (1998). Conscious and unconscious emotional learning in the human amygdala. *Nature, 393*, 467–470.

Mowrer, O. H. (1948). Learning theory and the neurotic paradox. *American Journal of Orthopsychiatry, 18*, 571–610.

Mowrer, O. H. (1950). *Learning theory and personality dynamics*. New York: Arnold Press.

Mowrer, O. H. (1960). *Learning theory and the symbolic processes*. New York: Wiley.

Mowrer, O. H., & Mowrer, W. M. (1938). Enuresis: A method for its study and treatment. *American Journal of Orthopsychiatry, 8*, 436–459.

Mudrik, L., Breska, A., Lamy, D., & Deouell, L. Y. (2011). Integration without awareness: Expanding the limits of unconscious processing. *Psychological Science, 22*, 764–770.

Mukherjee, S. (2011). *Post-Prozac Nation*. The New York Times Magazine. April 22, 2012. pp. 48–54.

Munder, T., Brütsch, O., Leonhart, R., Gerger, H., & Barth, J. (2013). Researcher allegiance in psychotherapy outcome research: An overview of reviews. *Clinical Psychology Review, 33*(4), 501–511.

Munro, G., Ditto, P., Lockhart, L., Fagerlin, A., Gready, M., & Peterson, E. (2002). Biased assimilation of sociopolitical arguments: Evaluating the 1996 U.S. presidential debate. *Basic and Applied Social Psychology, 24*, 15–26.

Muris, P., & Field, A. P. (2008). Distorted cognition and pathological anxiety in children and adolescents. *Cognition and Emotion, 22*, 395–421.

Muris, P., & Field, A. P. (2010). The role of verbal threat information in the development of childhood fear. *"Beware the Jabberwock!" Clinical Child and Family Psychology Review, 13*, 129–150.

Muris, P., Kindt, M., Bögels, S., Merckelbach, H., Gadet, B., & Moulaert, V. (2000a). Anxiety and threat perception abnormalities in normal children. *Journal of Psychopathology and Behavioral Assessment, 22*, 183–199.

Muris, P., Luermans, J., Merckelbach, H., & Mayer, B. (2000b). "Danger is lurking everywhere". The relationship between anxiety and threat perception abnormalities in normal children. *Journal of Behavior Therapy and Experimental Psychiatry, 31*, 123–136.

Muris, P., Merckelbach, H., & Damsma, E. (2000c). Threat perception bias in nonreferred socially anxious children. *Journal of Clinical Child Psychology, 29*, 348–359.

Muris, P., Merckelbach, H., & Van Spauwen, I. (2003a). The emotional reasoning heuristic in children. *Behaviour Research and Therapy, 41*, 261–272.

Muris, P., Rapee, R., Meesters, C., Schouten, E., & Geers, M. (2003b). Threat perception abnormalities in children: The role of anxiety disorders symptoms, chronic anxiety, and state anxiety. *Journal of Anxiety Disorders, 17*, 271–287.

Muris, P., Meesters, C., & Rompelberg, L. (2007). Attention control in middle childhood: Relations to psychopathological symptoms and threat perception distortions. *Behaviour Research and Therapy, 45*, 997–1010.

Murphy, M. L. M., Slavich, G. M., Rohleder, N., & Miller, G. E. (2013). Targeted rejection triggers differential pro- and anti-inflammatory gene expression in adolescents as a function of social status. *Clinical Psychological Science, 1*, 30–40. http://dx.doi.org/10.1177/2167702612455743.

Murphy, S. T., & Zajonc, R. B. (1993). Affect, cognition, and awareness: Affective priming with optimal and suboptimal stimulus exposures. *Journal of Personality and Social Psychology, 64*(5), 723–739.

Myers, F. (1893). The subliminal consciousness. *Proceedings of the Society for Psychical Research, 9*, 3–128.

Nabi, R. L. (2003). Exploring the framing effect of emotion. Do discrete emotions differentially influence information accessibility, information seeking, and policy preference? *Communication Research, 30*, 224–247.

Nargeot, R., Baxter, D. A., & Byrne, J. H. (1999a). In vitro analog of operant conditioning in Aplysia. I. Contingent reinforcement modifies the functional dynamics of an identified neuron. *The Journal of Neuroscience, 19*, 2247–2260.

Nargeot, R., Baxter, D. A., & Byrne, J. H. (1999b). In vitro analog of operant conditioning in Aplysia. II. Modifications of the functional dynamics of an identified neuron contribute to motor pattern selection. *The Journal of Neuroscience, 19*, 2261–2272.

Nathan, P. E., & Gorman, J. M. (2002). *A guide to treatments that work* (2nd ed.). New York: Oxford University Press.

Nawas, M. M., Welsch, W.V., & Fishman, S. T. (1970). The comparative effectiveness of pairing aversive imagery with relaxation, neutral tasks and muscular tension in reducing snake phobia. *Behaviour Research and Therapy, 6*, 63–68.

Nemeroff, C. B., & Schatzberg, A. F. (2002). Pharmacological treatments for unipolar depression. In P. E. Nathan, & J. M. Gorman (Eds.), *A guide to treatments that work* (2nd ed.) (pp. 229–243).

Nestler, E. J. (2011). Hidden switches in the mind. *Scientific American, 305*(6), 76–83. Dec.

Neuliep, J. W., & Crandall, R. (1990). Reviewer bias against replication research. *Journal of Social Behavior and Personality, 5*, 85–90.

Neuliep, J. W., & Crandall, R. (1993). Reviewer bias against replication research. *Journal of Social Behavior and Personality, 8*, 21–29.

Newcomer, J. W., & Krystal, J. H. (2001). NMDA receptor regulation and behavior in humans. *Hippocampus, 11*, 529–542.

Newell, A., & Simon, H. A. (1972). *Human problem solving*. Englewood Cliffs, NJ: Prentice-Hall.

Nisbett, R. E., & Wilson, T. D. (1977). Telling more than we can know: Verbal reports on mental processes. *Psychological Review, 84*, 231–259.

Nishitani, N., Avikainen, S., & Hari, R. (2004). Abnormal imitation-related cortical activation sequences in Asperger's syndrome. *Annals of Neurology, 55*, 558–562.

Nithianantharajah, J., & Hannan, A. J. (2006). Enriched environments, experience-dependent plasticity and disorders of the nervous system. *Nature Reviews Neuroscience*, 7, 697–709.

Njiokiktjien, C., Verschoor, A., de Sonneville, L., Huyser, C., Op het Veld, V., & Toorenaar, N. (2001). Disordered recognition of facial identity and emotions in three Asperger type autists. *European Child & Adolescent Psychiatry, 10*, 79–90.

Nolan, J. D., Mattis, P. R., & Holliday, W. C. (1970). Long-term effects of behavior therapy: A 12-month follow-up. *Journal of Abnormal Psychology, 76*, 88–92.

Nolen-Hoeksema, S., Wisco, B. E., & Lyubomirsky, S. (2008). Rethinking rumination. *Perspectives in Psychological Science, 3*, 400–424.

Norberg, M. M., Krystal, J. H., & Tolin, D. F. (2008). A meta-analysis of D-cycloserine and the facilitation of fear extinction and exposure therapy. *Biological Psychiatry, 63*, 1118–1126.

Norcross, J. C., & Goldfried, M. R. (1992). *Handbook of psychotherapy integration*. New York: Basic Books.

Norcross, J. C. (2011). *Psychotherapy relationships that work: Evidence-based responsiveness* (2nd ed.). New York: Oxford University Press.

Norcross, J. C., & Goldfried, M. R. (2005). *Handbook of psychotherapy integration* (2nd ed.). New York: Oxford University Press.

Norcross, J. C., & Karpiak, C. P. (2012). Clinical psychologists in the 2012s: 50 years of the APA Division of Clinical Psychology. *Clinical Psychology: Science and Practice, 19*, 1–12.

Nurnberger, J. I., & Hingtgen, J. N. (1973). Is symptom substitution an important issue in behavior therapy? *Biological Psychiatry, 3*, 221–236.

Nyklíček, I., & Denollet, J. (2009). Development and evaluation of the Balanced Index of Psychological Mindedness (BIPM). *Psychological Assessment, 21*, 32–44.

O'Brien, G., & Jureidini, J. (2002). Dispensing with the dynamic unconscious. *Philosophy, Psychiatry & Psychiatry, 9*, 141–153.

O'Reilly, R. C., & Munakata, Y. (2000). *Computational explorations in cognitive neuroscience: Understanding the mind by simulating the brain*. Cambridge, MA: The MIT Press.

Ober, D. C. (1968). Modification of smoking behavior. *Journal of Consulting and Clinical Psychology, 32*, 543–549.

Oberman, L. M., & Ramachandran, V. S. (2007). The simulating social mind: The role of the mirror neuron system and simulation in the social and communicative deficits of autism spectrum disorders. *Psychological Bulletin, 133*, 310–327.

Oberman, L. M., Hubbard, E. M., McCleery, J. P., Altschuler, E. L., Ramachandran, V. S., & Pineda, J. A. (2005). EEG evidence for mirror neuron dysfunction in autism spectrum disorders. *Brain Research, 24*, 190–198.

Oberman, L. M., Pineda, J. A., & Ramachandran, V. S. (2007). The human mirror neuron system: A link between action observation and social skills. *Social Cognitive and Affective Neuroscience, 2*, 62–66.

Oberman, L. M., Ramachandran, V. S., & Pineda, J. A. (2008). Modulation of mu suppression in children with autism spectrum disorders in response to familiar or unfamiliar stimuli: The mirror neuron hypothesis. *Neuropsychologia, 46*(5), 1558–1565.

Ochsner, K. N., Ray, R. R., Hughes, B., McRae, K., Cooper, J. C., Weber, J., Gabrieli, J. D. E., & Gross, J. J. (2009). Bottom-up and top-down processes in emotion generation: Common and distinct neural mechanisms. *Psychological Science, 20*, 1322–1331.

Ohlson, K. (2012). The cooperation instinct. *Discover,* December, 77(12), 34–41.

Öhman, A. (2002). Automaticity and the amygdala: Nonconscious responses to emotional faces. *Current Directions in Psychological Sciences, 11*(2), 62–66.

Oja, E. (1982). A simplified neuron model as a principle component analyzer. *Journal of Mathematical Biology, 15*, 267–273.

Olds, D. D. (1994). Connectionism and psychoanalysis. *Journal of the American Psychoanalytic Association, 42*, 581–611.

Olton, D. S., & Noonberg, A. R. (1980). *Biofeedback: Clinical applications in behavioral medicine.* Englewood Cliffs, NJ: Prentice-Hall.

Oreskes, W. (1999). *Rejection of continental drift.* New York: Oxford University Press.

Orr, M. G., Thrush, R., & Plaut, D. C. (2013). The theory of reasoned action as parallel constraint satisfaction: Towards a dynamic computational model of health behavior. *PLoS ONE, 8*(5), e62490.

Osgood, C. E., Suci, C. J., & Tannenbaum, P. H. (1957). *The measurement of meaning*. Urbana: University of Illinois Press.

Ottati, V. C., & Isbell, L. M. (1996). Effects on mood during exposure to target information on subsequently reported judgments: An on-line model of misattribution and correction. *Journal of Personality and Social Psychology, 71*, 39–53.

Ottenbacher, K., & Ottenbacher, M. (1981). Symptom substitution: A case study. *American Journal of Psychoanalysis, 41*, 173–175.

Overmier, J. B., & Seligman, M. E. P. (1967). Effects of inescapable shock upon subsequent escape and avoidance learning. *Journal of Comparative and Physiological Psychology, 63*, 28–33.

Ozer, E. J., Best, S. R., Lipsey, T. L., & Weiss, D. S. (2008). Predictors of posttraumatic stress disorder in symptoms in adults: A meta-analysis. *Psychological Trauma: Theory, Research, Practice, and Policy, S*, 3–36.

Ozer, E. J., Best, S. R., Lipsey, T. L., & Weiss, D. S. (2003). Predictors of posttraumatic stress disorder and symptoms in adults: A meta-analysis. *Psychological Bulletin, 129*, 52–73.

Paddock, J. R., Joseph, A. L., Chan, F. M., Terranova, S., Manning, C., & Loftus, E. F. (1998). When guided visualization procedures may backfire: Imagination inflation and predicting individual differences in suggestibility. *Applied Cognitive Psychology, 12*, S63–S75.

Paivio, S. C., & McCulloch, C. R. (2004). Alexithymia as a mediator between childhood trauma and self-injurious behaviors. *Child Abuse & Neglect, 28*, 339–354.

Paivio, S. C., & Pascual-Leone, A. (2010). *Emotion-focused therapy for complex trauma: An integrative approach.* Washington, DC: American Psychological Association.

Panksepp, J. (1998). *Affective neuroscience: The foundations of human and animal emotions.* New York: Oxford University Press.

Panksepp, J. (2005). Affective consciousness: Core emotional feelings in animals and humans. *Consciousness and Cognition: An International Journal: Special Issue on the Neurobiology of Animal Consciousness, 14*(1), 30–80.

Panksepp, J. (2008). The affective brain and core consciousness: How does neural activity generate emotional feelings? In M. Lewis, J. M. Haviland-Jones, & L. F. Barrett (Eds.), *Handbook of emotions*(3rd ed.) (pp. 47–67). New York: Guilford.

Panksepp, J. (2011). Cross-species affective neuroscience decoding of the primal affective experiences of humans and related animals. *PLoS ONE, 6*(8), e21236.

Park, D., & Gutchess, A. (2006). The cognitive neuroscience of aging and culture. *Current Directions in Psychological Science, 15*, 105–108.

Parker, M. T., & Isbell, L. M. (2010). How I vote depends on how I feel: The differential impact of anger and fear on political information processing. *Psychological Science, 21*, 549–550.

Parks, C. D., Joireman, J., & Van Lange, P. A. M. (2013). Cooperation, trust, and antagonism: How public goods are promoted. *Psychological Science in the Public Interest, 14*(3), 119–165.

Parks, R. W., & Levine, D. S. (1998). Neural network modeling of Wisconsin card sorting and verbal fluency tests: Applications with frontal lobe-damage and Alzheimer's disease patients. In R. W. Parks, D. S. Levine, & D. L. Long (Eds.), *Fundamentals of neural network modeling: Neuropsychology and cognitive neuroscience* (pp. 357–380). Cambridge, MA: The MIT Press.

Parnas, A. S., Weber, M., & Richardson, R. (2005). Effects of multiple exposures to D-Cycloserine on extinction of conditioned fear in rats. *Neurobiology of Learning and Memory, 83*, 224–231.

Pashler, H., & Harris, C. R. (2012). Is the replicability crisis overblown? Three arguments examined. *Perspectives on Psychological Science, 76*(6), 531–536.

Patterson, G. R., Reid, J. B., & Dishion, T. J. (1992). *Antisocial boys.* Eugene, OR: Castalia.

Paul, G. (1967). Strategy of outcome research in psychotherapy. *Journal of Consulting Psychology, 31*, 109–118.

Paul, G. L. (1968). Two-year follow-up of systematic desensitization in therapy groups. *Journal of Abnormal Psychology, 73*, 119–130.

Pavio, S. C., & Pascual-Leone, A. (2010). *Emotion-focused therapy for complex trauma: An integrative approach.* Washington, DC: American Psychological Association.

Pavlov, I. P. (1960). *Conditioned reflexes: An investigation of the physiological activity of the cerebral cortex.* In G. V. Anrep, & Trans. (Eds.). New York: Dover. (Original work published 1927).

Payne, B. K., & Gawronski, B. (2010). A history of implicit social cognition: Where is it coming from? Where is it now? Where is it going? In B. Gawronski, & B. K. Payne (Eds.), *Handbook of implicit social cognition: Measurement, theory, and applications* (pp. 1–15). New York: Guilford.

Paz, R., Gelbard-Sagiv, H., Mukamel, R., Harel, M., Malach, R., & Fried, I. (2010). A neural substrate in the human hippocampus for linking successive events. *Proceedings of the National Academy of Sciences of the United States of America (PNAS), 107*(13), 6046–6051.

Perner, J., Aichhorn, M., Kronbichler, M., Staffen, W., & Ladurner, G. (2006). Thinking of mental and other representations: The roles of left and right temporo-parietal junction. *Social Neuroscience, 1*, 245–258.

Perry, C., & Jean-Roch, L. (1984). Mental processing outside of awareness: The contributions of Freud and Janet. In K. S. Bowers, & D. Meichenbaum (Eds.), *The unconscious reconsidered* (pp. 9–48). New York: Wiley.

Pessoa, L., Thompson, E., & Noë, A. (1998). Finding out about filling-in: A guide to perceptual completion for visual science and the philosophy of perception. *Behavioral and Brain Sciences, 21*, 723–802.

Peterson, C., Maier, S. F., & Seligman, M. E. P. (1993). *Learned helplessness: A theory for the age of personal control*. New York: Oxford University Press.

Phaf, R. H., & Rotteveel, M. (2012). Affective monitoring: A generic mechanism for affect elicitation. *Frontiers in Psychology, 3, Article, 47*, 1–17.

Phelps, E. A. (2006). Emotion and cognition: Insights from studies of the human amygdala. *Annual Review of Psychology, 57*, 27–53.

Phillips, J., & Woody, J. M. (1994). Commentary on "Connectionist hysteria". *Philosophy, Psychiatry, & Psychology, 1*(2), 89–90.

Piaget, J. (1952). *The origins of intelligence in children*. New York: International Universities Press.

Piaget, J. (1983). Piaget's theory. In P. H. Mussen (Ed.), *Handbook of child psychology* (4th ed.) *History, theory, and methods: Vol. 1*. pp. 103–128). New York: Wiley.

Piaget, J. (1985). *The equilibration of cognitive structures*. In T. Brown, K. J. Thampy, & Trans (Eds.). Chicago: University of Chicago Press (Original work published in 1975).

Piaget, J., & Inhelder, B. (1969). *The psychology of the child*. New York: Basic Books.

Pierce, W. D., & Epling, W. F. (1994). Activity anorexia: An interplay between basic and applied behavior analysis. *The Behavior Analyst, 17*, 7–23.

Pillsbury, W. (1908). *Attention*. New York: Macmillan.

Pinaquy, S., Chabrol, H., Simon, C., Louvet, J. P., & Berbe, P. (2003). Emotional eating, alexithymia and binge-eating disorder in obese women. *Obesity Research, 11*, 195–201.

Pinsker, S. (1994). *The language instinct: How the mind creates language*. New York: Harper-Collins.

Pitman, R. K., & Orr, S. P. (1990). The black hold of trauma. *Biological Psychiatry, 27*, 469–471.

Pitman, R. K., Sanders, K. M., Zusman, R. M., Healy, A. R., Cheema, F., Lasko, N. B., Cahill, L., & Orr, S. P. (2002). Pilot study of secondary prevention of posttraumatic stress disorder with propranolol. *Biological Psychiatry, 51*, 189–192.

Plomin, R. (1990). *Nature and nurture: An introduction to human behavioral genetics*. Pacific Grove, CA: Brooks/Cole.

Plutchik, R., & Conte, H. R. (Eds.). (1997). *Circumplex models of personality and emotions*. Washington, DC: American Psychological Association.

Plutchik, R. (1958). Outlines of a new theory of emotions. *Transactions of the New York Academy of Sciences, 20*, 394–403.

Plutchik, R. (1980). *Emotion: A psychoevolutionary synthesis*. New York: Harper & Row.

Plutchik, R. (1997). The circumplex as a general model of the structure of emotions and personality. In R. Plutchik, & H. R. Conte (Eds.), *Circumplex models of personality and emotions* (pp. 17–45). Washington, DC: American Psychological Association.

Plutchik, R. (2001). The nature of emotions. *American Scientist, 89*, 344–350.

Plutchik, R. (2003). *Emotions and life: Perspectives from psychology, biology, and evolution*. Chapter 4: The language of emotions. Washington, DC: American Psychological Association. 61–90.

Polivy, J., & Herman, C. P. (2002). Causes of eating disorders. *Annual Review of Psychology, 53*, 187–213.

Polk, E., & Liss, M. (2007). Psychological characteristics of self-injurious behavior. *Personality and Individual Differences, 43*, 567–577.

Pollock, J. L. (1991). OSCAR: A general theory of rationality. In P. J. Cummins, & J. L. Pollock (Eds.), *Philosophy and AI: Essays at the interface* (pp. 189–213). Cambridge, MA: MIT Press.

Porrill, J., Dean, P., & Stone, J.V. (2004). Recurrent cerebellar architecture solves the motor-error problem. *Proceedings of the Royal Society, London, B, 271*, 789–796.

Porter, S., Yuille, J. C., & Lehman, D. R. (1999). The nature of real, implanted, and fabricated memories for emotional childhood events: Implications for the recovered memory debate. *Law and Human Behavior, 23*, 517–537.

Pos, A. E., Greenberg, L. S., Goldman, R. N., & Korman, L. M. (2003). Emotional processing during experiential treatment of depression. *Journal of Consulting and Clinical Psychology, 71*, 1007–1016.

Posner, M. I., & Boies, S. J. (1971). Components of attention. *Psychological Review, 78*, 391–408.

Posner, M. I., & Keele, S. W. (1968). On the genesis of abstract ideal. *Journal of Experimental Psychology*, 77, 353–363.

Power, M. J., Brewin, C. R., Stuessy, A., & Mahony, T. (1991). The emotional priming task: Results from a student population. *Cognitive Therapy and Research, 15*, 21–31.

Principe, G. F., Kanaya, T., Ceci, S. J., & Singh, M. (2006). Believing is seeing: How rumors can engender false memories in preschoolers. *Psychological Science, 17*, 243–248.

Prochaska, J. O., & DiClemente, C. C. (2005). The transtheoretical approach. In J. C. Norcross, & M. R. Goldfried (Eds.), *Handbook of psychotherapy integration*(2nd ed.) (pp. 147–171). New York: Oxford University Press.

Proctor, R. W., & Capaldi, E. J. (2001). Empirical evaluation and justification of methodologies in psychological science. *Psychological Bulletin, 127*, 759–772.

Pronin, E., Gilovitch, T., & Ross, L. (2004). Objectivity in the eye of the beholder: Divergent perceptions of bias in self versus others. *Psychological Review, 111*, 781–799.

Quian Quiroga, R. (2012). Concept cells: The building blocks of declarative memory functions. *Nature Reviews Neuroscience, 13*, 587–597.

Quian Quiroga, R., Reddy, L., Koch, C., & Fried, I. (2007). Decoding visual inputs from multiple neurons in the human temporal lobe. *Journal of Neurophysiology, 98*(4), 1997–2007.

Quian Quiroga, R., Kreiman, G., Koch, C., & Fried, I. (2008). Sparse but not "grandmother-cell" coding in the medial temporal lobe. *Trends in Cognitive Sciences, 12*(3), 87–91.

Quian Quiroga, R., Fried, I., & Koch, C. (2013). Brain cells for Grandmother. *Scientific American, 308*(2), 31–35.

Rachman, S. (1980). Emotional processing. *Behaviour Research and Therapy, 18*, 51–60.

Rachman, S. (1990). *Fear and courage.* New York: W. H. Freeman.

Raichle, M. E. (2009). A paradigm shift in functional brain imaging. *The Journal of Neuroscience, 29*(41), 12729–12734. http://dx.doi.org/10.1523/JNEUROSCI.4366-09.2009.

Raichle, M. E., & Snyder, A. Z. (2007). A default mode of brain function: A brief history of an evolving idea. *NeuroImage, 37*(4), 1083–1090.

Raichle, M. E., MacLeod, A. M., Snyder, A. Z., Powers, W. J., Gusnard, D. A., & Shulman, G. L. (2001). Inaugural article: A default mode of brain function. *Proceedings of the National Academy of Sciences of the United States of America (PNAS), 98*(2), 676–682.

Ramachandran, V. S. (2000). *Mirror neurons and imitation learning as the driving force behind "the great leap forward" in human evolution.* Retrieved August 25, 2006, from http://www.edge.org/documents/

Ramachandran, V. S., & Oberman, L. M. (2006). Broken mirrors: A theory of autism. *Scientific American, 295*(5), 62–69.

Ramachandran, V. S., & Ramachandran, D. R. (2008). Sensations referred to a patient's arm from another subjects intact arm: Perceptual correlates of mirror neurons. *Journal of Medical Hypotheses, 70*(6), 1233–1234. http://dx.doi.org/10.1016/j.mehy.2008.01.008.

Ramachandran, V. S., Rogers-Ramachandran, D., & Cobb, S. (1995). Touching the phantom limb. *Nature, 377*, 489–490.

Rankin, C. H., Abrams, T., Barry, R. J., Bhatnagar, S., Clayton, D. F., Colombo, J., Coppola, G., Geyer, M. A., Glanzman, D. L., Marsland, S., McSweeney, F. K., Wilson, D. A., Wu, C. F., & Thompson, R. F. (2009). Habituation revisited: An updated and revised description of the behavioral characteristics of habituation. *Neurobiology of Learning and Memory, 92*(2), 135–138.

Rapaport, D. (1959). The structure of psychoanalytic theory: A systematizing attempt. In S. Koch (Ed.). *Psychology: A study of a science: Vol. 1.* (pp. 55–183). New York: McGraw-Hill.

Raz, A., Shapiro, T., Fan, J., & Posner, M. I. (2002). Hypnotic suggestion and the modulation of Stroop interference. *Archives of General Psychiatry, 59*, 1155–1161.

Razran, G. H. S. (1939). Quantitative study of meaning by a conditioned salivary technique (semantic conditioning). *Science, 90*, 89–90.

Razran, G. H. S. (1940). Conditioned response changes in rating and appraising sociopolitical slogans. *Psychological Bulletin, 37*, 481.

Razran, G. H. S. (1949). Sentential and propositional generalizations of salivary conditioning to verbal stimuli. *Science, 109*, 447–448.

Read, S. J., & Miller, L. C. (1998). *Connectionist models of social reasoning and social behavior.* Mahwah, New Jersey: Lawrence Erlbaum.

Read, S. J., & Miller, L. C. (1994). Dissonance and balance in belief systems: The promise of parallel constraint satisfaction processes and connectionist modeling approaches. In R. C. Schank, & E. Langer (Eds.), *Beliefs, reasoning, and decision-making: Psychologic in honor of Bob Abelson* (pp. 209–235). Hillside, NJ: Lawrence Erlbaum.

Read, S. J., & Miller, L. C. (2002). Virtual personalities: A neural network model of personality. *Personality and Social Psychology Review, 6*, 357–369.

Read, S. J., & Monroe, B. M. (2009). Using connectionist networks to undersand neurobiological processes in social and personality psychology. In E. Harmon-Jones, & J. S. Beer (Eds.), *Methods in social neuroscience* (pp. 259–294). New York: Guilford.

Read, S. J., & Montoya, J. A. (1999). An autoassociative model of causal learning and causal reasoning. *Journal of Personality and Social Psychology, 76*, 728–742.

Read, S. J., Vanman, E. J., & Miller, L. C. (1997). Connectionism, parallel constraint satisfaction processes, and Gestalt principles: (Re) Introducing cognitive dynamics to social psychology. *Personality and Social Psychology Review, 1*, 26–53.

Read, S. J., Monroe, B. M., Brownstein, A. L., Yang, Y., Chopra, G., & Miller, L. C. (2010). A neural network model of the structure and dynamics of human personality. *Psychological Review, 117*, 61–92.

Reber, A. S. (1993). *Implicit Learning and Tacit Knowledge.* Oxford: University Press.

Redelmeier, D. A., & Tversky, A. (1996). On the belief that arthritis pain is related to the weather. *Proceedings of the National Academy of Sciences of the United States of America (PNAS), 93*(7), 2895–2896.

Reeves, A. G., & Roberts, D. W. (Eds.). (1995). *Epilepsy and the corpus callosum 2.* New York: Springer.

Reid, J. B., Patterson, G. R., & Snyder, J. (Eds.). (2002). *Antisocial behavior in children and adolescents: A developmental analysis and model for intervention.* Washington, DC: American Psychological Association.

Reisenzein, R. (1983). The Schachter theory of emotion: Two decades later. *Psychological Bulletin, 94*, 239–264.

Rescorla, R. A. (1987). A Pavlovian analysis of goal-directed behavior. *American Psychologist, 42*, 119–129.

Rescorla, R. A. (1988). Pavlovian conditioning: It's not what you think it is. *American Psychologist, 43*, 151–160.

Rescorla, R. A., & Wagner, A. R. (1972). A theory of Pavlovian conditioning: Variations in the effectiveness of reinforcement and nonreinforcement. In A. H Black, & W. F. Prokasy (Eds.), *Classical conditioning II: Current research and theory* (pp. 64–99). New York: Appleton-Century-Crofts.

Ressler, K. J., Rothbaum, B. O., Tannenbaum, L., Anderson, P., Graap, K., Zimand, E., Hodges, L., & Davis, M. (2004). Cognitive enhancers as adjuncts to psychotherapy: Use of D-Cycloserine in phobic individuals to facilitate extinction of fear. *Archives of General Psychiatry, 61*, 1136–1144.

Riess, B. F. (1940). Semantic conditioning involving the GSR. *Journal of Experimental Psychology, 36*, 238–240.

Riess, B. F. (1946). Genetic changes in semantic conditioning. *Journal of Experimental Psychology, 36*, 143–152.

Riley, W. T., Schumann, M. F., Forman-Hoffman, V. L., Mihm, P., Applegate, B. W., & Asif, O. (2007). Responses of practicing psychologists to a web site developed to promote empirically supported treatments. *Professional Psychology: Research and Practice, 38*, 44–53.

Rizzolatti, G., & Craighero, L. (2004). The mirror-neuron system. *Annual Review of Neuroscience, 27*, 169–192.

Rizzolatti, G., & Destro, M. F. (2007). Understanding actions and the intentions of others: The basic neural mechanism. *European Review, 15*(2), 209–222.

Rizzolatti, G., & Luppino, G. (2001). The cortical motor system. *Neuron, 31*(6), 889–901.

Rizzolatti, G., Fadiga, L., Fogassi, L., & Gallese, V. (1996). Premotor cortex and the recognition of motor actions. *Cognitive Brain Research, 3*, 131–141.

Robertson, S. S. (1985). Cyclic motor activity in the human fetus after midgestation. *Developmental Psychobiology, 18*, 411–419.

Robertson, S. S. (1987). Human cyclic motility: Fetal-newborn continuities and newborn state differences. *Developmental Psychobiology, 20*, 425–442.

Robinson, D. N. (1984). Psychobiology and the unconscious. In K. S. Bowers, & D. Meichenbaum (Eds.), *The unconscious reconsidered* (pp. 212–226). New York: Wiley.

Robinson, G. E., Grozinger, C. M., & Whitfield, C. W. (2005). Sociogenomics: Social life in molecular terms. *Nature Reviews Genetics, 6*, 257–270. http://dx.doi.org/10.1038/nrg1575.

Robinson, M. D., Watkins, E. R., & Harmon-Jones, E. (2013). *Handbook of cognition and emotion*. New York: Guilford.

Roediger, H. L., III, & McDermott, K. B. (1995). Creating false memories: Remembering words not presented in lists. *Journal of Experimental Psychology: Learning, Memory, & Cognition, 21*, 803–814.

Rogers, C. R. (1946). Significant aspects of client-centered therapy. *American Psychologist, 1*(10), 415–422.

Rogers, C. (1951). *Client-centered therapy: Its current practice, implications and theory*. Boston: Houghton Mifflin.

Rogerson, M. D., Gottlieb, M. C., Handlesman, M. M., Knapp, S., & Younggren, J. (2011). Nonrational processes in ethical decision making. *American Psychologist, 66*, 614–623.

Rogler, L. H., Malgady, R., & Tryon, W. W. (1992). Evaluation of mental health issues of memory in the Diagnostic Interview Schedule. *Journal of Nervous and Mental Disease, 180*, 215–222.

Rolls, E. T., & Treves, A. (1998). *Neural networks and brain function*. Oxford: Oxford University Press.

Rosen, G. M., & Davison, G. C. (2003). Psychology should list empirically supported principles of change (ESP's) and not credential trademarked therapies or other treatment packages. *Behavior Modification, 27*, 300–312.

Rosenberg, M. (1965). *Society and the adolescent self-image*. Princeton, New Jersey: Princeton University Press.

Rosenblum, L. D. (2013). A confederacy of senses. *Scientific American, 308*(1), 72–79.

Rosenthal, M. Z., Gratz, K. L., Kosson, D. S., Cheavens, J. S., Lejuez, C. W., & Lynch, T. R. (2008). Borderline personality disorder and emotional responding: A review of the research literature. *Clinical Psychology Review, 28*, 75–91.

Rosenzweig, M. R. (1996). Aspects of the search for neural mechanisms of memory. *Annual Review of Psychology, 47*, 1–32.

Rosenzweig, S. (1936). Some implicit common factors in diverse methods of psychotherapy. *American Journal of Orthopsychiatry*, *6*, 412–415.

Ross, H. E., & Young, L. J. (2009). Oxytocin and the neural mechanisms regulating social cognition and affiliative behavior. *Frontiers in Neuroendocrinology*, *30*(4), 534–547.

Ruckmick, C. A. (1921). A preliminary study of the emotions. *Psychological Monograph*, *30*(3), 30–35 (Whole No. 136).

Rumelhart, D. E., & McClelland, J. L. (1986). On learning the past tenses of English verbs. In J. L. McClelland, & D. E. Rumelhart (Eds.), *Parallel distributed processing: Explorations in the microstructure of cognition* (Vol. 2). (pp. 216–271). Cambridge, MA: MIT Press.

Rumelhart, D. E., McClelland, J. L., & the PDP Research Group (1986). *Parallel distributed processing: Explorations in the microstructure of cognition, Vol. 1: Foundations*. Cambridge, MA: MIT Press.

Russell, J. A. (1989). Measures of emotion. In R. Plutchik, & H. Kellerman (Eds.), *The measurement of emotions* (pp. 83–112). New York: Academic Press.

Ryan, R. M., & Deci, E. L. (2000). Self-determination theory and the facilitation of intrinsic motivation, social development, and well-being. *American Psychologist*, *55*, 68–78.

Ryan, R. M., & Deci, E. L. (2002). An overview of self determination theory: An organismic-dialectical perspective. In E. L. Deci, & R. M. Ryan (Eds.), *Handbook of self determination research* (pp. 3–36). Rochester, NY: University of Rochester Press.

Rychlak, J. F. (1968). *A philosophy of science for personality theory* (1st ed.). Boston: Houghton Mifflin Co.

Rychlak, J. F. (1981a). *A philosophy of science for personality theory* (2nd ed.). Malabar, FL: Robert E. Krieger.

Rychlak, J. F. (1981b). *Introduction to personality and psychotherapy: A theory-construction approach*. Boston: Houghton Mifflin Co.

Rychlak, J. F. (1988). Unification in psychology: My way! Our way! No way! *Contemporary Psychology*, *34*, 999–1001.

Rychlak, J. F. (1993). A suggested principle of complementarity for psychology: In theory, not method. *American Psychologist*, *48*, 933–942.

Sachs, O. (1985). *The man who mistook his wife for a hat*. London: Duckworth; New York: Summit Books.

Safer, D. L., & Chen, E.Y. (2011). Anorexia nervosa as a disorder of emotion dysregulation: Theory, evidence, and treatment implications. *Clinical Practice: Science and Practice*, *18*(3), 203–207.

Saffran, J. R., Aslin, R. N., & Newport, E. L. (1996). Statistical learning by 8-month-old infants. *Science*, *274* (13 December), 1926–1928.

Sale, A., Berardi, N., & Maffei, L. (2009). Enrich the environment to empower the brain. *Trends in Neurosciences*, *32*, 382–388.

Salzman, C. D., & Fusi, S. (2010). Emotion, cognition, and mental state representation in amygdale and prefrontal cortex. *Annual Review of Neuroscience*, *33*, 173–202.

Saunders, B. T., & Robinson, T. E. (2010). A cocaine cue acts as an incentive stimulus in some but not others: Implications for addiction. *Biological Psychiatry*, *67*, 730–736.

Sawyer, R. K. (2002). Emergence in psychology: Lessons from the history of non-reductionist science. *Human Development*, *45*, 2–28.

Saxe, R., & Kanwisher, N. (2003). People thinking about thinking people. The role of the temporo-parietal junction in "theory of mind". *NeuroImage*, *19*, 1835–1842.

Saxe, R., & Powell, L. (2006). It's the thought that counts: Specific brain regions for one component of Theory of Mind. *Psychological Science*, *17*, 692–699.

Saxena, S., Brody, A. L., Schwartz, J. M., & Baxter, L. R. (1998). Neuroimaging and frontal-subcortical circuitry in obsessive-compulsive disorder. *British Journal of Psychiatry Supplement*, *35*, 26–37.

Saxena, S., Gorbis, E., O'Neill, J., Baker, S. K., Mandelkern, M. A., Maidment, K. M., Chang, S., Salamon, N., Brody, A. L., Schwartz, J. M., & London, E. D. (2009). Rapid effects of brief intensive cognitive-behavioral therapy on brain glucose metabolism in obsessive-compulsive disorder. *Molecular Psychiatry*, *14*(2), 197–205.

Schachter, S. (1964). The interaction of cognitive and physiological determinants on emotional state. In L. Berkowitz (Ed.). *Advances in experimental social psychology: Vol. 1.* (pp. 49–80). New York: Academic Press.
Schachter, D. L. (1999). The seven sins of memory: Insights from psychology and cognitive neuroscience. *American Psychologist, 54*, 182–203.
Schachter, S., & Singer, J. E. (1962). Cognitive, social and physiological determinants of emotional state. *Psychological Review, 69*, 379–399.
Schaefer, E. S., & Plutchik, R. (1966). Interrelationships of emotions, traits, and diagnostic constructs. *Psychological Reports, 18*, 399–410.
Schatten, H. T., & Tryon, W. W. (2012). *Do individuals with Asperger's Syndrome also have alexithymia?* Manuscript under review.
Schatten, H. T., & Tryon, W. W. (2014). *Are individuals with Asperger's Syndrome also alexithymic?* (Manuscript submitted for publication).
Schlosberg, H. (1941). A scale for the judgment of facial expressions. *Journal of Experimental Psychology, 29*, 497–510.
Schlosberg, H. (1952). The description of facial expressions in terms of two dimensions. *Journal of Experimental Psychology, 44*(4), 229–237.
Schlosberg, H. (1954). Three dimensions of emotion. *Psychological Review, 61*, 81–88.
Schmajuk, N. (2010). *Computational models of conditioning.* Cambridge: Cambridge University Press.
Schmidt, F. (1992). What do data really mean? Research findings, meta-analysis, and cumulative knowledge in psychology. *American Psychologist, 47*, 1172–1181.
Schmidt, U., Jiwany, A., & Treasure, J. (1993). A controlled study of alexithymia in eating disorders. *Comprehensive Psychiatry, 34*, 54–58.
Schnabel, K., & Asendorpf, J. B. (2010). The self-concept: New insights from implicit measurement procedures. In B. Gawronski, & B. K. Payne (Eds.), *Handbook of implicit social cognition: Measurement, theory, and applications* (pp. 408–425). New York: Guilford.
Schneider, W., & Shiffrin, R. M. (1977). Controlled and automatic human information processing: I. Detection, search, and attention. *Psychological Review, 84*(1), 1–66.
Schoneberger, T. (2000). A departure from cognitivism: Implications of Chomsky's second revolution in linguistics. *The Analysis of Verbal Behavior, 17*, 57–73.
Schumann, C. M., Hamstra, J., Goodlin-Jones, B. L., Lotspeich, L. J., Kwon, H., Buonocore, M. H., Lammers, C. R., Reiss, A. L., & Amaral, D. G. (2004). The amygdala is enlarged in children but not adolescents with autism: the hippocampus is enlarged at all ages. *Journal of Neuroscience, 24*, 6392–6401.
Schwartz, G. E., & Beatty, J. (Eds.). (1977). *Biofeedback: theory and research.* NY: Academic Press.
Schwartz, J. M. (1998). Neuroanatomical aspects of cognitive-behavioural therapy response in obsessive-compulsive disorder. An evolving perspective on brain and behaviour. *British Journal of Psychiatry Supplement, 35*, 38–44.
Schweder, R. A., & Hoidt, J. (2002). The cultural psychology of the emotions: Ancient and new. In M. Lewis, & J. M. Haviland-Jones (Eds.), *Handbook of emotions* (pp. 397–414). New York: Guilford Press.
Scott, T. R. (1991). A personal view of the future of psychology departments. *American Psychologist, 46*, 975–976.
Seeman, T. E. (1996). Social ties and health: The benefits of social integration. *Annals of Epidemiology, 6*, 442–451.
Segalowitz, S. J. (1983). *Two sides of the brain: Brain lateralization explored.* Englewood Cliffs, N. J.: Prentice-Hall.
Segalowitz, S. J., & Bernstein, D. (1997). Neural networks and neuroscience: What are connectionist simulations good for? In D. M. Johnson, & C. E. Erneling (Eds.), *The future of the cognitive revolution* (pp. 209–216). New York: Oxford University Press.
Sejnowski, T. J., & Rosenberg, C. R. (1986). NETtalk: A parallel network that learns to read aloud. *The Johns Hopkins University Electrical Engineering and Computer Science Technical Report JHU/EECS-86/01*, 32.

Sejnowski, T. J., & Rosenberg, C. R. (1987). Parallel networks that learn to pronounce English text. *Complex Systems, 1*, 145–168.

Sekaquaptewa, D., Vargas, P., & von Hippel, W. (2010). A practical guide to paper-and-pencil implicit measures of attitudes. In B. Gawronski, & B. K. Payne (Eds.), *Handbook of implicit social cognition: Measurement, theory, and applications* (pp. 140–155). New York: Guilford.

Seligman, M. E. P., & Maier, S. F. (1967). Failure to escape traumatic shock. *Journal of Experimental Psychology, 74*, 1–9.

Seligman, M. E. P. (1970). On the generality of the laws of learning. *Psychological Review, 77*, 406–418.

Seligman, M. E. P. (1971). Phobias and preparedness. *Behavior Therapy, 2*, 307–321.

Seligman, M. E. P. (1995). *Helplessness: On depression, development, & death* (2nd ed.). San Francisco: Freeman.

Seligman, M. E. P., & Hager, J. L. (Eds.). (1972). *Biological boundaries of learning*. New York: Appleton-Century-Crofts.

Seligman, M., Railton, P., Baumeister, R., & Sripada, C. (2013). Navigating into the future or driven by the past: Prospection as an organizing principle of mind. *Perspectives on Psychological Science, 8*, 119–141.

Seung, H. S. (2003). Learning in spiking neural networks by reinforcement of stocastic synaptic transmission. *Neuron, 40*, 1063–1073.

Seung, S. (2012). *Connectome: How the brain's wiring makes us who we are*. Boston: Houghton Mifflin Harcourt.

Shaffer, R. (1978). *Language and insight*. New Haven: Yale University Press.

Shah, A. K., & Oppenheimer, D. M. (2008). Heuristics made easy: An effort-reduction framework. *Psychological Bulletin, 134*(2), 207–222.

Shannon, C. E. (1949). *The mathematical theory of information*. Urbana, Illinois: The University of Illinois Press.

Sharma, R. (2010). Carrying forward: Explicating Gendlin's experiential phenomenological philosophy and its influence on humanistic psychotherapy. *Journal of Humanistic Psychology, 50*, 1–23.

Shatz, C. J. (2009). MHC Class I: An unexpected role in neuronal plasticity. *Neuron, 64*(1), 40–45.

Shedler, J. (2010). The efficacy of psychodynamic therapy. *American Psychologist, 65*, 98–109.

Sherman, S. J., Cialdini, R. B., Schwartzman, D. E., & Reynolds, K. D. (1985). Imagining can heighten or lower the perceived likelihood of contracting a disease: The mediating effect of ease of imagery. *Personality & Social Psychology Bulletin, 11*, 118–127.

Sherrington, C. S. (1961). *Integrative action of the nervous system*. New Haven, CT: Yale University Press (Original work published 1906).

Shidlovski, D., & Hassin, R. R. (2011). When pooping babies become more appealing: The effects of nonconscious goal pursuit on experienced emotions. *Psychological Science, 22*(11), 1381–1385.

Shill, M. A., & Lumley, M. A. (2002). The Psychological Mindedness Scale: Factor structure, convergent validity and gender in a nonpsychiatric sample. *Psychology and Psychotherapy: Theory, Research and Practice, 75*, 131–150.

Shultz, T. R., & Lepper, M. R. (1996). Cognitive dissonance reduction as constraint satisfaction. *Psychological Review, 103*(2), 219–240.

Shultz, T. R., Leveille, E., & Lepper, M. R. (1999). Free choice and cognitive dissonance revisited: Choosing "Lesser Evils" versus "Greater Goods". *Personality and Social Psychology Bulletin, 25*, 40–48.

Siegle, G. J. (1999). A neural network model of attention biases in depression. In J. A. Reggia, E. Ruppin, & D. L. Glanzman (Eds.), *Disorders of brain behavior and cognition: The neurocomputational perspective* (pp. 415–441). NJ: Elsevier.

Siegle, G. J. (2001). Connectionist models of psychopathology: Crossroads of the cognitive and affective neuroscience of disorder. *Cognitive Processing, 2*, 455–486.

Sifneos, P. (1967). Clinical observations on some patients suffering from a variety of psychosomatic diseases. In *Proc. 7th European Conference on Psychosomatic Research*. Basel: Karger.
Sifneos, P. (1973). The prevalence of "alexithymic" characteristic mechanisms in psychosomatic patients. *Psychotherapy and Psychosomatics*, *21*, 133–136.
Sigelman, L., & Sigelman, C. (1984). Judgments of the Carter-Reagan debate: The eyes of beholders. *Public Opinion Quarterly*, *48*, 624–628.
Silberman, Y., Miikkulainen, R., & Bentin, S. (2001). Semantic effect on episodic associations. In J. D. Moore, & K. Stenning (Eds.), *Proceedings of the Twenty-Third Annual Conference of the Cognitive Science Society* (pp. 934–939). Mahwah, NJ: Erlbaum.
Silberman, Y., Miikkulainen, R., & Bentin, S. (2005). Associating unseen events: Semantically mediated formation of episodic associations. *Psychological Science*, *16*(2), 161–166.
Silva, A. J., Kogan, J. H., Frankland, P. W., & Kida, S. (1998). CREB and memory. *Annual Review of Neuroscience*, *21*, 127–148.
Silver, D. (1983). Psychotherapy of the characterologically difficult patient. *Canadian Journal of Psychiatry*, *28*, 513–521.
Silver, R., Boahen, K., Gillner, S., Kopell, S., & Olsen, K. L. (2007). Neurotech for neuroscience: Unifying concepts, organizing principles, and emerging tools. *The Journal of Neuroscience*, *27*(44), 11807–11819.
Simon, D., Pham, L. B., Le, Q. A., & Holyoak, K. J. (2001). The emergence of coherence over the course of decision making. *Journal of Experimental Psychology: Learning, Memory, and Cognition*, *27*, 1250–1260.
Simon, H. A. (1990). Invariants of human behavior. *Annual Review of Psychology*, *41*, 1–19.
Sinaceur, M., Heath, C., & Cole, S. (2005). Emotional and deliberative reactions to a public crisis: Mad Cow disease in France. *Psychological Science*, *16*(3), 247–254.
Sirigu, A., Daprati, E., Ciancia, S., Giraux, P., Nighoghossian, N., Posada, A., & Haggard, P. (2004). Altered awareness of voluntary action after damage to the parietal cortex. *Nature Neuroscience*, 7(1), 80–84.
Skeem, J. L., Polaschek, D. L. L., & Patrick, C. J. (2011). Psychopathic personality: Bridging the gap between scientific evidence and public policy. *Psychological Science in the Public Interest*, *12*, 95–162.
Skinner, B. F. (1938). *The behavior of organisms*. New York: Appleton-Century-Crofts.
Skinner, B. F. (1953). *Science and human behavior*. New York: Macmillan.
Skinner, B. F. (1957). *Verbal behavior*. New York: Appleton-Century-Cofts.
Skinner, B. F. (1966). The phylogeny and ontogeny of behavior. *Science*, *153*, 1205–1213.
Skinner, B. F. (1971). *Beyond freedom and dignity*. Indianapolis Indiana: Hackett Publishing Co.
Skinner, B. F. (1975a). The shaping of phylogenetic behavior. *The Journal of the Experimental Analysis of Behavior*, *24*, 117–120.
Skinner, B. F. (1975b). The steep and thorny way to a science of behavior. *American Psychologist*, *30*. 42–29.
Skinner, B. F. (1977). Why I am not a cognitive psychologist. *Behaviorism*, *5*, 1–10.
Skinner, B. F. (1981). Selection by consequences. *Science*, *213*, 501–504.
Skinner, B. F. (1984a). The evolution of behavior. *Journal of the Experimental Analysis of Behavior*, *41*, 217–221.
Skinner, B. F. (1984b). Selection by consequences. *The Behavioral and Brain Sciences*, 7, 477–510.
Skinner, B. F. (1989). The origins of cognitive thought. *American Psychologist*, *44*, 13–18.
Skinner, B. F., Solomon, H. C., Lindsley, O. R., & Richards, M. E. (1954). *Studies in behavior therapy*. Metropolitan State Hospital, Waltham: Massachusetts. Status Report II, May.
Skodol, A. E., Gunderson, J. G., Pfohl, B., Widiger, T. A., Livesley, W. J., & Siever, L. J. (2002). The borderline diagnosis I: Psychopathology, comorbidity, and personality structure. *Biological Psychiatry*, *51*, 936–950.
Slavich, G. M., & Cole, S.W. (in press). The emerging field of human social genomics. Clinical Psychological Science.

Slife, B. D., & Williams, R. N. (1997). Toward a theoretical psychology: Should a subdiscipline be formally recognized? *American Psychologist, 52*, 117–129.

Sloman, S. A. (1996). The empirical case for two systems of reasoning. *Psychological Bulletin, 119*, 3–22.

Smith, A. J. M., Kleijn, W. C., Trijsburg, R. W., Segaar, J. A., van der Staak, C. P. F., & Hutschemaekers, G. J. M. (2009). The psychological mindedness assessment procedure - Validation study of a Dutch version. Psychology and Psychotherapy: Theory. *Research and Practice, 82*, 185–197.

Smith, E. R. (1996). What do connectionism and social psychology offer each other? *Journal of Personality and Social Psychology, 70*, 893–912.

Smith, E. R. (1998). Mental representation and memory. In (4th ed.) D. T. Gilbert, S. T. Fiske, & G. Lindsey (Eds.), *Handbook of social psychology* (Vol. 2. pp. 391–445). New York: McGraw Hill.

Smolensky, P. (1988). On the proper treatment of connectionism. *Behavioral and Brain Sciences, 11*, 1–74.

Snyder, M., & Cantor, N. (1979). Testing hypotheses about other people: The use of historical knowledge. *Journal of Experimental Social Psychology, 15*, 330–342.

Sokolov, E. N. (1963). *Perception and the conditioned reflex*. In S. W. Waydenfold, & Trans. (Eds.). Oxford, England: Pergamon Press.

Soon, C. S., Brass, M., Heinz, H. J., & Haynes, J. D. (2008). Unconscious determinants of free decisions in the human brain. *Nature Neuroscience, 11*(5), 543–545.

Spearman, C. (1904). "General intelligence," objectively determined and measured. *American Journal of Psychology, 15*, 201–292.

Speed, J. (1996). Behavioral management of conversion disorder: Retrospective study. *Archives of Physical Medicine & Rehabilitation, 77*, 147–154.

Spek, V., Nyklícek, I., Cuijpers, P., & Pop, V. (2008). Alexithymia and cognitive behaviour therapy outcome för subthreshold depression. *Acta Psychiatrica Scandinavica, 118*, 164–167.

Spelke, E. S. (1994). Initial knowledge: Six suggestions. *Cognition, 50*, 431–445.

Spellman, B. A., Ullman, J. B., & Holyoak, K. J. (1993). A coherence model of cognitive consistency: Dynamics of attitude change during the Persian Gulf War. *Journal of Social Issues, 49*(4), 147–165.

Spence, J. T. (1987). Centrifugal versus centripetal tendencies in psychology: Will the center hold? *American Psychologist, 42*, 1052–1054.

Spencer, G. E., Syed, N. I., & Lukowiak, K. (1999). Neural changes after operant conditioning of the aerial respiratory behavior in Lymnaea stagnalis. *The Journal of Neuroscience, 9*, 1836–1843.

Spencer, H. (1855). *Principles of psychology*. London: Longman, Brown, Green, and Longmans.

Spencer, H. (1870). *Principles of psychology* (2nd ed.). London: Williams and Norgate.

Spencer, H. (1910). *Works: Principles of psychology*. New York: D. Appleton and Company.

Sperry, R. W. (1961). Cerebral organization of behavior. *Science, 133*, 1749–1757.

Sperry, R. W. (1968). Hemisphere deconnection and unity in conscious awareness. *American Psychologist, 23*, 723–733.

Sperry, R. W. (1969). A modified concept of consciousness. *Psychological Review, 76*, 532–536.

Spiegler, M. D., & Guevremont, D. C. (1993). *Contemporary behavior therapy* (2nd ed.). Pacific Grove, CA: Brooks/Cole Publishing Co.

Spitz, R. A. (1946). Anaclitic depression: An inquiry into the genesis of psychotic conditions in early childhood. *The Psychoanalytic Study of the Child, 2*, 313–342.

Spitzer, M. (1999). *The mind within the net: Models of learning, thinking, and acting*. Cambridge, MA: The MIT Press.

Sporns, O. (2011). *Networks of the brain*. Cambridge, MA: Massachusetts Institute of Technology Press.

Springer, S. P., & Deutsch, G. (1981). *Left brain, right brain.* San Francisco, CA: Freeman.

Spunt, R. P., & Lieberman, M. D. (2013). The busy social brain: Evidence for automaticity and control in the neural systems supporting social cognition and action understanding. *Psychological Science, 24*(1), 80–86.

Squire, L. R., Berg, D., Bloom, F. E., du Lac, S., Ghosh, A., & Spitzer, N. C. (2008). *Fundamental neuroscience* (3rd ed.). New York: Elsevier.

Squire, L. R., Knowlton, B., & Musen, G. (1993). The structure and organization of memory. *Annual Review of Psychology, 44,* 453–495.

Sripada, C., Railton, P., Baumeister, R. F., & Seligman, M. E. P. (2013). Reply to comments. *Perspectives on Psychological Science, 8*(2), 151–154.

Staats, A. W. (1968). *Learning, Language and Cognition.* New York: Holt.

Staats, A. W. (1975). *Social Behaviorism.* Homewood, Illinois: Dorsey Press.

Staats, C. K., & Staats, A. W. (1957). Meaning established by classical conditioning. *Journal of Experimental Psychology, 54,* 74–80.

Staats, A. W. (1983). *Psychology's crisis of disunity: Philosophy and method for a unified science.* New York: Praeger Publishers.

Staats, A. W. (1991). Unified positivism and unification psychology: Fad or new field? *American Psychologist, 46,* 899–912.

Staats, A. W. (1993). Unifying psychology requires new infrastructure, theory, method, and a research agenda. *Review of General Psychology, 3,* 3–13.

Staats, A. W. (2012). *The marvelous learning animal: What makes human nature unique.* Amherst, NY: Prometheus Books.

Staats, A. W., & Staats, C. K. (1958). Attitudes established by classical conditioning. *Journal of Abnormal and Social Psychology, 57,* 37–40.

Staats, A. W., Staats, C. K., & Biggs, D. A. (1958). Meaning of verbal stimuli changed by conditioning. *American Journal of Psychology, 51,* 187–192.

Staats, A. W., Staats, C. K., Heard, W. G., & Nims, L. P. (1959). Replication report: Meaning established by classical conditioning. *Journal of Experimental Psychology, 57,* 64.

Steele, C. M., & Southwick, L. (1985). Alcohol and social behavior I: The psychology of drunken excess. *Journal of Personality and Social Psychology, 48*(1), 18–34.

Stein, M. B., Kerridge, C., Dimsdale, J. E., & Hoyt, D. B. (2007). Pharmacotherapy to prevent PTSD: Results from a randomized controlled proof-of-concept trial in physically injured patients. *Journal of Traumatic Stress, 20*(6), 923–932.

Steiner, J. E. (1973). The gustofacial response: Observation on normal and anencephalic newborn infants. *Symposium on Oral Sensation and Perception, 4,* 254–278.

Sternberg, D. A., & McClelland, J. L. (2011). Two mechanisms of human contingency learning. *Psychological Science, 23*(11), 59–68.

Sternberg, R. J., & Grigorenko, E. L. (2001). Unified psychology. *American Psychologist, 56,* 1069–1079.

Stewart-Williams, S., & Podd, J. (2004). The placebo effect: Dissolving the expectancy versus conditioning debate. *Psychological Bulletin, 130,* 324–340.

Stinson, C. H., & Palmer, S. E. (1991). Parallel distributed processing models of person, schemas, and pathologies. In M. J. Horowitz (Ed.), *Person schemas and maladaptive interpersonal patterns* (pp. 334–378). Chicago: University of Chicago Press.

Stockhorst, U., Klosterhalfen, S., Klosterhalfen, W., Winkelmann, & Steingrueber (1993). Anticipatory nausea in cancer patients receiving chemotherapy: Classical conditioning etiology and therapeutical implications. *Integrative Physiological and Behavioral Science, 28,* 177–181.

Storbeck, J., & Clore, G. L. (2007). On the interdependence of cognition and emotion. *Cognition and Emotion, 21,* 1212–1237.

Strack, F., & Deutsch, R. (2004). Reflective and impulsive determinants of social behavior. *Personality and Social Psychology Review, 8,* 220–247.

Stricker, G. (2010). *Psychotherapy integration*. Washington, DC: American Psychological Association.

Stricker, G. (2013). On building walls. *Clinical Psychology: Science and Practice, 19*(4), 381–384.

Stricker, G., & Gold, J. R. (1993). *Comprehensive handbook of psychotherapy integration*. New York: Plenum.

Stroop, J. R. (1935). Studies of interference in serial verbal reactions. *Journal of Experimental Psychology, 18*, 643–662.

Strupp, H. H. (1963). The outcome problem in psychotherapy revisited. *Psychotherapy, 50*(1), 3–11. http://dx.doi.org/10.1037/h0094491.

Sullivan, H. S. (1953). *The interpersonal theory of psychiatry*. New York: Norton.

Summers, R. F., & Barber, J. P. (2010). *Psychodynamic therapy: A guide to evidence-based practice*. New York: The Guilford Press.

Sun, R. (Ed.). (2008). *The Cambridge handbook of computational psychology*. Cambridge: Cambridge University Press.

Sunstein, C. R. (2005). Moral heuristics. *Behavioral and Brain Sciences, 28*(4), 531–542.

Suthana, N., & Fried, I. (2012). Percepts to recollections. Insights from single neuron recordings in the human brain. *Trends in Cognitive Sciences, 16*(8), 427–436.

Sutton, R. S., & Barto, A. G. (1981). Toward a modern theory of adaptive networks: Expectation and prediction. *Psychological Review, 88*, 135–170.

Taber, C. S., & Lodge, M. (2006). Motivated skepticism in the evaluation of political beliefs. *American Journal of Political Science, 50*(3), 755–769.

Taber, C., Lodge, M., & Glather, J. (2001). The Motivated Construction of Political Judgments. In J. Kuklinski (Ed.), *Citizens and Politics: Perspectives from Political Psychology* (pp. 198–226). New York: Cambridge University Press.

Taghavi, M. R., Neshat-Doost, H. T., Moradi, A. R., Yule, W., & Dalgleish, T. (1999). Biases in visual attention in children and adolescents with clinical anxiety and mixed anxiety depression. *Journal of Abnormal Child Psychology, 27*, 215–223.

Taghavi, M. R., Moradi, A. R., Neshat-Doost, H. T., Yule, W., & Dalgleish, T. (2000). Interpretation of ambiguous emotional information in clinically anxious children and adolescents. *Cognition and Emotion, 14*, 809–822.

Tallis, F. (2002). *Hidden minds: A history of the unconscious*. New York: Arcade Publishing.

Tamir, M. (2009). What do people want to feel and why? Pleasure and utility in emotion regulation. *Current Directions in Psychological Science, 18*, 101–105.

Tamir, M., Chiu, C. Y., & Gross, J. J. (2007). Business or pleasure? Utilitarian versus hedonic consideration in emotion regulation. *Emotion*, 7, 546–554.

Tang, T. Z., & DeRubeis, R. J. (1999). Sudden gains and critical sessions in cognitive-behavioral therapy for depression. *Journal of Consulting and Clinical Psychology, 67*(6), 894–904.

Tang, Y. P., Shimizu, E., Duba, G. R., Hampon, C., Kerchner, G. A., Zhuo, M., Liu, G., & Tsien, J. Z. (1999). Genetic enhancement of learning and memory in mice. *Nature, 401*, 63–69.

Tani, P., Lindberg, N., Joukamaa, M., Nieminen-von Wendt, T., von Wendt, L., Appelberg, B., Rimón, R., & Porkka-Heiskanen, T. (2004). Asperger syndrome, alexithymia and perception of sleep. *Neuropsychobiology, 49*, 64–70.

Tashiro, T., & Mortensen, L. (2006). Translational research: How social psychology can improve psychotherapy. *American Psychologist, 61*, 959–966.

Tataryn, D. J., Nadel, L., & Jacobs, W. J. (1989). Cognitive therapy and cognitive science. In A. Freeman, K. M. Simon, & L. E. Beutler (Eds.), *Comprehensive handbook of cognitive therapy* (pp. 83–98). New York: Plenum Press.

Taylor, G. J. (1984). Alexithymia: Concept, measurement and implications for treatment. *American Journal of Psychiatry, 141*, 725–732.

Taylor, G. J., & Taylor, H. L. (1997). Alexithymia. In M. McCallum, & W. E. Piper (Eds.), *Psychological mindedness: A contemporary understanding* (pp. 77–104). Mahwah, New Jersey: Lawrence Erlbaum.

Taylor, G. J., Ryan, D., & Bagby, R. M. (1986). Toward the development of a new self-report alexithymia scale. *Psychotherapy and Psychosomatics*, *44*, 191–199.

Taylor, G. J., Bagby, M., & Parker, J. (1989). Psychological-mindedness and the alexithymia construct. *British Journal of Psychiatry*, *154*, 731–732.

Taylor, G. J., Parker, J. D., Bagby, R. M., & Bourke, M. P. (1996). Relationships between alexithymia and psychological characteristics associated with eating disorders. *Journal of Psychosomatic Research*, *41*, 561–568.

Teachman, B. A., Cody, M. W., & Clerkin, E. M. (2010). Clinical applications of implicit social cognition theories and methods. In B. Gawronski, & B. K. Payne (Eds.), *Handbook of implicit social cognition: Measurement, theory, and applications* (pp. 489–521). New York: Guilford.

Teasdale, J. D., & Fogarty, S. J. (1979). Differential effects of induced mood on retrieval of pleasant and unpleasant events from episodic memory. *Journal of Abnormal Psychology*, *88*, 248–257.

Tee, J., & Kazantzis, N. (2011). Collaborative empiricism in cognitive therapy: A definition and theory for the relationship construct. *Clinical Psychology: Science and Practice*, *18*, 47–61.

Teige-Mocigemba, S., Klauer, K. C., & Sherman, J. W. (2010). A practical guide to implicit association tests and related tasks. In B. Gawronski, & B. K. Payne (Eds.), *Handbook of implicit social cognition: Measurement, theory, and applications* (pp. 117–139). New York: Guilford.

Teo, T. (2012). Psychology is still a problematic science and the public knows it. *American Psychologist*, *67*(9), 807–808.

Terr, L. C. (1991). Childhood traumas: An outline and overview. *American Journal of Psychiatry*, *148*, 10–20.

Tesauro, G. (1990). Neural models of classical conditioning: A theoretical viewpoint. In S. J. Hannson, & C. R. Olson (Eds.), *Connectionist modeling and brain function: The developing interface* (pp. 74–104). Cambridge, MA: The MIT Press.

Thagard, P. (1989). Explanatory coherence. *Behavioral and Brain Sciences*, *12*, 435–502.

Thagard, P. (2000). *Coherence in thought and action*. Cambridge, MA: MIT Press.

Thagard, P. (2006). Evaluating explanations in law, science, and everyday life. *Current Directions in Psychological Science*, *15*, 141–145.

Theoret, H., Halligan, E., Kobayashi, M., Fregni, F., Tager-Flusberg, H., & Pascual-Leone, A. (2005). Impaired motor facilitation during action observation in individuals with autism spectrum disorder. *Current Biology: CB*, *15*(3), R84–R85.

Thoma, N. C., McKay, D., Gerber, A. J., Milrod, B. L., Edwards, A. R., & Kocsis, J. H. (2012). A quality based review of randomized controlled trials of cognitive behavioral therapy for depression: An assessment and metaregression. *American Journal of Psychiatry*, *169*(1), 22–30.

Thomas, M. S. C., & McClelland, J. L. (2008). Connectionist models of cognition. In R. Sun (Ed.), *The Cambridge handbook of computational psychology*. New York: Cambridge University Press.

Thompson, R. F., & Spencer, W. A. (1966). Habituation: A model phenomenon for the study of neuronal substrates of behavior. *Psychological Bulletin*, *73*, 16–43.

Thornton, E. M. (1984). *The Freudian Fallacy: An alternative view of Freudian theory*. Garden City, NY: Doubleday & Co.

Tononi, G., & Cirelli, C. (2013). Perchance to prune. *Scientific American*, *309*(2), 34–39.

Toulmin, S. (1987). On not overunifying psychology: A response to Kranz. *New Ideas in Psychology*, *5*, 351–353.

Troop, N. A., Schmidt, U. H., & Treasure, J. L. (1995). Feelings and fantasy in eating disorders: A factor analysis of the Toronto Alexithymia Scale. *International Journal of Eating Disorders, 18*(2), 151–157.

Trudeau, K., & Reich, R. (1995). Correlates of psychological mindedness. *Personality and Individual Differences, 19*, 699–704.

Tryon, W. W. (1976a). A system of behavioral diagnosis. *Professional Psychology, 7*, 495–506.

Tryon, W. W. (1976b). Models of behavior disorder. A formal analysis based on Woods's taxonomy of instrumental conditioning. *American Psychologist, 31*, 509–518.

Tryon, W. W. (1978). An operant explanation of Mowrer's neurotic paradox. *Behaviorism, 6*, 203–211.

Tryon, W. W. (1986). The convergence of Cognitive Behaviorism and Ego-Psychology. *Theoretical and Philosophical Psychology, 6*, 90–96.

Tryon, W. W. (1990). Why Paradigmatic Behaviorism should be retitled Psychological Behaviorism. *The Behavior Therapist, 13*, 127–128.

Tryon, W. W. (1993a). Neural Networks: I. Theoretical unification through connectionism. *Clinical Psychology Review, 13*, 341–352. http://dx.doi.org/10.1016/0272-7358(93)90017-G.

Tryon, W. W. (1993b). Neural Networks: II. Unified learning theory and behavioral psychotherapy. *Clinical Psychology Review, 13*, 353–371.

Tryon, W. W. (1994). Synthesis not complementarity. *American Psychologist, 49*, 892–893.

Tryon, W. W. (1995). Synthesizing animal and human behavior research via neural network learning theory. *Journal of Behaviour Therapy and Experimental Psychiatry, 26*, 303–312.

Tryon, W. W. (1995a). Neural networks for behavior therapists: What they are and why they are important. *Behavior Therapy, 26*, 295–318. http://dx.doi.org/10.1016/S0005-7894(05)80107-8.

Tryon, W. W. (1995b). Resolving the cognitive behavioral controversy. *The Behavior Therapist, 18*, 83–86.

Tryon, W. W. (1995c). Resolving the cognitive behavioral controversy. *The Behavior Therapist, 18*, 83–86.

Tryon, W. W. (1995d). Synthesizing psychological schisms through connectionism. In A. Gilgen, & F. Abraham (Eds.), *Chaos theory in psychology* (pp. 247–263). Westport, CT: Praeger.

Tryon, W. W. (1996a). Observing contingencies: Taxonomy and methods. *Clinical Psychology Review, 16*, 215–230.

Tryon, W. W. (1996b). Yes – Neural network learning theory can resolve the behavioral-cognitive controversy. *The Behavior Therapist, 19*(70), 72–73.

Tryon, W. W. (1998). A neural network explanation of posttraumatic stress disorder. *Journal of Anxiety Disorders, 12*, 373–385.

Tryon, W. W. (1999). A bidirectional associative memory explanation of posttraumatic stress disorder. *Clinical Psychology Review, 19*, 789–818.

Tryon, W. W. (2000a). Behavior therapy as applied learning theory. *The Behavior Therapist, 23*, 131–134.

Tryon, W. W. (2000b). Neural network learning theory integrates behavior therapy and behavior genetics. *The Behavior Therapist, 23*, 3–21.

Tryon, W. W. (2001). Evaluating statistical difference, equivalence, and indeterminacy using inferential confidence intervals: An integrated alternative method of conducting null hypothesis statistical tests. *Psychological Methods, 6*, 371–386.

Tryon, G. S. (2002). *Counseling based on process research: Applying what we know*. Boston, MA: Allyn & Bacon.

Tryon, W. W. (2002a). Contributions of connectionism to postmodern psychology. *American Psychologist, 57*, 455–456.

Tryon, W. W. (2002b). Network models contribute to cognitive and social neuroscience. *American Psychologist, 57*, 728.

Tryon, W. W. (2002c). Neural network learning theory: Unifying radical behaviorism and cognitive neuroscience. *The Behavior Therapist, 25*, 53–57.

Tryon, W. W. (2005). Possible mechanisms for why desensitization and exposure therapy work. *Clinical Psychology Review, 25*, 67–95.

Tryon, W. W. (2008a). History and theoretical foundations. In M. Hersen, & A. M. Gross (Eds.), *Adults Handbook of clinical psychology: Vol 1.* (pp. 3–37). New York: John Wiley & Sons.

Tryon, W. W. (2008b). Whatever happened to symptom substitution. *Clinical Psychology Review, 28*, 963–968.

Tryon, W. W. (2009a). Cognitive processes in cognitive and pharmacological therapies. *Cognitive Therapy and Research, 33*, 570–584.

Tryon, W. W. (2009b). Darwin's eclipse: Function vs. mechanism. *American Psychologist, 64*, 622–623.

Tryon, W. W. (2009c). Missing mechanisms information. *American Psychologist, 64*, 273–274.

Tryon, W. W. (2009d). Sensitivity of parent reports in the MTA. *Journal of the American Academy of Child and Adolescent Psychiatry, 48*, 1124.

Tryon, W. W. (2010a). Learning as core of psychological science and clinical practice. *The Behavior Therapist, 33*, 10–11.

Tryon, W. W. (2010b). Professional identity based on learning. *The Behavior Therapist, 33*, 9.

Tryon, W. W. (2012). A connectionist network approach to psychological science: Core and corollary principles. *Review of General Psychology, 16*(3), 305–317.

Tryon, W. W. (2013). *Comprehensive clinical practice: Unifying the Big Five clinical orientations.* Manuscript submitted for publication.

Tryon, W. W., & Briones, R. G. (1985). Higher-order semantic counterconditioning of Filipino women's evaluations of heterosexual behaviors. *Journal of Behavior Therapy and Experimental Psychiatry, 16*, 125–131.

Tryon, W. W., & Cicero (1989). Classical conditioning of meaning – I. A replication and higher-order extension. *Journal of Behavior Therapy and Experimental Psychiatry, 20*, 137–142.

Tryon, W. W., & Lewis, C. (2008). An inferential confidence interval method of establishing statistical equivalence that corrects Tryon's (2001) reduction factor. *Psychological Methods, 13*, 272–277.

Tryon, W. W., & McKay, D. (2009). Memory modification as an outcome variable in anxiety disorder treatment. *Journal of Anxiety Disorders, 23*, 546–556.

Tryon, W. W., & Misurell, J. R. (2008). Dissonance induction and reduction: A possible principle and connectionist mechanism for why therapies are effective. *Clinical Psychology Review, 28*, 1297–1309.

Tryon, W. W., & Tryon, G. S. (2011). No ownership of common factors. *American Psychologist, 66*, 151–152. http://dx.doi.org/10.1037/a0021056.

Tsai, G. E., Falk, W. E., Gunther, J., & Coyle, J. T. (1999). Improved cognition in Alzheimer's Disease with short-term D-Cycloserine Treatment. *The American Journal of Psychiatry, 156*, 467–469.

Tsankova, N., Renthal, W., Kumar, A., & Nestler, E. J. (2007). Epigenetic regulation in psychiatric disorders. *Nature Reviews Neuroscience, 8*, 355–367.

Tsien, J. Z. (2000). Building a brainier mouse. *Scientific American, 282*, 62–68.

Turk, C. L., Heimberg, R. G., Luterek, J. A., Mennin, D. S., & Fresco, D. M. (2005). Emotion dysregulation in generalized anxiety disorder: A comparison with social anxiety disorder. *Cognitive Therapy and Research, 29*, 89–106.

Turkle, S. (1988). Artificial intelligenceand psychoanalysis: A new alliance? *Daedalus, 117*, 213–240.

Tversky, A., & Kahneman, D. (1974). Judgment under uncertainty: Heuristics and biases. *Science, 185*, 1124–1130.

Umiltà, C. (2001). Mechanisms of attention. In B. Rapp, & B. Rapp (Eds.), *The handbook of cognitive neuropsychology: What deficits reveal about the human mind* (pp. 135–158). New York, NY: Psychology Press. Retrieved from http://search.-ebscohost.com/login.aspx?direct=true&db=psyh&AN=2001-16360-006&site=ehost-live.

Uttal, W. R. (2001). *The new phrenology: The limits of localizing cognitive processes in the brain.* Cambridge, MA: MIT Press.

Vaiva, G., Ducrocq, F., Jezequel, K., Averland, B., Lestavel, P., Brunet, A., & Marmar, C. R. (2003). Immediate treatment with propranolol decreases posttraumatic stress disorder two months after trauma. *Biological Psychiatry*, *54*, 947–949.

Valentino, N. A., Hutchings, V. L., Banks, A. J., & Davis, A. K. (2008). Is a worried citizen a good citizen? Emotions, political information seeking, and learning via the Internet. *Political Psychology*, *29*, 247–273.

Van Egeren, L. F. (1971). Psychophysiological aspects of systematic desensitization: Some outstanding issues. *Behaviour Research and Therapy*, *9*, 65–77.

Van Egeren, L. F., Feather, B. W., & Hein, P. L. (1971). Desensitization of phobias: Some psychophysiological propositions. *Psychophysiology*, *8*, 213–228.

Van Opstal, F., de Lange, F. P., & Dehaene, S. (2011). Rapid parallel semantic processing of numbers without awareness. *Cognition*, *120*, 136–147.

Van Oudenhove, L., & Cuypers, S. E. (2010). The philosophical "mind-body problem" and its relevance for the relationship between psychiatry and the neuroscience. *Perspectives in Biology and Medicine*, *53*(4), 545–557.

Van Overwalle, F. (2007). *Social connectionism: A reader and handbook for simulations.* New York: Psychology Press.

Van Overwalle, F. (2011). Connectionist simulation as a tool for understanding social cognition and neuroscience. In K. C. Klauer, A. Voss, & C. Stahl (Eds.), *Cognitive methods in social psychology* (pp. 391–419). New York: Guilford.

Van Overwalle, F., & Baetens, K. (2009). Understanding others' actions and goals by mirror and mentalizing systems: A meta-analysis. *NeuroImage*, *48*, 564–584.

Van Overwalle, F., & Jordan, K. (2002). An adaptive connectionist model of cognitive dissonance. *Personality and Social Psychology Review*, *6*, 204–231.

Van Praag, H., Kempermann, G., & Gage, F. H. (2000). Neural consequences of environmental enrichment. *Nature Reviews Neurosciences*, *1*, 191–198. http://dx.doi.org/10.1038/35044558.

van Strien, T., & Ouwens, M. A. (2007). Effects of distress, alexithymia and impulsivity on eating. *Eating Behaviors*, *8*, 251–257. http://dx.doi.org/10.1016/j.eatbeh.2006.06.004.

Vasey, M. W., Daleiden, E. L., Williams, L. L., & Brown, L. M. (1995). Biased attention in childhood anxiety disorders: A preliminary study. *Journal of Abnormal Child Psychology*, *23*, 267–279.

Vasey, M. W., El-Hag, N., & Daleiden, E. L. (1996). Anxiety and the processing of emotionally threatening stimuli: Distinctive patterns of selective attention among high- and low-test anxious children. *Child Development*, *67*, 1173–1185.

Vedantam, S. (2010). *The hidden brain: How our unconscious minds elect presidents, control markets, wage wars, and save our lives.* New York: Spiegel & Grau.

Villalobos, M. E., Mizuno, A., Dahl, B. C., Kemmotsu, N., & Muller, R. A. (2005). Reduced functional connectivity between V1 and inferior frontal cortex associated with visuomotor performance in autism. *NeuroImage*, *25*(3), 916–925.

Viney, W. (1989). The Cyclops and the twelve-eyed toad: William James and the unity-disunity problem in psychology. *American Psychologist*, *44*, 1261–1265.

Viney, W. (1996). Disunity in psychology and other sciences: The network or the block universe? *The Journal of Mind and Behavior*, *17*, 31–44.

Volk, S. (2013). In defense of free will. *DiscoverMagazine*, pp. 52–57. November.

Voss, J. L., & Paller, K. A. (2006). Fluent conceptual processing and explicit memory for faces are electrophysiologically distinct. *Journal of Neuroscience, 26*, 926–933.

Vul, E., Harris, C., Winkielman, P., & Pashler, H. (2009). Puzzlingly high correlations in fMRI studies of emotion, personality, and social cognition. *Perspectives on Psychological Science, 4*, 274–290.

Vyazovskiy, V.V., Olcese, U., Hanlon, E. C., Nir, Y., Cirelli, C., & Tononi, G. (2011). Local sleep in awake rats. *Nature, 472*, 443–447.

Wachtel, P. L. (1977). *Psychoanalysis and behavior therapy: Toward an integration*. New York: Basic Books.

Wachtel, P. L. (1997). *Psychoanalysis, behavior therapy, and the representational world*. Washington, DC: American Psychological Association.

Wagner, T. D., Rilling, J. K., Smith, E. E., Sokolik, A., Casey, K. L. ., Davidson, R. J., Kosslyn, S. M., Rose, R. M., & Cohen, J. D. (2004). Placebo-induced changes in fMRI in the anticipation and experience of pain. *Science, 303*, 1162–1167.

Waiter, G. D., Williams, J. H., Murray, A. D., Gilchrist, A., Perrett, D. I., & Whiten, A. (2005). Structural white matter deficits in high-functioning individuals with autistic spectrum disorder: A voxel-based investigation. *NeuroImage, 24*(2), 455–461.

Waller, N. G., & Meehl, P. E. (1998). *Multivariate taxometric procedures: Distinguishing types from continua*. New York: Sage.

Walsh, B. T., Seidman, S. N., Sysko, R., & Gould, M. (2002). Placebo response in studies of major depression: Variable, substantial, and growing. *Journal of the American Medical Association, 287*, 1840–1847.

Wampold, B. E. (2001). *The great psychotherapy debate: Models, methods, and findings*. Mahwah, NJ: Lawrence Erlbaum.

Wargo, E. (2012). The inner workings of decision making. *Association for Psychological Science Observer, 25*, 12–18.

Waters, W. F., McDonald, D. G., & Koresko, R. L. (1972). Psychophysiological responses during analogue systematic desensitization and non-relaxation control procedures. *Behaviour Research and Therapy, 10*, 381–393.

Watkins, M. J. (1984). Models as toothbrushes. *Behavioral & Brain Sciences*, 7, 86.

Watson, D., Clark, L. A., & Tellegen, A. (1988). Development and validation of brief measures of positive and negative affect: The PANAS scales. *Journal of Personality and Social Psychology, 54*, 1063–1070.

Watson, J. B. (1919). *Psychology from the standpoint of a behaviorist*. Philadelphia: Lippincott.

Watson, J. B. (1924). *Psychology from the standpoint of a behaviorist* (2nd ed.). Philadelphia: Lippincott.

Watson, J. B. (1929). *Psychology from the standpoint of a behaviorist* (3rd ed.). Philadelphia: Lippincott.

Watson, J. C., Gordon, L. B., Stermac, L., Kalogerakos, F., & Steckley, P. (2003). Comparing the effectiveness of process-experiential with cognitive-behavioral psychotherapy in the treatment of depression. *Journal of Consulting and Clinical Psychology*, *71*, 773–781.

Watson, J. M., Bunting, M. F., Poole, B. J., & Conway, A. R. A. (2005). Individual differences in susceptibility to false memory in the Deese-Roediger-McDermott paradigm. *Journal of Experimental Psychology: Learning, Memory, and Cognition, 31*, 76–85.

Watts, F. N., McKenna, F. P., Sharrock, R., & Trezise, L. (1986). Colour naming of phobia elated words. *British Journal of Psychology*, 77, 97–108.

Watts, S. E., & Weems, C. F. (2006). Associations among selective attention, memory bias, cognitive errors and symptoms of anxiety in youth. *Journal of Abnormal Child Psychology, 34*, 841–852.

Waydo, S. (2008). *Explicit object representation by sparse neural codes. Doctoral Dissertation*. California Institute of Technology.

Waydo, S., Kraskov, A., Quian Quiroga, R., Fried, I., & Koch, C. (2006). Sparse representation in the human medial temporal lobe. *Journal of Neuroscience, 26*(40), 10232–10234.

Weaver, I. C. G., Meaney, M. J., & Szyf, M. (2006). Maternal care effects on the hippocampal transcriptome and anxiety-mediated behaviors in the offspring that are reversible in adulthood. *Proceedings of the National Academy of Sciences*, *103*(9), 3480–3485.

Weaver, I. C. G., D'Alessio, A. C., Brown, S. E., Hellstrom, I. C., Dymov, S., Sharma, S., Szyf, M., & Meaney, M. J. (2007). The transcription factor nerve growth factor-inducible protein A mediates epigenetic programming: Altering epigenetic marks by immediate-early genes. *Journal of Neuroscience*, *27*(7), 1756–1768.

Webb, C. A., DeRubeis, R. J., & Barber, J. P. (2010). Therapist adherence/competence and treatment outcome: A meta-analytic review. *Journal of Consulting and Clinical Psychology*, *78*(2), 200–211.

Weder, N., & Kaufman, J. (2010). Critical periods revisited: Implications for intervention with traumatized children. *Journal of the American Academy of Child & Adolescent Psychiatry*, *50*, 1087–1089.

Wegner, D. M. (2003). The mind's best trick: How we experience conscious will. *Trends in Cognitive Sciences*, *7*(2), 65–69.

Wegner, D. M. (2005). Who is the controller of controlled processes? In R. Hassin, J. S. Uleman, & J. A. Bargh (Eds.), *The new unconscious* (pp. 19–36). New York: Oxford University Press.

Weinberger, J. (1993). Common factors in psychotherapy. In G. Stricker, & J. R. Gold (Eds.), *Comprehensive handbook of psychotherapy integration* (pp. 43–56). New York: Plenum.

Weinberger, J. (1995). Common factors aren't so common: The common factors dilemma. *Clinical Psychology: Science and Practice*, *2*, 45–69.

Weir, K. (2012). Overcoming temptation. *Monitor*, *43*(9), 52.

Weisman, M. M., Markowitz, J. C., & Klerman, G. L. (2000). *Comprehensive guide to interpersonal psychotherapy*. New York, NY: Basic Books.

Weitzman, B. (1967). Behavior therapy and psychotherapy. *Psychological Review*, *74*, 300–317.

Wentura, D., & Degner, J. (2010). A practical guide to sequential priming and related tasks. In B. Gawronski, & B. K. Payne (Eds.), *Handbook of implicit social cognition: Measurement, theory, and applications* (pp. 95–116). New York: Guilford.

Wertz, F. J. (1993). The phenomenology of Sigmund Freud. *Journal of Phenomenological Psychology*, *24*(2), 101–129.

Westen, D. (1999). The scientific status of unconscious processes: Is Freud really dead? *Journal of the American Psychoanalytic Association*, *47*, 1061–1106.

Westen, D. (2000). Commentary: Implicit and emotional processes in cognitive-behavioral therapy. *Clinical Psychology: Science and Practice*, *7*, 386–390.

Westen, D., & Gabbard, G. O. (2002). Developments in cognitive neuroscience: I. Conflict, compromise, and connectionism. *Journal of the American Psychoanalytic Association*, *50*, 53–98.

Whalen, P. J., Rauch, S. L., Etcoff, N. L., McInerney, S. C., Lee, M. B., & Jenice, M. A. (1998). Masked presentations of emotional facial expressions modulate amygdale activity without specific knowledge. *Journal of Neuroscience*, *18*(1), 411–418.

Wheeler, S. C., DeMarree, K. G., & Petty, R. E. (2007). Understanding the role of the self in prime-to-behavior effects: The active-self account. *Personality and Social Psychology*, *11*, 234–261.

White, H. (1989). Learning in artificial neural networks: A statistical perspective. *Neural Computation*, *1*, 425–464.

Wholert, A. B. (1993). Event-related brain potentials preceding speech and nonspeech oral movements of varying complexity. *Journal of Speech and Hearing Research*, *36*, 897–905.

Whyte, L. L. (1960). *The unconscious before Freud*. New York: Basic Books.

Whyte, L. L. (1978). *The unconscious before Freud*. New York: St. Martin's Press.

Wiggins, J. S. (1973). *Personality and predictions: Principles of personality assessment*. Reading, MA: Addison-Wesley.

Wiggins, J. S. (1979). A psychological taxonomy of trait-descriptive terms: The interpersonal domain. *Journal of Personality and Social Psychology*, *37*, 395–412.

Wilker, S., & Kolassa, I.-T. (2013). The formation of a neural fear network in posttraumatic stress disorder: Insights from molecular genetics. *Clinical Psychological Science, 1*(4), 452–469.

Wilkins, W. (1973). Expectancy of therapeutic gain: An empirical and conceptual critique. *Journal of Consulting and Clinical Psychology, 40*, 69–77.

Wille, S. (1994). Primary nocturnal enuresis in children. Background and treatment. *Scandanivan Journal of Urology & Nephrology Supplement, 156*, 1–48.

Wille, S., & Anveden, I. (1995). Social and behavioural perspectives in enuretics, former enuretics and non-enuretic controls. *Acta Paediatrica, 84*, 37–40.

Williams, J. H., Waiter, G. D., Gilchrist, A., Perrett, D. I., Murray, A. D., & Whiten, A. (2006). Neural mechanisms of imitation and "mirror neuron" functioning in autistic spectrum disorder. *Neuropsychologia, 44*, 610–621.

Williams, J. H., Whiten, A., & Singh, T. (2004). A systematic review of action imitation in autistic spectrum disorder. *Journal of Autism and Developmental Disorders, 34*(3), 285–299.

Williams, J. M. G. (2001). *Suicide and attempted suicide*. London: Penguin.

Williams, J. M. G., Watts, F. N., MacLeod, C., & Mathews, A. (1988). *Cognitive psychology and emotional disorders*. New York: Wiley.

Williams, J. M. G., Mathews, A., & MacLeod, C. (1996). The emotional Stroop task and psychopathology. *Psychological Bulletin, 120*, 3–24.

Wilson, E. O. (1998). *Consilience: The unity of knowledge*. New York: Knopf.

Wilson, G. T. (1997). Behavior therapy at century close. *Behavior Therapy, 28*, 449–457.

Wilson, T. D. (2002). *Strangers to ourselves: Discovering the adaptive unconscious*. Cambridge, MA: Harvard University Press.

Wilson, T. D., Lisle, D., Schooler, J. W., Hodges, S. D., Klaaren, K. J., & LaFleur, S. J. (1993). Introspecting about reasons can reduce postchoice satisfaction. *Personality and Social Psychology Bulletin, 19*, 331–339.

Wilson, T. D., & Schooler, J. W. (1991). Thinking too much: Introspection can reduce the quality of preferences and decisions. *Journal of Personality and Social Psychology, 60*, 181–192.

Winkielman, P., & Berridge, K. C. (2004). Unconscious Emotion. *Current Directions in Psychological Science, 13*, 120–123.

Winkielman, P., Halberstadt, J., Fazendeiro, T., & Catty, S. (2006). Prototypes are attractive because they are easy on the mind. *Psychological Science, 17*, 799–806.

Wohldmann, E. L., Healy, A. F., & Bourne, L. E., Jr. (2007). Pushing the limits of imagination: mental practice for learning sequences. *Journal of Experimental Psychology: Learning, Memory, and Cognition, 33*, 254–261.

Wolitzky, D. L., & Reuben, R. (1974). Psychological mindedness. *Journal of Clinical Psychology, 30*, 26–30.

Wolpe, J. (1958). *Psychotherapy by reciprocal inhibition*. Stanford, CA: Stanford University Press.

Wolpe, J. (1969). *The practice of behavior therapy*. Elmsford, NY: Pergamon Press.

Wolpe, J. (1995). Reciprocal inhibition: Major agent of behavioral change. In W. O'Donohue, & L. Krasner (Eds.), *Theories of behavior therapy: Exploring behavior change* (pp. 23–57). Washington, DC: American Psychological Association.

Wolpe, J., & Lazarus, A. A. (1966). *Behavior therapy techniques: A guide to the treatment of neuroses*. New York: Pergamon.

Wood, J. M., Lilienfeld, S. O., Nezworski, M. T., & Garb, H. N. (2001). Coming to groups with negative evidence for the comprehensive system for the Rorschach: A comment on Gacono, Loving, and Bodholdt; Ganellen; and Bornstein. *Journal of Personality Assessment, 77*, 48–70.

Woods, P. J. (1974). A taxonomy of instrumental conditioning. *American Psychologist, 29*, 584–597.

Woods, R. P., Brass, M., Bekkering, H., Mazziotta, J. C., & Rizzolatti, G. (1999). Cortical mechanisms of human imitation. *Science, 286*, 2526–2528.

Woodworth, R. S. (1938). *Experimental psychology*. New York: Henry Holt.

Yanchar, S. C. (2004). Some discontents with theoretical unification: A response to Henriques' psychology defined. *Journal of Clinical Psychology, 60*, 1279–1281.

Yanchar, S. C., & Slife, B. D. (1997). Pursuing unity in a fragmented psychology: Problems and prospects. *Review of General Psychology, 1*, 235–255.

Yates, A. J. (1958). Symptoms and symptom substitution. *Psychological Review, 65*, 371–374.

Yates, A. J. (1975). *Theory and practice in behavior therapy* (pp. 152–182). New York: Wiley.

Young, J. E. (1998). *Young Schema Questionnaire: Short form* (1st ed.). New York: Cognitive Therapy Center.

Young, L., Camprodon, J. A., Hauser, M., Pascual-Leone, A., & Saxe, R. (2010). Disruption of the right temporoparietal junction with transcranial magnetic stimulation reduces the role of beliefs in moral judgments. *Proceedings of the National Academy of Sciences of the United States of America (PNAS), 107*(15), 6753–6758.

Zajonc, R. B. (1980). Feeling and thinking: Preferences need no inferences. *American Psychologist, 35*, 151–175.

Zajonc, R. B. (1984). On the primacy of affect. *American Psychologist, 39*, 117–124.

Zeigler-Hill, V., & Jordan, C. H. (2010). Two faces of self-esteem: Implicit and explicit forms of self-esteem. In B. Gawronski, & B. K. Payne (Eds.), *Handbook of implicit social cognition: Measurement, theory, and applications* (pp. 392–407). New York: Guilford.

Zeiss, A. M., Lewinsohn, P. M., & Munoz, R. (1979). Nonspecific improvement effects in depression using interpersonal, cognitive, and pleasant events focused treatments. *Journal of Consulting and Clinical Psychology, 47*, 327–439.

Zhang, T.-Y., & Meaney, M. J. (2010). Epigenetics and the environmental regulation of the genome and its function. *Annual Review of Psychology, 61*, 439–466.

Zlotnick, C., Mattia, J., & Zimmerman, M. (1996). Clinical correlates of self-mutilation in a sample of general psychiatric patients. *The Journal of Nervous & Mental Disease, 187*, 296–301.

Zonnevylle-Bender, M. J., Goozen, S. H., Cohen-Kettenis, P. T., Elburg, A., Wildt, M., Stevelmans, E., & van Engeland, H. (2004). Emotional functioning in anorexia nervosa patients: Adolescents compared to adults. *Depression and Anxiety, 19*, 35–42.

Zonnevylle-Bender, M. J., van Goozen, S. H., Cohen-Kettenis, P. T., van Elburg, A., & van Engeland, H. (2002). Do adolescent anorexia nervosa patients have deficits in emotional functioning? *European Child & Adolescent Psychiatry, 11*, 38–42.

Zuckerman, M. (1991). *Psychobiology of personality*. Cambridge: Cambridge University Press.

INDEX

Note: Page numbers with "*f*" denote figures; "*t*" tables.

A

B

F

M

R

S

U

- cognition, affect and behavior are distributed, networked and parallel [(not serial) (occur at same time)]

- They change together: it is not the case that a change in one "causes" changes in the others

- music therapy: cognition, affect and behavior at the same time, in parallel processes

Edwards Brothers Malloy
Ann Arbor MI. USA
February 23, 2015